SUPERVISION
for
TODAY'S SCHOOLS

Fifth Edition

Peter F. Oliva
Author: *Developing the Curriculum*

George E. Pawlas
University of Central Florida

 LONGMAN

An imprint of Addison Wesley Longman, Inc.

New York • Reading, Massachusetts • Menlo Park, California • Harlow, England
Don Mills, Ontario • Sydney • Mexico City • Madrid • Amsterdam

Supervision for Today's Schools, Fifth Edition

Copyright © 1997, 1993, 1989, 1984, 1976 by Longman Publishers USA,
A Division of Addison Wesley Longman, Inc.
All rights reserved.
No part of this publication may be reproduced,
stored in a retrieval system, or transmitted
in any form or by any means, electronic, mechanical,
photocopying, recording, or otherwise,
without the prior permission of the publisher.

Longman, 10 Bank Street, White Plains, N.Y. 10606

Acquisitions editor: Virginia L. Blanford
Production editors: Linda Witzling, Barbara Gerr
Editorial assistant: Michael Lee
Cover design: Richard Dombrowski
Text art: Fine Line, Inc.
Production supervisor: Edith Pullman
Compositor: University Graphics
Credits begin on page C-1.

Library of Congress Cataloging-in-Publication Data

Oliva, Peter F.
    Supervision for today's schools / Peter F. Oliva, George E.
Pawlas.—5th ed.
        p.   cm.
    Includes bibliographical references and index.
    ISBN 0-8013-1650-2
    1. School supervision—United States.   I. Pawlas, George.
II. Title.
LB2806.4.043   1997
371.2—dc20   96-6458
                                                     CIP

1 2 3 4 5 6 7 8 9 10-MA-0099989796

TO RUTH AND SHARON

Contents

PART II   LEADERSHIP IN INSTRUCTIONAL DEVELOPMENT   89

CHAPTER 3   HELPING TEACHERS PLAN FOR INSTRUCTION   91

CHAPTER 4   HELPING TEACHERS PRESENT INSTRUCTION   131

Preface

The fifth edition of this book remains an overview of the field of instructional supervision. A major new ingredient is the presence of co-author Dr. George E. Pawlas, associate professor, University of Central Florida, who brings a wealth of experience in administration and supervision to these pages.

This textbook was planned to acquaint the student not only with our views on supervision but with those of other specialists in the field as well. Although we have sought to integrate theory and practice, the book continues to lean toward practice, with heavy emphasis on the supervisor's responsibilities as instructional leader.

We present in these pages not only what we believe to be best practice but also what we see as the prevailing practice in the schools. We accept the mountains of research conducted on instruction, curriculum, and supervision over the past twenty-five years. We have not attempted to present a new, idiosyncratic, philosophical approach to instructional supervision. Nor is the book a treatise on principles of educational leadership in general nor on managerial supervision. Rather, our focus is on the *instructional* supervisor; hence, there is special emphasis on the supervisor's role in helping teachers to improve instruction.

We adhere to the belief that supervisors should look at *teaching* before looking at the *teacher*. We focus on generic instructional skills that we believe can be learned and improved. We believe the supervisor should look at the classroom and school environment within the context of instruction. We continue to believe that supervisors should strive to assess teacher performance as objectively as possible, minimizing subjective judgment.

The text introduces the reader to three domains of supervision: instructional development, curriculum development, and staff development. Training programs for supervisors normally follow the overview course with one or more specialized courses in each of the three domains.

GOALS OF THE TEXT

We would like students to achieve the following goals as a result of reading *Supervision for Today's Schools*:

1. To develop a concept of supervision compatible with the needs of students, teachers, the community, society at large, and their own personalities.
2. To become aware of what to look for in each of the topics discussed in the book.
3. To find suggestions for measures that can be taken to improve areas of supervision discussed in the text.
4. To become sensitive to the instructional needs of teachers.
5. To confront recent developments, thought, and research within the domains of supervision discussed in this text.
6. To gain ideas for training programs for teachers.
7. To feel the need for becoming proficient in areas discussed in the text and to take what measures are needed to improve their own competence in each of the areas.
8. To become aware of some of the trends and issues in the field of supervision.
9. To become familiar with the work of some of the specialists in the field.

NEW FEATURES OF THE FIFTH EDITION IN ADDITION TO UPDATING

- Greater emphasis on curriculum development
- Sharper focus on staff development
- More emphasis on school-based management
- More emphasis on empowering teachers
- Discussion of national standards for teachers
- The use of portfolios as a tool for teaching and evaluating student achievement
- Newer job descriptions

We should point out that a continuing, unique feature of this text is the treatment of the supervisor's role in helping teachers with the very difficult area of classroom management.

HOW THIS TEXT IS ORGANIZED

This textbook is organized into six parts. Part I sets forth the role of the supervisor and raises a number of issues in supervision. Part II discusses the instructional process and ways in which the supervisor can help teachers in the planning, presentation, and evaluation of instruction. Part III presents ways in which supervisors engage in curriculum development. Part IV describes the supervisor's role in working with teachers both in groups and individually. Part V discusses summative evaluation of teacher performance. Part VI considers the evaluation of both the supervisor and the supervisory program and future directions in supervision.

At the beginning of each chapter we have specified desired objectives. Objectives are of two types: cognitive, specifying intellectual tasks; and affective, designed to bring out the reader's personal positions and attitudes. We have consciously tried to provide examples of all the major points discussed in the text. In so doing, we have made a special effort to provide illustrations from actual school systems whenever possible.

At the end of each chapter, you will find a generous number of activities for further study. Some are simple cognitive exercises. Others are complex, calling for research and considerable thought. These activities have two purposes: (1) to clarify and review the content of the chapter and (2) to extend study beyond the chapter. Instructors and students can select the activities that are most pertinent to them and to their courses.

At the conclusion of each chapter, we have assembled extensive bibliographies for those wishing to do further research on the topics presented in the chapter. Whenever possible, we have included media other than books that may help instructors illuminate the topics presented in the chapter.

Two appendixes conclude the book. Appendix A is a list of competencies that the preservice and in-service supervisor should be able to demonstrate after completing a course using this text as a basic textbook. Appendix B presents examples of job descriptions of supervisory positions.

Throughout this text, as well as in the notes and bibliographies, we have cited both old and new references. Older references in the chapter texts provide a sense of history to the field; the newer references, current thought.

This text, which has found wide acceptance among trainers of supervisors and practitioners in its previous editions, reflects positions held by many, perhaps the majority of, practicing supervision specialists. The textbook reflects the status of instructional supervision as it currently functions in school systems throughout the country and as it is practiced by many dedicated, experienced individuals at local school, district, and state levels.

We want to thank all the professors, students, and practitioners who have used the previous editions of this text. Special thanks go to the many people who have kindly expressed satisfaction with the book and have made helpful suggestions.

We would like to extend special thanks to Dr. Virginia L. Blanford, our editor at Longman, for her encouragement and for making this fifth edition possible. We are grateful to all the people who read drafts and offered advice and comments:

- Frank D. Adams, Wayne State College
- Gerald R. Firth, University of Georgia
- Larry W. Hughes, University of Houston
- Joyce E. Killian, Southern Illinois University
- Jerry L. Pulley, University of Texas–Pan American
- Martin W. Schoppmeyer, University of Arkansas
- Antonia L. Sims, California State University at Northridge

PART I

Nature of Supervision

Roles of the School Supervisor

Objectives

After studying Chapter 1 you should be able to accomplish the following objectives:
1. Outline the historical development of the field of supervision.
2. Formulate a working definition of supervision.
3. Describe a conceptual model of supervision.
4. Identify supervisors in a school system.
5. List common tasks of supervision.
6. Describe various roles of supervisors.
7. State what you believe to be minimal qualifications of a supervisor.
8. Show your position on supervision as a career.

SUPERVISION DEFINED

One of the best-kept secrets outside the education profession and, to a degree, even within the profession is the existence of a large shadow army of school personnel known by the collective title of supervisors. Parents and sometimes teachers profess not to know of the presence of these specialists in the school systems of the nation. Although laypersons may be aware that school systems employ a variety of personnel such as custodians, secretaries, cafeteria workers, and counselors, the concept of school personnel held by a typical layperson is a teacher in every classroom and a principal in every school. Were members of the community asked to identify a school supervisor, they would probably indicate the principal, who may or may not be the sole supervisor. Or they might refer to the superintendent, who plays a very small part in the type of supervision discussed in this book, namely, instructional supervision.

Yet, as the alien watchers say about extraterrestrial beings, supervisors are "out there." In fact, they are all around us. We could discover to what degree they are present if we had the power to equip every supervisor for one day with a coal miner's hat and to turn on all the light beams. If we could then photograph the light trails, we would trace a pattern of motion as astounding as any graphics drawn by a computer. We'd see almost endless movement as supervisors journey from class to class, school to school, and school system to school system. Whereas teachers are usually place-bound, supervisors are in periodic motion. A distinguishing feature of true supervisors is that they leave their offices frequently for the purpose of helping other school personnel do their jobs better.

Considering the veritable army of supervisors on local and state levels of schooling throughout the country, it is surprising to find that the role of the supervisor in education remains rather ill defined. Business and industry are not troubled by this same malady. The position of commercial or industrial supervisor is highly visible and well defined in the managerial structure of the organization. Educational supervisors may or may not be a part of the managerial structure of school systems. Whether they should be a part of management is, as we discover later, a storm center among specialists in supervision.

Responsibilities of educational supervisors are not at all clear from locality to locality and from state to state. Even within localities, supervisory roles are often poorly delineated. To compound the problem, the titles of supervisors are almost as varied as their roles.

Ben M. Harris attributed the variations in roles to differing theoretical perspectives:

> Supervision, like any complex part of an even more complex enterprise, can be viewed in various ways and inevitably is. The diversity of perceptions stems not only from organizational complexity but also from lack of information and absence of perspective. To provide perspective, at least, the total school operation must be the point of departure for analyzing instructional supervision as a major function.[1]

To varying degrees, many occupations outside education use the services of supervisors, whether as office boss, telephone supervisor, floor manager, construction foreman, department store head, or assembly-line supervisor. These individuals carry out the task of supervision in the original sense of the Latin word *supervideo*, "to oversee." They demonstrate techniques, offer suggestions, give orders, evaluate employees' performance, and check on results (products).

HISTORICAL APPROACHES

Supervision has gone through many metamorphoses. If we look at some of the changes that have occurred in this field since the early days of the republic, we can, a bit arbitrarily, establish historical time frames for the evolution of instructional supervision. In analyzing the development of most aspects of education, we should keep in mind what we might call "axioms."[2] Applied to curriculum development, these could include "School curriculum not only reflects but is a product of its time" and "Curriculum changes made at an earlier period of time can exist concurrently with newer curriculum changes at a later period of time." The same axioms are valid if we substitute *supervision* for *curriculum.*

Supervisory behaviors and practices are affected by political, social, religious, and industrial forces existent at the time. Further, traces of supervisory behaviors and practices that existed in earlier days of our country can be found, even today, among highly divergent practices and behaviors. History is forever with us. However, supervision has come far since colonial days as we can see in Table 1.1, which outlines the major periods in the historical development of supervision.

Not until the establishment of organized schools did the need for specialized school supervisors materialize. When parents, "dames," and tutors instructed youngsters in the home, these people were, in effect, both teacher and supervisor, but as the population grew, early colonists realized that they needed some formal structure for the education of their young. The Commonwealth of Massachusetts passed the famed "Old Deluder Law" of 1647 that required communities with fifty or more

TABLE 1.1. MAJOR PERIODS IN THE HISTORICAL DEVELOPMENT OF SUPERVISION

Period	Type of Supervision	Purpose	Persons Responsible
1620–1850	Inspection	Monitoring rules, looking for deficiencies	Parents, clergy, selectmen, citizens' committees
1850–1910	Inspection, instructional improvement	Monitoring rules, helping teachers improve	Superintendents, principals
1910–1930	Scientific, bureaucratic	Improving instruction and efficiency	Supervising principals, principals, general and special central-office supervisors, superintendents
1930–1950	Human relations, democratic	Improving instruction	Principal, central-office supervisors
1950–1975	Bureaucratic, scientific, clinical, human relations, human resources, democratic	Improving instruction	Principals, central-office supervisors, school-based supervisors
1975–1985	Scientific, clinical, human relations, human resources, collaborative/collegial, peer/coach/mentor, artistic, interpretive	Improving instruction, increasing teacher satisfaction, expanding students' understanding of classroom events	Principals, central-office supervisors, school-based supervisors, peer/coach/mentor
1985–present	Scientific, clinical, human relations, human resources, collaborative/collegial, peer/coach/mentor, artistic, interpretive, culturally responsive, ecological	Improving instruction, increasing teacher satisfaction, expanding students' understanding of classroom events; analyzing cultural and linguistic patterns in the classroom	School-based supervisors, peer/coach/mentor, principals, central-office supervisors

families to provide instruction in reading and writing and communities with one hundred or more families to establish a grammar school. Thus, educated young people would not be led astray by the Old Deluder, Satan. Note the powerful effect of the church on early education in the colonies. Though church and state are more or less separated today, strong controversy still exists about the role of religion in the public schools.[3]

As schools became established, local school committeemen fulfilled the function of supervisors by giving directions, checking for compliance with teaching techniques, and evaluating results of instruction by the teachers in their charge. In an authoritarian mode, early supervisors set strict requirements for their teachers and visited classrooms to observe how closely the teachers complied with stipulated instructions. Departure from these instructions was cause for dismissal.

Even in the eighteenth century, school people were anxious to appear at their best when visited by selectmen. Walter Herbert Small observed that as early as 1733 schools provided a dinner for schoolmasters, selectmen, and certain public officials on the occasion of the selectmen's visit to their schools.[4] Taking a cue from their eighteenth-century predecessors, today's school faculty, administrators, and board members extend the hospitality of an initial breakfast or dinner meeting to visiting teams from regional accrediting associations.

Limited schooling, primarily for boys, was the prevailing pattern through most of the seventeenth and eighteenth centuries. Benjamin Franklin's Philadelphia Academy and Charitable School, which opened in 1751, extended the curriculum and provided opportunities not found in the earlier Latin grammar schools. A growing population necessitated more schools, and an expanding curriculum revealed the need for specialists in instructional supervision.

Universal public education for boys and girls, poor and rich, was a phenomenon of the nineteenth century. The common elementary school grew rapidly in the first half of the nineteenth century, imitating Prussian and military models of graded organization. Horace Mann, secretary of the Massachusetts State Board of Education from 1837 to 1848, pushed the cause of public schools and created the first normal school in the United States for the training of teachers. He defined the state's responsibility for public education. During the same period, Henry Barnard, first secretary of the Connecticut State Board of Education, was also promoting public education.

The number of high schools in the country grew rapidly, spurred by political, social, and educational developments of the time. Among these developments were the creation of the first high school in Boston in 1821, the Massachusetts law of 1827 requiring a high school with a two-month program in towns of 500 or more families, and the famous Kalamazoo, Michigan, case of 1874 that affirmed the right of communities to tax for secondary education. New institutions, new programs, expanded student bodies, and increased population called for new ways of supervising instruction. Selectmen, citizens' committees, clergy, and parents gave way to trained educators.

In the nineteenth century, local committees began looking to professionally trained persons to administer and supervise the schools. As early as 1837, Buffalo, New York, and Louisville, Kentucky, employed school superintendents. By 1870, some twenty-nine school systems were headed by superintendents.[5] Superintendents in the early nineteenth century spent considerable time visiting and supervising schools, though their focus changed from looking for deficiencies meriting dismissal of teachers to helping teachers overcome difficulties.

Inspection, often derided as "snoopervision," was the prevailing approach in the nineteenth century. The appeal to authority was very evident in the widely reproduced set of instructions to teachers in Harrison, South Dakota, in 1872, shown below in Figure 1.1. To some extent school supervisors, or inspectors as they are called in other countries, continue to fulfill their tasks with an authoritarian approach. The classic illustration of this—although not entirely true—is France, of which it has often been said that the Minister of Education can tell on any day exactly where each teacher is in any textbook anywhere in the country. Such a situa-

1872

Instruction to the Teacher

Harrison, S.D.

1. Teachers will fill lamps, clean chimneys and trim wicks each day.

2. Each teacher will bring a scuttle of coal and a bucket of water for the day's use.

3. Make your pens carefully. You may whittle nibs for the individual tastes of children.

4. Men teachers may take one evening each week for courting purposes or two evenings a week if they go to church regularly.

5. After ten hours in school, the teacher should spend the remaining time reading the Bible and other good books.

6. Women teachers who marry or engage in other unseemly conduct will be dismissed.

7. Every teacher should lay aside from every pay a goodly sum of his earnings for his declining years so that he will not become a burden on society.

8. Any teacher who smokes, uses liquor in any form, frequents pool or public halls, or gets shaved in a barber shop will give good reasons to suspect his worth, intentions, integrity and honesty.

9. The teacher who performs his labors faithfully without fault for five years will be given an increase of 25ᶜ a week in his pay—providing the Board of Education approves.

Figure 1.1. 1872 Instruction to the Teacher. *Source: Board of Education, Harrison, South Dakota and Leo W. Anglin, Richard Goldman, and Joyce Shanahan Anglin,* Teaching: What It's All About *(New York: Harper & Row, 1982), p. 11. Reprinted by permission of Board of Education, Harrison, South Dakota.*

tion implies a highly structured form of instruction and a highly centralized system of supervision.

In America, we have no instructional inspectors in the foreign sense of the word. There are no inspectors from the United States Department of Education whose duty it is to check on teachers and schools. Some states do provide or have provided a limited type of inspection of teachers prior to full certification in a subject or grade level, but this is more uncommon than common. Even today, however, some individuals behave like inspectors although their job specifications do not call for such behavior.

Our system of education does not begin to approach foreign systems in degree of centralization, but during the 1970s and 1980s we saw considerable centralization at the state and school district levels. Some states either recommended or mandated minimal competencies that students were (and to some degree still are) expected to achieve in certain subjects at each grade level. Some school districts, engaging in a process called "curriculum alignment," specified detailed objectives that students were expected to master each marking period in each subject. Learning activities and test items based on the objectives were designed for each marking period. In states that conducted student-assessment programs, local curriculum guides were keyed into the objectives assessed on the states' examinations. In the 1990s, the movement toward centralization has abated and in its place have come decentralization and empowerment of teachers and lay people.[6]

As the population grew and schools increased in number, the superintendent could no longer supervise individual schools closely. In the late nineteenth century, principals and central office supervisors shared a major part of the burden of everyday supervision.

With the advent of the Industrial Revolution and the influence of people like Frederick W. Taylor and Max Weber in the late nineteenth and early twentieth centuries, scientific and bureaucratic approaches to supervision replaced inspection. Scientific management and efficiency were bywords of the new approach. The assumption of these strategies was that if organizations followed established principles for efficiency, production would presumably be high. Supervisors had only to assure the rigorous application of the principles.

While Taylor was expounding on scientific management, Weber was promoting the concept of bureaucratic management of organizations as the ideal model for achieving efficiency and productivity. The model provided for a hierarchy of authority and responsibility—from the chief executive officer at the top of the pinnacle to the lowliest worker at the bottom. The bureaucratic model became the pervasive organizational structure in all human institutions—business, industry, government, social organizations, church, and schools. In fact, the bureaucratic model has become so entrenched in our lives that *bureaucracy* has become, under some circumstances, a derogatory term.

Thus, in the early part of the twentieth century, the bureaucratic model of organization became firmly rooted in our school systems with the superintendent at the top and the teacher at the bottom. In between came a whole echelon of generalist and specialist personnel. Although philosophies, attitudes, and operating procedures have changed since the early twentieth century, the bureaucratic model remains the dominant, universal form of school organization in spite of predictions of an "emerging, pluralistic, collegial" concept of administrative organization.[7]

Describing the attitude of scientific managers during the early 1900s, William H. Lucio and John D. McNeil said that "teachers were regarded as instruments that should be closely supervised to insure that they mechanically carried out the methods of procedure determined by administrative and special supervisors."[8] "Scientific" supervisors look for fixed principles of teaching, drawn from research, that can be prescribed for teachers. The teachers' performances can then be judged on how well they follow the instructional principles in their teaching. To supervisors of this persuasion, teaching is a science rather than an art, and they believe that by following a prescribed set of rules, teachers are bound to be successful. Does this sound familiar to you in the 1990s?

Following research on instruction carried out through the 1960s and 1970s many educators still perceive teaching as a science whose component skills—generic competencies—can be identified, learned, and mastered.

Under the influence of people like Elton Mayo, Mary Parker Follett, Kurt Lewin, Ronald Lippitt, Ralph K. White, Kenneth D. Benne, Paul Sheats, and Warren G. Bennis at mid-twentieth century, supervision turned in the direction of human relations and group dynamics. Stress on the democratic process and the application of the behavioral sciences commanded the attention of supervisors. No longer did supervision constitute handing down methods to teachers, then monitoring their performance. Collaboration and partnership between supervisors and teachers became important. Supervisors began to realize that their success was dependent more on interpersonal skills than on technical skills and knowledge; they had to become sensitive to the behavior of groups and individuals within groups. They became more aware that they must respond to needs as determined by the people they served—the teachers—as opposed to satisfying their own needs based on their supposedly superior judgments. The prefix "super" on supervision declined in importance. The word *supervision* itself became modified by such words as *collaborative, cooperative, democratic,* and *consultative.* This change of focus has continued and intensified into the present.

What we are seeing today is an amalgamation of practices and attitudes. True, we can find holdovers of the inspection mentality and we can still encounter the boss-employee mind-set, but we are experiencing more cases of cooperation and collaboration between supervisors and teachers than in the past. We find a definite acceptance of the idea that instructional supervisors are employed to help teachers build on their strengths, improve, and remain in the profession instead of probing teachers' deficiencies and seeking their dismissal.

We are finding principles of scientific supervision within a clinical yet supportive context. Even within a scientific framework, supervisors place heavy reliance on human relations. Too, we note that teachers themselves are acting as instructional supervisors to their peers. We are also experiencing newer focuses of supervision—human resources, artistic, interpretive, and ecological approaches. We return to these later in the text.

Before exploring the new directions of supervision, however, it is helpful to see the old ways that are no longer considered effective. Three approaches discussed below are among those that competent supervisors would reject today.

- **The Authoritarian-Inspectorial Approach.** Professional supervisors realize that teachers, as professionals, can be persuaded but not coerced; many times, they have better answers to their own problems than do the supervisors.
- **Laissez-faire.** To some, supervision is a laissez-faire task. Supervisors who are thus inclined agree with many teachers that with supervision, less is better. Nondirective in their approach, they may visit the teachers' classrooms or stop by the teachers' lounge for a cup of coffee. They tend to consider a classroom visit and an appearance in the teachers' lounge as equally important; some might rate the chat in the lounge the more important of the two interactions. They see their task as giving the teacher a benevolent pat on the back now and then.
- **Group Dynamics.** To others, supervision is a never-ending exercise in group process. They see improvement of instruction as a continuing exercise in human relations. Viewing themselves as resource persons to the group, they spend considerable time fostering a positive group climate, using social affairs to establish a happy, cooperative frame of mind among teachers. They hope that after a period of deliberation, groups will reach consensus on points under discussion.

Neither an authoritarian nor a laissez-faire approach is adequate or suitable for today's schools, nor is an exclusively "scientific" or group-process approach. Though supervisors may lean toward a scientific approach to supervision, the human relations dimension cannot be ignored. Supervisors may favor group processes, but they will be called on to work with both groups and individuals. They must be mindful that many of the innovations in schools are products of experimentation by one or two individuals rather than groups.

VARYING INTERPRETATIONS

This discussion, however, still leaves us unsure of what supervision is or should be. To create a sharp, clear-cut definition of supervision is extremely difficult, as acknowledged by Ralph L. Mosher and David E. Purpel.

> The difficulty of defining supervision in relation to education also stems, in large part, from unsolved theoretical problems about teaching. Quite simply, we lack sufficient understanding of the process of teaching. Our theories of learning are inadequate, the criteria for measuring teaching effectiveness are imprecise, and deep disagreement exists about what knowledge—that is, what curriculum—is most valuable to teach. . . . When we have achieved more understanding of what and how to teach, and with what special effects on students, we will be much less vague about the supervision of these processes.[9]

Looking at the way specialists in supervision have defined the term may help us in our quest for a viable definition. William H. Burton and Leo J. Brueckner gave supervision a broad interpretation, viewing it as a technical service requiring expertise, the goal of which is improvement in the growth and development of the learner.[10]

Stressing the helping nature of supervision, Jane Franseth stated, "Today supervision is generally seen as leadership that encourages a continuous involvement of all school personnel in a cooperative attempt to achieve the most effective school program."[11] Ross L. Neagley and N. Dean Evans pointed to the democratic nature of modern supervision in their definition:

> Modern supervision is considered as any service for teachers that eventually results in improving instruction, learning, and the curriculum. It consists of positive, dynamic, democratic actions designed to improve instruction through the continued growth of all concerned individuals—the child, the teacher, the supervisor, the administrator, and the parent or other lay person.[12]

Contemporary definitions of supervision stress *service*, *cooperation*, and *democracy*. In this book, you will find the emphasis placed on *instructional* supervision. For that reason, it helps if we look at ways in which some of the experts view this term. Harris wrote: "Supervision of instruction is what school personnel do with adults and things to maintain or change the school operation in ways that directly influence the teaching process employed to promote pupil learning."[13] Robert J. Alfonso, Gerald R. Firth, and Richard F. Neville offered a slightly different definition: "Instructional supervision is herein defined as: Behavior officially designated by the organization that directly affects teacher behavior in such a way as to facilitate pupil learning and achieve the goals of the organization."[14]

John T. Lovell, in revising the earlier work of Kimball Wiles, looked at instructional supervisory behavior as behavior that "is assumed to be an additional behavior system formally provided by the organization for the purpose of interacting with the teaching behavior system in such a way as to maintain, change, and improve the design and actualization of learning opportunities for students."[15] Don M. Beach and Judy Reinhartz defined "instructional supervision as the process of working with teachers to improve classroom instruction."[16]

Note how many definitions focus on (1) the behavior of supervisors (2) in assisting teachers (3) for the ultimate benefit of the student. Robert Krey and Peter J. Burke offered a comprehensive definition of supervision:

> Supervision is instructional leadership that relates perspectives to behavior, clarifies purposes, contributes to and supports organizational actions, coordinates interactions, provides for maintenance and improvement of the instructional program, and assesses goal achievements.[17]

Thomas J. Sergiovanni and Robert J. Starratt redefined supervision in terms of an emerging theory they referred to as *normative* supervision. Expanding on the concept of human resources supervision, this approach would alter the traditional role of the supervisor by promoting the school as a community of learners in which teachers gain satisfaction through identifying and sharing professional and moral values.[18]

John C. Daresh and Marsha A. Playko offered a concise definition, viewing supervision as "the process of overseeing the ability of people to meet the goals of the organization in which they work."[19]

Supervision, as presented in this text, is conceived as a service to teachers, both as individuals and in groups. To put it simply, supervision is a means of offering to teachers specialized help in improving instruction. The words *service* and *help* should be underscored, and they are used repeatedly in this text.

PROBLEMS THAT COMPLICATE THE SUPERVISORY ROLE

Definitions by themselves do not reveal the complexities of the supervisory role. Supervision today is complicated by a number of factors, including diversity of conceptions of supervision and good teaching, mandates from the state level, and tensions between teachers and administrators/supervisors.

Continuing Diversity of Conceptions of Supervision

Realizing that the term *supervision* by itself is subject to so many different interpretations, some specialists in the field have found it expedient to add modifiers. Thus, in the literature we encounter *administrative, clinical, consultative, developmental, differentiated, educational, general, instructional,* and *peer.* Each of the adjectives offers a special interpretation of the term *supervision.*

Administrative supervision covers the territory of managerial responsibilities outside the fields of curriculum and instruction. *General supervision* is perceived by some as synonymous with *educational supervision* and by others as that type of supervision that takes place outside the classroom. *Differentiated supervision* allows teachers to choose the types of developmental activities in which they will engage.

Whereas *educational supervision* suggests responsibilities encompassing many aspects of schooling, including administration, curriculum, and instruction, *instructional supervision* narrows the focus to a more limited set of responsibilities, namely, supervision for the improvement of instruction. *Clinical, consultative, developmental,* and *peer supervision* are subsumed under *instructional supervision.*

Whether the supervisor perceives teaching as a science or as an art further colors the supervisor's role. The supervisor who follows a scientific approach believes that generic teaching skills can be identified and that all teachers at all levels should be able to demonstrate them. Such a supervisor believes that those skills can be described, observed, and analyzed. The supervisor who follows an artistic approach believes that teaching is a highly individualized activity that bears the stamp of the teacher's inimitable personality. This type of supervisor believes that the entire setting for instruction, the persons involved in the teaching act, and the general atmosphere of the classroom must be considered.

Some specialists would maintain that supervisors should devote all or most of their emphasis to a single approach or type of supervision. Others, including ourselves, see room for a more eclectic approach. We return to some of these varying conceptions of supervision in later chapters of the book.

Differing Conceptions of Effective Teaching

Some specialists ascribe difficulty in defining the term *supervision,* as did Mosher and Purpel, to a lack of understanding of the teaching process, impreciseness of the criteria for assessing teacher performance, and lack of agreement on what should be taught.[20] Those who follow an interpretive or hermeneutic approach to supervision look at the unique characteristics of a particular learning situation and, with the teacher, seek to interpret the events that have taken place during a lesson. Some supervisors look at *process,* that is, the demonstration of teaching skills. Some focus on *product,* such as test scores of students. Others include the teacher's personal and professional attributes in their description of effective teaching. Certain supervisors are partial to particular models and styles of teaching. Some smile, for example, on discovery learning and frown on lecturing. Some favor direct instruction of entire groups, some champion cooperative learning, and others advocate individualized instructional techniques.

These differing conceptions of what constitutes effective teaching make the supervisory process difficult for both the teacher and the supervisor. Many research studies on effective teaching have been conducted in recent years. These studies furnish partial answers to some of the pedagogical questions. They do not, however, provide answers to differing philosophical premises held by supervisors. We discuss some of that research in Chapter 4.

Mandates from the State Level

State legislatures in state after state during the past two decades passed legislation calling for sweeping reforms in public education. They raised teacher salaries, mandated state testing of teachers, instituted on-the-job assessment, established student assessment programs, prescribed aspects of the curriculum, and ordered annual evaluation of all school personnel. State departments of education have implemented and administered the many reforms mandated by their legislatures and state boards of education.

Although room remained for some local decision making, increased direction from the state level has certainly reduced the flexibility of local school systems to make decisions based on their assessment of local needs and on their own philosophies of education. Local school systems have had to give priority to state mandates. After meeting state requirements, they may and often did go beyond the state directives.

The supervisor's role is heavily affected by state mandates: by state tests for both teachers and students, by state model instruments for evaluating teachers, by state-developed curriculum guides, and by state specification of teaching competencies. Supervisors who are in disagreement with state reforms are faced with intrarole conflicts. State assessments of student achievement, for example, are almost exclusively cognitive in nature. The supervisor who has a commitment to affective and psychomotor as well as cognitive learning will feel uncomfortable with testing restricted to only the cognitive domain. Nevertheless, the supervisor owes it to the teachers to help them produce high student test scores. State mandates have established priorities for local school personnel, including supervisors. Fortunately, state mandating has peaked and the responsibility for administration, supervision, curriculum, and instruction is more and more being shifted to the local schools. Site-based or school-based management, teacher empowerment, and parental participation in decision making are clearly movements toward decentralization that place more responsibility and authority on the individual schools and less on the district and state levels.

Tensions between Teachers and Administrators/Supervisors

Evaluation of one individual by another is in itself a stressful activity. Increased emphasis on student achievement, accountability of teachers, and teacher competence have brought about increased stress (in both senses of the word: emphasis and discomfort) on evaluation of performance.

The public and, to an increasing degree, the profession have expressed dissatisfaction with student achievement and with incompetent teaching. They are demanding improvement in instruction to enhance student achievement. Consequently, evaluation of teaching has loomed large in recent years.

Teachers, especially through their organizations, have not wholeheartedly embraced current processes of evaluation. They have raised valid questions concerning the competencies on which they will be judged, who will do the evaluating, how the evaluation will be conducted, and what use will be made of the results.

Teachers question the reliability of the data collected on their performances and the competence of the administrators or supervisors in making assessments. Further, they want to be involved in the creation of the evaluation process.

The inability to separate supervisory service from evaluation, an issue addressed in Chapter 2, adds to the tensions. Teachers, as a rule, welcome real supervisory help. Yet many teachers view supervisors with contempt, feeling, sometimes rightly and sometimes wrongly, that they are more capable than the supervisor or that the supervisor has nothing of value to offer them. Many teachers simply ignore supervisors, choose not to ask for their help, and avoid opportunities to work with them.

Arthur Blumberg pictured the tensions between supervisors and teachers in the following passage:

> . . . the character of relationships between teachers as a group and supervisors as a group can be described as somewhat of a cold war. Neither side trusts the other and each side is convinced of the correctness of its position. Supervisors seem to be saying, "If they would just listen to us, things would really get better." Teachers seem to be saying, "What they give us doesn't help. It would be better if they left us alone."[21]

These negative, fearful, or hostile attitudes are symptoms of the malaise brought on by uncertainties about the role, function, and efficiency of the supervision profession. Great needs exist to clarify duties and responsibilities of supervisors, to discover the most effective techniques and skills, and to identify who the supervisors are.

WHO ARE THE SUPERVISORS?

In the traditional meaning of supervision, anyone who oversees the work of another is a supervisor. Hence, every administrator is ipso facto a supervisor. If we limit the concept of supervision to management of resources and personnel, we are on firm ground in labeling the administrator a supervisor. Yet if we delimit supervision to the means of improving the curriculum and instruction, we may not conclude that every administrator is an instructional supervisor.

Logically, it would seem that any school official who assists teachers in improving curriculum and instruction is a supervisor. In practice, however, some individuals in the school system are charged with the management of resources and personnel as their primary task whereas others are assigned the improvement of curriculum and instruction as their major function.

Many arguments are waged over whether the building principal, for example, is a supervisor. Although principals have responsibility for the curriculum and instruction of the school, supervision of those aspects is only one of their many tasks. Unfortunately, instructional supervision is often a secondary task for many school principals, who commonly lament that they do not have time to devote to curriculum and instructional leadership because they are too busy with the day-to-day operation of the school.

We must hasten to add that in those small schools throughout the country that employ several teachers, a principal, and no one to assist him or her, the principals do, by necessity if not by desire, perform the function of instructional supervisor. We might more accurately refer to those principals by a title used in earlier days, *supervising principals*, to distinguish them from *instructional supervisors*. We are witnessing, however, a desire for change if not change itself in the role of the building principal—from manager to instructional supervisor. The profession has begun to recognize the individual school as the locus of change, placing responsibility for instructional leadership squarely on the principal. Though some principals will continue to devote less time to instructional supervision than to other duties and may, if possible, delegate much of the task to others, more and more principals are accepting responsibility for the role of instructional supervisor. Such developments as state-mandated curricula, evaluation systems, merit pay, and career ladder programs further push the principal into fulfilling instructional supervisory responsibilities.

"By their fruits ye shall know them" is more pertinent in the world of supervision than "by their titles ye shall know them." Controversy swirls around the issue, which we examine in Chapter 2, concerning whether supervisors should assume administrative responsibilities. We should note at this point that the issue is not ordinarily reversed—that is, there is seldom discussion of whether administrators should assume supervisory responsibilities. For both legal and practical reasons, administrators already have these responsibilities.

As we try to identify supervisors, it might be helpful to depict the degree to which administrators and supervisors take on the role of guiding instructional improvement. Figure 1.2 illustrates how we can chart varying degrees of supervisory responsibility.

A full-time administrator (e.g., superintendent of schools; many principals, especially of large schools) is deep into budgeting, transportation, staffing, pupil personnel services, and public relations. He or she devotes little or no time to curricular and instructional supervision but delegates that duty to others. Some administrators, however, although preoccupied with managerial problems, expend some time and energy on supervisory activities. They may visit—and in many cases

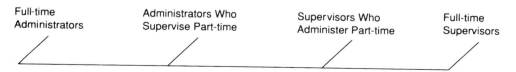

Figure 1.2. Continuum of Supervisory Responsibility.

they are required by law to visit—teachers in their classrooms, observe their teaching, make judgments, and offer advice. When they behave in this fashion, administrators become supervisors, if only for a portion of their time.

Some school personnel who by job description are classified as supervisors are charged with or assume on their own initiative administrative duties such as annual assessments of teacher performance. When they accept managerial tasks, they join the ranks of the administrators. Finally, those personnel who spend all their time and efforts in helping teachers directly with the improvement of instruction may be called full-time supervisors. Thus, with a nod to Izaak Walton, we have the Compleat Administrator on one side of the spectrum and the Compleat Supervisor on the other.

Types of Supervisors

The American system of education is a confusing diversity of systems that confounds people from abroad who attempt to study it. In fact, at times our system even perplexes Americans. This confusion extends to the provision of special services like supervision.

In this book, we talk about a person whom we call the supervisor. Unless otherwise specified, we are talking about the instructional supervisor. In agreement with many specialists, we include curriculum supervision within the context of instructional supervision.

Because of the great diversity in roles and duties of supervisors we urge the reader to keep in mind the distinction between the *supervisor*, with *supervisor* emphasized, and *the* supervisor, with *the* emphasized. In discussing the *supervisor* we make the assumption that principles and practices of supervision may apply *generally, to most, but not to all situations nor to all persons* who wear the hat of supervisor. This book concentrates on the *supervisor*. Were we to talk about *the* supervisor, we would be conveying the erroneous notion that there is a single, accepted role that supervisors can, do, or should play. The effort to identify a single role applicable under all circumstances is akin to searching for that elusive will-o'-the-wisp, the best model of teaching.

Supervisors are special service personnel to be found on the staffs of administrators at the state, district, and school levels. In administrative parlance these service personnel are *staff* employees, whereas the administrators, equipped with the mantles of status and authority, are *line* employees. Staff personnel are hired by and responsible to the line employees. Line personnel below the top position (e.g., superintendent) are hired by and responsible to other line employees in the chain of command.

Supervisors are often referred to as auxiliary personnel or staff. Although titles and responsibilities of these auxiliary personnel differ from state to state and from school district to school district, we can identify the major types of supervisors. Figure 1.3 shows some of the varieties of supervisors on different levels. Included among the types of supervisors are administrators who spend a portion of their time in supervising instruction as well as full-time supervisors. Figure 1.3 also distinguishes generalist supervisors, whose duties cut across disciplines and grade levels, from specialist supervisors, whose responsibilities fall within a subject or grade level.

Figure 1.3. Types of Supervisors.

State Supervisors. The chief supervisor on the state level is the assistant superintendent for curriculum and instruction. Although this position may bear other titles, this person's responsibility is to supervise the entire curricular and instructional program of the public schools in the state, with the help of staff members. The assistant superintendent interprets state department of education and state legislative mandates concerning education and is directly responsible to the state superintendent of public instruction. The assistant superintendent's office frequently directs teachers in the preparation of certain curricular materials and often supervises textbook adoptions. That office also provides consultant service to the schools, sponsors conferences on curriculum and instruction, and acts as liaison with the federal government in the preparation of proposals for grants for federal projects. This office encourages experimentation in curriculum design and instructional techniques.

The assistant superintendent for curriculum and instruction is aided by a staff of specialists who may be designated supervisors, directors, consultants, or coordinators. Frequently these include specialists in curriculum and instruction such as directors or supervisors of elementary, middle, and secondary education. These staff members aid in fulfilling the assistant superintendent's tasks. They generally confine themselves, however, to providing leadership at their own levels.

Well-developed state departments of education provide a variety of specialists in particular areas or disciplines such as science, English, social studies, and reading. These supervisors operate throughout the state in their own areas of specialization, assisting teachers, suggesting materials, giving advice, and demonstrating effective methods of teaching their specialties. They are generally responsible to the director of elementary education or director of middle schools, junior high schools, or senior high schools, depending on their level of responsibility. We sometimes find, for example, a supervisor of elementary language arts and a supervisor of secondary language arts on the assistant superintendent's staff.

Local Supervisors. The presence and effectiveness of the supervisor is felt more keenly on the local than on the state level. The state supervisors' areas are so large and responsibilities so many that they cannot possibly make the rounds of all the schools and teachers demanding services. Consequently, local supervisors become key people in the school system.

DISTRICT LEVEL. On the school district level, supervisors are on the staff of the local school superintendent. They are referred to in the literature and in practice as central office personnel, a designation that distinguishes them from school-based personnel employed to serve in particular schools.

On the central office staff, customarily an assistant superintendent for curriculum and instruction or sometimes a director of instruction provides curricular and instructional leadership throughout the local district. This key local official aids teachers in developing materials, encourages experimentation and research, provides schools with up-to-date materials and consultants, leads the district in the continuous task of curriculum development, and meets with teachers and administrators on problems of curriculum and instruction.

Helping the assistant superintendent are personnel of various types. Often these include one or more general supervisors, responsible for supervision from kindergarten through twelfth grade. They are frequently in the schools assisting individual teachers and groups of teachers in a variety of fields. These persons are familar with learning theory, adolescent psychology, methods of handling groups and individuals, and new ways to organize for instruction. Some of the smaller school districts limit their central office personnel to positions of this type.

Larger school systems employ supervisors or directors of elementary, middle, and secondary education. Whereas the general supervisor must be spread thin over the entire school system, these three specialists may concentrate on their individual levels.

Large school districts often provide a variety of supervisors or consultants in special fields such as reading, guidance, foreign languages, and vocational education. Some of the special-area supervisors divide their time between the elementary, middle, and secondary levels as, for example, in art, music, and physical education; others confine their work to one level. These specialists are in a strategic position for effecting change in individual classrooms. They have expertise in a particular field and may devote their full time and energies to the development of curriculum and instruction in their specialties. They can be knowledgeable about the latest content, materials, and methods in their fields of specialization.

SCHOOL LEVEL. Within the individual schools of a district are people who could be labeled supervisors. Often, a school will employ an assistant principal whose main duty is the supervision of curriculum and instruction. This person devotes full energies to developing the curriculum of his or her own school and helping teachers improve instruction.

Curriculum coordinators or lead teachers are sometimes found in the individual schools either as assistants to or replacements for the assistant principal for curriculum and instruction. It is their task to assist teachers with curricular and instructional problems and to give leadership to the development of the curriculum and the improvement of instruction

Team leaders, grade coordinators, and department heads in the individual schools can, should, and sometimes do serve as supervisors. With the team staffing patterns followed by many schools at all levels, the person who heads an instructional team plays a significant role as supervisor for that team. The department head in middle, junior high, and senior high schools fulfills for a department a supervisory function similar to that fulfilled by the team leader. Because elementary schools are ordinarily not departmentalized, the grade coordinators for all sections of a grade level and the team leaders for each section of a grade level serve as quasi-department heads who carry supervisory responsibilities. In the middle, junior high, and senior high schools, we may find both team leaders and department heads, with team leaders who are within departments responsible to the department heads.

School-based supervisors should lead in curriculum development, assist teachers in the production of instructional and curricular materials, arrange for staff development, and help teachers to improve their teaching methods. Principals have the obligation of freeing their coordinators and leaders so that they will not become bogged down, as so often happens, with either administrative details of running their grades, teams, or departments or with full-time teaching schedules. These activities can prohibit them from giving adequate time to instructional and curricular leadership. Newer practices in supervision enlist the services of peers, coaches, and mentors in the process to help avoid this overload.

You may question whether those personnel shown in Figure 1.3 who hold line or administrative positions are truly supervisors—for example, the assistant superintendents and directors on both state and district levels who often work only minimally with teachers. The assistant superintendent for curriculum and instruction and frequently the directors on the local district level occupy line rather than staff positions. Depending on the school district, line personnel may or may not work directly with teachers. In Figure 1.3, however, these line officials are classified as supervisors as they devote at least part of their time to supervisory duties. Whereas some specialists in supervision restrict their concept of a supervisor to those staff persons who work full time directly with teachers, others include within their concept line officers who have responsibilities for curriculum and instruction. Because many line administrators do engage in supervision, they should be trained in supervision as are those who pursue full-time careers in supervision. It is an unfortunate commentary on the licensing process in many states that the requirements for preparation of administrators and supervisors, which are often minimal, are identical. By taking a handful of college courses in educational administration and supervision, a person can become certified in both administration and supervision.

However delightful such an arrangement is for prospective administrators and supervisors, as one preparation program opens up two job markets, differentiation in training programs for administrators and supervisors remains a crying need of the profession. The training requirements of these two related careers are not identical.

TASKS OF SUPERVISION

We can gain a clearer insight into the field of supervision by focusing our attention on what supervisors actually do. As long ago as 1922, William H. Burton listed the tasks he saw as pertinent to the supervisor. These tasks, which some might label *arenas*, are delineated here.

1. The improvement of the teaching act (classroom visits, individual and group conference, directed teaching, demonstration teaching, development of standards for self-improvement, etc.).
2. The improvement of teachers in service (teachers' meetings, professional readings, bibliographies and reviews, bulletins, intervisitation, self-analysis and criticism, etc.).
3. The selection and organization of subject-matter (setting up objectives, studies of subject-matter and learning activities, experimental testing of materials, constant revision of courses, the selection and evaluation of supplementary instructional materials, etc.).
4. Testing and measuring (the use of standardized and local tests for classification, diagnosis, guidance, etc.).
5. The rating of teachers (the development and use of rating cards and checklists, stimulation of self-rating).[22]

A. S. Barr, William H. Burton, and Leo J. Brueckner considered Burton's listing "the first modern statement and concept" of supervision.[23] Burton's list looks surprisingly current when we examine the numerous tasks that today's supervisors actually perform.

Writing a half century later, Harris enumerated ten tasks of supervision in the following rather detailed list:

Task 1. *Developing curriculum.* Designing or redesigning that which is to be taught, by whom, when, where, and in what pattern. Developing curriculum guides, establishing standards, planning instructional units, and instituting new courses are examples of this area.

Task 2. *Organizing for instruction.* Making arrangements whereby pupils, staff, space, and materials are related to time and instructional objectives in coordinate and efficient ways. Grouping of students, planning class schedules, assigning spaces, allocating time for instruction, scheduling, planning events, and arranging for teaching teams are examples of the endeavors associated with this task area.

Task 3. *Providing staff.* Assuring the availability of instructional staff members in adequate numbers and with appropriate competencies for facilitating instruction. Recruiting, screening, selecting, assigning, and transferring staff are endeavors in this task area.

Task 4. *Providing facilities.* Designing or redesigning and equipping facilities for instruction. The development of space and equipment specifications is included in this task area.

Task 5.   *Providing materials.* Selecting and obtaining appropriate materials for use in implementing curricular designs. Previewing, evaluating, designing, and otherwise finding ways to provide appropriate materials are included in this task area.

Task 6.   *Arranging for in-service education.* Planning and implementing learning experiences that will improve the performance of the staff in instruction-related ways. This involves workshops, consultations, field trips, and training sessions, as well as formal education.

Task 7.   *Orienting staff members.* Providing staff members with basic information necessary to carry out assigned responsibilities. This includes getting new staff members acquainted with facilities, staff, and community, but it also involves keeping the staff informed of organizational developments.

Task 8.   *Relating special pupil services.* Arranging for careful coordination of services to children to ensure optimum support for the teaching process. This involves developing policies, assigning priorities, and defining relationships among service personnel to maximize relationships between services offered and instructional goals of the school.

Task 9.   *Developing public relations.* Providing for a free flow of information on matters of instruction to and from the public while securing optimum levels of involvement in the promotion of better instruction.

Task 10.   *Evaluating instruction.* Planning, instrumenting, organizing, and implementing procedures for data gathering, analysis, and interpretation, and decision making for improvement of instruction.[24]

Harris classified tasks 1, 3, and 4 as preliminary, 6 and 10 as developmental, and the others as operational.[25] You will note both similarities and differences in the Burton and Harris listings. We can find supervision specialists who would be willing to accept either compilation of supervisory tasks. On the other hand, we can find experts in the field who would reject both lists. Those who view supervision as a one-to-one, clinical relationship between the teacher and supervisor would eliminate many of the tasks from both lists. Those who view supervision as a field distinct from administration would delegate administrative tasks like scheduling, staffing, and public relations to the administrator rather than to the instructional supervisor.

What is more revealing about the functions of supervisors are the statements of expectations as shown in the job descriptions of various school personnel. In Appendix B are several examples of actual job descriptions of supervisory personnel at the school, district, and intermediate unit level. Were we to compare these examples with illustrations from other school systems, we would inevitably discover differences in the duties assigned to the various personnel even though they may bear the same titles. What is universally true throughout school systems, however, is that much is expected of all supervisors.

A MODEL OF SUPERVISION

The supervisor plays a variety of roles within certain domains, and the expertise demonstrated in the particular domains is derived from a number of bases or foundations. One way to explain the dimensions of supervisory behavior is in the form of a schematic model. Figure 1.4 (page 22) depicts the concept of supervision followed in this text.

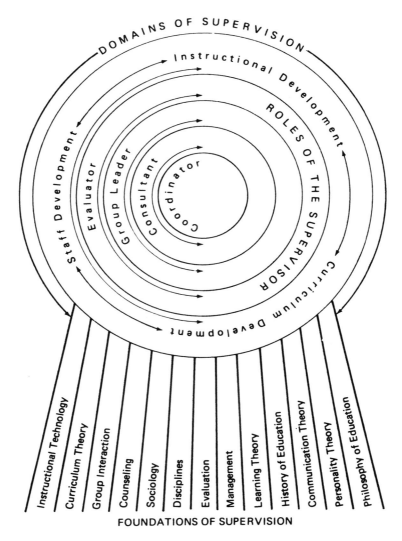

Figure 1.4. A Conceptual Model of Supervision.

The model shows three large domains or territories within which supervisors work. Within the model, several concentric wheels rest on a foundational bed. The four inner wheels show four primary roles of the supervisor, and the outer wheel surrounds the three supervisory domains. The foundational bed undergirds the whole system and indicates the sources of the supervisor's knowledge and skills.

The conceptual design of this model conveys the notion that supervision is both dynamic and service-oriented. The dynamic nature of the model is shown by the arrows, which indicate that any of the wheels may turn in either direction. This conceptual model depicts the supervisor's playing four major roles—coordinator, consultant, group leader, and evaluator—in three domains—instructional development, curriculum development, and staff development.

A model of this nature can quickly reveal the concepts held by the person who designs it. We can show this by taking the same basic design and following a different set of assumptions about the role(s) of the supervisor. Some people, for example, might take issue with the three domains, cut them to one or two, or expand them beyond three. They might eliminate supervisory duties in curriculum development, leaving instructional development and staff development. They might restrict supervision to instructional development and delimit it to clinical supervision. They might delete instructional development as well as curriculum development, allowing only staff development to remain. They might feel in so doing that instructional development—that is, improvement in the classroom—is a by-product or part of staff development. To them, staff development would mean assistance to teachers in improving personal and professional qualities.

In restricting the domains to staff development alone, these people might perceive the roles of the supervisor as two in number: consultant to individual teachers and consultant to groups of teachers. Some might even go further and restrict the supervisor to one role: consultant to individual teachers, or simply, trusted colleague.

In presenting the model of supervision shown here, we have taken the position that supervisors do and should work in all three domains and carry out at least the four roles. This model can accommodate limited and required administrative functions of supervisory personnel through the four roles already charted.

Domains of Supervision

The supervisor exercises various roles within each of three domains: instructional, curricular, and staff development. Following one or more of these major areas, the supervisor assists teachers in the improvement of instruction, curriculum planning and improvement, and personal and professional growth and development. In fulfilling the various roles within these domains the supervisor must bring to bear a wide repertoire of knowledge, skills, and techniques. Floyd C. Mann referred to the skills needed by supervisors as a "skill-mix," consisting of technical, managerial, and human relations skills.[26] Alfonso, Firth, and Neville have also given attention to the skill-mix necessary to instructional supervision.[27]

In Figure 1.4, two-headed arrows connect the three domains to show that all are interrelated and overlap. Staff development activities may focus on personal growth, instructional development, or curriculum development. When a supervisor works, for example, as a group leader in curriculum development, he or she may at the same time work in the domain of instructional development and/or staff development.

Edward Pajak headed a recent study on identification of supervisory proficiencies sponsored by the Association for Supervision and Curriculum Development. Through reviewing the literature on supervision and surveying instructional leaders, Pajak affirmed twelve domains with relevant knowledge, attitudes, and skills in each domain.[28] These domains and their definitions are cited below:

- Community Relations—Establishing and maintaining open and productive relations between the school and its community;

- Staff Development—Developing and facilitating meaningful opportunities for professional growth;
- Planning and Change—Initiating and implementing collaboratively developed strategies for continuous improvement;
- Communication—Ensuring open and clear communication among individuals and groups through the organization;
- Curriculum—Coordinating and integrating the process of curriculum development and implementation;
- Instructional Program—Supporting and coordinating efforts to improve the instructional program;
- Service to Teachers—Providing materials, resources, and assistance to support teaching and learning;
- Observation and Conferencing—Providing feedback to teachers based on classroom observation;
- Problem Solving and Decision Making—Using a variety of strategies to clarify and analyze problems and to make decisions;
- Research and Program Evaluation—Encouraging experimentation and assessing outcomes;
- Motivating and Organizing—Helping people to develop a shared vision and achieve collective aims;
- Personal Development—Recognizing and reflecting upon one's personal and professional beliefs, abilities, and action.[29]

Eleven of the twelve domains—essentially ways of working with individuals and groups within the schools—are central to this text. The external aspects of the supervisor's job—that is, community relations, which is certainly an important domain not only for supervisors but also for administrators, teachers, and other school personnel—find less treatment here. For help in the domain of community relations, the reader should consult some of the literature on public relations, building community support, and power structure.[30] Building positive community relations is extremely important for every school person. However, the designated administrator should assume the primary task of leadership in community relations and allow the instructional supervisor to concentrate on the task for which he or she is uniquely equipped: service to teachers.

Varying Roles

The roles supervisors play vary from locality to locality and from state to state. They are defined by the superintendents or principals to whom the supervisors are responsible and, as happens in most positions of leadership, by the supervisors themselves. Although some variation will be found in the roles supervisors may fulfill, more than likely the service-oriented supervisor will perform at varying times each of the four roles shown in the model.

Coordinator. The supervisor serves as a coordinator of programs, groups, materials, and reports. It is the supervisor who acts as a link between programs and people. He or she knows the disparate pieces of the educational process and directs the actions of others to make the pieces blend. As a director of staff development, the supervisor plans with teachers, arranges, evaluates, and often conducts in-service programs for teachers.

Consultant. The supervisor serves in a consulting capacity as a specialist in curriculum, instructional methodology, and staff development. In this capacity, he or she renders service to both individual teachers and groups. At times, the supervisor may simply furnish necessary information and suggestions. At other times, he or she may help teachers to define, set, and pursue goals. The supervisor should be a prime source of assistance to teachers wishing to improve either their generic or specialized teaching skills. Though some will disagree with us, we believe the supervisor-consultant should be able to demonstrate a repertoire of teaching strategies.

Group Leader. The supervisor as group leader works continuously to release the potential of groups seeking to improve the curriculum, instruction, or themselves. To perform this role the supervisor must be knowledgeable about group dynamics and must demonstrate leadership skills. The supervisor assists groups in consensus building, in moving toward group goals, and in perfecting the democratic process. As a group leader, the supervisor seeks, identifies, and fosters leadership from within the group.

Evaluator. As an evaluator, the supervisor provides assistance to teachers in evaluating instruction and curriculum. The supervisor helps teachers find answers to curricular and instructional problems, identify research studies that may have a bearing on their problems, and conduct limited research projects. Additionally, the supervisor helps teachers evaluate their classroom performance, assess their own strengths and weaknesses, and select means of overcoming their deficiencies.

Foundations of Supervision

The supports that constitute the bed for the wheel of supervision are areas of learning from which the supervisor derives expertise. The large number of areas from which a knowledgeable and skilled supervisor must draw suggests the need for a broad training program in preparation for work as a supervisor.

When we study the conceptual model of supervision, with its domains, roles, and foundations, we can deduce competencies that supervisors should be able to demonstrate. Supervisors should possess (1) certain personal traits and (2) certain types of knowledge and skills.

Personal Traits. The literature on supervision is remarkably silent on what personal characteristics are necessary for successful supervisory behavior. Perhaps this silence can be attributed to one or more of the following reasons.

1. Personal characteristics can be inferred from the skills supervisors should possess. Thus, if supervisors are expected to demonstrate a high degree of skill in human or interpersonal relations, they should exhibit human and humane traits like empathy, warmth, and sincerity.
2. Educational research has been notably unsuccessful in identifying personal qualities common to all successful administrators and supervisors. The presence of generally valued personal traits in a leader does not guarantee suc-

cess on the job, nor does the absence of these traits assure failure. Because the search for universal traits has been unproductive, the experts have concentrated on the more certain requisite knowledge and skills.

3. Personal traits necessary for success in positions of leadership appear so obvious that they need no elaboration. Some specialists in the field may feel that a compendium of supervisory traits is similar to the oath that Boy Scouts take, promising to be trustworthy, loyal, helpful, friendly, and so on.

4. The search for personal traits is a somewhat dated activity at a time when researchers are attempting to identify competencies that school personnel should demonstrate. Nevertheless, in spite of these encumbrances, let's briefly consider the question of personal characteristics needed by supervisory personnel. The successful supervisor is in constant contact with people and should possess those personal traits of warmth, friendliness, patience, and a sense of humor that are essential not only to supervision but also to teaching. As a service-oriented agent for improvement, the supervisor must be imbued with the spirit counselors refer to as "the helping relationship," the desire to give of oneself in order to be of assistance to others. Beyond this, the supervisor needs a type of persuasiveness and infectious enthusiasm to cause teachers to want to make changes for the better.

The supervisor should be an "idea person," one who leads people to think about new and improved ways of doing things. He or she needs to convey the attitude of valuing and seeking the ideas of others while not appearing to have answers to all the problems teachers face.

The supervisor who is a helper to teachers is able to effect a democratic environment in which the contributions of each participating member are valued. Above all, the supervisor needs to possess a predisposition to change and must constantly promote improvement. If supervisors, whose chief responsibility is to bring about improvements, are satisfied with the status quo, they can be sure that the teachers will be too. The supervisor must be able to live with change and help teachers adapt to changing needs of society and of children and youth. To accomplish this mission the supervisor should be able to work effectively in both one-to-one relationships and in groups.

Knowledge and Skills. Although personal traits of supervisors are not often discussed, we can find an abundance of statements about the knowledge and skills successful supervisors need. There is general agreement that supervisors should have

- A sound general education program
- A thorough preservice professional education program
- A major field of study
- A solid graduate program in supervision
- Three to five years of successful teaching at the elementary, middle, or secondary school level

In preservice and in-service training programs, supervisors should develop a grounding in

- Learning theory and educational psychology
- Philosophy of education
- History of education, especially of curriculum and instructional development
- The role of the school in society
- Curriculum development
- Instructional design and methods
- Group dynamics
- Conferencing and counseling
- Assessment of teacher performance

Lovell and Wiles pointed to necessary knowledge and skills when they wrote that supervision is

- Releasing human potential
- Leadership
- Communications
- Coordinating and facilitating change
- Curriculum development
- Facilitating human development[31]

Alfonso, Firth, and Neville drew implications for instructional supervisory behavior from organization leadership, communication, decision making, and change theories.[32]

Read the table of contents of any textbook on supervision and you will see the broad knowledge and special skills demanded by the profession. To identify knowledge and skills required for effective supervision, we may also turn to Figure 1.4 and analyze the domains, roles, and foundations presented in the conceptual model. To perform effectively, the supervisor must possess broad knowledge of both a general and professional nature and be able to translate that knowledge into skillful practice. At appropriate points in this book, you will encounter further discussion of the knowledge and skills essential to instructional supervisors.

People considering the job of supervisor might begin by taking a look at themselves. They should decide whether they possess the fund of knowledge and skills required by the job. Prospective supervisors should ponder whether they have the personality for dealing with teachers in a supervisory capacity. They should know whether they enjoy working intimately with people in a helping relationship. A beginning point in supervision is the determination by the prospective supervisor of his or her adequacy to fill the roles demanded.

SUMMARY

The roles and titles of supervisory personnel vary among the school systems of the nation. Supervision is defined in this text as a service provided to teachers for the purpose of improving instruction, with the student as the ultimate beneficiary.

A supervisor is a trained auxiliary or staff person whose primary function is the provision of service according to a conceptual model. The model presented in this chapter portrays the supervisor as fulfilling the roles of coordinator, consultant, group leader, and evaluator within the domains of instructional, curricular, and staff development.

The supervisor should possess personal traits that will enable him or her to work harmoniously with people and sufficient knowledge and skills to perform all functions effectively. Leadership, interpersonal, and communications skills appear to be especially important to successful supervision. Supervisors should possess a judicious mix of technical, managerial, and human relations skills.

Supervisors perform a wide variety of tasks, which may or may not include administrative duties. The focus of this book is on instructional supervision, which is an inclusive term to signify service to teachers in developing the curriculum, instruction, and themselves.

QUESTIONS FOR DISCUSSION

1. Are there other domains of supervision besides those shown in Figure 1.4 or cited from the Pajak study?
2. Do supervisors have roles besides those shown in Figure 1.4?
3. Are there other foundations of supervision besides those shown in Figure 1.4?
4. How would you describe the status of instructional supervision?
5. Are there too many supervisors in our school systems?

ACTIVITIES FOR FURTHER STUDY

1. Cite at least four definitions of supervision to be found in references at the end of this chapter, show their similarities and differences, state whether you agree or disagree with each definition, and give reasons for your position.
2. Formulate your own definition of supervision.
3. Design your own conceptual model of supervision.
4. Poll a sample of teachers and inquire (a) whether they know what supervisory help is available to them and (b) how they perceive the functions of each supervisor.
5. Identify at least two improvements in curriculum and/or instruction that have been made in a particular school system in the last three years and postulate on how these came about.
6. State your position on the following questions:
   a. Is the principal a supervisor? Why or why not?
   b. Would our system of education be better if the U.S. Department of Education employed inspectors to check on instruction throughout the country? Give reasons for your answer.
   c. Would our system of education be better if state departments of education regularly sent out inspectors to check on instruction throughout their states? Why or why not?
   d. How much teaching experience is essential for a person to be an effective supervisor?
7. Inquire of several teachers how often supervisors visited them in their classrooms during the past school year. Identify the supervisors by title, such as assistant principal for curriculum, supervisor of language arts, and so on.

8. Interview and obtain a job description, if available, for one or more of the following supervisors and write a brief description of their chief duties based on the interview:
   a. Assistant superintendent for curriculum and instruction
   b. General supervisor
   c. Team leader
   d. Grade coordinator (grade chairperson)
   e. Lead teacher
   f. Department head
   g. Director of elementary, middle, junior, or senior high schools
9. Describe supervisory assistance available to teachers in your field from the following sources:
   a. State department of education
   b. Cooperative (regional) educational service agencies (intermediate school district level)
   c. School superintendent's office
10. Write a short paper, using references in the bibliography at the end of this chapter, expanding on the list of qualifications of supervisors discussed in the chapter.
11. Write a short paper, using references in the bibliography at the end of this chapter, expanding on the functions, roles, or tasks of supervisors discussed in the chapter.
12. Outline a desirable university training program for supervisors and compare it with a training program with which you are familiar.
13. Tape an interview with a supervisor on the central office staff and write a summary covering the following points: (a) How does the supervisor perceive his or her role? (b) What are major problems in supervision as he or she sees them? (c) What training is required for the job?
14. Outline the state requirements for certification as (a) a school principal and (b) a supervisor. Write a brief summary contrasting the differences, if any, and comparing the similarities.
15. Examine the staffing pattern of a school system you know well and list as many different types of supervisors as you can discover.
16. Following the concept of a skill-mix, list specific (a) technical, (b) managerial, and (c) human relations skills that you believe are needed by a supervisor.
17. Write an analysis of your own knowledge, skills, and personal traits as they bear on the role of the supervisor. Describe your strengths and indicate areas in which you feel you need improvement.
18. Use Appendix A, "Exit Competencies," as a self-diagnosis instrument by rating yourself on each competency to determine the degree to which you believe you can now demonstrate the particular competency. Rate yourself by applying this scale: 5—completely competent; 4—high degree of competence; 3—average degree of competence; 2—limited degree of competence; 1—lack of competence.

NOTES

1. Ben M. Harris, *Supervisory Behavior in Education*, 3rd ed. (Englewood Cliffs, N.J.: Prentice-Hall, 1985), pp. 1–2.
2. Peter F. Oliva, *Developing the Curriculum*, 3rd ed. (New York: HarperCollins, 1992), pp. 30–45.

3. See ibid., pp. 554–57.

4. Walter Herbert Small, *Early New England Schools* (Boston: Ginn and Company, 1941), p. 340. Reprinted by Arno Press and *The New York Times*, New York, 1969.

5. Elwood P. Cubberley, *Public School Administration* (Boston: Houghton Mifflin, 1922), pp. 58–59.

6. See G. Alfred Hess, Jr., *Empowering Teachers and Parents: School Restructuring through the Eyes of Anthropologists* (Westport, Conn.: Bergin & Garvey, 1992).

7. Edgar L. Morphet, Roe L. Johns, and Theodore L. Reller, *Educational Organization and Administration*, 4th ed. (Englewood Cliffs, N.J.: Prentice-Hall, 1982), pp. 79–82.

8. William H. Lucio and John D. McNeil, *Supervision: A Synthesis of Thought and Action*, 2nd ed. (New York: McGraw-Hill, 1969), p. 3.

9. Ralph L. Mosher and David E. Purpel, *Supervision: The Reluctant Profession* (Boston: Houghton Mifflin, 1972), p. 3.

10. William H. Burton and Leo J. Brueckner, *Supervision: A Social Process*, 3rd ed. (New York: Appleton-Century-Crofts, 1955), p. 11.

11. Jane Franseth, *Supervision as Leadership* (Evanston, Ill.: Row, Peterson, 1961), p. 19.

12. Ross L. Neagley and N. Dean Evans, *Handbook for Effective Supervision of Instruction*, 3rd ed. (Englewood Cliffs, N.J.: Prentice-Hall, 1980), p. 20.

13. Harris, *Supervisory Behavior*, pp. 10–11.

14. Robert J. Alfonso, Gerald R. Firth, and Richard F. Neville, *Instructional Supervision: A Behavioral System*, 2nd ed. (Boston: Allyn & Bacon, 1981), p. 43.

15. John T. Lovell and Kimball Wiles, *Supervision for Better Schools*, 5th ed. (Englewood Cliffs, N.J.: Prentice-Hall, 1983), p. 4.

16. Don M. Beach and Judy Reinhartz, *Supervision: Focus on Instruction* (New York: Harper & Row, 1989), p. 8.

17. Robert D. Krey and Peter J. Burke, *A Design for Instructional Supervision* (Springfield, Ill.: Charles C. Thomas, 1989), p. 22.

18. Thomas J. Sergiovanni and Robert J. Starratt, *Supervision: A Redefinition*, 5th ed. (New York: McGraw-Hill, 1993), p. 18.

19. John C. Daresh and Marsha A. Playko, *Supervision as a Proactive Process: Concepts and Cases*, 2nd ed. (Prospect Heights, Ill.: Waveland Press, 1995), p. 26.

20. Mosher and Purpel, *op. cit.*

21. Arthur Blumberg, *Supervisors and Teachers: A Private Cold War* (Berkeley, Calif.: McCutchan, 1980), pp. 5–6.

22. William H. Burton, *Supervision and the Improvement of Teaching* (New York: D. Appleton-Century, 1922), pp. 9–10.

23. A. S. Barr, William H. Burton, and Leo J. Brueckner, *Supervision: Democratic Leadership in the Improvement of Learning*, 2nd ed. (New York: Appleton-Century-Crofts, 1947), p. 5.

24. Harris, *Supervisory Behavior*, pp. 10–12.

25. Ibid., p. 13.

26. Floyd C. Mann, "Toward an Understanding of the Leadership Role in Formal Organization," in *Supervision and Productivity*, ed. Robert Dubin (San Francisco: Chandler, 1965), pp. 773–77.

27. Alfonso, Firth, and Neville, *Instructional Supervision*, pp. 12–13, 14, 73–74, 322–67, 452, 457–59, 480–81.

28. Edward Pajak, *Identification of Supervisory Proficiencies Project* (Athens, Ga.: College of Education, University of Georgia, 1989).

29. Ibid., pp. 4–5.

30. See, for example, George E. Pawlas, *Administrator's Guide to School-Community Relations* (Princeton, N.J.: Eye on Education, 1995); Ralph B. Kimbrough and Michael Y. Nunnery,

Educational Administration: An Introduction, 3rd ed. (New York: Macmillan, 1988); and Don Bagin, Donald R. Gallagher, and Leslie W. Kindred, *The School and Community Relations*, 5th ed. (Boston: Allyn & Bacon, 1994).

31. Lovell and Wiles, *Supervision for Better Schools*, pp. 3–6, 8, 10.
32. Alfonso, Firth, and Neville, *Instructional Supervision*, Part II.

BIBLIOGRAPHY

Alberty, Harold B., and V. T. Thayer. *Supervision in the Secondary School*. Boston: D. C. Heath, 1931.

Alfonso, Robert J., Gerald R. Firth, and Richard F. Neville. *Instructional Supervision: A Behavior System*, 2nd ed. Boston: Allyn & Bacon, 1981.

Bagin, Don, Donald R. Gallagher, and Leslie W. Kindred. *The School and Community Relations*, 5th ed. Boston: Allyn & Bacon, 1994.

Barr, A. S., and William H. Burton. *The Supervision of Instruction: A General Volume*. New York: D. Appleton & Company, 1926.

Barr, A. S., William H. Burton, and Leo J. Brueckner. *Supervision: Democratic Leadership in the Improvement of Learning*, 2nd ed. New York: Appleton-Century-Crofts, 1947.

Beach, Don M., and Judy Reinhartz. *Supervision: Focus on Instruction*. New York: Harper & Row, 1989.

Blumberg, Arthur. *Supervisors and Teachers: A Private Cold War*, 2nd ed. Berkeley, Calif.: McCutchan, 1980.

Bobbitt, Franklin. *The Supervision of City Schools*. Chicago: University of Chicago Press, 1913.

Burnham, Reba, and Martha L. King. *Supervision in Action*. Alexandria, Va.: Association for Supervision and Curriculum Development, 1961.

Burton, William H. *Supervision and the Improvement of Teaching*. New York: D. Appleton and Company, 1922.

Burton, William H., and Leo J. Brueckner. *Supervision: A Social Process*, 3rd ed. New York: Appleton-Century-Crofts, 1955.

Cooper, James M., ed. *Developing Skills for Instructional Supervision*. White Plains, N.Y.: Longman, 1984.

Cubberley, Elwood P. *Public School Administration*. Boston: Houghton Mifflin, 1922.

Daresh, John C., and Marsha A. Playko. *Supervision as a Proactive Process*, 2nd ed. Prospect Heights, Ill.: Waveland Press, 1995.

Duke, Daniel L. *School Leadership and Instructional Improvement*. New York: Random House, 1987.

Dull, Lloyd W. *Supervision: School Leadership Handbook*. Columbus, Ohio: Merrill, 1981.

Eye, Glen G., Lanore A. Netzer, and Robert D. Krey. *Supervision of Instruction*, 2nd ed. New York: Harper & Row, 1971.

Firth, Gerald R., and Edward Pajak, eds. *Handbook of Research on School Supervision*. New York: Macmillan (in press).

Franseth, Jane. *Supervision as Leadership*. Evanston, Ill.: Row, Peterson, 1961.

Glatthorn, Allan A. *Differentiated Supervision*. Alexandria, Va.: Association for Supervision and Curriculum Development, 1984.

———. *Supervisory Leadership: Introduction to Instructional Supervision*. Glenview, Il.: Scott, Foresman, 1990.

Glickman, Carl D., ed. *Supervision in Transition*. 1992 Yearbook. Alexandria, Va.: Association for Supervision and Curriculum Development, 1992.

Glickman, Carl D., Stephen P. Gordon, and Jovita M. Ross-Gordon. *Supervision of Instruction: A Developmental Approach*, 3rd ed. Boston: Allyn & Bacon, 1995.

Goldstein, William. *Supervision Made Simple.* Bloomington, Ill.: Phi Delta Kappa Educational Foundation, 1982.

Greenfield, William, ed. *Instructional Leadership: Concepts, Issues, and Controversies.* Boston: Allyn & Bacon, 1986.

Grimsley, Edith E., and Ray E. Bruce. *Readings in Educational Supervision from Educational Leadership*, 2nd ed. Alexandria, Va.: Association for Supervision and Curriculum Development, 1987.

Gwynne, J. Minor. *Theory and Practice of Supervision.* New York: Dodd, Mead, 1961.

Harris, Ben M. *Supervisory Behavior in Education*, 3rd ed. Englewood Cliffs, N.J.: Prentice-Hall, 1985.

Harrison, Raymond H. *Supervisory Leadership in Education.* New York: American Book Company, 1968.

Hess, G. Alfred, Jr., ed. *Empowering Teachers and Parents: School Restructuring through the Eyes of Anthropologists.* Westport, Conn.: Bergin & Garvey, 1992.

Hicks, Hanne J. *Educational Supervision in Principle and Practice.* New York: Ronald Press, 1960.

Hoy, Wayne K., and Patrick B. Forsyth. *Effective Supervision: Theory into Practice.* New York: Random House, 1986.

Kimbrough, Ralph B., and Michael Y. Nunnery. *Educational Administration: An Introduction*, 3rd ed. New York: Macmillan, 1988.

Krey, Robert D., and Peter J. Burke. *A Design for Instructional Supervision.* Springfield, Ill.: Charles C. Thomas, 1989.

Kyte, George C. *How to Supervise: A Guide to Educational Principles and Progressive Practices of Educational Supervision.* Boston: Houghton Mifflin, 1930.

Leeper, Robert R., ed. *Role of Supervisor and Curriculum Director in a Climate of Change.* Alexandria, Va.: Association of Supervision and Curriculum Development, 1965.

Leeper, Robert R., and Fred T. Wilhelms, eds. *Supervision: Emerging Profession.* Alexandria, Va.: Association for Supervision and Curriculum Development, 1969.

Lewis, Arthur J., and Alice Miel. *Supervision for Improved Instruction: New Challenges, New Responses.* Belmont, Calif.: Wadsworth, 1972.

Lovell, John T., and Kimball Wiles. *Supervision for Better Schools*, 5th ed. Englewood Cliffs, N.J.: Prentice-Hall, 1983.

Lucio, William H., ed. *Supervision: Perspectives and Propositions.* Alexandria, Va.: Association for Supervision and Curriculum Development, 1967.

Lucio, William H., and John D. McNeil. *Supervision: A Synthesis of Thought and Action*, 2nd ed. New York: McGraw-Hill, 1969.

———. *Supervision: A Synthesis of Thought and Action*, 3rd ed. New York: McGraw-Hill, 1979.

Mann, Floyd C. "Toward an Understanding of the Leadership Role in Formal Organization." In *Supervision and Productivity*, edited by Robert Dubin, pp. 773–77. San Francisco: Chandler, 1965.

McKean, Robert C., and H. H. Mills. *The Supervisor.* New York: Center for Applied Research in Education, 1964.

McNerney, Chester T. *Educational Supervision.* New York: McGraw-Hill, 1951.

Maeroff, Gene. *The Empowerment of Teachers: Overcoming the Crisis of Confidence.* New York: Teachers College Press, 1988.

Marks, James R., Emery Stoops, and Joyce King-Stoops. *Handbook of Educational Supervision: A Guide for the Practitioner*, 3rd ed. Boston: Allyn & Bacon, 1985.

Melchior, William T. *Instructional Supervision: A Guide to Modern Practice.* Boston: D. C. Heath, 1950.

Morphet, Edgar L., Roe L. Johns, and Theodore L. Reller. *Educational Organization and Administration*, 4th ed. Englewood Cliffs, N. J.: Prentice-Hall, 1982.

Mosher, Ralph L., and David E. Purpel. *Supervision: The Reluctant Profession*. Boston: Houghton Mifflin, 1972.

Neagley, Ross L., and H. Dean Evans. *Handbook for Effective Supervision of Instruction*, 3rd ed. Englewood Cliffs, N.J.: Prentice-Hall, 1980.

Nutt, Hubert Wilbur. *The Supervision of Instruction*. Boston: Houghton Mifflin, 1920.

Oliva, Peter F. *Developing the Curriculum*, 4th ed. New York: HarperCollins, 1997.

Pajak, Edward. *The Central Office Supervisor of Curriculum and Instruction: Setting the Stage for Success*. Boston: Allyn & Bacon, 1989.

———. *Identification of Supervisory Proficiencies Project*. Athens, Ga.: College of Education, University of Georgia, 1989.

Pawlas, George E. *Administrator's Guide to School-Community Relations*. Princeton, N. J.: Eye on Education, 1995.

Pfeiffer, Isobel, and Jane Dunlap. *Supervising Teachers: A Guide to Supervising Instruction*. Phoenix, Ariz.: Oryx Press, 1982.

Sergiovanni, Thomas J., ed. *Supervision of Teaching*. 1982 Yearbook. Alexandria, Va.: Association for Supervision and Curriculum Development, 1982.

Sergiovanni, Thomas J., and Robert J. Starratt. *Supervision: A Redefinition*, 5th ed. New York: McGraw-Hill, 1993.

Small, Walter Herbert. *Early New England Schools*. Boston: Ginn and Company, 1941. Reprinted by Arno Press and *The New York Times*, New York, 1969.

Stoller, Nathan. *Supervision and the Improvement of Instruction*. Englewood Cliffs, N.J.: Educational Technology Publications, 1978.

Swearingen, Mildred E. *Supervision of Instruction: Foundations and Dimensions*. Boston: Allyn & Bacon, 1962.

Tanner, Daniel, and Laurel N. Tanner. *Supervision in Education: Problems and Practices*. New York: Macmillan, 1987.

Unruh, Adolph, and Harold E. Turner. *Supervision for Change and Innovation*. Boston: Houghton Mifflin, 1970.

Wiles, Jon, and Joseph Bondi. *Supervision: A Guide to Practice*, 4th ed. Englewood Cliffs, N. J.: Merrill, 1995.

Videotape

The Principal as Instructional Leader. 1984. Approximately one hour. Teachers, principals of four schools, and three researchers discuss five leadership patterns common to effective school leaders. Association for Supervision and Curriculum Development, 1250 North Pitt Street, Alexandria, Va. 22314.

2

Issues in Supervision

Objectives

After studying Chapter 2 you should be able to accomplish the following objectives:

1. Identify several issues in supervision.
2. Explain varying positions on each issue.
3. Choose and defend your position on each issue.

NUMEROUS UNRESOLVED ISSUES

The educational world seems to attract unresolved problems or issues. Whether we are talking about learning theories or curriculum or methodology, there are no certainties to which we can subscribe. Take, for example, the specification of behavioral objectives. This procedure is roundly attacked by its opponents and strongly supported by its adherents. As with many issues, a polarity has developed, with vocal camps on both sides. One camp holds the writing of behavioral objectives to be a waste of time; extremists in the opposite camp feel that teaching can scarcely survive unless teachers design behavioral objectives.

Somewhere between these poles are groups who champion portions of an issue and reject other aspects. For instance, some educators encourage behavioral objectives in the cognitive and psychomotor domains but not the affective; others insist on behavioral objectives in all three. Some claim that it is impossible to write behavioral objectives in the affective domain; others assert that affective objectives must be specified. Some advocate a formulalike approach to writing objectives; others are willing to be more permissive. Some accept general goals in place of specific objectives; others accept only objectives that can be observed and measured. When we discuss helping teachers plan for instruction, we will return to the issue of behavioral objectives. We introduce it at this point solely as an illustration of one controversial issue in professional education, of which there are many. If we were to compile a quick list of current controversies in education relative to curriculum or instruction, our list would surely include those listed below.

- Corporal punishment
- Behavior modification
- Mainstreaming full inclusion of handicapped children
- Charter schools
- Multicultural education
- Inquiry learning
- Bilingual education
- Integration of subject matter
- Minimal competencies for graduation
- Alternative assessment options
- State assessment of student achievement
- Methods of teaching reading
- Alternative scheduling
- Placement of subject matter
- Grouping learners
- Role of vocational education

This list, far from being a complete set of issues in education, illustrates unresolved problems with which supervisors must contend. Like its companion disciplines, sociology and psychology, education is besieged with problems because by their very nature, education, sociology, and psychology are imprecise sciences. These social and behavioral sciences lack precision primarily because they deal with human beings. Unlike machines, people are notoriously unpredictable. Whereas natural scientists may manipulate elements and equipment in the laboratories, the social and behavioral scientists have difficulty manipulating people. People, especially in a literate, democratic environment, tend to reject manipulation. Of course, we can all point to exceptions, as studies of mob behavior, demagoguery, and totalitarianism readily show. People living in a democracy, however, prefer to think through answers to problems themselves. As a result, we often find that there are multiple answers to specific problems. The presence of multiple answers causes consternation for many people in education who are seeking *the* definitive answers to particular problems. We cannot even be sure, for example, that 5 plus 4 equals 9. If we are working with a base of 6 instead of 10, 5 plus 4 equals 13. Perhaps John Dewey and his progressive followers were right after all when they averred that truth was relative.

To know whether 5 plus 4 equals 9 or 13, we must know, as they say in that esoteric language called psychobabble, "where you're coming from." If you're working in base 6 and trying to communicate with a person who thinks in base 10—and who believes 10 is the only base possible—the message does not get through. Thus, for those who see a supervisor only as a specialist who works with individual teachers, many of the issues in the field are either nonexistent or spurious.

Because supervision, along with teaching, counseling, and administration, is one of the subsystems of the enterprise of education, we should not be surprised to find it embroiled in a number of unresolved problems. Supervision may even be confronted with more issues than the other subsystems because the role of the supervisor is drawn so ambiguously. Teachers, counselors, and administrators usually have a clearer perspective of their behavior systems and the roles expected of them than do supervisors. We can show the relationships among these four major behavior systems in Figure 2.1.

All systems interact with each other. The four behavior systems shown here meet, relate, reinforce, and sometimes lock horns. The educational commons where the four come together (shaded area on the diagram) is both bedecked with roses and strewn with nettles. The supervisory behavior system is enclosed with a broken circle to indicate that its borders are less firm than those of the other three subsystems. Whereas the uncertainty of the supervisor's role creates some problems, at the same time it has the saving grace of permitting specialists the opportunity to refine the role. In this respect, supervision is more malleable than the other systems.

Working Group of the Association for Supervision and Curriculum Development (ASCD)

The Executive Council of the Association for Supervision and Curriculum Development (ASCD) in 1975 created the Working Group on Supervisory Practices, which identified issues in supervision. The Working Group surveyed 163 public

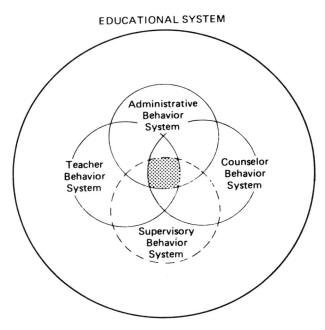

Figure 2.1. Relationships among Four Major Behavior Systems.

school supervisors and others associated with colleges and universities, all of whom were members of ASCD. The public school personnel made up 70 percent of the respondents. Those surveyed ranked the following seven statements[1] (which we have restated as questions) as high-priority issues.

1. Should supervisors evaluate teachers or should they evaluate instruction only?
2. Should supervisors help individual teachers or should they provide leadership for instructional change?
3. Should the teacher and the school's program be the central focus of supervision or should the emphasis be on the child and learning?
4. Should supervisors be proactive in initiating change or should they be reactive and respond to needs?
5. Should the supervisor's authority be based on expertise and interpersonal relationships or should it be based on conferred status and decision-making responsibility?
6. Should supervisors work to develop curricula and materials or should they work to improve instruction?
7. Should supervisors rely on teachers to promote their own improvement or should they work cooperatively with teachers toward fulfilling goals?

The respondents viewed another ten issues, listed next, as significant but less important.

1. Should supervision be carried out by generalists or by specialists?
2. Should supervisors be assigned instructional program responsibilities only or should they be members of the administrative staff?
3. Should supervisors maintain collegial relationships with principals or should they be members of the staff?
4. Should supervisors have assignments within a single school or should they be assigned to several schools?
5. Should the supervisor's schedule be highly structured or should it be flexible?
6. Should supervisors' assignments focus on program or subject tasks or on broad issues?
7. Should responsibility for supervision be diffused or should it be concentrated in the hands of the supervisory staff?
8. Is the supervisors' task to model, advise, and suggest or is it to facilitate, interest, and collaborate?
9. Should supervisors represent management in collective negotiations, should they represent teachers, or should they represent neither?
10. Should supervision be a team approach or should it be an individual assignment?

The seventeen issues identified by the ASCD Working Group showed some of the problems that members of the profession considered important. All these issues, and more, are still with us. Some persons may be inclined to say that the either/or dichotomy of these issues is unrealistic. They would conclude that supervisors must be occupied with both sides of the issue. They would take the position that you cannot, for example, evaluate instruction without evaluating teacher performance.

Yet affirming that supervisors must fulfill responsibilities on both sides of every issue is as simplistic as rejecting out of hand one side or the other. We do find supervisors devoting energies to both sides of some issues. In some few cases, they expend equal energies on the dual tasks. On the other hand, some supervisors throw greater efforts into one dimension of an issue than into the other. Generally, supervisors tend to lean toward one side of an issue, even if only slightly past the midpoint. They may not be Leaning Towers of Pisa with pronounced inclinations, but they lean far enough to show their preference.

An even larger question than where do supervisors spend their time is where *should* supervisors spend their energies? To answer the normative question *should*, we must bring to bear not only a knowledge of prevailing practice but also the philosophical assumptions we hold about supervision. We find so many conflicting views on what supervision is because the viewers start with varying sets of assumptions. This textbook, of course, is no exception. We present here certain positions for your consideration and analysis. We would be the last to say that every position—yes, and bias—in this book represents *the right answer*. "Right" answers are hard to come by. What is right for one situation may hopefully be right generally. On the other hand, what is right in one situation may not be right in other situations. We need to think in terms of *situational supervision* in much the same way we think of *situational leadership*. Leadership is a function of both the characteristics of the leader and of the situation in which the leader demonstrates his or her abilities. Successful supervision is the judicious application of the supervisor's knowledge and skills in a particular setting.

Practitioners, therefore, must exercise professional judgment in determining what is right in a given situation. However, practitioners must know what the options are, and if they reject a practice that has been found to be generally effective elsewhere, they should be able to explain their reasons.

In this chapter, we examine what we see as some of the more pressing issues in supervision:

1. Is supervision necessary?
2. For whom should supervision be provided?
3. Should the supervisor's authority be based on expertise and interpersonal relationships or on conferred status and decision-making responsibilities?
4. Should the supervisor be an administrator?
5. Is supervision staff development?
6. Is supervision curriculum development?
7. Is supervision evaluation?
8. Should supervisors work with groups of teachers or with individual teachers?
9. Should supervision be carried out by supervisors based in the central office or in the individual schools?
10. Should the supervisor use a directive or nondirective approach?
11. Should school systems organize for supervision by employing generalists or by hiring specialists?

12. Should there be national professional standards for teachers?

By their very nature, issues are problems whose answers are not fully settled and on which specialists may disagree. In the case of each issue you will see a figure representing a scale.

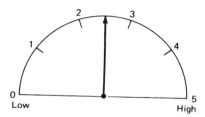

The reading shows graphically the position we have taken on each issue. The indicator moves from a low of zero to a high of five. Unless the indicator is all the way over to one side and touching, latitude has been left for some degree of responsibility on the other side of the issue. If the indicator remains in the middle, the reading should be interpreted as giving equal weight to both sides of the issue—taking the middle ground.

In the following pages, the positions we have taken apply to the instructional staff supervisor, the protagonist of this book. The positions may or may not be the same for line supervisors (administrators). When there are differences of this nature, we have noted it in the narrative. It is not the purpose of this discussion to persuade supervisors and prospective supervisors to accept the positions presented here but rather to help them think through the issues and reach their own decisions.

ISSUE 1: IS SUPERVISION NECESSARY?

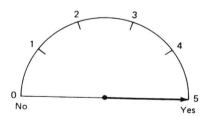

The question "Is supervision necessary?" may seem out of place in a text on supervision. The mere fact that there are supervisors and a body of literature on supervision would seem to indicate its necessity. Yet this fundamental question has probably not been given enough consideration. Teachers, administrators, and supervisors assume the necessity for supervision as a given. In their memory, supervisors have been like the firmament; they have always existed and so presumably they will always exist.

We might phrase the question in another way. Can we do without supervisors? As the system now operates, the answer is apparently that we cannot. Supervisors meet a need in our current educational structure and will undoubtedly continue to do so for a long time to come. Theoretically, however, we could dispense with the services of supervisors *if*—a very improbable if—all teachers were dynamic, knowledgeable, and skillful. In one sense, the supervisor is like the preacher who strives to make his or her parishioners into sinless beings. When all churchgoers have reached that happy, utopian state, the need for the minister will have been obviated. Because it is not likely that all humans will achieve this state of sinlessness, however, the task of the preacher will not be relegated to obsolescence. As not all teachers have reached a state of perfection, the need for supervision remains.

An assumption in this issue is that preservice programs do not turn out finished teachers. The typical training program consists of general education, concentration in a teaching field, and professional education. In a time of rapid development in all fields of knowledge, prospective teachers cannot begin to learn in college all that they will need to know when teaching. Nor can they gain a full mastery of techniques of instruction; study of curriculum and teaching constitutes only a beginning point. In many college programs, the work in curriculum and instruction occurs in a hypothetical context, which students may translate into practice only in limited participation programs and in student teaching. Student teaching gives the preservice teacher merely a taste of teaching—ten to twelve weeks in a school under the direction of a supervising teacher. It is impossible for teacher education institutions to assure perfection in their products. To the limited program must be added the differences among individuals themselves. Teachers develop their capacities at different rates of speed. Some are ready to move into the classroom with a sense of confidence and demonstrable ability at the end of—sometimes even before—the student teaching experience. Others will need a few years to develop their potential; some, unfortunately, will never become really good teachers. The assumption can be made then that teachers need the help of supervisors because they have not been fully prepared by their teacher education programs and because there is a great difference in their abilities and needs. Recognizing these differing abilities and needs, some teacher education institutions have offered "warranties," pledges that they will assist their graduates on the job in the beginning years of their career.[2]

Limitations of Teaching

By providing supervision, the educational system is declaring, in effect, that teachers are not completely free to run their own classrooms as they see fit. Limitations are imposed by school regulations, state legislative regulations, types of students, and types of communities. A supervisor is often more aware of or more sensitive to these limitations than teachers and can help teachers work within the restrictions.

Supervision skirts dangerously close to the issue of academic freedom, teachers' right to teach as they deem appropriate within their particular realm of competence. The doctrine of academic freedom, however, raises many questions. Do teachers have the right to teach topics that have been explicitly forbidden by the school board or administrators? Can teachers reject textbooks that have been adopted by a state textbook commission or by colleagues in their own grade or department?

May a teacher follow a curricular program that disrupts the sequence from one grade level to another?

Academic freedom has its limitations. Realistically, it is more limited on the public school level than in institutions of higher education. For a number of reasons, public schools are more susceptible to pressures from the community than are colleges and universities. This means that a public school teacher must live within certain limitations and must seek individuality within a context generally accepted in the school system. The supervisor helps teachers understand the context of their positions and find their own ways of teaching within that context. A simple illustration is the case of the teacher who does not like a particular textbook that is used in the school. The teacher cannot simply ignore the school's investment in the textbook or arbitrarily declare that pupils must buy a different textbook. If the textbook is part of a sequence, that teacher cannot disrupt this sequence without destroying previous planning of colleagues and without confusing students. The supervisor can help the teacher find ways to use the textbook; expand on the textbook; provide supplementary, original activities that go beyond it; and use additional text materials.

When the teacher and supervisor discuss the thorny issue of academic freedom, they should not ignore a dimension that some teachers overlook, namely, that academic freedom does not exist for the teacher alone. Not only does academic freedom provide an environment in which a teacher is free to teach—within established parameters—but it should also provide a climate in which the learner is free to learn—within the same parameters.

In providing a program of supervision, the assumption is made that change is desirable, necessary, and indeed, inevitable. School programs and methods of instruction must keep pace with changing times. If all teachers were professionally dedicated enough to keep up-to-date in their fields, the need for supervision might diminish. Unfortunately, teaching has not fully reached a professional status. Consider, for example, the continuing debate in educational circles on whether teaching is a profession. Individuals choose to go into teaching for a number of reasons. Some are dedicated to teaching and over the years become devoted teachers. Others enter teaching because they have majored in a particular field and, by adding some professional education courses, can be certified to teach. They may have no great interest in teaching but reason that teacher training will equip them for the job market. Still others in teaching are marking time until they can move into another profession. Some are in teaching because of the sense of power they hold over the lives of young people. For these reasons, a considerable degree of supervision will need to be provided for teachers.

Need for the Supervisor

One assumption in supervision is that without assistance, some teachers will not make changes. We make the further assumption, therefore, that supervisors are able to help teachers to bring about changes. Whether this assumption is translated into fact depends on the supervisor, the teacher, and the interaction between the two. Possibly, if existing patterns of educational organization were changed, means other than the presence of a live supervisor might—stress *might*—help teachers to effect change. Dissemination of professional literature from the central office or other teacher/administrator and self-evaluation techniques, including the use of media, also might enable the teacher to change faster than a supervisor is able to stimulate change. So far, the evidence seems to point to the need for supervisors to help people change.

Educators agree that there should be some internal consistency to sequences of subject matter and that there should be articulation between grades of a school and levels of the school system. A supervisor is the one person in a school system who can help achieve these goals. The district supervisor, for example, moving from school to school, knows what materials are being used in each class and what the objectives of teachers are in the various schools. The supervisor of language arts in the elementary school, for example, helps teachers coordinate their sequences, avoid duplication of content, define goals, and work cooperatively.

The district supervisor is concerned with sequences across levels—that is, with the problem of articulation. The supervisor of language arts in the elementary school works with the supervisor of language arts in the middle or secondary school to develop coordinated, sequential programs between the elementary and middle or secondary levels. The provision of coordinated sequences of subject matter between levels—elementary and middle school or junior high, middle school or junior high and senior high, senior high and college—is a problem in need of solution in many communities. Solution requires joint planning by teachers at the various levels. The supervisor can act as a catalyst in getting teachers together so they can cooperatively work out sequences whose parts will bear some relationship to one another.

At the individual school building level, the principal, assistant principal, lead teacher, curriculum coordinator, or curriculum resource teacher can oversee the planning for continuous sequences among courses or grades within a particular school with help from team leaders, grade coordinators, and department heads. At both the school level and the district level, someone needs to be assigned to work with teachers so they are not going off in different directions. The learner should be able to go through an orderly progression of study from the elementary school through high school. This orderly progress is a well-planned, well-formulated sequence in each area of study. To achieve this sequence requires the cooperation of teachers at all levels. The supervisor serves to bring these teachers together and to acquaint them with the problems of sequence and articulation.

Ross L. Neagley and N. Dean Evans explained the need for supervision in the following way:

> Supervision, then, seems destined to be essential to deciding the nature and content of the curriculum, to selecting the school organizational patterns and learning materials to facilitate teaching, and to evaluating the entire educational process. Effective coordination of the total program, kindergarten through high school, has never been achieved in most school systems, although this is one of the most pressing needs in American public education today.
>
> We can no longer afford the waste of human resources in overlapping courses, duplication of teaching effort, and lack of continuity from one school level to the next. A careful curriculum plan embracing the entire school experience from entry to graduation is imperative and long overdue. An effective supervisory program is needed in every school district—small, intermediate, or large—to launch or coordinate this effort.[3]

Supervision is, therefore, a necessary service to teachers for a number of reasons. The stage has not yet been reached when the services of these specialized personnel may be eliminated. In fact, there is a present need for more supervisors who are better trained and more highly skilled in the performance of their tasks than most supervisors currently working.

ISSUE 2: FOR WHOM SHOULD SUPERVISION BE PROVIDED?

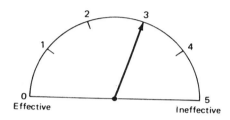

Should supervision be provided for new teachers only? For older as well as newer teachers? For experienced as well as inexperienced? For poor as well as able teachers? Ostensibly, supervision is made available to all teachers, and supervisors make choices about where they will spend most of their time and energies.

Naturally, most effort is devoted to those who seem to need the help most: the new, the inexperienced, and the less able teachers. Teachers who are new to the school system need help in learning how the particular system operates. The supervisor introduces them to the resources of the school and community and helps them to understand the types of students and parents in the system. The teacher new to a school district has special needs, different from the needs of those who have been in the system a while. A supervisor must be tuned in to these special needs and must make an effort to help new teachers become familiar with the system.

The supervisor will spend more time assisting teachers who are inexperienced. He or she knows that the inexperienced teacher is not a finished product. Although those who are in their first years of teaching are often uncertain of themselves, they usually make up in enthusiasm what they may lack in experience. They will probably be eager to receive whatever help is extended to them. They are often more approachable and more receptive to suggestions than more experienced teachers, who are convinced that they know the answers from years of service. It is understandable that many supervisors choose to spend most of their efforts on new and inexperienced teachers.

The less able teacher requires particular help from the supervisor. This teacher may or may not be a new or inexperienced teacher and may or may not seek help from the supervisor. There are, of course, less competent teachers among the new and inexperienced. In many cases, the supervisor can help these less effective but new or inexperienced teachers to improve their teaching. Familiarity with the school system and a few years of teaching experience often resolve the problems of some teachers who were initially ineffective.

On the other hand, we can sometimes find the less able among experienced teachers and among those who have been in a school system for years. These teachers fall into several categories. There is first the teacher who is ineffective in the supervisor's judgment but sees himself or herself as effective. This teacher is identified by the poor progress of his or her students, by lack of rapport with students, by a lack of knowledge of the material being taught, by lack of skill in presenting the material, and by lack of classroom control. A supervisor can help this type of individual take an inventory of personal strengths and weaknesses. In this particular case, the supervisor is supported in his or her judgment of the teacher because the teacher is considered ineffective by the school principal and by colleagues as well. A much more difficult problem for the supervisor is the second category of teachers; these are teachers the supervisor considers ineffective, but the supervisor's judgment is not shared by either the principal or the teacher's colleagues. Such a teacher considers himself or herself to be effective, even superior. To put it simply, the teacher does a great job of teaching the wrong things in the wrong way.

In the opinion of some teachers and some principals, rigid discipline is a virtue. Strict disciplinarians keep all learners under their thumbs, allowing no freedom for childhood or adolescent exuberance. Some teachers and principals believe that the subject matter is king and the learner should be adjusted to the subject matter rather than vice versa. Some feel that the "old ways" of teaching are better than the "new ways," if we may so distinguish between subject-centered and learner-centered approaches to presenting content. Thus, the teacher who is a stern disciplinarian, a subject-centered personality, and a follower of tradition is often labeled effective, indeed superior.

If the supervisor believes that some allowances should be made for young learners, this same "effective" teacher would be considered ineffective. The supervisor would consider an authoritarian, regimented classroom inappropriate, a type of educational climate more suitable to a totalitarian than a democratic society.

If the supervisor believes that the learner should take precedence over subject matter and that subject matter ought to be tailored to fit the learner rather than vice versa, he or she will consider the subject-centered teacher ineffective. The supervisor works with such a teacher to bring about an understanding of the motivation of learners and to review learning theories. The supervisor will recall with the teacher some of the principles of educational psychology with which the teacher became acquainted during preservice training and will try to point out to the teacher that these psychological principles were not simply truisms for college students but have their applications in the classroom.

In working with a strictly subject-centered teacher, the supervisor may find the route to change in teacher behavior slow going, for the weight of tradition is on the side of the teacher. Tradition is a powerful block, especially when it is supported by school administrators and other teachers who resist change. Experienced teachers are often in greater need of supervision with respect to rigidity and subject-centeredness than are inexperienced teachers. Inexperienced teachers who have just recently completed their preparation programs know some of the latest methods and strategies in education and in their teaching field and are not set in fixed ways. They are still flexible and have not developed particular techniques, plans, and procedures to which they are committed and which they repeat from year to year, nor have they as yet become tainted by the cynicism that some experienced teachers develop. The supervisor will have less difficulty working with inexperienced teachers who have open minds than with experienced teachers who are certain they have all the answers.

A third category of ineffective teachers is those who are clearly ineffective and know it. Supervisor, principal, and colleagues may agree that the teacher is ineffective. A willingness on the part of the teacher to improve is a first step. Yet ineffective teachers who recognize their ineptness are often defensive about their instruction and refuse to seek the help of the supervisor or other resource people. Declining to participate in teachers' workshops or institutes for fear of revealing their own inadequacies, they develop defensive excuses for their lack of competence. Often they blame the students, claiming they are unmotivated. Or they blame uncooperative administrators for their difficulties. They claim that they are placed in the wrong grade or in their minor teaching field or in the wrong school. But deep within, they know they lack the preparation or other qualifications to be effective teachers. They see improvement in their instruction as an insurmountable barrier and often exhibit the same lack of motivation that they ascribe to their learners. Tenure regulations and lifetime certificates make it difficult to correct situations like this no matter how hard a supervisor tries unless the teacher is willing to be helped. The documentation and paperwork required to substantiate that a teacher is ineffective remain the responsibility of the school principal, but the supervisor may be involved in the development of the documentation.

The supervisor can work with any teacher who is willing to cooperate, but first he or she must develop a trusting relationship in which that teacher will not be fearful of disclosing inadequacies. The teacher must know that no retribution will result from revealing problem areas. Since retribution can be harsh—a change of grade level or school or even dismissal—no teacher will willingly make personal inadequacies known if punishment is expected to follow.

Numbered among the ineffective teachers are those who are "burned out." Teachers may or may not be aware of their ineffectiveness or willing to admit that they are suffering from burnout. Some of those who confront the problem resolve it by leaving teaching. Others stay on and mark time.

Teacher burnout is characterized by disenchantment with teaching, fatigue, frustration, impatience, rationalization, decreased motivation, cynicism, day-to-day existence, and alienation from the system, especially from administrators and supervisors who are perceived as additional burdens. Figures from the "Teacher Questionnaire" for 1987–88 and 1988–89, surveys done by the National Center for Education Statistics of the U.S. Department of Education, revealed clear evidence of burnout. These responses indicated that more than 27 percent of the public school secondary teachers who responded would "probably not" become teachers, given the opportunity to make the decision again. Fourteen percent of the private school secondary teachers indicated the same feelings. Similar responses were reported by more than 24 percent of the public school elementary teachers and more than 10 percent of the private school elementary teachers.[4] The 1990 study on teaching conditions by the Carnegie Foundation for the Advancement of Teaching also revealed widespread dissatisfaction on the part of teachers. Forty-five percent of the more than 21,000 elementary and secondary public school teachers surveyed expressed a feeling of lack of control over their own professional lives. Whereas 75 percent had reported satisfaction with the degree of control they felt they had over their professional lives in 1987, that figure had dropped rather significantly to 55 percent—slightly over half of the teachers—by 1990.[5] Such dissatisfaction is bound to spill over into the classroom.

Teacher burnout arises from stressful situations brought on by unruly and, in some cases, unmanageable students; massive amounts of paperwork and record keeping; low pay; inadequate budgets; high teacher–pupil ratios; uncaring or perceived as uncaring administrators and supervisors; school facilities in need of repair; parental demands; restrictions on freedom to plan and teach; and overemphasis on student test scores.

Supervisors have attempted to combat teacher burnout by providing staff development activities on management of time and stress. Administrators can help alleviate some of the pressures by assuring reasonable class size, helping teachers with discipline problems, and keeping required paperwork to a minimum.

Civility and positive reinforcement from administrators and supervisors go a long way toward making the job more satisfying to the teacher. Teaching must be made to appear attractive if young people are to enter the profession. Teachers' ego needs, like the administrator's and supervisor's ego needs, must be fulfilled if teachers are to do an effective job and remain in the profession.

Supervisors must not act surprised at whatever low level of preparation or skill is shown by teachers they supervise. They begin with the fact that like Mount Everest, the teacher is there. It does little good for supervisors to wring their hands and lament that ineffective teachers are found in many school systems, for it is unrealistic to believe that every school system in the United States could fill all its vacancies with effective teachers. Supervisors can work with these individuals only after allaying all the teachers' fears that exposure of their difficulties will result in unpleasant repercussions.

Supervision should be available to all teachers, not just the new, the inexperienced, and the ineffective. Supervisors can be of help to experienced and effective teachers. Those who are capable and see themselves as capable tend to welcome advice and suggestions and go out of their way to seek new ideas. These are the teachers who urge supervisors to drop in to see them and talk to them. These teachers are completely at ease when supervisors, administrators, and colleagues step into their classrooms and observe. Some enjoy the experience of demonstrating to others that they are effective teachers. These teachers can serve as demonstration models for others to observe.

Supervisors should be concerned with helping teachers not only to overcome their deficiencies but also to grow, develop, and build on their strengths. Supervisors can help the better teachers by offering suggestions drawn from visits to other classrooms and from personal experiences. They can assist the more able teachers by introducing them to new publications and materials these teachers have not had a chance to examine. Supervisors can be timesavers for teachers. In some ways the supervisor may get "better mileage" from suggestions they make to the more able teachers than from those they offer to the less able. The more able will take the suggestions seriously and try them out whereas the less able will be reluctant or hesitant to try new ideas. Because they possess the self-confidence to surmount failures, the more able teachers do not fear failure of a new plan or technique. Cooperative, able teachers are a joy to the supervisor. Whereas some uncooperative or ineffective teachers keep their doors shut to the supervisor, teachers who are eagerly looking for assistance throw open their doors and welcome any observer.

The supervisor will have to decide where the priorities for help lie. One priority may be to concentrate on troubleshooting. This would yield short-term results but would do little for the long term. If leadership is to be given in improving instruction, the supervisor must do more than troubleshoot. He or she must work with individuals and groups in developing the curriculum and improving instruction. Together they must study goals, means of reaching the goals, and ways of evaluating what they have accomplished, a process that requires considerable time. The supervisor must achieve some balance between short-term and long-term projects. There must also be balance in workload between helping teachers individually and working with them in groups. Like the teacher who has thirty-five students in a class, the supervisor cannot give complete attention to one individual who has a problem; he or she has to devise ways to handle both individuals and groups. Just as the teacher cannot follow a single strategy and expect all learners to be successful as a result, the supervisor cannot use an identical approach with every teacher or group of teachers.

Ideally, supervisors should provide help to all teachers, experienced and inexperienced, effective and ineffective. In reality, though, they will need to spend more time with the inexperienced and ineffective.

ISSUE 3: SHOULD THE SUPERVISOR'S AUTHORITY BE BASED ON EXPERTISE AND INTERPERSONAL RELATIONSHIPS OR ON CONFERRED STATUS AND DECISION-MAKING RESPONSIBILITIES?

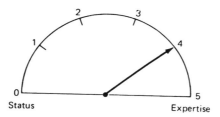

Authority is derived from various sources. Although we tend to think of conferred power as the only source of authority, many leaders actually derive their authority from their ability to influence other people. A role is prescribed either directly or indirectly for each position in an organization. With each role go certain expectancies. Power to varying degrees undergirds positions so that leaders may fulfill their role expectancies. Thus, role expectations are often met because of the power attached to them.

On the other hand, some leaders fulfill their roles without resorting to the use of power. Some leaders by the force of reason, persuasiveness, and personality can achieve their goals without exerting power and flaunting status. These leaders would be able to perform their duties even if the props of power and status were removed.

Other leaders, lacking the ability to reason, to demonstrate vision, or to relate to other people must fall back on bestowed power to get their tasks done. Some of these leaders spend more time preserving the authority of their office than solving the problems of the organization.

Robert J. Alfonso, Gerald R. Firth, and Richard F. Neville took the position that status and power conferred on the supervisor by the organization are necessary if he or she is to be effective.[6] In considering this issue, we must again distinguish between line supervisors (administrators) and staff supervisors. The line supervisors, like the assistant superintendent, the principal, and the assistant principal, possess certain powers conferred on them through law and state and local regulations; the staff supervisor possesses only those powers narrowly prescribed by regulation and by the administrator. The supervisor's power is greatly circumscribed. One need only look at a school system's table of organization to realize that supervisors are not high in the power structure; as a result, their jobs are not high-status positions. We believe that the staff person who serves as instructional supervisor needs neither conferred power nor exalted status. Supervision, like teaching, has an importance of its own.

Line supervisors (administrators) can fall back on power and status if they must to effect their orders. The staff supervisor cannot command nearly as much power. That is not to say that the supervisor has no power. In fact, supervisors bask in the reflected power of the administrator and the organization. Teachers may follow a supervisor's direction *because* they perceive supervisors to possess powers that, in reality, the supervisors do not have.

We will next examine the issue of whether the supervisor should *be* an administrator. At this point, we need to decide whether supervisors should seek to use the limited powers they may have, call on the administrator's power, or convey the impression of possessing derived administrative powers in fulfilling their roles.

William H. Lucio and John D. McNeil maintained that the authority of office and influence cannot be separated and that there are times when supervisors must use the authority of their position.

> Popularly, supervisors are seen as those who justify themselves as they are able to influence fellow executives at all levels by virtue of their factual or technical mastery, consultative skill, advisory persuasiveness—in short, by their educational effectiveness.... We question the notion that within a line-and-staff organization school leaders are administrators and not supervisors when they exercise initiative in movements for the improvement of teaching and learning, making decisions, coordinating the work of others, and issuing directions. They are supervisors when using authority as well as supervisors when exerting influence.... Supervisors are sometimes delegated authority and held responsible for results. Hence, they must hold others responsible for carrying out instructions.[7]

Resorting to authority of office, however, can interfere with helping teachers. If the teacher fails to respond to the supervisor's directions and the supervisor resorts to using power, this action implies punishment of some kind and creates a threatening climate. Like most human beings, teachers perform more effectively in a non-threatening environment.

Wayne K. Hoy and Patrick B. Forsyth saw formal authority and status as getting in the supervisor's way:

> Supervisors are staff—master teachers. They are expected to provide advice and support to colleagues, not to discipline them. The staff position has little formal authority; authority is primarily informal and earned—arising from the supervisors' expertise and personal skills. Teachers must have confidence in those to whom they turn for help, and trust can more readily be built when status distinctions among supervisors and teachers are limited. In fact, formal authority and status can be dysfunctional for supervisors as they seek to establish colleague relationships. Such status distinctions are likely to curtail authentic interactions and productive problem solving because they hinder social support and restrict and distort communication of information.*

Numerous studies have shown that if teachers seek help at all—and many do not[8]—they want the supervisor to demonstrate the type of expertise that will help them in the classroom.[9] They also expect the supervisor to be able to develop rapport with them and to work with them in a cooperative way.

It probably does not matter to teachers whether the supervisor possesses power if the supervisor is able to help them do their jobs better. If the supervisor is able to provide teachers with the help they need, he or she will not find it necessary to call on power. We should make an exception, of course, in the case of the incompetent teacher, as contrasted with the ineffective teacher. The ineffective teacher can be helped; the incompetent teacher should be removed from the classroom.

ISSUE 4: SHOULD THE SUPERVISOR BE AN ADMINISTRATOR?

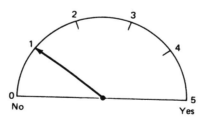

In Chapter 1, we noted the uncertainty and ambiguity concerning whether the supervisor should be an administrator and vice versa. Administrators by the very nature of their positions have supervisory responsibilities. Many administrators unfortunately are not able to give primary attention to the main purpose for which schools have been established—instruction of the young. They are too busy with plant maintenance, record keeping, personnel management, scheduling, auxiliary services, and public relations. On the surface, we can certainly distinguish between administration and supervision. William H. Burton and Leo J. Brueckner described the difference in the following way:

---

*Excerpt from Wayne K. Hoy and Patrick B. Forsyth, *Effective Supervision: Theory into Practice* (New York: Random House, 1986). Reproduced with permission of The McGraw-Hill Companies.

50

1. Administration is *ordinarily* concerned with providing material facilities and with operation in general.
2. Supervision is *ordinarily* concerned with improving the setting for learning in particular.
3. Administration and supervision considered *functionally* cannot be separated or set off from each other. The two are coordinate, correlative, complementary, mutually shared functions in the operation of educational systems.[10]

Though administration may be distinguished from supervision, an ongoing controversy centers on whether supervision *should* be an arm of administration. In the small school, where the principal has no assistants or supervisory help from the central office, the principal *must* serve in the dual roles of administrator and supervisor. On the other hand, where additional supervisory resources exist, distinctions in roles and functions can be made. The question remains of whether supervisors are or should be administrators. On one side of the issue are those who view supervision as a fundamental appendage of administration. On the other side are those who would divorce supervision from administration. Some forty years ago, Harold Spears stated the issue clearly, pointing out the lack of success in resolving the problem.

> Ever since supervisors were added to school management, there has been a concerted attempt to draw a line of demarcation between administration and supervision, between the job of administering and that of supervising. But this campaign for strict interpretations is still far short of its goal, for those who have dared to set the stakes have reached no common agreement.[11]

The issue remains with us. Historically, supervision has been a part of administration. In the first edition of their textbook entitled *Supervision of Instruction: A Phase of Administration*, Glen G. Eye and Lanore A. Netzer defined supervision as "that phase of administration which deals primarily with the achievement of the appropriate selected instructional expectations of educational service."[12]

James P. Esposito, Gary E. Smith, and Harold J. Burbach have created a four-part taxonomy of the supervisor's role that encompasses both administrative and supervisory responsibilities. Their taxonomy is reproduced in Table 2.1.

Only in recent years has supervision branched out from its parent, administration. In the early years of our country, supervision was decidedly one of the functions of the administrator—the person with status and power. Thus, the administrator was the person with super-superior vision about education and it was he (since early administrators were universally males) who hired, directed, demanded, inspected, examined, and dismissed.

From the mid-1950s to the present, specialists in supervision have been inclining toward reducing the administrative roles of the supervisor—some on philosophical grounds, some on the basis of role definition, and some for the very practical reason that supervisors have too much to do when they take on administrative as well as supervisory duties.

Underscoring the conflict and tension between administrative and supervisory functions, Hoy and Forsyth proposed a differentiated model of supervision in which administrative and supervisory roles are distinct but complementary (see Table 2.2, page 52).[13]

The problem might be resolved if the administrator assumed more of a super-

TABLE 2.1. TAXONOMY OF THE SUPERVISORY ROLE

Helping Role		Administrative Role	
Factor Indirect I Service to Teachers	*Factor IV Direct Service*	*Factor II Administrator*	*Factor III Evaluator*
Plan and arrange in-service education programs and workshops	Assist in the orientation of new and beginning teachers	Coordinate instructional programs	Plan and arrange in-service education programs and workshops
Participate in-service education programs and workshops	Assist teachers in the location, selection, and interpretation of materials	Assist in the evaluation and appraisal of education programs	Participate in in-service education programs and workshops
Coordinate instructional programs	Visit and observe in the classroom	Routine administrative duties	Assist in the evaluation and appraisal of school programs
Assist in the orientation of new and beginning teachers	Teach demonstration lessons	Participate in the formulation of policy	Arrange intersystem visitations to observe promising practices
Assist teachers in the location, selection, and interpretation of materials	Hold individual conferences with teachers	Engage in public relations	Arrange intrasystem visitations to observe promising practices
Collect and disseminate current curriculum materials		Work with citizens' or lay groups	
Develop curriculum designs and coordinate curriculum improvement efforts		Arrange intersystem visitations to observe promising practices	
Assist in the development of curriculum guides and other publications			
Assist textbook selection committees			
Develop and prepare new instructional media			
Assist in the evaluation and appraisal of school programs			

Source: James P. Esposito, Gary E. Smith, and Harold J. Burbach, "A Delineation of the Supervisory Role," Education 96, *No. 1 (Fall 1975): 66. Reprinted with permission of* Education.

visory role and turned over to assistants some managerial aspects of running a school system. Most administrators are unwilling to relinquish management responsibilities. They may, therefore, concentrate on administrative and operational matters and delegate responsibilities for curricular and instructional leadership to a subordinate. Or they may call in outside help, specifically staff persons who are employed to perform the supervisory roles they cannot fill.

TABLE 2.2. A DIFFERENTIATED MODEL OF SUPERVISION OF INSTRUCTION

Role	Position	Level	Authority Relationship	Orientation	Supervisory Function
Supervisor	Staff (Supplies advice)	Technical	Informal authority from expertise and personal skills (no formal authority)	—Professional —Long-term perspective —Theoretical —Change	To improve the teaching-learning process by direct and cooperative work with teachers on: —Joint planning of instruction —Classroom observation —Joint analysis of teaching and learning —Renewed planning and change
Principal	Line (Issues directives)	Managerial	Formal authority from position (informal authority can be developed)	—Bureaucratic —Short-term perspective —Pragmatic —Stability	To improve the organizational climate of the school by fostering: —Open, authentic interactions —Professional autonomy of teachers —Orderly teaching environment —High performance and achievement standards —Participative and supportive leadership —Shared decision making and high motivation —Colleague control —High morale —Security —Trust

Source: Wayne K. Hoy and Patrick B. Forsyth, Effective Supervision: Theory into Practice *(New York: Random House, 1986), p. 15. Reproduced with permission of The McGraw-Hill Companies.*

The question is not so much whether administrators should assume supervisory tasks as they already do this to one degree or another and as they already possess responsibility for supervision. We must examine more carefully the opposite side of the coin. The question is whether the supervisor should assume administrative tasks and responsibilities. Should the administrator require or permit a person charged with leadership in curriculum and instructional development to perform administrative duties? Should teachers recognize the supervisor as one who has direct line authority over them, determines promotions, passes on salary increments, decides on retention, makes decisions on expenditures for materials and equipment, and determines specifications for construction of new facilities teachers will use?

Should supervisors think of themselves as administrators? If administrative authority is not delegated to the supervisor per se, should the supervisor act as the agent of the administrator who reports back to the administrator? Are the supervisor and administrator in cahoots, so to speak? Is the supervisor the administrator's alter ego when setting foot in the teacher's classroom?

If we conceive of supervision as service, it is difficult to see how supervisors can maintain rapport with teachers if teachers perceive them as people who control their destinies. For supervision to be successful, teachers must want the services of the supervisor. They must feel that the supervisor is there to serve them and to help them become more effective teachers.

We find ourselves in a real dilemma with respect to rating teacher effectiveness, an issue discussed more fully in Chapter 13. Shall the supervisor rate the teachers and, having rated them, report to the administrator? When this happens, what does it do to the teachers' willingness to call on the supervisor for help and to reveal their inadequacies?

Supervisors are often required by their administrators to perform administrative tasks, such as rating teachers. By their close proximity to the superintendent, frequently sharing office space in the same building, they fall heir to administrative duties they might not have if they were housed away from the center of administrative power. The supervisor, as a subordinate, cannot refuse to accept assigned administrative duties. The fact that supervisors must accept such tasks prompts the suggestion—perhaps impractical—to house central office supervisors away from the administrator's headquarters.

Such a move would be understood by teachers as affirming that supervisors are really employed primarily to help them and not to assist the administrator. Although such a move might not appeal to supervisors who see themselves as administrators, those who see themselves as service-oriented people might welcome it. We might hypothesize that supervisors who maintain they have no time to visit schools and are unduly loaded with paperwork see themselves as administrators rather than as supervisors. They have become involved in administrative decision-making activities assigned to them by the administrator or assumed on their own initiative.

To take the extreme position that the supervisor must never accept administrative tasks would be unrealistic. Sometimes the administrator requires the supervisor to fulfill administrative duties. At other times, as in the case of teacher evaluation, for example, the supervisor is in a most advantageous position to assess performance and to suggest remedial measures to the teacher when necessary.

What is needed by today's supervisors is a desire to emphasize supervisory behavior and to deemphasize administrative behavior. We must admit that there are individuals who enjoy being near the center of power without sharing the responsibilities borne by the administrator. There are also supervisors who are closet administrators. If so, they should admit it and seek to join the ranks of the administrators. Like many teachers, some supervisors are administrators-in-waiting, looking forward to the day when they might be able to trade in their staff job for a line position. Those supervisors who view instructional leadership as their career will try to keep administrative responsibilities to a minimum.

ISSUE 5: IS SUPERVISION STAFF DEVELOPMENT?

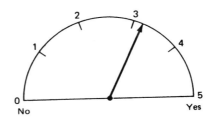

As conceptualized in this book, staff development is one of the three domains of supervision. It is not, however, as it appears in some school systems, the sole domain. The role of the supervisor as shown in Figure 1.4 involves instructional development on which there is little or no controversy; curriculum development, on which there is disagreement; and staff development, on which there is also argument.

In large school systems, more than one person may be employed to carry out the multiple tasks of supervision. Their responsibilities may range across all three domains, or individuals may devote themselves entirely to one or two domains. There are, for example, directors of staff development, directors of curriculum development, and directors of both staff and curriculum development. These directors are often subordinate to an assistant superintendent for curriculum and/or instructional development.

If supervision is a service designed to help teachers become more effective so that their students will benefit, then staff development is an important domain of supervision. In describing staff development, Leslee J. Bishop said that it

> focuses upon professional growth rather than upon credentialing or maintaining . . . the emphasis here is upon those attitudes, competencies, and knowledges that enhance learning, program effectiveness, and professional adequacy. These are related to the systematic efforts to improve the conditions, objectives, resources, and processes that are the responsibility of the school district.[14]

Many people equate staff development with in-service education. Lloyd W. Dull, for example, used the terms *in-service education* and *staff development* synonymously. He defined in-service education as "the sum of all activities designed for the purpose of improving, expanding, and renewing the skills, knowledge, and abilities of staff personnel."[15]

Ben M. Harris took the position that a distinction should be made between staff development and in-service education. He divided staff development into two aspects: staffing and training. The staffing aspect he viewed as the assignment of the best qualified person to a task. The training aspect he separated into in-service education and advanced preparation. By in-service education he meant "any planned program of learning opportunities afforded staff members of schools, colleges, or other educational agencies for purposes of improving the performance of the individual in already assigned positions."[16] Advanced preparation, according to Harris, is training for a different and higher position.

Although the literature frequently uses the terms *staff development* and *in-service education* synonymously, Donald C. Orlich saw staff development as a broader term, subsuming in-service education. Explaining the difference, Orlich said:

> Whereas in-service education is oriented toward immediate training objectives, staff development implies persistent and personally significant activities. In essence, staff development subsumes in-service education projects and also addresses the larger issue of developing organizational problem-solving capacities and leadership skills. The totality of building human and institutional resources in the organization becomes the goal of staff development.[17]

Not only is staff development often equated with in-service education but also it is sometimes used interchangeably with instructional development. We might say that instructional development or improvement is one hoped-for result of staff development. Although we concede that staff development is a somewhat broader term, we equate staff development with in-service education. We define in-service education as a program of organized activities of both a group and individual nature planned and carried out to promote the personal and professional growth of staff members—in this case, teachers. In Chapter 9, we discuss the supervisor's role in staff development.

Instructional development consists of those staff-development activities that focus directly on the improvement of instruction—for example, perfecting testing techniques. Instructional development focuses on *instructional* design, implementation, and evaluation. Another way of viewing instructional development is to consider it a specialized domain of staff development. We do not include within the concept of instructional development those staff-development activities that aim primarily at the personal growth of the teacher, such as learning to demonstrate empathy, to be more cooperative in group settings, and to treat parents courteously and professionally.

Because we are examining the specialized field of supervision, our discussion emphasizes activities that are organized and planned by the supervisor. We would be remiss if we did not note that a good deal of staff development is much less structured; it is planned and engaged in by the individual teacher for that teacher's self-improvement.

As we shall see when we consider issue 6, we encounter a problem with curriculum development similar to the question of distinguishing between staff development and instructional development. Staff-development activities relate to curriculum development when they consist of organized, planned activities of a group or individual nature that focus on *curriculum* design, implementation, and evaluation.

In effect, staff development, instructional development, and curriculum development flow into each other. To paraphrase Gertrude Stein, we might say that staff development is instructional development is curriculum development is staff development . . . ad infinitum. Each set of two domains is like a pair of Siamese twins; it is very difficult and sometimes impossible to separate them. Perhaps we need not separate them if we are aware of the extent and limitations of each. Supervisors will find staff development high on their agenda.

ISSUE 6: IS SUPERVISION CURRICULUM DEVELOPMENT?

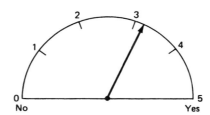

When supervisors help teachers either individually or in groups to make decisions about programs as opposed to methods, they are working in the domain of curriculum development. As curriculum leaders, supervisors direct teachers in the study of scope and sequence, of balance, and of articulation.[18] When they chair curriculum councils or serve as resource persons to them, supervisors engage in curriculum development. When they direct a curriculum needs assessment involving students, teachers, administrators, and parents, they are exerting curriculum leadership. They are in the curriculum arena when they help faculties try out innovative programs like learning centers, integrated thematic instruction, remedial laboratories, and nongrading.

Helping teachers make decisions about programs can be a full-time job. The scope of curriculum development is so vast that supervisors once committed to the domain may never exit. There is constant need for review and revitalization of the curriculum to keep it current with rapidly developing knowledge.

Those who feel that people who direct or coordinate curriculum are not really supervisors point out that these staff people spend so much time in curriculum development, running from school to school and group to group, that they never have time to get into the classrooms where the real action is. Teachers who desperately need help with improving instruction go without assistance. Because some supervisors put all their eggs in the curriculum basket, those who reject curriculum development as a domain of supervision believe that students would benefit more if supervisors worked in a clinical setting on a one-to-one basis with classroom teachers.

Yet programmatic decisions must be made daily and continually. The decisions are usually difficult and complex. They call for a knowledge of the research and intelligent deployment of human and physical resources. They require a match between the school's philosophy and its practice, and they must be accompanied by an appropriate evaluation plan.

Groups must be assembled to study ramifications of curriculum problems, make recommendations, and translate plans into operation. Leadership is essential for successful completion of these tasks.

We can argue about whether it is better for school systems and for education in general to limit supervision exclusively to one domain or to provide attention to two or three domains. We have no evidence to prove conclusively that restricting supervision to one domain would result in a better product. By limiting help to one domain we could do a respectable job in one area while neglecting other areas. Consequently, we believe supervision must be provided in all three domains. Whether we assign supervisors to each one or whether all supervisors work in all domains is not the major question. Supervision becomes questionable when the supervisory staff, no matter how large or how small, restricts itself to one area, whether it is staff development, instructional development, or curriculum development.

The supervisory job can be done by (1) choosing priorities carefully, (2) managing time wisely, (3) placing energies where they will be of most benefit, and (4) making better use of personnel, even if they have to be trained on the job. School systems could make far better use of assistant principals, department heads, team leaders, grade coordinators, and teachers themselves in the roles of coaches and mentors. We are sitting on a largely untapped gold mine of supervisory talent that is eager to be released.[19] These people could be of enormous help to administrators, curriculum directors, and other instructional supervisors.

Supervisors must set their objectives, manage their time, and direct their energies to enhance their efficiency. Some supervisors move frantically at top speed from one problem to another without asking whether the problem is serious, without delegating authority and responsibility for its resolution, and without completing one task before they leap to the next.

A review of the literature on supervision reveals many specialists who include curriculum development within the responsibilities of the supervisor. John T. Lovell and Kimball Wiles asserted that "supervision is curriculum development . . . an important function of instructional supervisory behavior."[20] Kathryn V. Feyereisen, A. John Fiorino, and Arlene T. Nowak stressed curriculum change in their book *Supervision and Curriculum Renewal: A Systems Approach*.[21] Lucio and McNeil assigned a large leadership role for the supervisor. In a chapter on curriculum planning and change entitled "Strategies and Tactics for Program Improvement," they wrote, "The public relies on supervisors who possess certain professional competencies to present to the elected representative body definite recommendations for improving the curriculum for children and youth."[22] Morris Cogan, however, narrowed the definition of supervision to clinical supervision, which focuses on ways of helping teachers improve their performance in the classroom. Cogan labeled all supervisory activities that occur outside the classroom general supervision.[23] However desirable it might seem to throw all the supervisory forces into either staff development or instructional development, we believe the supervisor must continue to function in curriculum development as well as in the other two domains.

ISSUE 7: IS SUPERVISION EVALUATION?

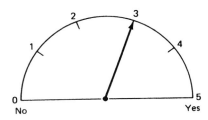

Whenever one individual makes a judgment of any kind about another individual, he or she is engaging in evaluation. It makes little difference whether that judgment is called *assessment, appraisal,* or *evaluation.* The issue of whether supervision is evaluation touches on four questions that you have already encountered: What is the purpose of supervision? Is supervision administration? Who should carry out supervisory functions? What is the role of the principal in supervision?

Those who maintain that supervision is not evaluation are thinking in terms of a process involving observation of the teacher's classroom performance for the purpose of helping the teacher improve instruction without the necessity for making personnel decisions. We'd call this type of supervision *consultative* or *formative evaluation.*

On the other hand, some see supervision in terms of evaluation and have in mind administrative assessments based on data obtained both within and outside the classroom for purposes of making personnel decisions, such as contract renewal, tenure, merit pay, teaching assignments, and placement on a career ladder. We'd call this type of supervision *administrative* or *summative evaluation.* Whether consultative or administrative, evaluation is always present.

Gary Embretson, Ellen Ferber, and Terry Langager drew a clear line between supervision and evaluation.

> Supervision and evaluation are quite distinct from one another and this distinction is recognized. Supervision is a developmental process which promotes continuing growth and development of staff members in the art of teaching; continued and increased staff motivation; and an improved instructional program. Evaluation on the other hand is a management function designed to maintain organizational efficiency; establish standards for staff performance; and appraise staff performance.[24]

They described a process wherein the supervisor would "*observe* performance in order to improve it (supervision) and *judge* performance on the basis of accepted criteria of good teaching (evaluation)."[25]

G. H. Fredrich, too, saw supervision and evaluation as different concepts. "Too often the terms *evaluation* and *supervision* are used synonymously when, in fact, they represent different concepts. Supervision is a formative, supportive approach to improving teaching competence: evaluation is a summative process that should culminate a period of supervision."[26] Fredrich added that the responsibility for supervision and evaluation should rest with different personnel; that department heads, supervisors, consultants, and colleagues should take primary responsibility for supervision whereas the principal should handle evaluation. Using secondary school principals as an example, Fredrich commented:

The principal's role as evaluator is well established, but what about his role in supervision? In many jurisdictions one of the stated primary expectations of a principal is to be a curriculum leader. If this role description were consistent with the practice, then the principal would play a primary part in teacher supervision. However, whether by choice or time restrictions, few principals at the secondary school level can claim that their *primary* function is to act as curriculum leaders.

Nor is this undesirable. I believe that the principal would be much more effective as a *coordinator of supervision.*[27]

Thomas A. Petrie, on the other hand, maintained that contemporary practice in schools refutes the belief that supervision and evaluation are incompatible. He believed that principals do and should have the responsibility for supervision and evaluation. "The principal is the person in the best position to orient new teachers to the needed instructional skills, observe instruction, provide information about the instructional repertoire, arrange opportunities to improve, and to make evaluation judgments."[28]

If the purpose of supervision is to help teachers improve their performance and the data collected are not used for making personnel decisions, supervision is less an evaluation process. We say "less" because supervision can never be completely free of this dimension.

If the purpose of supervision is the collection of data for making decisions about the teacher's career, supervision is an administrative evaluation process. If a staff supervisor carries out the supervisory task and does not supply the data for personnel decisions, supervision is a consultative evaluation process. If a line supervisor performs the supervisory function, the element of administrative evaluation is always there, for the data can, will, and should be used in making personnel decisions.

If a staff person serves as the supervisor, the evaluation can be formative in nature—that is, assessment of progress for the purpose of diagnosing difficulties and suggesting remediation during the course of the year. If a line administrator serves as the supervisor, the evaluation may be formative as well as summative, culminating in an annual written evaluation of the teacher's performance. What disturbs some people, and rightfully so we believe, is that supervision is sometimes perceived as summative evaluation only, with little or no effort at formative evaluation.

John C. Daresh spoke to this point when he said,

> Educators often assume that *educational supervision* is virtually synonymous with *evaluation*—that supervisors do little more than evaluate teachers and curricular programs. . . . To be sure, a strong relationship exists between supervision and evaluation. Supervisors *do* have a responsibility to carry out evaluation . . . evaluation is simply one important aspect of the effort to match individual human abilities with organizational goals, objectives, and priorities, and we will try to defuse the notion that educational evaluation automatically and necessarily involves evaluation of the teaching staff for the purpose of making employment decisions.[29]

Evaluation, then, is an integral part of supervision. Supervisors will collect data on teacher performance. The key is what is done with the data. A robot that feeds data in and spills data out can avoid the task of making judgments. Supervisors, being human, do more than process data; they analyze and interpret data and render judgments, which is the essence of evaluation. When a supervisor decides, for example, that a teacher needs help with certain skills, he or she is engaging in evaluation.

Those who argue that supervision is not evaluation would have us separate the helping relationship from the administrative dimension. As discussed later in this book, certain approaches to supervision emphasize the helping relationship and deemphasize the administrative function.

ISSUE 8: SHOULD SUPERVISORS WORK WITH GROUPS OF TEACHERS OR WITH INDIVIDUAL TEACHERS?

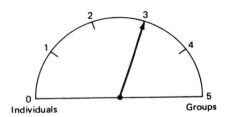

Supervisors must decide repeatedly whether their time is best used when allocated to groups of teachers or to individual teachers who need and want their help. As much as our sentiments lean to the individual side of the scale, our judgment counsels us that such a rating is not practical. If individualization of supervision implies assisting all or even most teachers in a school system, very few school districts have either the funds or the personnel to serve every teacher or the majority of teachers on an individualized basis.

Traditionally, supervisors have worked with groups of teachers in an in-service mode with workshops, conferences, and the like. If you read Edward Pajak's analysis of the role of the central office supervisor of curriculum and instruction, you were probably struck by how often supervisors, at least at the central-office level, are working in and with groups of one kind or another.[30]

The work of a number of specialists in recent years in the field of clinical supervision has resulted in bringing this issue to the forefront. The specialists in clinical supervision encourage us to move the pendulum toward the individual side of the scale. Both group and individual work have advantages, as shown in the lists below.

Working with groups has the following merits:

1. It is less costly in the supervisor's time; it eliminates excessive travel from classroom to classroom.
2. It is a more efficient use of resources. For example, if we are offering training in the classroom use of computers, it would be foolhardy to provide this instruction to teachers on an individual basis.
3. In a time when there is a great deal of concern with the phenomenon of burnout, we can reduce the wear and tear on supervisors when they do not have to repeat learning experiences for teachers individually.

4. Some activities necessitate group decisions, as in the case of curriculum proposals.
5. Some activities require the efforts of more than one person, as in conducting a curriculum needs assessment for a school system.
6. Some activities cannot achieve their objectives if they are to be attempted on an individual basis, such as training in group dynamics.

Individualized supervision also has advantages:

1. It meets the special needs of the individual teacher; it is, therefore, tailor-made supervision.
2. It demonstrates the supervisor's personalized interest in the teacher.
3. If it meets the teacher's need, it overcomes some of the hostility teachers feel toward unproductive group sessions.
4. If conducted properly, it permits teachers to reveal inadequacies without fear of exposure.
5. It allows personal relationships to build between the supervisor and teacher that are not possible in a group setting.

Unless we are talking about very small schools with a handful of teachers, adequate individualized supervision for all teachers is unlikely. As a result, some compromises are necessary. Supervisors can continue to spend more than half their time working with and through groups. They can provide individualized help to (1) those teachers who call for it; (2) those teachers for whom administrative assessments reveal deficiencies; and (3) inexperienced teachers who need help initially. Whereas good, effective experienced teachers would welcome individual help that would contribute to their professional development, time in most school systems does not permit supervisors to render a great deal of that aid. Although we may lament it, it is perhaps fortuitous that not all teachers seek help, for if they did the demand would exceed the supply of helpers.

To fulfill the need for individual help to every teacher would require a greater army of supervisors than now exists. In a time of tight money, when staff personnel are among the first to be cut, it would be unrealistic to expect boards of education to expand the cadre of supervisors. Given the typical makeup of our democratically elected boards of education, we cannot look forward to a posture of largesse in expending public money. Board members are notoriously tightfisted with the dollar, aware as they are that an increase in the property tax—the source of local support for the schools—could remove them from the position on the school board that they may desire to keep for various reasons.

Supervisors must plan for a judicious mixture of both group and individual activities. They can often plan training that combines both features—for example, group instruction in using higher-order questions followed by observation and advisement in the classrooms of those teachers who participated in the group training session.

From the standpoint of cost effectiveness, school administrators show partiality to group-oriented supervisory activities. They want as much "bang for the buck" as possible. In working with groups, supervisors can reach more people with more training in a shorter period of time than would be feasible in sessions with individuals.

We would laud school systems that exhibit effective, completely or predominantly individualized programs of supervision. These school systems would be rarities that should receive national recognition as models for emulation. Until such a time, however, when the horn of plenty reappears, as it did in the 1950s, supervisors will devote most of their time to working with groups. The balance of their time will be devoted to helping teachers on an individual basis. An effective program of supervision consists of a combination of both group and individualized activities.

ISSUE 9: SHOULD SUPERVISION BE CARRIED OUT BY SUPERVISORS BASED IN THE CENTRAL OFFICE OR IN THE INDIVIDUAL SCHOOL?

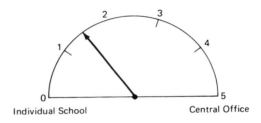

In practice today, supervisory services to the local schools are furnished by supervisors who are headquartered at one of four locations: (1) the state level, (2) an intermediate level between the state and local school, (3) the school district (central office) level, and (4) the individual school level.

State Level
Education is one of the powers reserved to the states by the Tenth Amendment to the U.S. Constitution. In principle, the state has the authority to manage and supervise all public schools within its boundaries. For practical and political reasons, with the notable exception of Hawaii, states choose not to oversee the daily operations of their school systems. Though some may disagree, state education officials by and large restrict their roles to activities they can handle with a degree of efficiency.

State Departments of Education. Instructional supervision from the state level is extremely limited. Leaders from the state department of education may direct research studies, supervise state assessments of student achievement, and help define statewide educational goals. They may assemble groups to work on statewide curricular and instructional issues and problems. Some examples are reviewing and recommending textbooks and related materials, identifying minimal competencies for high school graduation, or specifying important generic teaching competencies. State-level supervisors may organize groups to write curriculum guides, which unify the scope and sequence of disciplines and which can be (though are not necessarily required to be) used throughout the state. Some state departments of education offer limited consultative help to local school systems. We can visualize, however, the modicum of help a state supervisor of mathematics education, for example, could give to any one local school system in the state.

State supervision is often of an administrative rather than an instructional nature, as in checking compliance with state-mandated programs. Instead of being broadly based, if it is provided at all, state supervision concentrates on the concerns of the moment indicated by the state legislature, the state board of education, or the state department of education. Examples of these might be prekindergarten, early childhood education, language arts, mathematics, or exceptionalities. Georgia, as a case in point, furnishes the services of a few (presently, six) highly specialized employees of the Georgia Department of Education known as regional school service center directors. They are distributed throughout the state and offer administrative support to schools in their assigned territories. A school service center director may serve a geographical area that includes fourteen to thirty county and city school systems. The function of these consultants is to provide assistance exclusively to the K–4 level, grades the state has selected to receive special attention.

Learning Resource Systems. The various states, through federal funding, have created agencies known as learning resource systems. These are part of a nationwide network of special education resource centers.

Each state network, comprising a number of centers, is a teacher support system for people working with children who have special needs. Again using Georgia as an example, that state maintains eighteen centers within its network. These centers, which come under the jurisdiction of the Georgia Department of Education, provide a number of services to special educators, including the ones listed here.

1. Maintenance of instructional materials, which may be borrowed on a short-term basis for diagnosis, teacher training, and children's use
2. In-service training of teachers
3. Sponsorship of innovative projects
4. Dissemination of information
5. Help with diagnosis and referral

Practically speaking, the state level is too far removed from the scene to be of significant help to teachers and schools directly and consistently. To many people, the state capital, where most state agencies are housed, is at the far side of the globe, even though modern transportation links exist between the capital and local communities. We must look to lower levels for more adequate supervisory services.

Intermediate Level

When we come to the intermediate level of school organization and administration, we become entangled in a veritable maze. No example of the organizational structure of American education shows so vividly the effects of decentralization as the permutations and commutations of this level.

Most of us are aware that responsibility for education in America rests with the states. The prevailing pattern of school administration within a state places school systems under the direction of an appointed or elected state commissioner or superintendent who is, as a general rule, responsible to some type of state board of education. We also are even more aware that there are local school districts administered by a superintendent who is elected by the people or appointed by a local school board. The board itself may be either appointed (by a grand jury, for example) or elected by the people. Local school superintendents are responsible to the local school board. However, both local school administrators and the boards of education serve as agents of the state.

County Superintendents. Thirteen states administer schools (K–12) through the county-unit system. In those states, the school territory is congruent with the political entity called a county. County-unit school systems are governed by a county school board and administered by a county school superintendent. The models for the county-unit system vary state by state. Florida, for example, is divided into sixty-seven counties, in each of which are a county superintendent and board who exercise jurisdiction over all public schools in the county. One of these is Dade County, the largest county in Florida. With over twenty incorporated communities within its borders, including populous Miami, some 250 schools and over 10,000 teachers, this county gets along with only one school board and one superintendent of schools. Holmes County, in the rural panhandle of Florida, likewise has one board and one superintendent to govern its seven schools. Each county is a single school district. School systems of this type are local school districts, not intermediate units.

The pattern in Georgia, another county-unit state, is slightly different. In Georgia, there are 186 school districts, of which 159 are county units and 27 are city districts. The city districts operate independently from the county units.

Outside the county-unit states, the patterns of school organization vary widely. Hawaii forms a single school district. In Illinois there are close to 1,100 school districts (out of some 15,000 nationally). In an Illinois community you can find an elementary school district and a secondary school district, each with its own board, administrators, faculties, and facilities.

We must explore the position of county superintendent to understand the intermediate unit. County superintendents come in three varieties, which are somewhat difficult to describe. First, there is the *county* county superintendent. These are the superintendents of schools in the thirteen states that have the county-unit system. They are elected by the people or hired and fired by the local school board. They are responsible to the local board of education. We have little difficulty understanding this species of county superintendent. He or she heads a local school district whose boundaries are coterminous with those of the county.

Second, there is the *state* county superintendent. The state of New Jersey has complicated the picture of the intermediate unit with county superintendents who are appointed by the state commissioner.[31]

Third, there is the *intermediate* county superintendent, once a plentiful but now a dying species. The intermediate county superintendency has a long history. This official functions somewhere between the state level and the local school level. His or her jurisdiction, as in the case of New York State, may not be coterminous with the county boundaries. In cases where these administrators' territories expanded beyond the confines of a county, they were often called *intermediate district superintendents*. We'll not burden you with a lengthy discussion of the fact that units smaller than the counties, called *townships*, formed intermediate units prior to the establishment of the county superintendency.

Roald F. Campbell, Luvern L. Cunningham, Raphael O. Nystrand, and Michael D. Usdan reported thirty-nine states with intermediate units.[32] Stephen J. Knezevich pointed out that intermediate units can have several different names.

> intermediate school district (in Michigan), county school district (in California), cooperative educational services agency (in Wisconsin), multicounty educational services unit (in Nebraska), board of cooperative educational services (in New York), education service regions (in Illinois), area educational agencies (in Iowa), and regional educational service agency (in West Virginia).[33]

What is important for our purposes is to remember that the *intermediate* county superintendent has fewer powers than the *county* county superintendent or the *state* county superintendent. The intermediate units are by-products of a rural society. Although the functions of the intermediate unit are undergoing study and change in the states where they exist, the typical intermediate unit does not manage schools or programs; it does not hire and fire teachers; it does not mandate curricula, provide transportation to students, or handle disciplinary problems. Its traditional mission is to furnish the local districts with services they cannot afford or choose not to perform themselves. Among these services are centralized purchasing of supplies; pupil testing; school health; reporting; research; and what interests us most, curriculum development, staff development, and instructional supervision. As the intermediate units continue to change they may take on some limited operational responsibilities in addition to their traditional service functions.

Cooperative Educational Service Agencies. Over the years, the intermediate units have undergone transformation. The intermediate unit in New York State, for example, evolved from deputy superintendency appointed by a county board of supervisors, to town superintendency, to elected county superintendent, to supervisory district superintendent, to district superintendent hired by a district board of school directors, to district superintendent selected by a board of cooperative educational services.

The intermediate county unit has evolved in some states like New York into cooperative educational service agencies, which encompass wide service areas. The Board of Cooperative Educational Services (BOCES) in the state of New York provides service through its forty-four centers to most of the 740 local school districts of the state. In Georgia, sixteen Regional Educational Service Agencies (RESAs) serve some 170 school systems.

The cooperative educational service agencies are funded by the state or through a combination of state and local money. In New York, the BOCES unit is administered by a district superintendent who serves as executive officer of the district board of cooperative educational service. At the same time, the BOCES superintendent reports to the state commissioner of education. In Georgia, the head of each RESA is a director responsible to a board of control, which consists of all the superintendents of the participating school districts and lay persons elected by caucuses of members of the participating school boards. Laypersons must make up one-third of the RESA board of control and must not be educators or holders of public office.

Emery Stoops, Max Rafferty, and Russell E. Johnson suggested that local school districts could look to the intermediate units for the services listed below.

1. Direct supervision of classroom teachers (This diminishes as school districts grow larger.)
2. Coordination of area programs among districts
3. In-service education of certificated and classified personnel
4. Preparation of communication and publication aids
5. Adoption and preparation of courses of study
6. Provision of audiovisual, library, educational TV, and other materials or programs
7. Consultant help with pupil personnel services
8. Operation of federal programs, such as Title III (Elementary-Secondary Education Act [ESEA]), and assistance to districts that apply for federal programs under the several titles of ESEA
9. Cooperation with business and industry to improve vocational education
10. Scoring, interpreting, and summarizing standardized testing
11. Furnishing leadership toward innovations such as flexible scheduling, programmed instruction, team teaching, Head Start and preschool education, collective bargaining or professional negotiation, continuing education in business and industry, citizenship, and skills in human relations
12. Coordination and cooperation with problem departments, law enforcement agencies, legislative committees, character-building organizations, and community support groups.[34]

A considerable amount of instructional supervision is provided by the intermediate level. What we have said about supervision from the state and intermediate levels is prologue to consideration of the heart of issue 9: whether local school districts should make use of central office supervisors or assign supervisors full time to individual schools.

A related issue, which time and space do not permit us to discuss, is whether supervision should be provided by the intermediate unit or by the local school districts. Is service from the intermediate unit the only way small school systems can conduct supervisory programs? Can only the larger and wealthier local school districts establish their own staff, curriculum, and instructional development programs?

Local School Districts

An example of the organization of a large urban school district is shown in Figure 2.2. This figure depicts the organization of the public school system in Orange County, Florida. Note that the deputy superintendent of instruction supervises a large number of administrators/coordinators in a variety of disciplines and specialties. These administrators/coordinators assume leadership for program development in their assigned fields. As such, they represent a typical staffing pattern for a large school system.

The effective central office supervisor must be an itinerant staff member, which means that he or she cannot spend a great deal of time with any one teacher or in any one school. He or she will more likely concentrate on working with groups than with individual teachers.

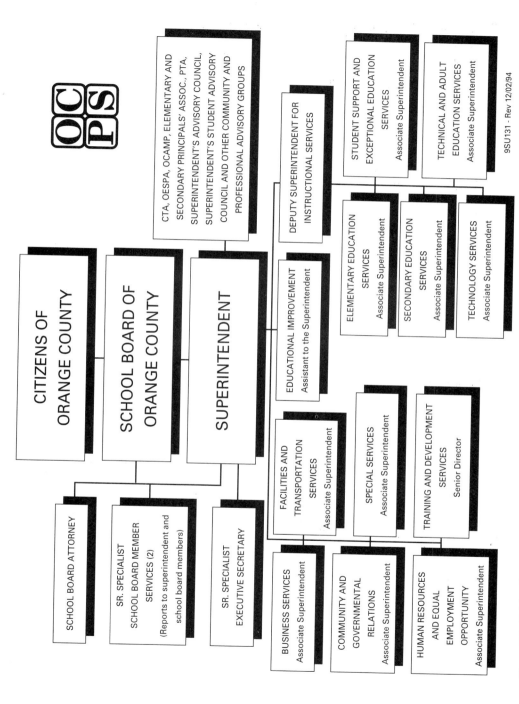

Figure 2.2. Table of Organization, Orange County, Florida, Public Schools. *Source: Orange County Public Schools, Orlando, Florida. Reprinted with permission of the Orange County Public Schools.*

67

Neagley and Evans outlined the major duties of the K–12 office subject-area co-ordinator, as shown below.

1. Visits classrooms and works with teachers from K–12 on instructional and curricular matters peculiar to the discipline or subject area.
2. Includes teachers in decision making and change.
3. Works with the principals and coordinators of elementary and secondary education in a staff relationship and shares particular knowledge and competence as needed.
4. Reports to the assistant superintendent and informs this person of the developing curriculum and new trends and research in the area of specialization.
5. Chairs the district curriculum committees in the discipline or subject area.
6. Makes recommendations to the appropriate officials of instructional and curricular materials and resources.
7. Works closely with the appropriate curriculum consultants in the intermediate unit office or the regional curriculum center, and keeps abreast of the latest research and trends in the field.
8. Conducts parent and community meetings for the lay public and interprets the latest methods and content in the subject area.
9. Prepares written materials for the lay public on topics related to the discipline.
10. Participates actively in the sessions of the curriculum council, especially when the coordinator's area of concern is on the agenda.
11. Meets and works with the other subject-area coordinators, under the leadership of the assistant superintendent in charge of instruction, in order that a balanced curriculum may be developed.[35]

In his study, Edward Pajak confirmed the variety of responsibilities of the central office supervisor. He noted that

> the responsibilities of central office supervisors, curriculum coordinators, and directors of instruction may be described without exaggeration as being extremely diverse and global. . . . While no two job descriptions are exactly the same, those associated with supervisory positions typically include instruction-related tasks, such as coordinating the educational program, ensuring continuity in the kindergarten-through-twelfth-grade curriculum, supervising curriculum planning and development, coordinating program evaluation at the district level, coordinating staff supervision and evaluation, identifying staff development and in-service needs of teachers, planning for staff meetings and workshops for the improvement of instruction, and selecting and recommending textbooks and other teaching materials.[36]

Pajak observed that many other duties required of central-office supervisors go beyond instructional responsibilities into administrative and management activities: collecting information, writing reports, managing budgetary tasks, and engaging in public relations.[37]

Historically, instructional and curricular supervision at the individual building level throughout the country has generally been very limited. Most supervisory service within school systems has come from the central office. Until recent years, the small amount of supervision that can be identified as an individual school activity has been carried out by the principal or assistant principal, occasionally with the help of lead teachers, team leaders, grade coordinators, and department heads.

The lead teacher is a newer position roughly equivalent to a school-based curriculum coordinator. Many schools are employing lead teachers, curriculum coordinators, and resource personnel as members of the staff.

Team leaders, grade coordinators, and department heads are, as a rule, allocated so little released time for supervisory duties as to make their roles in supervision meaningless. As noted earlier, these leaders represent a reservoir of talent that should be developed and put to use in a supervisory capacity.

Arthur J. Lewis and Alice Miel proposed a solution to the central office/individual school issue by separating responsibilities for curriculum leadership and instructional leadership. They suggested that central-office supervisors should carry heavy responsibility for curriculum development whereas the staff of the individual school should concentrate on instructional development.

> The separation of curriculum and instruction lends itself well to this view of a useful sharing of responsibility and authority between central office and semi-autonomous individual schools. Certain kinds of curricular decisions may be made at the school system level in the interests of a broad range of young people. The decisions may be refined and implemented or greatly modified at the building level where those to be educated can be known quite well.
>
> Initiative for curriculum change can be exercised by anyone at any level and provision for coordination makes it more likely that innovative ideas will be shared. Responsibility for instruction clearly belongs in the individual school.[38]

Lovell observed that if we separated curriculum leadership from instructional leadership we might designate the two categories of personnel "curriculum supervisors" and "instructional supervisors."[39] Although the notion of separating curriculum from instruction may be appealing and can be done for purposes of analysis, we find it extremely difficult to do in practice.

Writing for the Working Group of the Association for Supervision and Curriculum Development (ASCD) on the roles and responsibilities of supervisors, A. W. Sturges recommended that school systems recognize two types of instructional supervisors: the *consultative* instructional supervisor and the *administrative* instructional supervisor.

> The *consultative* instructional supervisor is primarily concerned with the improvement of instruction and works closely with teachers. Teachers prefer this type of supervisor be assigned to a specific building. . . . The *administrative* instructional supervisor is also concerned with the improvement of instruction, but more from a controlling and coordinating level. More often housed at a central office, duties will include administrative functions such as requesting and administering Federal grants, acquisition of materials, quality control of the learning environment, and the overall coordination of the instructional program. Responsibilities of the administrative instructional supervisor are often assigned to a principal or department head at the building level or directors/assistant superintendents/coordinators at the district level.[40]

Decentralization of authority and responsibility for the operation of schools has gained in popularity in recent years. Although state direction and power over local schools continue strong, the practice of state mandating prominent in the 1970s and 1980s may have peaked. For example, in the spring of 1991 the state legislature of Florida considered a proposal made by the Commissioner of Education and endorsed by the governor to suspend some state mandates for a period of three years and allow local schools to devise their own plans for meeting state goals.

In a similar vein, in keeping with the philosophy of such influential educators as John I. Goodlad who saw the school as the unit for improvement, more responsibility has shifted from the school district level to the individual school level.[41] The movement toward allowing parents to choose their children's schools, whether public or private, may well impel schools further toward school-based management as competition among schools increases and faculties strive to make their schools more effective. At the same time, pressures are growing for "empowering" teachers—that is, granting them the right to share in decision making.[42] If empowerment is to become reality, shared decision making will need to take place at the individual school level.

In recent years administrators have recognized the value of school-based management. School-based supervision is a concomitant result of school-based management with the individual school staff accepting responsibility for bettering the school's programs and for helping teachers improve instruction. In this approach, school principals, supporting staff, and teachers all join forces to promote the school's goals.

Although figures documenting the increase in the number of school-based supervisors are not available, empirical data reveal many schools supplementing their administrative staff with resource persons, consultants, coordinators, and teachers on special assignment as instructional supervisors. Arthur Costa and Charles Guditus noted that the number of central-office supervisors has declined in recent years.[43] The decrease in number at the district level does not necessarily mean that the increase in school-based supervisors has come about at the expense of central-office supervisors. Costa and Guditus ascribed the decline to diminishing school enrollments as well as a lower priority for curriculum and instructional management from the district level. Central-office supervisory positions are often the first to be terminated when school systems must make budget cuts. The public often harbors the perception—sometimes justified, sometimes not—that administrative staffs at both the state and district levels are top heavy. They prefer to see more resources where their children are—in the individual schools.

Lack of clarity in the central-office supervisor's role also creates problems. Pajak observed, "The absence of a clear conception of the role makes the position of central office supervisor vulnerable when resources are scarce, but it is tenuous even in prosperous times."[44]

The use of school-based supervisors offers several advantages. They are on duty in the school building full time. They can devote all their energies to assisting teachers. They can respond to teachers when they are needed and can serve as the schools' designated leaders in curriculum and instruction.

Although schools cannot and should not duplicate the kinds of supervision the central office can provide, school systems do need to find additional ways for individual schools to create their own supervisory programs in conjunction with central office assistance. If this were done, schools could provide more of the clinical type of supervision recommended by experts like Cogan. What is needed is a well-planned team approach that carefully divides supervisory responsibilities between central office and individual school staff, with a somewhat heavier share of the responsibility falling on the supervisors of the individual school. Both central-office and individual school personnel would work in all three domains of supervision.

In passing, we should observe that the department head of the secondary school is in a precarious position. The department head is often perceived as a member of the administrative team. In systems bound by teachers' union contracts, however, the department head—that is, a teacher—may be designated a member of the bargaining unit and as such is prohibited from conducting or participating in formal evaluations of teacher performance, a function reserved to the administrator. In spite of contractual limitations, department heads can still be available to assist teachers at their request and can work with them on an informal basis. Such an approach might be even more productive in the long run than the traditional department head function.

Significant developments that can greatly and effectively expand supervisory services on the local school level are the movements toward use of teachers to serve as coaches to their peers and of experienced mentors to assist less-experienced teachers. These collegial practices in supervision are discussed later in the text.

ISSUE 10: SHOULD THE SUPERVISOR USE A DIRECTIVE OR NONDIRECTIVE APPROACH?

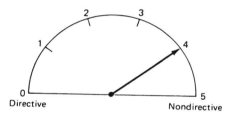

Should the supervisor adopt a direct approach or an indirect approach in working with teachers? Is it the supervisor's mission to tell teachers how to go about their tasks or does the supervisor attempt to effect change by persuasion and example?

Some supervisors see their role as a highly directive one and prescribe content, materials, and techniques for teachers to follow. Others prefer to help teachers to come to their own decisions about content and methods.

An indirect approach in supervision is similar to the nondirective approach followed by guidance personnel and psychologists. The nondirective counselor refrains from claiming to know the answers. Such a counselor does not listen to a client and write a prescription but rather allows the client to express his or her own concerns and ideas. Often the teacher merely wants the reassurance the supervisor is in a position to give. The teacher wants help in thinking through problems and wishes to try out solutions on another person whose judgment can be trusted. An effective supervisor is ready with suggestions for a teacher to consider, knowing that until the teacher has accepted the suggestions and has, in effect, incorporated them into his or her behavior, the suggestions fall on barren land.

Of course, teachers expect the supervisor to be of help to them and to have *some* answers. But they do not expect always to receive the "right" or "approved" or "only" answers; they want the freedom to feel that their solution to an instructional problem is as good as or better than the supervisor's solution.

Teachers can argue with the nondirective supervisor who serves as a sounding board but not with the directive supervisor, the one who tells them what and how they must teach. We are raising a basic question in human relations: Are people motivated to change, cooperate, and work effectively by being told, demanded, or ordered? In the case of supervision, can we tell or demand or order highly trained professionals?

Directive Administrators and Supervisors

Even the administrator who possesses the sanction of society and the law for telling or demanding or ordering finds that in dealing with people a cooperative approach is far more effective in most cases than the hard-nosed approach.

The hard-nosed administrator says, "You must do this because I say so," and may fall back on status and legal authority for enforcing compliance. Individuals commonly react to the highly directive approach in one of a number of ways. They may comply with the administrator's wishes because they happen to be in accord with them and choose to ignore the manner in which they have been made known. If they take issue with the directive manner of an administrator, they may, and probably will, still comply, though in a sullen, resentful way. They will do just enough to meet the minimal requirements of the administrator's edict. They will be cooperative on the surface and uncooperative deep down inside.

Still another type of individual may simply throw in the towel and withdraw in body or spirit from teaching. The creative teacher who feels compelled to accept the administrator's or supervisor's prescribed methods down to the last detail may despair and give up teaching entirely. Others silently ignore edicts, remain in teaching, and resign themselves to the knowledge that their reluctant behavior will lead to penalties for them in assignments, recognition, salary, and promotions.

Bolder individuals will speak out, resist prescriptions of the administrator, and actively rebel. If they have not achieved tenure, the administrator may deny it to them. If they are already on tenure, continuing animosity may exist between the hard-nosed administrator and these rebellious teachers.

Of course, administrators should have the authority to be directive when they need such authority. If a teacher contemplates an activity that might be dangerous to the bodies and minds of students, the administrator has not only the right but the duty to be directive. Teachers recognize this authority as necessary to the administrator's job. It is more often the manner of the administrator than the actual requests that antagonize teachers. The same is true of the directive supervisor whose manner may rub a teacher the wrong way and destroy rapport even when the validity of specific suggestions is not disputed.

Those supervisors who behave in a highly directive fashion are more likely to perceive supervision as a function of administration than those who behave in a nondirective fashion. Directive supervisors tend to see themselves as line administrators rather than as staff service personnel.

If a supervisor is not an administrator, in effect, he or she does not have the implied sanction of status and legal position to be prescriptive. Prescriptive behavior may turn out to be particularly ineffective if teachers realize that the supervisor has no administrative authority and cannot compel them to behave in specific ways. To effect change, the prescriptive supervisor must then appeal to the administrator to apply considerable administrative authority to make recalcitrant teachers see things the supervisor's way. If the supervisor frequently appeals to the authority of the administrator to effect change, the supervisor then becomes aligned in the teachers' minds with the administrator and is no longer perceived as a service-oriented person whom they can count on, confide in, and trust. The supervisor has destroyed the very fabric that should have been maintained—rapport with the persons to be served and assisted.

"Have you ever thought of . . . ?" "Why don't you try . . . ?" "What would you think of . . . ?" are much better ways to phrase suggestions to a teacher than "Do it this way," "Never mind your way," and "It is required." It is a simple psychological principle that individuals will go out of their way to comply with a directive they feel they have helped formulate, about which they made a choice. Whether they indeed had a choice is not nearly as significant as whether they feel that they did. They need to feel also that it is not just the beliefs of one individual that necessitate their compliance with requirements in curriculum and instruction, but that compliance is necessary for the best interest of all concerned—the students, the community, and colleagues.

Blumberg contrasted the direct and indirect approaches in supervision, noting the effects of each style.

> A supervisor using predominantly direct behavior might well be assuming that:
> - The control of a situation is based on the authority of one's position in an organizational hierarchy.
> - People in higher organizational positions have more expertise.
> - People in lower organizational positions can best be evaluated by those who are higher.
> - The most important external rewards of a job come to a person primarily from a person who holds a higher position.
> - Empathic listening to the teacher is not a necessary dimension of helping.
> - People learn best by being told what to do by someone in a higher organizational position.
> - Work is rational; there is little place in supervision for discussion of feelings or interpersonal relationships.
> - Collaborative problem solving between supervisor and teacher is not a critical concern in supervision.
> - Teaching as a skill can generally be separated into the right and wrong ways of doing things.
>
> The assumptions about people that appear to accompany a supervisor's heavily loading indirect behavior are that:
> - Control of the situation depends on the demands of the problem. The problem determines the direction that events take.
> - Expertise is a function of knowledge and experience, not necessarily of organizational position.
> - The product of a teacher's work is the best evaluative tool to use in measuring his performance.
> - The important rewards of teaching are intrinsic to the job, but they need to be supplemented by external rewards.

- People learn best by being confronted with a situation and, with help, finding their own solution.
- It is important for teachers to feel that they have been listened to and understood.
- Work is both rational and emotional; that discussion of feelings and interpersonal relations may be as important as discussion about the job.
- Collaborative problem solving between supervisor and teacher is an important concern of supervision.
- Teaching is a complex process and what works well for one person may not for another, so that most of what goes on in a classroom needs to be viewed experimentally.[45]

Supervisors who follow a nondirective approach treat teachers as intelligent, professional, and valued persons. Room must be left, however, for a directive approach under two circumstances: (1) when a teacher's actions may be detrimental to students, to other faculty, to the program, or to the school; and (2) when the teacher wants or responds only to directive supervisory behavior. Some teachers prefer the direct approach. They want to be told what to do. They feel that a nondirective approach wastes their time and the supervisor's. Further, some teachers believe that a nondirective approach is a subtle way of manipulating them.

Carl D. Glickman referred to a third approach, which he termed *collaborative*. This approach is neither directive nor nondirective, or conversely, both directive and nondirective on the parts of both the teacher and supervisor. Following this concept, the supervisor and teacher work together and take turns at listening, analyzing, and making suggestions.[46] It is the supervisor's task to adapt an individual approach to each teacher's style. We examine directive, collaborative, and nondirective approaches more closely in Chapter 10.

ISSUE 11: SHOULD SCHOOL SYSTEMS ORGANIZE FOR SUPERVISION BY EMPLOYING GENERALISTS OR SPECIALISTS?

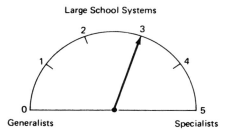

The chief school administrator—the superintendent—must make some difficult decisions on what qualifications to look for in hiring supervisors and how to use personnel. The administrator must decide how many supervisors and what kind will be needed and develop a plan for organizing supervision in the district.

The administrator takes into consideration a number of factors in making these decisions, including the size and financial resources of the district. Each administrator is aware of not only the number of teachers in the system but also their particular strengths and needs as well as their attitudes toward supervision.

The superintendent will have personal views regarding organizational patterns for supervision but must also take into consideration the philosophy of the board of education and the attitudes of the public. Because the employment of specialized personnel will have to be justified to the public, the administrator will have to offer strong reasons for adopting supervisory programs, particularly if they entail a sizable staff. The patterns of organization that are adopted will have to conform to limitations by the school district and to resources available.

Granted the freedom to adopt whatever pattern of organization seems wisest, the superintendent must decide on the kinds of personnel desired: director of instruction, consultants, coordinators, and so forth. But perhaps more basic than the kinds and titles of supervisory personnel is a question that has been debated inside and outside curriculum circles for many years. Should the superintendent employ generalists or specialists to perform the supervisory functions?

Generalists

The generalist may be described as a supervisor who has responsibilities for supervising teachers in a number of grades or in a variety of subjects. Possessing expertise and experience in at least one teaching field, the generalist may and usually does supervise in areas in which he or she does not have special training or has had no training at all. The generalist is an expert at teaching and knows what constitutes good general methods. Each generalist can recognize, for example, a good classroom environment, knows when a teacher is presenting a lesson well, and can judge the effectiveness of planning.

The generalist understands learning theory, is conversant with principles of evaluation and measurement, understands the use of audiovisual materials, has a good background in resources and materials, and knows where to locate additional sources.

The generalist has a broad view of curriculum and can compare what teachers in various grades, classes, subjects, and schools do. The generalist supervisor can assist the teacher with problems of discipline and may be able to help the teacher develop techniques of counseling. The able generalist has a good overall knowledge of curriculum and instruction. By helping teachers of different grades and subjects to work together, this leader can serve as a unifying force.

Personnel who are generalists possess titles such as assistant superintendent of curriculum and instruction, director of instruction, director of elementary education, director of middle schools, director of secondary education, and general supervisor.

Specialists

The specialist supervisor has depth of preparation and experience in a particular level or subject. Each supervisor not only knows the level or subject thoroughly but also knows modern techniques and latest trends in teaching.

The specialist possesses some of the same knowledge and skills as the generalist. The person understands learning theory and can help a teacher with discipline, classroom climate, and guidance. The specialist's forte lies in his or her ability to relate principles and techniques to a particular grade level or field.

The specialist can help a teacher apply techniques of evaluation to a particular subject, or can discuss the use of audiovisual materials with the teacher in relation to a specific grade or field. Planning is considered with the teacher in relation to a specific field rather than to principles of planning in the abstract.

The specialist knows sources of specific materials useful to teachers and can help them to detect and correct mistakes made in teaching particular topics. The specialist has a more limited view of curriculum and instruction than the generalist, as the specialist works within one area and the generalist works across areas. Special supervisors bear such titles as supervisor of language arts, supervisor of science, coordinator of foreign languages in the elementary school, and consultant in social studies.

Look for a moment at the Table of Organization of the Orange County, Florida, Public Schools shown in Figure 2.2; you will note a number of generalists who are responsible for the major operations of the school district. A large number of specialists (coordinators/directors) report to them. A typical arrangement for generalist and specialist supervisors at the district level appears in Figure 2.3.

At the school level, a schematic representation of a school in a typical district, as in Figure 2.4, might show the principal administering a supervisory staff composed of one or two generalists, with team leaders, grade coordinators, or department heads performing the roles of specialist supervisors.

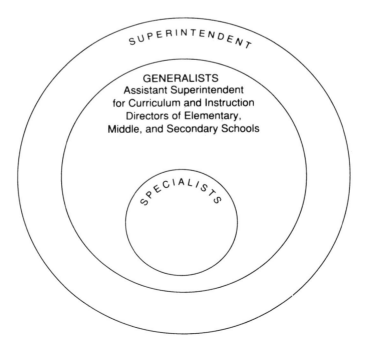

SUPERINTENDENT

GENERALISTS
Assistant Superintendent
for Curriculum and Instruction
Directors of Elementary,
Middle, and Secondary Schools

SPECIALISTS

Figure 2.3. Generalist and Specialist Supervisors at the District Level.

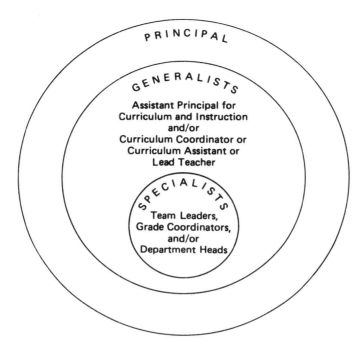

Figure 2.4. Generalist and Specialist Supervisors in an Individual School.

Should teachers be supervised by generalists or specialists? Which type of supervision is the most effective? This is one of the more difficult issues to resolve. Both types of supervision are found throughout the country. Although some school systems provide the services of both generalists and specialists, others must limit their choice to one or the other.

Because they normally have limited financial resources, small school systems tend to employ generalists who can work in a number of areas and across grade levels. Thus, the general supervisor is a common position in those small school districts that can afford the services of a supervisor. If their resources permit, small school systems may employ one or two specialists to help the generalist, particularly in those fields that require a fairly high degree of technical skill such as reading, guidance, exceptionalities, vocational education, science, and mathematics. In a large school system with its greater financial resources, however, the choice may be open to the superintendent, and the chief school officer must decide whether to provide supervisory help through general supervisors or special supervisors or both.

There are without doubt roles for both the generalist and specialist in school supervision. A school system that can afford the services of a full staff of both generalists and specialists is a fortunate system. The generalists provide broad, unifying supervision, and the specialists, narrow, in-depth supervision.

The critical problem arises when a choice has to be made, when a school system must elect one type or the other. The superintendent's philosophy and the wishes of teachers will loom large in solving this problem. At the elementary level, because most elementary classrooms are self-contained, the superintendent may wish to begin a supervisory program by using generalists. Generalists can work very effectively at the elementary school level. They have a breadth that corresponds to the breadth of training provided for elementary school teachers.

Need for Specialists

Elementary teachers, however, are increasingly in need of help from specialists. Mathematics, science, and reading programs have posed problems both for teachers and general supervisors who are not trained in the latest techniques of these programs. Instructing exceptional children, along with the inclusion of these children in regular classrooms, teaching foreign languages, and implementing programs of bilingual and multicultural education have created the need for specialized supervision. General supervisors often lack the depth of training to help teachers write objectives, select appropriate methods, and evaluate results in the specialized fields. They may work effectively in the phases of the program that are more generic in nature, such as language arts, social studies, or humanities. Probably they feel more at home supervising in fields for which they have had preparation and experience. Given this condition, they may minimize or omit assistance to teachers in some critical areas of the school's program.

As school systems move into newer programs and patterns of curriculum organization, the need for special supervisors becomes increasingly clear. Whereas an elementary school might get along satisfactorily with the use of generalists, we believe that it is imperative today to provide specialists in supervision at the secondary level. Content and methods have changed—and continue changing—so rapidly that no generalist can possibly keep up with the changes in all fields.

What school systems really need are specialists who are, in effect, generalists, or conversely, generalists who are, in effect, specialists. A specialist who is well trained should have had at least the usual preparation in principles of teaching. Each will ordinarily have had work in the foundations of education and should be able to identify a suitable learning environment as readily as a generalist. The specialist should know the necessity for teachers to maintain rapport with their students. From prior training and experience, the specialist should know principles of discipline, evaluation, and counseling.

Specialist supervisors who are professional will not push their own vested interest any more than enthusiastic teachers will promote theirs. An administrator always has the power to maintain controls that would prohibit anyone's particular interests from being stressed disproportionately.

Some generalists are both generalist and specialist. They have responsibilities in a number of areas and have depth in one or two. They can provide the coordinating function of generalists while at the same time providing skillful supervision in one or two fields. It would be a mistake to conclude that all specialists are so narrow that they cannot offer more general types of supervision or that all generalists are so shallow that they cannot provide any supervision in depth. In fact, we could mount a defense for the elementary school supervisor as both a generalist and a specialist, the specialty being elementary education.

Generalists such as the director of instruction may assume more responsibilities for coordinating the work of the specialists. They may devote their energies to working with groups of representatives from different fields. Specialists may work with individual teachers and groups of teachers in the same field.

Little if any solid research exists on the relative merits of using general or special supervisors. Barring experimental evidence concerning which type of supervision is better for which teachers and in what kinds of situations, administrators might poll their teachers to learn what type of supervision they would respond to best. The administrator might ask, If there were both a generalist and a specialist in your middle school or secondary field or a specific field of the elementary school program available, which one would you call on first for help? The teachers would be directed to assume that both kinds of supervisors are competent and easy to work with.

Some Parallels

The issue of generalist versus specialist is encountered in other situations within and outside the profession of education. Universities continue to wrestle with this problem in providing faculty supervision of student teachers. Some teacher training institutions have set up their programs in such a way that generalists supervise student teachers at all school levels; others turn to specialists.

It is easier to employ generalists than specialists and it is easier for a university to administer a student teaching program in which supervision is conducted by generalists. Generalists are easier to schedule and can be used more flexibly. Specialists are harder to come by and assignment in their cases is more difficult. Administrative considerations in operating the student teaching program play a more prominent role than efficacy in supervision.

Outside the field of education, medicine has long since resolved the question of generalist versus specialist in favor of specialists over general practitioners. It is sometimes difficult for a patient to know which type of specialist should be consulted. With the mighty strides made in medicine, it has become extremely difficult for the general practitioner to keep up to date in all fields of specialization. Medicine, however, has preserved a role for the generalist. The medical profession's solution to the generalist versus specialist dilemma parallels to some extent the education profession's answer, using generalists who refer particular problems to specialists. The family practitioner, an updated version of the general practitioner, treats common maladies in his or her office but refers patients to specialists as the need arises.

How then shall we organize for supervision? Shall we provide wide-sweeping supervision or supervision in depth?

ISSUE 12: SHOULD THERE BE NATIONAL PROFESSIONAL STANDARDS FOR TEACHERS?

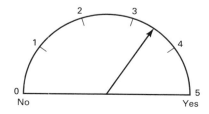

If we are to raise the level of school performance, one important action we can take is to strengthen classroom teaching. That is the purpose of the National Board for Professional Teaching Standards (NBPTS). NBPTS is a private, nonprofit organization, formed in 1987 as a result of a recommendation from the Carnegie Forum on Education and the Economy. The sixty-three-member governing board oversees the program to establish high and demanding standards for what accomplished teachers should know and be able to do as they teach. NBPTS also wants to develop and operate a voluntary national system to assess and certify teachers who meet those standards.

The foundation for National Board certification is expressed in five core propositions:

- Teachers are committed to students and their learning.
- Teachers know the subjects they teach and how to teach them to students.
- Teachers are responsible for managing and monitoring student learning.
- Teachers think systematically about their practice and learn from experience.
- Teachers are members of learning communities.

Currently, standards are being written that cover subject matter and developmental age of students in more than thirty fields. Some examples are Early Childhood (ages 3–8)/Generalist; Middle Childhood (ages 7–12)/Social Studies-History; and Early Adolescence (ages 11–15)/Mathematics.[47]

Increasing support for the mission of NBPTS is coming from federal legislation, the Council of Chief State School Officers, states and local school districts, and contracts negotiated between teachers and local school boards. The negotiated contracts allow reimbursement for NBPTS fees and/or a salary increase, or special endorsement as lead teacher on this national certification. Major education organizations, including the National Education Association, the American Federation of Teachers, the National Association of Elementary School Principals, and the National Association of Secondary School Principals, are supporting the efforts of NBPTS. Financial support from private corporations and foundations has been increasing in recent years.

The first group of eighty-one teachers from twenty-three states to pass the Early Adolescence/Generalist certificate field test was announced in January 1995. They were among the larger group of 290 teachers who completed the rigorous national assessment exercises for that specific certificate.[48]

In August 1995, a second group of ninety teachers from twenty-three states received National Board certification in Early Adolescence/English Language Arts. These English Language Arts teachers of middle grade students started the quest for the certification from a larger group of 230 teachers who sought the certification. Additional certificates planned in the immediate future by the National Board will focus on Early Childhood/Generalist and Middle Childhood/Generalist, with others to follow.[49]

To be considered a candidate for National Board certification, a teacher must have a baccalaureate degree from an accredited institution and three years of elementary, middle, or high school teaching experience. National Board certification differs from state licensure, sometimes referred to as certification, because a state license focuses on entry-level requirements for teaching in a state. National Board certification is designed to recognize experienced and accomplished teachers who practice at a high level. Teachers are evaluated on knowledge of their subjects, understanding of students and teaching, and actual classroom practice.[50]

We believe the heart of education is teaching. Providing each student in our schools with the best teacher should be the focus of every supervisor working in those schools. Ensuring that the professionals working with the students are committed to the students and their learning is essential. It appears that one way of realizing the goal of developing a truly excellent educational system is through the efforts of the National Board for Professional Teaching Standards. Supervisors, school principals, school board members, and the general public need to unify their efforts to support NBPTS in raising teaching standards so as to improve the quality of instruction in America's classrooms. The support can be financial (helping to pay the board's fee, providing salary supplements, allowing the teacher participants paid professional leave), or by sharing information about the NBPTS standards, by encouraging teachers to seek National Board certification, and by offering incentives to participate in the process. Nettie Webb is a school principal and NBPTS board member. She observed that

> traditionally, the principal has been viewed as the instructional leader. But in today's schools, with their complex array of problems and diverse student body, this must be a shared role. Our promise to the community is to improve student learning. With a National Board Certified Teacher on the faculty, that promise can become a reality.[51]

SUMMARY

In this chapter, we have explored twelve issues in supervision. First, supervision is seen as a continuing and necessary service to teachers. Second, the supervisor can provide help to all teachers whether they are experienced or inexperienced, effective or ineffective; more time should be allocated to the inexperienced and the ineffective. Third, the supervisor's authority should be derived from expertise and interpersonal relationships. Fourth, the supervisor is likely to maintain a higher degree of rapport with teachers and render more effective service if not perceived as an administrator and if the supervisor does not perceive himself or herself in that role. Fifth and sixth, staff development and curriculum development are legitimate domains of supervision. Seventh, supervision encompasses two types of evaluation: formative, for the purpose of helping the teacher, and summative, for the purpose of making personnel decisions.

Eighth, supervisors should work with both individuals and groups of teachers, with a somewhat greater allocation of time to working with groups. Ninth, supervision is best carried out by a judicious combination of central office and individual school supervisors, with greater weight given to the supervisory program of the individual school. Tenth, supervisors should, as a rule, manifest a nondirective approach in working with teachers. Eleventh, supervision requires the services of both generalists and specialists, with a slightly greater preponderance of specialists in the larger school systems that can afford them. Twelfth, the supervisor's responsibilities will be enhanced as more teachers achieve certification from the National Board for Professional Teaching Standards.

QUESTIONS FOR DISCUSSION

1. Which of the twelve issues in supervision is the most influential one impacting supervision in your school district?
2. Should a supervisor work primarily with inexperienced teachers or with experienced teachers?
3. Should a supervisor work primarily with ineffective teachers or effective teachers? Why?
4. Should supervisors have had administrative experience? Why?
5. Should a supervisor spend the majority of time working with groups of teachers or with individual teachers? Explain.

ACTIVITIES FOR FURTHER STUDY

1. For each of the twelve issues discussed in this chapter, draw a scale similar to the one shown with each issue and on each scale draw an arrow that shows your position.
2. Interview several practicing supervisors and determine the types of teachers with whom they spend most of their time: new, inexperienced, experienced, effective, or ineffective.
3. Poll a group of teachers at the school level in which you are most interested and ask them whether they prefer help from generalists or specialists.
4. Poll a group of teachers to learn whether they believe that supervisors in their school system are directive or nondirective and ask them which approach they prefer.
5. Find out what Ben M. Harris (*Supervisory Behavior in Education*, 3rd ed.) means by *tractive* and *dynamic* supervision.
6. Find out what Carl D. Glickman (see the chapter bibliography) means by developmental, directive, collaborative, and nondirective supervision.
7. Study the objectives of local chapters of the National Education Association and the American Federation of Teachers. How many of these objectives concern curriculum and instruction? How would the actions of these organizations affect the status and duties of supervisors?
8. Describe characteristics of ineffective teachers and state how you would work as a supervisor with ineffective teachers.
9. Select one characteristic of an ineffective teacher (identified in activity 8) and describe how you would help the teacher diminish that characteristic.
10. Conduct a limited research study in a local school system to confirm or negate the hypothesis that experienced teachers are more effective teachers than inexperienced teachers.
11. Write a brief paper on one of the following questions:
    a. Should the supervisor of elementary education be a specialist or generalist? Why? Is there an area of specialization called elementary education?
    b. Should the supervisor of secondary education be a specialist or generalist? Why? Is there an area of specialization called secondary education?
12. Talk with a sample of school principals and learn what percentage of their time is devoted to supervision of instruction. Determine whether they would prefer to spend more or less time on this task and why they gave the answers they did.
13. Interview one of the top administrators of the school system you know best and

tape his or her comments and views on the role of supervisors on the staff. Among other things, ask how the administrator rates supervisors.

14. Participate in small group discussions in class on each of the twelve issues examined in this chapter. Try to reach consensus on which issue is the most important in the small group and then with the class as a whole.

15. Prepare a position statement on any one of the seventeen issues identified by the ASCD's Working Group on Supervisory Practices that has not been examined in this chapter.

16. Obtain and analyze the staffing pattern of a school system you know well and make a critique of its strengths and weaknesses.

17. Learn whether your state has intermediate units and report on their organizational structure and the services they provide to local schools.

18. Cite one or more issues other than those discussed in this chapter and show your position on each.

NOTES

1. ASCD Working Group on Supervisory Practices, "Issues in Supervisor Roles: What Do Practitioners Say?" *Educational Leadership* 34 (December 1976): 217–20.
2. See George Antonelli, "The Educational Warranty: Refocusing Teacher Education," *Kappa Delta Pi Record* 23 (Fall 1986): 16–19.
3. Ross L. Neagley and N. Dean Evans, *Handbook for Effective Supervision of Instruction*, 3rd ed. (Englewood Cliffs, N.J.: Prentice-Hall, 1980), p. 4.
4. U.S. Department of Education, *America's Teachers: Profile of a Profession* (Washington, D.C.: U.S. Department of Education, 1993), p. 142.
5. Carnegie Foundation for the Advancement of Teaching, *The Conditions of Teaching, 1990* (Princeton, N.J.: Carnegie Foundation for the Advancement of Teaching, 1990), p. 12.
6. Robert J. Alfonso, Gerald R. Firth, and Richard F. Neville, *Instructional Supervision: A Behavior System*, 2nd ed. (Boston: Allyn & Bacon, 1981), pp. 124–25.
7. William H. Lucio and John D. McNeil, *Supervision in Thought and Action*, 3rd ed. (New York: McGraw-Hill, 1979), pp. 26–27.
8. Arthur Blumberg, *Supervisors and Teachers: A Private Cold War*, 2nd ed. (Berkeley, Calif.: McCutchan, 1980), pp. 19–20.
9. A. W. Sturges, *The Roles and Responsibilities of Instructional Supervisors* (Alexandria, Va.: ASCD Working Group on the Roles and Responsibilities of Supervisors, Association for Supervision and Curriculum Development, 1978).
10. William H. Burton and Leo J. Brueckner, *Supervision: A Social Process*, 3rd ed. (New York: Appleton-Century-Crofts, 1955), p. 85.
11. Harold Spears, *Improving the Supervision of Instruction* (Englewood Cliffs, N.J.: Prentice-Hall, 1953), p. 27.
12. Glen G. Eye and Lanore A. Netzer, *Supervision of Instruction: A Phase of Administration* (New York: Harper & Row, 1965), p. 12.
13. Hoy and Forsyth, *Effective Supervision*, pp. 9–16.
14. Leslee J. Bishop, *Staff Development and Instructional Improvement: Plans and Procedures* (Boston: Allyn & Bacon, 1976), p. 1.
15. Lloyd W. Dull, *Supervision: School Leadership Handbook* (Columbus, Ohio: Merrill, 1981), p. 110.
16. Ben M. Harris, *In-Service Education for Staff Development* (Boston: Allyn & Bacon, 1989), p. 18.

17. Donald C. Orlich, *Staff Development: Enhancing Human Potential* (Boston: Allyn & Bacon, 1989), pp. 5–6.

18. See Peter F. Oliva, *Developing the Curriculum*, 3rd ed. (New York: HarperCollins, 1992).

19. See Harold E. Turner, "The Department Head: An Untapped Source of Instructional Leadership," *NASSP Bulletin* 67 (September 1983): 25–28.

20. John T. Lovell and Kimball Wiles, *Supervision for Better Schools*, 5th ed. (Englewood Cliffs, N.J.: Prentice-Hall, 1983), p. 143.

21. Kathryn V. Feyereisen, A. John Fiorino, and Arlene T. Nowak, *Supervision and Curriculum Renewal: A Systems Approach* (New York: Meredith, 1970), p. 15.

22. Lucio and McNeil, *Supervision in Thought and Action*, p. 155.

23. Morris Cogan, *Clinical Supervision* (Boston: Houghton Mifflin, 1973), p. 9.

24. Gary Embretson, Ellen Ferber, and Terry Langager, "Supervision and Evaluation: Helping Teachers Reach Their Maximum Potential," *NASSP Bulletin* 68 (February 1984): 27.

25. Ibid.

26. G. H. Fredrich, "Supervision and Evaluation: Recognizing the Difference Can Increase Value, Effectiveness," *NASSP Bulletin* 68 (November 1984): 12.

27. Ibid., p. 13.

28. Thomas A. Petrie, "Ideas That Hinder Education—Debunking the Myths," *NASSP Bulletin* 64 (December 1982): 53–54.

29. John C. Daresh, *Supervision as a Proactive Process* (White Plains, N.Y.: Longman, 1989), p. 195.

30. Edward Pajak, *The Central Office Supervisor of Curriculum and Instruction: Setting the Stage for Success* (Boston: Allyn & Bacon, 1989).

31. See Roald F. Campbell et al., *The Organization and Control of American Education*, 6th ed. (Columbus, Ohio: Merrill, 1990), p. 136.

32. Ibid., p. 132.

33. Stephen J. Knezevich, *Administration of Public Education*, 4th ed. (New York: Harper & Row, 1984), p. 190.

34. Emery Stoops, Max Rafferty, and Russell E. Johnson, *Handbook of Educational Supervision* (Boston: Allyn & Bacon, 1975), pp. 72–73. See also Ralph B. Kimbrough and Michael Y. Nunnery, *Educational Administration: An Introduction*, 3rd ed. (New York: Macmillan, 1988), pp. 209–17.

35. Neagley and Evans, *Handbook for Effective Supervision of Instruction*, p. 107; adapted from Ross L. Neagley and N. Dean Evans, *Handbook for Effective Curriculum Development* (Englewood Cliffs, N.J.: Prentice-Hall, 1967), pp. 137–38.

36. Pajak, *The Central Office Supervisor*, pp. 4–5.

37. Ibid., p. 5.

38. Arthur J. Lewis and Alice Miel, *Supervision for Improved Instruction: New Challenges, New Responses* (Belmont, Calif.: Wadsworth, 1972), p. 47.

39. John T. Lovell, "Instructional Supervision: Emerging Perspective," in Sturges, *Roles and Responsibilities*, p. 32.

40. Sturges, *Roles and Responsibilities*, pp. 72–73.

41. John I. Goodlad, *A Place Called School: Prospects for the Future* (New York: McGraw-Hill, 1984), p. 31.

42. See Gene Maeroff, *The Empowerment of Teachers: Overcoming the Crisis of Confidence* (New York: Teachers College Press, 1988).

43. Arthur Costa and Charles Guditus, "Do Districtwide Supervisors Make a Difference?" *Educational Leadership* 41 (February 1984): 84.

44. Pajak, *The Central Office Supervisor*, p. 3.

45. Blumberg, *Supervisors and Teachers*, pp. 88–89.

46. Carl D. Glickman, Stephen P. Gordon, and Jovita M. Ross-Gordon. *Supervision of Instruction: A Developmental Approach*, 3rd ed. (Boston: Allyn & Bacon, 1995), Chap. 10.

47. Barbara C. Shapiro, *National Standards for Teachers. Streamlined Seminar* (Alexandria, Va.: National Association of Elementary School Principals, vol. 13, February 1995).

48. Joanne Kogan Krell, Press Release. "National Board Recognizes First 81 Teachers Who Meet National Certification Standards" (Detroit, Mich.: National Board for Professional Teaching Standards, January 5, 1995).

49. Joanne Kogan Krell, Press Release. "90 Teachers Nationwide Join Elite Group of Top Honorees" (Detroit, Mich.: National Board for Professional Teaching Standards, August 21, 1995).

50. Ibid.

51. Shapiro, *National Standards for Teachers*, pp. 3–4.

BIBLIOGRAPHY

Alfonso, Robert J., Gerald R. Firth, and Richard F. Neville. *Instructional Supervision: A Behavior System*, 2nd ed. Boston: Allyn & Bacon, 1981.

Antonelli, George. "The Educational Warranty: Refocusing Teacher Education." *Kappa Delta Pi Record* 23 (Fall 1986): 16–19.

ASCD Working Group on Supervisory Practices. "Issues in Supervisor Roles: What Do Practitioners Say?" *Educational Leadership* 34 (December 1976): 217–20.

Association for Supervision and Curriculum Development. "Instructional Supervision: Trends and Issues." *Educational Leadership* 34 (May 1977): 563–618.

Bishop, Leslee J. *Staff Development and Instructional Improvement: Plans and Procedures*. Boston: Allyn & Bacon, 1976.

Blumberg, Arthur. *Supervisors and Teachers: A Private Cold War*, 2nd ed. Berkeley, Calif.: McCutchan, 1980.

Bradley, Ann. "Pioneers in Professionalism." *Education Week* (April 20, 1994): 19–27.

Briggs, Thomas, and Joseph Justman. *Improving Instruction through Supervision*, rev. ed. New York: Macmillan, 1962.

Burton, William H., and Leo J. Brueckner. *Supervision: A Social Process*, 3rd ed. New York: Appleton-Century-Crofts, 1955.

Campbell, Roald F., Luverne L. Cunningham, Raphael O. Nystrand, and Michael D. Usdan. *The Organization and Control of American Schools*, 6th ed. Columbus, Ohio: Merrill, 1990.

Carnegie Foundation for the Advancement of Teaching. *The Conditions of Teaching, 1990*. Princeton, N.J.: Carnegie Foundation for the Advancement of Teaching, 1990.

Caswell, Hollis L. "The Generalist—His Unique Contribution." *Educational Leadership* 24 (December 1966): 213–15.

Cogan, Morris. *Clinical Supervision*. Boston: Houghton Mifflin, 1973.

"Collective Bargaining." *Phi Delta Kappan* 63 (December 1981): 231–56.

Costa, Arthur, and Charles Guditus. "Do Districtwide Supervisors Make a Difference?" *Educational Leadership* 41 (February 1984): 84.

Daresh, John C. *Supervision as a Proactive Process*. White Plains, N.Y.: Longman, 1989.

Douglass, Harl R., Rudyard K. Bent, and Charles W. Boardman. *Democratic Supervision in Secondary Schools*, 2nd ed. Boston: Houghton Mifflin, 1961.

Dull, Lloyd W. *Supervision: School Leadership Handbook*. Columbus, Ohio: Merrill, 1981.

Embretson, Gary, Ellen Ferber, and Terry Langager. "Supervision and Evaluation: Helping Teachers Reach Their Maximum Potential." *NASSP Bulletin* 68 (February 1984): 27.

Esposito, James P., Gary E. Smith, and Harold J. Burbach. "A Delineation of the Supervisory Role." *Education* 96 (Fall 1975): 63–67.

Eye, Glen G., and Lanore A. Netzer. *Supervision of Instruction: A Phase of Administration*. New York: Harper & Row, 1965.

Eye, Glen G., Lanore A. Netzer, and Robert D. Krey. *Supervision of Instruction*, 2nd ed. New York: Harper & Row, 1971.

Feyereisen, Kathryn V., A. John Fiorino, and Arlene T. Nowak. *Supervision and Curriculum Renewal: A Systems Approach*. New York: Meredith, 1970.

Fredrich, G. H. "Supervision and Evaluation: Recognizing the Difference Can Increase Value, Effectiveness." *NASSP Bulletin* 68 (November 1984): 12.

Glanz, Jeffrey, and Richard F. Neville, eds. *Educational Supervision: Perspectives, Issues, and Controversies*. Norwood, Mass.: Christopher-Gordon, 1996.

Glickman, Carl D. *Development Supervision: Alternative Practices for Helping Teachers Improve Instruction*. Alexandria, Va.: Association for Supervision and Curriculum Development, 1981.

Glickman, Carl D., Stephen P. Gordon, and Jovita M. Ross-Gordon. *Supervision of Instruction: A Developmental Approach*, 3rd ed. Boston: Allyn & Bacon, 1995.

Goodlad, John I. *A Place Called School: Prospects for the Future*. New York: McGraw-Hill, 1984.

Gwynn, J. Minor. *Theory and Practice of Supervision*. New York: Dodd, Mead, 1961.

Harris, Ben M. *Improving Staff Performance through In-Service Education*. Boston: Allyn & Bacon, 1980.

———. *In-Service Education for Staff Development*. Boston: Allyn & Bacon, 1989.

———. *Supervisory Behavior in Education*, 3rd ed. Englewood Cliffs, N.J.: Prentice-Hall, 1985.

Harrison, Raymond H. *Supervisory Leadership in Education*. New York: American Book, 1968.

Hoy, Wayne K., and Patrick B. Forsyth. *Effective Supervision: Theory into Practice*. New York: Random House, 1986.

Kimbrough, Ralph B., and Michael Y. Nunnery. *Educational Administration: An Introduction*, 3rd ed. New York: Macmillan, 1988.

Knezevich, Stephen J. *Administration of Public Education*, 4th ed. New York: Harper & Row, 1984.

Krell, Joanne Kogan. Press Release. "National Board Recognizes First 81 Teachers Who Meet National Certification Standards." Detroit, Mich.: National Board for Professional Teaching Standards, January 5, 1995.

———. Press Release. "90 Teachers Nationwide Join Elite Group of Top Honorees." Detroit, Mich.: National Board for Professional Teaching Standards, August 21, 1995.

Leeper, Robert R., and Fred T. Wilhelms, eds. *Supervision: Emerging Profession*. Alexandria, Va.: Association for Supervision and Curriculum Development, 1969.

Lewis, Arthur J., and Alice Miel. *Supervision for Improved Instruction: New Challenges, New Responses*. Belmont, Calif.: Wadsworth, 1972.

Lovell, John T. "Instructional Supervision: Emerging Perspective." In *The Roles and Responsibilities of Instructional Supervisors*, chairman A. W. Sturges. Alexandria, Va.: ASCD Working Group on the Roles and Responsibilities of Supervisors, Association for Supervision and Curriculum Development, 1978.

Lovell, John T., and Kimball Wiles. *Supervision for Better Schools*, 5th ed. Englewood Cliffs, N.J.: Prentice-Hall, 1983.

Lucio, William H. *The Supervisor: New Demands, New Dimensions*. Alexandria, Va.: Association for Supervision and Curriculum Development, 1969.

Lucio, William H., and John D. McNeil. *Supervision in Thought and Action*, 3rd ed. New York: McGraw-Hill, 1979.

McKean, Robert C., and H. H. Mills. *The Supervisor*. New York: The Center of Applied Research in Education, 1964.

Maeroff, Gene. *The Empowerment of Teachers: Overcoming the Crisis of Confidence.* New York: Teachers College Press, 1988.

Marks, James R., Emery Stoops, and Joyce King-Stoops. *Handbook of Educational Supervision: A Guide for the Practitioner*, 3rd ed. Boston: Allyn & Bacon, 1985.

Mosher, Ralph L., and David E. Purpel. *Supervision: The Reluctant Profession.* Boston: Houghton Mifflin, 1972.

Neagley, Ross L., and N. Dean Evans. *Handbook for Effective Supervision of Instruction*, 3rd ed. Englewood Cliffs, N.J.: Prentice-Hall, 1980.

Oliva, Peter F. *Developing the Curriculum*, 4th ed. New York: HarperCollins, 1997.

Ordovensky, Pat. "National Certification Sounds Sweet All Right, but Will It Fly?" *The Executive Educator* 12 (January 1990): 18–20, 30.

Orlich, Donald C. *Staff Development: Enhancing Human Potential.* Boston: Allyn & Bacon, 1989.

Pajak, Edward. *The Central Office Supervisor of Curriculum and Instruction: Setting the Stage for Success.* Boston: Allyn & Bacon, 1989.

Petrie, Thomas A. "Ideas That Hinder Education—Debunking the Myths." *NASSP Bulletin* 64 (December 1982): 53–54.

Raths, James, and Robert R. Leeper, eds. *The Supervisor: Agent for Change in Teaching.* Alexandria, Va.: Association for Supervision and Curriculum Development, 1966.

Sergiovanni, Thomas J., ed. *Supervision of Teaching*, 1982 Yearbook. Alexandria, Va.: Association for Supervision and Curriculum Development, 1982.

Sergiovanni, Thomas J., and Robert J. Starratt. *Supervision: A Redefinition*, 5th ed. New York: McGraw-Hill, 1993.

Shapiro, Barbara C. *National Standards for Teachers. Streamlined Seminar.* Alexandria, Va.: National Association of Elementary School Principals, vol. 13 (February 1995).

Spears, Harold. *Improving the Supervision of Instruction.* Englewood Cliffs, N.J.: Prentice-Hall, 1953.

Stoops, Emery, Max Rafferty, and Russell E. Johnson. *Handbook of Educational Administration.* Boston: Allyn & Bacon, 1975.

Sturges, A. W., chairman. *The Roles and Responsibilities of Instructional Supervisors.* Alexandria, Va.: ASCD Working Group on the Roles and Responsibilities of Supervisors, Association for Supervision and Curriculum Development, 1978.

Subcommittee on National Security and International Operations. *Specialists and Generalists, a Selection of Readings.* Washington, D.C.: U.S. Government Printing Office, 1968.

Turner, Harold E. "The Department Head: An Untapped Source of Instructional Leadership. " *NASSP Bulletin* 67 (September 1983): 25–28.

Unruh, Adolph, and Harold E. Turner. *Supervision for Change and Innovation.* Boston: Houghton Mifflin, 1970.

U.S. Department of Education. *America's Teachers: Profile of a Profession.* Washington, D.C.: U.S. Department of Education, 1993.

Vail, Kathleen. "Raising the Bar." *The American School Board Journal* 182 (April 1995): 48–49.

Wiles, Jon, and Joseph Bondi. *Supervision: A Guide to Practice*, 4th ed. Englewood Cliffs, N.J.: Merrill, 1995.

Williams, Stanley W. *New Dimensions in Supervision.* Scranton, Pa.: Intext, 1972.

Wilson, L. Craig, T. Madison Byar, Arthur S. Shapiro, and Shirley H. Schell. *Sociology of Supervision: An Approach to Comprehensive Planning in Education.* Boston: Allyn & Bacon, 1969.

PART II
Leadership in Instructional Development

Helping Teachers Plan for Instruction

Objectives

After studying Chapter 3 you should be able to accomplish the following objectives:

1. Describe your own preferred model of instruction.
2. Demonstrate skill in following a systematic approach to instructional design.
3. Demonstrate skill in following a model of instruction.
4. Demonstrate skill in writing instructional goals and objectives.
5. Demonstrate skill in applying taxonomies of instructional objectives.
6. Demonstrate skill in describing and analyzing learning tasks.
7. Demonstrate skill in organizing instructional plans.

MODELS OF INSTRUCTION

Years ago a postcard arrived at the university address of one of the co-authors. The card came from an elementary school teacher who requested that a plan for the year's work be sent to her for use with her first graders. It apparently had not occurred to her in spite of whatever preservice training she had had that planning for instruction was her responsibility. She sought a ready-made, complete year's plan—to be given to her—by someone with no knowledge of her school, her community, her pupils, and her own objectives.

Surprisingly, with state and district mandates on curriculum during the 1970s and 1980s, we almost reached that point. As a matter of fact, we have gone through a period when curriculum and instructional planners sought to create curricula that would be "teacher-proof."

With varying degrees of success, every teacher education institution provides instruction in planning, primarily in its preservice training program. Students learn basic techniques of planning and usually experience opportunities for demonstrating their plans and putting them into practice.

The teacher education institution, however, can simply offer an introduction to instruction, providing a foundation and limited practice in demonstrating teaching skills. These skills become refined as a teacher gains experience on the job. Central to this book is the belief that all teachers, no matter how long they have taught, can develop new skills and improve old ones. As more becomes known about the instructional process with every passing year, newer and better ways of providing instruction continuously develop. The supervisor's function is to assist teachers in becoming familiar with newer approaches to instruction and in developing and improving instructional skills.

The alert supervisor becomes aware of the extent of planning and the degree of proficiency in this skill shown by teachers who are to be supervised. Supervisors encounter, for example, some teachers with no written plans for instruction. Given the complexities of education today, surely some sort of written plan is in order and should be expected for each lesson a teacher presents.

Supervisors might begin to examine the problem of planning as they try to ascertain what kinds of plans teachers are making. As they spot deficiencies in planning, they may work with individuals or groups in devising better ways to go about this fundamental task.

The supervisor may encounter resistance to planning in a variety of forms. There are teachers who fully believe that they need not write anything down because they have sufficient mastery of the content of the program. They overlook the value of a written plan as a communication device that allows the *learner* to know what to expect from subsequent instruction.

Some teachers view their role in the Socratic tradition, hoping that young people will flock around them to gather unorganized bits of wisdom. Other teachers will readily admit that they realize the value of planning but rationalize that they do not have sufficient time to write plans. The supervisor needs to show them that planning is a much more complicated and important phase of instruction than many teachers believe. Conscientious teachers will have to consider many variables as they begin to plan. Each group of pupils has varying abilities, needs, and interests. Among the newer challenges is planning that takes into consideration the inclusion of children with exceptionalities in the regular classroom and the increasing linguistic and cultural diversity among students.

A seemingly inexhaustible pool of content exists from which teachers can draw. Certain parameters such as the school's schedule and budgetary limitations must be considered, as well as expectations of other teachers, the public, school administrators, and even the state legislature. Faced with many methods or strategies for presenting a given lesson, the teacher must make choices, knowing that some of these strategies are likely to be more effective than others for certain purposes, with certain groups, with certain individuals, in certain settings, and for the teacher's particular personality. Consequently, when the teacher jots down in a small plan book a reference to a particular chapter or exercise or topic and views that as an adequate lesson plan, he or she is ignoring many significant variables. All teachers at all levels can improve their planning skills, and one of the supervisor's tasks is to help them do so.

Simplified Model

Planning is the first stage of a continuum, followed by the implementation or presentation stage and then the evaluation stage. Some specialists in instruction would diagram the phases of the continuum as follows:

$$\text{Planning} \longrightarrow \text{Presentation} \longrightarrow \text{Evaluation}$$

They would refer to the diagram as a simplified model of instruction, which is a pattern providing teachers with a guide for following certain aspects of behavior. The model indicates simply that the teacher begins the instructional process with initial planning, proceeds through the strategies of presentation, and moves finally to evaluating what the plan set out to achieve.

CLASSROOM PLANNING: A SIX-POINT PROGRAM

In practice, teachers become involved in planning on a school, district, state, regional, and national level—and on rare occasions, on an international level. In this text, stress is placed on planning that relates to curriculum and instruction at the classroom, school, and district levels and on the role of the supervisor in fostering curricular and instructional planning at those levels. This chapter considers techniques for the improvement of instruction in the individual teacher's classroom. Chapter 7 discusses faculty involvement in curriculum development on the various levels.

Effective classroom presentation requires a great deal of thought and preparation by teachers. To assist them with the task of planning, the supervisor may provide training in the development of six competencies, shown here.

1. Skill in following a systematic approach to instructional design
2. Skill in following a model of instruction
3. Skill in writing instructional goals and objectives
4. Skill in applying taxonomies of instructional objectives
5. Skill in describing and analyzing learning tasks
6. Skill in organizing instructional plans

The supervisor should begin by surveying the degree to which these skills are possessed by the various teachers. Some teachers may have a high level of expertise in all these competencies. If that is the case, the supervisor, after verifying the fact that the teachers demonstrate these skills, would encourage those teachers to continue their good work and give more attention to teachers who need assistance in perfecting one or more of the skills. The supervisor may use the skilled teachers as models and may call on them to serve as resource persons to teachers who need assistance.

Following a Systematic Approach to Instructional Design

A systematic approach to instruction is guided by four questions: What do you wish to achieve? What resources do you have and need to achieve your objectives? How will you go about achieving your objectives? How well have you accomplished your objectives?

Whenever a teacher creates a course outline or lesson plan, he or she is engaging in instructional design. The teacher can make the design process more efficient and more effective by approaching the task systematically. A systematic approach replaces haphazard planning by requiring a careful examination of all the parts of a plan and how the parts relate to each other.

The basic principles of a systematic approach are simple. For our purposes, this approach is a planned, integrated, complete design for the use of materials, media, and personnel to accomplish certain predetermined objectives. Each of the component parts interrelates with the others, providing continuous feedback for modification of the design. A systematic approach to instruction is the process of creating a learning design in which all the component parts are specified, assembled, and interrelated.

There are eight steps in the process. Let us suppose for illustration that we wish to design a year's program in a particular subject or for a particular grade level. We might equally illustrate the process with a sequence of a particular curriculum extending over several years—for example, the language arts curriculum; or we could plan for a portion of a program—a unit—extending over a few weeks; or in abbreviated form, we could plan for a day or a class period. The steps that follow will give us a global look at the process. We have singled out steps 1, 2, 3, and 5 for more extended treatment in this chapter. Because of their complexity we devote greater attention to steps 6 and 7 separately in Chapter 4, and steps 4 and 8 in Chapter 6. The process of systematic planning entails the following steps.

1. *Taking stock of the present program.* The teacher reviews the present program, analyzes what has been covered in the past, and reexamines the current goals and objectives. He or she examines the procedures for presenting the content, the varied resources that have been available, and the existing limitations. The teacher must decide whether the program fits into the total scheme of the curriculum and whether it meets the needs of the learners for whom the program is intended. Before redesigning an old program or designing a new program, the teacher must consider the past and the present.

2. *Specifying the goals of instruction.* The teacher decides on the general purposes of the program. The goals provide a sense of direction for subsequent instruction and help the teacher define the specific objectives.

3. *Specifying the objectives of instruction.* One of the most important phases of systematic design is the specification of objectives, the specific outcomes of instruction. The objectives state what the learner is expected to learn, to accomplish, or to do, under what conditions, and with what degree of mastery. They serve as the source of the evaluation process.

4. *Designing an evaluation plan.* The instructor must determine whether the presentations have been successful, that is, whether students have mastered the content and whether they have reached the objectives set out at the beginning. The teacher may choose from a variety of evaluation techniques to learn how well students have achieved.

5. *Describing and analyzing the learning tasks.* If the learning tasks are complex, the teacher must break them down and describe the sequence in which instruction is to be presented. He or she must know what skills the learners must bring to the tasks to achieve the objectives; the teacher must analyze the tasks and decide whether they are appropriate for the particular group of learners who will be confronted with the material. The teacher must call on his or her knowledge of learning theory and decide what types or conditions of learning are involved in the pursuit of the tasks.

6. *Designing instructional procedures.* The teacher makes decisions about the strategies of instruction to be employed, choosing the instructional procedures that appear to have the best chance for success given the nature of the program, any constraints that have been imposed, and the nature of the learners. Techniques of instruction must be compatible with the teacher's own abilities and personality.

7. *Implementing the instructional procedures.* At this stage, the design moves from thinking and planning to the actual process of instruction. The instructor meets with the learners and leads them in study of the content, then enters into a process of interaction—the learners interacting with the teacher and with each other and both the learners and the teacher interacting with the content.

8. *Implementing the evaluation plan.* Both during implementation of the instructional procedures and at the end of implementation, the teacher puts the evaluation plan into operation and seeks to obtain continuous feedback concerning whether the students are, indeed, learning the material and mastering the tasks. We must discover whether students are successful not only for traditional purposes of evaluation but also for the purpose of modifying the instructional process.

The teacher uses feedback from evaluation in making revisions in the design and modifying the program. If the objectives are inappropriate for any reason, they must be redesigned. If the data show that instructional procedures have been ineffective, different procedures must be tried. A systematic approach permits, in fact mandates, that continuous redesign take place.

If we were to contrast older approaches to planning with a systematic approach, we could note the following differences.

SYSTEMATIC APPROACH	OLDER APPROACH
Focus on learner's objectives, what the learner does	Focus on teacher's objectives, what the teacher does
Objectives apparent before instruction begins	Objectives not apparent or apparent during or after instruction
Continuous feedback	No feedback or feedback at the end of instruction
Continuous redesign	Redesign after instruction and for the next group of learners
Evaluation of all objectives	Evaluation of selected objectives
Achievement of the learner related to mastery of the objectives	Achievement of the learner related to achievement of other learners

The supervisor may wish to offer an in-service training program that takes teachers through the eight steps of a systematic approach to instruction.

Following a Model of Instruction

Instructional designers follow a sequence of steps that they refer to as a model of instruction. A model is a pattern that provides a logical progression from one step to the next. Earlier in this chapter, you became acquainted with a simplified model of instruction consisting of three components: planning, presentation, and evaluation. Models are normally shown in the literature on instruction as charts or schematic representations using a series of boxes, lines, or arrows. The preceding simplified model of instruction can be diagrammed as shown in Figure 3.1.

A model serves as a guide to the teacher for instructional design. It reveals both the essential elements of the instructional process and the sequence in which these elements are put into practice. Figure 3.1, the simplified model of instruction, however, is not an adequate guide. It is not detailed enough. It omits one or more essential elements and it does not show the important characteristic of feedback. Figure 3.1 can be expanded into a four-part model that is slightly more explicit in form and substance (see Figure 3.2).

Other experts in instruction have advocated four-part models. Robert J. Kibler, Donald J. Cegala, David T. Miles, and Larry L. Barker discussed a four-part model that they referred to as the General Model of Instruction[1] while W. James Popham and Eva L. Baker labeled their four-part model a Goal-Referenced Instructional Model.[2] We might convert the four-part model shown in Figure 3.2 by adding one block at the beginning labeled Formulation of Goals, as in Figure 3.3, thus creating a five-part model.

The five-part model of instruction calls for the formulation or specification of the goals and objectives of instruction. It incorporates an assessment of the learner's skills prior to initiating study of the subject matter. Evaluation of student achievement follows implementation or presentation of instruction. Feedback lines cycle back from evaluation to the preceding stages.

Figure 3.1. Simplified Model.

Figure 3.2. Four-Part Model.

Figure 3.3. Five-Part Model.

Models found in the literature show many similarities in essential elements. They differ mainly in their detail and in the choice of components they emphasize. Some vary the sequence of components slightly; others are a bit more sophisticated. Some attempt to sketch every instructional act in the model itself.

The differences in models are not so great as to recommend one over the other. The important responsibility of the teacher is to select a model compatible with his or her style of teaching or to create a model and follow that model in the design of instruction. The teacher could combine components of various models and create one such as that shown in Figure 3.4.

We could even recast the steps in the process of systematic planning discussed earlier in this chapter in the form of a model of instruction. Such a model would look like the one in Figure 3.5 (page 98). The feedback lines at the top and bottom of the model show that as a result of evaluation the component parts of the design may be modified.

Which of the models of instruction a teacher follows does not matter greatly, but for perfecting the skill of following a model, the teacher should select one carefully and stick with it for a period of time. In this way, he or she can develop an easy familiarity with the model, and this familiarity will simplify the planning process.

Figure 3.4. Oliva Model. *Source: Peter F. Oliva,* The Secondary School Today, *2nd ed. (New York: Harper & Row, 1972), p. 292.*

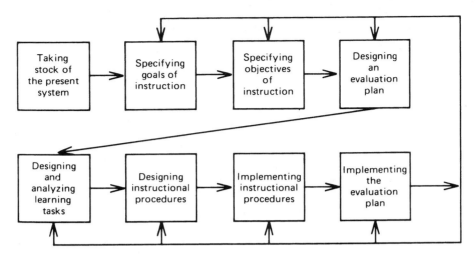

Figure 3.5. Alternative Systematic Model.

If supervisors are going to help teachers work with models of instruction, they should try out various models for themselves to see how they work in the actual process of instructional design. After analyzing models of instruction, supervisors should help teachers become acquainted with various ones, assist them in selecting models compatible with their own needs, and encourage them to try their own hands at creating a model.

Writing Instructional Goals and Objectives

Instructional Goals. The educational literature is peppered with the words *aims, purposes, goals,* and *objectives*. We hear and read about "the aims of education," "the purposes of American education," "goals of education for the twenty-first century," and "objectives of secondary education." The terms are used interchangeably and loosely. Although the dictionary equates *objective* with *goal*, in instructional planning *goal* and *objective* are not necessarily the same and in our opinion they should not be used interchangeably. For purposes of instructional design, the words *aims* and *purposes* should be avoided. These terms should be relegated to philosophical discussions of education on a broader scale.

When some people speak of goals, they mean the broad aims or purposes of education, which we might also refer to as *educational goals*. In this chapter, we are not concerned with broad educational goals but rather with more limited instructional goals. Whereas educational goals may apply to the whole process of education and schooling, instructional goals apply only to particular content. We make a sharp distinction between goals and objectives in instructional design. Both relate to the instructional process and both are concerned with specific content.

Instructional goals are general statements of hoped-for learning on the part of the student. Goal statements contain such language as "The student should become familiar with . . . ," "The student should become aware of . . . ," "The student should gain an understanding of . . . ," and "The student should develop an appreciation for . . . ." These expressions cannot be evaluated with any degree of precision. In fact, they may contain statements of outcomes that are not even observable, such as "to develop an appreciation for . . ." A teacher may or may not be able to discover whether a student has indeed developed an appreciation for the particular subject matter.

Goals provide the teacher with a general sense of direction. They are rough indicators of where instruction is taking the student. As such, they are written in terms of the learner and not the teacher. The teacher's goals may or may not be the same as the learner's goals. The whole thrust of instructional design should be on the achievement of the learner. For this reason, statements of goals of instruction are cast into the form of expectations on the part of the learner. We can illustrate this with some goal statements from a variety of disciplines.

- The student should develop an appreciation for the music of Mozart by listening to recordings of his works performed by the London Philharmonic Orchestra.
- As a result of study of Darwin's *Origin of Species,* the student should better understand the basic principles of Darwin's theory of evolution.
- The student should understand the role of a citizen in a democratic society.
- When encountering persons of an ethnic group different from his or her own, the student should have empathy for them.
- The student should become acquainted with a variety of linguistic pattern drills.
- The learner should understand the system of checks and balances written into the U.S. Constitution.
- The pupil should learn the nines multiplication table.
- The child should enjoy reading Dr. Seuss's books.
- The student should develop an understanding of his or her role as a member of a family.
- The learner should recognize the hazards of cigarette smoking.
- The student should develop the ability to solve mathematics problems.
- The student should comprehend the necessity for conservation of natural resources.
- The pupil should learn to take responsibility as a member of a committee.
- The pupil should understand why it is necessary to wash his or her hands before eating.
- The student should know the differences between goals and objectives.

The verbs used in these statements—*understand, know, learn, appreciate,* and *recognize,* for example—are nonbehavioral. They do not tell exactly what the learner must demonstrate or do to show the teacher that the learner has accomplished what the teacher expected to be accomplished. Goals serve the useful purpose of giving direction to instruction, but their breadth, their lack of specific learner behavior, and their vagueness do not permit evaluation of the learner's mastery of content. The writing of instructional goals, however, is an important exercise, for it aids the teacher in deriving instructional objectives.

After pointing out the general direction of instruction by specifying the goals, the teacher turns to the task of deciding on instructional objectives—the specific outcomes of learning.

Instructional Objectives. Instructional objectives, alternately known as behavioral or performance objectives, state clearly expected behavior on the part of the learner. Instructional objectives differ from goals in that they are written in terms of student performance that can usually be observed and measured. We say *usually* advisedly, for when we enter the unexplored world of the affective domain, it is not always possible to observe or measure expected student behavior.

Most instructional planners recommend that behavioral objectives possess three characteristics:

1. *Expected behavior on the part of the learner*. The teacher must answer the question "What will the student actually do to show that he or she has learned the material?" The teacher decides on the expected behavior by examining the goals, by describing and analyzing the learning task, and by considering the world outside this class where the expected behavior may be applied. Following the discussion of writing objectives, we will examine the process of describing and analyzing learning tasks. A description and analysis of a learning task may cause a teacher to revise the behavioral objectives already specified.

The teacher should give some thought to the applicability of the behavior in situations outside the classroom both in the present and in the future. We are talking here about the transfer of training. We must ask ourselves in what way the expected behavior may be of value to the learner either in other school situations or outside the school.

Whether the objectives are in the *cognitive* domain (the area of knowledge), the *affective* domain (the area of feeling), or the *psychomotor* domain (the area of perceptual-motor skills), the teacher should consider their usefulness beyond the walls of the classroom. Many objectives, particularly those of a cognitive nature, are useful at the next higher levels of education. They are useful in the next grade, in an advanced sequence, or in a higher institution of learning. As such they are preparatory to additional and continuing education. Other objectives are useful in the learner's day-to-day life in the school, in the home, and in the community. Still others are useful in part-time jobs while the learner is in school or in a full-time career after he or she finishes school. You can easily see the transferability of instruction in auto mechanics, for example. Provided the instruction in auto mechanics has been adequate, the learner can leave school, accept a job as an auto mechanic, and apply the skills learned in school. More difficult to explain to many learners is the transferability—or relevance—of the study of Pizarro's conquest of Peru or of Giuseppe Verdi's opera *Rigoletto*.

Whenever possible, verbs used in statements of instructional objectives should reflect some overt behavior on the part of the learner. The words chosen should be action verbs such as *list, define, interpret, draw, analyze, compare, construct, organize, write, explain, produce, decide, classify, synthesize, type, summarize,* and *report.* While writing the objectives, the teacher should be thinking of ways to determine whether the learners achieve them. The teacher's evaluation plan should begin to take shape in his or her mind while selecting the objectives.

The supervisor can help individual teachers and groups of teachers write goals and objectives by collecting and showing the teachers examples of nonbehavioral goals and behavioral objectives and asking teachers to distinguish between goals and objectives. The supervisor should demonstrate ways in which nonbehavioral goals can be translated into behavioral objectives by means of action words.[3]

2. *Conditions under which the learning takes place.* A complete behavioral objective stipulates the situational elements in which the learner works to fulfill the objective. The teacher specifies the tools the learner will use or the setting in which the learning occurs. For example, a mathematics teacher might decide on the following behavioral objective. Given a pencil, ruler, paper, and compass, the student will construct an isosceles triangle in five minutes. The pencil, ruler, paper, and compass, the tools with which the learner performs the task, are the conditions necessary for accomplishing it. A business education teacher might wish the learners to be able to process forty-five words per minute using a specific word-processing program with a maximum of two errors. The word-processing program is the condition written into this objective. Or a science teacher may write the following objective: "In the science laboratory, using paper, matches, a small ashtray, and a glass tumbler, the student will demonstrate that oxygen is necessary for combustion to take place."

Some experts in constructing performance objectives show a preference for expressing conditions by starting with the word *given*. Thus, you find such statements as "Given a set of problems . . . ," "Given a list of authors . . . ," "Given a paper and pencil test . . ." Although the use of the word *given* followed by the conditions is one satisfactory way of stating conditions, it is by no means the only way. Following this pattern exclusively can make the construction of behavioral objectives border on writing formulas rather than creative ideas. Indeed, when the conditions are obvious, there is no need to state them. For example, it is not necessary for the teacher to state, "Given a paper and pencil test . . ." When the teacher prepares the test and distributes it, obviously that is the condition imposed. Behavioral statements should include the conditions when they are not readily apparent. The supervisor should avoid the pedantic or dogmatic position of insisting that all behavioral objectives contain written statements of conditions. Belaboring the obvious turns off teachers and discourages them from writing behavioral objectives.

3. *Level of mastery.* A behavioral objective should show or imply a level of mastery of the behavior sought. The teacher should determine what quality of performance to expect of the learner. The teacher needs to specify the standard of performance unless that standard is an obvious one. Standards of performance may be expressed in the form of time to complete a task, number of correct responses, number of errors permitted, or percentage of correct demonstrations of the behavior. For example, the earlier illustration "Given a pencil, ruler, paper, and compass the student will construct an isosceles triangle in five minutes" contains a time standard— five minutes. The illustration from the business education curriculum, "The student will process forty-five words per minute using a specific word-processing program with a maximum of two errors," requires a two-part standard—forty-five words per minute with a maximum of two errors. The following example calls for a degree of mastery in terms of number of correct responses and percentage: "On this test of twenty-five items, the student will achieve a score of at least twenty (80 percent)."

The teacher could make the objective more demanding by adding a time element, as "On this test of twenty-five items the student will achieve a score of at least twenty (80 percent) in ten minutes."

When the standard is implied or obvious, there is no need to write it into the objective. Take the following example from the field of Spanish: "The student will be able to write with correct spelling the names of the months of the year." The statement includes two levels of mastery, one specified (correct spelling) and one implied (all twelve months). No standard need be written into this objective: "Define the word *ethnic*." The student's answer is either right or wrong. It would be superfluous or artificial to tack on "with 100 percent accuracy." Unless a teacher indicates differently, 100 percent mastery is expected, as in the illustration "Given a series of measures in miles, the student will convert them to kilometers." The teacher is requiring the correct conversion of all items in the series.

Some objectives are so complex that it is a difficult or forced procedure for teachers to stipulate levels of mastery. It would require a rather lengthy description to write a standard for this objective: "Draw a graph showing the growth of the population of California for the last decade." To spell out a standard for this objective, the teacher would have to say something about the accuracy of figures used, the learner's skills in graphing, even the learner's artistic ability. There comes a point of diminishing return in terms of the time it would take a teacher to refine an objective to the point of including all standards. We must rely on the teacher's judgment for determining whether this objective has been achieved. A similar problem exists in a typical social studies learning task: "The student will present to the class his or her views on welfare payments." This objective involves personal views, informational content, and skills of oral presentation.

Sometimes it is not possible to write a level of mastery. This is particularly true of objectives in the affective domain. The impression is often given that writing affective objectives is analogous to writing objectives of a cognitive or psychomotor nature. Both conditions under which behavior is demonstrated and level of mastery can evade the teacher in the affective domain. What level of mastery might be required from the objective "Respond to an appeal from fellow students by helping to collect food and clothing for needy families of the community"? This could be a very important learning. The appeal might be seen as the condition, but how much help and what kinds of help should be expected? You could say simply that any degree of help would fulfill this objective. A teacher of environmental studies might want students to "appreciate the consequences of actions that pollute the air and water supplies." Under what conditions should this appreciation take place? What degree of appreciation is required?

The affective domain, in which attitudes, feelings, and values are paramount, begs the question of indoctrination. Whose values should be taught? The learners'? The teacher's? The community's? The nation's? The world's? Are all values of equal worth? Supervisors need to help teachers identify those values that are generally accepted by American society and that can be safely promoted. Writing affective objectives is much more difficult than writing cognitive and psychomotor objectives. The expected behavior of the learner cannot always be observed when we are dealing with the affect. We cannot always be sure of the learner's feelings and attitudes.

You cannot always know under what conditions or to what degree he or she may show the desired behavior. The expected behavior, if it takes place at all, often takes place outside the classroom and outside the school. Sometimes the expected behavior does not occur until a long time after the learning experiences that sought to produce the behavior. These conditions should not dissuade teachers from writing affective objectives, but the conditions should make teachers realize that they need not strain to write conditions and levels they can neither control nor predict with accuracy.

COMPONENTS OF BEHAVIORAL OBJECTIVES. Most of the instructional specialists who have written on the subject of behavioral objectives have recommended three components: (1) the expected or terminal behavior, (2) the conditions under which the behavior takes place, and (3) the level of mastery that the learner is expected to demonstrate. Robert H. Davis, Lawrence T. Alexander, and Stephen L. Yelon suggested a fourth component.[4] They distinguished between performance standards—that is, level of mastery—and performance stability. They believed that a stability standard or criterion should be included to indicate the number of times the learner must perform the behavior at or above the performance standard. They provided examples of objectives that contain both a performance standard and performance stability. One of these is "The student will run the 100-yard dash in fifteen seconds, three out of five times." The expected behavior is "run the 100-yard dash." The performance standard is one of time—"in fifteen seconds." The stability criterion is "three out of five times." The conditions under which the behavior is to be performed, incidentally, have been left out of the statement. It is assumed that the student will have a place to run and will probably have to dress properly for the activity. A supervisor may wish to acquaint teachers with the distinction between performance standard and performance stability and suggest that they write a stability criterion into an objective when doing so seems plausible.

Planning for instruction begins with the writing of instructional objectives. Because objectives are detailed and numerous in many cases, setting them down on paper is essential to avoid overlooking important ones and omitting significant learnings. Writing objectives is essentially a creative and thought-provoking activity. Different teachers will decide on different objectives. Each teacher brings to this task all he or she knows about the learner, the subject, instruction, and society. Writing instructional objectives is no simple task. It is an extremely important job, however, because all subsequent steps of the instructional process hinge on the objectives that have been specified.

To help teachers with the planning process, the supervisor might institute an in-service program on the writing and use of instructional objectives. He or she might consider dividing this program into two distinct phases: (1) writing objectives following criteria described in this text or in other sources, and (2) using objectives already developed elsewhere.

Some practice in writing objectives would be desirable to help teachers perfect the skill. Teachers have probably had some exposure (perhaps in some cases overexposure) to writing instructional objectives in their preservice training. If they are already familiar with the technique, they may apply it and develop objectives for their particular courses and grade levels. The objectives they develop may be retained to build a local bank of objectives from which they may later draw. As a group activity, the process of writing objectives can be beneficial when teachers examine, exchange, and present critiques of objectives written by their peers.

Because teachers, state departments of education, and organizations in various parts of the country have long been involved in developing instructional objectives in a variety of disciplines, the supervisor should acquire and share with teachers curriculum materials containing objectives that have already been written. The teachers could examine objectives in their fields of interest to see whether they meet the criteria for instructional objectives and to decide whether specific objectives would be useful in their own programs. This activity would be essentially a process of selecting objectives from a pool of objectives that have already been prepared. We should note that some state- and district-mandated curricula prescribe instructional objectives that are to be mastered by students in various disciplines and grades. For those disciplines in which mandated curricula exist, the teacher's opportunities to specify objectives are reduced. However, teachers would still have the freedom to go beyond the prescribed curricula and, indeed, should do so.

Applying Taxonomies of Instructional Objectives

Earlier in this chapter we used the terms *cognitive domain*, *affective domain*, and *psychomotor domain*. Each domain implies a large area of related learnings. The cognitive domain encompasses learning of a factual and intellectual nature; cognitive tasks are mental exercises leading to knowledge. The affective domain takes in learnings of an emotional nature; affective tasks produce feelings and attitudes toward things and people. The psychomotor domain comprises learnings that may require some cognition but are primarily skills that demand movement of parts of the body. Because psychomotor learnings involve both mental and bodily activity, they are often called perceptual-motor skills.

A task description and analysis, discussed later in this chapter, will reveal whether the learning tasks are primarily those of the cognitive, affective, or psychomotor domain. The content of a given course may include learnings from all three domains. The supervisor should encourage teachers to write objectives in all three domains whenever all are applicable. Because cognitive and psychomotor objectives are the most apparent, affective objectives are often overlooked. Of course, not all content will lead to outcomes in all three domains. On the other hand, much of the content studied in school is of such a nature that learnings in at least two and often all three of the domains should be sought.

An experienced teacher soon learns that not all learnings of a given domain are of equal merit. Some learnings are more complex than others. Some are more important than others in terms of their significance to the learner and their permanence. Some learnings are clearly of a lower level of competence than other learnings.

The three domains have been subjected to study for the purpose of answering these questions: What categories of learnings may be classified in each domain? What is the order of importance of each category? In 1956, Benjamin S. Bloom and his associates published a classification system—a taxonomy—of educational, that is, instructional, objectives in the cognitive domain.[5] David R. Krathwohl, Bloom, and

Bertram B. Masia produced a system in 1964 for classifying objectives in the affective domain.[6] A taxonomy of objectives in the psychomotor domain by Elizabeth Jane Simpson appeared in 1972.[7] These taxonomies have been widely cited and implemented.

In the following discussion, we describe each domain and give three examples of instructional objectives in each major category. The first example in each category of all three domains is drawn from the same learning unit so you can trace objectives on one theme through all levels of all three domains. To follow a topic through all three domains, we have had to choose a unit from a discipline in which psychomotor, as well as cognitive and affective, learnings are sought. We have, therefore, turned to a unit at the secondary school level on impressionist painters.

The second set of examples illustrates a theme through all levels of two domains: the cognitive and affective. For this series of illustrations we have selected the topic of federal income tax applicable to a course in consumer education at the junior or senior high school level. Psychomotor learnings are of little importance in studying federal income tax. This same theme, therefore, cannot be carried through the psychomotor taxonomy. A unit on tumbling in physical education at the elementary, middle, or senior high school level furnishes the second set of examples of psychomotor objectives.

The third set contains examples taken from many disciplines of the elementary, middle, and secondary school; there is no relationship among the third set of examples across domains or at any levels within a domain. These last examples are a miscellaneous collection of objectives that serve as additional illustrations.

The Bloom Taxonomy. The Bloom taxonomy of the cognitive domain sets forth a hierarchy of six major categories.[8] From the lowest level to the highest these categories are

1. Knowledge
2. Comprehension
3. Application
4. Analysis
5. Synthesis
6. Evaluation

The taxonomy further subdivides each of the categories into subcategories according to levels of importance, but it will serve our purposes to confine discussion to the six major categories. The taxonomy says, in effect, that those instructional objectives that are designed to seek only the acquisition of knowledge are at the lowest level of both complexity and importance. Most lay people feel that the cognitive domain is or should be what schools are all about. It is no secret to anyone who has ever gone to school that most of the learnings sought have been, still are, and will likely continue to be in the cognitive domain and that most of those learnings hover around the low end of the taxonomy. All a supervisor needs to do to verify this point is to examine several tests given by teachers and he or she will see how frequently learners are asked to recall specific factual information as opposed to interpreting, applying, analyzing, synthesizing, and evaluating data. A supervisor needs to help teachers to write higher-level objectives. We illustrate below what behavioral objectives look like at each level of the Bloom system of classification.

1. Knowledge
   a. The student will name four impressionist painters.
   b. The student will give the number of the short form used for filing his or her federal income tax statement.
   c. On an outline map of the United States showing the Great Lakes, the student will print the name of each lake in its proper location.
2. Comprehension
   a. The student will explain what is meant by *impressionism*, citing the chief characteristics of this school of painting.
   b. The student will tell the difference between an *exemption* and a *deduction* as applied to the federal income tax.
   c. Given a graph showing the increase in population of the state of Arizona over the last thirty years, the student will interpret to his or her classmates the facts shown by the graph.
3. Application
   a. From a series of reprints of classical and modern paintings and applying characteristics studied in class, the student will select those that are the works of impressionist painters.
   b. Given a set of data, the student will correctly calculate the tax due the federal government by using the appropriate tax table.
   c. The student will correctly solve eight out of ten problems in long division.
4. Analysis
   a. The student will examine reprints of one painting of an impressionist painter and one painting of a nonimpressionist painter and contrast the differences in the styles.
   b. Given a completed 1040 tax form, the student will determine whether there are any errors in filling out the form and whether the tax due has been calculated correctly.
   c. The student will watch several commercials on television and decide whether they meet the standard of "truth in advertising."
5. Synthesis
   a. The student will write a biography of an impressionist painter.
   b. The student will fill out a 1040A tax form by using data furnished by the teacher.
   c. The student will produce a documented research paper on the effects of drugs on the human body.
6. Evaluation
   a. The student will examine a reprint of a painting by a lesser-known impressionist and evaluate the quality of the work, applying characteristics studied in this unit.
   b. From background data about a fictitious taxpayer and a completed income tax return, the student will evaluate the deductions taken by the taxpayer and decide whether he or she was entitled to all the deductions claimed. The student will give reasons for all decisions.

   c. The student will read a short story by O. Henry and evaluate it in respect to (1) mood, (2) vocabulary, and (3) impact on the reader.

Although we have used the style "The student will . . ." in each of the preceding examples, teachers may prefer an abbreviated style that is equally acceptable. "The student will" can simply be omitted, leaving, for example, "Name four impressionist painters"; "Given a graph showing the increase in population of the state of Arizona over the last thirty years, interpret to your classmates the facts shown by the graph."

A teacher or group of teachers can develop their own classification system. They might create, for example, a simplified system consisting of two levels: low-order objectives and high-order objectives.[9] However, because the Bloom taxonomy has been with us for many years and has been widely followed with considerable success, it provides a ready-made guide that teachers might well choose to follow. In either case, the object is to raise the level of behavioral objectives to a higher order than is commonly found in many classrooms. Curricular efforts today place great emphasis on thinking skills. If teachers are ever to develop learners' ability to think, they must move instruction to the higher levels of learning. Parenthetically, we must note that thinking skills cannot be demonstrated in a vacuum. The thinker must possess a cognitive base to use those skills effectively.

We should point out that in all three taxonomies discussed in this chapter objectives may overlap levels of each domain. Each level within a domain builds on the preceding level, adding a degree of complexity with each ascending step in the hierarchy. It is difficult, sometimes impossible, and generally not necessary for a given objective to fit precisely and clearly within one level. The important understanding we should hold is that the thrust of the objectives should be upward in each hierarchy.

The Krathwohl Taxonomy. Krathwohl and his colleagues enumerated five levels in their classification of objectives in the affective domain:

   1. Receiving
   2. Responding
   3. Valuing
   4. Organization
   5. Characterization by value or value complex[10]

Like the Bloom taxonomy, the Krathwohl classification breaks each major category into subcategories in a hierarchy from low to high level. As in our discussion of the Bloom taxonomy, we illustrate by referring only to the major categories and rely on the reader to consult the taxonomies themselves for the detailed subdivisions of each category. Following are examples of objectives for each of the five categories.

   1. Receiving
      a. The student will demonstrate in conversation an awareness of impressionistic art that he or she encounters in daily life.
      b. The student will evidence an awareness of the need for paying one's federal income tax and the consequences of not filing when required to do so.

    c. The student will show an awareness that the Native American has suffered at the hands of the white settlers of America.

2. Responding

    a. The student will choose and read a book on impressionism.

    b. The student will observe the deadline for filing his or her tax return.

    c. The student will volunteer to serve on a committee for a class project.

3. Valuing

    a. The student will express an appreciation for the contributions of the impressionists to our aesthetic life.

    b. The student will support the income tax system by pointing out worthwhile government expenditures financed by tax revenues.

    c. The student will defend physical fitness exercises.

4. Organization

    a. The student will decide whether he or she likes impressionist painting and what the characteristics are that cause him or her to like it or dislike it.

    b. The student will analyze the reasons some people cheat on their income tax returns and decide whether he or she approves or disapproves of this behavior.

    c. The student will account for his or her reasons for subscribing to a particular moral value.

5. Characterization by value or value complex

    a. The student will express a positive predisposition toward the fine arts as an enrichment for our lives.

    b. The student will consistently demonstrate honesty in paying his or her income tax.

    c. The student will develop the habit of collecting facts before making a decision.

The preceding illustrations show some of the inherent problems of affective objectives. As we noted earlier, objectives in the affective domain are often both unobservable in school and unmeasurable. We cannot know for sure whether the student in affective category 2b, for example, will, indeed, file an income tax return. The student can tell the teacher that he or she is aware of the laws requiring the filing of income tax returns and can express agreement with the need for a federal income tax and measures to enforce the laws. We have no way of knowing, however, whether the student has complied with the law. We do know, of course, that there is often a discrepancy between what people profess to do and what they actually do. For some of us, the affective domain may dwarf the cognitive in regard to payment of income taxes. It was tempting to give examples such as "The student will refrain from groaning when income tax time comes around."

Few people would argue the importance of learnings such as those illustrated in the five categories of the affective domain. Affective objectives can point the way toward hoped-for ends. Because students may achieve the affective objectives, if not immediately, perhaps in the future, these types of objectives are worth writing. We do raise a caution at this point, however, and will return to it in the discussion of evaluating instruction in Chapter 6. Because it is difficult and often impossible to structure affective objectives in such a way that they can be both observed and measured and because they reflect values, opinions, and attitudes, they cannot be evaluated and scored in the same way as cognitive and psychomotor learnings.

The Simpson Taxonomy. More recent than the taxonomies of the cognitive and affective domains is the Simpson classification of instructional objectives in the psychomotor domain. Simpson recommended a classification system consisting of seven categories.[11] Her major categories from lowest to highest are

1. Perception
2. Set
3. Guided response
4. Mechanism
5. Complex overt response
6. Adaptation
7. Origination

Anita J. Harrow, who also created a taxonomy of the psychomotor domain, suggested that Simpson's category of perception may be considered as interpreting; set, as preparing; guided response, as learning; mechanism, as habituating; complex overt response, as performing; adaptation, as modifying; and origination, as creating.[12] The following examples serve to illustrate the Simpson scheme for classifying psychomotor objectives.

1. Perception
   a. The student will perceive the visual impact (blurred effect, dots) of impressionist painting.
   b. The student will recognize the mat as appropriate equipment for demonstrating skill in tumbling.
   c. The student will identify the sound of the piano.
2. Set
   a. The student will demonstrate how to hold a paintbrush.
   b. The student will demonstrate the correct stance from which to begin tumbling.
   c. The student will demonstrate the proper way to hold the clarinet.
3. Guided response
   a. The student will imitate the teacher's demonstration of mixing water colors.
   b. The student will imitate the teacher's demonstration of tumbling.
   c. Following directions on the box the student will mix a batch of batter for pancakes.
4. Mechanism
   a. The student will mix water colors to prepare the shades he or she will use in copying a reprint of a classical landscape or seascape.
   b. The student will perfect proper form by practicing several tumbles, each of which the teacher will critique.
   c. The student will sand manually the top of a small wooden table.
5. Complex overt response
   a. The student will copy a reprint of a classical landscape or seascape.

    b. The student will do a triple tumble, demonstrating proper form at the beginning, while tumbling, and in regaining standing position.

    c. The student will transcribe dictation that has been recorded on a dictating machine.

6. Adaptation

    a. The student will paint a second copy of the same reprint of a classical landscape or seascape, converting it to impressionist style.

    b. The student will introduce a variation on the tumbling exercise taught by the teacher.

    c. The student will convert a popular ballad or classical theme to disco beat (using any musical instrument).

7. Origination

    a. The student will do an original painting in water color or in oils in impressionist style.

    b. The student will create a new exercise using the mat without additional props.

    c. The student will create and build a model house of original design and of unusual building materials.

Each succeeding category from perception to organization demands a higher degree of skill, from the simplest to the most complex. Some of the psychomotor objectives—mainly in the category of perception—are mastered during the preschool years. With psychomotor skills as with cognitive learnings, it is somewhat easier to write conditions and levels of mastery into these objectives than into affective objectives. Some of the examples specify conditions; others merely imply them. Many of the examples imply a level of mastery—right or wrong, correct or incorrect.

When you examine all three taxonomies, you can readily see that they are not discrete and mutually exclusive. Learnings often cut across all domains. All perceptual-motor skills contain elements of cognition and often of the affect. Affective objectives require mastery of cognitive and often psychomotor learnings. The cognitive domain may reach into the affective and many times the psychomotor. The whole area of language learning, for example, may bounce back and forth among the three domains. When the student completes a sentence correctly, whether written or oral, he or she may be in all domains at the same time. Knowledge of the correct grammatical form and sentence structure places the student in the cognitive domain. Pleasure at giving the right response and being rewarded for it by the teacher's approval leads the student into the affective domain, whereas the physical action of writing or moving vocal chords, tongue, and lips puts the student in psychomotor territory.

The teacher should, therefore, classify instructional objectives under the domain that seems to be the primary nature of the task. A workshop on the classification of instructional objectives and the application of a system of classification to instructional planning could be a valuable in-service program for a supervisor to organize.

Describing and Analyzing Learning Tasks

Task Description. A task description and analysis of each instructional objective (i.e., the task) are helpful to the teacher in refining planning. Some instructors combine the concepts of task description and task analysis and think in terms simply of task analysis; others distinguish between them. Davis, Alexander, and Yelon clearly separated description of a task from analysis.[13] A task description is a determination of the steps or sequence in which a learning task is studied. A task analysis, according to Davis et al., is the identification of characteristics of the learner, the types of learning involved, and the conditions or constraints imposed. This distinction between description and analysis is a useful one.

Certain tasks must be taught in a step-by-step procedure. The teacher should describe that procedure before attempting to present the content. The concept of task description is more useful in some content areas than in others, being particularly helpful in developing competencies in the psychomotor domain. Complex perceptual-motor skills must often be taught in a particular sequence of steps. For example, there are generally accepted sequences for teaching activities like the ones shown here.

- Baking a cake
- Refinishing a table top
- Parallel parking
- Cleaning a rifle
- Repairing an automobile generator
- Drawing a blood specimen
- Making a papier-mâché figure
- Laying vinyl tiles
- Filling out an airline ticket and reserving space for a customer
- Developing film
- Cutting a piece of lumber with an electric handsaw

These tasks involve both mental and manual skills. To accomplish the tasks correctly the learner must follow a particular or fixed sequence of steps. As an example, we can describe the task of parallel parking by listing the steps that must be followed. Assume that we have the car in motion. The driver's handbook furnished by a state's department of motor vehicles furnishes an excellent description of the task of parallel parking. The required steps are clearly specified, and woe be to the applicant for a driver's license who does not follow them exactly:

1. Stop even with car ahead and about two feet away from it.
2. Turn wheels sharply right and back slowly toward the car behind.
3. As your front door passes the back bumper of the car ahead, quickly straighten the wheels and continue to back straight.
4. When clear of car ahead turn wheels sharp left and back slowly to car behind.
5. Turn wheels sharp right and pull toward center of parking space.
6. Put gear in park position.
7. Set parking brake.
8. Shut off motor.
9. Remove key from switch.

We hypothesized a car in motion for a specific reason—to show a single sequence of steps. Suppose for a moment that the car is parked in the driveway and that we wish to give our offspring—who has a learner's permit—a real test before going for the driver's license examination by having our child drive downtown and parallel park. Our driver-to-be would have to demonstrate several series of steps in a fixed order:

1. Start the car
2. Back out of the driveway
3. Drive straight ahead
4. (Possibly) Pass a car
5. Make right and left turns
6. Respond to signal lights and road signs
7. Parallel park

Each of these skills requires its own particular sequence of steps. A driver-training instructor would need to describe each sequence.

Task descriptions are less common, less necessary, and less readily apparent in the cognitive and affective domains. The task description is obvious when a student is called on to "list the names of the five leading oil-producing nations of the world." There is no sequence involved in a simple cognitive task of this type. An element of sequence might be provided by asking the student to list the nations in the order of number of barrels of oil they produce annually, but that is not a sequence of steps to be followed in mastering the objective.

In the affective area of learning it is almost impossible to describe a fixed sequence of steps. What would be the sequence of steps for the affective objective that seeks to have a student "demonstrate empathy for an ethnic group different from his or her own by writing an essay that supports the ethnic group's desire for improved economic and political opportunities"? Students will approach this task in a variety of ways.

Some of the more complex cognitive tasks may lend themselves to task description if there is a generally accepted sequence that most experts follow. Solving types of mathematical problems is an illustration of a complex cognitive task that can be described. For example, suppose that we wish to teach pupils to multiply one factor (the multiplicand) by another factor (the multiplier) of three digits. We might ask the student to demonstrate ability to perform this task by requiring him or her to multiply 2,326 by 247.

$$
\begin{array}{r}
2326 \\
\times\ 113 \\
\hline
16282 \\
9304 \\
4652 \\
\hline
574522
\end{array}
$$

Though the operation can be done mechanically, the learner should be taught that a particular sequence of steps is being followed:

Step 1: multiply 2326 by 7 $2326 \times\ \ 7 = \ 16282$
Step 2: multiply 2326 by 40 $2326 \times\ 40 = \ 93040$
Step 3: multiply 2326 by 200 $2326 \times 200 = \underline{465200}$
Step 4: add 16282, 93040, and 465200 574522

There is likely to be agreement among mathematicians that these four steps are the proper ones in teaching this learning task. If there is no agreed-upon correct sequence for performing a learning task, the teacher can still make his or her own task description that would show the learner the sequence to follow.

A foreign language specialist in a teacher education institution, for example, might wish students in a methods class to teach some principles of grammar by means of a selected number of oral pattern drills. Although there is no particular sequence to this task, and variations in sequence might occur from instructor to instructor, the specialist would undoubtedly want the students to begin the study of this task with the simpler kinds of drills and proceed to the more complex.

The instructor might phrase the performance objective: "In the methods class before peers, the student will demonstrate during one class period four different types of pattern drills for teaching points of grammar." For students to reach this stage the instructor must teach them the various types of pattern drills and break the task down into four steps.

Step 1: Work on simple analogy drills.
Step 2: Work on item-substitution mutation drills.
Step 3: Work on fixed-increment drills.
Step 4: Work on paired-sentence drills.

The instructor next recasts the steps of the description into behaviorally stated subobjectives, which are often referred to as enabling objectives or, simply, enablers. They are the subcompetencies that must be mastered before the major objective, the competency, itself is attempted. In behavioral terms, enabling objectives in this case may be stated as shown here.

1. The student will construct and present orally in class a simple analogy drill.
2. The student will construct and present orally in class an item-substitution mutation drill.
3. The student will construct and present orally in class a fixed-increment drill.
4. The student will construct and present orally in class a paired-sentence drill.

Highlighting the steps in a learning task makes it easier to identify the subobjectives that must first be achieved by the learners. The description also helps to refine the major learning task itself.

Though a teacher may often write task descriptions even if the experts in the discipline are in disagreement on the order in which learning should be presented, it is not always possible or desirable for the teacher to attempt a task description for every kind of learning task. It is questionable whether there can be or should be a fixed progression of steps in such activities as suggesting ways to solve the nation's environmental problems, writing a poem, designing the floor plan of a house, doing an original painting in water colors, or composing a song. These learnings appear to be of a creative nature, cutting across the cognitive, affective, and psychomotor domains. To try to establish a fixed order for which learnings of this type are undertaken could result in squelching the very creativity they are designed to foster.

Task Analysis. Task analysis follows task description. After the steps of the task have been determined, the teacher examines the nature of the task, seeking answers to such questions as these: What is the background of the learners who will encounter the task? Do they have the necessary prerequisite skills for beginning study of the topic? What skills do learners really need to be successful in mastering the content? In this regard, the supervisor should help teachers develop the ability to assess prerequisite (entry) skills, a topic considered in Chapter 6 when we discuss evaluation of instruction.

The teacher's analysis proceeds by identifying the kind of learning involved in the task so the best choice of teaching procedures for presenting the content can be made. Some preservice or in-service training in learning theories and their application in the classroom is essential for this task. Learning theory would be a very appropriate topic for an in-service program arranged by a supervisor. To help the supervisor recognize types of learning, Robert M. Gagné's categories might be used as a guide.[14] Gagné has classified what he referred to as conditions of learning from simplest to most complex types. His classification includes eight types of learning. These types are presented briefly here.

1. *Signal learning.* This is classical conditioning—the formation of conditioned responses to planned or unplanned stimuli. Experiments of the Russian scientist Ivan Pavlov to train a dog to salivate at the ringing of a bell are the classic illustrations of this type of learning. Fear of thunder is a conditioned response. Somewhere in the past the individual heard a sudden clap of thunder that was followed by a fright reaction—perhaps a scream—of another person, which provoked a fear reaction in the individual. Although teachers need to be aware of both positive and negative kinds of conditioning that may be going on in school, signal learning has little place in planned school instruction.

2. *Stimulus-response learning.* This type of learning is also known as *operant conditioning* and appears to be particularly relevant to the development of motor learning of animals and young children. Gagné illustrated this type of learning with examples of a person teaching a dog to shake hands and someone teaching a child to say "mama." He pointed out that reinforcement of the desired response is an important feature. Gagné observed that it is difficult to find pure examples of this type of learning in humans. What appears to be stimulus-response learning in humans is more likely to be chaining (type 3) or verbal association (type 4).

3. *Chaining.* Gagné limited chaining to motor learning and described it as connecting a series of stimulus-response links. To perform a complex motor skill successfully, the learner must complete the individual stimulus-response links—or subskills—in a particular order. Applying a tourniquet to stop bleeding furnishes a good illustration of chaining. To stop the bleeding, each of the stimulus-response links must be followed in order:

STIMULUS	RESPONSE
Sight of person bleeding	Desire to stop the bleeding
Pad and strip of cloth or piece of cloth alone if no pad available	Place pad over artery that is bleeding; put cloth over pad and around limb between wound and body; tie cloth over pad.
Stick	Slip stick under the cloth next to the limb and turn stick, tightening cloth until bleeding stops.

Bleeding stopped	Note time tourniquet applied and take person to doctor.

4. *Verbal association.* This type of learning is similar to chaining but differs in that it applies to verbal learning. Verbal association involves the connecting of a series of verbal links—a verbal chain. The naming of objects and the memorization of passages are examples of verbal association. A two-link verbal chain can be shown in teaching students the name of the geometric figure rectangle.

STIMULUS	RESPONSE
Picture of a rectangle or an actual rectangular object	Observation of the picture or object
Teacher says the word *rectangle.*	Pupils repeat the word *rectangle.*

The test of the pupils' learning would be to determine whether they recognize rectangles when these are next presented.

A three-part verbal chain can be illustrated in teaching both a noun and its definite article in Spanish.

STIMULUS	RESPONSE
Picture of a church	Pupils observe picture.
Teacher says *iglesia.*	Pupils repeat *iglesia.*
Teacher says *la iglesia.*	Pupils repeat *la iglesia.*

If the pupils have mastered the noun and the article, they will be able to repeat *la iglesia* when the teacher next shows them a picture of a church.

5. *Discrimination learning.* Human beings master a large number of motor and verbal chains, many of which, though distinct, are at the same time similar. Learners discriminate, for example, when they learn to distinguish the different skills required in driving a car with an automatic transmission, a car with a standard stick transmission, a car with "four on the floor," and a tractor-trailer. Pupils who have learned separate verbal chains for *rectangle, square,* and *triangle* must learn to discriminate among these figures. Pupils who have been taught that *iglesia* means *church* and *la iglesia* means *the church* must distinguish churches from other buildings, must recognize churches as a class even though each church may be architecturally different, and must repeatedly use *la* with the noun and not *el,* which they have seen in other verbal chains. They must further recognize that *la* when used as an article means *the* and not something else. Even though they have been exposed to hundreds of other verbal chains for other words, they must always remember that the word *iglesia* means *church.*

6. *Concept learning.* We get into a higher order of learning when we seek to teach learners concepts. Concepts are abstractions—some more abstract than others—which require the medium of language for their learning. The property of a rectangle—its rectangularness—is a concept. The color blue and the number three are concepts. An office building is a concept that differs from the concept school building. First, last, and always are concepts, as are north and south, up and down, large and small, left and right. Concepts may refer to concrete objects such as a football, to properties of objects such as the color red, and to ideas such as democracy.

Brotherhood, excellence, and honesty are concepts. Students must have the necessary mastery of language to be able to understand concepts. The beauty of language is that it permits us to talk about concepts and to communicate these abstractions to others. We do not need the football to talk about it. We do not have to be in the presence of an office building to discuss it. We cannot even see the concept of honesty but we know what traits an honest person exhibits and can communicate those traits to others. Much of the instruction in school involves teaching concepts.

7. *Rule learning.* A rule is a chain of concepts. The learner puts together the relationship between concepts and formulates a rule or principle. We are constantly teaching rules in school. The science instructor teaches learners that litmus paper turns red when dipped into an acid. Three concepts are involved in this rule: litmus paper, acid, and red. The relationship between the litmus paper and the acid is the action of turning red. We teach the principle that yellow plus blue makes green. We teach that $a^2 + b^2 = c^2$. Students learn that life insurance is a way of protecting one's family. We teach that some drugs have a harmful effect on the health of the individual. Rule learning brings out the relationships and applications of the concepts that are linked together to form the rule.

8. *Problem solving.* This is the highest-order and most complex type of learning. The problem-solving process is the development of the ability to think. The learner puts to use all the rules learned that have a bearing on a particular problem in order to seek a solution to that problem, and in the process generates new rules and new knowledge. Problem solving is the process of reasoning. In other contexts, problem solving is equated with the scientific method. Each attempt at problem solving reveals new ideas and adds to the store of knowledge, which may in turn be applied to the solution of subsequent problems. The various disciplines teem with illustrations of both successful and unsuccessful attempts to solve problems, such as the discovery of vaccines for contagious diseases, the search for ways to convert garbage into energy, more effective means of providing for the nation's housing needs, combating crime, growing disease-resistant grain, and piecing together the origin of the human species.

We have reviewed these eight types of learning to help teachers recognize the different types of learning evident in their learning tasks. A supervisor should study a classification system of types of learning such as that of Gagné to help teachers make task analyses.[15]

In addition to a review of the learners' characteristics and identification of type of learning, a task analysis should include an appraisal of any special conditions or constraints under which the learning tasks will occur. The teacher should ask, Do the tasks require special equipment or other resources? Can the tasks be performed in the space provided? Are there time constraints? Are there limitations imposed by the school, the community, or the state? If we may go back to the example of parallel parking and place it as a topic in a driver education course, we might analyze this task in the following manner:

1. *Nature of the learners.* The learners must be of age to obtain a learner's permit to drive. They must possess sufficient physical coordination skills to handle an automobile. They must know the rules of the road and recognize road signs.

2. *Type of learning.* This task is primarily chaining, the development of a series of perceptual-motor skills.
3. *Special conditions and constraints.* The students must have obtained their learners' permits. In a class of twenty-five students, the teacher can allot only one-half hour of actual practice in parallel parking to each student. The school must have a driver education automobile that is fully insured and equipped with dual controls.

By understanding the nature of the task, the teacher is more likely to realize the goal of instruction—mastery of the content by the learners. Task description and analysis aid the teacher in designing enabling objectives and in perfecting the main objective itself. The supervisor can serve as a consultant to teachers who wish to develop the skills of task description and analysis.

The professional literature of the 1980s and 1990s abounds with articles and books advocating the development of thinking skills as the primary goal of education. Not since 1961 when the Educational Policies Commission declared that the central purpose of education is the development of the ability to think has there been such a flurry of interest and research into thinking skills.[16] Certainly, problem solving or, as some people call it, "reflective thinking" or "the scientific method" is one dimension of the thinking process.

Jozef Cohen identified productive, novel, and chimerical thinking as the principal cognitive or thinking processes.[17] Some educators lump all thinking skills under the rubric of problem solving or critical thinking. Barry K. Beyer distinguished critical thinking from other thinking skills, describing critical thinking as "the process of determining the authenticity, accuracy, and worth of information of knowledge claims."[18]

Recent research has delved into the functioning of the brain and into metacognition, which Arthur Costa defined as "being conscious of our own thinking and problem solving while thinking . . . a uniquely human ability occurring in the neocortex of the brain."[19] Costa elaborated on metacognition when he said: "Metacognition is our ability to formulate a plan of action, monitor our own progress along that plan, realize what we know and don't know, detect and recover from error and reflect upon and evaluate our own thinking processes."[20] In one sense metacognition is thinking about thinking.

The study of the functions of the brain, including research into the functions of the left and right hemispheres, is fascinating. Some evidence seems to indicate that one side of the brain predominates in individuals. When the left side is dominant, people learn best through logical and linear thinking processes. When the right side is paramount, the individual learns best through creative and intuitive processes. Assuming the validity of the left-brain/right-brain research, we can note that most of the school's curriculum is designed for left-hemisphere learners.

Interpreting the left-brain/right-brain research, educators have concluded that the right hemisphere has been neglected, that teachers should determine, through checklists and other means, learners' hemispheric predominance, that teachers should tailor the curriculum to the means by which individuals learn best, and that the curriculum should include more content and experiences oriented to right-brain learning. One goal would be the development of both halves of the brain.

Susan Dobbs cautioned, however, against oversimplification of the concept of hemispheric predominance. She called attention to evidence that complex mental functions are not necessarily symmetrically divided between the brain's hemispheres. She observed that "the terms 'left and right brained' are largely metaphoric, based on an overextension of available data," and warned against "interpreting this metaphor literally in the classroom."[21] Dobbs advocated developing many types of thinking skills, especially higher-order ones, following both logical and creative processes without concern for the location of the processes within the brain.

Identification of thinking skills is germane to development of the ability to think. Many researchers have developed lists of thinking skills. Bloom's taxonomy of the cognitive domain is but one of these.[22] Barbara Z. Presseisen presented a useful model of basic thinking processes drawing on the work of Bloom and J. P. Guilford (see Figure 3.6).[23]

Knowledge about thinking and strategies for encouraging thinking can go only so far. The teaching of thinking is as much an attitude on the part of the teacher as it is a set of skills. Thinking can only be taught when pupils are placed in a posture of thinking. Simple recall learning, which makes up the major part of a typical school

---

A Model of Thinking Skills: Basic Processes

CAUSATION—*establishing cause and effect, assessment:*
   Predictions
   Inferences
   Judgments
   Evaluations
TRANSFORMATIONS—*relating known to unknown characteristics, creating meanings:*
   Analogies
   Metaphors
   Logical inductions
RELATIONSHIPS—*detecting regular operations:*
   Parts and wholes, patterns
   Analysis and synthesis
   Sequences and order
   Logical deductions
CLASSIFICATION—*determining common qualities:*
   Similarities and differences
   Grouping and sorting, comparisons
   Either/or distinctions
QUALIFICATIONS—*finding unique characteristics:*
   Units of basic identity
   Definitions, facts
   Problem/task recognition

Figure 3.6. A Model of Thinking Skills: Basic Processes. *Source: Barbara Z. Presseisen, "Thinking Skills: Meanings and Models," in* Developing Minds: A Resource Book for Teaching Thinking, *Arthur L. Costa, ed. (Alexandria, Va.: Association for Supervision and Curriculum Development, 1985), p. 45. Reprinted with permission from the Association for Supervision and Curriculum Development and Barbara Z. Presseisen. Copyright © 1985 by the Association for Supervision and Curriculum Development. All rights reserved.*

curriculum, cannot elicit thinking. Thinking is encouraged when probing questions replace recall, divergent questions substitute for convergent, why? and how? replace who? what? where? and when?, alternative answers are sought in place of single responses, originality is stressed over conformity, intuition is fostered, and higher-order learning displaces lower-order cognition.

We need to remind ourselves that thinking does not occur in a vacuum. Albert Einstein did not pull his famous formula for atomic energy, $E = mc^2$, out of thin air. He had to have mastered a large store of knowledge from which to derive the facts presented in the formula. We cannot, therefore, play down the necessity for students' mastery of cognitive learnings which provide the tools for thinking.

Organizing Instructional Plans

At some point the teacher must assemble the various products of planning, must put them all together in some form of comprehensive plan. We are concerned in the remaining pages of this chapter with types of plans that will be put to immediate use in the classroom, and defer discussion of broader plans such as curriculum guides to Chapter 7.

To begin to organize his or her plans, the teacher looks at the content: knowledge, skills, and affective outcomes as a whole and the time available for presenting that content to the students. A year, a half year, nine weeks, or possibly six weeks may be available for dealing with the particular subject matter. The next step is to break that content into its principal topics. A teacher may need the entire time to treat one topic. Most likely, however, if the period of time is a long one, several topics can be covered. The teacher should estimate the amount of time necessary for most—and hopefully all—students to master the material.

Unit Plans After identifying the topics and the time available for each topic, the teacher proceeds to create a type of plan known as a unit, learning unit, or teaching unit. A unit is a segment of an instructional program. If mastery of one unit depends on mastery of previous units, the units must be put into sequence. The unit could follow a number of formats. Drawing on the earlier discussion of models of instruction we can devise a functional format such as the following.

1. *Goals.* At the beginning of each unit the teacher should state the nonbehavioral instructional goals.
2. *Objectives.* Following the goals should come the instructional objectives. The objectives and subobjectives should be stated behaviorally, classified, and grouped by domain.
3. *Preassessment.* The teacher should indicate what procedures are to be used to answer this question: Do the students already possess the knowledge and skills that the teacher plans to develop in the unit? This information is needed so that the teacher may alter the content or choose different content if the pupils demonstrate they have already sufficiently mastered the content to be studied. The teacher must also specify the entry skills, if any, needed to begin study of the unit and the means by which possession of the prerequisite skills would be determined.
4. *Instructional procedures.* In this part of the unit the teacher should detail the learning strategies to be used to present the material and the human and ma-

terial resources needed. The following chapter of this text, on presentation of instruction, is designed to help the supervisor work with teachers in the selection of instructional procedures.

5. *Resources*. The teacher should list the physical and human resources that will be used in the unit.

6. *Evaluation*. The final section of the unit is devoted to evaluation techniques. The teacher chooses those techniques most appropriate to the content and the learners and writes whatever tests are to be used to measure student achievement.

The unit outline suggested here is general enough to be adaptable to a broad range of the curriculum: elementary and middle school content; segments of a high school discipline; minicourses (for example, Purchasing Life Insurance); interdisciplinary topics (for example, Homes of the Colonial Period); and even phases of the extra-class program of the middle, junior high, and senior high schools.

Although the six points covered in the suggested unit format may apply in planning in most fields and at most levels of learning, there will be variations in the substance, extent, and complexity of plans from teacher to teacher and from program to program. Although a unit plan in social studies, for example, would be quite different from a unit plan in skill areas such as word processing, gymnastics, or instruction in playing the clarinet and in creative areas such as art, writing, and other crafts, teachers in all areas need to spell out goals, objectives, preassessment techniques, instructional procedures, resources, and evaluation techniques on more than a day-to-day basis. A unit plan requires the teacher to look at instruction on a longer-range basis than the next day's work. The supervisor should help teachers to find a planning format that is compatible with their own disciplines or grade levels.

If the unit is primarily for the teacher's use and is not to be put into the hands of the pupils, the teacher has the choice of incorporating tests under the appropriate section—preassessment or evaluation—or placing them in appendixes or keeping them separate from the unit itself.

Some instructors who teach mature learners, particularly at the college level, like to give an entire unit plan to the students. In that case, tests cannot be made a part of the unit. The students do not need a copy of the entire unit but instead may receive an abbreviated version that outlines goals, objectives, entry skills needed, and resources to be used. Whether students receive a copy of the plan or not, the teacher must be certain to communicate the goals and objectives of the units.

Lesson Plans. The unit serves as a basis for day-to-day planning. It is from the unit that the teacher derives daily lesson plans. The word *daily* should be stressed. If study of a particular unit in a high school course is to last six weeks, a course that meets five days per week would require thirty lesson plans. The elementary school teacher in a self-contained classroom will find it necessary not only to outline the work of an entire day but also to develop minilesson plans for each subject area or topic studied during the day.

A lesson plan need not be lengthy. The supervisor must remember that planning is a continuing activity of teachers and the demands on teachers' time are many. Each lesson plan should include at least the following elements:

1. *Objectives of the particular lesson plan.* Not all objectives can necessarily be accomplished in one day's time. Some will carry over to the next day or for several days. Some daily plans, in practice, will require more than one day's presentation. What the teacher must do is review the plan at the conclusion of the day and make whatever revisions are needed for the next day. That teachers must make a plan for every class every day does not mean that each plan must be totally new; it may legitimately be a revised plan based on the accomplishments of the preceding day.

2. *Instructional procedures and resources.* The teacher will select from the unit plan those procedures pertinent to the particular day's activities and will use those resources applicable for that day.

3. *Evaluation.* The teacher should employ some evaluation techniques no matter how simple, to reveal whether the day's lesson has "gone over."

We have omitted from the lesson plan the goals, which normally apply to the entire unit, and preassessment, which is conducted before beginning the unit and relates to the whole unit.

The formats of a unit and lesson plan can be seen in the following abbreviated unit and lesson plan entitled "The Use of the Dictionary" for an upper middle school class (pages 122–24).

The foregoing outlines of two types of instructional plans—the unit plan and the lesson plan—offer ways to organize products of the planning process into a logical and intelligible form. A great deal of thought and creativity go into constructing instructional plans. Plans may and should differ from teacher to teacher even when topics are the same; no two teachers approach the task of planning in the same way, a fact that makes the planning process such a highly creative endeavor. The supervisor may aid teachers in developing unit and lesson plans by showing them models of well-constructed plans. In so doing, he or she should make clear to them that plans are not written to please the administrator or supervisor but to enable the teachers to carry out instruction more effectively.

SUMMARY

Instructional planning is seen as the first step in a continuum whose subsequent steps are presentation and evaluation of instruction. Plans must be continuously revised as feedback from learner achievement shows modifications that should be made.

The supervisor can implement a six-point program to help teachers develop and improve skills in following a systematic approach to instructional design, using a model of instruction as a guide to planning, writing nonbehavioral goals and behavioral objectives, describing and analyzing tasks, applying taxonomies of instructional objectives, and organizing instructional plans.

A major goal of schooling is the development of the ability to think. Among the principal thinking skills are problem solving, decision making, critical thinking, and creative thinking. Teachers should select content and plan activities utilizing higher-order processes. Two types of instructional plans are recommended: the lesson plan,

Illustrative Unit Plan: The Use of the Dictionary

Goals

The child should become familiar with the kinds of help that can be found in a dictionary.

The child should gain an appreciation of the dictionary as a useful tool in language learning.

Objectives

Cognitive and Psychomotor

Using a dictionary supplied in class, the child will look up words given orally by the teacher and will write the correct spelling of those words.

Using a dictionary supplied in class, the child will look up words given in written form by the teacher or encountered in books or magazines and will write definitions of the words.

Using a dictionary supplied in class, the child will look up words given in written form by the teacher or encountered in books or magazines and will pronounce them correctly.

Using a dictionary supplied in class, the child will look up words given in written form by the teacher or encountered in books or magazines and will find synonyms for those words.

Using a dictionary supplied in class, the child will look up words given in written form by the teacher and will tell the language origin of those words.

Given words in written form that cannot be found in the dictionary supplied in class, the child will go to the library and look up the definition and pronunciation and will verify the spelling in *Webster's Unabridged Dictionary*.

Given three different dictionaries, the child will state the differences in systems for noting division of words into syllables, differences in marking pronunciation, and differences in preferred definitions.

Affective

When asked by his or her parents to look up the spelling, meaning, pronunciation, or origin of words not familiar to them, the child will find pleasure in carrying out this task.

On encountering a new word while reading, the child will find satisfaction in being able to find out what the word means.

Preassessment

A pretest [not included in this illustrative unit] will be administered that requires the children to look up the spelling, meaning, pronunciation, and origin of selected words. A mastery level of 90 percent accuracy will indicate that a child already possesses the competencies to be learned in the unit.

The child will be able to read most of the materials of the fifth grade, will be able to write the letters of the alphabet in sequence, and will be able to alphabetize a word to four letters (as, *dict*ionary).

Instructional Procedures

The children will take a spelling test of words dictated by the teacher and will look up in the dictionary words they misspell.

The children will read passages from a book, identify words whose meanings they do not know, and look up in the dictionary the definitions of those words.

The children will be taken on a tour of the school library by the librarian, who will show them the various kinds of dictionaries the library has, discuss the value of dictionaries, and show them how to use *Webster's Unabridged Dictionary.*

The children will listen to a presentation by the teacher on how to read the pronunciation of words in the dictionary. The teacher will use transparencies on the overhead projector for explanations and will distribute a dittoed sheet that shows words broken into syllables and marked for sounds and stress.

The child will look up the same word in three dictionaries supplied in class and compare differences in noting syllables, in indicating pronunciation, and in preferred definitions.

Resources

Dictionaries such as the latest edition of *Webster's Collegiate Dictionary*, paperback dictionaries, *Webster's Unabridged Dictionary*, overhead projector and transparencies, librarian.

Time allotted for the unit: forty-five minutes per day for five days.

Evaluation

The children will attempt to achieve a 90 percent mastery level on a performance test [not included in this illustrative unit] that requires them to look up words in the dictionary and give their correct spelling, definition, pronunciation, and origin. Students who score less than 90 percent will need individualized help in mastering the content of the unit.

Illustrative Lesson Plan

Objectives

The children will write twenty words dictated by the teacher, look up the correct spelling of the words in a dictionary supplied in class, and verify their spelling of the words.

Instructional Procedures and Resources

Set Induction:[24] The teacher will ask pupils whether they have ever used the dictionary, whether they have ever wanted to know how to spell words correctly, whether *recieve* or *receive* is the correct spelling of the word, and why it is important to know the correct spelling of words. (5 min.)

The children will write words dictated by the teacher. (10 min.)

The children will use a dictionary supplied in class to verify the spelling of each word and to correct words misspelled. (20 min.)

Illustrative Lesson Plan continued

Closure:[25] (last 2 min.) The teacher will summarize the pupils' success in finding and correcting words they had misspelled and will stress the usefulness of the dictionary for helping them with spelling unfamiliar words.
Resources: dictionaries; dittoed sheet with correct spellings.

Evaluation

The children will double-check the correct spelling of the words from a dittoed sheet distributed by the teacher giving spellings they should have found in the dictionary and will report to the teacher how many words they had written correctly after looking them up. (8 min.)

which shows the planning for one day, and the unit plan, which shows the planning for longer periods of time and from which the lesson plans are derived. Planning requires a good deal of thought and time but it is an essential process with the ultimate aim of enhancing student learning.

QUESTIONS FOR DISCUSSION

1. What knowledge and skills are necessary for teachers to plan effectively?
2. Is any one of the three taxonomies more important than the other? If so, which one and why?
3. What effect should the presence of exceptional students in the regular classroom have on planning?
4. How would you evaluate a teacher's planning for instruction?
5. Should administrators review teachers' lesson plans? If Yes, when and how often?

ACTIVITIES FOR FURTHER STUDY

1. Define the following terms:

   instructional design
   model of instruction
   instructional goal
   instructional
      (behavioral) objective

   taxonomy of instructional objectives
   cognitive domain
   affective domain
   psychomotor domain

2. Diagram a model of instruction and explain its parts.
3. Select a learning task, and describe and analyze it.
4. Apply the taxonomies of the three domains of learning by writing one behavioral objective for each of the major categories of each domain.

5. Locate definitions of the following terms and document the sources:

problem solving	intuitive thinking
decision making	logical thinking
critical thinking	cognition
creative thinking	metacognition
linear thinking	epistemic cognition
holistic thinking	hemisphericity

6. Describe ways teachers can develop thinking skills.

7. Give examples of low-order questions and higher-order questions in your subject field or grade level.

8. Locate and report on a list of thinking skills that differ from those mentioned in this chapter.

9. Review and critique one or more research studies on functions of the left and right hemispheres of the brain.

10. Describe the relationship between brain hemispheres and handedness.

11. Construct one unit plan and one lesson plan.

12. Locate one model of instruction that is different from any model in the text and compare it to the five-part model of instruction described in this chapter.

13. Describe the differences between task description and task analysis.

14. Write one instructional goal for a particular topic that you might teach in school and three instructional objectives derived from the instructional goal.

15. Describe the following types of learning and give one illustration of each:

chaining	rule learning
concept learning	problem solving

16. List two behavioral terms (verbs) that might be used in stating cognitive objectives in each of the six categories of the Bloom taxonomy.

17. List two behavioral terms (verbs) that might be used in stating affective objectives in each of the five categories of the Krathwohl taxonomy.

18. List two behavioral terms (verbs) that might be used in stating psychomotor objectives in each of the seven categories of the Simpson taxonomy.

19. Compare Anita J. Harrow's taxonomy of the psychomotor domain (see bibliography for this chapter) with the Simpson taxonomy in (a) categories and (b) use.

20. Compare the taxonomy of the psychomotor domain found in Kibler, Barker, and Miles, *Behavioral Objectives and Instruction*, Chapter 3 (see bibliography for this chapter), with the Simpson taxonomy in (a) categories and (b) use.

21. State three components of complete behavioral objectives.

22. Distinguish a performance standard from a stability standard in writing an instructional objective.

23. Describe ways in which a supervisor can decide whether teachers are doing adequate planning.

24. Observe two teachers in their classrooms and try to determine from their presentations whether there is evidence of planning. If you believe there is such evidence, attempt to judge the quality of planning that went into the presentation.

25. Talk with the teachers you selected for activity 24 and report to the class on planning procedures they use. Determine whether the teachers follow planning procedures discussed in this chapter or other techniques.

26. Classify the following instructional objectives as to domain and category within the domain (answers follow). The student will
   a. Evaluate and compare the nutritive value of six breakfast cereals.
   b. Demonstrate how to hold a tennis racket and ball in order to serve.
   c. Listen to a native speaker of a foreign language that he or she is studying and summarize what the speaker has said.
   d. Respond to a call for a contribution to a leading charity.
   e. Assemble a kite following instructions on the wrapper.
   f. Using a twelve-inch ruler, measure and record in inches and fractions of inches the lengths of several straight lines on a handout distributed by the teacher.
   g. Regularly demonstrate sensitivity in his or her relationships with other people.
   h. Write a biography of a famous political or military leader on either side in World War II.
   i. Practice cutting chunks of raw cabbage into pieces for cole slaw.
   j. Name the president and vice-president of the United States.
   k. Express admiration for the fine work that has been put into a handmade afghan.
   l. Identify basil leaves by their smell.
   m. Demonstrate an awareness that vandalism is hurting the school's image.
   n. Create an original fruit punch.
   o. Decide whether a proposed solution to a community problem is likely to work.
   p. Change a tire (leaving it on the rim) by substituting the spare for the front left tire.
   q. Decide whether saving money "for a rainy day" is worthwhile or not.
   r. Using a dresser that has been painted a solid color, refinish it in antique white.

Answers to activity 26:
   a. cognitive-evaluation
   b. psychomotor-set
   c. cognitive-comprehension
   d. affective-responding
   e. psychomotor-guided response
   f. cognitive-application
   g. affective-characterization by value or value complex
   h. cognitive-synthesis
   i. psychomotor-mechanism
   j. cognitive-knowledge
   k. affective-valuing
   l. psychomotor-perception
   m. affective-receiving
   n. psychomotor-origination
   o. cognitive-analysis
   p. psychomotor-complex overt response
   q. affective-organization
   r. psychomotor-adaptation

27. For each of the following behaviors identify the type of learning with Gagné's classification of types (answers follow).
   a. Defining charity
   b. Repeating a sound. Baby repeats *Da-Da* on hearing his or her father say *Da-Da*

    c. Choosing the right computer for the needs of the office
    d. Showing fear of high places
    e. Learning that smoking may be hazardous to your health
    f. Learning a word. An adult points to an animal in a zoo and says to a child "elephant." When seeing an elephant again, the child says "elephant"
    g. Pitching a baseball
    h. Distinguishing oak from other woods.

Answers to activity 27:
    a. concept learning
    b. stimulus-response learning
    c. problem solving
    d. signal learning
    e. rule learning
    f. verbal association
    g. chaining
    h. discrimination learning

NOTES

1. Robert J. Kibler, Donald J. Cegala, David T. Miles, and Larry L. Barker, *Objectives for Instruction and Evaluation* (Boston: Allyn & Bacon, 1974), pp. 20–27.
2. W. James Popham and Eva L. Baker, *Systematic Instruction* (Englewood Cliffs, N.J.: Prentice-Hall, 1970), pp. 11–18.
3. For additional help in writing instructional objectives, consult Benjamin S. Bloom, J. Thomas Hastings, and George F. Madaus, *Handbook on Formative and Summative Evaluation of Student Learning* (New York: McGraw-Hill, 1971); Benjamin S. Bloom, George F. Madaus, and J. Thomas Hastings, *Evaluation to Improve Learning* (New York: McGraw-Hill, 1981); Norman E. Gronlund, *Stating Objectives for Classroom Instruction*, 2nd ed. (New York: Macmillan, 1978); Robert F. Mager, *Preparing Instructional Objectives*, 2nd ed. (Belmont, Calif.: Fearon, 1975); Newton S. Metfessel, William B. Michaels, and Donald A. Kirsner, "Instrumentation of Bloom's and Krathwohl's Taxonomies for the Writing of Educational Objectives," *Psychology in the Schools* 6 (July 1969): 227–31; W. James Popham and Eva L. Baker, *Establishing Instructional Goals* (Englewood Cliffs, N.J.: Prentice-Hall, 1970).
4. Robert H. Davis, Lawrence T. Alexander, and Stephen L. Yelon, *Learning System Design: An Approach to the Improvement of Instruction* (New York: McGraw-Hill, 1974), p. 41.
5. Benjamin S. Bloom, ed., *Taxonomy of Educational Objectives: The Classification of Educational Goals: Handbook I: Cognitive Domain* (White Plains, N.Y.: Longman, 1956).
6. David R. Krathwohl, Benjamin S. Bloom, and Bertram B. Masia, *Taxonomy of Educational Objectives: The Classification of Educational Goals: Handbook II: Affective Domain* (White Plains, N.Y.: Longman, 1964).
7. Elizabeth Jane Simpson, "The Classification of Educational Objectives in the Psychomotor Domain," *The Psychomotor Domain*, vol. 3 (Washington, D.C.: Gryphon House, 1972), pp. 43–56. See also Anita J. Harrow, *A Taxonomy of the Psychomotor Domain: A Guide for Developing Behavioral Objectives* (White Plains, N.Y.: Longman, 1972).
8. Bloom, *Taxonomy*, p. 18.
9. See VIMCET filmstrip-audio tape program, *Selecting Appropriate Educational Objectives*, 1967, Vimcet Associates, Los Angeles, Calif.
10. Krathwohl, Bloom, and Masia, *Taxonomy*, p. 35.
11. Simpson, "Classification of Educational Objectives."
12. Harrow, *A Taxonomy*, p. 27.

13. Davis, Alexander, and Yelon, *Learning System Design*, chs. 5 and 7.
14. Robert M. Gagné, *The Conditions of Learning*, 2nd ed. (New York: Holt, Rinehart and Winston, 1970).
15. For a useful discussion of three types of learning (humanistic, cognitive, and behavioral), see Carl D. Glickman, *Developmental Supervision: Alternative Practices for Helping Teachers Improve Instruction* (Alexandria, Va.: Association for Supervision and Curriculum Development, 1981), pp. 3–5.
16. Educational Policies Commission, *The Central Purpose of American Education* (Washington, D.C.: National Education Association, 1961).
17. Jozef Cohen, *Thinking* (Chicago: Rand McNally, 1971), pp. 26–43.
18. Barry K. Beyer, "Critical Thinking: What Is It?" *Social Education* 49 (April 1985): 276.
19. Arthur L. Costa, "Teaching for, of, and about Thinking," in *Developing Minds: A Resource Book for Teaching Thinking*, ed. Arthur L. Costa (Alexandria, Va.: Association for Supervision and Curriculum Development, 1985), p. 21.
20. Costa, "The Principal's Role in Enhancing Thinking Skills," in *Developing Minds*, p. 31.
21. Susan Dobbs, "Some Second Thoughts on the Application of Left Brain/Right Brain Research," *Roeper Review* 12 (December 1989): 121.
22. See also Georgia Department of Education, *Essential Skills for Georgia Schools* (Atlanta, Ga.: Georgia Department of Education, 1980), pp. 87–88, for list of thinking skills based on the Bloom taxonomy.
23. Barbara Z. Presseisen, "Thinking Skills: Meanings and Models," in *Developing Minds*, pp. 43–48. See also Barbara Z. Presseisen, "Thinking Skills: Meanings and Models Revisited," in *Developing Minds: A Resource Book for Teaching Thinking*, rev. ed., Arthur L. Costa, ed. (Alexandria, Va.: Association for Supervision and Curriculum Development, 1991), p. 58.
24. See Chapter 4 for discussion of this term.
25. See Chapter 4 for discussion of this term.

BIBLIOGRAPHY

Armstrong, Robert J., Terry O. Cornell, Robert F. Kraner, and E. Wayne Roberson. *The Development and Evaluation of Behavioral Objectives*. Worthington, Ohio: Charles A. Jones, 1970.

Baker, Eva L., and W. James Popham. *Expanding Dimensions of Instructional Objectives*. Englewood Cliffs, N.J.: Prentice-Hall, 1973.

Banathy, Bela H. *Instructional Systems*. Belmont, Calif.: Fearon, 1968.

Becker, Wesley C., Siegfried Engelmann, and Don R. Thomas. *Teaching 2: Cognitive Learning and Instruction*. Chicago: Science Research Associates, 1975.

Beyer, Barry K. "Critical Thinking: What Is It?" *Social Education* 49 (April 1985): 276.

———. "Improving Thinking Skills—Defining the Problem," *Phi Delta Kappan* 65 (March 1984): 486–90.

Bloom, Benjamin S., ed. *Taxonomy of Educational Objectives: The Classification of Educational Goals: Handbook I: Cognitive Domain*. White Plains, N.Y.: Longman, 1956.

Bloom, Benjamin S., J. Thomas Hastings, and George F. Madaus. *Handbook on Formative and Summative Evaluation of Student Learning*. New York: McGraw-Hill, 1971.

Bloom, Benjamin S., George F. Madaus, and J. Thomas Hastings. *Evaluation to Improve Learning*. New York: McGraw-Hill, 1981.

Briggs, Leslie J. *Handbook of Procedures for the Design of Instruction*. Washington, D.C.: American Institutes for Research, 1970.

Cohen, Jozef. *Thinking*. Chicago: Rand McNally, 1971.

Cooper, James M., ed. *Classroom Teaching Skills*, 4th ed. Lexington, Mass.: D. C. Heath, 1990.

Costa, Arthur L. *Developing Minds: A Resource Book for Teaching Thinking.* Alexandria, Va.: Association for Supervision and Curriculum Development, 1985.

———. *Developing Minds: A Resource Book for Teaching Thinking,* rev. ed. Alexandria, Va.: Association for Supervision and Curriculum Development, 1991. vol. 1.

———. *Developing Minds: Programs for Teaching Thinking,* rev. ed. Alexandria, Va.: Association for Supervision and Curriculum Development, 1991. vol. 2.

———. "The Principal's Role in Enhancing Thinking Skills." In *Developing Minds: A Resource Book for Teaching Thinking,* ed. Arthur L. Costa. Alexandria, Va.: Association for Supervision and Curriculum Development, 1985.

———. "Teaching for, of, and about Thinking." In *Developing Minds: A Resource Book for Teaching Thinking,* ed. Arthur L. Costa, pp. 20–23. Alexandria, Va.: Association for Supervision and Curriculum Development, 1985.

Davies, Ivor K. *Objectives in Curriculum Design.* London: McGraw-Hill, 1976.

Davis, Robert H., Lawrence T. Alexander, and Stephen L. Yelon. *Learning System Design: An Approach to the Improvement of Instruction.* New York: McGraw-Hill, 1974.

Dick, Walter, and Lou Carey. *The Systematic Design of Instruction,* 2nd ed. Glenview, Ill.: Scott, Foresman, 1985.

Dobbs, Susan, "Some Second Thoughts on the Application of Left Brain/Right Brain Research," *Roeper Review* 12 (December 1989): 119–21.

Educational Policies Commission. *The Central Purpose of American Education.* Washington, D.C.: National Educational Association, 1961.

Gagné, Robert M. *The Conditions of Learning,* 2nd ed. New York: Holt, Rinehart and Winston, 1970.

Gagné, Robert M., and Leslie J. Briggs, *Principles of Instructional Design.* New York: Holt, Rinehart and Winston, 1974.

Georgia Department of Education. *Essential Skills for Georgia Schools.* Atlanta, Ga.: Georgia Department of Education, 1980.

Glickman, Carl D. *Developmental Supervision: Alternative Practices for Helping Teachers Improve Instruction.* Alexandria, Va.: Association for Supervision and Curriculum Development, 1981.

Gronlund, Norman E. *Stating Objectives for Classroom Instruction,* 2nd ed. New York: Macmillan, 1978.

Harrow, Anita J. *A Taxonomy of the Psychomotor Domain: A Guide for Developing Behavioral Objectives.* White Plains, N.Y.: Longman, 1972.

Henson, Kenneth T. *Methods and Strategies for Teaching in Secondary and Middle Schools,* 2nd ed. White Plains, N.Y.: Longman, 1993.

Hunter, Madeline, and Douglas Russell. "How Can I Plan More Effective Lessons?" *Instructor* 87 (September 1977): 74–75f.

Kibler, Robert J., Larry L. Barker, and David T. Miles. *Behavioral Objectives and Instruction.* Boston: Allyn & Bacon, 1970.

Kibler, Robert J., Donald J. Cegala, David T. Miles, and Larry L. Barker. *Objectives for Instruction and Evaluation.* Boston: Allyn & Bacon, 1974.

Krathwohl, David R., Benjamin S. Bloom, and Bertram B. Masia. *Taxonomy of Educational Objectives: The Classification of Educational Goals: Handbook II: Affective Domain.* White Plains, N.Y.: Longman, 1964.

Lee, Blaine Nelson, and M. David Merrill. *Writing Complete Affective Objectives: A Short Course.* Belmont, Calif.: Wadsworth, 1972.

Mager, Robert F. *Developing Attitude toward Learning.* Belmont, Calif.: Fearon, 1968.

———. *Preparing Instructional Objectives,* 2nd ed. Belmont, Calif.: Fearon, 1975.

Metfessel, Newton S., William B. Michaels, and Donald A. Kirsner. "Instrumentation of Bloom's and Krathwohl's Taxonomies for the Writing of Educational Objectives." *Psychology in the Schools* 6 (July 1969): 227–31.

Morine-Dershimer, Greta. "Instructional Planning." In *Classroom Teaching Skills*, 4th ed., ed. James M. Cooper, pp. 17–49. Lexington, Mass.: D. C. Heath, 1990.

O'Brien, Lynn. "Learning Styles: Make the Student Aware." *NASSP Bulletin* 73 (October 1989): 85–89.

Pfeiffer, Isobel, and Jane Dunlap. *Supervising Teachers: A Guide to Supervising Instruction.* Phoenix, Ariz: Oryx Press, 1982.

Popham, W. James. "Practical Ways of Improving the Curriculum via Measurable Objectives." *The Bulletin of the National Association of Secondary School Principals* 55 (May 1971): 76–90.

Popham, W. James, and Eva L. Baker. *Establishing Instructional Goals.* Englewood Cliffs, N.J.: Prentice-Hall, 1970.

———. *Systematic Instruction.* Englewood Cliffs, N.J.: Prentice-Hall, 1970.

Presseisen, Barbara Z. "Thinking Skills: Meanings and Models." In *Developing Minds: A Resource Book for Teaching Thinking*, ed. Arthur L. Costa. Alexandria, Va.: Association for Supervision and Curriculum Development, 1985, pp. 43–48.

———. "Thinking Skills: Meanings and Models Revisited." In *Developing Minds: A Resource Book for Teaching Thinking*, rev. ed., vol. 1, pp. 56–62. Alexandria, Va.: Association for Supervision and Curriculum Development, 1991.

Simpson, Elizabeth Jane, "The Classification of Educational Objectives in the Psychomotor Domain." *The Psychomotor Domain* 3 (1972).

Tenbrink, Terry. "Instructional Objectives." In *Classroom Teaching Skills*, 4th ed., ed. James M. Cooper, pp. 51–83. Lexington, Mass.: D. C. Heath, 1990.

"Thinking Skills in the Curriculum." *Educational Leadership* 42 (September 1984): 3–87.

Tyler, Ralph W. *Basic Principles of Curriculum and Instruction.* Chicago: University of Chicago Press, 1949.

Videotapes

Tactics for Thinking. 1988–90. Eight hours of videotape (four cassettes), Teacher's Manual, Blackline Activities. Written by Robert Marzano, Diane Paynter, and Daisy Arredondo. Features Robert Marzano presenting tactics for teaching thinking skills. Association for Supervision and Curriculum Development, 1250 North Pitt Street, Alexandria, Va. 22314.

Teaching Skillful Thinking. 1986. Four videocassettes featuring Ernest Boyer, Arthur Costa, Robert Sternberg, David Perkins, Matthew Lippman, et al. Tapes are Issues in Teaching Thinking (30 min.); The Skillful Thinker (21 min.); Teaching for Thinking (40 min.); Teaching of and about Thinking (22 min). Association for Supervision and Curriculum Development, 1250 North Pitt Street, Alexandria, Va. 22314.

4

Helping Teachers
Present Instruction

Objectives

After studying Chapter 4 you should be able to accomplish the following objectives:

1. Describe characteristics of effective teaching.
2. Select resources by applying appropriate criteria.
3. Select teaching strategies by applying appropriate criteria.
4. Demonstrate set induction.
5. Demonstrate appropriate lecturing techniques.
6. Demonstrate skill in conducting a class discussion.
7. Demonstrate nonverbal cues.
8. Demonstrate oral questioning techniques.
9. Provide for variation of stimuli.
10. Provide for variation of learning activities.
11. Demonstrate closure.
12. Apply a checklist for observing lesson presentations.
13. Express a desire to master skills of presentation so that in your capacity as a supervisor you can help teachers become more effective at lesson presentation.

RESEARCH ON EFFECTIVE TEACHING

An observation was made in Chapter 1 that educators disagree on what constitutes effective teaching. In the past twenty or so years, a large number of studies known collectively as the "effective schools research" have sought to identify characteristics of effective schools and effective teaching. Among those who have conducted research on this topic are David C. Berliner, Wilbur B. Brookover, Jere E. Brophy, Ronald R. Edmonds, C. M. Evertson, Thomas L. Good, Lawrence W. Lezotte, Donald M. Medley, Barak V. Rosenshine, and Jane A. Stallings. You will find references to studies by these and other researchers in the bibliography.

The effective schools research has made clear that some long-held beliefs about effective teaching do, indeed, make a difference in student achievement. Though stated in different ways by different researchers, the research says to the teacher that student achievement is likely to be higher when the teacher

- Sets clear goals for the class
- Holds high expectations of students
- Focuses on the academics
- Maintains an orderly classroom
- Uses suitable materials for instruction
- Monitors student performance
- Provides feedback to students about their performance
- Uses positive reinforcement

We can view these findings as generic (i.e., generally accepted principles of effective teaching applicable to all teachers at all levels). In fact, what the research has done is to affirm strategies many teachers have followed for many years.

The research describes an effective teacher as one who uses class time wisely and keeps learners engaged in purposeful activities. Time on task has become almost a slogan in recent years, but for good reason. Effective teachers pay close attention to the factor of academic engaged time, that is, the time during which students are occupied with learning activities.

Donald M. Medley summarized almost 300 studies of teacher effectiveness and concluded that the following variables are related to student achievement: an orderly and supportive learning environment, time on task, instruction in large groups, and, surprisingly, the use of low-level questioning.[1] Barak V. Rosenshine identified engaged time, content covered, and direct instruction as factors in teacher effectiveness.[2] Other researchers affirmed the importance of direct instruction and academic focus for student achievement.[3]

Some educators are disturbed by the findings that student achievement is higher when teachers use direct instruction, teach whole groups, engage in low-level questioning, and follow a teacher-centered approach. Direct instruction (that is, techniques such as teacher's presentation to the group, questions with a factual basis, and focus on subject matter) and teaching an entire class as a total group run counter to widely espoused beliefs about individualizing instruction, forming subgroups, involving students more actively in the learning process, and paying heed to the affective and psychomotor domains of learning as well as the cognitive area. Low-level questioning clashes with notions about the importance of higher-order questioning and the development of thinking skills. A teacher-directed approach conflicts with teaching methods that are basically student centered. What seems to be clear is that direct instruction, teaching the class as a total group, the use of low-level questioning, and teacher-centeredness can raise student achievement in some areas of the curriculum.

The effective teaching research has pointed to some basic principles on which most teachers can agree, such as setting goals, having high expectations, monitoring, giving feedback, and keeping students on task. It has also established other principles—such as direct instruction, teaching whole classes, and teacher-centeredness—which teachers can follow under certain conditions and for certain instructional purposes. However, teachers should not rule out strategies like cooperative learning, discovery learning, small-group discussion, individualized techniques, higher-order questioning, and student-centered activities for other instructional purposes.

Effective teaching principles are based on what is termed *process-product* research. The instructional strategies that teachers employ are the process; the product is student achievement as measured by standardized tests. You can immediately see the limitations of this type of research. Some instructional objectives—for example, higher-order cognition, creative activities, affective and psychomotor skills—do not lend themselves as readily or at all to standardized testing.

Within its process-product parameters, the effective teaching research demonstrates well certain principles of instruction that apply generally. What it does not reveal are those characteristics idiosyncratic to individual effective teachers. Ascertained only by observation of particular teachers, those traits may or may not offer clues generalizable to other teachers.

At the moment, effective teaching research has apparently reached a plateau and leveled off. Perhaps this particular research emphasis has gone as far as it can go, or perhaps we are in a gestation period during which its principles are being digested and incorporated into teaching practice. If effective teaching research accomplished nothing else, it confirmed the effectiveness of didactic teaching under certain conditions and for certain purposes. It also affirmed common sense principles such as time on task and holding pupils to high expectations. Although discussion of effective teaching research has tapered off, the principles attributed to this body of research remain valid.

Similar to the research on effective teaching, a body of studies known collectively as effective schools research has identified schoolwide characteristics like those demonstrated by effective teachers—namely, maintenance of an orderly school climate, high expectations of students and staff, emphasis on academics, monitoring of student progress, and one additional, very important ingredient—strong leadership by the principal.

STEPS IN IMPLEMENTATION

An old saw prescribes the steps for presenting a lesson. It directs the teacher to

1. Tell them what you are going to tell them.
2. Tell them.
3. Tell them what you told them.

Like old wives' tales, old saws sometimes have a ring of truth. Today we couch our ideas in more technical language, but this old prescription is not completely off target. We talk now of set induction instead of the pedestrian "tell them what you're going to tell them," of explaining instead of the pointed "tell them," and of closure instead of the mundane "tell them what you told them."

To initiate the discussion of ways to help teachers present instruction, we can use the five-part model of instruction discussed in Chapter 3 as our reference point. Recall that the fourth block of the model is implementation of instruction. In the ensuing discussion, implementation of instruction is seen as including the selection of resources and the selection and implementation of teaching strategies.

The selection of resources and the decisions about strategies are parts of the planning phase whereas implementation of the resources and strategies is the actual presentation phase. The task of selecting resources and strategies prior to presentation reinforces a concept discussed in the previous chapter, namely, that the instructional process is a continuum. There are no sharp divisions between planning and presentation, between planning and evaluation, and between presentation and evaluation. The components of a model of instruction glide into and double back on each other.

SELECTION OF RESOURCES

The great disparities in school financing are nowhere more readily visible in a school system than in the case of instructional resources. The resources at the teacher's command vary considerably from community to community, from state to state, even from school to school within a community. Some schools have only the barest essentials whereas others have a superabundance of materials and equipment, some of which lie dormant in media storage rooms. A few fortunate schools are blessed with an instructional materials center that produces audiovisual aids in support of instruction throughout the school.

A major task of the teacher is to identify whatever resources are available for instructional purposes. A central task of the supervisor is to assist the teacher in locating, obtaining, and creating instructional aids. There are very few teachers who would not like additional resources and who do not feel that they would be more effective if these resources were available to them. The task of selecting resources is twofold. First, teachers must make effective use of the resources they do have, and second, teachers must uncover resources that are available but untapped.

Generally, even the most poorly financed classrooms possess some limited instructional resources. Most classrooms contain a blackboard, bulletin board, textbooks, dictionary, and often maps and a globe. In some classrooms these time-honored aids could be put to more effective use.

One of the first jobs of teachers new to a school system is to learn what instructional materials and equipment are available, not only in the school itself but also from the central office. A supervisor can speed up this initial orientation process by providing in written form lists of available resources, their location, and how to obtain them.

Teachers must develop the habit of thinking beyond the confines of the school for aids in instruction. Some communities are rich in educational resources. To varying degrees, all communities can provide significant educational experiences for young people. We must get away from the old notion that the only educational experiences that are important are those that take place within the walls of the school; we need to develop the corollary notion that the community is the school's campus. A supervisor can do much to break down the traditional barriers between the school and the community by suggesting sources of aid and by encouraging teachers to make full use of what is available. One helpful technique for promoting the use of community resources is an organized tour of the community for teachers who are new to the system. This would give teachers an early chance to see the neighborhoods from which their students come and to pinpoint places that might be of future help to them in instruction.

Teachers must think in terms of human as well as physical resources. They should identify individuals and groups inside and outside the school system who might help them present particular topics. People with unique and pertinent experiences should be invited into the classroom or have classes taken to them so they may share their experiences with students. Today, with great frequency, parents and others from the community serve schools in the capacity of volunteer aides and resource persons. Retired specialists, for example, can provide a valuable service when their fields are under study. They are often eager to share their knowledge and skills with young people.

Some alternative educational arrangements take students outside the school's walls into the community, calling on the voluntary services of artists, tradespeople, bankers, salespeople, writers, farmers, and scientists for supplementing the traditional curriculum. Teachers customarily identify libraries, museums, and art galleries as sources of educational experiences for students, but except for the field of vocational education, teachers often overlook experiences that can be derived from stores, banks, garages, hospitals, prisons, insurance agencies, or travel agencies.

Schools in recent years have made great strides in establishing partnerships with businesses and industries in the community. Through these partnerships, a business or industry "adopts" a particular school and cooperates with it to enhance the education of students in that school. Supervisors will find it beneficial to develop and promote these kinds of linkages to the community. They will need to orient new teachers to community organizations and agencies that cooperate with their schools.

The supervisor might recommend that teachers who are engaged in the process of selecting resources apply a checklist such as the one shown here for evaluating resources and making choices.

CHECKLIST FOR SELECTING RESOURCES	YES	NO
1. The resources relate directly to the objectives.	____	____
2. The resources are in keeping with the abilities of the learners.	____	____
3. The resources are in keeping with the age level of the learners.	____	____
4. The resources will be of interest to the learners.	____	____
5. The resources are varied enough to accommodate individual differences in learners.	____	____

6. The resources are accurate and up to date.   ____   ____
7. The resources are without bias, or if with
   bias, the bias is clearly stated and the
   resources are balanced to reveal different
   biases.   ____   ____
8. The resources are easily accessible to the
   learners.   ____   ____
9. The resources are without cost to the learners.   ____   ____

Clearly, the resources must relate to the predetermined objectives, for the resources are the vehicles that carry the learners to their destination. There will undoubtedly be agreement that the resources selected should match the learners' abilities, age level, and interests. If at all possible, the resources chosen should be stimulating and motivating and should enable the teacher to provide age-appropriate learning experiences.

While searching for resources for the class as a whole, the teacher should also seek resources that might appeal to individuals within the group. Some materials should be relatively easy, others more difficult. Some should be concrete, others more abstract. Whatever resources are selected—whether in the form of media or in the form of resource persons—all should make available accurate and relevant knowledge.

Some teachers may take issue with the use of biased materials. Yet many of the problems facing humankind are controversial ones with no clear-cut, factual solutions. People differ on the resolution of controversial issues. You cannot study opposing views on controversial subjects without examining biased points of view. Whenever an individual takes a side in a controversial issue, he or she is presenting a bias. When dealing with controversial content, the teacher may offset the bias of one side by presenting the biases of other sides.

The checklist suggests that resources be readily accessible and without cost to the learners. In the public schools, where learners are an immature and captive population, it is the teacher's responsibility to see that the instructional resources chosen are at the command of the learner. The teacher must also assure that the materials to be used will be either without cost or of insignificant cost to the learners and their parents. The public school is not like a college or university, where a professor may order mature students who choose to be there to purchase books and other instructional materials and to pay a variety of laboratory fees.

The checklist offers the teacher some guidelines for selecting resources. The alert teacher is constantly on the lookout for new instructional materials, particularly those that are free or inexpensive. It is a duty of the supervisor to supply teachers continuously with references to new resources that have come to his or her attention and that appear worthwhile. Further, teachers can be encouraged to evaluate resources they might use by applying criteria such as those suggested in the preceding checklist.

SELECTION OF STRATEGIES

When teachers consider the problem of selecting strategies for presenting content to students, they might well paraphrase the poet: "How shall I teach thee? Let me count the ways. . . ." Many strategic avenues are open to them. Like the streets of any city, some avenues are more traveled than others, some thoroughfares receive little traffic, and some are unknown except to those in the neighborhood.

Pedagogy has borrowed the word *strategy* from the armed services. We can envision the military brass mapping out a campaign and planning tactics. Some teachers might well point out that there is another analogy in the use of the word strategy—it applies to the field of battle. We prefer not to conceptualize the classroom as a battlefield, with the teacher and students on opposing sides, but rather as a team effort, with the teacher as the leader and both teacher and students working together for a common cause.

The terms *procedures* or *strategies* appear with some of the models of instruction you saw earlier. Whichever term is used, we are talking about methods—the means of providing age-appropriate opportunities for students to encounter content. We find not only these terms in the pedagogical literature but also *tactics, techniques*, and *modes of instruction*.

Some specialists in instruction see differences in the concepts mentioned in the preceding paragraph. We could, if we wished, make some subtle distinctions in these concepts. For example, we could identify the use of nonprint media as a strategy whereas the use of a specific medium—a videotape—could be labeled a technique. But we shall not make these fine distinctions in our discussion. We will use the aforementioned terms when they apply to teaching or instruction as synonymous and interchangeable.

We do need to distinguish, however, between a teaching strategy and a learning strategy. In this text, we emphasize teaching or instructional strategies—those methods teachers select and use to present subject matter. We are further concerned with the supervisor's ability to help teachers select and use appropriate strategies.

Learning strategies are personalized ways by which a learner internalizes content, that is, learns the subject. Some learners will outline subject matter so they can grasp the points in logical sequence. Some memorize words or sentences as keys to learning. Can any schoolchild forget the palindrome "Able was I ere I saw Elba," which has the dubious virtue of not only reminding the learner of Napoleon's first place of confinement but also being a completely reversible sentence? Some pupils put together both real and nonsensical words that have meaning only to them to help them recall facts. Some pupils like to read a passage in its entirety quickly, then go back and study segments in depth. Some students subject themselves to silent question-and-answer sessions on content they are studying. These are all learning strategies, not teaching strategies. When we use the word *strategy* by itself in this text, we mean teaching or instructional strategy and equate it with procedure, method, technique, mode, or tactic.

The process of selecting strategies is part of the planning process. Not until the teacher walks into the classroom and initiates a lesson does he or she move out of the sphere of planning and into the area of implementation or presentation.

A teaching strategy may be defined as a procedure or set of procedures for using resources and for deploying the central figures in the instructional process—the teacher and the learners. With this definition in mind, we can list some of the many strategies a supervisor might suggest to teachers:

lecturing   oral reports
discussion   written reports
textbook exercises   drill
recitation   audio media
grouping by ability,   video media
   achievement, or interest   laboratory
questioning   portfolios
discovery   field trips
role-playing   tests
tutoring   homework
problem solving   independent study

    This list is far from complete, but it indicates the variety of strategies teachers may use in presenting content. Variations are possible in a number of these strategies. For example, the teacher might lecture to large groups or small groups. Discussion might be conducted in small groups or even smaller seminars. Textbook exercises might be written or oral. Students may be grouped for learning according to varying criteria; subgroupings are possible within larger groups; given a team of teachers, groupings may be arranged around team teaching or differentiated staffing patterns; collaborative and cooperative learning techniques may be employed. You can see that the range of procedures open to teachers is broader than they sometimes realize.

    The difficult task is to select that strategy or those strategies that would be most productive for the learners. By way of illustration, suppose an elementary school teacher wishes the pupils during science study to become familiar with the concept of the nitrogen cycle, the process whereby nitrogen undergoes change, nitrites and nitrates are formed for nourishment of green plants, and nitrogen returns to its original state, a process vital to the maintenance of life on earth. How can this content be placed before the learners in such a way that they will readily master the principles involved? A number of alternatives run through the teacher's mind:

1. Prepare a lecture and use only written notes.
2. Prepare a lecture and use an overhead projector to sketch the nitrogen cycle for the students.
3. Prepare a lecture and use charts that have been prepared by the teacher or former students or an instructional materials center.
4. Show a film on the nitrogen cycle.
5. Ask the class to open textbooks to the section on the nitrogen cycle and have students read aloud the passages in the text. The teacher could follow each reading with oral questions to determine whether pupils understand the concept.
6. An alternative to 5 is to have the students open their books and the teacher read to them—a still far too common procedure in many classrooms.
7. Introduce the content by raising questions such as What is nitrogen? Is there more nitrogen in the air than oxygen? Animals, bacteria, and green plants play a part in the nitrogen cycle—what are their roles? The teacher may ask

students to look up the nitrogen cycle in the textbook and/or reference books either as class work or homework. Pupils report their findings to class.

8. Lecture and ask pupils to follow up the lecture with drawings of the nitrogen cycle.

9. Use a programmed text to teach the content.

10. Appoint a committee to study the nitrogen cycle and prepare a report to be given to the class.

11. Bring in a small bag of fertilizer—for example, 6-6-6 100 percent organic. The class could discuss the difference in meaning between organic and inorganic. The teacher can show them the label on the bag that describes the contents and explain to them that 6-6-6 means 6 percent nitrate, 6 percent phosphate, and 6 percent potash. The teacher explains that growing plants need these chemicals, singles out the nitrate, and relates it to the nitrogen cycle, which the class will then study.

12. Lead the class up to study of the nitrogen cycle over a period of time during which the class experiments with growing plants in the classroom. Several plants are given proper water and chemicals; other plants are given proper water and inadequate chemicals; some plants are given proper water and no chemicals. Students will observe the necessity for plants to get sufficient food.

13. Take the class on a field trip to a farmer's pasture that is complete with cows, manure, green plants, and decaying plants. The teacher can point out the nitrogen cycle at work.

14. Organize the class into small cooperative groups with responsibilities for helping each other master the content.

How can the teacher know which of the alternative strategies would be most effective? Surely, more than one road leads to Rome. Contrary to the classic expression, however, not all roads do lead to Rome, or certainly some roads are more circuitous than others.

The teacher can choose one strategy at random and try it. If it doesn't work, he or she can try another strategy, and then another until one that will work is found. To some extent, all teachers follow a trial-and-error procedure. Intuitively, they select a strategy that seems on the surface as if it would be effective. These teachers would verify the notion that experience is the best teacher. Over the years, after considerable trial and error they have learned which strategies have been most effective under which conditions.

But what guidance can the supervisor give the new teacher to avoid the lengthy process of trial and error? Or what help can the supervisor give the experienced teacher who wants to test intuition against some criteria? How can a teacher judge in advance whether a given strategy will work? Although you can never be absolutely sure that a given procedure will work until it is put to the test in the classroom, chances for success will be greatly enhanced if the supervisor will help the teacher develop some simple guidelines such as the following:

1. *The strategy must be right for the learners.* The teacher must consider the age level of the students and the interests of that age level, remaining cognizant of the

learners' achievement levels. If we refer to the presentation of the nitrogen cycle to elementary school pupils, a formal lecture by the teacher using written notes could be a disaster. Short minutes after the lecture has begun, the teacher may well be confronted with a classroom full of wiggling, twisting, uninterested urchins. If the teacher has a room full of poor readers, requiring them to go to reference works and encyclopedias to dig out information may be an unrewarding approach. Teachers should select strategies that look beyond the common concepts of just linguistic and mathematical intelligence to the concepts of, as Howard Gardner termed them, *multiple intelligences*—for example, interpersonal and musical.[4]

2. *The strategy must be right for the teacher.* Each teacher is a unique personality. Some function well in certain situations and not so well in others. Some teachers, for example, are master lecturers. Others work more effectively in small groups. Teachers who adopt a counseling point of view toward education and life are more effective in one-to-one situations than teachers who are more remote and detached. Some teachers, holding constructivist views of learning, see themselves as facilitators who provide authentic learning experiences so students may create their own knowledge.[5]

Some teachers have a knack for dramatizing content whereas other teachers are more matter of fact. Some teachers are extroverted and others are introverted. Some have more background and skill in a particular subject than others. Teachers need to be aware of their strengths and limitations. In Chapter 12, we examine ways in which a supervisor may help teachers evaluate themselves. Whatever strategy teachers select must be compatible with their skills, knowledge, values, and personality.

3. *The strategy must be right for the subject matter.* This guideline is such an obvious one that violating it seems impossible. Yet how often do teachers teach about the content of a subject rather than the subject itself? How often do teachers accept pupils' verbalization of rules, for example, without probing to see if they understand the rules? How often do teachers accept memorization of content for mastery of content? How often do teachers structure tests in such a way that students can cram for them, regurgitate the content, then immediately let the content float off into oblivion?

How many supervisors and other visitors have walked into modern language classrooms, for example, and wondered whether the teacher was teaching a foreign language or English? When English is consistently substituted for the foreign language in the modern language classroom, the strategy does injustice to the subject matter.

Teachers violate this guideline if they use inaccurate resources. The teacher must exercise care in the selection of printed and other resources that may present as fact something that is no longer true, as in the use, for example, of out-of-date atlases. The teacher must be discriminating about materials placed before the learners.

An injustice is done to the subject matter when the teacher either intentionally or unintentionally directs learners to one-sided treatments of the content. For example, if the teacher selects a research paper as a strategy for studying the racial problem in America, students should be directed to books and articles written by both black and white authors. If we are studying poverty in Latin America and looking at pictures of slum areas of some Latin American cities, we should at the same time study problems of the poor and homeless in urban and rural areas of our own country. Teaching controversial topics calls for careful selection of resources and strategies to bring out all dimensions of the topics.

Because their resources are often limited—sometimes to a single textbook—teachers frequently but unintentionally present a distorted picture of content. Only in recent years have social studies teachers begun to dispel some of the myths that have surrounded great personalities of history. We have begun to see famous men and women from the past as real, once living, breathing human beings, not as larger than life supermen and superwomen. How many of us still believe that Washington chopped down the cherry tree and threw his half-dollar across the Potomac? How many schoolchildren were ever made aware that the nation's first president was rather tight-fisted with a nickel, had slaves working at his splendid home at Mount Vernon, and was, perhaps, a bit pompous? How many children believe that when Abraham Lincoln wasn't splitting rails, he was wandering around in top hat and tails? How many children learned that Abraham Lincoln had an earthy sense of humor and enjoyed a salty joke? The teacher must select strategies that bring out the essence and preserve the integrity of the subject matter.

4. *The strategy must be right for the time available.* The amount of practice, follow-up, review, independent study, and research that will be conducted on a topic will depend on its relative importance and the time allotted for its study. Some procedures take more time and move more slowly. Study in depth will require more time than a superficial survey. Achievement by the learners of active mastery of the content will require more time than passive acquaintance. Time frames have already been established in every school system in terms of the number of hours in the school day and the number of days in the school year and marking periods.

Whatever the strategies selected, the teacher must make the best use of the time available. As noted earlier in this chapter, recent studies have confirmed what many educators have long observed—that a great deal of time is lost in a typical classroom.[6] John I. Goodlad reported that research funded by the Kettering Foundation and conducted over a period of eight years in some thirty-eight schools, primarily at the elementary school level, revealed a considerable amount of time wasted in such activities as recess and cleaning up. As a result, students are deprived of an adequate amount of instructional time for some of the disciplines.[7] Goodlad reported averages of 72 percent to 77 percent of the school day devoted to instruction, with the balance of time going to routines, behavior control, and social activity.[8] Roughly an average of one and one-half hours per day or seven and one-half hours per week are lost to noninstructional activities. Goodlad's findings parallel an earlier report by Jack L. Davidson and Freda M. Holley. Davidson and Holley, summarizing a study in the Austin, Texas, public schools, reported a considerable amount of time lost during the school day to noninstructional activities, with less than four hours per day devoted to actual instruction.[9] Time must be conserved for instructional rather than noninstructional purposes. Barak V. Rosenshine noted the negative impact of nonacademic activities on students' academic achievement.[10]

Using a technique such as that described by Keith A. Acheson and Meredith Damien Gall, supervisors in classroom visits should observe the amount of time teachers keep the learners on task and should help teachers analyze where they went off task, how to remain on task, and how to focus on content.[11]

Teachers must consider whether they can or should permit an element of self-pacing to enter the picture. The concept of self-pacing allows learners to take varying amounts of time to complete a particular learning task. Some students may take a shorter period of time than average; others may take longer. Time, then, becomes a variable. The traditional approach to instruction is to hold time constant and vary content. All learners work within the same time framework. Some learners master the learning task, but others never achieve the objective. When a teacher introduces the notion of self-pacing, content is held constant and time is variable.

Self-pacing is a feature of most competency-based approaches to instruction. Certain objectives (competencies or learning tasks) are stipulated for the learner to master. This approach acknowledges that some individuals take more time to master specific content than other learners. The important aim is the attainment of the objectives by all learners, even if some learners take longer than others.

A companion concept of self-pacing is criterion-referenced measurement, which is discussed in Chapter 6. In a competency-based approach to instruction, a learner earns credit and receives a grade when the objectives have been mastered. When the criterion, the minimal level of competence, is met, the learner receives full credit. In a more traditional approach, the teacher follows a norm-referenced system of measurement and compares students to each other rather than to the criterion. The teacher considers the degree to which various learners have accomplished the task. Whether individual learners have had sufficient time to complete a learning task is not considered an important factor under a norm-referenced system. We return to these distinctions later.

Ideally, if a teacher subscribes to the concept of self-pacing, learners should be able to take all the time they need to accomplish a task. One consequence of such a procedure would be completely individualized learning. Under these conditions, the teacher's role would be much different, for he or she would work in different ways with different learners.

There is always a gap between the ideal and the practical. An instructional staff must live within certain institutional parameters. Unlimited time is simply not available to any teacher or class. A published school calendar shows the dates when the school year and terms within the year begin and end. Classes change, teachers change, and content changes at the beginning of new instructional periods. Therefore, if teachers wish to introduce self-pacing, certainly a defensible practice, they will have to institute a modified self-pacing plan that allows some variation in time within the larger time parameters set by the school. Instead of unlimited time to complete a task, a learner may have more than the average amount of time up to a fixed limit established by the teacher. A teacher might give the learner several opportunities to achieve an objective, permitting the learner to attempt a task more than one time, a process some educators refer to as "recycling." The teacher may permit the learner to recycle only a reasonable number of times—say, two or three—after which the press of time forces the teacher to move on. A modified self-pacing plan will permit more learners to achieve objectives than is possible when time is held constant.

Some learners will still fail to attain the objectives, even if they are permitted several attempts, unless they receive remedial work and tutoring.

5. *The strategy must be right for the resources available.* A decision to use a number of reference books to explore a topic is contingent on the availability of those reference books. The finest film or tape in the world is useless without equipment to show it. Duplicated practice worksheets are possible only if the school has the supplies and duplicating equipment to reproduce them.

Earlier in this chapter, we cautioned that resources must be accessible and without cost to the learners. A teacher cannot take for granted that resources outside the school are always available to students. A home economics teacher cannot, for example, expect that all homes are equipped with sewing machines. The language arts teacher cannot make the assumption that all homes have magazines and books. The social studies teacher cannot count on reference books and encyclopedias being available in homes of the students. Teachers cannot assume the availability of useful equipment like the typewriter, computer, VCR, television set, or even telephone in the home. Because most teachers are products of the middle class, they sometimes forget that children from many homes, particularly those of the lower socioeconomic levels, do not have the educational resources to which children of upper socioeconomic levels are accustomed.

Nor can the teacher assume that if resources are not available in the home students can locate them somewhere in the community. Even if the desired resources are available, many students will be prevented from reaching them because the students lack transportation, have part-time jobs after school, or have duties at home. Lack of resources will reduce the range of strategies open to the teacher.

6. *The strategy must be right for the facilities.* A strategy that calls for laboratory experiences in a particular discipline implies appropriate materials, equipment, and space. Learning centers, clinics, and remedial areas require resources similar to those needed for laboratories.

To put into practice, for example, a plan that requires large group instruction, small group discussion, and independent study, space problems must be resolved. Meeting rooms of varying sizes are needed. Library facilities are required. Sliding partitions may have to be installed. Faculty may have to be deployed differently. Existing facilities must be considered when a strategy is being selected.

7. *The strategy must be right for the objectives.* Perhaps the most important guideline of all is that there must be a direct fit between the strategy chosen and the objectives the strategy is designed to achieve. If teachers have specified objectives at higher levels of the taxonomies, they must choose strategies for reaching the higher levels. A strategy to achieve the cognitive level of evaluation will differ from one to achieve the level of knowledge. A strategy to achieve the affective level of valuing will be different from one for reaching the level of responding. A procedure that would bring about attainment of the psychomotor level of adaptation would differ from one to reach the level of set. The relationship between the objectives and strategies is direct and intimate. Alone, the objectives are nothing but ideas from the teacher's mind. The strategy is the vehicle for carrying the objectives from the teacher's mind to the learner's mind and body.

By engaging in periodic analysis and discussion of these seven guidelines with teachers, the supervisor may assist the teachers to develop the skill of selecting appropriate strategies and to avoid the uneconomical process of trial and error.

LESSON PRESENTATION

The goals are written, the objectives are stated, the tasks are analyzed and described, resources and strategies are selected, entry skills of learners are assessed, the unit plan is developed, the first lesson plan is created, and the planning process phases out. The implementation process is about to begin: The teacher starts the first lesson of the unit by initiating study of the unit's topic.

When the teacher steps into the classroom, the hours of prior planning should result in an effective lesson. They provide a sense of confidence that all systems are "go." Can any experienced teacher ever forget the first time soloing in front of a group of students? Can the butterflies in the stomach be compared to the actor's stage fright? Did the teacher wonder how the audience would react? How would the lesson go over?

Sometimes the teacher conducts a silent dress rehearsal the night before each lesson, running through the unit and reviewing how the lesson plan fits into the unit plan. Each part of the lesson plan must be checked to fix clearly in mind the details of each of the components. The teacher makes an inventory of the materials and equipment needed and tries to anticipate problems likely to be encountered.

In practice, of course, teachers do not carry out a full-scale review of each lesson prior to presentation the following day. They do not have time for exhaustive checks, but in a cursory or abbreviated fashion they do make a quick check. They will probably spend somewhat more time readying the lesson plan for the introductory class of each unit than on succeeding plans as the unit moves along lesson by lesson.

Each day's lesson provides feedback for review and modification of the next day's lesson plan. The competent instructional supervisor who has helped the teacher plan for instruction must now help the teacher translate the plans into action.

The discerning supervisor who visits a class in session should be able to tell with little difficulty whether the teacher has done any planning for instruction. The clues are there for any perceptive visitor to see.

- Are there any visible written plans to which the teacher refers?
- Does the teacher exhibit confidence?
- Does the teacher appear to know where learners are going?
- Has the teacher communicated the objectives to the learners?
- Is there a flow to the day's activities?
- Are there blocks of time during which nothing constructive seems to be taking place?
- Are the learners kept busy at productive tasks?
- Does the teacher rely on worthwhile learning tasks for managing the class or on threats and reprimands?
- Are the needed materials and equipment on hand and ready to use?

- Does the teacher appear to be improvising, moving from one tangent to another, prolonging activities beyond their productive time?
- Does the teacher repeat content after it is apparent that all the learners have mastered it?
- Does the teacher achieve closure, summarizing the learning by involving the learners?

The experienced supervisor can attest that adequate planning does make a difference in both teacher behavior and student behavior during the course of a lesson presentation. We can use a theatrical model to examine more closely the elements of a well-conducted lesson. For a lesson presentation to be effective, the teacher attends separately to the beginning, the middle, and the end of the lesson. For each of these three parts the teacher uses different strategies. Several of the most frequently used strategies will be examined in our analysis of lesson presentation.

Beginning the Lesson

The skilled teacher realizes that the problem of starting a lesson is a little like the problem faced by a storyteller in the initial paragraphs of a story. The storyteller knows that the reader's interest must be stimulated at the very beginning. The master storyteller knows how to grab the reader's attention in the first few sentences. The first two verses of Genesis make us want to read on: "In the beginning God created the heaven and the earth. And the earth was without form, and void; and darkness was upon the face of the deep. And the Spirit of God moved upon the face of the waters."

Who can resist reading Agatha Christie's *The Mystery of the Blue Train*, which starts:

> It was close on midnight when a man crossed the Place de la Concorde. In spite of the handsome fur coat which garbed his meager form, there was something essentially weak and paltry about him.
> A little man with a face like a rat.[12]

An author attempts at the very beginning of a story to arouse the reader's interest and establish a particular frame of mind or "set." The author seeks to influence the reader to respond to the message in such a way that the reader will want to learn more. An aura of mystery and suspense lures the reader on, sometimes to the point that he or she cannot put the book down until the last page is finished. Many have read a fascinating book until the wee hours of the morning! Some enduring books and movies have had such an impact on readers and viewers that they have read or seen them again and again.

On a smaller scale, we see the phenomenon of set in our daily lives as we attempt to influence others' predispositions about people, places, or things. Two girls are talking, for example, and one tells the other, "I met the most handsome boy last night. I want you to meet him." The drama critic writes in a review, "The new musical that opened last night was a smash hit." Our neighbors invite us into their home to see slides of their recent trip to Switzerland and use words such as "If you ever go to Switzerland, you mustn't miss Lucerne." The endless television commercials exhort us to rush out to buy the sweetest-smelling soap, the longest-lasting deodorant, and the softest toilet tissue. Daily we try to put others into a certain frame of mind or we are recipients of others' attempts to motivate us to take certain actions.

A teacher shares a similar need to stimulate learners to put themselves in a frame of mind receptive to pursuing the content of the lesson. The teacher wants to pique the learners' interest and cause them to want to learn more. The teacher wants to make the forthcoming content interesting to learners as well as to give them some notion of the relationship of the ensuing content to previous content and some idea of its relevance to them and their lives. When planning, the teacher should design some means of eliciting student interest at the start of the lesson.

The techniques a teacher uses to put the learners in a receptive frame of mind are referred to by some specialists on instruction as set induction.[13] Madeline Hunter and Douglas Russell referred to this skill as "anticipatory set."[14] *Set induction* is a pedagogical term used to label various techniques employed by teachers to gain students' attention, stimulate their interest, and make them receptive to further instruction.

We have all sat in classes where the teacher's opening ploy has been deadening. What kind of reactions may we expect from the following classic openings?

- "Open your books to page 113."
- Calling the roll, consuming five minutes of valuable class time.
- "O.K., who's scheduled to give a report today?"
- Handing out corrected exam papers, the teacher comments, "This was a terrible set of examinations."
- "Class, today we're going to study about volcanoes." The teacher then plunges into the lesson plan.
- "Take out your workbooks and work the problems on page 30."

What kind of mind-set may be expected from the learners? Will they react with a "Ho-hum, just another day"? Will the class who did poorly on the examinations react positively when they are told how bad their papers were? Will calling the roll bring them to attention and create the expectation of learning something interesting? Is the teacher's statement that the class is going to study volcanoes sufficient to motivate the learners to proceed with the topic?

Teachers need to inject an element of the dramatic or semidramatic into an introduction. They should ask themselves questions like "What technique—or stunt, if you wish—will be likely to attract the students' interest?" "What do I know about my students that I can capitalize on to make them want to learn this material?"

Techniques of set induction can be quite personal. Some teachers can carry off some techniques better than others. Some teachers have an innate flare for the dramatic. Others find a modicum of just plain hamminess a useful tool in dealing with children and adolescents. No supervisor should expect that every lesson of every day will be a polished gem and that teachers will succeed in making students become wildly excited and eager for each day's study. But supervisors have a right to expect that teachers will make more than a token gesture toward putting the learners into the proper frame of mind for studying the material. There are several guidelines any teacher may follow in an effort to establish set. Even if the teacher is not able to put all learners into a receptive state of mind, at the very least he or she can point them in the right direction.

Let us assume first that we wish to establish an appropriate set for studying a topic new to the class. After examining several suggested ways of arousing interest in the new topic, we will consider ways of inducing set with continuing topics. Each lesson, whether it is the first or part of a series, should incorporate a planned introduction. What techniques can we borrow from the repertoire of experienced, skilled teachers to motivate learners to pursue the topic of a unit we have planned for them?

The teacher can bring in an article from a current magazine or recent edition of the daily newspaper pertinent to the topic and read it to the class. If the article is controversial, so much the better. Using a story reported in the press immediately shows that the topic has currency and relevance to the students' daily lives. A report on the discovery of asbestos filings in the drinking water of a city on one of the Great Lakes would stimulate interest in a study of the Great Lakes much more effectively than the teacher's announcement, "Today we're going to study the Great Lakes." Such an article could introduce not only a unit on geography of the Great Lakes region but also a unit on water or other pollution. A chart from a magazine article showing stock market cycles could be used to introduce either a unit on the stock market or a unit on graphing. The timelier the article, the better it will serve its purpose. Some students may already have read the article; this will strengthen your introductory strategy by underscoring that what they will study has importance to them. This technique can bring the past and the future as well as the present to the students' attention. A news account of the damage being done to the Colosseum by pollution from modern-day traffic in Rome could be used to introduce a variety of units, including the significance of the Colosseum itself and ancient Rome's contributions to the present. A unit on space could begin with a dramatic article on the Venus probes, which revealed that Venus's atmosphere is mainly carbon dioxide and its surface temperature 900 degrees Fahrenheit, or on the Galileo probes of Jupiter and its mysterious moons, or on the dramatic clues about the birth of the universe revealed by the Hubble Space Telescope. The cooperation of American astronauts and Russian cosmonauts in space can introduce not only a unit on space exploration but also one on the dramatic political changes brought about by the end of the Cold War.

The teacher can introduce a lesson with physical objects or pictures that may provoke a reaction. Geographical units can be initiated with samples of arts and crafts from various countries. A jade necklace, an onyx chess set, a hand-tooled leather purse, and a straw hat can arouse curiosity about the places where they originated and the people who created them. Samples of foreign currency can be used to start a unit on international money and banking. Three-dimensional geometric figures that may be taken apart and reassembled have proved helpful in beginning mathematical units.

If it is not practical or feasible to carry physical objects to the classroom, photographs, slides, or filmstrips can be used effectively to induce set. Pictures of breadfruit, papaya, and passion fruit, edibles not customarily seen in most parts of the United States, can replace the fruits themselves at the start of a unit on products of the tropics. The photograph of Marines raising the American flag on Iwo Jima symbolizes the war in the Pacific, 1941–1945. Pictures of the destruction of the Berlin Wall can be used to begin a unit on the unification of Germany, the restoration of democracy, or human values.

Audio impressions can be as effective as visual impressions. Recordings of the voices of John F. Kennedy, Franklin D. Roosevelt, Martin Luther King, Jr., and other men and women of history help learners think of these personalities of the past as real people rather than myths. A particular atmosphere can be created in class by the judicious selection of recorded music or poetry or drama. The teacher's aim is to provide just enough stimulation to make students want to study the topic.

A simple means of creating curiosity is the technique teachers use when they write an unfamiliar word or expression on the board and let students ponder it. The word *cloning* written across the blackboard can bring about a discussion of both philosophical and biological dimensions when students debate whether it is possible or desirable for human beings to be able to reproduce themselves asexually. Significant words of low familiarity will serve as brain teasers. The teacher might scrawl *deoxyribonucleic acid* on the board and ask the learners to define it. Some bright student may know or guess it to be DNA, the main complex compound found in chromosomes. From there the teacher can move into a unit on heredity and genetics. The words *habeas corpus* can instigate a unit on fundamental freedoms. It is unlikely that history students will at first recognize the names Vladimir Ilyich Ulyanov or Iosif Vissarionovich Dzhugashvili, but world history would have been far different without Lenin and Stalin, names by which they were better known. Unfamiliar though significant words and names may be found in all subject fields. The device of writing such words on the board to bring forth questions and discussion offers a simple and effective way of introducing a lesson.

The teacher may stage an action that may even startle the learners. To introduce a unit on psychology, he or she may spend the first few minutes of class berating them, calling them "dumb," telling them they are the worst class ever, and predicting no good for all of them. Then with a smile, the teacher lets them in on the secret that it was just playacting to illustrate a point and proceeds to ask them how it felt to be on the receiving end of such a harangue. An endless variety of role-playing situations can be concocted with the aid of other teachers, parents, and students. For example, an angry parent (whose role is played by an adult friend of the teacher) barges into the classroom and accuses the teacher of using obscene, Communist, irreligious, and unpatriotic textbooks. The parent storms out of the room to the bewilderment of the learners. At this point, the teacher breaks the shock effect and starts them on a study of censorship, freedom of the press, or church-state relationships. As another illustration, a class in journalism or criminal justice might have its powers of observation tested when (by prearrangement) two boys who resemble each other rush into the classroom. One angrily accuses the other of "ratting" on him and threatens to "beat him up." The teacher shoos them out of the room and then asks the class to relate what they saw and heard. These contrived situations can make the topic to be studied very dramatic.

The teacher cannot, of course, fruitfully employ dramatic means of introducing every lesson. After a unit has been started, more routine methods of beginning a lesson will be in order. Yet each lesson should have some planned introduction, even if it is only an explanation of the transition to the particular lesson from the previous day's lesson. Some of the more routine but highly effective introductory procedures are discussed next.

1. *An explanation of the reasons for studying the content.* The teacher will tell the students why the content is important to them and how it can have meaning in their daily lives. Some content is easily justified on the basis that it meets both immediate and long-range needs of students. Other content is more difficult to justify but remains important; some content is not justifiable at all and would be better removed from the curriculum.

2. *A review of yesterday's lesson.* A quick review can be conducted in a number of ways. The teacher can summarize what took place the day before and how it relates to today's lesson. A student can be asked to summarize what was learned in class yesterday. The teacher can pose some questions based on the previous day's work and see how well the students comprehended the material. Sometimes only a very few minutes of review will be necessary. Other times the entire work of the preceding day must be repeated to ensure mastery of the content.

3. *An analysis of results of a test taken the preceding day.* If the preceding day's work included a test or examination and the papers have been scored, the teacher should give them back immediately and go over them. The test should be used as a learning device and a review. The teacher should show students where they made their mistakes and how to correct them.

The supervisor should help the teacher devise effective procedures for initiating lessons and provide the teacher with feedback on how the introductory procedures appear to be received by the students. The supervisor should make the teacher aware that half the battle is won if students are interested, have developed a receptive frame of reference, understand the value of the content to be studied, comprehend the relationship of the present day's lesson to the previous day's and to future lessons, and are oriented to the direction their study will take.

Moving through the Middle of the Lesson

When the teacher feels that the class is in the proper frame of mind, it is time to move into the heart of the lesson. The word *feels* is stressed here not only in connection with lesson presentation but also in relationship to the entire teaching process. Though the teaching act strives to be as scientific as possible, much of teaching still remains an art. A great deal of teaching is intuitive. We cannot say, for example, that set induction should occupy the first five minutes of each class. The teacher has to develop almost a sixth sense to judge when the learners are ready. With experience, the teacher can detect the nuances and know when to start, change pace, recapitulate, and end. Teachers must learn when to switch from one technique to another, which techniques most frequently achieve the best results, and which procedures are adaptable to which types of students.

Ordinarily, many strategies are available to present any given lesson and many combinations of those strategies are possible. As any experienced supervisor can attest, not all teachers are equally skilled in implementing all strategies. One of the big advantages of some team-teaching plans is that they capitalize on the strengths of teachers. Those who are skilled at lecturing to large groups, for example, may put those skills to use when team teaching and differentiated staffing patterns are employed. When the individual teacher is alone in the self-contained classroom, however, he or she must develop at least a passable level of performance in the most frequently used strategies.

Efforts have been made by teacher educators over the years to identify the component skills of the teaching process. These skills are generic competencies, which all teachers at all levels should be able to demonstrate. Dwight Allen and Kevin Ryan identified fourteen of these skills:

1. Stimulus variation
2. Set induction
3. Closure
4. Silence and nonverbal cues
5. Reinforcement of student participation
6. Fluency in asking questions
7. Probing questions
8. Higher-order questions
9. Divergent questions
10. Recognizing attending behavior
11. Illustrating and using examples
12. Lecturing
13. Planned repetition
14. Completeness of communcation[15]

Madeline Hunter and Douglas Russell recommended seven steps, essentially generic teaching competencies, for more effective lessons:

1. Anticipatory set
2. Perceived objective and its purpose
3. Input (task analysis)
4. Modeling
5. Checking for understanding
6. Guided practice
7. Independent practice[16]

To this list we would add an eighth skill: closure.

In recent years, buoyed up by the effective teaching research, a number of states have engaged in specifying generic teaching skills that teachers in their states should be expected to demonstrate. Some of these states have created tests and/or on-the-job assessments of these skills for purposes of certification.

In this chapter we will concern ourselves primarily with six generic teaching competencies. One of these skills has already been introduced: opening the lesson, or set induction. The chapter will terminate with a discussion of the skill of closing the lesson, or closure. To help the teachers with the presentation of the central part of a lesson, the supervisor may assist them in developing four major skills: (1) lecturing, (2) conducting a discussion, (3) questioning, and (4) providing for variation. A seventh skill (or set of skills), evaluation, is discussed in Chapter 6.

Lecturing. Included in the concept of lecturing are telling, explaining, describing, demonstrating, and teacher talk generally, skills that are grossly overworked. It is a fact of school life that teachers by and large talk far too much. Yet lecturing is a time-honored technique not soon to be shunned by instructors. It can be an efficient means of imparting large quantities of information to a large group of students in a short period of time. It can also be an extremely inefficient mode of instruction and one unsuited to many learners. The strategy of lecturing can be improved if the teacher will follow a few guidelines:

1. *The learners should be mature enough to accept the mode of lecturing.* As a general rule, the younger the child, the less receptive he or she is to the technique of lecturing. Young children do not have the powers of concentration possessed by older students. Lecturing requires a self-discipline not yet developed by young children, who must be active rather than passive. Consequently, straight lecturing—that is, sustained talk—has been the stock in trade of the college professor. Whether college professors should indulge in relentless lecturing is another story, but because college students are older, more disciplined, more motivated, and not a captive audience, the strategy of lecturing is at least passable at the college level. Some professors, of course, use other strategies like small group work and student reports.

2. *The learners should have developed adequate listening skills.* The development of listening skills is a function of both maturity and training. In recent years, the language arts have incorporated instruction in the skills of listening. There is general agreement that listening skills can be learned and improved. One needs only to attend some adult committee meetings to realize that maturity alone is no guarantee that listening skills have been perfected. Through faulty instructional procedures, teachers sometimes encourage the development of poor rather than good listening skills. The teacher must know whether the learners have sufficient skill in listening before choosing lecturing.

3. *The teacher must use language the learners understand.* The teacher must neither talk over their heads nor down to them—either case will lose listeners. The teacher must be careful of the vocabulary burden, making sure that all students understand the words in the lectures. If students are puzzled after the teacher uses an unfamiliar word, the teacher should stop and define it. Teachers need to exert some caution in the use of children's slang and street language. Some teachers feel that to communicate they must use the current slangy or trendy expressions. A little argot goes a long way. Children do not expect teachers to use their language; they expect teachers to play their roles as adults, and they often resent or are amused by adults' attempts to mimic them. Judicious use of selected words may help the teacher get the message across, but overworking the jargon may lose the audience.

4. *Every lecture should be planned.* The teacher should have prepared a written outline that sets forth the key points to be made, key questions to be raised, and relevant illustrations or life examples to amplify key points. Like a good lesson plan, a lecture should have an introduction, a middle, and an end. Amusing illustrations will help carry the lecture. A summarization of the main points is essential.

5. *Talk alone is not sufficient.* A lecture should be supplemented whenever possible with actions (demonstration) and visual aids. Slides, charts, pictures, and transparencies help create interest. Even the use of the blackboard for a "chalk talk" is superior to talk by itself.

6. *Provision should be made for feedback and follow-up.* Time should be allotted for questions from the class. The teacher should conduct some sort of evaluation to make sure that learners have mentally digested the points made in the lecture. The technique of following up a lecture to a large group with small discussion groups has much to recommend it.

Supervisors may find it helpful in working with teachers on the strategy of lecturing to apply a checklist such as the one presented by Keith A. Acheson and Meredith Damien Gall, shown here as Table 4.1. The supervisor should counsel teachers who have a penchant for lecturing to help them decide whether lecturing is indeed the most effective way to teach and, if so, what measures can be taken by the teachers to achieve the maximum advantages of this strategy.

Conducting a Discussion. Discussion and lecturing are often confused. Many teachers claim to be conducting a discussion when, indeed, they are lecturing to students. Discussion implies an interaction between the teacher and learners. We have used the term *discussion* somewhat loosely in referring to the narration in this text. We do

TABLE 4.1. CHECKLIST FOR LECTURE-EXPLANATION TEACHING

Behaviors to Be Rated	good		needs improvement		
Organization					
1. Lecture has clear organization and sequence	5	4	3	2	1
2. Uses blackboard, handout, etc., to show organization of lecture	5	4	3	2	1
3. Tells students what (s)he expects students to remember from lecture	5	4	3	2	1
4. Repeats key points and summarizes them at end	5	4	3	2	1
5. Avoids digressions	5	4	3	2	1
	good		needs improvment		
Delivery					
1. Speaks slowly and clearly	5	4	3	2	1
2. Conveys enthusiasm	5	4	3	2	1
3. Avoids reading from lecture notes	5	4	3	2	1
4. Avoids filler phrases such as "you know"	5	4	3	2	1
5. Avoids nervous gestures	5	4	3	2	1
6. Maintains eye contact with students	5	4	3	2	1
7. Uses humor	5	4	3	2	1

Source: Keith A. Acheson and Meredith Damien Gall, Techniques in the Clinical Supervision of Teachers: Preservice and Inservice Applications, *2nd ed. (White Plains, N.Y.: Longman, 1987), p. 137. Reprinted with permission of Longman, Inc.*

so with the assumption that the instructor who adopts this text will use the narration in developing discussions with the students. An effective discussion involves not only certain individual mental and oral skills but also skills in group participation, for discussion is a group activity, not a lecture or a dialogue. The subcomponents of the generic skill of discussion, student participation and nonverbal cues, should be brought to the attention of teachers by the supervisor.

STUDENT PARTICIPATION. The teacher should provide continuous and frequent opportunities for students to express themselves. Discussion time should give students a chance to develop skills of listening, thinking, speaking, and participating as members of a group. Maximum student participation should be sought. Teachers often have difficulty restraining themselves and giving students a chance to express their thoughts, but this is a must. In conducting a discussion, the teacher is concerned not only with illuminating the material under study but also with perfecting the discussion skills themselves. So much of the world's social and business activities are transacted through discussion that these skills cannot be slighted in any course or grade.

Teachers should attempt to provide opportunities for all learners to participate and not be content with participation by only a few students. They should not let individuals dominate a discussion but should seek to develop a kind of atmosphere in which students feel free to state their opinions and to raise questions. Students should be encouraged to volunteer responses and to contribute illustrations and anecdotes from their own experiences. The teacher needs to make the students feel that class participation is an important part of the day's lesson. Students will participate more frequently when they are reassured that their opinions count for something and when they do not fear ridicule or disapproval by the teacher or their classmates.

One of the teacher's tasks in conducting a discussion is to keep it under control and focused on the main topic. Students must learn to take turns talking and to listen while others are speaking. The teacher generally serves as moderator but can often turn over this function to students so they can gain additional skills. The teacher should help the students evaluate the significance of their own responses and questions by urging them to support their positions with facts and logical argument.

When sitting in on a discussion lesson, the supervisor should observe which students are actively participating and which ones are sitting back, which ones the teacher calls on repeatedly and which ones are never involved. The supervisor should observe whether the discussion stays on its course, whether participants listen to and understand each other, and whether they accept each other's ideas. If problems are detected in these areas, the supervisor should confer with the teacher about ways the discussions can be improved.

NONVERBAL CUES. Messages are often conveyed through means other than the spoken or printed word. A look, a nod, a frown, or just silence may transmit meaning to the listener. A discussion can be started, stopped, moved along, or turned in another direction by the judicious use of gestures or movement. A nod and a smile from the teacher can reinforce a student's contribution. A frown at a student who is not paying attention can bring him or her back into participation. A period of complete silence can often quiet a group and cause it to return to the subject at hand. The old technique of tapping on the chalkboard or overhead projector can call for increased attention to the topic under consideration.

The teacher is conveying a message to students when he or she is moving around the room and directing discussion from varying vantage points. The message may be "I want to see everybody participating" or "The noisy clique in the corner must pay attention to the discussion" or "I am just as interested in the participants in the back row as in the front row." The teacher's movement and proximity to the learners acts as stimuli for the learners to continue participating.

When the teacher adopts a puzzled expression, the student who is responding knows that the response is not clear. Teachers who are adept at charades can often draw out responses from students. Audiolingual foreign language teachers, for example, have developed a whole range of nonverbal signals for specific types of student responses.

Using silence and nonverbal cues is a little like directing an orchestra. The teacher can point to the students who are to respond, can appear to follow a student's comment with an accepting "uh huh" or nod of the head, can show bewilderment with an audible "hmmmmm," and can show amusement with a broad smile and rolling eyes. The analogy of teaching to dramatics comes forth again as we employ movement, gesture, and silence to convey certain meanings. To some individuals these are habitual traits; some may learn the cues by watching other teachers and by studying their own performance. A supervisor should help teachers analyze their use of silence and nonverbal cues by watching them in action and providing them with feedback on their performances. We return to the topics of nonverbal language in Chapter 11.

Questioning. What is often called lecturing or discussion in reality turns out to be an oral question-and-answer session. The teacher poses questions and the students are expected to furnish the right answers. Of all classroom strategies, questioning may well be the most overworked and the most often abused.

Contrary to common practice, questioning sessions should be planned. The supervisor can readily tell when a teacher is firing questions at students from the "top of the head." The questioning session should have a specific purpose and an internal consistency, which can be achieved only through advance planning. In any question-and-answer session the teacher should write key questions into the lesson plan to avoid forgetting essential points. Questioning is a skill that can be developed by following the rules presented next.

1. *Because questioning is essentially a verbal, cognitive type of activity, the teacher should strive to raise the questions to the highest possible level of the cognitive domain.* Reference is made to the six levels of the Bloom taxonomy: knowledge, comprehension, application, analysis, synthesis, and evaluation.[17] Whenever possible, teachers should pose questions at the higher end of the classification spectrum. Too often they settle for simple recall or yes-no types of responses. Such responses neither encourage thought nor give students practice in formulating their ideas and opinions.

Though the teacher may seek to raise the level of the questions to those of a higher order, certainly we would not eliminate the lower levels completely. There are times when lower-level questions are perfectly legitimate, particularly in drill sessions on materials of a repetitive nature. Under some circumstances, questioning at the low level of the Bloom taxonomy may be more productive than higher-order questioning.[18] The important consideration, however, is that the teacher's questioning not remain at the lower levels of the taxonomy but consciously and deliberately move toward the higher levels. Questions at the lower level may sharpen the memory process but they do little to develop the more important abilities—to think and to express one's thoughts. We can illustrate this with questions at the six levels in the teaching field of English.

- *Knowledge*: Name three novels by Charles Dickens.
- *Comprehension*: Give me a résumé in your own words of the first chapter of *David Copperfield.*
- *Application*: Is there any moral lesson in any of the novels by Dickens you have read that would apply to our society today?
- *Analysis:* What is there about *A Christmas Carol* that has made it a favorite story for more than 100 years?
- *Synthesis*: What human values run through these three novels: *David Copperfield, Oliver Twist,* and *Great Expectations*?
- *Evaluation*: In your judgment which is the better novel: *David Copperfield* or *Great Expectations*? Why?

It is not always possible, depending on the content, to structure higher-order questions. Nor is it always possible to run the full gamut of questioning from lowest level to highest. The teacher's goal, as a rule, is to raise the level of questioning to the highest order possible whenever possible.

2. *The teacher should phrase questions clearly and in language the learner will understand.* The importance of using language geared to the level of the learner has already been stressed in the section on lecturing. The same principle holds true with the strategy of questioning. Not only should questions be clear but they should also be in the teacher's own words, not those of the text materials. Questioning should be considered supplementary to text materials, an approach to content different from that used by authors of the text materials. By the same token, students should be expected to paraphrase or respond in their own words instead of repeating the language of the text materials.

3. *The teacher should first address a question to the entire group.* A brief wait-time of three to five seconds should follow while the students give some thought to the question. The teacher may then direct the question to an individual student. This practice encourages all students to listen to the questions. If the teacher calls on a student before posing a question, the others may tune out both the question and the response. On the other hand, the teacher can sometimes draw inattentive students back to the lesson by calling their names before the questions are framed. Recognize that the latter procedure is a control practice rather than an instructional one.

4. *The teacher should avoid uttering a series of questions (i.e., multiple questions) at the same time before anyone has had the opportunity to respond.* Though the teacher may mean to clarify a question, multiple questions can confuse the students. To which question, they wonder, should they respond? Which is the more important question?

5. *Because the teacher is concerned with the development of listening skills as well as speaking and comprehending skills, he or she should not develop the habit of repeating the questions and the answers given by students.* The teacher should speak loudly and clearly enough that all students can hear. Repetition encourages students to allow their attention to wander and permits them to wait for the second go-around. Only if it is apparent that students have not understood the question should it be repeated or, preferably, rephrased. Students should be taught to develop the habit of listening the first time and to make their own responses clear and audible so their classmates can understand them.

6. *The teacher should distribute questions around the group to gain maximum participation.* The teacher needs to resist the temptation to confine questioning exclusively to those students whose hands are waving in the air or to those who assure the teacher of a correct answer. The teacher should direct questions to students in the back of the room as well as in the front and to the students on the teacher's left as well as right. The teacher must guard against conscious and unconscious biases in favor of bright students, one gender over another, or one ethnic group over others.

7. *A questioning session should consume only a portion of a lesson.* Long, extended question-and-answer periods can cause the teacher to lose the audience and defeat the purposes for which the questioning was intended. One help in livening up questioning sessions is to cast them in the form of games. For example, by creating teams to field questions, the teacher can introduce a pleasant group competitive spirit. This technique, however, is adaptable only for the lower-level questions and is too awkward for more complex and probing questions.

8. *The teacher should keep in mind the affective learning that takes place along with the cognitive.* Student responses should be positively reinforced by the teacher with words or gestures of approval when the responses are satisfactory. When the responses are not correct, the student's attempt at responding should be encouraged even though the content of the response itself may have to be corrected. The teacher is responsible for maintaining a classroom climate that permits students to respond, encourages all to participate, and develops a spirit of acceptance for each other's ideas. Supervisors should encourage teachers to examine their questioning technique to be sure it meets these guidelines.

Providing for Variation. In the fields of literature, drama, and television, a fast-moving story commands attention. A television producer who wants to hold an audience through the commercials knows how important it is to present the actors in varying situations, provide action, change scenery, and use appropriate audio and visual effects. The teacher can borrow some of the producer's tricks, for like the producer, the teacher must attempt to prevent boredom and lack of interest from setting in.

Unlike the producer, the teacher is up against the inexorable laws of human growth and development. Children tend to be restless and in need of movement and change. Their attention span is much shorter than that of adults, and the younger the child, the shorter is the span of attention. Because not all young people are intrinsically motivated to encounter the material the teacher is presenting, the teacher must design age-appropriate activities and devise extrinsic means of attempting to arouse interest in the topic of study.

Variation is a key word in the task of stimulating interest. The teacher must vary the content, the pace of learning, the activities of the lesson, even his or her own style of teaching. The supervisor may observe in the teacher's performance three components of the generic teaching skill called variation: (1) variation of the stimuli, (2) variation of learning activities for the group, and (3) variation of learning activities for the individual.

VARIATION OF THE STIMULI. In every second of every class hour, countless stimuli effect certain responses in the learners and in the teacher. The human beings in the classroom, the lighting, the color of the paint on the walls and ceiling, the furniture and equipment in the room, the loudspeaker and clock, and the activity that takes place outside the doors and windows all have a bearing on the learning or lack of learning in the classroom. By far the most significant stimuli are the teacher and the learners, each of whom interacts with the other and provokes certain responses in the other.

The teacher who sits or stands motionless; makes no gestures; and talks in a monotone with no variation in pitch, tone, volume, and intonation; is unaware of the impact of nonverbal cues; and leads the class through a single, long, unchanging learning activity is violating a premise of good teaching, namely, frequent altering of the stimuli. This means, of course, that a teacher must be able to detect stimuli that affect learning in the classroom and must be able to read the impact of these stimuli. When spotting the telltale signs of boredom, the teacher needs to shift gears quickly in the hope that the change will refuel the learners and bring them back to life.

An earlier section of this chapter on conducting a discussion considered the effectiveness of movement, the use of gestures to transmit meaning, and the use of silence (pausing) to secure the attention of the students. Allen and Ryan suggested that teachers master the skills of focusing, using interactional styles, and shifting sensory channels as well as the skills of movement, gestures, and pausing.[19] By focusing, these authors mean directing attention to particular objects or concepts. Typically, focusing is done with a statement such as "Keep this point in mind" or "Let's look at the table on page 25." The teacher zeroes in on an item and gives it special emphasis.

The term *interaction* has been used elsewhere in this text, and many researchers have postulated that learning is an interactive process. Allen and Ryan supported this view by cautioning against teacher monologs and recommending training in varying interactional styles.[20] The monologist may hold an honored place in the entertainment world but that style is decidedly out of place in the classroom, where learner achievement is the goal. Teachers should not only interact with the learners but also change the style of interaction frequently. Teachers customarily interact with groups but may also interact with individuals within a group and may direct interaction between students. All three of these interactive styles are superior to the monolog.

Shifting sensory channels as described by Allen and Ryan is a simple skill that is often overlooked. The most common sensory channel in teaching is the path from the teacher's mouth to the student's ears—spoken communication. Allen and Ryan recommended switching stimuli from oral to visual and back again. There may even be times when the senses of smell and touch may become the primary modes of communication.

The teacher's objective is to maintain, hold, or recapture, if necessary, the learners' attention. Manipulating and varying the stimuli can more readily gain and keep student interest.

VARIATION OF GROUP LEARNING ACTIVITIES. If we identify all the learning activities that take place in class as stimuli, this second point in our discussion of providing for variation is identical to the first: Stimuli must be varied; therefore, learning activities, which are stimuli, must be varied. By employing the stimulus variation of focusing, we need to distinguish between the specific stimuli previously mentioned and more general learning activities or strategies. The supervisor should suggest to teachers that they build into their lesson plans a variety of activities for each lesson. Teachers should be encouraged to use many kinds of media. As a general rule, a single, prolonged activity—whether lecture, panel discussion, videotape, or film— will not hold a group's attention and interest as well as a variety of activities. Key activities should be written into the teacher's lesson plans along with the estimated amount of time the class should devote to each activity. The object of variation of group activities is learner motivation.

1. *Subgrouping within the class.* The teacher may create special interest groups, ability groups, or remedial groups. By subgrouping learners the teacher reduces the range of abilities or interests and makes instruction more individualized, although not completely individualized. Students may be grouped and regrouped for specific tasks and for special purposes. The teacher can more effectively help individuals within smaller subgroups to realize their own personal goals. Subgrouping is simpler and possibly more successful in schools where teachers are assisted by aides or where teachers are members of a teaching team.

2. *Cooperative learning.* Within the last decade, cooperative, also known as collaborative, learning has proved a popular variant of subgrouping. Robert E. Slavin, a leading advocate of cooperative learning, defined this technique as "a form of classroom organization in which students work in small groups to help one another learn academic material."[21] A key characteristic that distinguishes it from other forms of grouping is emphasis on the group's performance and success as well as the more traditional individual performance within the classroom.

Organizing for cooperative learning, teachers structure small heterogeneous groups whose task is to assist each other in mastering the specified objectives. Individuals share responsibilities for instructing each other. Cooperative learning, with its emphasis on pupils' aiding each other, differs from the traditional, competitive models in which individuals vie for success in the classroom.

Varying classroom organization as circumstances dictate is a sound principle of instruction. Teachers should implement organizational plans to meet their particular objectives with particular groups at a particular time. No single pattern of classroom organization is likely to achieve all objectives. Total group instruction as opposed to subgroupings may well be the most viable and most efficient method for accomplishing certain objectives. Independent study has its purposes. The teacher's repertoire must encompass various techniques of grouping pupils for instruction.

VARIATION OF INDIVIDUAL LEARNING ACTIVITIES. Not only must activities be varied for the group as a whole but also special activities are necessary for individuals who make up that group. With this skill, we enter the difficult realm of individualizing instruction. The individualization of instruction is a noble teaching goal and it has been described, analyzed, and advocated in countless books and articles. It is often made to seem like a simple task to which easy formulas can be applied. In reality, individualizing instruction is extremely difficult. The ultimate would be an individualized curriculum, individual programming, and tutorial instruction using either human or machine tutors. However, education is a mass venture quite unlike the one-to-one relationship of doctor to patient or lawyer to client. We must handle individuals within groups and as members of a larger group, the student body. Given the mass nature of education, we can partially adapt instruction to individual differences as we attempt to move toward the ideal of individualization.

Learning is, indeed, an individual activity. No one can learn for another; one human being can help another learn, but what goes on in the mind of the individual is an intensely personal affair. The teacher, who is the principal helper during the formal education process, will put into practice whatever skillful means he or she can employ to help differentiate instruction and make it more personal to the learner. The supervisor may point out that instruction moves toward individualization when the teacher engages in the following strategies.

1. *Allows choices*. The teacher should make a habit of extending the opportunities for selection to students whenever possible during the school year. Students can be given a choice, for example, of subgroups to which they wish to belong. They can be offered choices of learning activities that have equal value, approaches they would like to take to the study of a topic, and resources they would prefer to use.

2. *Provides for independent study*. Students who are mature and interested enough to pursue a topic of study independently should be allowed to do so. The teacher may allot a portion of the student's time to independent study under supervision.

3. *Differentiates questions to individuals on the basis of their particular interests and abilities*. When conducting an oral question-and-answer session, the teacher can tailor the complexity of questions according to varying abilities represented in the class.

4. *Provides differentiated assignments*. Minimal assignments may be set for slower students and more difficult assignments for faster students. The teacher may distinguish among a series of tasks those that are most difficult and assign them to the brighter students. Some extrinsic device may need to be used to motivate the faster learners to do the more difficult tasks, but the practice of bonus tasks or honors assignments sometimes helps.

5. *Uses resources of varying levels of difficulty*. Learning resources should be provided beyond a single adopted textbook. There should be supplementary text

materials available for varying levels of readers. There should be various types of instructional materials that present the topic being studied in different ways so that if the treatment in the textbook is not clear, students may approach the topic in another way.

6. *Makes use of learning resources outside the classroom.* The teacher will want to call on the services of the reading clinic, if there is one, and learning resource centers, where students may study more or less on their own. Worthwhile community resources should be used.

In individualizing instruction, the teacher should attempt to capitalize on students' particular learning styles. Some pupils learn better orally; others, visually; still others, tactilely. Some need quiet; some learn more readily with background noise or music. Some need many concrete materials; others can work with abstractions.[22]

The supervisor should strongly reinforce the efforts of teachers who try to individualize or personalize instruction. In spite of the importance and value in individualizing instruction, however, for some purposes it is acceptable and sometimes a better practice to hold the class together and instruct the students as a large group. In short, there is a place for large group instruction, small group instruction, and individualized learning activities.

The Place of Motivation.[23] Two of the generic skills discussed in this chapter—set induction and providing for variation—are aspects of the broader skill of motivating learners. The term *motivation* has two meanings. The first and primary meaning of motivation as related to the process of learning is the disposition or desire of the learner to learn. The second meaning is found in those actions teachers take to arouse a desire on the part of the learner to learn. The most effective form of motivation, perhaps the only form of motivation in its true meaning, is the desire that lives within the learner, which is referred to as intrinsic motivation.

One can easily observe the presence or absence of motivated learners in the classroom and school. Some students look alert, respond quickly, and show enthusiasm for what they are doing. Others appear bored, are inattentive, and are impatient for the school day to end. The highly motivated learner enjoys school and learning. The converse is true of the unmotivated learner.

More often than not, the highly motivated learner is a good reader, can handle abstractions, possesses verbal aptitude, and is intelligent. This is not to say that all intelligent pupils are highly motivated. Far from it. One of the tragedies of the modern school is that some intelligent pupils are not at all motivated. They see little purpose in what they are doing. They do a minimum to get by. They may be so bright that the curriculum offers them no challenge. Creative minds are often squelched by the formalism of education.

Learners are motivated when they conceive of themselves as capable individuals. They feel that their peers, teachers, and others in their environment recognize them as able to achieve. Students possess the desire to learn when they are dealing with materials that they understand and that are geared to their level. They are motivated when they see purpose in their activities and study.

Learners are motivated if they live in a safe, orderly, and attractive environment. They are motivated if they have opportunities to express their psychological needs for success, recognition, and approval. Students must feel that the learning experiences are for them, not for the teacher. They need to understand why the content is important, what application it may have in their lives, and why the subject matter they are studying should take precedence over other activities.

Learners are motivated when the teacher promotes a climate in which both students and teacher respect and respond positively to social and cultural differences present in the classroom. Learners are motivated when they feel a sense of pride in their backgrounds. Their self-worth is enhanced in an environment that is free of cultural, ethnic, and gender biases.

Learners are motivated when the teacher is motivated and upbeat about the subjects to be learned. Enthusiasm is contagious. The disengaged teacher cannot expect students to express interest in the subject matter, school, or learning in general.

Learners are motivated when they experience success more often than failure. The feeling of achievement that accompanies success motivates the student to want to learn more.

We would be fortunate if we could prescribe a bag of tricks that would be surefire means of motivation. But impelling motives differ from person to person. Consequently, the techniques that work with one individual may not work with other individuals or other groups. We should be neither surprised nor discouraged if we cannot arouse enthusiasm and interest in all learners at all times. Boredom is bound to creep in from time to time. The conditions of learning may not always be optimal. The teacher may turn in a poor performance on a certain day. The students may be tired after a school event the preceding evening. Some local, state, national, or international crisis may have leaped to the forefront to shut out all attempts at school studies. The best teachers can hope for is that they may reach most of the learners most of the time.

Teachers often resort to extrinsic forms of motivation to promote the development of intrinsic motivation. The use of awards in schools is a time-honored practice. If rewards for learning are positive and kept within reasonable limits, they often succeed in encouraging students to learn. Simple rewards such as a smiling face on a piece of work well done or the teacher's praise for a student's accomplishments can go a long way toward motivating learners.

In our evident pleasure with students who achieve in school, we as teachers should seek to distinguish between achievement that results from positive, healthy motivation and achievement that comes from negative, destructive motivation. We should be aware of the intense pressures placed by some parents on their children to achieve, perform, and succeed. The teacher needs to be understanding and not add to the negative motivation.

Closing the Lesson

Each lesson should have not only a beginning, a middle, and an end, but a *planned* beginning, middle, and end. The closing of the class lesson should be controlled by the teacher and actively involve the learners; it should not be determined by the ringing of the bell or the passing of groups or classes.

Toward the end of the day's lesson, teachers customarily make the assignment for the next day. In analyzing a lesson presentation with a teacher, the supervisor should not neglect the skill of assignment making. The classic distortions of assignment making are the hurried directives from the teacher, "Read the next chapter," "Study pages 115 to 135," and "Work the next 10 problems in your book." Such assignments are common and far too simplistic for the most effective learning. The supervisor might encourage teachers to take a sampling of the assignments they have given their class the last few days and see how they stack up against the guidelines below.

1. *The assignments should be clear to all students.* This means that the teacher must take enough time during the lesson to make the task understood. The directions must be in language the learners understand. Time should be allotted for questions about the assignment from the students.
2. *The assignments should be on work the class has already covered or the teacher is sure the learners are able to do.* If the assignment involves new principles the teacher has not yet explained to the students, it is best that they not go ahead without adequate instruction. If students attempt work ahead of instruction, they may do the work incorrectly and develop wrong learnings, which are then difficult to correct.
3. *Difficulties students may have in the assignment should be anticipated and suggestions given by the teacher on how to overcome them.* The teacher may review the points of difficulty and direct the students to resources that will be helpful.
4. *Assignments should be differentiated for varying interests and abilities.* The element of choice can often enter at this point. Though more difficult to plan than a single, blanket assignment for all, multiple assignments have the advantage of appealing to a wider number of learners.
5. *The assignments should be reasonable in terms of the amount of out-of-class work expected.* Middle and high school teachers in particular must be aware of the amount of homework they are assigning.
6. *Assignments should be not only reasonable in length but also necessary.* "Busy work"—assignments for assignments' sake—should be avoided. Busy work serves only to discourage rather than promote interest. If there is no real need for an assignment, none should be made.
7. *Resources for accomplishing the assignment must be available.* The teacher cannot assume the availability of resources in the home. Consequently, the teacher must know what resources are called for and direct students to their location.
8. *It is helpful if assignments are given through more than one sensory channel.* Instead of relying exclusively on an oral direction, the teacher can supply instruction in written form as well. An oral explanation based on written instructions makes the task to be done that much clearer, for the student not only hears but also sees the assignment and, as a result, is better able to carry out the instructions.
9. *Teachers may allot a portion of the class time to allow students to begin homework assignments.* In that way the teacher may circulate among the students to help them, if necessary, and to verify whether they can perform the assignments.

Before the class ends, the teacher will want to know whether the objectives of each lesson have been achieved. Success with the lesson may have been evident all through the activity. However, before the group leaves for the day, the teacher should evaluate their achievement of the objectives, no matter how limited these may be. He or she can accomplish this by posing a few summary questions to learn whether the students have understood the work of the day and by encouraging questions from the group. The teacher can be misled, however, if the group has no questions. The customary teacher's remark, "Any questions?" does not always bear fruit. Students may not have understood enough of the lesson to ask intelligent questions. They may not know what they don't know and therefore cannot raise questions. Further, they may be tired or ready to leave class and not want to prolong the lesson.

The teacher should allow at least a few minutes before the end of the class for a wrap-up or closure. In this time, the students will reexamine what they have achieved that day and attempt to fix the more important learnings in their minds. The teacher may effect closure by reviewing the main points of the day's lesson or by asking one of the students to summarize the main points. The teacher should review with the class what they have learned—or at least what he or she expected them to learn. The teacher should not only look back over the day's work but should also show the learners the connections with previous lessons and with future lessons, particularly the next day's lesson. The supervisor should look for lesson closure when visiting teachers and observing them in action.

A CHECKLIST

The checklist that follows is based on the principles discussed in this chapter and is supplied to help the supervisor evaluate lesson presentations. The more items the supervisor can check in the "Yes" column when observing a teacher teaching, the better that lesson presentation may be said to be. "No" responses indicate points needing dialog between the supervisor and the teacher.

A CHECKLIST ON LESSON PRESENTATION

On the basis of classroom observation, the supervisor will check "Yes" for those items observed in the lesson presentation and "No" for those items not observed.

Selection of Resources

	Yes	No
Related to objectives	___	___
In keeping with abilities of learners	___	___
In keeping with age of learners	___	___
Of interest to learners	___	___
Varied for individual differences	___	___
Accurate and up to date	___	___
Without bias or balanced as to biases	___	___
Easily accessible to learners	___	___
Without cost to learners	___	___

Selection of Strategies

Right for learners	___	___
Right for teacher	___	___

Right for subject matter ——— ———
Right for time available ——— ———
Right for resources available ——— ———
Right for facilities ——— ———
Right for objectives ——— ———

Teacher's Conduct of the Lesson

General
  Has written plans ——— ———
  Exhibits confidence ——— ———
  Appears to know where class is going ——— ———
  Communicates objectives to learners ——— ———
  Maintains flow in the day's activities ——— ———
  Keeps students on task ——— ———
  Avoids unnecessary repetition of content ——— ———
  Learners attentive; absence of student misbehavior ——— ———
  Materials and equipment on hand ——— ———

Beginning of lesson
  Establishes set ———

Middle of lesson
  Lecturing ——— ———
    Ensures that learners are mature enough ——— ———
    Ensures that learners are developing listening skills ——— ———
    Ensures that learners understand language ——— ———
    Gives evidence of advance planning ——— ———
    Supplements with aids ——— ———
    Provides for feedback and follow-up ——— ———
  Securing student participation ——— ———
    Gives continuous opportunity for student expression ——— ———
    Uses silence and nonverbal cues ——— ———
    Uses effective questioning ——— ———
      Asks higher-order questions ——— ———
      Asks probing questions ——— ———
      Asks divergent questions ——— ———
      Ensures that learners understand language ——— ———
      Avoids repeating questions and answers ——— ———
      Consumes only a portion of lesson ——— ———
      Is aware of affective learning ——— ———
  Provision for variation ——— ———
    Varies stimuli ——— ———
    Varies activities for the group ——— ———
    Varies activities for individuals ——— ———

End of lesson
  Provides for evaluation ——— ———
  Allows time for assignment making ——— ———
    Makes assignments clear ——— ———
    Reviews work covered or students are able to do ——— ———
    Anticipates difficult points ——— ———
    Differentiates for varying student interests and abilities ——— ———
    Is reasonable length ——— ———
    Is necessary ——— ———
    Ensures that needed resources are available ——— ———
    Uses more than one sensory channel ——— ———
  Achieves closure ——— ———

Comments/Summary

SUMMARY

The research on effective teaching underscores the necessity for setting clear goals, holding high expectations, focusing on academics, maintaining an orderly climate, using appropriate materials, and using time productively.

Lesson presentation involves a complex variety of component skills. The supervisor can be a help to teachers as they translate their unit and lesson plans into action. The supervisor determines whether the teacher has chosen suitable resources and selected appropriate strategies. This chapter provides guidelines for selecting both resources and strategies. The supervisor helps teachers in developing generic skills of instruction, which include effective ways of beginning, carrying through, and closing a lesson.

The supervisor should encourage teachers to increase student participation and incorporate a variety of stimuli and activities in both their planning and actual presentation. To help the supervisor work with teachers on lesson presentation, we have examined the specific skills (generic competencies) of set induction, lecturing, discussion, questioning, providing for variation, and closure. Supervisors should help teachers discover whether they are using time most productively for instructional purposes. In selecting instructional strategies teachers need to be mindful of the problem of motivation.

It is in the presentation stage that the carefully laid plans come to fruition—or fail. Lesson presentation is the phase of instruction the public knows as teaching, as it is often unaware of or ignores the hours of planning, grading papers, and other miscellaneous duties required of today's teacher. The presentation phase is the most rewarding to the teacher and is what keeps most teachers in the classroom. It is during this stage that ideas leap from mind to mind, skills are mastered by those who lacked them before instruction, and knowledge is stored in the brain—primarily because of the efforts of the teacher.

QUESTIONS FOR DISCUSSION

1. Should cooperative learning replace individualized learning? If so, why and how?
2. About which should teachers be more concerned: content and skills or students' self-concept?
3. Should all students be expected to master all basic knowledge and skills?
4. What is the place of direct teaching?
5. What knowledge and skills are necessary for teachers to make effective presentations?

ACTIVITIES FOR FURTHER STUDY

1. Define these terms:

generic teaching competency	anticipatory set
probing question	teaching strategy
stimulus variation	higher-order question
set induction	closure
convergent question	divergent question

2. Summarize common errors made by teachers in presenting a lesson and describe ways in which you, as a supervisor, could help teachers to overcome the errors.
3. Prepare a lecture/demonstration such as you would give to an in-service group of teachers on one of the following topics: selection of strategies, set induction, lecturing, conducting a discussion, questioning, stimulus variation, or closure.
4. Summarize two or three recent articles in professional journals on ways to individualize instruction and the (a) applicability elsewhere, (b) soundness of approach, and (c) cost of each.
5. Observe a teacher who is presenting a lesson and apply the checklist included at the end of this chapter. As a result of the observation, decide how effective you believe the presentation was with respect to each of the items on the checklist.
6. Write a fifty-minute lesson plan that incorporates skills studied in this chapter.
7. Select a topic, choose three strategies for presenting that topic to a particular group of learners, and decide which one of the three would be most effective as an initial strategy.
8. Examine the text materials used at one grade level or in one subject and apply the criteria for resources cited in this chapter.
9. Choose a topic and demonstrate set induction.
10. Describe or outline ways of evaluating the development of listening skills by the students.
11. Prepare and demonstrate effective lecturing following the guidelines presented in this chapter.
12. Prepare and demonstrate a discussion lesson using at least four nonverbal cues.
13. Select a topic that could be taught to a particular group of learners and write two questions (which you would present to a class orally) at each level of the Bloom taxonomy of cognitive objectives.
14. Write a report on adapting instruction to students' individual learning styles. (See Dunn and Dunn in chapter bibliography.)
15. Write a brief description of each of Madeline Hunter and Douglas Russell's seven steps for effective lessons (see chapter bibliography).
16. Summarize one or more reports of the "effective teaching research" of the past fifteen years. (See Berliner, Brookover, Brophy and Evertson, Brophy and Good, Edmonds, Lezotte, Medley, and Rosenshine in chapter bibliography.)
17. Prepare and conduct a short question-and-answer session and point out how frequently you used higher-order questions.
18. Observe a teacher conducting a questioning session and evaluate the effectiveness of the questioning, applying guidelines presented in this chapter.
19. Write a lesson plan and indicate where you incorporate variation of learning activities for the group.
20. Observe a teacher presenting a lesson and decide whether the teacher varied the stimuli and in what ways.
21. Demonstrate closure.
22. Critique at least two assignments given by teachers and decide whether each assignment meets the guidelines presented in this chapter.
23. Describe the seven intelligences according to Howard Gardner. (See chapter bibliography.)

NOTES

1. See Donald M. Medley, "The Effectiveness of Teachers," in *Research in Teaching: Concepts, Findings, and Implications*, ed. Penelope L. Peterson and Herbert J. Walberg, pp. 11–27

(Berkeley, Calif.: McCutchan, 1979). See also Donald M. Medley, "Research in Teacher Effectiveness—Where It Is and How It Got There," *Journal of Classroom Interaction* 13 (Summer 1978): 20.

2. See Barak V. Rosenshine, "Academic Engaged Time, Content Covered, and Direct Instruction," *Journal of Education* 160 (August 1978): 38–66; and Barak V. Rosenshine, "Content, Time, and Direct Instruction," in *Research in Teaching: Concepts, Findings, and Implications*, eds. Penelope L. Peterson and Herbert L. Walberg (Berkeley, Calif.: McCutchan, 1979), p. 52.

3. See N. L. Gage, *The Scientific Basis of the Art of Teaching* (New York: Teachers College Press, 1978). See also references in note 7.

4. Howard Gardner, *Multiple Intelligences: The Theory in Practice* (New York: Basic Books, 1993).

5. For discussion of constructivist principles and practices, see Jacqueline Grennon Brooks and Martin G. Brooks, *In Search of Understanding: The Case for Constructivist Classrooms* (Alexandria, Va.: Association for Supervision and Curriculum Development, 1993).

6. See David C. Berliner et al., *Phase III of the Beginning Teacher Effectiveness Study* (San Francisco: Far West Laboratory for Educational Research and Development, 1976); J. E. Brophy and C. M. Evertson, *Process-Product Correlation in the Texas Teacher Effectiveness Study* (Austin: University of Texas, 1974); Diana Hiatt, "Time Allocation in the Classroom: Is Instruction Being Shortchanged?" *Phi Delta Kappan* 61 (December 1979): 289–90; John D. McNeil, "A Scientific Approach to Supervision," in *Supervision of Teaching*, 1982 Yearbook, ed. Thomas J. Sergiovanni (Alexandria, Va.: Association for Supervision and Curriculum Development, 1982); Donald M. Medley, "The Effectiveness of Teachers," in *Research in Teaching: Concepts, Findings, and Implications*, ed. Penelope L. Peterson and Herbert L. Walberg, pp. 11–27 (Berkeley, Calif.: McCutchan, 1979). See also notes 8, 9, and 10.

7. See the following articles: John I. Goodlad, Kenneth A. Sirotnik, and Bette C. Overman, "An Overview of 'A Study of Schooling,' " *Phi Delta Kappan* 61 (November 1979): 174–78; M. Frances Klein, Kenneth A. Tye, and Joyce E. Wright, "A Study of Schooling: Curriculum," *Phi Delta Kappan* 61 (December 1979): 244–48; Barbara J. Benham, Phil Giesen, and Jeannie Oakes, "A Study of Schooling: Students' Experiences in Schools," *Phi Delta Kappan* 61 (January 1980): 337–40; Mary M. Bentzen, Richard C. Williams, and Paul Heckman, "A Study of Schooling: Adult Experiences in Schools," *Phi Delta Kappan* 61 (February 1980): 394–97; John I. Goodlad, "A Study of Schooling: Some Findings and Hypotheses," *Phi Delta Kappan* 64 (March 1983): 465–70; John I. Goodlad, "A Study of Schooling," *Educational Leadership* 40 (April 1983): 4–37. See also John I. Goodlad, *A Place Called School: Promise for the Future* (New York: McGraw-Hill, 1984).

8. Goodlad, *A Place Called School*, p. 97.

9. Jack L. Davidson and Freda M. Holley, "Your Students May Be Spending Only Half the School Day Receiving Instruction," *American School Board Journal* 166 (March 1979): 40–41.

10. Rosenshine, "Content, Time, and Direct Instruction," p. 52. See also Goodlad, *A Place Called School*, p. 365, n. 4 of chap. 4 for additional references on the relationship between student achievement and time spent.

11. See Keith A. Acheson and Meredith Damien Gall, *Techniques in the Clinical Supervision of Teachers: Preservice and Inservice Applications*, 2nd ed. (White Plains, N.Y.: Longman, 1987), pp. 98–105 for description of At Task Technique.

12. Agatha Christie, *The Mystery of the Blue Train* (New York: Dodd, Mead, 1928), p. 1.

13. See H. E. Aubertine, *An Experiment in the Set Induction Process and Its Application*, doctoral diss., Stanford University, 1964; Committee on Establishing Set, Metcalf Laboratory School, Illinois State University, "Set Induction Materials," mimeographed, n.d.; Dwight Allen and Kevin Ryan, *Microteaching* (Reading, Mass.: Addison-Wesley, 1969), pp. 18–19.

14. Madeline Hunter and Douglas Russell, "How Can I Plan More Effective Lessons?" *Instructor* 87 (September 1977): 74–75, 88.
15. Allen and Ryan, *Microteaching*, p. 15.
16. Hunter and Russell, "More Effective Lessons," pp. 74–75, 88.
17. See Chapter 3 of this text.
18. See Medley, "Effectiveness of Teachers."
19. Allen and Ryan, *Microteaching*, pp. 15–18.
20. Ibid., p. 16.
21. Robert E. Slavin, "Cooperative Learning and Student Achievement," in *School and Classroom Organization*, ed. Robert E. Slavin (Hillsdale, N.J.: Lawrence Erlbaum, 1989), p. 129.
22. For discussion of students' learning styles, see Rita Dunn and Kenneth Dunn, *Teaching Students through Their Individual Learning Styles: A Practical Approach* (Reston, Va.: Reston Publishing, 1978).
23. Adapted from Peter F. Oliva, *The Secondary School Today*, 2nd ed. (New York: Harper & Row, 1972), pp. 266–73.

BIBLIOGRAPHY

Acheson, Keith A., and Meredith Damien Gall. *Techniques in the Clinical Supervision of Teachers: Preservice and Inservice Applications*, 2nd ed. White Plains, N.Y.: Longman, 1987.

Allen, Dwight, and Kevin Ryan. *Microteaching*. Reading, Mass.: Addison-Wesley, 1969.

Aubertine, H. E. *An Experiment in the Set Induction Process and Its Application*. Doctoral dissertation, Stanford University, 1964.

Benham, Barbara J., Phil Giesen, and Jeannie Oakes. "A Study of Schooling: Students' Experiences in Schools." *Phi Delta Kappan* 61 (January 1980): 337–40.

Bentzen, Mary M., Richard C. Williams, and Paul Heckman. "A Study of Schooling: Adult Experiences in Schools." *Phi Delta Kappan* 61 (February 1980): 394–97.

Berenson, David H., Sally R. Berenson, and Robert B. Carkhuff. *The Skills of Teaching: Content Development Skills*. Amherst, Mass.: Human Resource Development Press, 1978.

Berenson, Sally R., David H. Berenson, and Robert R. Carkhuff. *The Skills of Teaching: Teaching Delivery Skills*. Amherst, Mass.: Human Resource Development Press, 1979.

Berliner, David C. et al. *Phase III of the Beginning Teacher Effectiveness Study*. San Francisco: Far West Laboratory for Educational Research and Development, 1976.

Brookover, Wilbur B. *A Study of Elementary School Social Systems and School Outcomes*. East Lansing: Michigan State University Center for Urban Affairs, 1977.

Brooks, Jacqueline Grennon, and Martin G. Brooks. *In Search of Understanding: The Case for Constructivist Classrooms*. Alexandria, Va.: Association for Supervision and Curriculum Development, 1993.

Brophy, Jere E., and C. M. Evertson. *Process-Product Correlation in the Texas Teacher Effectiveness Study*. Austin: University of Texas, 1974.

Brophy, Jere, and Thomas L. Good. "Teacher Behavior and Student Achievement." In *Handbook of Research on Teaching*, 3rd ed., ed. Merlin C. Wittrock, pp. 328–75. New York: Macmillan, 1986.

Carkhuff, Robert R., David H. Berenson, and Sally R. Berenson. *The Skills of Teaching: Lesson Planning Skills*. Amherst, Mass.: Human Resource Development Press, 1978.

Carkhuff, Robert R., David H. Berenson, Richard M. Pierce, Andrew H. Griffin, and Carolyn H. Schoenecker. *The Skills of Teaching: Interpersonal Skills*. Amherst, Mass.: Human Resource Development Press, 1977.

"Collegial Learning," *Educational Leadership* 45 (November 1987): 3–75.

Committee on Establishing Set. "Set Induction Materials." Mimeographed. Illinois State University, n.d.

Cooper, James M., ed. *Classroom Teaching Skills*, 4th ed. Lexington, Mass.: D. C. Heath, 1990.

"Cooperative Learning," *Educational Leadership* 47 (December 1989/January 1990): 3–66.

Davidson, Jack L., and Freda M. Holley. "Your Students May Be Spending Only Half the School Day Receiving Instruction." *American School Board Journal* 166 (March 1979): 40–41.

Dunn, Rita, and Kenneth Dunn. *Teaching Students through Their Individual Learning Styles: A Practical Approach*. Reston, Va.: Reston Publishing, 1978.

Edmonds, Ronald R. "Programs of School Improvement: An Overview." *Educational Leadership* 40, no. 3 (November 1982): 4–11.

Flinders, David J. "Supervision as Cultural Inquiry." *Journal of Curriculum and Supervision* 6 (Winter 1991): 87–106.

Gage, N. L. *The Scientific Basis of the Art of Teaching*. New York: Teachers College Press, 1978.

Gardner, Howard. *Multiple Intelligences: The Theory in Practice*. New York: Basic Books, 1993.

Garrett, Sandra Sokolove, Myra Sadker, and David Sadker. "Interpersonal Communication Skills." In *Classroom Teaching Skills*, 4th ed., ed. James M. Cooper, pp. 185–228. Lexington, Mass.: D. C. Heath, 1990.

Goodlad, John I. *A Place Called School: Promise for the Future*. New York: McGraw-Hill, 1984.

———. "A Study of Schooling." *Educational Leadership* 40 (April 1983): 4–37.

———. "A Study of Schooling: Some Findings and Hypotheses." *Phi Delta Kappan* 64 (March 1983): 465–70.

Goodlad, John I., Kenneth A. Sirotnik, and Bette C. Overman. "An Overview of 'A Study of Schooling.'" *Phi Delta Kappan* 61 (November 1979): 174–78.

Gunter, Mary Alice, et al. *Instruction: A Models Approach*. Boston: Allyn & Bacon, 1990.

Henson, Kenneth T. *Methods and Strategies for Teaching in Secondary and Middle Schools*, 2nd ed. White Plains, N.Y.: Longman, 1993.

Hiatt, Diana. "Time Allocation in the Classroom: Is Instruction Being Shortchanged?" *Phi Delta Kappan* 61 (December 1979): 289–90.

Hunter, Madeline, and Douglas Russell. "How Can I Plan More Effective Lessons?" *Instructor* 87 (September 1977): 74–75, 88.

Hutchins, C. L., Barbara Dunning, Marilyn Madsen, and Sylvia Rainey. *Minicourses Work*. San Francisco: Far West Laboratory for Educational Research and Development, n.d.

Intermediate Science Curriculum Study. *Individualizing Teacher Preparation: Individualization*. Morristown, N.J.: Silver Burdett, 1972.

———. *Individualizing Teacher Preparation: Questioning*. Morristown, N.J.: Silver Burdett, 1972.

Johnson, David W., and Roger T. Johnson. *Learning Together and Alone: Cooperation, Competition, and Individualization*. Englewood Cliffs, N.J.: Prentice-Hall, 1975.

Johnson, David W., Patricia Roy, and Edythe Holubec. *Circles of Learning: Cooperation in the Classroom*. Alexandria, Va.: Association for Supervision and Curriculum Development, 1980.

Joyce, Bruce, and Marsha Weil. *Models of Teaching*, 3rd ed. Englewood Cliffs, N.J.: Prentice-Hall, 1986.

Kim, Eugene C., and Richard D. Kellough. *A Resource Guide for Secondary School Teaching: Planning for Competence*, 6th ed. Englewood Cliffs, N.J.: Merrill, 1995.

Klein, M. Frances., Kenneth A. Tye, and Joyce E. Wright. "A Study of Schooling: Curriculum." *Phi Delta Kappan* 61 (December 1979): 244–48.

Leighton, Mary S. "Cooperative Learning." In *Classroom Teaching Skills*, 4th ed., ed. James M. Cooper, pp. 307–35. Lexington, Mass.: D. C. Heath, 1990.

Lezotte, Lawrence W., and Beverly A. Bancroft. "Growing Use of the Effective Schools Model for School Improvement." *Educational Leadership* 42 (March 1985): 23–27.

McNeil, John D. "A Scientific Approach to Supervision." In *Supervision of Teaching*, 1982

Yearbook, ed. Thomas J. Sergiovanni. Alexandria, Va.: Association for Supervision and Curriculum Development, 1982.

Martorella, Peter H. "Teaching Concepts." In *Classroom Teaching Skills*, 4th ed., ed. James M. Cooper, pp. 149–84. Lexington, Mass.: D. C. Heath, 1990.

Medley, Donald M. "The Effectiveness of Teachers." In *Research in Teaching: Concepts, Findings, and Implications*, ed. Penelope L. Peterson and Herbert J. Walberg, pp. 11–27. Berkeley, Calif.: McCutchan, 1979.

———. "Research in Teacher Effectiveness—Where It Is and How It Got There." *Journal of Classroom Interaction* 13 (Summer 1978): 20.

Miltz, Robert. *How to Explain: A Manual for Teaching*. Palo Alto, Calif.: Stanford Center for Research and Development in Teaching, 1972.

Nichols, Ralph G. *Listening and Speaking: A Guide to Effective Oral Communication*. New York: McGraw-Hill, 1972.

O'Brien, Lynn. "Learning Styles: Make the Student Aware." *NASSP Bulletin* 73 (October 1989): 85–89.

Oliva, Peter F. *The Secondary School Today*, 2nd ed. New York: Harper & Row, 1972.

Oliva, Peter F., and Kenneth T. Henson. "What Are the Essential Generic Teaching Competencies?" *Theory into Practice* 19 (Spring 1980): 117–21.

Orlich, Donald C. *Teaching Strategies: A Guide to Better Instruction*, 2nd ed. Lexington, Mass.: D. C. Heath, 1985.

Peter, Laurence J. *Competencies for Teaching*, vols. 1, 2, and 3. Englewood Cliffs, N.J.: Prentice-Hall, 1975.

Peterson, Penelope L., and Herbert J. Walberg, eds. *Research on Teaching: Concepts, Findings, and Implications*. Berkeley, Calif.: McCutchan, 1979.

Popham, W. James, and Eva L. Baker. *Planning an Instructional Sequence*. Englewood Cliffs, N.J.: Prentice-Hall, 1970.

———. *Systematic Instruction*. Englewood Cliffs, N.J.: Prentice-Hall, 1970.

Postman, Neil. *Teaching as a Conserving Activity*. New York: Delacorte, 1979.

Postman, Neil, and Charles Weingartner. *Teaching as a Subversive Activity*. New York: Delacorte, 1969.

Rosenshine, Barak V. "Academic Engaged Time, Content Covered, and Direct Instruction." *Journal of Education* 160 (August 1978): 38–66.

———. "Content, Time, and Direct Instruction." In *Research on Teaching: Concepts, Findings, and Implications*, ed. Penelope L. Peterson and Herbert J. Walberg, pp. 28–56. Berkeley, Calif.: McCutchan, 1979.

Sadker, Myra, and David Sadker. "Questioning Skills." In *Classroom Teaching Skills*, 4th ed., ed. James M. Cooper, pp. 111–48. Lexington, Mass.: D. C. Heath, 1990.

Sharan, Shlomo, ed. *Cooperative Learning: Theory and Research*. New York: Praeger, 1990.

Shostak, Robert. "Lesson Presentation Skills." In *Classroom Teaching Skills*, 4th ed., ed. James M. Cooper, pp. 85–109. Lexington, Mass.: D. C. Heath, 1990.

Slavin, Robert E. *Cooperative Learning*. White Plains, N.Y.: Longman, 1983.

———. "Cooperative Learning." *Review of Educational Research* 50 (Summer 1980): 315–42.

———. "Cooperative Learning and Student Achievement." In *School and Classroom Organization*, ed. Robert E. Slavin. Hillsdale, N.J.: Lawrence Erlbaum, 1989.

———. *Cooperative Learning: Theory, Research, and Practice*. Englewood Cliffs, N.J.: Prentice-Hall, 1990.

———, ed. *School and Classroom Organization*. Hillsdale, N.J.: Lawrence Erlbaum, 1989.

Smith, B. Othanel, in collaboration with Saul B. Cohen and Arthur Pearl. *Teachers for the Real World*. Washington, D.C.: American Association of Colleges for Teacher Education, 1969.

Squires, David A., William G. Huitt, and John K. Segars, eds. *Effective Schools and Classrooms:*

A Research-Based Perspective. Alexandria, Va.: Association for Supervision and Curriculum Development, 1983.

Stallings, Jane A. "Using Time Effectively: A Self-Analytical Approach." In *Improving Teaching,* 1986 Yearbook, ed. Karen K. Zumwalt, pp. 15–27. Alexandria, Va.: Association for Supervision and Curriculum Development, 1987.

Tillman, Murray. *Learning to Teach.* Lexington, Mass.: D. C. Heath, 1976.

———. *Troubleshooting Classroom Problems: A Practical Guide.* Glenview, Ill.: Scott, Foresman, 1982.

Wittrock, Merlin C., ed. *Handbook of Research on Teaching,* 3rd ed. New York: Macmillan, 1986.

Zumwalt, Karen K., ed. *Improving Teaching,* 1986 Yearbook. Alexandria, Va.: Association for Supervision and Curriculum Development, 1986.

Audiotapes

Ronald R. Edmonds. *The Characteristics of Schools That Are Instructionally Effective for All Pupils.* 1981. Association for Supervision and Curriculum Development, 1250 North Pitt Street, Alexandria, Va. 22314.

John I. Goodlad, Kenneth A. Tye, and M. Frances Klein. *About a Study of Schooling.* 1979. Ninety minutes. Association for Supervision and Curriculum Development, 1250 North Pitt Street, Alexandria, Va. 22314.

Videotapes

Cooperative Learning. A series of five videotapes featuring David Johnson, Roger Johnson, Robert Slavin, and Britt Vasquez, 1990. Demonstrates how to conduct a cooperative learning program. With Facilitator's Manual. Association for Supervision and Curriculum Development, 1250 North Pitt Street, Alexandria, Va. 22314.

Effective Instruction, 1987. Series 1: A series of five videotapes, including Decisions in Teaching, The Instructional Objective, Motivation and Positive Reinforcement, Retention, and Critical Attribute and Lesson Design. Orange County Department of Education, P.O. Box 9050, Costa Mesa, Calif. 92628–9050. These tapes are part of Clinical Supervision: A Videotape Series for Instructional Leadership. For Series 2, Instructional Conference, see Bibliography, Videotapes, Chapter 12.

Effective Teaching for Higher Achievement. 1981. Two hours of videotape and Leader's Guide. Features Barak Rosenshine, Jane Stallings, Jere Brophy, Georgea Sparks Langer, and Dennis Sparks. Steps in using time, managing classroom behavior, and planning lessons. Association for Supervision and Curriculum Development, 1250 North Pitt Street, Alexandria, Va. 22314.

Instructional Decisions for Long-Term Learning. 1987. Developed by Patricia R. Wolfe and Pam Robbins, this program consists of four videotapes and accompanying materials that integrate Madeline Hunter's principles of classroom decision making with research on how students process information. The four parts are as follows:
1. *The Student's Mind: Focus for Decisions,* Tape: sixty minutes, Workshop: two hours.
2. *Guidelines for Instructional Decisions,* Tape: sixty minutes, Workshop: three hours.
3. *Increasing Student Participation in Learning,* Tape: forty minutes, Workshop: ninety minutes.
4. *Support for Effective Teaching,* Tape: thirty minutes, Workshop: sixty minutes.
Association for Supervision and Curriculum Development, 1250 North Pitt Street, Alexandria, Va. 22314.

Learning—A Matter of Style. 1980. Thirty-minute videotape featuring Rita Dunn. Discussion Guide. Presentation on elements of student learning styles. Association for Supervision and Curriculum Development, 1250 North Pitt Street, Alexandria, Va 22314.

Mastery Teaching: Increasing Instructional Effectiveness in Secondary Schools, Colleges, and Universities. 1982. A set of twenty videotapes narrated by Madeline Hunter on teaching techniques. Instructional Dynamics, Inc., Pacific Palisades, Calif.

Teacher and School Effectiveness. 1981. Twenty-one minutes. Discussion of characteristics of effective teachers and schools. Barak V. Rosenshine discusses the importance of academic focus, selection of activities, grouping of students, demonstration-practice-feedback, and mastery. Ronald Edmonds discusses five characteristics: principal's leadership style, instructional emphasis, climate, expectation, and assessment of pupil progress. Peter Mortimore reinforces these characteristics. Association for Supervision and Curriculum Development, 1250 North Pitt Street, Alexandria, Va. 22314.

The Teaching Strategies Library. Parts One and Two. 1987–89. Eight videotapes of forty to fifty minutes each, featuring Richard Strong, Harvey Silver, and Robert Hanson on mastery lecture, concept attainment, concept formation, peer practice, compare and contrast, reading for meaning, "Synectics,"™ and circle of knowledge. Thirty-minute overview tape. Two training manuals. Programs focus on mastery, understanding, synthesis, and involvement. Association for Supervision and Curriculum Development, 1250 North Pitt Street, Alexandria, Va. 22314. Synectics is a registered trademark for Synectics, Inc., Cambridge, Mass.

Time on Task. 1983. Twenty-six minutes. Discussion of an important aspect of effective teaching: keeping learners on task. American Association of School Administrators, 1801 North Moore Street, Arlington, Va. 22209.

Workshop

Teacher Expectations and Student Achievement (TESA). An in-service training program consisting of five workshops on fifteen teacher behaviors designed to encourage nondiscriminatory behavior toward students and to raise the academic performance of low achievers. Participants' follow-up workshop observing each other in the classroom. Teacher handbooks and program coordinator's manual. Distributor in California: Los Angeles County Superintendent of Schools, 9300 Imperial Highway, Downey, Calif. 90242. Outside California: Phi Delta Kappa, Eighth & Union Streets, Box 789, Bloomington, Ind. 47402.

5

Helping Teachers
with Classroom Management

Objectives

After studying Chapter 5 you should be able to accomplish the following objectives:

1. Identify common sources of behavior problems.
2. Describe the characteristics of a fully functioning personality and its relationship to the problem of discipline.
3. Describe common teaching styles and their impact on discipline.
4. Describe common learning styles and their impact on discipline.
5. Describe several measures that can be taken to prevent disciplinary problems.
6. Describe several models of discipline.
7. Describe several approaches to discipline.
8. Contrast the strengths and weaknesses of behavior modification.
9. Contrast strengths and weaknesses of psychodynamic or diagnostic approaches to discipline.
10. List steps in behavior modification.
11. Analyze the methods of discipline you prefer.
12. Select appropriate corrective measures.
13. Explain the role of punishment.
14. Formulate your own views on discipline.

DISCIPLINE: A SERIOUS PROBLEM

A frazzled young elementary teacher holds her head at the end of a particularly rough day with her group of superactive children. As she fumbles for an aspirin in her handbag, it is obvious to the supervisor, who happened to drop in on this inauspicious occasion, that the children's behavior that day had been less than ideal. The supervisor empathizes with the teacher and hopes that the painkiller will relieve her headache. If only the problems of classroom management would respond to a simple formula like aspirin and then vanish overnight!

Even Socrates, one of the most famous teachers in history, must have been holding his head when he lamented, "Children now love luxury. They have bad manners, contempt for authority. They show disrespect for elders and love chatter in place of exercise. Children are now tyrants, not the servants of their households."[1]

Sometimes it seems that not much has changed since 400 B.C. Not even the venerable Socrates was able to concoct a formula that would serve as either a vaccine or a cure for misbehavior by young people. Fantasizing, harried teachers feel that student behavior problems would disappear if these conditions existed:

- If only children were mature—but they are not.
- If only children were as motivated as the teacher—but they are not.
- If only children could choose whether they wanted to come to school—but they cannot.
- If only children had no problems—but they do.

If only—teachers could go on and wistfully hope never to encounter a disciplinary problem, and proceed smoothly from planning to presentation to evaluation without stumbling on the pebbles and boulders of behavior problems. But the road is rocky and the stones are there. It is the teacher's task to clear the stones out of the way, go over them, go around them, or even push them out of the way if need be, and it is the supervisor's task to help the teachers in this arduous job.

The teacher's task in matters of discipline, control, and classroom management should not be minimized. These topics are constantly on the minds of most teachers, particularly new and inexperienced ones. The frustration of dealing with disciplinary problems has driven many teachers out of the classroom. Some have left the profession; others, ironically, have gravitated to administrative positions where they have responsibility for the disciplinary problems of an entire school instead of just the problems of their own classes. Some have taken on the mantle of the college professor, whose disciplinary problems are usually few and far between.

Discipline is a word that is easily understood by everyone but difficult to define. Perhaps the difficulty of defining the word stems from its resemblance to a Portuguese man-of-war: It has so many and such long tentacles. If we go back far enough—say 2,000 years—the little Roman *discipulus* was a pupil, a learner, who was subjected to *disciplina*—instruction, training, or education. Hence the use of the term discipline to mean an organized body of knowledge, a subject field. The *disciples* of Christ were those who had been instructed in the teachings of Christ.

Though the word *discipline* still refers to organized fields of specialization, *discipline* in its "training" sense has come to signify order, management, conduct, deportment, and even punishment. People talk about the discipline of the school and the discipline of the class. We say the teacher maintains good discipline and disciplines the pupils. This text defines discipline as a state of order in the class or school environment that permits learning to proceed smoothly and productively.

Behavior is another of those words that can be understood only in context. Previous chapters discussed learning behaviors, meaning, in that context, outcomes or objectives of learning in any of the three domains of learning. To speak of behavior in the context of discipline (as opposed to *a* discipline) is to equate it with conduct or deportment, just as *misbehavior* means misconduct. The student who has learned to take responsibility for his or her own actions in socially acceptable ways is said to possess self-discipline, a major goal not only of discipline but of the entire process of education in our society. Those who behave in socially unacceptable ways are said to have—or, in personified form, to be—behavior problems or disciplinary problems.

A teacher not only teaches classes but also manages them, or more properly, manages the learning environment in such a way that learning can occur. The skills the teacher employs for this purpose are called collectively *classroom management*. Included within the scope of this definition are classroom routines, prevention of misbehavior, and correction of behavior problems.

Both teachers and school administrators agree that discipline is the most serious problem faced by teachers, particularly inexperienced teachers. Harvey F. Clarizio observed that "classroom management has always been one of the foremost problems for teachers. Indeed, the adequate control of a class is a prerequisite to achieving instructional objectives and to safeguarding the psychological and physical well-being of students."[2]

Since 1969, Gallup polls have surveyed the public's attitudes toward the public schools. The results are published each fall in the *Phi Delta Kappan*, the journal of Phi Delta Kappa, the national society in education. Lack of discipline has consistently appeared at or near the top—until recent years, in first place—of the public's list of problems in the public schools. The public has generally ranked lack of discipline ahead of such other thorny issues as lack of proper financial support, poor curriculum/poor standards, difficulty in getting good teachers, teachers' lack of interest, and integration/busing. In the Gallup Polls of the late 1980s and early 1990s, the public ranked use of drugs as the major problem in public schools. Lack of discipline was second. The 27th Annual Phi Delta Kappa/Gallup Poll conducted in 1995 indicated that 15 percent of Americans considered lack of discipline to be the biggest problem with which the public schools must deal. Nine percent of the respondents indicated that fighting/violence/gangs were another important problem for school personnel.[3]

The students, in their role as potential misbehavers and recipients of disciplinary measures, are intimately concerned with the problem of discipline. Students expect teachers to foster a classroom environment where, whether productive learning goes on or not, at least their security and self-esteem are protected.

Students realize that they are a part of the American school culture. As such, they expect to encounter misbehavior on the part of their peers and they anticipate that they themselves may indulge in some infractions of the rules, if only to maintain their status in the culture. As a result, they expect the teacher to respond to misconduct. Earlier Gallup surveys showed that the majority of students felt the discipline of their school was about right. Only a small percentage believed the discipline was too strict, and a significant percentage considered the discipline not strict enough.[4] What students expect is not absence of response to their misbehavior but attitudes of concern and fairness for them as people.[5]

With all the stress placed by the constituents within the school and the community on discipline, the supervisor's work is cut out. Classroom management may well be the single most difficult task of public school teaching. If there is any one aspect of teaching with which beginning teachers especially need help from a supervisor, discipline fits that description. Fredric H. Jones observed that the problem of discipline "has gone noticed but unattended. . . . Administrators want teachers to take care of it, teachers want administrators to take care of it, and the universities ignore it as though the study of it would ruin their humanistic credentials."[6]

The principal, the assistant principal for administration, and the dean of students may well ponder the question of discipline in their school as they sit in their offices and receive a steady flow of "discipline problems" from the various classrooms. They note great variations among what teachers consider serious behavior problems—those sent to the administrators' offices. They observe that some of the teachers on the faculty have either a greater skill in handling disciplinary problems than other teachers or a greater tolerance for enduring them, for some teachers never send misbehaving pupils to an administrator's office; they prefer, as the saying goes, to "skin" their own skunks. Other teachers repeatedly send children out of their classrooms because of misconduct. The administrators realize with a touch of amusement that the teachers who send them their misbehaving students expect them to handle the problems where the teachers have failed; the teachers expect them to take some drastic action on each case, whether the culprit has simply sassed the teacher or pulled a weapon.

As they walk through the corridors of the school, these administrators cannot help noticing great differences in teaching styles among the faculty. They conjecture that there must be some relationship between teaching style and the presence or absence of behavior problems in the classroom. And yet, no single variable can be found to be a sure predictor of skill in discipline except perhaps for the reality that the beginning teacher seems to have more difficulty with discipline than the experienced teacher.

Even the variable of experience, however, is not an accurate predictor of a teacher's success or failure in handling disciplinary problems. No one can say with certainty that an inexperienced teacher is always less skillful in maintaining discipline than an experienced teacher, for that is not always the case. Neither is an older teacher always better at maintaining discipline than a younger teacher. Male teachers are not always more skillful at discipline than female teachers; quite often the opposite is true. At times it seems as if some mysterious body chemistry of a teacher is the secret of discipline. Among teachers in the same school, working with the same students, some teachers have few or no disciplinary problems whereas others have constant problems. Administrators may finally conclude that those teachers who are having difficulties with discipline lack certain understandings about behavior—both the student's behavior and their own—and certain skills in classroom management.

What kind of program, then, can a supervisor institute to help teachers develop and improve both their understanding of behavior and their skills in classroom management? The program should include at least three components:

- Teachers should be engaged in discussions of causes of behavior problems and helped to develop basic understandings about discipline.
- Teachers should be helped to develop skills for preventing disciplinary problems.
- Teachers should be helped to choose suitable corrective measures.

CAUSES OF BEHAVIOR PROBLEMS

The disciplinary problems of the schools today range from the trivial to the terrifying and from the casual to the criminal. Since the days of the Latin Grammar School, teachers in America have had to contend with children who scrapped with each other, carved their initials on school furniture, scribbled on the walls, failed to pay attention, were impertinent, and disrupted learning in a variety of ingenious ways. Many of the troublemakers in American schools have gone on to become prominent and productive citizens. Only in recent times have teachers had to cope with students who bring handguns to school, use drugs, threaten, and sometimes inflict bodily harm on both teachers and other students. A pessimist might conclude that young people and society have gone to hell, hedonism is in the saddle, religion has failed, and we have entered an era of darkness.

Such a pessimistic outlook makes the mistake of generalizing that a large percentage of children in all schools are serious troublemakers. True, some schools do have more than their share of serious offenders, but these schools are not the norm of our educational operation. The extent of this enterprise we call public education can be seen in some recent statistics. Our children are schooled in almost 59,000 elementary public schools and 20,120 secondary public schools.[7] It takes more than 2 million teachers to instruct these young people: Over 1,680,000 teachers are engaged in the education of approximately 30 million elementary school children, and some 1,073,000 teachers work to educate approximately 14,651,000 secondary school students.[8]

Great variations in disciplinary climate exist among these 79,000-plus schools, some of which are located in rural and small-town America; some in urban settings, including the inner city; and some in suburbia. Some of these schools are characterized by relatively few behavior problems and only a very small percentage of serious problems; other schools have many behavior problems, a sizable percentage of which are serious. The serious problems such as the use of drugs, violence, and sex offenses tend to be highlighted and featured in the news media. Although the serious problems are numerous—more numerous than we would wish them to be—the truth is that most children and youth are law abiding and cooperative. Although the headlines of the daily press feature rising crime rates throughout the nation, the majority of our population still subscribes to the rule of law. Certainly, in those schools where serious problems are frequent, strict measures must be taken to cope with them. What plagues most teachers, however, is the continuing, repeated, frustrating behavior of students who impede not only their own learning but the learning of others.

Well-disciplined schools share two characteristics: (1) the absence of disciplinary problems and (2) a total program that promotes the teaching of self-discipline. Both these characteristics are goals that schools should strive to achieve even though both are difficult to realize. Self-discipline means the individual's ability to exercise self-control and to take responsibility for his or her own conduct. When self-discipline is present in a school, behavior problems disappear.

The absence of disciplinary problems per se is, however, no guarantee that self-discipline is present. Behavior problems can be held in check—at least temporarily—by strict regimentation. Stern disciplinary measures by the faculty can repress behavior problems, but at the same time they prevent the development of self-discipline by the students.

Because discipline is such a pervasive problem and teachers are eager for answers, supervisors sometimes initiate the discussion of discipline with a case study approach. Teachers share anecdotes of misbehavior with their colleagues and jointly try to recommend the best strategies for dealing with each case. Though this procedure is a useful and practical approach to the study of discipline, the case study approach is more effective after the teachers have developed some understanding of the causes of behavior problems. When they can form some hypotheses about why a child has behaved in a certain way, they can more intelligently recommend solutions to the problem. Understanding causes of behavior problems may indicate additional information teachers must gather before they can attempt to resolve a problem. The supervisor should help teachers clarify the reasons children become disciplinary problems.

Some years ago in researching the subject of discipline, Oliva classified causes of behavior problems under six broad categories: causes originating with the child, causes originating with the child's group, causes originating with the teacher, causes originating with the school, causes originating with the home and community, and causes originating in the larger social order.[9] Analysis and discussion of each of these categories can contribute to the teachers' understanding of pupil behavior. The six categories of this classification scheme are in reality sources or roots of disciplinary problems. An early conclusion teachers will reach is the understanding that behavior may be manifested in class but its origins may lie somewhere else. Teachers will come to realize that problems in the classroom may very well be symptoms of trouble rather than the trouble itself. Teachers are usually already aware that there are causes of behavior problems over which they have little or no control. For that reason our discussion of prevention and correction of behavior problems later in this chapter emphasizes those measures that are within the powers of the teachers to affect. As a prelude to an examination of what the teacher may do about disciplinary problems, let's consider why pupils exhibit misbehavior.

Causes Originating with the Child

Personal Problems. Children experience a variety of physical, mental, social, and emotional problems that can create disciplinary difficulties in the classroom. A typical class includes children with physical handicaps, slower intellectual capacities, and social and psychological problems. Defects in hearing and vision are common handicaps, and they sometimes go undetected for years. A child who cannot see well or hear well can easily become a disciplinary problem for the teacher. Malnutrition is a more common problem than we sometimes realize. Not only is malnutrition a problem among children of parents who cannot afford to provide a nutritious diet but it is also a problem in middle- and upper-class families who can afford nutritious diets but for one reason or another do not follow sound principles of nutrition. If there is some truth to the saying, "You are what you eat," a good many classroom behavior problems can be traced to faulty diets. The general health of the child, the presence or absence of fatigue, endocrine deficiencies, and past diseases may all be factors in the child's performance and behavior in class.

Of all the physical factors that contribute to disciplinary problems, the most common and most obvious is the child's stage of growth and development. The handling of concepts, the ability to solve problems, the ability to sit still, the ability to listen, the ability to pay attention, the ability to take turns in speaking, and the ability to get along with others are all functions of growth and development. Biological determiners join with sociocultural determiners to make growing up in America a protracted experience for children and adolescents. Biologically, children develop in a fixed pattern—they learn to walk before they learn to talk; they learn to talk before they learn to read; they learn simple number concepts before they can solve equations. Ultimately, the majority of them learn to take responsibility for their own behavior. Culturally, the American public keeps its children in school for longer periods of time than many other societies. One reason is that the American public accepts the dictum that education opens the doors for its youth. Doesn't every American mother or father secretly wish he or she could proudly say, "My child, the doctor"? Don't repeated public opinion polls show doctors, lawyers, and engineers at the top of lists of preferred occupations—all calling for prolonged education? (Teaching, which once ranked among the most preferred of occupations, has moved down somewhat, but in spite of all its problems it still enjoys a wide popularity, as evidenced by the numbers of young people aspiring to be teachers.)

The American public keeps its children in school longer and therefore in a less than mature status to reduce competition of young people with adults for jobs. Raising the age for compulsory school attendance over the years has been a direct function of the efforts of the public to safeguard jobs for the adult breadwinners of the family. Though growth and development are significant factors in discipline at all levels, many teachers seem to feel that the middle school and junior high years are the most difficult. Caught as they are between puberty and adolescence, preadolescents, or transescents, as they are sometimes called, often exhibit simultaneously problems of childhood and adolescence.

An analysis of the mental abilities of children in any heterogeneous class will show a range from very slow to gifted. Any of these levels—slow, average, or fast—can become behavior problems given an inappropriate learning environment. When slow learners are frustrated by their inability to cope with their studies, when average learners find nothing stimulating about their studies, and when bright students do not find their studies a challenge, they can create disciplinary problems for the teacher.

Self-Concept. All human beings have common sociopsychological needs. All need love, security, recognition, approval, and success, and the lack of awareness, the frustration, even the squelching of these needs breed countless behavior problems. William Glasser, exponent of Reality Therapy, identified love and self-worth as the most important needs of all humans.

> Love and self-worth are so intertwined that they may properly be related through the use of the term *identity*. Thus we may say that the single basic need that people have is the requirement for an identity: the belief that we are someone in distinction to others, and that the someone is important and worthwhile. Then *love and self-worth may be considered the two pathways* that mankind has discovered lead to a successful identity.[10]

Perceptual psychologists have called educators' attention to the necessity for recognizing the importance of the self-concept. Every human being has the need to become, as Carl R. Rogers termed it, "a fully functioning personality,"[11] or as A. H. Maslow called it, "a self-actualizing"[12] person, or as Arthur W. Combs labeled it, "a truly adequate person."[13]

Don E. Hamachek described how the self-concept is formed. "How we view ourselves is determined partially by how we perceive ourselves as really being, partially through how we view ourselves as ideally wanting to be, and partially through the expectations we perceive that others have for us."[14]

Combs identified four characteristics that seemed to underlie the behavior of truly adequate persons. "These characteristics are: (a) a positive view of the self, (b) identification with others, (c) openness to experience and acceptance, and (d) a rich and available perceptual field."[15] Of the self-concept Combs wrote,

> The self concept, we know, is learned. People *learn* who they are and what they are from the ways in which they have been treated by those who surround them in the process of their growing up. . . . People develop feelings that they are liked, wanted, acceptable and able from *having been* liked, wanted, accepted and from *having been* successful. One learns that he is these things, not from being told so, but only through the experience of *being treated as though he were so*. Here is the key to what must be done to produce more adequate people. To produce a positive self, it is necessary to provide experiences that teach individuals they are positive people.[16]

Maslow placed self-actualization at the top of a hierarchy of basic needs.[17] Self-actualizing persons hold a positive view of the self. Many children, however, in their association with "significant others" have learned self-doubt, low self-esteem, and fearfulness. "The self is built almost entirely, if not entirely," said Earl C. Kelley, "in relationship to others. . . . Unfortunately, many people in the world today suffer from inadequate concepts of self. . . . An inadequate concept of self, so common in our culture, is crippling to the individual."[18]

In contrasting behaviors commonly observed in students Hamachek noted that students with high, positive self-concepts get along well with others, are friendly, and show self-confidence. Students with low, negative self-concepts generally worry, exhibit shyness, and can be overassertive.[19]

Self-Fulfilling Prophecy. Many students who hold inadequate self-concepts have become victims of what is known as the *self-fulfilling prophecy*. Friends, relatives, or teachers (or possibly all) have led them to believe that they are inadequate, and as a result, they have come to believe in their own inadequacies. They may have been told that they cannot read, they cannot do math, they cannot draw, they cannot excel in sports; they *cannot* . . . you name it. If told enough times, they agree they are inadequate. This belief leads to failure, which deepens their conviction that they cannot achieve, which leads to more failure.

On the other hand, if they are told that they are adequate and that they can do the tasks asked of them, they are more often successful. With success comes the belief that they are adequate, which leads to continued success. Somehow negative attitudes toward the self need to be replaced by positive ones. Teachers are in a vital position to help young people gain a sense of adequacy, which is fundamental to living and learning. Therefore, it is sound pedagogy for teachers to hold learners to high expectations.

Supervisors should help teachers to realize that when a child takes a seat the first day of class, he or she has brought along certain physical, mental, social, and emotional attributes, which during the course of the year may lead to disciplinary problems.

Causes Originating with the Child's Group

Children act not only as individuals but also as members of groups. Most notably, all children are members of their classes and react with one another in their classes. To varying degrees the behavior of one individual in a class shapes the behavior of other individuals in that class. The learning environment of which the teacher is the chief manipulator can contribute to behavior problems in the group.

Children are not only members of their classes but they participate as members of other peer groups both inside and outside school. Unless they are "loners," they will have a small circle of intimate friends with whom they constantly associate. Subgroups develop within classes and can become powerful shapers of student behavior. Some young people are more gregarious than others and are members of many groups: school clubs, church organizations, community groups, and street gangs. For many, youth groups outside school permit them to achieve a sense of identity they cannot find in school.

The peer groups to which a child belongs exercise a potent influence on every group member's behavior. This influence can be positive or negative depending on whether the aims of the group are social or antisocial. Peer-group pressures, particularly among adolescents, force children often into patterns of behavior that may be against their own best inner judgments. Long ago Allison Davis made an observation that still holds true:

> The example of the adolescent's play group and of his own kin, however, is the crucial determinant of his behavior. Even where the efforts of the parent to instill middle-class mores in the child are more than half-hearted, the power of the street culture in which the child and adolescent are trained overwhelms the parent's verbal instruction. The rewards of gang prestige, freedom of movement, and property gain all seem to be on the side of the street culture.[20]

We cannot blame youth alone for responding to group pressures. The handshaking, back-slapping, gregarious, conforming Organization Man is still an ideal of our society. Those who are critical of social customs and practices are not always appreciated. American society has placed a great emphasis on outer-direction, as evidenced by advertisers who attempt to make us feel inadequate if we do not use their products and by the joining syndrome, which the Frenchman Alexis de Tocqueville observed about Americans in the nineteenth century.

Neither conformity to a particular group's pressures nor nonconformity should be considered an end in itself. Conformity to the rule of law and to conventions subscribed to by society as a whole is a must—whether in the classroom or out. Conformity of thought, of ideas, and of opinions is not a goal to be sought—whether in the classroom or out.

Teachers need to be aware that there are groups, such as youth gangs, outside the class group vying for the interests of members of the class. They need to be aware also that the aims and activities of those outside groups are often more appealing to the members of their classes than is membership in the class group. They are literally in competition with other forces that demand the time, interest, and loyalty of members of their class. The textbook answer to this problem is the creation of a learning environment so appealing that children will choose academic pursuits over other interests. Whether this can be achieved is highly problematical. Even the experienced supervisor may be hard pressed to advise the teacher how to make learning more attractive to young people than avocational, recreational, and other out-of-class activities. The supervisor sometimes feels like the grasshopper who envied the household roach for its good fortune at being able to live inside where it could find food and be sheltered from bad weather. The grasshopper asked the roach, "How can I share your good fortune?" The roach answered, "That's easy. Just turn yourself into a roach." The grasshopper, perplexed, inquired, "But how can I do that?" The roach replied, "Well, I've given you the principle. Now you work out the details."

The supervisor can advise the teacher to create as favorable and positive a classroom climate for learning as possible. Some of the dimensions of this positive climate are examined later in this chapter. The supervisor can advise the teacher, at the risk of being accused of tautology, to try to develop groups of nonconforming conformists or, vice versa, conforming nonconformists by providing a climate where there is freedom to learn. But freedom, the supervisor hastens to add, is accompanied by restraint on the part of all members who make up the groups. Without restraint, preferably self-restraint, there can be no freedom for anyone.

Causes Originating with the Teacher

A complete change of thought will be required before the majority of teachers will be willing to admit that teachers themselves can be causes of pupil behavior problems. A teacher must have an open, introspective personality to look within and recognize that he or she can be a source of student problems. Such introspection flies in the face of tradition, for it has been the custom since schools were first established to place the blame for misbehavior on the offender. It is the pupil, after all, who is not behaving properly. We may on occasion look beyond the child and lament, as the refrain goes, "Poor helpless child, he's not to blame, his father's folks are just the same." From time to time we might listen instead to Cassius's words, "The fault, dear Brutus, is not in our stars, but in ourselves." Or we may recall that the comic strip character Pogo identified the enemy as us. Chapter 12 develops the theme of teacher behavior and suggests ways in which a supervisor can help teachers evaluate themselves.

A common source of disciplinary problems can be found in the methods of instruction employed by the teacher. Objectives that are inappropriate to the learners (or lack specified objectives) or poorly conceptualized, haphazard planning, ineffective presentations, unsuitable materials, inadequate evaluation, and lack of provision for feedback—dealt with at length in previous chapters—create and magnify pupil behavior problems. Although many behavior problems are caused by poor method, this aspect of teaching fortunately can be improved with training. It is far easier and less threatening for a teacher to admit that methods of instruction are causing disciplinary problems than it is to admit that something about his or her personality provokes problems. The supervisor should continuously work with teachers in helping them to improve their methods of instruction. William B. Glasser's control theory contends that no one can make anyone do anything. He suggests that it is the job of the manager (the teacher) to manage so that it is easy for workers (the students) to see a strong connection between what they are asked to do and what they believe to be worth doing.[21] Fortunately too, improvement in methods of teaching can be observed and measured by both the teacher and the supervisor. Improvement—translate this *success*—spurs the teacher on to continued improvement and helps develop rapport between the teacher and supervisor.

Unfortunately, not all teacher-caused faults lie in the methods of instruction. The attitudes teachers reveal about students, learning, the school, the community, morality, democracy, and life in general can create a climate that either produces or reduces behavior problems, depending on whether these attitudes are negative or positive. There has been a more consistent shift in the proportion of new teachers who agree strongly that a significant number of children come to school with so many problems that it is difficult for them to be good students. Twenty-eight percent of the teacher respondents to *The Metropolitan Life Survey of The American Teacher 1992* agreed that students come to school with so many problems that their learning is impeded. However, after one year of teaching more than 47 percent said so, and 50 percent agreed with the statement after two years of teaching experience.[22] Teachers who care about their students and show it will have fewer disciplinary problems than teachers who dislike their students, their school, and their job.

Teachers' attitudes toward education and life are shaped to a great extent by their socioeconomic and cultural origins. Teachers as a group are usually middle-class products espousing middle-class values. Students in our public schools manifest a cultural diversity with differing values. Teachers need training in coping with this diversity. Teacher education institutions may provide limited training in teaching in a multicultural environment. Supervisors should expand on that training by arranging for in-service education on problems of teaching in multicultural settings. Teachers must understand the history of subcultures represented in their classes; social, economic, educational, and health problems that their students face; home environments; special learning problems; differing beliefs and values; even such behavior as nonverbal language, which often varies from culture to culture.

Beyond a genuine interest and affection for the level of learners they are teaching, teachers should possess certain common personal characteristics without which successful school teaching is impossible. Both a sense of humor and a sense of confidence are essential attributes of a teacher. Some people seem to be born with both these characteristics, though we know they have developed them over the years through contacts with other people. If a sense of humor and a sense of confidence are lacking in an individual, they are both exceedingly difficult to develop. Of the two traits, a sense of confidence may be developed more easily than a sense of humor. Good planning, for example, can give a teacher a sense of confidence. When a teacher knows how to go about the instructional process, fears of floundering disappear. The teacher can develop confidence by managing instruction in such a way that students achieve their objectives. A supervisor can help a teacher develop a sense of confidence by pointing out ways to plan for instruction and present lessons effectively and by building the teacher's sense of confidence with frequent and positive reinforcement.

Whether the supervisor can help a teacher develop a sense of humor if the teacher has none is doubtful. The lack of a sense of humor may be symptomatic of personal problems that will only respond to the kind of therapy a supervisor neither can nor should attempt to provide. In some cases, if the supervisor displays a sense of humor and cajoles the teacher a little, a latent seed of humor may blossom forth.

Much has been written in recent years about students' rights to dress and groom themselves as they see fit. Certainly teachers should have similar rights to select their wardrobes and wear their hair in a manner pleasing to them. Yet some bounds of propriety are essential. Though many beginning teachers are scarcely out of their teens themselves, they are still adults and must dress and conduct themselves as adults. Further, young people want to look to them as adults, not as their peers. The teacher's choice of dress and language should be such as to command the respect of young people. Teachers who attempt to imitate the lifestyle of students in the mistaken notion that this is the way to show their interest in the students run the risk of becoming ridiculous in their eyes. Whether they want the role or not, teachers are parent substitutes and as such have a certain culturally determined role they must play. To forsake this role is to invite disciplinary problems.

One attribute that must be mentioned is the teacher's voice. Confidence is communicated to students through what the teacher says and how it is said as well as through what the teacher does and how it is done. The teacher's voice must be strong enough to be heard—the first time—if students are to be taught listening skills. Teachers with a speech impediment have a tough row to hoe, for at times students can be intolerant to the point of cruelty. A grating or shrill voice fails to command either attention or respect. What the teacher should seek to develop is a calm, well-modulated, resonant voice and well-articulated, grammatically correct speech patterns. The supervisor might recommend that teachers who have problems in speaking and voice projection take some training in speech and if necessary undergo speech therapy.

The supervisor must ask teachers to look at themselves as possible sources of some of the behavior problems they encounter in their classrooms. Later in this chapter we return to the role of the teacher in preventing and correcting disciplinary problems.

Causes Originating with the School

A number of conditions beyond the boundaries of the classroom combine in the school to create disciplinary problems. Among these are the culture or ecology of the school and the curriculum. Individuals manifest characteristics that identify them as persons. Some are short; some tall; some are graceful; some clumsy; some possess a sense of humor; some are taciturn; some are handsome; some plain. The totality of personal traits makes up the individual.

In much the same way, organizations, of which the school is a prominent example, reveal traits of their own, aside from the characteristics of the individuals and groups that work within the organization. To use an inept metaphor, we can say that organizations have their own "personalities."

Schools as organizations may be happy places or dreary institutions. They may evidence cohesiveness and high morale among faculty and students or they may house a dispirited group of individuals. They may be on the move or apathetic and static. They may mirror a democratic society or they may serve as examples of authoritarianism in action. They may be sharing, caring institutions or they may be islands of disregard for people.

Each school possesses a culture of its own. Some set high standards and expect persons within the institution to live up to those standards, whether intellectual, social, or moral. Schools demonstrate what Michael Rutter, Barbara Maughan, Peter Mortimore, and Janet Ouston referred to as "overall ethos," the attitudes, values, and other behaviors exhibited by persons within the organization.[23] Others refer to this institutional phenomenon as "school climate" or "atmosphere."

The ethos of the school affects students' behavior both in school and out. Positive ethos can lead to positive attainments by students, as Rutter and others discovered in conducting research in twelve secondary schools in the inner London area.[24]

School climate impinges on pupil behavior in much the same way as the climate in the individual classroom affects pupil conduct. The perceptive visitor to a school can sense the morale of students. A visitor can tell whether students feel a pride in their school and a sense of identity with it and can judge whether there exists that intangible something called "school spirit." The care of the building and grounds by its inhabitants sometimes speaks louder than words. The school should be a place where students enjoy not only learning but also living. Charles E. Silberman made some harsh judgments about the schools of the 1970s when he said,

> It is not possible to spend any prolonged period visiting public school classrooms without being appalled by the mutilation everywhere—mutilation of spontaneity, of joy in learning, of pleasure in creating, of sense of self. . . . Because adults take the schools so much for granted, they fail to appreciate what grim, joyless places most American schools are, how oppressive and petty are the rules by which they are governed, how intellectually sterile and esthetically barren the atmosphere, what an appalling lack of civility obtains on the part of teachers and principals, what contempt they unconsciously display for children as children.[25]

Glasser felt that instead of stressing success, schools emphasize failure. He hit hard the failure orientation of the schools. He pointed out that the child enters school in a successful and optimistic frame of mind: "Very few children come to school failures, none come labeled failures; *it is the school and the school alone which pins the la-*

bel of failure on children. . . . The shattering of this optimistic outlook is the most serious problem of the elementary schools."[26]

The school climate of nine secondary schools was studied by Carl Nordstrom, Edgar Z. Friedenberg, and Hilary A. Gold.[27] They found extensive presence of a negative attitude, which they called *ressentiment*. Their study of attitudes of teachers and students in these schools showed ressentiment deriving from the presses or limitations on students' behavior and from the premium schools place on conformity. Little evidence points to quantum leaps in improvement in school climate since these studies were conducted. In fact, with stress on testing, budget constraints, ethnic tensions, health and nutrition problems of young people, and parental dissatisfactions, the climate of many schools is far from what we might call healthy. Theodore R. Sizer was commenting on at least one dimension of school climate when he said, "Most middle- and upper-income Americans would be both shocked and afraid of some of the places where the young citizens of the poor are now in school."[28]

Administrators and faculty should look at the type of climate they are fostering. If a school has a large number of behavior problems, its climate may very well be at fault and in need of revitalizing.

Sarah Lawrence Lightfoot carried out an interesting study of six public and private high schools.[29] She selected six schools that professional and lay persons had identified as "good." Through visits to the schools, Lightfoot sought to discover the variables that accounted for the positive image portrayed by these schools. Common to all six were administrators who set a positive tone, faculties who cared for the students, rapport between teachers and students, a sense of pride in the schools' achievements, administrators' respect for their teachers, a sense of community, and a desire to improve.

Following an ecological approach, Roger G. Barker and Paul V. Gump studied the impact of size of secondary schools.[30] Taking a somewhat different tack from other studies of the school as a social culture that focused on individuals and groups, Barker and Gump sought to identify "behavioral settings" within the school that have an impact on individuals and groups. These researchers found a negative correlation between size of school and participation of students in school activities.

In advocating an ecological approach to the study of the school culture, Seymour B. Sarason underscored the importance of describing the behavior settings: "Within the school culture (as well as in a lot of other places) problem behavior is wrongfully viewed as a characteristic of the individual rather than as an interaction of individual and particular setting."[31] An investigator following an ecological approach would describe the many behavior settings found in the school.

The development of a healthy school climate is everybody's business in the school, not just the responsibility of an administrator or small groups of teachers. The supervisor should engage teachers in a study of the school and classroom learning climate and in identification of areas that need correcting.

A study of the school's curriculum from the academic program to the extraclass program to the pupil personnel services will show that the curriculum contributes to and causes many behavior problems. When the curriculum is "out of joint," to use Shakespeare's expression, disciplinary problems can spring up like toadstools.

The curriculum can be out of joint in several ways. Though much has been said about individualized instruction, education remains a mass operation, with most instruction aimed at a hypothetical average child. The curriculum often misses the large numbers of students who fall below or above the average. Couple the curriculum—the program itself—with methods of instruction that fail to meet the needs of the slow and fast ends of the spectrum and a breeding ground for behavior problems is created. When students cannot cope with the program, they find other ways to distract themselves, much to the teacher's consternation.

The word *relevance* has been so abused and distorted that we almost hesitate to use it. Nevertheless, evidence of irrelevant content can be found in the schools. For some people relevance has come to mean catering to the immediate needs of students. Preferably, a relevant curriculum is one that will help students not only in the present but also in the future. Relevant subject matter helps pupils to make decisions—to think—and to carry out life activities. B. Othanel Smith, Saul B. Cohen, and Arthur Pearl indicated relevant subject matter as helping the learner to

- choose and follow a vocation,
- exercise the tasks of citizenship,
- engage in personal relationships,
- take part in culture-carrying activities.[32]

Glasser defined relevance as "the blending of one's own world with the new world of the school" and saw relevance working in two directions: The school curriculum must be relevant to the child's life and the child's life must be relevant to the curriculum.

Thus we have both parts of relevance.

1. Too much taught in school is not relevant to the world of the children. When it is relevant, the relevance is too often not taught, thus its value is missed when it does exist.
2. The children do not consider that what they learn in their world is relevant to the school.[33]

Glasser attacked the chronic disease of schools since time immemorial—the stress on memorization as opposed to thinking.

> Children discover that in school they must use their brains mostly for committing facts to memory rather than expressing their interests or ideas or solving problems . . . beginning in the first grade . . . thinking is less valuable than memorizing for success. . . . Memorizing is bad enough. . . . Worse is that most of what they are asked to memorize is irrelevant to their world; where it is relevant, the relevance is taught either poorly or not at all.[34]

Certainly, the current literature advocating the development of thinking skills, which we considered in Chapter 3, is in accord with Glasser's comments made over two decades ago. Like the school's culture, the curriculum may be a source of behavior problems.

Causes Originating with the Home and Community

The child's family, neighborhood, and community play a profound part in shaping behavior. During preschool years and on through school to adulthood, attitudes learned from closest associates affect the child's behavior. Parental love for their children is one of the most powerful determiners of behavior. That love is often missing, as can be seen in the number and growth of reports of child abuse in the United States. The number of such reports increased over seven years from just under 800,000 or some 3.5 per 1,000 population in 1980 to just over 2,000,000 or some 8.3 per 1,000 population in 1987—a problem of significant proportions.[35] Children who are abused or rejected by their parents or other adults are much more likely to become behavior problems than children who are loved.

The parents' attitude toward education influences children for good or for ill. Children who receive reassuring support from their parents are more likely to succeed in school and less likely to be behavior problems than children whose parents do not care whether they succeed or not. Parents err when they provide no reassurance or exert too much pressure on their children to succeed in school. Either extreme can contribute to behavior problems. Oversolicitous parents who insist their children bring home nothing but A's can induce feelings of guilt and anxiety, which can erupt as disciplinary problems in the school.

Disharmony in the home can produce pupil misconduct in school. A child's relationships with brothers and sisters and parental preferences for one child over the other can create difficulties. It is far too common for parents to hold up one child in the family as a model of behavior. Each child wants to create a personal identity and be valued as an individual. Teachers too often compound the problems by telling a child that an older brother or sister whom they may also have had in a class was a better student.

The neighborhood and immediate community in which a child lives make their impression on his or her behavior. Surveying some 60,000 teachers and 600,000 students in 4,000 elementary schools after passage of the Civil Rights Act of 1964, James S. Coleman found that children's families and peers have a greater impact on children's achievement than do teachers and material resources of the school.[36]

All children bring their problems to school. The teacher who is aware that some of a child's problems may be arising from the home environment can use this knowledge to advantage. For many children from unfavorable homes the school is, can be, or should be a warmer, more comfortable setting than their home or neighborhood.

The teacher will realize that there is usually little or nothing that can be done to change a child's home environment. The teacher can refrain from exacerbating a child's problems and from creating a classroom environment that in itself causes behavior problems.

Causes Originating in the Larger Social Order

Determining the effects of conditions on the social scene that contribute to disciplinary problems is difficult. Some students cheat, for example, because they hear and read about cases of cheating by adults and conclude that that is the accepted way of making one's way in the world. Unethical and illegal conduct by prominent people is featured in the press. The illicit drug trade with its lure of quick, though risky and criminal, rewards is more appealing to some young people than fighting the battle of the books to enter a socially accepted but far less lucrative job. The young person may have a tendency as a result to conclude that the problem in criminal behavior lies not in the conduct itself but in getting caught.

Studies of class in America have shown that mores differ from one socioeconomic class to another. Classes differ in moral and spiritual values, permissiveness, patterns of aggression, sexual habits, and even language. Our schools are middle-class institutions staffed largely by middle-class teachers. But the children in these schools are not all from middle-class environments. Children from lower socioeconomic backgrounds have been taught behavior patterns quite different from those taught children of middle-class backgrounds, and they must manifest these behavior patterns to survive in their environment. Change to middle-class values of cleanliness, industriousness, refined language, and so on—what we might call "gentlemanly behavior"—however laudable, cannot be effected overnight. Almost every teacher knows that behavior patterns are difficult and often impossible to change.

The effects of violence in everyday life on individual behavior are difficult to gauge. Violence seems to be a way of life on the contemporary American scene. Young people are bombarded with reports and stories of violence daily in the press, on television, and in films. According to the Federal Bureau of Investigation's crime report for 1990, violent crime in the United States jumped 10 percent between 1989 and 1990. Increases were recorded in the number of murders, rapes, robberies, aggravated assaults, and motor vehicle thefts. Only the instances of robberies declined slightly while larcenies remained at the same level. New York City alone piled up over 2,000 murders in 1992, an 18 percent increase over 1990. Washington, our nation's capital, pushed its number of murders in 1992 to nearly 500, up 10 percent over 1990, making it the leader in murders per capita. Muggers were busy in New York City in 1992, racking up about 325 robberies per day.[37]

Schools face an uphill battle in achieving what then President George Bush referred to as a "kinder, gentler" nation. The drug culture is pervasive throughout the country with Americans expending enormous sums per year on mood-altering substances. Street gangs flourish in our urban areas. Graphic violence, casual sex, and generous use of Anglo-Saxon expletives by both men and women are steady fare on our television and movie screens. More and more parental groups, psychologists, and government officials are becoming concerned with the large doses of sex and violence being served to children in books, recordings, television shows, and movies. There is a growing concern that preoccupation with either sex or violence can be destructive to the individual and can result in behavior that can be destructive to society.

The Patterson and Kim survey (mentioned in Chapter 6) found that our country lacks a moral consensus and individual Americans are living by their own moral codes, which often conflict both internally within themselves and externally with other people.[38] The chances of an individual teacher's making much of an impact on behavior problems that stem from the social scene are small. Teachers can and must restrain students who exhibit antisocial behavior, but fundamental changes in society are not within their power to make. On the other hand, suppose for a moment that every teacher, every administrator, and every supervisor in every school system of the country were aware of the impact of the larger social order on the behavior of pupils. Just think of the dramatic impact made when every person in a darkened football stadium strikes a match at the same time. Though each person contributes only one tiny match, their combined efforts turn the stadium from night into day. Could not teachers' combined efforts make a dent in the antisocial behavior of students? Could not a program be designed from kindergarten up that would help resolve some of these social problems and even result in changes in society? Would not relevance of content take on new meaning?

PREVENTING BEHAVIOR PROBLEMS

The prevention of behavior problems should be foremost in the minds of teachers. When measures to prevent disciplinary problems are successful, the teacher has little worry about corrective measures. From an examination of causes of behavior problems, can the supervisor derive ways of helping teachers to prevent problems from arising? The supervisor can help and encourage teachers to take a number of actions.

Analyze Attitudes

Attitudes toward Behavior Problems. Students exhibit a wide array of behaviors, from minor disorderliness to deep-seated personality problems. The seriousness with which teachers view varying behaviors affects their handling of behavior problems. Not surprisingly, teachers regard those behaviors that frustrate their teaching, such as talking, inattention, impudence, disinterest, and laziness, as more serious or more relevant than personality disorders like withdrawal, unsocialness, shyness, and suspiciousness. Looking at behavior problems from a perspective different from that of psychologists and counselors, teachers may even be unaware of the existence of some serious personality disorders.

Whereas behaviors that impede teaching may well disappear as the student matures, personality disorders may cripple the individual for life. This is not to say that teachers should ignore troublesome classroom behaviors. Nor does it say that teachers by and large possess the skills and knowledge to treat personality disorders. But teachers should be conscious of personality problems, should recognize the seriousness of such problems, and should refer students to appropriate counseling when they discover the presence of serious personality disorders.

Attitudes toward Children. Teachers need to know what attitudes they hold about young people. They need to assess the expectations they hold for each learner. The research of R. Rosenthal and L. Jacobson,[39] W. Burleigh Seaver,[40] J. Michael Palardy,[41] and Don E. Hamachek[42] provided evidence that teachers' expectations do make a difference in learners' achievement. An astute supervisor can detect that some teachers subconsciously interact more often and more positively with some students than with others. Teachers tend to favor brighter students, those from higher-socioeconomic levels, those seated near the front of the classroom, those at their favored hand (right or left)—in short, those who are nearest at hand, who please the teacher, and who give fewer problems of an academic or disciplinary nature. Barbara J. Weber and Les M. Omotani reported the results of two Rand Corporation studies that measured teacher efficacy—that when teachers believe they can influence student learning, they usually do. The research supported the self-fulfilling prophecy that when teachers have high expectations for the students, the students can be expected to live up to those expectations.[43] Manifestations of negative overt attitudes of teachers toward pupils' backgrounds, personal characteristics, and abilities stand as barriers to learning and exacerbate discipline problems. One of the generally accepted tenets of the effective teaching research in the past two decades is the teacher's holding of high expectations of learners.[44] Benjamin S. Bloom and others, in advocating mastery learning, subscribed to the belief that most pupils could learn most of the subject matter teachers present to them.[45] These two attitudes—high expectations and the belief that most learners are capable of achieving—can work to promote learning and reduce behavior problems.

Attitudes toward Themselves. Teachers need to develop a feeling of their own adequacy as both teachers and people. Because teachers are in charge of groups of young people, it is most important that they be fully functioning personalities. Teachers can have a powerful influence on the development of the learner's self-concept. They need to exhibit qualities of cheerfulness, fairness, and sensitivity. Not only do they need to be self-actualizing people, but they need also to be effective teachers, skillful at explaining and communicating.[46] Combs concluded that good teachers feel adequate, wanted, and worthy.[47]

The supervisor should invite freewheeling discussions of teacher attitudes toward types of learners, ethnic groups, the purposes of education, satisfactions from teaching as a career, and the relative seriousness of behavior problems. Discussion is likely to show that teachers generally view problems that disrupt their classes as more serious than deep-seated personality problems.

The supervisor, in observing classes, should look for evidence of negative attitudes held by teachers and should offer personal counseling, training in interpersonal skills or, when warranted, referral to counseling to help teachers develop more positive attitudes.

Analyze Teaching Styles and Students' Learning Styles

The supervisor should ask the teachers to look within themselves and try to decide whether their teaching styles provoke disciplinary problems. Are they autocratic martinets who repress every form of childish exuberance? Do they practice laissez-faire and let the students do as they please? Are they conscientious about planning or do they adopt a what-do-you-want-to-learn-today-kids approach to instruction? Do they project a counseling, facilitating approach to instruction as opposed to an authoritarian, dispenser-of-information approach? Do they exude confidence or do they let students intimidate them?

Barbara Bree Fischer and Louis Fischer identified six teaching styles, described here.

- *The task-oriented.* These teachers prescribe the materials to be learned and demand specific performance on the part of the students. . . .
- *The cooperative planner.* These teachers plan the means and ends of instruction with student cooperation. . . .
- *The child centered.* This teacher provides a structure for students to pursue whatever they want to do or whatever interests them. . . .

- *The subject centered.* These teachers focus on organized content to the near exclusion of the learner. . . .
- *The learning centered.* These teachers have equal concern for the students and for the curricular objectives, the materials to be learned. . . .
- *The emotionally exciting and its counterpart.* These teachers show their own intensive emotional involvement in teaching. They enter the teaching-learning process with zeal and usually produce a classroom atmosphere of excitement and high emotion. Their counterparts conduct classrooms subdued in emotional tone, where rational processes predominate, and the learning is dispassionate though just as significant and meaningful as in the classrooms of the emotionally more involved teachers.[48]

Teachers should attempt to identify the individual students' learning styles. It is quite possible that a clash between the instructor's teaching style and a student's learning style can result in disciplinary problems. Fischer and Fischer listed ten learning styles.

- *The incremental learner.* These students proceed in a step-by-step fashion, systematically adding bits and pieces together to gain larger understandings. . . .
- *The intuitive learner.* The learning style of these students does not follow traditional logic, chronology, or a step-by-step sequence. There are leaps in various directions, sudden insights, and meaningful and accurate generalizations derived from an unsystematic gathering of information and experience. . . .
- *The sensory specialist.* This student relies primarily on one sense for the meaningful formation of ideas. . . .
- *The sensory generalist.* These students use all or many of the senses in gathering information and gaining insights. . . .
- *The emotionally involved.* These are students who function best in a classroom in which the atmosphere carries a high emotional charge . . . through the teacher's use of poetry, drama, lively descriptions, and the teacher's own obvious enjoyment and involvement in the substance of learning [or] . . . in which the teacher and students carry on active, open discussions where disagreements are common.
- *The emotionally neutral.* Some students function best in a classroom where the emotional tone is low-keyed and relatively neutral.
- *Explicitly structured.* These students learn best when the teacher makes explicit a clear, unambiguous structure for learning. Limits and goals are carefully stated, guiding the intellectual tasks to be achieved as well as the behaviors that will be acceptable and unacceptable in the classroom.
- *Open-ended structure.* . . . The overall structure of the classroom is sufficiently visible, yet there is place for divergence, for exploration of relevant yet not explicitly preplanned phenomena.
- *The damaged learner.* While this category is too broad, too inclusive to be identified as a learning style, it is sufficiently important and commonplace to merit discussion. These are students who are physically normal but damaged in self-concept, social competency, aesthetic sensitivity, or intellect in such a way that they develop negative learning styles.
- *The eclectic learner.* Students who can shift learning styles and function profitably may find one or another style more beneficial, but can adapt to and benefit from others.[49]

Rita S. Dunn and Kenneth J. Dunn advocated identification of both the learner's and teacher's styles and the matching of the two.[50] Whenever possible, the teacher should use a teaching style that is compatible with the learner's style.

Analyze the Classroom Environment

Is there rapport between teacher and students and among the students themselves? Teachers will want to identify both the academic and social leaders in the class and those students who seem to be left out of classroom transactions. They will need to ask themselves whether they are encouraging a success orientation among the students as opposed to a failure orientation. They will want to develop an approach that is permissive enough to allow for pupil freedom but restrictive enough that learning can take place. They should ask themselves whether their classrooms are the "grim, joyless" places Silberman talked about.

In a healthy classroom climate the teacher avoids using learning as a threat or a punishment. The object of instruction is to make learning as enjoyable an experience as possible, a pursuit that young people will want to continue all their lives. Teachers have been known to penalize a rambunctious class by piling on homework, by administering tests to quiet a noisy class, by threatening students with examinations or low grades if they do not behave properly, and by making individuals perform meaningless academic tasks as a form of punishment. The pupil who has to write "Constantinople fell in 1453" 500 times may forever remember the date of the Turkish conquest of the Byzantine Empire, but he or she will probably also develop a dislike for history, for the teacher, for the school, and for learning itself. With such experiences as these, it is small wonder that many children cannot wait to get out of school so they can cease formal education and pursue learning that has meaning to them.

Analyze the Curriculum Continuously

Every teacher must examine the question of relevance and determine whether the curriculum can pass that test. Teachers must decide whether the particular curriculum meets the needs of the specific groups of which they have charge. Materials of instruction must be appropriate to the learners. Content that is either too difficult or too simple can cause behavior problems. The supervisor has the responsibility of helping teachers with planning, implementing, and evaluating the curriculum, which we discuss in Chapters 7 and 8.

Analyze the Methods of Instruction Employed

Teachers must be able to organize the content, sequence it properly, present it lucidly, and evaluate its mastery fairly. They must decide whether they have set realistic objectives. They must apply the principle of feedback and check their instructional design to make sure they are employing appropriate strategies and engaging learners in appropriate content. They should analyze pupils' successes and failures to see whether modifications in instruction are necessary.

Teachers should stress thinking over memorization. This procedure is both a curricular problem and an instructional problem. Teachers will need to decide when memorization is essential and when problem-solving techniques should be employed. This text has urged in previous chapters that teachers aim for higher levels of cognition and move away from pupils' regurgitation and recapitulation of sheer and often isolated facts. The noted educational philosopher John Dewey long ago recommended the adoption of the scientific method—or problem solving—as the principal route to learning. Dewey's recommendation still stands as a laudable goal.

Additional research is needed on the use of repetition as an instructional technique. Teachers at all levels repeat material ad infinitum as a means of reinforcing learning. What we need to determine is how many times we can or should repeat subject matter before we meet with mastery or, conversely, with negative results (ad nauseam, as they say). Jacob S. Kounin called attention to the phenomenon of satiation, that is, the students' tiring of subject matter because of too much repetition. Kounin advised teachers who want to avoid pupils' satiation to assure them a feeling of progress.

> A feeling of progress is the most essential variable influencing the rate of satiation. Satiation does not occur, or occurs very slowly, when there is a feeling of progress since the essential condition for producing satiation is repetitiousness: doing the same thing over and over without getting anywhere. When there is a feeling of progress there is no feeling of repetition and no consequent satiation.[51]

The class should be kept moving with meaningful tasks, not with "busy work," that is, repetitive, unnecessary, and often inconsequential activities designed to fill time. Students are justified in balking at busy work. Teachers must examine each activity required of students to make sure the work has meaning and purpose. They must distinguish between appropriate, necessary practice and unnecessary repetition.

Successful classroom management goes hand in hand with the elements of instructional design: thorough planning, effective presentation, and careful evaluation. Teachers must give attention to the factor of motivation and plan for a variety of activities. Daily lesson plans should always provide for more than enough meaningful activities so the teacher is never placed in a situation where time hangs heavy and, as a result, students become behavior problems. One backup or "sponge" technique that teachers can use to fill an unplanned void is an invitation to the class to discuss problems it is experiencing during the study of the unit or lesson.

Problems of classroom management are eased when teachers carry out classroom routines with skill and dispatch. Disorder can occur, for example, if materials and equipment are not ready for immediate use. Behavior problems frequently arise during distribution of materials, setting up of equipment, rearrangement of furniture, collection of materials, and taking of attendance.

Gather as Much Information as Possible about Individual Learners

Information about a child's background at home and in school can help the teacher understand some of the reasons for the child's behavior. Teachers must exert much caution, however, in evaluating and using information about a child's past history. Teachers are working with children in the present and must deal with problems in the present, not the past. Although a child's past history is important, teachers must find ways of helping children in the here and now.

Judgments of a negative nature about a child's work and behavior in previous classes may prove harmful if a teacher does not realize that children may change in the course of a year's time. Comments that can be found in children's cumulative records, for example, must often be discounted because they no longer apply or because they may represent the opinion of only one teacher. It is possible, too, that a personality conflict between a teacher and child has resulted in negative comments in a child's record.

With the legal moves that open students' records to students and their parents, teachers must be extremely careful and judicious about the remarks they place in pupils' cumulative files. A hasty, negative comment about a child has on too many occasions dogged that child through school and on into college and adulthood. We can recall reading an anecdote about a high school freshman—perhaps a harmless report and certainly trivial in the grand scheme of things—preserved presumably for posterity in the student's file: "Puts ink on tongue, sticks it out, and makes other pupils laugh." We cannot resist commenting that this childish behavior will surely eradicate itself. These observations about the dangers of using past data are not meant to imply that we should not study the past history of a child but rather that we should be wary about the data and how we use the information.

Analyze the Disciplinary Models Used

We can find considerable differences in the models of discipline and approaches to discipline followed by teachers. We can also find considerable argument about which models and approaches are the most appropriate and effective. Laurel N. Tanner described five models of discipline.[52] Two of these, *training* and *behavior modification*, she labeled as established. The other three, *psychodynamic*, *group dynamics*, and *personal-social growth*, she called emergent.

With the training model, children learn habits through repetition of the desired behaviors. Through drill pupils learn habitual responses such as the proper way of arranging their chairs, sharpening pencils, and going to the rest rooms. Though training is, of course, necessary, little reflection, thought, or self-direction is possible with this model.

Behavior modification is a procedure for bringing about or extinguishing specific behaviors through the use of appropriate reinforcement. Behavior can be shaped and controlled through this technique.

Proponents of the psychodynamic model encourage teachers to try to understand the underlying emotional causes of behavior problems. With roots in child-centered philosophy and psychoanalysis, the psychodynamic model poses problems for teachers' use. Many teachers, lacking the necessary training, are not able to uncover causes of learners' problems. Further, once they have discovered the reasons for a child's misbehavior, they have difficulty deciding how to use the information they have obtained to change the child's behavior.

The group dynamics model calls for the effective management of the class as a group. The teacher literally orchestrates the group. The personal-social growth model encourages the development of self-discipline by providing pupils with opportunities to decide for themselves what constitutes appropriate behavior. The behavior chosen by the learner conforms to the goals established. Tanner found the group dynamics model and the personal-social growth model to be particularly helpful.

Behavior Modification. One of the discipline models identified by Tanner, behavior modification is a technique for coping with common classroom problems. It is based on the premise that both appropriate and inappropriate behaviors are learned. It is the teacher's task to reinforce appropriate behaviors by the use of rewards and to eliminate inappropriate behaviors by withholding rewards and/or using punishment. Wilford A. Weber spoke of the assumptions underlying behavior modification.

> The behavior-modification approach is built on two major assumptions: (1) There are four basic processes that account for learning; and (2) learning is influenced largely, if not entirely, by events in the environment. Thus, the major task of the teacher is to master and apply the four basic principles of learning that behaviorists have identified as influencing human behavior. They are: positive reinforcement, punishment, extinction, and negative reinforcement.[53]

Clarizio outlined steps for modifying behavior, which he called the four phases of positive classroom discipline.

> a. Choosing the behavior [that needs to be changed].
> b. Doing the A, B, Cs—attention is focused on the A, B, Cs—the antecedents of behavior (A), the behavior itself (B), and the consequences attached to the behavior (C).
> c. Selecting strategies . . . (1) behavior formation techniques: positive reinforcement and social modeling, to restrict, reduce, or eliminate undesirable behaviors and to strengthen existent adaptive responses, to acquire new adaptive ones, and to extend desirable behaviors to other settings; (2) behavior elimination techniques: extinction, punishment, and desensitization, to weaken undesirable behaviors.
> d. Keeping track of the results.[54]

Clarizio made a strong case for the system he recommended:

> Because mental health or psychoeducational specialists (psychologists, psychiatrists, social workers, and counselors) have not fully understood the teacher's role, they have offered to teachers few specific and concrete practical suggestions pertaining to the management of the child's daily behavior. . . . Admonitions to be accepting, nonthreatening, and understanding of the child's needs have not helped teachers to cope with troublesome behavior. In giving advice to educators, mental health professionals seem to forget about the following aspects of the teacher's role, which make it difficult for a teacher to heed their advice:
>
> 1. The teacher is a group worker and, therefore, cannot usually work with just one child.
> 2. The teacher's primary goal is not to increase the child's personal insights but to achieve certain academic objectives.
> 3. The teacher must reflect cultural values and, hence, cannot be permissively accepting.
> 4. The teacher deals primarily with conscious or preconscious processes and materials.
> 5. Finally, the teacher must focus on the reality of problems as they exist in the present situation.[55]

J. Michael Palardy and James E. Mudrey defined four approaches to discipline: "the permissive, the authoritarian, the behavioristic, and the diagnostic."[56] They rejected the permissive and authoritarian approaches, found the behavioristic (behavior modification) wanting, and supported the diagnostic approach. Of the behavioristic approach they wrote,

> Does behavior modification work? We think it does, but not to the degree or with the frequency behaviorists predict. For the approach, in our opinion, has several se-

rious flaws. The most significant is that only the symptoms of behavior problems are dealt with, not their causes.

Stated bluntly, but not unjustly, proponents of behavior modification argue that teachers are wasting time in trying to discover and treat underlying causes of behavior. From the point of view of advocates of behavior modification, teachers can be effective if they deal only with the behavior itself. . . . As long as the cause of the child's problem is undiagnosed and untreated, he is hurting and sooner or later symptoms of that hurt will emerge.[57]

Palardy and Mudrey saw the diagnostic approach as "the most comprehensive and legitimate approach to discipline."[58]

Contrary to behavior modification, this approach assumes that there can be lasting effects on certain behavior problems only after their causes are ferreted out and treated. . . . There is no quick, easy, or fail-proof formula for diagnosing the causes of pupils' behavior problems. But there is one absolutely essential step: to learn as much as possible about the pupils. . . .

Most critics of this approach argue that the whole effort of diagnosis is a waste of time and energy because nothing can be done anyway . . . we disagree with this argument. First, because it assumes that the causes of behavior problems are never school related or school induced. Like it or not, many are.

Second, even if the diagnosis shows that the causes are not school related or school induced, much can still be done. Pupils' ego needs can be met in school, their self-respect enhanced, their enjoyment of life increased. In school, pupils can be given love and can learn to give it in return. Schools can provide food and clothing. They can make medical, dental, and psychological referrals. They can contact community action programs, welfare departments, civic organizations, churches, and even law-enforcement agencies. Schools can provide for adult education, sex education, and early education. We disagree that diagnosis is a waste of time because nothing can be done![59]

In spite of its limitations behavior modification is widely practiced in the schools.

A Teacher Behavior Continuum. Charles H. Wolfgang and Carl D. Glickman described behaviors commonly demonstrated by teachers in handling disciplinary problems. They placed these behaviors on a continuum from those over which the child has most control (Ct) to those over which the teacher exerts most control (cT), as in Figure 5.1.

Using their Teacher Behavior Continuum, Wolfgang and Glickman analyzed nine disciplinary models based on three perspectives. First is the relationship-listening approach, whose advocates "believe that the child develops by having a sup-

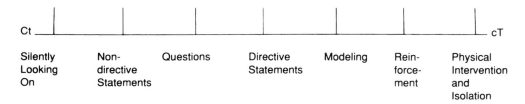

Figure 5.1. Teacher Behavior Continuum (TBC). *From: Charles H. Wolfgang and Carl D. Glickman,* Solving Discipline Problems: Strategies for Classroom Teachers, *2nd ed., p. 22. Copyright ©1986 by Allyn and Bacon. Reprinted by permission.*

portive atmosphere that encourages his or her own problem solving."[60] Included in this approach are the models of Thomas Gordon;[61] Thomas A. Harris;[62] and Louis E. Raths, Merrill Harmin, and Sidney B. Simon.[63] Second is the confronting-contracting approach, whose advocates "believe that a child develops through a constant give-and-take relationship with others."[64] Included in this category are such models as Rudolf Dreikurs's Discipline with Dignity[65] and William Glasser's Cooperative Discipline.[66] Third is the rules/rewards-punishment approach, whose advocates "believe that the child develops only by the conditioning of outside forces."[67] In this group are the models of Saul Axelrod,[68] Lee and Marlene Canter,[69] Siegfried Engelmann,[70] and James C. Dobson.[71] The supervisor and teacher may wish to examine these and other models.[72]

The effective teacher seeks to control the class and shape behavior by whatever legitimate techniques he or she is adept at using. While controlling and shaping behavior, however, the teacher will want to gather as much information about the student as possible, uncover possible causes of misbehavior, and do whatever is within his or her means to treat the causes.

Set and Enforce Minimum Expectations of Behavior

Rules of conduct should be made known at the beginning of the year. A key factor in setting rules of conduct is pupil participation in drawing up the rules. With each succeeding year of schooling and the accompanying increase in the learner's maturity, a greater degree of participation in determining the rules of behavior should be extended to the students. Boys and girls are much more likely to conform to standards they have helped set than to standards that are imposed on them.

We agree with Glasser that "children should have a voice in determining both the curriculum and the roles of their school. Democracy is best learned by living it."[73] Glasser recommended, wisely we believe, that once students have participated in formulating the rules, when they break the rules, the teacher should ask them to make a value judgment about their behavior, to select a better course of behavior, and to make a commitment to change.[74]

Pupils must be given time to practice unfamiliar behaviors. The teacher should be willing to spend sufficient time to help pupils develop routines and to get accustomed to classroom organization and procedures. The supervisor should advise teachers not to hasten into the content areas until they have the procedural learnings under control. This principle is particularly significant in dealing with students who come from communities where standards of behavior are greatly different from the standards expected by the school.

The supervisor should assist teachers in diagnosing the learning environments they maintain to determine whether they are doing everything within their power to prevent disciplinary problems. The old expression, trite as it is, "An ounce of prevention is worth a pound of cure" has special relevance to the problem of discipline.

CORRECTING BEHAVIOR PROBLEMS

No matter how much the teacher may understand about causes of behavior problems, no matter how healthy and wholesome the learning climate of a class or school may be, no matter how hard the teacher may try to prevent disciplinary problems, behavior problems will still arise. Teachers should enter public school teaching expecting a certain amount of youthful misbehavior, and they must rather quickly develop skills for coping with behavior problems. Some teachers are masters of discipline from the first day they set foot in the classroom. Others develop disciplinary skills as they gain experience and confidence at controlling the behavior of young people. Others are in need of help and support. Sooner or later the question will come from a teacher, often in desperation, "What shall I do?" That teacher may turn to a colleague for advice or, if he or she has sufficient rapport with the principal or supervisor, may turn to one of them. At that time the principal or supervisor must supply some kind of guidance if a state of rapport is to continue between them. The supervisor cannot come up with some hackneyed platitude like "Children will be children," "Just remember that all behavior is caused," and "Show them love." These platitudes are fine in perspective, in their place, and at the right time. When a teacher has an immediate behavior problem, more than a slogan is called for. On the other hand, the supervisor cannot sit like a physician and write out a prescription of action a teacher should take to cure the malady. How often has the experienced principal or supervisor heard a litany of offenses both minor and major and wished for some medicine that would effect a quick cure? How often has he or she wished to feed into the computer a description of a behavior problem and obtain an instant printout of the course of action that should be taken?

When a behavior problem arises in the classroom, the teacher must make some response. In fact, the students expect the teacher to make some response and often test the teacher to see what he or she will do. Assume for illustration that an African-American male student and a white male student in an eighth-grade English class suddenly leap out of their seats, call each other names, and start pummeling each other. Their teacher reacts almost instinctively, hastens to the boys, forcefully separates them, firmly orders them to take their seats, and sets the class back to work. The immediate situation has been effectively handled. But the teacher meditates on what corrective measure or punishment, if any, should be applied to these boys so neither they nor others will repeat the behavior. The teacher decides to talk with the principal. The teacher relates the incident to the principal and asks the principal what should be done as a follow-up to the incident.

The principal might say, "Send them to in-school suspension," or might suggest, "Send them to me and I'll suspend them out of school for three days"—but neither would be commendable. He or she might rather begin by commending the teacher for restoring order and preventing what could have become an inflammatory situation. And the principal could add that had more help been needed to restore order, the teacher should not have hesitated to call for immediate assistance. The principal should lead up to the question of correction or punishment by asking the teacher to reflect on the incident again before making a decision. Now that the heat of the moment has dissipated, the incident should be analyzed. The principal may raise a number of questions with the teacher.

- Who were the boys?
- Was this the first time anything like this has taken place in the class?
- Was this the first time these two boys have behaved in this way?
- Has either of the boys displayed antisocial behavior before?

- Was there any provocation on the part of either boy?
- Were any other students actively involved in the incident?
- Do you believe this was a racial incident or simply a case of two middle school boys having a fight?
- What was going on in the class at the time of the incident?
- Did the teacher do anything that could have contributed to the incident?
- Was anyone hurt?
- Was there any damage to property?
- How serious should we consider this incident?

A calm discussion of these questions might terminate with the decision to apply the same corrective measure the teacher or principal might have selected prior to any discussion.[75] On the other hand, consideration of questions like these might lead the principal and teachers to choose other forms of correction.

Early in the school year when the faculty is still fresh and the pupils have not yet created a plethora of disciplinary problems, it would be beneficial for the principal or assistant principal, department head, or other supervisor to assemble his or her group of teachers and have them develop a set of guidelines for implementing corrective measures. If teachers know what guidelines have faculty and administrative support at the time a behavior problem occurs, they can more readily and more intelligently decide what action they should take as a response. The supervisor might lead them to agree on the following points.

1. *The corrective measure applied should fit the offense.* Showing off should be treated differently from defiance. Skipping school merits lesser punishment than pushing drugs. Stealing twenty dollars is more serious than stealing twenty cents.

2. *The corrective measure applied should fit the offender.* The democratic practice would seem on the surface to treat all offenders equally, but mitigating circumstances are taken into consideration when imposing punishment, for example, in the case of a first offense. The goal of correction is a change in behavior—rehabilitation. For this goal to be realized, the corrective measure must be chosen with both the offense and the offender in mind.

3. *Minor, routine types of childish behavior should be met with the simplest of techniques:* a glare, a stare, silence, pointing a finger at the culprit, using proximity by standing beside a misbehaving pupil, a terse order of "Let's be quiet" or "Knock it off," suddenly increasing the volume of the voice, changing pupils' seats—any of a host of little personalized techniques that teachers have developed to maintain order and to keep the class on track. There are teachers who never have to go beyond these simple techniques of control but are able to maintain a productive learning environment without resorting to sterner means.

The common, garden-variety misbehavior that stems from excess childish energies should be treated with a minimum of fuss. The teacher should not make a big issue of petty misbehaviors. We find teachers who insist on continuous, complete, and absolute attention and quiet—a next-to-impossible goal for children and adolescents—and stamp hard on every infraction of their (the teachers') rules. From the classrooms of these teachers, children stream to the principal's office for punitive action. These teachers weaken their own image in the eyes of the children, the administrator, and the children's parents, and they may place themselves in a precarious position. When they encounter a serious problem and look for help, the administrator may conclude that they are once again "crying wolf" when there is no wolf in sight.

4. *Nonpunitive, remedial measures should be taken before resorting to punishment.* Teachers should be more concerned with helping a child to change behavior than with retribution for misconduct. If they can reason with a child and obtain results in that way, they should do so. A beginning approach in cases of pupil misbehavior is an individual conference with the child during which the teacher tries to get the child to evaluate his or her behavior, to see how the particular conduct has been detrimental to himself or herself and to others, and to choose a better way of behaving. The conference provides the teacher with an opportunity for learning more about the child and the reasons for the misbehavior. The conference is a chance for the teacher to show a child who is a behavior problem that some adult cares enough to want to help. These conferences should be entered into in a counseling frame of mind and should not be considered occasions for laying down the law and reprimanding the perpetrator.

The conference should be conducted in private, where teacher and pupil can talk freely. Individual conferences will not always be successful in producing a change in behavior. If an individual conference with the pupil is not successful in changing a pupil's behavior after a reasonable time, the teacher may then wish to confer with the child's parents or guardians. If the teacher chooses to go this route, the parent-teacher conference must be managed very carefully. Parents may be anxious to come to school to talk about their child's academic progress, but they are not so eager to visit the teacher to talk about their child's behavior problems. Many elementary school administrators expect their teachers to make contacts early in the school year. Administrators encourage teachers to relate to parents their positive comments about each student. By doing so, they can balance positive interactions with negative.

A polite invitation rather than a summons should be extended to the parents in the form of a letter or phone call from the teacher. The conference should be set up as a chance for the parents and teacher to communicate and share their knowledge about the child. The goal of the conference is to find ways in which the parents and teacher can cooperate to help the child improve his or her classroom behavior. Some teachers include the student in the conference discussion because the student can add personal reasons and information about why he or she exhibited certain behaviors in the classroom. At all costs, the teacher must avoid an antagonistic view toward the parents, for this will generate ill will and result in the loss of their cooperation.

The teacher must also know what the parents' attitudes are toward discipline, as some parents may treat the child more harshly than would the school. A united wall of parent-teacher hostility toward a child may worsen behavior rather than improve it.

The teacher should call on the services of specialists and agencies both within the school and outside for help in working with behavior problems. Referrals to the guidance counselor, school psychologist, or school nurse are often first steps in the remediation process. Community agencies stand ready in most communities to provide certain kinds of help to schoolchildren—from needed eyeglasses to a Big Brother or Big Sister.

When seeking remedial help for children with problems, the teacher should not overlook the nonaggressive, docile, timid, fearful, despondent children in the classroom. These children may not complicate the teacher's life the way aggressive children do, but in their own way they have behavior problems, often as serious and as prolonged as the problems of overt, disruptive children.

5. *Punishment is in order if the teacher deems that there is no other way to correct an individual's behavior.* Wesley C. Becker, Siegfried Engelmann, and Don R. Thomas made a case for the use of punishment:

> Probably no area of behavioral psychology has generated more emotion, confusion, and misunderstanding than the topic of punishment. Some people believe that any use of punishment under any circumstances is immoral. . . . Teachers have been told that they should not use punishment because it doesn't work and that it produces only temporary suppression of behavior, not real change. . . . Punishment is an effective method of changing behavior.[76]

Punishment and the threat of punishment serve as deterrents to repetition of misconduct by the same offender or other offenders. It is utopian to hold that punishment will never be necessary in school. No matter how hard we strive to maintain an attractive learning environment, no matter how well disciplined the school, no matter how great an effort is made to counsel students, and no matter what preventive measures are taken, behavior problems will still arise, and some of these will be serious enough to merit punishment. Becker, Engelmann, and Thomas specified two circumstances when punishment may be required.

> The first is when behavior is so *frequent* that there is little or no incompatible behavior to reinforce. . . . The second circumstance where punishment may be required is when the problem behavior is so *intense* that someone might get hurt, including the child himself.[77]

When punishment must be administered, it should be done in a firm and calm manner. The teacher should wait until the heat of the moment dies down before applying punitive techniques. However, punishment should be certain. The pupil who chooses to misbehave should know that misbehavior will result in some kind of punishment. If punishment is fair and reasonable, the public will support the teacher and administrator. The supervisor should help teachers to identify and use punitive measures that can be considered fair and reasonable and to reject those measures that are unfair and unreasonable.

We can easily find illustrations of punitive measures that do not meet the standards of fairness, reasonableness, or soundness. Preservice and in-service education should build concepts about discipline and punishment so that teachers will employ disciplinary procedures that are both psychologically and pedagogically sound. Preservice training does not succeed in building an adequate foundation for this purpose because of the many variables involved, and in-service training under the leadership of a competent supervisor must continue the task.

The position the authors take on punishment consists of the following elements: (1) Every behavior problem that seems to be serious enough for punitive action should be thoroughly analyzed before any action is taken; (2) the punishment should be adjusted to both the offense and the offender; (3) the punishment should be fair, reasonable, and sound; (4) the punishment should be within the law; and (5) when punishment is clearly warranted, it is the teacher's and/or principal's responsibility to administer it. The teacher's or administrator's power derives from the fact that school personnel represent the power of the adult (mature) world over the child's (immature) world, and because the school is an agency of the state, school personnel are servants of the state and are charged with the responsibility of educating the young. Both cultural and legal factors permit school personnel to administer punishment.

Returning to the teacher's question to the principal ("What shall I do?"), what helpful guidance can be provided? The answer falls into two parts: What *do* teachers do? What *should* teachers do? The answers to these two questions are not always the same. Teachers can be found, sometimes in collaboration with the principal, who employ the following disciplinary measures. Some of these are only mildly punitive; others are rather severe: They threaten a class or an individual, scold a class or individual, force misbehavers to apologize to them or to their classmates, ridicule children, force children to repeat their offenses until they are weary, spank children (mostly boys), banish children from the classroom, send children to the principal's office, suspend children from school for varying periods of time, take away privileges, make children pay fines, give children demerits, subject children to personal indignities, humiliate children in front of their peers, turn children over to security guards or police, expel children from school permanently, transfer children to special schools, keep an individual or class after school, isolate misbehavers from the rest of the class, make children pay for items they have damaged, punish the whole class for an offense committed by an unidentified individual, use learning as punishment, and reduce the grades of children who misbehave. This by no means exhausts the list of punitive procedures found in the schools, for we teachers can be as ingenious at inventing punitive measures as young people are at demonstrating novel forms of misbehavior.

Whether any or all of the foregoing punitive measures are either justifiable or effective in changing behavior can provoke a debate among teachers. The supervisor should encourage teachers to discuss each punitive measure and try to reach some consensus on subordinate questions, such as What is the purpose of the measure? Is the measure more damaging than helpful to the individual? Is the measure more damaging than helpful to the group? What is the long-range effect of the measure? Will the measure serve as a deterrent? Has the measure proved effective in the past? What are the legal restrictions on the measure?

Though some teachers and administrators may disagree, we believe that a reasonable case can be made for the following punitive measures.

- Taking away school privileges
- Requiring a student to restore, repair, or pay for damage done
- Detaining a student after school
- Sending a student to the office
- Isolating a student within the class

- Assigning a student to in-school suspension
- Suspending a student from school or class for a period of time
- Referring a student to security guards or police
- Expelling a student permanently from school
- Transferring a student to a special school

The following types of punishment appear to us to be unreasonable.

- Subjecting students to personal indignities
- Threatening
- Humiliating
- Charging fines for misbehaving
- Using academic work as punishment
- Lowering a child's academic mark for misconduct

In a class by itself is corporal punishment. Though we personally reject corporal punishment as unsound and ineffective, a case for spanking can be made, it is acceptable to a large segment of the public, and it is legally permitted in some communities. In 1977, the U.S. Supreme Court upheld the right of schools to administer corporal punishment.[78]

Ten Reasonable Punishments

Let us take a brief look at each of the ten punitive measures for which a reasonable case may be made, and then consider the thorny problem of corporal punishment.

Taking Away School Privileges. The loss of privileges is a natural consequence of misbehavior, a form of punishment to which many children are accustomed at home. A child or group that creates a disruption at a school play, for example, may have the privilege of attending school assemblies taken away for a period of time. A group or child who causes a turmoil at a school dance or athletic event may be denied attendance at future events for a period of time. The child who has been granted the privilege of doing independent study and who abuses that privilege may be reassigned to more closely supervised study. Children who have been appointed by the faculty or elected by their peers to positions of leadership or responsibility and who become behavior problems may be removed from these positions. Generally speaking, the loss of privileges should be a temporary punishment. Privileges should be restored when the student has demonstrated an ability to conform and the teacher is assured that the misconduct that provoked the loss will not recur.

Requiring a Student to Restore, Repair, or Pay for Damage Done. When a pupil takes property that belongs to someone else, he or she has the obligation of bringing that property back or reimbursing the individual or individuals from whom the property was taken. When a pupil damages or destroys another person's property, he or she has the obligation of repairing, restoring, or paying for that property or suffering other consequences of a more serious nature. Extensive destruction of schoolrooms and buildings by vandals is a major crime and must be dealt with in other ways.

Allowing for a student's age, physical condition, financial means, and the legal restrictions, the teacher or principal should seek to have the student rectify or at least help to rectify damage caused through misbehavior. If caught writing graffiti on the walls, for example, the student should be required to use some elbow grease and remove those graffiti. If discovered defacing a desk or table, the offender should be required to restore it as well as possible. If the offense is breaking a window, charges should be assessed for its replacement.

Because the acts of restoring and repairing materials may require the expenditure of work or money or both, the pupil's parents need to be consulted, give their consent, and be involved in the successful restoration or repair process. This punishment is practical only if a pupil has the necessary strength, skill, and knowledge to repair damage or the financial resources to pay for it. It is sometimes possible for those who do not have the funds to work off their debt at jobs in the school, by earning money in part-time jobs after school, or by repaying loans from their parents. This form of punishment has a direct bearing on the type of misconduct shown by a student and is a common measure used and accepted by society.

Detaining a Student after School. Detaining pupils after school has been a historic form of punishment in the schools. It is a relatively harmless type of punishment and not always an effective one in terms of changing pupils' behavior. The teacher is always faced with the problem of what kind of activity the pupil should be engaged in while being detained. Commonly, students work on their studies during the period of detention. This practice means that academic requirements are being used as a form of punishment and can create subsequent antagonism to studies for this reason.

Punishment should follow misbehavior as soon as possible, but it is not always possible for the teacher to detain a pupil the same day misconduct was demonstrated. In many school districts, school board policies require teachers to notify parents of their child's misbehavior and what punishment will be administered before it is done. Transportation home, part-time jobs, after-school lessons, and after-school student activities make immediate detention a problem. The teacher may create conflicts with parents and with other teachers who are making demands on the pupils' after-school time in attempting to enforce detention on the same day. Detention may have to be scheduled at a later date after the student has had a chance to readjust his or her schedule. Unfortunately, the delay diminishes the effectiveness of the punishment.

Some schools send all pupils who are given after-school detention to a central detention room, which teachers take turns supervising. Because detention is not a severe type of punishment, teachers tend to use it for a wide variety of relatively minor offenses. As a rule, the teacher who "sentences" a pupil to detention should supervise that student. This might provide an opportunity for some helpful dialogue between the teacher and the offender, and if the student works on studies pertinent to that teacher's class, the teacher might give the student some aid. The requirement that the teacher supervise his or her own behavior problems means that the teacher is detained as well as the pupil, a procedure that may hold as little appeal for the teacher as for the pupil. This requirement, however, could result in reducing the number of pupils who are kept after school and the use of detention for trivial offenses.

Unless it can be established that every child in a class has misbehaved, the detention of an entire class after school is neither wise nor fair. Mass punishment can result in rebellion, particularly of older children who have not misbehaved and who feel they are being unfairly treated. Punishment of an entire group for the offense of one or several members of a group, whether these offenders can be identified or not, is an abuse of the teacher's power. If rebellion and defiance result from an attempt to implement punishment, the teacher's status can be seriously eroded to the point that misbehavior will increase and learning will cease.

Sending a Student to the Office. When a child disrupts a group, it is perfectly within reason to remove the child at least temporarily from that group. The welfare of the group must take precedence over the welfare of an individual. Unfortunately, some teachers abuse this form of punishment and use it for minor offenses. Consistent use of this corrective measure weakens its effectiveness. For some students a reprieve from class may be more attractive than suffering through to the end of the hour or day.

When a teacher judges it essential that a child be removed from class, the child must be sent where supervision can be provided. The most logical place for that is the administrator's office. Administrators are inclined to support a teacher who on rare occasions sends an offender to their offices. They tend to view the teacher who sends many pupils to their offices as a poor disciplinarian. The supervisor should help teachers to clarify their views as to what measures they expect administrators to take with behavior problems that have arisen in their classes. Teachers must also realize that the administrator must have the full circumstances of the case before any corrective action can be taken. In some school districts teachers are expected to complete disciplinary forms before sending a student to the principal's office. This procedure allows the principal to have necessary background information while also causing some teachers to rethink the need to remove the student because of the extra work involved. As a result, many teachers have resorted to sending only the most serious offenders to the office.

Some teachers paint themselves into a corner when they banish a student from class with the command not to return. Although teachers may be permitted to suspend a student temporarily from class by sending him or her to the principal's office or to a special center for behavior problems within the school, they do not have the power to suspend or expel pupils from school. That power rests in the school board and is administered through the principal and superintendent. An order to a pupil not to return is unenforceable unless the administrator agrees with the teacher that the misconduct is severe enough to merit suspension or expulsion. The teacher loses "face" when the pupil is permitted to trot back to class because the teacher's order has been an empty threat.

Isolating a Student within the Class. Separating a misbehaving student from the other members of the class is a simple and justifiable procedure. The action demonstrates to the offender that the child's behavior is interfering with the work of the group and as such cannot be tolerated. We do not recommend standing the child in the corner or making the misbehaver sit on a stool with a dunce cap, common techniques of years ago, but the individual can be physically separated to a remote area in the room where disruptive activity will be less possible. When the offender appears to be ready to take part again in the group's activities, permission to rejoin the class should be granted. Removing a student to sit or stand in the hallway outside the classroom is ineffective and can result in a child's disappearing from the area. As a teacher is responsible for his or her students, this approach is a poor choice.

Assigning a Student to In-School Suspension. Some school systems employ alternatives to suspending students from school. Some elementary and secondary schools have established centers for special instruction that are, in effect, a form of in-school suspension. These centers within each school are rooms to which offenders are sent for the prescribed number of days during which they would ordinarily have been denied attendance at school. The centers are provided with a teacher as director and sometimes with the services of aides and part-time counselors. The director is expected to supervise an academic tutoring program and to conduct group counseling sessions.

Before children are assigned to the centers, their parents are advised of the action. The offenders are assigned to the centers only after other means of handling their behavior have been tried and failed. Students may be released from the center earlier than their assigned number of days if their behavior improves, and they may be held longer if they continue to misbehave. By using this in-school technique, the schools are able to decrease the number of students who would ordinarily be suspended from school. A great advantage of this program is that with its use students are not free to roam the streets but are kept in school under supervision and are engaged in some form of learning.

Suspending a Student from School or Class for a Period of Time. Suspension, the temporary denial of the privilege of attending school, is a corrective measure in widespread use in schools. It is a controversial measure, one of the more severe forms of punishment, and one that is limited by legal constraints. Suspension is a means that schools should not use lightly. Educators who reject suspension as a form of punishment point out that it does little good to turn offenders out on the streets, where they are denied learning and where they may get into more serious trouble. They argue that working parents are not able to supervise their children during working hours and the children are left to their own devices.

On the other hand, when an administrator decides an offense is serious enough to merit suspension of the offender, he or she has in mind the welfare of the group of which the student is a part and the welfare of the school generally. The administrator must resort to some measure to protect the other students from a serious offender. Suspension should be used only after remedial and less severe forms of punishment have been attempted without success.

A principal can typically suspend a student on his or her own initiative for periods of one to ten days. With the approval of the school board the principal may be permitted to suspend a student for a longer period of time. The longer pupils are suspended, the farther they usually fall behind in their school work and the more difficult it is for them to catch up when they return. Some provision for making up the work is necessary when they come back or else they are liable to continue as behavior problems. In many instances, school board policy requires the student to be given credit for assignments completed while he or she is suspended.

The U.S. Supreme Court has underscored the position that suspension of students should not be imposed arbitrarily. In two close (five to four) decisions, the Court held that students must be granted an informal hearing by the principal before they can be suspended and that school boards are liable for damages if they violate a student's constitutional right by administering suspension without a hearing.[79]

Referring a Student to Security Guards or Police. Though some educators may deplore the presence of security personnel in the schools, the security guard has become an established member of the staff of many of America's large urban secondary schools. The often necessary addition of security guards to the school staff has been a result of the rather shocking increase in school crime and violence since the middle 1960s. Offenses include assaults on teachers and other students, use of alcohol and drugs, weapons, arson, vandalism, robberies, and even murder.

Both older and newer studies have shown the continuing presence of crime in the schools. The National Institute of Education's study, *Violent Schools—Safe Schools: The Safe School Study Report to the Congress*, in 1978 revealed serious disorders in the public schools and estimated the cost of school crime at $200 million per year.[80] David Brooks commented, "It's impossible to estimate how many students arm themselves in school for the sake of self-defense, but in some schools, almost 70 percent of the students are said to be armed."[81] *Disorder in Our Public Schools*, a 1984 memorandum of the White House Cabinet Council, cited numerous instances of violence in the schools.[82] Publications of the National School Safety Center, a joint undertaking of the U.S. Departments of Justice and Education and Pepperdine University, reveal the seriousness of school violence, assaults on students and teachers, bullying, drug use, vandalism, and carrying of weapons into school.[83] George Nicholson, director and chief counsel of the National School Safety Center, et al. observed that "the level of violent crime perpetrated by juveniles in our society is three times greater today [1985] than it was in 1960."[84] The sixth annual survey conducted by *The Executive Educator* in 1993 reported that fights, bullying, and other violent acts are now commonplace among high school students and that more violence is infiltrating middle and elementary schools. Fifty-four percent of middle school principals and 56 percent of elementary school principals acknowledged an increase in the number of violent acts in their schools compared with five years earlier. More than 1,200 school principals responded to the survey.[85]

Recommendations for curbing the problems of crime and violence in the schools have been made by various groups; these range from the use of weapon detectors to establishing security departments in the schools to setting up special classes and schools for problem children to modifying teacher preparation to include more training in human relations and in working with emotionally disturbed children. A recent article in *Instructor* offered elementary teachers relevant suggestions for helping students live in a world with violence.[86] The goal to be achieved is a school climate free from violence.

Whereas a faculty works to create a climate in which the seeds of violence will not grow, the administrator must preserve the order and safety of all school personnel and must protect the school plant and facilities. When the necessity arises, both the teacher and the principal should be free to call in the services of either the school's security guard or the local police, and offenders should be turned over to appropriate authorities for hearings and further correction.

Expelling a Student Permanently from School. Expulsion is an extreme measure, an ultimate action of school authorities, and bound by legal restrictions. It is used to remove incorrigibles who menace the welfare of the group. Whereas suspension is a temporary denial of school attendance, expulsion is a permanent denial. Expulsion implies that the school has given up on the offender and that no further correction is possible under the school's jurisdiction. The power to expel rests in the school board. Parents must be involved, hearings must be held, and complete justification must be made for expulsion to be sanctioned.

Transferring a Student to a Special School. When it has been decided that a child can no longer function in a regular school and must be removed, the next question that must be raised is whether the pupil might make progress in another type of school. If a child is below the age of compulsory attendance and is to be removed from a school, other schooling must be arranged. Those above the age of compulsory attendance should have the option of attendance at a school that might be able to help them. Some school systems, especially large ones, operate types of social adjustment and alternative schools. These schools have been established to accommodate and educate children with behavior problems. Many of these schools are better equipped and staffed to handle a difficult teaching assignment. Special instructional programs, tutoring, and counseling are techniques used in working with children who manifest behavior problems. In some cases, if a child makes sufficient progress in a special school, transfer back to a regular school is possible.

Corporal Punishment

The debate over corporal punishment has raged ever since children were herded into institutions called schools and schoolmasters first whipped out the hickory stick. Whereas only two states prohibited corporal punishment in the early 1970s, today about twenty-seven states and a considerable number of localities ban this form of punishment.[87] Spanking is usually a last-ditch, desperate effort before suspension of a child, expulsion, or transferral. Whether it is effective is highly questionable. Jones made his view of corporal punishment clear when he said,

> Of all the discipline techniques in existence, corporal punishment distinguishes itself as having the fewest assets and the greatest number of liabilities. In terms of locking adult and child into a series of coercive cycles, it is the all-time champion. Those who rely on it swear by it—a testimonial to the addictive properties of quick short-term cures.[88]

The supervisor should urge teachers to study the efficacy of corporal punishment, if it is permitted in their school system. They should seek answers to questions such as these: How many children received corporal punishment during a school year? What were the ages, gender, and ethnic origin of the children? How severely were they spanked? Who administered the spankings? How many were spanked more than once during the year? For what offenses were they spanked? Do students view spanking as effective in changing their behavior? Do students actually fear corporal punishment? Do some students gain status in their peers' eyes as a result of being spanked? Is corporal punishment more effective in changing behavior than sending pupils to special rooms or suspending them?

The teachers must also familiarize themselves with the laws circumscribing corporal punishment. They must determine whether corporal punishment is legal in the community and state. They must learn the conditions under which spanking is permitted. For example, corporal punishment is generally administered in private and with an adult witness present. Parents usually have to be informed of the punishment. When corporal punishment is permissible, children can be spanked only on the posterior. The teachers will certainly want to learn whether any lawsuits have arisen over cases of corporal punishment, what the circumstances were, and what the courts' decisions were. If a disproportionate number of children of minority families and lower socioeconomic classes are spanked, teachers must be aware they skirt the possibility of being accused of discrimination. It is surprising, as corporal punishment is applied almost exclusively to boys, that school officials have not been charged more frequently with discrimination based on gender.

We believe that teachers should handle their own student behavior problems if at all possible, and this belief applies equally to corporal punishment. They must ascertain whether they are permitted to administer corporal punishment themselves or whether in their school system only an administrator may do so. When teachers are allowed to inflict corporal punishment, they must have the physical strength to do so. Incongruous situations sometimes develop when a teacher attempts to spank a boy who is physically stronger than the teacher. Female teachers and even some male teachers may have a problem paddling a strapping football player. Some educators have very strong views about the use of corporal punishment. For example, in October 1994, an elementary school principal in Ohio resigned his position rather than paddle students as he was directed under a new school district policy.[89]

Corporal punishment is effective only if the pupil has a fear or distaste for the punishment. Some students are quite willing to take a few swats of the paddle in place of other forms of punishment for which they may have a greater antipathy.

Corporal punishment is a severe measure; if it is used at all, it should be reserved for serious offenses. Because the intent of this punishment is to inflict pain on the offender, it should never be administered when the teacher or administrator is angry and likely to inflict serious pain or even injury. Like all forms of punishment, it should be administered in a dispassionate manner.

The supervisor should engage teachers in the clarification of their positions on the use of the various punitive measures. Further, because concern for students' rights and due process for the student is a growing issue, faculties must examine this concern.

In recent years, school systems, responding to the students' rights movement, have developed written codes of student conduct that are distributed to students, parents, and staff. Rules of conduct and possible remedial, corrective, and punitive measures that may be taken as a consequence of misconduct should be made known and should apply throughout the school system.[90] The supervisor should work with administrators, faculties, and students (as their maturity permits) to examine the school's disciplinary climate, analyze disciplinary measures, and develop codes of conduct.

SUMMARY

Classroom management is one of the more difficult aspects of public school teaching. It is an aspect that causes many teachers great concern and one with which teachers frequently need help. Preservice training programs barely scratch the surface of this complex phase of teaching, and therefore in-service training is essential to help teachers develop classroom management skills and understanding about discipline.

Parents, students, and teachers are in agreement that lack of discipline is a serious problem of the schools, and they expect the schools to take some action to prevent, reduce, or eliminate disciplinary problems. This chapter discusses six sources of disciplinary problems: the child, the child's group, the teacher, the school, the home and community, and the larger social order.

A number of models and approaches to discipline are in use in the schools. Among models that have been recommended by various authorities are the training, behavior modification, psychodynamics, group dynamics, personal-social growth, and diagnostic models. Varying approaches to discipline have been identified, including relationship-listening, confronting-contracting, and rules/rewards-punishment.

The school's culture and curriculum can contribute to pupils' behavior problems. A faculty should seek to order the class and school environment in such a way that disciplinary problems will be minimized. When behavior problems do arise, remedial, nonpunitive measures should be tried to correct those problems before punitive measures are taken.

The following corrective measures are suggested as reasonable: taking away school privileges; requiring a student to restore, repair, or pay for damage done; detaining a student after school; sending a student to the principal's office; isolating a student within the class; assigning a student to in-school suspension; suspending a student from school or class for a period of time; referring a student to security guards or police; transferring a student to a special school; expelling a student permanently from school.

Corporal punishment is a corrective measure acceptable to some educators and rejected by others. A school system must decide, laws permitting, whether to use corporal punishment. Within that context the faculties of individual schools of a district need to decide whether they wish to resort to corporal punishment.

The supervisor may profitably invite faculty study of four facets of the problem of discipline: causes of behavior problems, models and approaches to discipline, preventive measures, and corrective measures. The supervisor should keep before the teachers the understanding that the object of all discipline is the development of self-discipline on the part of the learner.

QUESTIONS FOR DISCUSSION

1. What are some of the reasons teachers have problems with student discipline and classroom management?
2. How can teachers improve the self-concept of their students?
3. What can a supervisor do to help teachers improve the culture of a school?
4. How can a teacher create a classroom environment in which every student comes to believe, "I count, I care, and I can"?
5. What did Alfie Kohn, researcher and author, mean when he said, "It is remarkable how often educators use the word motivation when what they mean is compliance"?

ACTIVITIES FOR FURTHER STUDY

1. Write a paper suggesting ways in which learners may be taught self-discipline.
2. Describe principal causes of student misbehavior.
3. Create an instrument for evaluating disciplinary climate and practices in the classroom.
4. Write a research paper on a number of court decisions (state and federal) on suspension and expulsion.
5. Visit four teachers in their classrooms, analyze the group climate in those classrooms, make a brief summary of each situation, and suggest ways in which you feel the group climate might be improved.
6. Talk with six teachers; compile statements of their beliefs on what they feel are the most serious behavior problems in their school and what they feel can be done about them. Drawing on these talks, summarize some teacher attitudes that a supervisor may be expected to contend with and suggest ways you would go about dealing with these attitudes.
7. Write a paper on the culture of the school and its impact on student behavior.
8. Identify several behavioral settings in a school and show how they affect either teachers or students or both. (See Barker and Gump in the chapter bibliography.)
9. Visit one or more schools and report on ressentiment practices you discover. Report how a supervisor might help teachers to correct the practices. (For reference on ressentiment, consult Nordstrom, Friedenberg, and Gold in the chapter bibliography.)
10. Make an audiotape recording of an interview with a group of students on their feelings about their school. Write a report showing how a supervisor would go about using student input such as this for making changes.
11. Write a paper on students' rights, explaining the meaning of due process and citing pertinent court cases. In your paper, show your position on student rights.
12. Discover and report three examples (on three different grade levels) of self-discipline being taught.
13. Make a classification of what you consider reasonable and unreasonable forms of punishment.

14. Write a paper on corporal punishment, citing state and federal court cases and stating your position.
15. Identify and report on schools that maintain special classes for children with behavior problems and special schools in the community for this purpose.
16. Specify possible steps to be considered by a teacher who is having the following behavior problems: (a) truancy, (b) excessive tardiness, (c) aggressive behavior in the classroom, (d) withdrawing behavior in the classroom.
17. Conduct a limited survey of parental attitudes on discipline.
18. Develop your own classification of causes of behavior problems.
19. Prepare a report on the relationship between pupil behavior and one of the following: (a) the teacher's attitudes on discipline, (b) instructional design, (c) grading practices, (d) peer-group relationships, (e) parental attitudes toward education, and (f) the curriculum.
20. Interview a sample of students and security guards (in schools that have security personnel) and report on the relationship between students and guards.
21. Obtain copies of the school board's policy manual and state school code and prepare a report on disciplinary measures permitted.
22. Gather and report data on assaults on teachers and students in schools of your community for the last two years.
23. Gather data on the cost of school crime in your community for the last two years.
24. Observe several experienced teachers and several inexperienced teachers and formulate a judgment about whether experienced teachers have fewer disciplinary problems than inexperienced teachers.
25. Sit in the assistant principal's (or principal's) office for several hours or a day and observe and keep a log of types of disciplinary problems sent to the assistant principal (or principal).
26. Analyze a school's records of behavior problems for one school year and tabulate the number of problems by age, intelligence test scores, gender, ethnic origin, social class, and status of the home.
27. Role-play with a peer a parent-teacher conference on a case in which the son has been caught smoking marijuana in the boys' rest room.
28. Write a paper showing whether you believe that Charles E. Silberman's assertion that schools are "grim, joyless places" still holds true and state your reasons. If you agree with Silberman (see bibliography), recommend ways to make schools more joyful places.
29. Role-play with a peer a conference between a teacher and a sixth-grade girl who has stolen a dollar from one of her classmates.
30. Write a review of Arthur W. Combs's book, *The Professional Education of Teachers* (see bibliography).
31. Report on the five models of discipline discussed by Laurel N. Tanner (see bibliography).
32. Prepare a position paper on behavior modification.
33. Describe the disciplinary model proposed by each of the following writers. (See bibliography. See also C. M. Charles (CMC) and Charles H. Wolfgang and Carl D. Glickman (W&G) for descriptions of these models.)
    a. Saul Axelrod (W&G)
    b. Lee and Marlene Canter (CMC; W&G)
    c. James C. Dobson (W&G)
    d. Rudolf Dreikurs (CMC; W&G)
    e. Siegfried Engelmann (W&G)

    f. Haim G. Ginott (CMC)

    g. William Glasser (CMC; W&G)

    h. Thomas Gordon (W&G)

    i. Thomas A. Harris (W&G)

    j. Fredric H. Jones (CMC)

    k. Jacob S. Kounin (CMC)

    l. Louis E. Raths, Merrill Hamrin, and Sidney B. Simon (W&G)

34. Describe the neo-Skinnerian model of discipline discussed in C. M. Charles (see bibliography).

35. If your school system has a written student code of conduct, obtain a copy and critique it. If your school system does not have a written code of conduct, sketch an outline of topics that should be covered in it. (This can be a group project.)

36. Determine what Jacob S. Kounin (see bibliography) meant by "withitness" and "overlapping."

37. Review *Teaching Students through Their Individual Learning Styles: A Practical Approach* by Rita S. Dunn and Kenneth J. Dunn (see bibliography) and draw implications for discipline.

38. Prepare a talk that you as a supervisor would give to a group of teachers on prevention of disciplinary problems.

NOTES

1. *The Education Digest* 19 (January 1954): 20.

2. Harvey F. Clarizio, *Toward Positive Classroom Discipline*, 3rd ed. (New York: Wiley, 1980), p. 1.

3. See the annual Phi Delta Kappa/Gallup Poll of the Public's Attitudes toward the Public Schools, published each fall in the *Phi Delta Kappan*. In 1995, this annual survey was in its twenty-seventh year.

4. Stanley Elam, ed., *The Gallup Poll of Attitudes toward Education 1969–1973* (Bloomington, Ind.: Phi Delta Kappa, 1973), pp. 57, 66–67.

5. See Kenneth T. Henson, *Secondary Teaching: A Personal Approach* (Itasca, Ill.: F. E. Peacock, 1974), pp. 3–4.

6. Fredric H. Jones, *Positive Classroom Discipline* (New York: McGraw-Hill, 1987), p. 9.

7. U.S. Department of Commerce, Bureau of the Census, *Statistical Abstract of the United States 1994*, 114th ed. (Washington, D.C.: U.S. Government Printing Office, 1994), p. 163. Figures include combined elementary and secondary public schools.

8. Ibid., pp. 128, 141.

9. Peter F. Oliva, "High School Discipline in American Society," *The National Association of Secondary School Principals Bulletin* 40 (January 1956): 1–103.

10. William Glasser, *Schools without Failure* (New York: Harper & Row, 1969), pp. 13–14.

11. Carl R. Rogers, "Toward Becoming a Fully Functioning Person," in *Perceiving, Behaving, Becoming*, 1962 Yearbook, ed. Arthur W. Combs (Alexandria, Va.: Association for Supervision and Curriculum Development, 1962), pp. 21–33.

12. A. H. Maslow, "Some Basic Propositions of a Growth and Self-Actualization Psychology," in *Perceiving, Behaving, Becoming*, 1962 Yearbook, ed. Arthur W. Combs (Alexandria, Va.: Association for Supervision and Curriculum Development, 1962), pp. 34–49.

13. Arthur W. Combs, "A Perceptual View of the Adequate Personality," in *Perceiving, Behaving, Becoming*, 1962 Yearbook, ed. Arthur W. Combs (Alexandria, Va.: Association for Supervision and Curriculum Development, 1962), pp. 50–64.

14. Don E. Hamachek, *Encounters with the Self*, 2nd ed. (New York: Holt, Rinehart and Winston, 1978), p. 33.
15. Combs, "A Perceptual View of the Adequate Personality," p. 51.
16. Ibid., p. 53.
17. A. H. Maslow, *Motivation and Personality*, 2nd ed. (New York: Harper & Row, 1970), pp. 35–58.
18. Earl C. Kelley, "The Fully Functioning Self," in *Perceiving, Behaving, Becoming*, 1962 Yearbook, ed. Arthur W. Combs (Alexandria, Va.: Association for Supervision and Curriculum Development, 1962), pp. 9–20.
19. Hamachek, *Encounters with the Self*, p. 222.
20. Allison Davis, "Socialization and Adolescent Personality," *Adolescence*, 43rd Yearbook, Part I (Chicago: National Society for the Study of Education, 1944), p. 210.
21. William Glasser, "The Quality School," *Phi Delta Kappan* 6 (February 1990): 425–35.
22. Humphrey Taylor, Robert Leitman, and Susan Barnett, *The Metropolitan Life Survey of The American Teacher 1992* (New York: Louis Harris and Associates, 1992).
23. Michael Rutter et al., *Fifteen Thousand Hours: Secondary Schools and Their Effects on Children* (London: Open Books, 1979), p. 56.
24. Ibid., pp. 145–62.
25. Charles E. Silberman, *Crisis in the Classroom* (New York: Random House, 1970), p. 10.
26. Glasser, *Schools without Failure*, p. 26.
27. Carl Nordstrom, Edgar Z. Friedenberg, and Hilary A. Gold, *Society's Children: A Study of Ressentiment in the Secondary School* (New York: Random House, 1967).
28. Theodore R. Sizer, *Horace's Compromise: The Dilemma of the American High School* (Boston: Houghton Mifflin, 1984), p. 179.
29. Sarah Lawrence Lightfoot, *The Good High School* (New York: Basic Books, 1983).
30. Roger G. Barker and Paul V. Gump, *Big School, Small School: High School Size and Student Behavior* (Palo Alto, Calif.: Stanford University Press, 1964).
31. Seymour B. Sarason, *The Culture of the School and the Problem of Change* (Boston: Allyn & Bacon, 1971), p. 93.
32. B. Othanel Smith, Saul B. Cohen, and Arthur Pearl, *Teachers for the Real World* (Washington, D.C.: American Association of Colleges for Teachers Education, 1969), p. 130.
33. Glasser, *Schools without Failure*, pp. 52–53.
34. Ibid., pp. 29–30.
35. Data from American Humane Association, "National Analysis of Official Child Neglect and Abuse Reporting," Denver, Colo., reported in *Statistical Abstract of the United States, 1990*, p. 176. See also James Patterson and Peter Kim, *The Day America Told the Truth: What People Really Believe about Everything That Really Matters* (New York: Prentice-Hall Press, 1991), pp. 125–27.
36. James S. Coleman et al., *Equality of Educational Opportunity* (Washington, D.C.: U.S. Office of Education, 1966). This study is often referred to as the Coleman Report.
37. See *Crime in the United States: Uniform Crime Reports* (Washington, D.C.: U.S. Department of Justice, Federal Bureau of Investigation, 1990 and 1992). The FBI annually publishes statistics on crime. For statistics on crime rate and child neglect and abuse cases, see *Statistical Abstract of the United States*, published annually.
38. Patterson and Kim, *The Day America Told the Truth*. (See p. 230 of this text)
39. See R. Rosenthal and L. Jacobson, *Pygmalion in the Classroom* (New York: Holt, Rinehart and Winston, 1968).
40. See W. Burleigh Seaver, "Effects of Naturally Induced Teacher Expectancies," *Journal of Personality and Social Psychology* 28 (December 1973): 333–42.

41. See J. Michael Palardy, "What Teachers Believe, What Children Achieve," *Elementary School Journal* 69 (April 1969): 370–74.
42. See Hamachek, *Encounters with the Self*, pp. 225–31.
43. Barbara J. Weber and Les M. Omotani, "The Power of Believing," *The Executive Educator* 16 (September 1994): 35–38.
44. See, for example, end notes of John H. Ralph and James Fennessey, "Science or Reform: Some Questions about the Effective Schools Model," *Phi Delta Kappan* 64 (June 1983): 689–94.
45. Benjamin S. Bloom, J. Thomas Hastings, and George F. Madaus, *Handbook of Formative and Summative Evaluation of Student Learning* (New York: McGraw-Hill, 1971), p. 46.
46. See Arthur T. Jersild and Frances B. Holmes, "Characteristics of Teachers Who Are Liked Best and Disliked Most," *Journal of Experimental Education* 9 (December 1940): 139–51. See also Paul Witty, "An Analysis of the Personality Traits of the Effective Teacher," *Journal of Educational Research* 40 (May 1947): 662–72.
47. Arthur W. Combs, *The Professional Education of Teachers: A Perceptual View of Teacher Preparation* (Boston: Allyn & Bacon, 1965), p. 71.
48. Barbara Bree Fischer and Louis Fischer, "Styles in Teaching and Learning," *Educational Leadership* 36 (January 1979), 251.
49. Ibid., pp. 246–50.
50. Rita S. Dunn and Kenneth J. Dunn, *Teaching Students through Their Individual Learning Styles: A Practical Approach* (Reston, Va.: Reston Publishing, 1978).
51. Jacob S. Kounin, *Discipline and Group Management in Classrooms* (New York: Holt, Rinehart and Winston, 1970), p. 127.
52. Laurel N. Tanner, *Classroom Discipline for Effective Teaching and Learning* (New York: Holt, Rinehart and Winston, 1978), pp. 5–18.
53. Wilford A. Weber, "Classroom Management," in *Classroom Teaching Skills*, 4th ed., ed. James M. Cooper (Lexington, Mass.: D. C. Heath, 1990), p. 257.
54. Clarizio, *Toward Positive Classroom Discipline*, pp. 8–16.
55. Ibid., p. 4.
56. J. Michael Palardy and James E. Mudrey, "Discipline: Four Approaches," in *Teaching Today: Tasks and Challenges*, ed. J. Michael Palardy (New York: Macmillan, 1975), pp. 315–24.
57. Ibid., pp. 318–19.
58. Ibid., p. 319.
59. Ibid., pp. 319, 323, 324.
60. Charles H. Wolfgang and Carl D. Glickman, *Solving Discipline Problems: Strategies for Classroom Teachers*, 2nd ed. (Boston: Allyn & Bacon, 1986), p. 22.
61. Thomas Gordon, *T.E.T.: Teacher Effectiveness Training* (New York: David McKay, 1974).
62. Thomas A. Harris, *I'm OK—You're OK: A Practical Guide to Transactional Analysis* (New York: Harper & Row, 1969).
63. Louis E. Raths, Merrill Hamrin, and Sidney B. Simon, *Values and Teaching: Working with Values in the Classroom*, 2nd ed. (Columbus, Ohio: Merrill, 1966).
64. Wolfgang and Glickman, *Solving Discipline Problems*, p. 22.
65. Rudolf Dreikurs and Pearl Cassel, *Discipline without Tears: What to Do with Children Who Misbehave*, rev. ed. (New York: Hawthorne Books, 1972).
66. Glasser, *Schools without Failure*.
67. Wolfgang and Glickman, *Solving Discipline Problems*, p. 22.
68. Saul Axelrod, *Behavior Modification for the Classroom Teacher*, 2nd ed. (New York: McGraw-Hill, 1983).
69. Lee Canter and Marlene Canter, *Assertive Discipline: A Take-Charge Approach for Today's Educator* (Seal Beach, Calif.: Canter and Associates, 1976).

70. Siegfried Engelmann, *Preventing Failure in the Primary Grades* (New York: Simon & Schuster, 1969).
71. James C. Dobson, *Dare to Discipline* (Wheaton, Ill.: Tyndale House Publishers, 1970).
72. See C. M. Charles, *Building Classroom Discipline: From Models to Practice*, 2nd ed. (White Plains, N.Y.: Longman, 1985).
73. Glasser, *Schools without Failure*, p. 37.
74. Ibid., pp. 22–23.
75. This text uses the term *corrective measure* as an inclusive term, which encompasses punishment. Punishment in this context is one form of correction. Suspension of a pupil, for example, is a punitive corrective measure. An individual conference with a pupil is a corrective measure of a remedial, nonpunitive nature.
76. Wesley C. Becker, Siegfried Engelmann, and Don R. Thomas, *Teaching 1: Classroom Management* (Chicago: Science Research Associates, 1975), pp. 255–61.
77. Ibid., p. 260.
78. *Ingraham v. Wright*, 430 US 651 (1977).
79. *Goss v. Lopez*, 419 US 565 (1975); *Wood v. Strickland*, 420 US 308 (1975).
80. National Institute of Education, *Violent Schools—Safe Schools: The Safe School Study Report to the Congress* (Washington, D.C.: National Institute of Education, 1978).
81. David Brooks, "Order in the Classroom—Forget the Fire—Just Keep Teaching," *National Review* 37 (December 13, 1985): 25.
82. Gary L. Bauer, Chairman, *Disorder in Our Public Schools* (Washington, D.C.: White House Cabinet Council, 1984).
83. See, for example, Stuart Greenbaum and Brenda Turner, eds., *Safe Schools Overview*. National School Safety Center Resource Paper (Malibu, Calif.: National School Safety Center, Pepperdine University, November 1990).
84. George Nicholson, Ronald Stephens, Rory Elder, and Vicky Leavitt, "Safe Schools: You Can't Do It Alone," *Phi Delta Kappan* 66 (March 1985): 496.
85. James Boothe, Leo Bradley, T. Michael Flick, Katherine Keough, and Susanne P. Kirk, "The Violence at Your Door," *The Executive Educator* 15 (February 1993): 15–22.
86. "How to Teach Children about Living in a World with Violence," *Instructor* 1 (July / August 1995): 64–79.
87. Robert C. Johnston, "Policy Details Who Paddles Students and with What," *Education Week* 14 (November 16, 1994): 5.
88. Jones, *Positive Classroom Discipline*, p. 344.
89. Johnston, "Policy Details Who Paddles Students and with What."
90. For a plan in which rules may vary from class to class, see Roland S. Barth, "Discipline: If You Do That Again—," *Phi Delta Kappan* 61 (February 1980): 398–400.

BIBLIOGRAPHY

American Humane Association. "National Analysis of Official Child Neglect and Abuse Reporting." Reported in U.S. Census Bureau, *Statistical Abstract of the United States, 1990*. Washington, D.C.: U.S. Census Bureau, 1990.

"Assaults on Teachers." *Today's Education* 61 (February 1972): 30–32ff.

Axelrod, Saul. *Behavior Modification for the Classroom Teacher*, 2nd ed. New York: McGraw-Hill, 1983.

Baker, Keith, and Robert J. Rubel, eds. *Violence and Crime in the Schools*. Lexington, Mass.: D. C. Heath, 1980.

Banks, James A., and Cheryl A. McGee Banks, eds. *Handbook of Research on Multicultural Education*. New York: Macmillan, 1995.

Barker, Roger G., and Paul V. Gump. *Big School, Small School: High School Size and Student Behavior*. Palo Alto, Calif.: Stanford University Press, 1964.

Barth, Roland S. "Discipline: If You Do That Again—." *Phi Delta Kappan* 61 (February 1980): 398–400.

———. *Improving Schools from Within*. San Francisco: Jossey-Bass, 1990.

Bauer, Gary L. *Disorder in Our Public Schools*. Washington, D.C.: White House Cabinet Council, 1984.

———, Chairman. "Restoring Order to the Public Schools." *Phi Delta Kappan* 66 (March 1985): 488–91.

Bauer, Gordon, Richard Dubanoski, Lois A. Yamuchi, and Kelly Ann M. Honbo. "Corporal Punishment and the Schools." *Education and Urban Society* 22 (May 1990): 285–99.

Becker, Wesley C., Siegfried Engelmann, and Don R. Thomas. *Teaching 1: Classroom Management*. Chicago: Science Research Associates, 1975.

Blau, Peter M., and W. Richard Scott. *Formal Organizations: A Comparative Approach*. San Francisco: Chandler, 1962.

Bloom, Benjamin S., J. Thomas Hastings, and George F. Madaus. *Handbook of Formative and Summative Evaluation of Student Learning*. New York: McGraw-Hill, 1971.

Boothe, James, Leo Bradley, T. Michael Flick, Katherine Keough, and Susanne P. Kirk. "The Violence at Your Door." *The Executive Educator* 15 (February 1993): 15–22.

Brooks, David. "Order in the Classroom—Forget the Fire—Just Keep Teaching." *National Review* 37 (December 13, 1985): 24–29.

Bybee, Roger W., and E. Gorden Gee. *Violence, Values, and Justice in the Schools*. Boston: Allyn & Bacon, 1982.

Canter, Lee, and Marlene Canter. *Assertive Discipline: A Take-Charge Approach for Today's Educator*. Seal Beach, Calif.: Canter and Associates, 1976.

Carson, Joan C., and Peter Carson. *Any Teacher Can!: Practical Strategies for Effective Classroom Management*. Springfield, Ill.: Charles C. Thomas, 1984.

Charles, C. M. *Building Classroom Discipline: From Models to Practice*, 2nd ed. White Plains, N.Y.: Longman, 1985.

Clarizio, Harvey F. *Toward Positive Classroom Discipline*, 3rd ed. New York: Wiley, 1980.

"Classroom Discipline: The Diagnostic Approach." *Streamlined Seminar*. Alexandria, Va.: National Association of Elementary School Principals, 1993.

Coleman, James S., et al. *Equality of Educational Opportunity*. Washington, D.C.: U.S. Office of Education, 1966.

Combs, Arthur W. "A Perceptual View of the Adequate Personality." In *Perceiving, Behaving, Becoming*, 1962 Yearbook, ed. Arthur W. Combs. Alexandria, Va.: Association for Supervision and Curriculum Development, 1962.

———. *The Professional Education of Teachers: A Perceptual View of Teacher Preparation*. Boston: Allyn & Bacon, 1965.

———, ed. *Perceiving, Behaving, Becoming*, 1962 Yearbook. Alexandria, Va.: Association for Supervision and Curriculum Development, 1962.

Combs, Arthur W., and Donald Snygg. *Individual Behavior: A Perceptual Approach to Behavior*, rev. ed. New York: Harper & Row, 1959.

Crime in the United States: Uniform Crime Reports. Washington, D.C.: U.S. Department of Justice, Federal Bureau of Investigation, 1990 and 1992.

Curwin, Richard L., and Allen N. Mendler. *Discipline with Dignity*. Alexandria, Va.: Association for Supervision and Curriculum Development, 1988.

Davis, Allison. "Socialization and Adolescent Personality." *Adolescence*, 43rd Yearbook, Part I. Chicago: National Society for the Study of Education, 1944.

Dobson, James C. *Dare to Discipline*. Wheaton, Ill.: Tyndale House Publishers, 1970.

Dreikurs, Rudolf, and Pearl Cassel. *Discipline without Tears: What to Do with Children Who Misbehave*, rev. ed. New York: Hawthorne Books, 1972.

Duke, Daniel L. *School Leadership and Instructional Improvement*. New York: Random House, 1987.

————, ed. *Helping Teachers Manage Classrooms*. Alexandria, Va.: Association for Supervision and Curriculum Development, 1982.

Dunn, Rita S., and Kenneth J. Dunn. "Learning Styles / Teaching Styles: Should They . . . Can They . . . Be Matched?" *Educational Leadership* 36 (January 1979): 238–44.

————. *Teaching Students through Their Individual Learning Styles: A Practical Approach*. Reston, Va.: Reston Publishing, 1978.

Education Digest 19 (January 1954): 20.

Elam, Stanley, ed. *The Gallup Polls of Attitudes toward Education 1969–1973*. Bloomington, Ind.: Phi Delta Kappa, 1973.

Elam, Stanley, Lowell C. Rose, and Alec M. Gallup. "The 23rd Annual Gallup Poll of the Public's Attitudes toward the Public Schools." *Phi Delta Kappan* 73 (September 1991): 41–56.

Elam, Stanley, and Lowell Rose. "The 27th Annual Phi Delta Kappa / Gallup Poll of the Public's Attitudes toward the Public Schools." *Phi Delta Kappan* 77 (September 1995): 41–56.

Fischer, Barbara Bree, and Louis Fischer. "Styles in Teaching and Learning." *Educational Leadership* 36 (January 1979): 245–54.

Furtwengler, Willis J. *Improving School Discipline: An Administrator's Guide*. Boston: Allyn & Bacon, 1982.

Georgiady, Nicholas, Ronald Sinclair, and Charlene Sinclair. "What Is the Most Effective Discipline?" *Principal* (September 1991): 49–50.

Getzels, Jacob W., and Egon C. Guba. "Social Behavior and the Administrative Process." *School Review* 65 (Winter 1957): pp. 423–41.

Glasser, William. "The Quality School." *Phi Delta Kappan* 6 (February 1990): 424–35.

————. *Reality Therapy: A New Approach to Psychiatry*. New York: Harper & Row, 1975.

————. *Schools without Failure*. New York: Harper & Row, 1969.

Gordon, Thomas. *T.E.T.: Teacher Effectiveness Training*. New York: David McKay, 1974.

Greenbaum, Stuart, and Brenda Turner, eds. *Safe Schools Overview*. National School Safety Center Resource Paper. Malibu, Calif.: National School Safety Center, Pepperdine University, November 1990.

Hamachek, Don E. *Encounters with the Self*, 2nd ed. New York: Holt, Rinehart and Winston, 1978.

Harris, Thomas A. *I'm OK—You're OK: A Practical Guide to Transactional Analysis*. New York: Harper & Row, 1969.

Henson, Kenneth T. *Secondary Teaching: A Personal Approach*. Itasca, Ill.: F. E. Peacock, 1974.

————. *Secondary Teaching Methods*. Lexington, Mass.: D. C. Heath, 1981.

Herndon, James. *How to Survive in Your Native Land*. New York: Bantam, 1971.

————. *The Way It Spozed to Be*. New York: Simon & Schuster, 1968.

Hill, Marie S., and Frank Hill. *Creating Safe Schools: What Principals Can Do*. Thousand Oaks, Calif.: Corwin Press, 1994.

"How to Teach Children about Living in a World with Violence," *Instructor* 1 (July / August 1995): 64–79.

Hoy, Wayne K., and Patrick B. Forsyth. *Effective Supervision: Theory into Practice*. New York: Random House, 1986.

Jersild, Arthur T., and Frances B. Holmes. "Characteristics of Teachers Who Are Liked Best and Disliked Most." *Journal of Experimental Education* 9 (December 1940): 139–51.

Johns, Frank A., and Robert H. McNaughton. "Spare the Rod: A Continuing Controversy." *The Clearing House* 63 (May 1990): 388–92.

Johnson, David W., and Roger T. Johnson. *Reducing School Violence through Conflict Resolution*. Alexandria, Va.: Association for Supervision and Curriculum Development, 1995.

Johnson, Lois V., and Mary A. Bany. *Classroom Management Theory and Skill Training*. New York: Macmillan, 1970.

Johnston, Robert C. "Policy Details Who Paddles Students and with What." *Education Week* 14 (November 16, 1994): 5.

Jones, Fredric H. *Positive Classroom Discipline*. New York: McGraw-Hill, 1987.

———. *Positive Classroom Instruction*. New York: McGraw-Hill, 1987.

Joyce, Bruce. *Changing School Culture through Staff Development*. Alexandria, Va.: Association for Supervision and Curriculum Development, 1990.

Kaufman, Bel. *Up the Down Staircase*. New York: Avon, 1964.

Kelley, Earl C. "The Fully Functioning Self." In *Perceiving, Behaving, Becoming*, 1962 Yearbook, ed. Arthur W. Combs. Alexandria, Va.: Association for Supervision and Curriculum Development, 1962.

Kennedy, J. Michael, and Patricia Williams. "Does It Matter Who Makes the Rules?" *Kappa Delta Pi Record* 29 (Winter 1993): 43–45.

Kindsvatter, Richard, and Mary Ann Levine. "The Myths of Discipline." *Phi Delta Kappan* 61 (June 1980): 690–93.

Kounin, Jacob S. *Discipline and Group Management in Classrooms*. New York: Holt, Rinehart and Winston, 1970.

Kozol, Jonathan. *Death at an Early Age*. Boston: Houghton Mifflin, 1967.

———. *Savage Inequalities*. New York: Crown Publishers, 1991.

Kritsonis, William Allan, and Sam Adams. *School Discipline: The Art of Survival*. Baton Rouge, La.: Land and Land Publishing Division, 1986.

Lemlech, Johanna Kasin. *Classroom Management*. New York: Harper & Row, 1979.

Lightfoot, Sarah Lawrence. *The Good High School*. New York: Basic Books, 1983.

Lindsey, Bryan L., and James W. Cunningham. "Behavior Modification: Some Doubts and Dangers." In *Discipline and Learning: An Inquiry into Student-Teacher Relationships*. Washington, D.C.: National Education Association, 1975.

McCarthy, Martha M. "How Can I Best Manage My Classroom?" *Instructor* 87 (September 1977): 72–73.

Madsen, Charles H., Jr., and Clifford K. Madsen. *Teaching/Discipline*, 2nd ed. Boston: Allyn & Bacon, 1974.

Marshall, James. *The Devil in the Classroom: Hostility in American Education*. New York: Shocken Books, 1985.

Maslow, Abraham H. *Motivation and Personality*, 2nd ed. New York: Harper & Row, 1970.

———. "Some Basic Propositions of a Growth and Self-Actualization Psychology." In *Perceiving, Behaving, Becoming*, 1962 Yearbook, ed. Arthur W. Combs. Alexandria, Va.: Association for Supervision and Curriculum Development, 1962.

———. *Toward a Psychology of Being*, 2nd ed. New York: D. Van Nostrand, 1968.

Mercure, Christine M. "Alternatives to Corporal Punishment." *Here's How*. Alexandria, Va.: National Association of Elementary School Principals, 1994.

National Institute of Education. *Violent Schools—Safe Schools: The Safe School Study Report to the Congress*. Washington, D.C.: U.S. Department of Health, Education, and Welfare, 1978.

Nicholson, George, Ronald Stephens, Rory Elder, and Vicky Leavitt. "Safe Schools: You Can't Do It Alone." *Phi Delta Kappan* 66 (March 1985): 491–96.

Nordstrom, Carl, Edgar Z. Friedenberg, and Hilary A. Gold. *Society's Children: A Study of Ressentiment in the Secondary School*. New York: Random House, 1967.

Novelli, Joan. "Better Behaviors for Better Learning." *Instructor* 103 (July/August 1993): 74–79.

Oakes, Jeannie. *Keeping Track: How Schools Structure Inequality*. New Haven, Conn.: Yale University Press, 1985.

Oliva, Peter F. "High School Discipline in American Society." *The Bulletin of the National Association of Secondary School Principals* 40 (January 1956): 1–103.

———. *The Secondary School Today*, 2nd ed. New York: Harper & Row, 1972.

Palardy, J. Michael. "What Teachers Believe, What Children Achieve." *Elementary School Journal* 69 (April 1969): 370–74.

———, ed. *Teaching Today: Tasks and Challenges*. New York: Macmillan, 1975.

Palardy, J. Michael, and James E. Mudrey. "Discipline: Four Approaches." In *Teaching Today: Tasks and Challenges*, ed. J. Michael Palardy. New York: Macmillan, 1975.

Patterson, James, and Peter Kim. *The Day America Told the Truth: What People Really Believe about Everything That Really Matters*. New York: Prentice-Hall Press, 1991.

Railsbach, Charles E. "Promoting Good Classroom Management." *Here's How*. Alexandria, Va.: National Association of Elementary School Principals, 1992.

Rajpal, Puran J. "What Behavior Problems Do Teachers Regard as Serious?" *Phi Delta Kappan* 53 (May 1972): 591–92.

Ralph, John H., and James Fennessey. "Science or Reform: Some Questions about the Effective Schools Model." *Phi Delta Kappan* 64 (June 1983): 689–94.

Raths, Louis E., Merrill Harmin, and Sidney B. Simon. *Values and Teaching: Working with Values in the Classroom*, 2nd ed. Columbus, Ohio: Merrill, 1966, 1978.

Rogers, Carl R. *Freedom to Learn*. Columbus, Ohio: Charles E. Merrill, 1969.

———. "Toward Becoming a Fully Functioning Person." In *Perceiving, Behaving, Becoming*, 1962 Yearbook, ed. Arthur W. Combs. Alexandria, Va.: Association for Supervision and Curriculum Development, 1962.

Rosenthal, R., and L. Jacobson. *Pygmalion in the Classroom*. New York: Holt, Rinehart and Winston, 1968.

Rutter, Michael, Barbara Maughan, Peter Mortimore, and Janet Ouston. *Fifteen Thousand Hours: Secondary Schools and Their Effects on Children*. London: Open Books, 1979.

Sanford, Julie, and Edmund T. Emmer. *Understanding Classroom Management: An Observation Guide*. Englewood Cliffs: Prentice-Hall, 1988.

Sarason, Seymour B. *The Culture of the School and the Problem of Change*. Boston: Allyn & Bacon, 1971.

Seaver, W. Burleigh. "Effects of Naturally Induced Teacher Expectancies." *Journal of Personality and Social Psychology* 28 (December 1973): 333–42.

Short, Paula M., Rick Jay Short, and Charlie Blanton. *Rethinking Student Discipline: Alternatives That Work*. Thousand Oaks, Calif.: Corwin Press, 1994.

Silberman, Charles E. *Crisis in the Classroom*. New York: Random House, 1970.

Silvernail, David L. *Developing Positive Student Self-Concept*. Washington, D.C.: National Education Association, 1981.

Simon, Sidney B., Leland W. Howe, and Howard Kirschenbaum. *Values Clarification: A Handbook of Practical Strategies for Teachers and Students*, rev. ed. New York: Hart, 1978.

Sizer, Theodore R. *Horace's Compromise: The Dilemma of the American High School*. Boston: Houghton Mifflin, 1984.

Skinner, B. F. *Skinner for the Classroom: Selected Papers*. Champaign, Ill.: Research Press, 1982.

Smith, B. Othanel, Saul B. Cohen, and Arthur Pearl. *Teachers for the Real World*. Washington, D.C.: American Association of Colleges for Teacher Education, 1969.

Stephens, Ronald. *Safe Schools: A Handbook for Violence Prevention*. Bloomington, Ind.: National Education Service, 1995.

Stone, James C., and Donald P. DeNevi, eds. *Teaching Multi-Cultural Populations: Five Heritages*. New York: D. Van Nostrand, 1971.

Sulzer, Beth, and G. Roy Mayer. *Behavior Modification Procedures for School Personnel*. Hinsdale, Ill.: Dryden Press, 1972.

Tanner, Daniel, and Laurel Tanner. *Supervision in Education: Problems and Practices*, chaps. 5 and 8. New York: Macmillan, 1987.

Tanner, Laurel N. *Classroom Discipline for Effective Teaching and Learning*. New York: Holt, Rinehart and Winston, 1978.

Taylor, Humphrey, Robert Leitman, and Susan Barnett. *The Metropolitan Life Survey of The American Teacher 1992*. New York: Louis Harris and Associates, 1992.

U.S. Department of Commerce, Bureau of the Census. *Statistical Abstract of the United States 1994*, 114th ed. Washington, D.C.: U.S. Government Printing Office, 1994.

Vail, Kathleen. "Unrepentant." *The Executive Educator* 16 (May 1995): 31–33.

Vestermark, Seymour D., Jr., and Peter D. Blauvelt. *Controlling Crime in the School: A Complete Security Handbook for Administrators*. West Nyack, N.Y.: Parker, 1978.

"Violence in Our Culture," *Newsweek*, April 1, 1991, 46–52.

Walker, Dean. "Preventing Violence in Schools." *Research Roundup*. Alexandria, Va.: National Association of Elementary School Principals, 1994/95.

Weber, Barbara J., and Les M. Omotani. "The Power of Believing." *The Executive Educator* 16 (September 1994): 35–38.

Weber, Wilford A. "Classroom Management." In *Classroom Teaching Skills*, 4th ed., ed. James M. Cooper, pp. 229–306. Lexington, Mass.: D. C. Heath, 1990.

Weiner, Elizabeth Hirzler. *Discipline in the Classroom*, 2nd rev. ed. Washington, D.C.: National Education Association, 1980.

Wickman, E. K. *Children's Behavior and Teachers' Attitudes*. New York: Commonwealth Fund, 1928.

Wilson, Ertha, June Alexander, and Barbara Spann. "How Do You Rate as a Classroom Manager?" *Instructor* 103 (July/August 1993): 30–37.

Witty, Paul. "An Analysis of the Personality Traits of the Effective Teacher." *Journal of Educational Research* 40 (May 1947): 662–72.

Wolfgang, Charles H., and Carl D. Glickman. *Solving Discipline Problems: Strategies for Classroom Teachers*, 2nd ed. Boston: Allyn & Bacon, 1986.

Films

For titles of thirty-two films, see Charles H. Wolfgang and Carl D. Glickman, *Solving Discipline Problems: Strategies for Classroom Teachers*, 2nd ed., refs. on pp. 44–45, 65–66, 81–83, 103–106, 126–28, 148–49, and 179. Boston: Allyn & Bacon, 1986.

Filmstrips

Improving School Climate. Based on the research of Robert Fox. Three sound filmstrips, two miniaudits, and a leader's guide. Alexandria, Va.: Association for Supervision and Curriculum Development.

For titles of twenty filmstrips, see Charles H. Wolfgang and Carl D. Glickman, *Solving Discipline Problems: Strategies for Classroom Teachers*, 2nd ed., refs. on pp. 66–67, 125–26, 162–63, and 180. Boston: Allyn & Bacon, 1986.

Guidebooks and Workbooks

See Charles H. Wolfgang and Carl D. Glickman, *Solving Discipline Problems: Strategies for Classroom Teachers*, 2nd ed., pp. 67, 163. Boston: Allyn & Bacon, 1986.

Multimedia

Assertive Discipline in Action (two filmstrips in color and two audiocassettes); *Assertive Discipline in the Classroom* (two filmstrips in color and two audiocassettes); *Assertive*

Discipline: A Take-Charge Approach (two guidebooks and one workbook). These materials describe the assertive discipline approach of Lee and Marlene Canter. Available from Social Studies School Service, 10,000 Culver Boulevard, Dept. E3, P.O. Box 802, Culver City, Calif. 90230.

Classroom Management. 1988. A one-hour videotape with facilitator's manual. Pat Wolfe explains stages of planning, implementing, and maintaining effective classroom management. Association for Supervision and Curriculum Development, 1250 North Pitt Street, Alexandria, Va. 22314.

Newsjournal

School Journal, published three times a year by the National School Safety Center, Pepperdine University, 24255 Pacific Coast Highway, Malibu, Calif. 90263.

Videotapes

Catch Them Being Good: Reinforcement in the Classroom. 1988. Two hours of videotape plus facilitator's manual. Techniques for minimizing behavior problems. Practice tapes contain classroom episodes at the kindergarten, elementary, and secondary school levels. Features Pat Wolfe. Association for Supervision and Curriculum Development, 1250 North Pitt Street, Alexandria, Va. 22314.

Classroom Management. 1988. One hour. Facilitator's manual. Shows a three-stage classroom management plan with segments in elementary, middle, and secondary school classrooms. Features Pat Wolfe. Association for Supervision and Curriculum Development, 1250 North Pitt Street, Alexandria, Va. 22314.

Dealing with School Violence and Student Confrontation: What Works, What Doesn't. 1994. 22 minutes. The video examines the growing trend of violence and confrontation in the schools, offering possible solutions and innovative ideas that have helped schools improve the climate for learning. National Association of Secondary School Principals Special Projects, 3 Regent Street, Suite 306, Livingston, N.J. 07039.

Discipline with Dignity. 1991. A three-video set—each video is 15–20 minutes in length. A comprehensive leader's guide is available for an additional charge. The three videos are titled "Overview," "Prevention," and "Action/Resolution." Based on the research of the presenters, Rick Curwin and Allen Mendler. National Educational Service/NASSP, P.O. Box 8, Station M7, Bloomington, Ind. 47402.

Early Childhood Education: Classroom Management—Curriculum Organization. 1991. 40 minutes. Facilitator's Manual. Part One depicts approaches to classroom management. Part Two shows teachers using individualized instructional techniques. Features Kay Drake and Markie Pringle. Barbara Day, consultant. Association for Supervision and Curriculum Development, 1250 North Pitt Street, Alexandria, Va. 22314.

Effective Classroom Management for the Elementary School. 1980. 30 minutes. Demonstrates effective techniques of classroom management in the elementary school. Based on the research of Carolyn Evertson. Association for Supervision and Curriculum Development, 1250 North Pitt Street, Alexandria, Va. 22314.

Learning Styles and the Learning Process. 1994. 32 minutes. This video focuses on the relationship between learning style theory and practice and their applications in the classroom. It provides practical examples and insights that open the door to personalizing education, motivating students, and accelerating learning. Features Dr. Marie Carbo. National Association of Secondary School Principals Special Projects, 3 Regent Street, Suite 306, Livingston, N.J. 07039.

Motivation to Learn. 1990. Two tapes, leader's manual, and accompanying book. Tape One portrays issues concerning unmotivated students. 25 minutes. Tape Two demonstrates guidelines for conferring with students. 28 minutes. Features Raymond J. Wlodkowski. Association for Supervision and Curriculum Development, 1250 North Pitt Street, Alexandria, Va. 22314.

Strategies for Classroom Management. 1990. Four tapes, each 15 to 20 minutes in length. Pam Robbins and Pat Wolfe discuss research-based techniques for improving students' attitudes and behavior. Includes several demonstrations by actual teachers in their classrooms. Leader's Guide. National Staff Development Council, P.O. Box 240, Oxford, Ohio 45056.

Success with Discipline: The Trials of Jenny Tippet. 1994. Three tapes and Comprehensive Training Guide. The three videos focus on Beliefs and Attitudes, Prevention, and Reacting to Discipline Problems. These videos form a comprehensive training program to meet the unique needs of a middle school faculty. National Middle School Association, Dept. #700. Columbus, Ohio 43265.

6

Helping Teachers Evaluate Instruction

Objectives

After studying Chapter 6 you should be able to accomplish the following objectives:

1. Explain the differences between evaluation, measurement, and testing.
2. Contrast norm-referenced and criterion-referenced measurement.
3. Define formative and summative evaluation and explain when to use each.
4. Describe purposes and techniques of preassessment.
5. Write and identify well-constructed essay-test items and explain the purposes for which they should be used.
6. Write and identify well-constructed objective-test items and explain the purposes for which they should be used.
7. Develop and lead faculties to adopt and apply guidelines for a sound marking system.
8. Develop and lead faculties to adopt and apply guidelines for a sound reporting system.
9. Formulate your philosophical position about evaluating student achievement.

EVALUATION: AN ESSENTIAL PHASE

From the day of birth until the day of death human beings are subjected to continuous evaluation by fellow human beings. In fact, a person's deeds may continue to be evaluated long after he or she is gone from the scene. The infant is told by parents, with appropriate gestures and tone of voice, "That was very naughty." The teenage girl views her boyfriend as a combination of Hercules and Apollo. The wife lets her husband know of her displeasure with the appraisal "You never help me around the house." The boss produces a feeling of elation in an employee by saying, "That was brilliant work. I'm going to give you a raise." The teacher is happy when the supervisor gives praise for a job well done: "That was a great class you had today." And the student, who is at the low end of the educational totem pole, knows that no day will go by without some kind of evaluation and hopes today will be the day to hear "You answered every question correctly on the test."

The evaluation of instruction requires a complex set of skills of the part of the teacher. It is an essential phase of the instructional process but a phase that can lead to inaccuracies and even abuse if not performed skillfully. This chapter examines some fundamental concepts of evaluation and suggests evaluation techniques that the supervisor should encourage.

PREASSESSMENT

Recall the boxes that represent the five-part model of instruction shown in Chapter 3. The third box has the label "preassessment" and the fifth box "evaluation." The model shows the feedback lines from evaluation to each of the other blocks: formulation of goals, formulation of objectives, preassessment, and implementation of instruction.

Terms other than *preassessment* and *evaluation* might be used, such as *preevaluation* and *evaluation*, or *pretesting* and *posttesting*. Whatever the terms used, both the third and fifth blocks of the five-part model of instruction are evaluation components. They are similar in that the teacher may use some of the same techniques to conduct a preassessment as to conduct the evaluation. They are different in respect to both timing and purpose.

As the name implies, preassessment takes place before instruction. The purpose of preassessing is twofold. First, the teacher wants to learn whether the students have already mastered the skills and knowledge planned for presentation. The teacher does not wish to perpetuate the arch mistake of elementary schools and force students to study Indians at every grade level. The scope and sequence of a curriculum should prevent this; however, students may well have mastered the content to be studied in other grades, at other times, and even outside the school. There is no sense requiring students to review and relearn content they already know, which is an evil that can take place when no preassessment is made.

Second, the teacher wants to know whether the students possess the requisite skills and knowledge to begin study of the material. The literature on instruction talks of entry skills or entry behavior. The lack of student entry skills is often apparent in programs that are part of a sequence. Students may enter into higher levels of the sequence (for example, fourth-grade language arts, sixth-grade arithmetic, second-year algebra, third-year French) without a sufficient level of mastery of the preceding skills and knowledge. The teacher must determine whether students are ready to begin the new study.

What *should* preassessment say to the teacher when the results are uncovered? First, if students do *not* know the content of the material to be studied, the teacher should be satisfied and permit them to encounter the material. If the students already have sufficiently mastered the content, the teacher should omit study of that material and move on to the next topic in the curriculum. Second, if students have the requisite entry skills, the teacher can confidently introduce them to the content to be studied. If they do not possess the necessary entry behaviors, remediation must be provided before students' encounter with the new material can begin.

The supervisor should encourage teachers to conduct a preassessment at the beginning of each unit. Preassessments can be conducted through the use of evaluation techniques such as teacher-made tests, standardized tests, or student essays; they can also be done with less formal means such as oral questioning and discussions. The supervisor should encourage teachers to go beyond the traditional forms of preassessment: prerequisite courses, grades in other courses, and other teachers' comments about the performance of students in their classes. The information from these sources may prove helpful, but there are no substitutes for teachers' own preassessment of learners' entry skills.

A favorite and commendable technique of teachers who conduct preassessments is the pretest–posttest. The terminal evaluation (posttest) is created at the beginning of the unit. Another version of the posttest is given to students as the pretest. Students take the pretest at the beginning of instruction and the posttest at the end of instruction. The teacher compares the results to see how much gain has been made during the period of instruction. If students have shown gain on the posttest, the teacher cannot always be sure that the gain has resulted from classroom instruction alone. The students may have picked up some of the skills and knowledge elsewhere, but unless the teacher is attempting to determine whether the instruction has alone made the difference, where students obtained the skills and knowledge is not paramount. The important fact is that they have performed at a satisfactory level of mastery on the posttest whereas they had performed less well on the pretest.

A pretest on the content to be studied may not reveal with certainty which entry behavior students lack. Consequently, further probing or testing may be necessary to pinpoint which entry behaviors must be learned before instruction begins on the new material.

The format of a unit described in Chapter 3 recommended that the teacher incorporate into the plan a statement of the entry skills necessary to begin study of the unit. This exercise forces the teacher to identify those skills and knowledge that the learners must have if they are to be successful with the ensuing content.

CONTINUING ASSESSMENT

A group of teachers, when asked why they assess or evaluate, would offer a variety of answers. Some teachers would say they evaluate so they may inform students of their progress in the subject. Others would say they evaluate to provide a basis for assigning marks. Still others would respond they evaluate so that they may send report cards home to parents and advise them of their children's work.

If asked what it is that they evaluate, they would likely again give multiple answers. Some teachers would say they evaluate the students' performance in class; others, that they evaluate students in relation to each other in the class. Fewer teachers state that they evaluate the instruction, the instructional procedures, or the instructor.

The process of evaluation may be viewed as assessing achievement of the objectives of instruction by each of the learners who make up a class. There should be a direct line from the objectives originally set forth at the beginning of a unit or course to the evaluation techniques before, during, and at the end of instruction. Evaluation seeks to determine whether students have mastered the objectives. The results of evaluation are also used to make necessary modifications in the instructional design. Whether the students achieve or not says something to the teacher about the effectiveness of the design itself and the effectiveness of the instructional procedures. When students fail to achieve the objectives of instruction, several hypotheses for this failure may be explored. It could well be that the students have failed through lack of effort, lack of study, lack of motivation, or combinations of these factors; but some reasons may be tied to the instruction.

- The objectives were not related to the task.
- The objectives were not clear to the learners.
- The objectives were not behaviorally stated and therefore not subject to accurate evaluation.
- Preassessment was poorly conducted.
- The teacher did not provide remediation before proceeding with the content.
- Resources were inappropriate or unavailable.
- Strategies were not appropriately selected.
- Content did not relate directly to the objectives.
- Continuing assessment was neglected.
- Terminal evaluation did not relate directly to the objectives.
- The teacher was ineffective in managing the group, keeping the members focused on the instruction, and presenting the content.
- Sufficient review of the material was lacking.

Evaluation should be thought of as an integral part of instruction, not an activity separate from instruction. For this reason, evaluation should always be present and continuing. In some manner, no matter how brief or informal, evaluation should take place every day with every lesson. The teacher wants to know not only how well students will perform at the end of a unit or course but also how well they have mastered each day's work. The supervisor can help teachers master a variety of formal and informal evaluation techniques that they can call on as the need arises.

Evaluation at the end of the lesson or day may be nothing more than several oral questions posed to the students by the teacher. It may be only silent observation of the way students tackle the work of the day. The alert teacher can tell by student actions and questions whether they seem to have understood and whether they are able to do the work. Calling for a summary of the day's lesson by students can be an evaluation technique. Daily reflections by the teacher about the instruction and learning that took place also can be very informative. Periodic progress checks during the course of the unit should be conducted to show whether the learners are staying with the teacher and what needs to be reviewed and perfected.

When evaluation is mentioned in a school setting, testing—largely of the paper-and-pencil variety—immediately leaps to mind. This reaction may be only natural as schools have traditionally administered paper-and-pencil tests, schooling is to a great extent cognitive in nature and assessment is most easily served by paper-and-pencil tests, and many teachers and the public are test conscious. Teachers devote a good deal of time to the construction and administration of paper-and-pencil tests; therefore, some time will be devoted in this chapter to principles of testing that the supervisor may wish to incorporate into an in-service training program. However, the supervisor must not overlook evaluation techniques other than testing, such as these:

- oral questioning
- observation of students at work
- portfolios
- oral and written reports
- evaluation of group work
- surveys and questionnaires
- attitude inventories
- evaluation conferences
- actual performance of skills
- self-evaluation
- anecdotal reports
- autobiographies
- projective techniques
- evaluation of class participation
- summaries and résumés

NORM-REFERENCED AND CRITERION-REFERENCED MEASUREMENT

Before proceeding further, we need some common agreement on the language of evaluation. As most teacher trainees are aware, many colleges and universities offer courses in tests and measurement or in measurement and evaluation. Unless the words in each pair of titles are redundant—a distinct possibility given the professorial penchant for embellishment—we must assume that each word in each pair signifies something different from the other word in each pair.

Although all three terms are related, *testing* is different from *measurement* and *measurement* is different from *evaluation* or *assessment*. In this text, the global concept is evaluation and is synonymous with assessment. Evaluation or assessment as it relates to instruction means the process of making judgments about specific aspects of a learner's behavior; it consists of a set of skills by which an instructor determines whether the learner has mastered the objectives established.

Measurement is a phase of evaluation during which the instructor quantifies instances of the learner's behavior; the quantitative data provide the teacher with a basis for assigning marks or grades—at least in the cognitive and psychomotor domains. A test is an instrument for measuring, for ascertaining the presence of expected behaviors and discovering the degree of mastery of those behaviors. Testing is the process of administering the test instrument.

The distinctions among evaluation, measurement, and testing are more than semantic ones and the supervisor will do well to explore these differences with teachers. The behavior of a learner can be evaluated without measuring; however, behavior cannot be measured without testing. In Chapter 3, we noted that it is not always possible to observe and to measure the achievement of objectives in the affective domain. We can measure mastery of cognitive objectives—at least learner achievement of these objectives can be sampled—and the presence of psychomotor skills can be measured; but in dealing with attitudes, feelings, interests, and emotions—the affect—it may or may not be possible to observe the attainment of these objectives. Less possible is measuring or quantifying the degree of mastery of affective outcomes. How enthusiastic must an attitude of enthusiasm be? How much willingness must the student show to earn a passing grade?

Attempts to measure and quantify the attainment of affective objectives exist in the form of personality tests and interest tests. More accurately, these instruments are personality inventories and interest inventories. Standardized inventories of personality and interest provide behavior norms for the groups that took the inventories. But these norms or standards should not be thought of as accurate measurements of individual behavior in the same way as reading skills can be measured and physical fitness demonstrated. With affective instruments, we encounter difficulty in attempting to label answers "right" or "wrong." The affective behaviors of an individual might be compared with socially stated norms. Those who do not agree with socially stated norms might be labeled "wrong" and those who do agree with them as "right." Failure to live up to middle-class norms might be called wrong, neurosis wrong, interest in illegal activities wrong, and racism wrong. The point is that these outcomes cannot be measured with any degree of certainty. There is no certainty that the socially stated norms are really the norms practiced by many—possibly even the majority—of the population, as Alfred Kinsey and later sex researchers discovered. In a 1991 study of behaviors and values held by Americans, Jim Patterson and Peter Kim discovered lack of consensus on values and respondents' admission of behaviors that depart from more traditional values often voiced in our society.[1]

What is possible in the domain of the affect is for the instructor to specify as well as possible objectives that he or she hopes to be able to observe in the classroom. Some of these objectives will not be visible during the time the learner spends with the teacher but may blossom in later years. Attitudes and feelings can be surveyed with various types of inventories asking for agreement or disagreement or for gradations of agreement and disagreement. Instructors may even, more or less, measure the achievement of affective outcomes if they are willing to accept a binary measure as a satisfactory indicator of presence or absence of the outcome. For those outcomes that are observable, they may evaluate their presence or absence with "yes, the outcome is present," or "no, the outcome is not present." They cannot use this crude measurement, however, to form a basis for marking students on the affect in the same way they rate them on the achievement of cognitive and psychomotor skills.

This discussion of evaluation of the affect is preliminary to observing that most of the measurement that takes place during schooling is assessment of achievement in the cognitive and psychomotor domains. Though we will return to the problems of evaluating and reporting the attainment of affective objectives, the major part of this chapter is devoted to the measurement of cognitive and psychomotor behaviors and to those aftermaths of measurement—marking and reporting pupil progress and achievement.

Norm-Referenced Measurement

In practice, schools use two different approaches to measurement: norm-referenced measurement and criterion-referenced measurement. Norm-referenced measurement is the historic approach to measurement in the schools. Both approaches to measurement weigh the student's achievement against some standard or norm. When following a norm-referenced approach, the instructor compares a learner's achievement with the norm of some group that was subjected to the same measuring instrument. That group may be and most frequently is the learner's own class. The teacher may, first of all, create a test, administer it, and score it, making judgments about individual performance relative to the performance of all members of the group. Using some mathematically acceptable statistical concept (see Chapter 8), the teacher determines an average around which the majority of scores cluster. Some students will achieve above that average and some below. The average group has, in effect, set the standard against which each individual's performance is compared. The average group may or may not have achieved the objectives specified at the beginning of instruction, and the teacher has the option to set the average on any given test as high or low as the group's performance seems to indicate. What the scores on a test may mean in terms of mastery of the objectives is not always clear.

If teachers administer the same test or equivalent forms of a test to successive groups of learners, they may over the years build up a set of standards or norms that show the performance of these previous groups. Teachers may then choose, as a second option, to measure an individual's achievement against these standards, called *local norms*. As a third alternative, teachers may choose to administer a standardized test, prepared and available from a commercial publisher. In this case, teachers compare the performance of their students on the test against the norms of the group or groups to which the test maker administered the test. These groups may be and commonly are groups far distant from the local scene and they may or may not be representative of the teacher's own current group of students. The standards achieved by these groups are reported as norms in the test manuals that accompany the test, and it is against these standards that the students' performance is compared.

As a fourth procedure, teachers may accumulate local norms on the standardized test and compare performance of learners in their current classes against the performance of previous learners on that same standardized test or equivalent form. Thus, teachers who follow a norm-referenced approach to measurement have four options as bases for comparison of student achievement:

1. The performance of all other individuals in the class on the basis of a teacher-made test
2. The performance of previous groups in past years to whom the teacher has administered the same teacher-made test or equivalent form thereof
3. The performance of groups to whom the standardized-test maker has administered the test
4. The performance of previous groups in the same subject in the same school on the same standardized test or equivalent form thereof

The key qualifiers of a norm-referenced system of measurement are *comparative*, *relative*, and *competitive*. Norm-referenced measuring compares learners with each other; its standards are relative rather than absolute; it recognizes degrees of mastery; and it encourages competition among learners. Our schools by and large have employed and championed the norm-referenced approach to measurement. This competitive approach to measurement has been espoused by the majority of the teaching profession, by the public at large, and, perhaps, though this is less certain, by the majority of students. The letter-grade system, A–F, discussed later, is an integral part of the norm-referenced system. The C grade represents a mystical (perhaps mythical) average. A and B reflect above-average performance, and D and F below-average.

The roots of the norm-referenced system lie in the statistical concept of the normal curve, which assumes that certain attributes such as intelligence are distributed among the population as a whole and the possession of these attributes can be depicted in the form of a bell-shaped curve. When a test of intelligence, for example, is administered to a large, random sample of the population, a mean score (the sum of all scores divided by the number of scores) may be determined. This mean score coincides with the median score (middle score) and the majority of those who took the test cluster around this mean/median score. Thus, it may be said, somewhat loosely and unscientifically, that a quotient of 100 determined as a result of dividing the mental age of a student shown on a test of intelligence by the chronological age of the student and multiplying by 100 represents average intelligence.

Of the four options that serve as bases for comparison of student achievement, the prevailing option has been the first one—comparison of an individual's achievement against the performance of all other individuals in the class on the basis of a teacher-made test. Because the performance of a particular group sets the standard, that standard may vary from section to section of the same subject and it may vary from year to year. The standard for a group that as a whole performed poorly may be lower than the standard for a group that performed well on the test. This is what is meant in saying the standards under a norm-referenced approach to measurement are relative.

The norm-referenced system can show how well students perform in relation to their peers and can provide data for assigning competitive marks. Because the nature of norm-referenced measurement is comparative and competitive, the norm-referenced approach must be used in situations in which screening individuals and selection are required.

Criterion-Referenced Measurement

Under a criterion-referenced system of measurement, an individual student's performance is compared not against the achievement of other learners but against the attainment of the objectives of instruction themselves. Following this approach, the teacher determines whether each student has mastered the objectives specified in the planning stage of instruction. The student either masters the objectives or does not. Once the student has mastered those objectives, the content is considered to have been passed and the next objectives are presented. If the student does not demonstrate mastery of the objectives, additional time for study and practice are needed.

The application of criterion-referenced measurement is seen most readily, perhaps, in the psychomotor domain. An elementary school pupil can demonstrate skill in tying shoes, writing letters of the alphabet, skipping or hopping, and using a crayon or marker. The secondary school student can show the ability to construct an angle of sixty degrees by using a pencil, paper, ruler, and protractor; type forty words a minute accurately on a word processor or an electric typewriter; remove, clean, properly gap an auto's spark plugs, and replace them; and chin on a horizontal bar ten times without stopping.

The application of criterion-referenced measurement in the cognitive domain is a little less apparent. On any test of cognitive outcomes, the teacher must set some level of mastery. For example, an objective in fifth-grade social studies might read: "Given a paper-and-pencil test on this unit, the pupil will achieve 80 percent mastery" (or will answer correctly eight of the ten questions). The 80 percent level of mastery is an arbitrary one set by the teacher after due reflection and consideration of what the group is likely to do. It may be based on the teacher's experience with previous classes. It is often overlooked in the literature of evaluation that levels of mastery on criterion-referenced tests are to a large extent determined by norm-referenced means. A level of mastery set on the basis of the teacher's experience with other groups at other times brings norm-referenced principles into play. Mastery in the cognitive domain, therefore, is somewhat different from mastery in the psychomotor domain. Mastery in the psychomotor domain represents the presence or absence of the particular skill. Mastery in the cognitive domain is revealed by an arbitrary percentage. Whatever percentage is set, even 100, represents only an approximation of mastery of the subject matter, for any cognitive test is only a sampling of the whole content. A score of 80 percent, for example, signifies that the learner has achieved a level of 80 percent on the test items that the teacher has chosen to put on the test.

As already noted, caution must accompany the use of the term *measurement* in respect to affective objectives. We believe that the attainment of affective outcomes may and should be evaluated, but these outcomes should not be subjected to statistical treatment, scoring, or marking with the traditional symbols of a grading system. The problem of reporting attainment of affective outcomes is dealt with in the section of this chapter on marking and reporting.

Criterion-referenced measurement has become an attractive alternative to norm-referenced measurement in recent years. The behavioral objectives movement, which has blossomed since the late 1960s, has given impetus to criterion-referenced measurement. Underlying concepts of this movement are a competency-based approach to instruction, self-pacing, and learning for mastery.

In discussing learning for mastery Benjamin S. Bloom, J. Thomas Hastings, and George F. Madaus clearly pictured the conflicting philosophical positions on measurement.

> Each teacher begins a new term or course with the expectation that about a third of his students will adequately learn what he has to teach. He expects about a third to fail or to just "get by." Finally, he expects another third to learn a good deal of what he has to teach, but not enough to be regarded as "good students." This set of expectations, supported by school policies and practices in grading, is transmitted to the students through the grading procedures and through the methods and materials of instruction. This system creates a self-fulfilling prophecy. . . .
>
> This set of expectations, which fixes the academic goals of teachers and students, is the most wasteful and destructive aspect of the present educational system. . . .
>
> Most students (perhaps more than 90 percent) can master what we have to teach them, and it is the task of instruction to find the means which will enable them to master the subject under consideration. A basic task is to determine what we mean by "mastery of the subject" and to search for the methods and materials which will enable the largest proportion of our students to attain such mastery.*

If teachers are teaching for mastery and students are learning for mastery, a measurement system must test for mastery. This situation implies a criterion-referenced approach whereby student achievement is compared to some standard of mastery of the content set by the teacher and not by group norms. State and local school district assessment programs have moved heavily into criterion-referenced measurement. Whether a student passes to the next grade level or is awarded a high school diploma is based in some states and localities on criterion-referenced tests. Some states and districts employ a combination of criterion-referenced and standardized norm-referenced tests.

Relation of Evaluation to Objectives

Evaluation begins with the statement of the objectives of instruction. Sometimes the objectives, which are stated in the form of learning tasks, are the test items themselves, as shown in the examples below.

- Define the words *cognitive, affective,* and *psychomotor.*
- Sight-read a musical passage.
- Balance a series of chemical equations.
- Compare the weekly cost of food for a family of four in different parts of the country and account for variations.
- Produce a documented research paper on the causes and effects of inflation.
- After studying several conflicting proposals for solving the country's drug problem, choose the proposal that seems to be the best solution to the problem, and state the reasons for your choice.

These six cognitive illustrations proceeded from the lowest to the highest levels of the Bloom taxonomy. Each objective is, in effect, a test itself, although the com-

---

* Excerpts from Benjamin S. Bloom, J. Thomas Hastings, and George F. Madaus, *Handbook on Formative and Summative Evaluation of Student Learning* (New York: McGraw-Hill, 1971). Reproduced with permission of The McGraw-Hill Companies.

plexity of each objective as a test is increasingly more involved as we go from the lowest order of knowledge to the highest order of evaluation.

In the psychomotor domain the following objectives may also serve as test items.

- Recognize a broken water pump in the automobile by the noise it causes.
- Demonstrate the proper way of holding the clarinet.
- Imitate the instructor's karate movement.
- Plant tomato seeds in a suitable container.
- Correctly operate a data-processing machine.
- Use traditional hula dance movements to express a story.
- Design and create a ceramic jar.

These psychomotor objectives are actually performance tests rather than verbal tests. The teacher can evaluate these kinds of performances by observing the learner in the act of demonstrating the perceptual-motor skills.

In the case of both the cognitive and the psychomotor illustrations given here, mastery of the objective can be measured. An acceptable level of mastery can be established by the teacher for each of the objectives. We cannot establish a level of mastery of affective objectives, however, for items such as these:

- Develop a sensitivity to the problems of the elderly.
- Enjoy reading historical novels.
- Express a positive school spirit.
- Judge persons of different ethnic groups as individuals rather than as groups.
- Develop the habit of collecting facts before making a decision.

Although some objectives in the cognitive domain may serve as tests of performance themselves, this is not always the case. The illustration "Given a paper-and-pencil test on this unit, the pupil will answer correctly eight out of ten questions" is not a test in itself. The teacher must carry this objective one step further and write the actual test items. The teacher may also have to refine the criteria for measuring accomplishment of some objectives. For example, the objective that calls for students to produce a research paper requires a statement of the bases for grading the paper, if the teacher wants more from the student than simply handing in a paper regardless of quality. The teacher may choose as criteria a minimum length, correct English usage, proper footnoting, and proper form for bibliography.

Many teachers—perhaps a majority—tend to write cognitive tests at the end of instruction. They wait to see what they have covered and then sample the content of that material. Experts in evaluation and instruction recommend the opposite—that teachers write cognitive tests at the beginning of instruction or early in the course. Some recommend that the terminal evaluation for a unit or course be written right after the objectives are written. The teacher would then have two tasks right after writing the objectives: preparing the preassessment instrument and preparing a preliminary terminal assessment instrument. Michael Scriven recommended the construction of a pool of test items in the early phase of instruction: "Even though the project is only at the stage of finishing the first unit of a projected ten-unit curriculum, it is entirely appropriate to be formulating questions of the kind that it is proposed to include in the final examination on the final unit or, for that matter, in a follow-up quiz a year later."[2]

By designing the test items before instruction starts or in the early phase of instruction, the teacher can more readily achieve consistency between the objectives and the test items. When the teacher waits until instruction is finished, some of the objectives specified at the beginning may be overlooked. It is not that the teacher must be compelled to accomplish every objective originally sought. The teacher may, anytime feedback is received, modify, add, or eliminate objectives. But there should be consistency between all remaining objectives and items on any final examination. The teacher and supervisor should not read into this discussion that a final examination on an entire course or a year's work is a must. The teacher may choose to administer a final examination covering only the final unit; but if the choice is made to administer a final examination covering the whole course, the pool of test items should be initiated at the very beginning of the course. In a like manner, if the teacher administers a final test on a unit of a program, construction of the test items should begin when the unit is introduced.

By starting the evaluation process at the beginning stage of instruction, the teacher can more readily conduct what Scriven called a "consistency analysis."[3] Scriven urged that there be consistency among the goals (i.e., objectives) of a course, the content of the course, and the pool of test items.

The supervisor should help teachers clarify the distinctions between norm-referenced measurement and criterion-referenced measurement and should point out the appropriate uses of each approach. The supervisor needs to help teachers define the meaning of *mastery* and identify ways of assessing it.

FORMATIVE AND SUMMATIVE EVALUATION

The literature on evaluation and research is rich with technical terms, some of which the reader will become familiar with in this text; others we leave to the specialists in measurement and evaluation. The focus of this text is on the needs of classroom teachers and the supervisor who works with them in carrying out evaluation for the improvement of instruction.

Two terms, *formative evaluation* and *summative evaluation*, have gained great currency in recent years and are concepts with which the supervisor should help teachers develop familiarity. Stripping the terms down to their essentials, *formative evaluation* as applied to instruction comprises those assessment procedures the teacher uses during the course of instruction, and *summative evaluation* those evaluation techniques the teacher uses at the end of instruction. In the cognitive domain, formative evaluation may be equated with progress tests and summative evaluation with final examinations. The reaction of many teachers to these terms may be "I've been doing that for years." What the teachers may not have been doing is refining the formative and summative processes to achieve maximum effectiveness.

An evaluation process is effective when the teacher can determine whether the learner has achieved mastery of the subject. The evaluation is less likely to show learners' mastery of the subject in the situations below.

- The teacher does not prespecify the instructional objectives
- The teacher does not relate test items directly to the objectives
- The teacher waits until the end of instruction to create the test items

- The teacher fails to capitalize on the results of formative evaluation and modify instruction
- The teacher writes tests that poorly sample the content and contain poorly written items.

Bloom, Hastings, and Madaus encouraged teachers to "break a course or subject into smaller units of learning" and to administer at the end of each unit "brief diagnostic progress tests," which they referred to as *formative evaluation*.[4] Though many teachers follow this practice, they often stop at this point and simply use the results of these progress tests to form part of the student's grade at the end of a marking period. Bloom, Hastings, and Madaus recommended frequent progress tests and saw their use as helping to "ensure that each set of learning tasks has been thoroughly mastered before subsequent tasks are started."[5] They described the purposes of these frequent tests:

> For the student who has thoroughly mastered the unit, the formative tests should reinforce the learning and assure him that his present mode of learning and approach to study are adequate.
> For the student who lacks mastery of the unit, the formative test should reveal the particular points of difficulty—that is, the specific questions he answered incorrectly and the ideas, skills, and processes he still needs to work on.[6]

Bloom, Hastings, and Madaus stressed the importance of using the formative tests for diagnosing learning difficulties and for prescribing what the student needs to do to overcome these difficulties. The authors took a position with which many teachers may not agree.

> We are of the opinion that formative tests should not be assigned grades or quality points. The tests are marked to show *mastery* and *nonmastery*. The nonmastery evaluation is accompanied by a detailed diagnosis and prescription of what has still to be done before mastery is complete. It is likely that the use of grades on repeated progress tests prepares students for the acceptance of less than mastery.[7]

They admit that there is limited evidence on this point, and certainly teachers who do use progress tests for the dual purpose of diagnosing and grading would not be remiss.

A major purpose of both formative and summative evaluation is to furnish feedback for redesigning the instructional model. Formative evaluation provides feedback for ongoing revision of objectives and instructional procedures, whereas summative evaluation provides feedback for later revision. Summative evaluation in the form of a final examination serves not only to provide a score that will be used in grading the learner's achievement but also to indicate changes that should be made in instruction with subsequent groups. Bloom, Hastings, and Madaus saw summative evaluation as less threatening to students if they have undergone frequent progress tests: "The student who consistently demonstrates mastery on the recurring tests should be able to reduce his anxiety about his course achievement."[8]

TESTING

Although tests may be described by the teacher as opportunities for students to demonstrate mastery of the content, to students they are usually distasteful hurdles, something to be tolerated as a part of this enterprise called education. Most students take testing in stride. Some small percentage of students even welcome tests as an opportunity to show what they know and as challenges to be met, but others regard each test as a traumatic experience. Certainly most students learn the power of tests in the early years of schooling and come to know full well the implications of performance on tests. These are the instruments that determine marks, scholastic status, promotions, entrance into higher levels of education, and employment. As the current expression goes, "They have consequences."

The impact of tests is readily apparent in any class. Having observed in countless classrooms of in-service and student teachers from the 1950s up to the time of writing this text in the mid-1990s, we can attest that tests remain the prime motivator of instruction at all levels. We have heard the teacher say thousands of times, "This will be on the test" or "Let's review for your test on Friday." It sometimes seems as if pupils are in a constant state of preparation with the test as be-all and end-all.

The supervisor might on some appropriate occasion with a group of teachers raise the question "Why do we test?" After the initial teacher reaction that this is an absurd question, the supervisor might start to get answers such as the ones here.

- To learn what students know
- To discover who are the best students in the class
- To discover who are the poorest students in the class
- To accumulate data for calculating marks
- To gather data to share with parents about their children's work

After some discussion it develops that teachers test

- To provide incentive for study
- To serve as a punitive device for controlling unruly classes
- To help students develop practice in the skill of taking tests

It may take some probing before the supervisor draws out responses like these:

- To learn whether the learners have attained the objectives
- To diagnose learning difficulties
- To appraise the effectiveness of instruction
- To judge the effectiveness of the teacher

The last response raises the specter of a concept in education today that is not too popular with teachers—namely, accountability. Historically, when students fail to achieve in school, the fault has always been assigned to the students themselves. It is said that they do not study, they are lazy, they are unmotivated, they don't have the proper background—any number of both legitimate reasons and rationalizations for learners' lack of achievement. Teachers in the past have been accountable for their teaching performance to their superintendent, principal, and school board, and in a rather indirect and vague way to parents and the public at large.

Today, the public has grasped the notion that learners' achievement is in direct relationship to the effectiveness of teachers as instructors and that some judgment should be made of the teachers' effectiveness. This has been an appealing concept to the taxpayers, who must foot the bill for public education and who in the past have had no reckoning of the effectiveness of their investment. Accountability implies that teachers are instrumental in the success or failure of students, and when students fail, teachers are as much or more responsible than the learners. Teachers' groups have resisted the accountability movement because they claim with some justification that they are unable to control all the variables that affect learners' achievements. They cite forces outside the school and sometimes years of educational neglect that are beyond the capacities of even the best instructors to overcome.

However, the concept of accountability cannot be completely eliminated. Most supervisors can attest that there are unsuccessful teachers as well as unsuccessful students. It is a fact of educational life that both effective and ineffective teachers are employed in the schools. The supervisor's primary task is to try to help ineffective teachers become effective ones.

One product of the accountability movement has been to make teachers more conscious of their responsibilities in respect to learners' achievement and to refrain from shrugging off learners' failure as completely the fault of the learner. Consequently, they strive harder so that their students will score well on both standardized achievement tests and on their own teacher-made tests. The norm-referenced approach to measurement in one way obstructs accountability, for by varying standards of performance some learners will always do poorly in relation to other learners. The concepts of criterion-referenced measurement and learning for mastery of content are compatible with accountability. If the objectives of instruction are clear and realistic, if content and methods directly relate to achieving the objectives, and if tests are designed to measure learners' attainment of the objectives, fewer students will do poor work. Bloom, Hastings, and Madaus reiterated the generalization that most students can master what we have to teach them.

> Thus, we are expressing the view that, given sufficient time and appropriate types of help, 95 percent of students . . . can learn a subject with a high degree of mastery. To say it another way, we are convinced that the grade of A as an index of mastery of a subject can, under appropriate conditions, be achieved by up to 95 percent of the students in a class.[9]

Success on tests, particularly standardized tests of achievement, has become more and more critical. Central to state reforms, efforts have been made to provide assessment of student performance at various grade levels. Along with statewide testing programs, some local school systems have set student achievement on criterion-referenced tests as one factor in the evaluation of the performance of both teachers and principals. Some school districts have responded to public accountability by publishing test results on a school-by-school basis, allowing the public to make judgments about the relative success of their children's schools.

The climate for school reform, brought about mainly by the dismal academic performance of boys and girls, has created a demand for parental choice of public or private school with governmental help to parents in the form of tax credits or vouchers for use at schools of their selection. Looming on the horizon in the mid-1990s is the development and administration of national examinations, once anathema to educators, but now much in line with current demands for accountability. Promoted by then President George Bush and the National Governors' Association (and reaffirmed by President Clinton), voluntary national examinations in English, mathematics, science, history, and geography at the 4th-, 8th-, and 12th-grade levels constitute one of six national goals supposed to be achieved between the date of their proclamation in 1990 and the year 2000.[10]

Standardized Tests

A fairly wide variety of standardized tests and inventories is available for use by school personnel. We can find standardized instruments to measure intelligence and achievement and to inventory interest, aptitude, attitude, and personality. Each of the tests comes with its manual of norms reporting the performance of the groups on which the tests were standardized.

The classroom teacher will have occasion to make use of some or all of these types of tests for general background information about the learner. If the teacher administers a standardized test, most likely it will be a test of achievement in a discipline. Other types of tests and inventories such as intelligence, interest, and the like are often administered by specialized school personnel and the results made available to teachers to help them plan instruction.

Standardized tests will be dealt with only briefly in this text for we believe them to be inappropriate instruments for measuring instructional objectives in particular classrooms and for serving as a basis for marks or promotion. Standardized tests of achievement do serve a very valid purpose, however, in permitting comparison of the local group's achievement with the achievement of the norm groups. It is helpful to the teacher to find out how well the students have done in comparison to groups elsewhere, and the data do provide some guidance to the teacher in terms of what content should be included in the scope of the program. Admittedly, it is good public relations to run an article in the local press to show the public that local students compare favorably with students elsewhere. The public is pleased when its students "measure up" to national norms and displeased when they do not. Though some schools attempt to squelch negative findings when their students score below national norms, in the long run it is best to report the situation as it is. This is especially true because test information is in the public domain and members of the media have access to the information.

As far as classroom teachers are concerned in the matter of standardized tests, they should know how to (1) select an appropriate standardized achievement test, (2) administer and score the test, and (3) interpret results. The supervisor should aid teachers in developing these skills and can direct them to catalogs of test publishers and to such standard references as *The Mental Measurements Yearbook*,[11] which contains reviews of various kinds of standardized tests and provides information on the reliability and validity of the tests as well as the adequacy of the norms reported and the costs. Manuals that accompany the tests describe procedures for administering and scoring them and for interpreting the results. Chapter 8 discusses some of the common statistical concepts the supervisor will wish teachers to be familiar with so that they may interpret test results.

Teacher-Made Tests

Each time a teacher feels it is appropriate to give a test, he or she must make a number of decisions. The teacher must decide whether to give a paper-and-pencil test or require the students to demonstrate actual physical performance of an objective; whether to administer a written test or an oral test; whether to administer the test to the group all at once or to students individually. If the decision is for written tests, the teacher must decide whether to give an objective test, an essay test, or a combination thereof. If a test is defined as a student's try at demonstrating achievement of specific objectives, oral and written reports or written papers may be substituted for objective- and essay-type examinations. The choices the teacher will make depend on the objectives students are to achieve and the nature of the content.

The tests must be an accurate reflection of what the teacher set out to achieve with the learners and what has been covered in the course. Therefore, the tests that accompany the textbook and other materials used in the instructional program should be used with caution. These published tests reflect the objectives of the author and not the classroom teacher. A test must reflect the objectives that have been taught by the teacher, not printed in the book. This caution extends to the use of computer banks as well, as illustrated by a chemistry teacher in a Central Florida high school who had a computer generate a twenty-five, multiple-choice-item test on a unit by selecting random items. The developed test did not contain a single item on the major topics that the class had studied for two full days. Oral tests are clearly called for in assessing a student's ability to speak in courses in speech and dramatics and in foreign languages. Both aural (hearing and auditory discrimination) and oral skills must be assessed in phases of instruction in music and foreign languages.

Both the actual demonstration of skills and tangible products of instruction must be evaluated in phases of the fine arts, business education, industrial arts, and vocational and technical education. No written report or paper-and-pencil examination can substitute for actual performance when the teacher wishes to know whether a student can create an attractive piece of pottery, take shorthand at a certain speed with a minimum number of errors, put paneling on the walls of a room, or swim the length of a pool.

When tests of actual performance or authentic assessment are to be used, teachers must make known to the students in advance what the criteria are that constitute a level of mastery of the particular skills. The time it takes to complete a job and the number of errors that will be permitted may be appropriate criteria. Qualitative judgments of a finished product are also necessary. A piece of pottery, for example, may be judged on such characteristics as originality, symmetry, size, finish, and color. The evaluation of tangible end products and psychomotor skills is more difficult than the scoring of paper-and-pencil objective tests. In some ways it is analogous to scoring essay tests. The task of evaluating both actual performance and essay tests is made easier and more reliable if teachers specify in advance the criteria they as experts will apply and communicate these criteria to the learners.

In all fields of study there are times when tests of actual performance may be more appropriate than paper-and-pencil tests and when oral examinations may be more pertinent than written examinations. Generally, the type of test the typical classroom teacher will use most frequently is the paper-and-pencil group test. Given the exigencies of mass education and the cognitive nature of most instruction, the paper-and-pencil, group variety of test is the most economical and practical solution to testing cognitive achievement. Individual tests, though highly desirable, are impractical except for certain diagnostic and remedial purposes. Individual conferences covering the content could conceivably be substituted for examinations, but however laudatory, they are too time-consuming to be practical. Lengthy written reports place too much of a demand on teacher time to represent a routine solution to the problem of assessing achievement. Nor is there sufficient time for either individual or group oral reports from all members of a class on all the content of a program. Consequently, teachers must resort to administering group, written tests as indications of performance in the cognitive domain.

Essay Tests. Two major types of paper-and-pencil tests are in wide use in the schools—the essay test and the objective test; these are also called the subjective test and the objective test. However, essay tests are not completely subjective, nor are objective tests completely objective: Subjectivity comes into play in the construction of both types of tests. In scoring these two types of tests, objective tests reduce the element of judgment on the part of the scorer and for that reason may be labeled objective.

If the supervisor provokes a discussion with teachers on the use of essay and objective tests, teachers will disclose attitudes from antipathy to essay tests to almost exclusive use of this type of test, and from complete rejection of objective tests to their exclusive use. What discussions of this nature sometimes omit is the recognition that the two types of tests serve different purposes. Although both types are designed to measure students' mastery of content, they do not have the same functions.

An essay test may measure a limited amount of content but in addition may evaluate a student's ability to write coherently, to organize thoughts, to describe situations, to make comparisons, to use English properly, to make applications of content, to demonstrate writing style, to summarize content, to cite research, and to elaborate reasons for positions taken. Essay tests sample a limited portion of the content, whereas objective tests sample a much wider range of content. An essay test may consist of only one or a few test items; an objective test may consist of many items. Some balance needs to be struck between essay testing and objective testing. Consistent use of objective tests from elementary school through secondary school can leave the learner deficient in sustained writing, a deficiency lamented by many college professors who receive the products of the high schools. Consistent essay testing would, on the other hand, leave instructors uncertain of the learners' breadth of mastery of content.

Essay tests are more difficult to construct than many teachers believe and they are certainly difficult to score. In the press for time, some teachers have a tendency to dash off both essay and objective test items. Such a practice is much more harmful in the case of essay tests than in the case of objective tests, for an objective test allows learners many opportunities to reveal knowledge of the subject whereas essay tests limit the number of items and therefore the learners' chances of demonstrating achievement.

Essay-test items should communicate to learners exactly what they have to do and what degree of mastery is considered an acceptable performance. A common and unsatisfactory essay-test item is seen in the example "Discuss current relationships between the United States and Japan." The supervisor might ask a group of teachers what is wrong with such an item. Those teachers who have had training in measurement and evaluation may quickly respond that the question is not specific enough. It does not indicate to the students what they must do to give a complete answer and to achieve maximum credit for the question. Unfortunately, far too many essay-test items are of this caliber. Even training in measurement and evaluation does not prevent teachers from writing inadequate essay items. Thus, there is value in a supervisor's calling for analysis of test questions, if only to serve as a reminder to teachers that it is possible to improve test items.

An interesting exercise that a supervisor may conduct with a group of teachers is to administer an essay item such as the previous example to the teachers and then ask teachers to score each other's answers. This is often an illuminating activity to many teachers, for if their experiences run parallel to those of other groups, the scores they have assigned to each other's answers will range from failing to outstanding, from F to A, and probably all grades in between. If the teachers are short of time or if the supervisor feels that answering a test item themselves will inject too much personal involvement in the exercise (for example, if individuals did not have sufficient command of the content called for), the supervisor may duplicate the response made by a student to an essay item and ask teachers to grade that response. We have on occasion used an editorial written by a school principal for the school paper for this purpose, and without any identification, the unnamed principal has consistently been graded from failing to superior.

This little exercise shows the unreliability of many essay tests. A test should yield the same score or close to the same score regardless of who scores it or when it is scored. A group of teachers should be expected to come up with the same or close to the same scores on a test item, especially if they are all experts in the field being tested. The unreliability of essay-test items can also be demonstrated when the same scorer grades the items at different times. A particular mood at a particular time can affect the grade the scorer gives a learner. Almost everyone who has ever taken essay tests has suffered at some time from this abuse. If an essay item is subject to such variation in its scoring, we cannot say that that item measures mastery of content. It measures only those aspects of content and learner behavior the teachers subjectively determine it to measure at the time they are scoring the item.

The example given could be sharpened and thereby made a more reliable item by expanding it and specifying what the teacher desires for a full answer. An improvement in the item can be made as follows:

- Discuss current relationships between the United States and Japan. In your answer state two points of agreement and two points of disagreement between the two countries. State what has been reported in the sources you have read to be the position of each of the following on the points of disagreement: (1) the president of the United States, (2) the prime minister of Japan, and (3) the U.S. Congress. Finally, state your own position on each of the four points of agreement and disagreement and the reasons for your position.

This revised version will help increase the reliability of scoring of the item. However, it will still not eliminate the problem, for some teachers will still score other behaviors in addition to the content called for. Some will grade spelling, grammar, style of writing, length of response, even handwriting. The teacher's prerogative to grade these additional behaviors is not in dispute; but if these behaviors are being graded, that information must be communicated to the learner as well as the relative weights to be assigned to each behavior.

A task of the teacher preliminary to any scoring is the construction of a key that outlines the points the learners should touch on in their answers. Constructing a key is a step many teachers short-circuit, and the absence of a key contributes to the unreliability of the grading. Without a key against which to compare a student's response, the teacher is liable to forget significant points that he or she is supposed to be looking for; without a key, the teacher can also be unduly swayed and sidetracked by students who write well or at length but who fail to include significant points of content. The supervisor could ask the teachers once again to score an answer to an essay question and this time supply a key to each member of the group to learn whether using it decreases the range of scores.

A student's chances of demonstrating mastery of content are improved when the teacher increases the number of test items on any given essay test. As a general rule, it is an unwise procedure to give an essay test consisting of only one test item. The more test items there are on a given test, the wider is the sampling of the content. A student may "bomb out" on a particular test item of which he or she has an inadequate command or which he or she has neglected to study, but additional test items can provide an opportunity for the student to demonstrate at least some degree of mastery. The single-item test induces unnecessary anxiety in the learner, who wonders whether he or she will be lucky enough to be able to respond to the item the teacher selects.

More test items will require shorter answers, which is not necessarily a bad feature. If a teacher wishes to test for sustained writing, an occasional or term paper that students do outside class may serve this purpose much better than an essay test. Let us illustrate a few variations of essay-test items, following the classification in Bloom's taxonomy of the cognitive domain. Essay-test items may be constructed for each of the six major categories of the taxonomy as the following illustrations show:

1. *Knowledge:* State the steps by which a federal bill becomes a law.
2. *Comprehension:* Explain in fifty words or fewer what message John Donne was conveying when he wrote, "Never send to know for whom the bell tolls, it tolls for thee."
3. *Application:* Briefly describe what is meant by the economic law of supply and demand and give three examples of the operation of this law in the American marketplace in the last five years.
4. *Analysis:* Contrast the characteristics of a developed nation and an underdeveloped nation by citing four ways in which a developed nation differs from an underdeveloped nation. Following your statement of differences tell whether you would classify each of the following as an underdeveloped nation or a developed nation: (1) United States, (2) El Salvador, (3) Thailand,

(4) Israel, (5) Great Britain, (6) Ethiopia. Select one additional nation of your own choice that meets the characteristics of an underdeveloped nation and describe efforts that nation is making to become a developed nation.

5. *Synthesis:* If you were the chief of police of this community, describe what actions you would recommend to reduce the number of automobile accidents in the community. In your answer show that you are familiar with principal causes of accidents and data on fatalities, injuries, and property damage from automobile accidents in the community.

6. *Evaluation:* A legislator of our state, which has no state income tax, proposed that an income tax of 2.5 percent on taxable income above $10,000 be levied. Evaluate this proposal as to (1) the need for such a tax, (2) possible uses to which the tax might be put, (3) effects of the tax on various socioeconomic classes of the state, and (4) likelihood of its acceptance by the people. Compare the benefits and disadvantages of the proposed income tax with the benefits and disadvantages of increasing the state sales tax from 5 to 6 percent.

The supervisor should encourage teachers to write full and clear essay-test items and to avoid the common, inadequate "Discuss. . . ." Generally some elaboration is necessary beyond the simple command to "discuss." Essay-test items can be given a particular twist by substituting other words for *discuss*, including *describe, compare, contrast, outline, analyze, apply, summarize, evaluate, state the reasons,* and *show the relationships*.

One final suggestion might be offered to teachers on scoring essay tests. When a test consists of more than one item, many teachers prefer to rate each item for all the papers before going to the next item. In that way, they avoid skipping around from item to item and are able to keep in mind the specific points they are looking for in each response. Essay tests have a definite place in the instructional process, but they must be carefully constructed and used for the purposes they serve best.

Objective Tests. Whereas essay tests sample limited content in depth, objective tests can sample breadth but not depth of content. The length of answers to essay-test items sometimes deludes the teacher into thinking that breadth of content is being tested. If a teacher wishes to test for knowledge of a subject, the supervisor should recommend an objective test as a far better instrument for this purpose than the essay test. The objective test can cover much more ground and can sample a field of study in a much shorter time.

A test is said to be objective if it eliminates a need for judgment on the part of the scorer. Any person—or a machine for that matter—should be able to take the key of an objective test and arrive at the same score as any other person. Consequently, the reliability of objective tests is much higher than that of essay tests. Subjectivity does enter into objective testing, however, in two ways. At the beginning, the teacher must make subjective decisions on which items to include on a test. The first step is to refer to the objectives and then analyze the content. Because each test at best represents a sampling of content, the teacher will incorporate only certain items of content in a test, deciding which are the more important items. Subjectivity can also enter into the process of scoring objective tests. There are times, for example, when a student will give a correct response to an item that is different from the response expected by the teacher. The wording or construction of a test item sometimes leaves the item open for judgment by the student and fails to elicit the response indicated by the teacher.

In their own way good objective-test items are as difficult to write as are good essay-test items. It is difficult but not at all impossible to write objective-test items that measure cognitive behavior above the lowest levels of the Bloom taxonomy. A fruitful exercise for the supervisor to carry out with a group of teachers is to ask them to bring in for analysis and discussion an assortment of objective-test items that have appeared on their tests. The supervisor must assure the teachers that the discussion and analysis will be carried on in a friendly, positive manner so that they will not feel threatened by the exercise. Through this exercise, the teachers will ordinarily come to realize that many of the items confine themselves to low-level cognition, many items are worded ambiguously, some do not relate to the unit or course objectives, and some call for obvious answers.

A collection of teachers' objective-test items will usually consist of at least five major types of items: (1) recall, (2) multiple choice, (3) alternative response, (4) matching, and (5) rearrangement. We will describe and illustrate each of these types of items and then apply the Bloom taxonomy of the cognitive domain to objective testing.

RECALL ITEMS. A recall item offers no choice of responses for the test taker and requires a direct answer that must be retrieved from the learner's memory. In its varied forms it is probably the most common type of objective item used, one of the easiest to construct, and the one that is subject to original answers if the teacher has not carefully structured the item. The types used most often are direct questions, commands, and statements to be filled in, which are also called completion items. The student's life is filled with both oral and written recall items in the form of direct questions that require short answers.

- Where did the Mayan Indians live?
- Who succeeded President Kennedy as president of the United States?
- What is the sum of 12 plus 9?
- What colors are found at the extremes of the color spectrum?
- When did Columbus first reach the New World?

To be an objective item, the question must yield a single or separate short answer. The direct question "Why did we fight in Vietnam?" would lead to an essay answer and would not be appropriate as an objective item.

Recall items may be structured as commands:

- Name the present U.S. secretary of state.
- Give the nickname of New York State.
- List three sources of protein in the diet.
- Translate the word *agricola*.
- Mention four contributions of ancient Rome.

Each of these commands can be responded to in brief form. No elaboration is necessary or wanted. The student must draw on his or her own fund of information to supply the correct answers.

Recall items may also be written as statements to be completed.

- The result obtained when we divide 12 by $1/2$ is _____.
- The chemical formula for table salt is _____.
- _____ is the name of the capital of France.
- "The Gift of the Magi" was written by _____.
- The fiftieth state admitted to the United States is _____.

Questions, commands, and completion are three styles of recall items. Note that all the illustrations call for low-level cognition—specific factual data. Note also that recall items reduce the chronic problem of objective items—guessing by the student. Naturally, students can guess at the whole answer but they do not have alternative responses presented that may suggest answers. An active command of the knowledge is necessary to answer recall items.

Subjectivity can enter into the scoring of recall items when the items call for more than one response. For example, one of the preceding illustrations asks students to mention four contributions of ancient Rome. Let us suppose the teacher expected the responses *laws, roads, aqueducts,* and *military weapons.* A student might respond *architecture, military tactics, language,* and *literature* as well as a number of other possible acceptable answers. In each case the teacher must judge whether the unexpected answer is correct, and if it is, give the student credit for it. If a teacher gets correct responses to an item that are different from the responses expected, the fault lies with the test item and not with the students. For this reason the teacher must exercise care to write items so that students will respond in the way desired.

Students' answers can sometimes contain surprises for the teacher if the teacher's test items are poorly constructed. The following example is an ambiguous item: "George Washington was born in _____." The teacher might be looking for the answer 1732 but might receive the answer Virginia, an equally creditable response. Would it help, assuming that a date is the expected answer, to write, "George Washington was born on _____"? Probably not, for the student could answer Pope's Creek Farm or February 22 or February 22, 1732. A real sharpie might answer February 11 or February 11, 1732, which was the actual date according to the calendar in use at that time. To avoid ambiguity, completion items sometimes must be cued, as "George Washington was born in _____ (year)," or written more fully, "George Washington was born in the year _____." The recall item must be directed to the specific response or responses that the teacher desires the students to make. A student who gives a correct answer regardless of where that answer has been learned should be given full credit for the answer.

The teacher will not, of course, give credit for frivolous answers, as *pest* instead of *German roach* or *German cockroach* in completing the item, "The common name for *Blatella germanica* is _____."

The supervisor should help teachers detect ambiguity in test items and suggest ways to avoid this problem by pointing out to them that the function of the test item is to determine whether the students know that particular item of content. Teachers sometimes inadvertently provide clues to the correct responses by varying the length of the blanks in completion items and by using *a* or *an* unwisely. If a student is debating, for example, whether to respond "Nile" or "Amazon" to the statement "The longest river in the world is the _____," the short blank would sway him or her to write the correct response and would be especially noticeable if subsequent completion items had blanks of varying lengths. All blanks on a completion test should be of uniform length to prevent students from guessing. Similarly, the correct answer might be suggested by the article *a* or *an* in an item such as "A house made of blocks of ice and inhabited by Eskimos is called an _____." If the student is conscious of language, he or she knows the correct answer must start with a vowel. An improved version of this item would be "Houses built of blocks of ice and inhabited by Eskimos are called _____." A single blank should always be used rather than a number of blanks equal to the number of words in the correct response. Would not the student be likely to respond "Saudi Arabia" to the item "_____ _____ is the nation in the Middle East that produces the most barrels of oil annually"?

Some measurement specialists recommend that the blank come at the end of the item. Although that format is desirable and perhaps most common, there may be times when the teacher wishes to vary it.

Though even objective tests should strive to measure higher levels of cognition, it is necessary many times to test for lower-level cognition. Recall items perform that function admirably.

MULTIPLE CHOICE. A multiple-choice test item provides students with a statement or question and a number of responses from which the student selects one or more responses according to the directions with the items. This type of item is favored by most teachers and professional test makers for its versatility and for its ability to sample content in a limited time. The multiple-choice item is subject to guessing to a much greater degree than is a recall item. However, compared to some types of objective items discussed later in this section the multiple-choice test item reduces the student's ability to guess the correct response. When there are four responses, for example, from which a student must select one, the chances of guessing are one in four; with five responses, one chance in five; and so on.

Multiple-choice items can be used in any cognitive field and may range from very simple to very complex in nature. They may be used to test for low-level cognition and for higher levels, as you will see later in this section. They come in a number of varieties, such as "Select the right answer," "Select the incorrect answer," and "Select the best answer." They may call for one response or many responses and they may require considerable thought, as anyone who has wrestled with responses such as "all of the above," "none of the above," "a, c, and d but not b" can attest. Let's examine a few of these items from a number of subjects.

12 + 4 = 3 +
a. 12
b. 13
c. 14
d. 15

Las gafas are
a. Gloves
b. Groves
c. Glasses
d. Gallons

Day: Night = _____: Black
a. Blue
b. White
c. Green
d. Red

Mark Twain is author of all the novels except
a. *Huckleberry Finn*
b. *Tom Sawyer*
c. *Pudd'nhead Wilson*
d. *Henry Esmond*

If $x = 2$ and $y = 4$, $2x + 2y =$
a. 6
b. 12
c. 4
d. 10

The opera *Madame Butterfly* takes place in
a. Italy
b. China
c. France
d. Japan
e. Spain

The formula for water is
a. H_2SO_4
b. H_2O
c. H_2O_2
d. HCl

The proper response a driver should make when his or her auto begins
to skid on ice is
a. jam on the brakes and slide through
b. throw the shift into neutral and coast
c. hold the wheel tight and keep steady
d. turn the wheel in the direction of the skid
e. turn the wheel in the opposite direction
f. step hard on the accelerator

A person with *savoir-faire* is
a. reticent
b. knowledgeable
c. impressionable
d. contagious

Note that for readability, each choice starts on a different line. We want to assess what a student knows or understands and do not want to confuse the person with choices that run together. For this reason, the ACT, SAT, and other tests use separate lines. Teacher-made tests should do the same.

More than likely, as the supervisor and teachers examine sample test items, they will find some common errors of construction. Analysis of these errors will suggest some guidelines, such as those below, that the supervisor may suggest to teachers to help them write multiple-choice items.

1. *As a rule of thumb, it is a good idea to provide at least four responses for each item.* The more responses there are, the fewer opportunities the student has for guessing. There comes, of course, a point of diminishing return in terms of time for pupils to read items and respond to them and in terms of actual space required to duplicate the items. A general practice is the use of four or five responses. Usually, multiple-choice tests will offer the same number of responses for each test item.

2. *The answers to a multiple-choice test consisting of many items should not follow a consistent pattern that the student can guess.* Although it expedites scoring if the answers are a, b, c, d, a, b, c, d, for example, many students can decipher the pattern and respond accordingly. The teacher wants to know whether the students have mastered the content, not whether they are good at breaking codes.

3. *Responses should all be the same or almost the same length and consistent in form.* For example, let's take the preceding Mark Twain item. Suppose it read this way:

> Mark Twain is author of all the novels except
> a. *Huckleberry Finn*
> b. *Innocents Abroad*
> c. *Pudd'nhead Wilson*
> d. *Call of the Wild*

Which response would you have made if you did not know the title of the novel Twain did not write? Chances are you would select *Call of the Wild*, which is different in form—four words instead of two, as in all the others. The tendency of the test taker is to select a response that is different in length or form from the other responses. If the different form is the correct response, the student may guess it and be rewarded for the guess. Dostoevsky sticks out like a sore thumb in the item below.

> *Crime and Punishment* was written by
> a. Capote
> b. Dostoevsky
> c. Lewis
> d. Doyle

The student who did not know would likely guess Dostoyevsky and would be right. On the other hand, the teacher may play the game with the student a bit and make one of the incorrect responses different, as shown here:

> All were famous generals of ancient times except
> a. Caesar
> b. Hannibal
> c. Cicero
> d. Scipio Africanus

If the student chooses Scipio Africanus because it is different in form from the others, the choice would be incorrect, as Cicero is the correct answer. The purpose of writing an item like this is not to trick a student deliberately; there is no trick, as these were all personages of history and Scipio Africanus was, indeed, a general. The teacher wants to reward knowledge and not the ability to guess.

The supervisor should encourage teachers to build up a pool of test items so they can mix them on subsequent testing. They should strive to create items with increasing complexity and those that test more than low-level cognition. Teachers who work within the same field of study can help each other critique test items and can even share items where applicable.

ALTERNATIVE RESPONSE. Alternative-response items, as the name implies, gives the test takers two choices from which they must select one. The most common form of this type is the true-false item, a much overworked kind of objective item. A major advantage of alternative-response items is their ability to sample an extensive amount of content in a short space and short time. Their major disadvantage is that students have a fifty-fifty chance of guessing correctly. Typical of a multitude of true-false items are the following, to which students would respond by circling the T for true or F for false.

T F   Thomas Jefferson was the third president of the United States.
T F $6 \times 9 = 54$
T F   The seasons of the northern hemisphere are the reverse of the seasons in the southern hemisphere.
T F   Leap year comes every other year.

True-false items can be made more difficult and therefore less objective if the student is required to state the reason for any false answer. Asking a student to state why an answer is false is a perfectly acceptable testing procedure, but the teacher will soon realize that this slows down the scoring process and often leads to the necessity for making judgments about the stated reason.

Alternative-response items may appear in forms other than true-false. Language concepts, for example, can be tested in the following ways:

(Its, It's) time to go.

The student may circle or underline the correct response or strike out the incorrect response. The teacher may simplify scoring by placing blanks after each item in a column and asking students to write the correct responses on the blanks.

The language arts teacher might ask students to tell whether the italicized words are prepositions.

	Yes	No
After he left, I found the note.	_____	_____
I saw *her* come in.	_____	_____
The man spoke *to* his dog.	_____	_____
I couldn't hear, *for* he had turned his head.	_____	_____

The pupil checks "Yes" if the italicized word is a preposition, "No" if it is not.

One of the vowel sounds of the English language is tested in this example of an alternative-response item.

Are the sounds of *a* in each of the following words the same as in the word *cat*?

	Same	Different
hat	_____	_____
hate	_____	_____
jar	_____	_____

had   _____   _____
hall   _____   _____

Alternative-response items hover around the low levels of cognitive learning, particularly with true-false items. The language arts illustrations at least move up to the level of application. True-false items seem especially easy to create, and as a result, the teacher stumbles into pitfalls—or it should be said the learner stumbles into pitfalls dug by the teacher.

A supervisor might collect or write examples of true-false items such as those below and ask teachers what the problem is in their construction.

T F   It is always cold in Alaska.
T F   It never snows in Florida.
T F   It is sometimes permissible in the United States to make a right turn on a red light.
T F   Every country of South America has Spanish as its official language.
T F   No country of South America has two official languages.

Discussion will reveal that all these statements have qualifiers that make it easy for a learner to guess the answer. This same deficiency can be found in the construction of other types of objective-test items. Words like *always, never, sometimes, every, all,* and *no* should be avoided. If the question cannot be restructured, it should not be placed on a test. The student already has a fifty-fifty chance of guessing, and the teacher does not want to give away the items.

Another common error is illustrated in these examples.

T F   Agriculture is the most important business of California.
T F   Watergate was the worst political scandal in U.S. history.
T F   It is warm in Hawaii all year round.

Each of these items calls for some judgment on the part of the test taker. Qualifiers like *important* or *most important* should be avoided unless they are clearly spelled out: Agriculture is most important in what way? Dollars generated? Number of persons employed? Number of people affected? Possibly, historians will judge Watergate to be the worst political scandal, but we did have the Teapot Dome and the Iran-Contra affair. By whose criteria is Watergate the worst or not the worst scandal? The example "It is warm in Hawaii all year round" may be designed to test knowledge of Hawaii's tropical climate but warm is a relative term. Warm to whom? How many degrees is warm? If anyone has been in Hawaii when the thermometer occasionally hits sixty degrees in February, he or she might wish for a touch of heat in the house.

Alternative-response items, like all objective items, must be clear. The double negative does not lend clarity to an item, as "It is not uncommon to find snow in Yellowstone National Park in the summer." The teacher should avoid involved, obtuse, and convoluted statements. They should be direct, clear, and precise and yield only one correct answer.

Because of the problem of guessing, alternative-response tests should not be used consistently or exclusively. When they are used, it is advisable to construct a test with a fairly good number of items. One additional guideline should be mentioned: By no means should the teacher copy statements verbatim from the textbook for tests. Students who are familiar with the text may remember the passages from the book and receive unwarranted help from this familiarity.

MATCHING AND REARRANGEMENT ITEMS. Matching and rearrangement items are two varieties of objective items that provide a little stimulation and challenge on the order of puzzles and make for good variation. Both are somewhat difficult to construct and both require more time to score than any of the three other types of items, with the possible exception of recall items. The matching-test item seeks to show whether students can recognize and pair up a specific stimulus with a specific response. A single theme runs through the pairs of stimuli and responses, as in the case of writers and their novels.

1. Swift   _____   *The Vicar of Wakefield*
2. Scott   _____   *Gulliver's Travels*
3. Carroll   _____   *The Forsyte Saga*
4. Goldsmith   _____   *Ivanhoe*
5. Galsworthy   _____   *Alice in Wonderland*
                    _____   *Little Women*

In this matching item, students write the numbers they find to the left of the authors' names in the appropriate blank to the left of the titles. To reduce guessing by the process of elimination the teacher should provide at least one more response than there are stimuli, otherwise if a student knows all the responses except one, the last response would be a "freebie."

In the next example, students are required to solve each math problem before pairing them.

           _____ $2 \div 1/2$
1. 54   _____ $21 \div 1/7$
2. 9   _____ $24 \div 2/3$
3. 4   _____ $12 \div 3/4$
4. 32   _____ $18 \div 1/3$
5. 16   _____ $8 \div 1/4$
           _____ $6 \div 2/3$

In constructing matching items, the teacher should take care that members of the pair are not opposite each other and that the correct answers do not form a pattern, as 1, 2, 3, 4, 5 in succession.

Rearrangement items test for knowledge of a particular sequence. If order is an important feature to the teacher, the rearrangement item fulfills this requirement. The teacher provides a statement or command and a set of responses out of sequence. The student must put the items into their proper sequence by writing 1 beside the first item in the sequence, 2 next, and so on, as in the next two examples.

Rank the states from 1 to 7 according to the latest U.S. Census population figures:
    ( ) Ohio
    ( ) Pennsylvania
    ( ) Michigan

(   ) California
(   ) New York
(   ) Texas
(   ) Illinois

In listing a book that has a single author in a bibliography there is a standard order in which items are written. Mark from 1 to 6 the order in which the items should appear.

(   ) city of publisher
(   ) number of pages
(   ) name of author
(   ) name of publisher
(   ) title of work
(   ) date of publication

Recall, multiple-choice, alternative-response, matching, and rearrangement questions all have their place on objective tests. They each have their distinct advantages and disadvantages. Students should be exposed to all types of items if for no other reason than for stimulus variation, which serves to heighten student interest.

The Bloom Taxonomy and Objective-Test Items

The question may be raised concerning whether objective-test items can measure achievement in the highest levels of cognitive learning. Let's take a look at some illustrations of objective-test items for each of the major categories of the Bloom taxonomy.

KNOWLEDGE

A synonym for lethargic is
a. cool
b. taut
c. slow
d. long

Of the planets listed, the one that is closest to our sun is
a. Pluto
b. Jupiter
c. Venus
d. Saturn
e. Mars

COMPREHENSION

The question "Do you mean American time or Latin time?" implies
a. North Americans have the custom of arriving late for appointments.
b. Latin Americans have the custom of arriving late for appointments.
c. North America lies in time zones different from South America.
d. Time zones in South America are the reverse of those in North America.

The moral of Daphne Du Maurier's short story "The Birds" is
a. People can triumph over anything.
b. Nature can get out of balance.

    c. Birds are vital to humankind's existence.
    d. Birds are rapidly becoming extinct.
    e. People should help their feathered friends.

APPLICATION

If a man loads 50 kegs of nails on a truck in 1 hour, to find out how many cases he could load in 8 hours you would
    a. subtract 8 from 50
    b. divide 50 by 8
    c. add 8 to 50
    d. multiply 50 by 8

Underline all the Spanish nouns that follow the regular rule for identifying feminine nouns.
    a. casa
    b. mano
    c. cosa
    d. mesa
    e. pelo
    f. pozo

ANALYSIS

The following sentence contains an error:
My friend Jimmy Lane don't know how to read.
The error is
    a. absence of commas
    b. use of the apostrophe
    c. agreement of the verb
    d. spelling of *friend*

The snake in the picture shown you by the teacher has all the characteristics of a
    a. king snake
    b. chicken snake
    c. coral snake
    d. milk snake

SYNTHESIS

Add the fifth step in the sequence of steps for multiplication on the pocket calculator that we used in class.
    a. Punch "clear" button
    b. Punch the number to be multiplied
    c. Punch the (multiplication) button
    d. Punch the number of the multiplier
    e. _____
    f. Read the product in the window.

A boy went into a store with 25 cents. He wanted to buy lollipops, which cost 3 cents each, and bubble gum, which costs 2 cents each. He decided to buy six lollipops and spend the remainder for as many pieces of bubble gum as he could buy. To find out how much change he would receive you would need to follow certain steps. Mark from 1 to 5 the steps you would

take to solve this problem in the order in which you would take them.
( ) Multiply 3×2.
( ) Subtract 18 from 25.
( ) Multiply 6×3.
( ) Subtract 6 from 7.
( ) Divide 7 by 2.

EVALUATION

Of the four test items that follow, select the one that meets the characteristics of a well-constructed T–F item as described in this text:
a. T F   It is not uncommon to find mountain streams that are polluted.
b. T F   Apples are the most important product of the state of Washington.
c. T F   Milk is the best beverage.
d. T F   Washington, D.C., is the capital of the United States.

The students will preview three films made for children. On the basis of criteria studied in class, the students will assign each film a rating of 1, 2, 3, or 4 stars (four is the highest rating). The rating for the first film is
a. one star
b. two stars
c. three stars
d. four stars

Although it is common and acceptable practice for both teacher-made and standardized tests to consist of a single type of objective-test item, as multiple choice, we would recommend as a general rule that teacher-made tests include a variety of objective-test items. Tests should be considered an instructional strategy. To use tests effectively as instructional techniques the teacher should score them and convey the results to the learner as rapidly as possible.

Some teachers have students use Scantron® or other optically scanned answer sheets to record their responses to multiple choice or matching test items. The Scantron® forms are similar to those used for standardized tests that require students to use a pencil and confine their responses to neatly filled in circles, ovals, rectangles, or squares.

A special machine is needed to scan, mark, and summarize responses given by each student. After the form containing the answer key is sent through the machine, the students' forms can be graded in a matter of minutes. In addition to learning how each student did on the exam, a teacher can have a composite made of all students' scores along with an item analysis of right/wrong responses.

EVALUATING AFFECTIVE OBJECTIVES

Earlier in this chapter, we observed that cognitive objectives may be measured by essay and objective tests and psychomotor skills by tests of actual performance. Standards of mastery may be set and observed for learning in these two domains. Judgmental kinds of decisions must be made for cognitive essay tests and for performance of psychomotor skills. In both these cases, the standards against which the cognitive and psychomotor performance will be weighed should be established beforehand, written down, and communicated to the test takers.

You will find it difficult or impossible to observe mastery of many affective objectives, and for that reason it is preferable to think of assessment of affective objectives as evaluation rather than measurement. Though we may administer instruments to assess attainment of affective objectives and even subject the results to statistical treatment, the assessment of affective objectives should be used for purposes other than marking and reporting in the traditional sense of marking and reporting.

The affective domain, which comprises feelings, emotions, and attitudes, may be assessed in a variety of ways. Among these techniques are the following:

1. *Observation.* Observation is the most common technique for evaluating performance in any domain. The experienced teacher develops skills in observing the performance of individuals and groups both in and out of class. Affective behavior is shown through comments students make in class, by their behavior in school and out, by the enthusiasm they show, and by questions they raise. The teacher may elicit certain kinds of behavior by placing students in particular situations, by asking them to role-play, and by posing controversial issues.

2. *Essays.* Students may be asked to write compositions that will reveal their feelings and positions on issues. The teacher may suggest personalized topics such as "My Favorite Subject in School," "The Worst Experience of My Life," and "What It Means to Be Cooperative." The teacher might also suggest topics that are more cognitive in nature but still designed to bring out attitudes of the learner, as "The Role of Welfare in Our Society," "Equal Rights for Women," and "Opportunities for Service in the Community."

3. *Opinionnaires.* Attitudes of students may be surveyed with alternative response items.

> Circle the letter A if you agree with the statement and D if you disagree.
> A D   Handguns should be outlawed.

Some teachers and professional inventories provide for a continuum of responses from "strongly agree" to "strongly disagree."

> Circle SA if you strongly agree, A if you agree, U if you are undecided, D
> if you disagree, and SD if you strongly disagree with the statement.
> SA A U D SD   The personal use of marijuana should be a criminal offense.

Attitude inventories may yield scores, but these scores should be considered simply compilations of responses to give a picture of the positions taken by individuals and the group (and not considered correct and incorrect responses).

To construct items and exercises for evaluating affective objectives, the teacher goes back to the objectives in the same way as for assessing objectives of the cognitive and psychomotor domains and tries to design assessment items that come as close as possible to showing whether the learner has met the affective objectives.

The supervisor should engage the teachers in discussion of ways to evaluate affective objectives and should raise questions such as "Which affective objectives should we seek?" "In what ways can accomplishment of these objectives be observed?" "Which affective objectives should be stressed over others?" "What shall we do with the results of evaluation of affective objectives?" "Are there any affective objectives that we should insist on for every student or do all affective objectives pertain only to the individual? For example, if a student believes that dishonesty is the only way to get along in life, should this attitude be of any concern to the teacher?" Evaluation of objectives in the affective domain presents problems quite different from evaluation of objectives in the cognitive and psychomotor domains.

OTHER EVALUATION TECHNIQUES

The major portion of this chapter concerns testing. Yet evaluation through means other than testing occupies a far greater portion of a teacher's time.

Observation of Class Participation

Although tests are not and should not be given every day, observation of pupil achievement, usually the most common evaluation technique, occurs daily. Most observation is informal and unstructured. Teachers gain impressions about the work of pupils in their classes. By carefully examining how pupils go about their work, the depth of their understanding of the content, and the quality of their questions and responses, the teacher can make judgments about their achievement.

The teacher is concerned not only with the pupils' achievement but also with their participation—how they interact with each other and with the teacher. Some other student behaviors the teacher looks for are attentiveness and interest shown, frequency with which pupils participate, and responsiveness. If active class participation by all class members is a goal, the teacher can devise a systematic way of observing and evaluating class participation. The rating instrument shown in Figure 6.1 is one means of providing subjective individual feedback to the pupil on class participation as judged by the teacher.

Oral Reports

Oral reports by individuals, committees, panels, and the like provide the teacher with another way to assess student performance. The teacher should provide pupils who are to present oral reports with the criteria against which they will be rated. Common standards include clarity of presentation, correct language usage, supporting data, enunciation, and evidence of preparation. Both individual and group oral reports can be rated by using instruments such as those shown in Figures 6.2 (page 260) and 6.3 (page 261). Whenever evaluation instruments are used, the teacher should make the results known to the pupils so they may improve their future presentations.

Written Assignments

As common as oral reports are written assignments of varying types, from a set of problems to be worked or questions to be answered to brief compositions to research papers. In each case, the teacher should provide the learners in advance with a set of standards by which the work will be judged. For routine written homework, that standard may simply be completion of the assignment, for it is impossible for teachers to grade all written assignments. On the other hand, the teacher must take the time to grade major written assignments and report the results to the learners.

Portfolio Assessment

Portfolio assessment calls for a collection of student work samples that demonstrate achievement of objectives. Portfolios have been used by art teachers for some time. Teachers in other areas now collect samples of student work. The examination of samples of work the students have assembled in portfolio form helps the teacher to determine whether students have achieved planned objectives. The teacher may wish to place value on the work samples, based on announced criteria, and may calculate their value along with tests in the assignment of a grade.

In some instances the items placed in a student's portfolio have been prescribed by the state or local school district. Teachers often have opportunities to suggest which items would reflect an accurate portrayal of student achievement. In some cases, where some latitude and encouragement exists, teachers allow students to select items to be included in their portfolios.

EVALUATION OF CLASS PARTICIPATION

Student:_____ Date: _____

CHARACTERISTIC	A Excellent	B Good	C Fair	D Poor	F Failing
Attentiveness and interest shown					
Frequency of participation					
Merit (quality) of answers and questions raised					
Extent of volunteering					
Contributions of significant anecdotes, illustrations, and facts to assist in topics under discussion					

Comments:

Composite Grade: _____

Figure 6.1. Evaluation of Class Participation. *Adapted from Peter F. Oliva,* The Secondary School Today, *2nd ed. (New York: Harper & Row, 1972), p. 528.*

One important asset of a portfolio is in self-evaluation. Portfolio assessment offers students a way to take charge of their learning; it also encourages ownership, pride, and high self-esteem. We have worked with elementary education interns who have assembled a class portfolio that was a composite of works reflecting the students' achievements of the district's goals. The composite portfolio contains information that can be used for program assessment. Portfolios further provide an opportunity for parents to view samples of their children's work.

Creative Assignments

Creative assignments such as scrapbooks and artwork give evidence of certain types of learning. Many of the areas of the curriculum offer opportunities for pupils to create some tangible products that demonstrate various skills and knowledge. Whether each of the creative assignments is to be graded, pupils must know in advance the criteria on which they will be judged.

Group Work

When pupils work on assignments in groups, efforts should be made by the teacher and the members of the group to evaluate their work as a group. Evidence should be obtained concerning how effectively each member of the group carried out individual responsibilities. From time to time, it is possible and desir-

---

INDIVIDUAL ORAL PRESENTATION OR REPORT

Student: _____ Date: _____

CHARACTERISTIC	Low 1	2	3	4	High 5
The speaker was prepared.					
The speaker's presentation was clear to the listeners.					
The speaker's voice was audible.					
The speaker's voice was not monotonous.					
The speaker's language usage was correct.					
The speaker was animated and enthusiastic.					

Comments:

Composite Grade: _____

Figure 6.2. Individual Oral Presentation or Report. *Adapted from Peter F. Oliva,* The Secondary School Today, *2nd ed. (New York: Harper & Row, 1972), p. 533.*

GROUP ORAL PRESENTATION OR REPORT

Group Members: _____

_____

CHARACTERISTIC	Low 1	2	3	4	High 5
There was evidence of preparation in respect to content.					
There was evidence of preparation in respect to organization and presentation of the material.					
All the students in the reporting group had the opportunity to participate in the report					
All the students spoke audibly.					
All the students used language correctly.					

Comments to the group:

Composite Grade: _____

Figure 6.3. Group Oral Presentation or Report. *Adapted from Peter F. Oliva,* The Secondary School Today, *2nd ed. (New York: Harper & Row, 1972), p. 534.*

able for the class to participate in evaluating the work of individuals and groups in the class. This technique requires the teacher to lay certain ground rules for students' evaluation of the performance of other students. They must be taught to do so in a positive, constructive way. Figure 6.4 (page 262) is an example of an instrument that permits pupils to evaluate their own work as members of a committee or group.

This particular instrument uses the letter grading system. Should the teacher not wish to couple the evaluation with letter grades, a numerical scale or categories such as excellent, very good, good, fair, and poor could be used.

Self-Evaluation and Joint Evaluation

A total evaluation plan should include opportunities for pupils to develop the skill of evaluating their own performance. Pupils can benefit from sharing their own perceptions of their work with the teacher. Not that the pupils' self-evaluations would substitute for the teacher's evaluation of their work nor ultimately determine a mark, but the self-appraisals would provide the teacher with a type of information often otherwise missed and with clues for assisting individual students. Pupils—particularly those at the secondary school level—might be asked to rate themselves on such criteria as their performance on tests, quality and regularity of homework, partici-

---

SELF-EVALUATION FOR COMMITTEE MEMBER

Please rate yourself on each of the following phases of your committee's work by encircling the appropriate letter.

PLANNING   (Extent of your participation in planning sessions)

A   B   C   D   F

Rationale for this rating:

PREPARATION   (Library research, search for materials, committee work outside of planning and class sessions)

A   B   C   D   F

Rationale for this rating:

TEACHING   (Performance during class periods devoted to your topic)

A   B   C   D   F

Rationale for this rating:

Composite Grade: _____
                 Write A, B, C, D, or F

Student: _____   Date: _____

Figure 6.4. Self-Evaluation for Committee Member. *Adapted from Peter F. Oliva,* The Secondary School Today, *2nd ed. (New York: Harper & Row, 1972), p. 537.*

pation in class discussions, participation in a small group, effort expended, cooperation with teacher and fellow pupils, ability to listen, and conduct in class. It can prove helpful to discover how realistic students' perceptions are of their own work and how far apart are their appraisals and the teacher's appraisal of their work.

A self-appraisal instrument can be designed that reflects the various criteria the teacher deems important. It can be made into a joint evaluation process, which would necessitate appraisal conferences with each pupil. The form could be completed independently by the student and teacher, shared at a conference, and a composite evaluation jointly determined. Such an instrument is shown in Figure 6.5.

A key characteristic of cooperative learning models is performance of the group as a whole. Teachers can provide some mechanism for group members to assess their performance as a group. Figure 6.6 enables the teacher and group members,

```
┌─────────────────────────────────────────────────────────────────────┐
│                  JOINT EVALUATION OF STUDENT ACHIEVEMENT              │
│                                                                       │
│  Student: _____  Date: _____  │
│                                                                       │
│  Teacher: _____  Subject: _____  Period: ___ │
│                                                                       │
│  Place an A, B, C, D, or F in each blank.                             │
│                                                                       │
│                                      Student's      Teacher's         │
│                                      Appraisal      Appraisal   Weight │
│  Achievement (tests)                 _____      _____    2/6   │
│                                                                       │
│  Quality of written assignments (homework,  _____  _____  1/6 │
│  class work, research papers, term reports,                           │
│  book reports)                                                        │
│                                                                       │
│  Preparation for class               _____      _____    1/6  │
│                                                                       │
│  Assigned readings (completed, understood)  _____  _____  1/6 │
│                                                                       │
│  Participation in class discussions (value of  _____  _____ 1/6 │
│  contributions, frequency, attentiveness)                             │
│                                                                       │
│  Comments:                                                            │
│                                                                       │
│                              Composite Grade: _____ │
└─────────────────────────────────────────────────────────────────────┘
```

Figure 6.5. Joint Evaluation of Student Achievement. *Adapted from Peter F. Oliva,* The Secondary School Today, *2nd ed. (New York: Harper & Row, 1972), p. 537.*

```
┌─────────────────────────────────────────────────────────────────────┐
│                  INDIVIDUAL EVALUATION OF GROUP'S PERFORMANCE         │
│                                                                       │
│  Group Members: _____ │
│                                                                       │
│  Title: _____  Date: _____  │
│                                                                       │
│                                                    YES        NO      │
│  1. Group members mastered the specified objectives.  _____    _____  │
│  2. The group remained on task.                       _____    _____  │
│  3. The group used time efficiently.                  _____    _____  │
│  4. The group met established deadlines.              _____    _____  │
│  5. The group organized its work efficiently and fairly. _____  _____ │
│  6. Group members made positive contributions.        _____    _____  │
│  7. Group members fulfilled their responsibilities.   _____    _____  │
│  8. Group members helped each other.                  _____    _____  │
│  9. Group members presented a quality finished product. _____  _____  │
│                                                                       │
│  Comments:                                                            │
│                                                                       │
└─────────────────────────────────────────────────────────────────────┘
```

Figure 6.6. Individual Evaluation of Group's Performance. *Adapted from Peter F. Oliva,* Supervision for Today's Schools, *4th ed. (New York: Longman, 1993), p. 203.*

each rating separately, to assess the *group's* performance. The ratings can be a simple Yes or No; letter or numerical symbols; or words such as excellent, good, and so on. In all cases, as you will see in the next section on marking, when symbols are used, they must be defined. Items on any evaluation form for student use must be tailored to the maturity level of the students.

The teacher may elect to ask students to sign the evaluation, which provides some insights into the attitudes and skills of the evaluator as well as the group's performance. The teacher may wish to make a composite summary of the members' evaluations and share that summary as well as his or her own with the group. Whether students sign the evaluations or not, individual evaluations should not be shared with the group.

Theoretically, teachers can devise an instrument by which members of a group can rate each other's performance. We do not advocate such a process because negative results from one's peers—some young people can be harsh critics—can be too destructive of the ego and serve to discourage rather than motivate learners. Peer evaluations, even if used with adults, must be structured, conducted, and controlled with great caution.

Although testing may occupy a prominent place in the instructional program, the teacher should not rely exclusively on testing as a means of evaluation. Some of the outcomes of education cannot be assessed by ordinary testing. The teacher's evaluation skills should include more than expertise in the construction and administration of essay and objective tests and should include a variety of techniques other than testing. When the supervisor discovers that teachers need to develop their evaluation skills, some in-service training is in order.

Pop quizzes, book reports, and countless other devices can be part of a total formal assessment program. It is wise to remember that frequent and multiple assessment opportunities enhance the learning process.

MARKING STUDENT ACHIEVEMENT

At the end of each marking period every teacher engages in a pseudoscience known as *marking*. Marking, or *grading*, as it is also called—a concept that conjures up visions of a steamroller leveling a road—has all the appearance of a science. Teachers administer tests, collect data, subject the data to statistical treatment, and finally come up with a symbol—the letter grade. They place that grade on some sort of reporting form and give it to the student and parents. The school divides its years into a number of marking periods, and teachers repeat the grading process at the end of each marking period and wrap up student achievement in one symbol that represents performance for the year. The most common system of grades, particularly at the secondary school level, is a five-letter system: A, B, C, D, F. We know that the student who receives an A will be a much happier person than the student who receives an F. If a student or parents ask a teacher what a given symbol means—say a B—some teachers will give answers akin to Humpty Dumpty's line in *Through the Looking Glass*: "It means just what I choose it to mean."

Assume for a moment the role of the mathematics department head in a secondary school that has no consistent policy on marking—that is, on grading practices—and leaves such decisions entirely in the hands of each individual teacher. This department head is concerned about the grading practices among the teachers of the department. At the end of the current marking period, she made the rounds of the six teachers' classrooms and discovered a variety of practices, including these:

- A teacher adding up all numerical scores compiled by each student during the marking period, dividing by the number of scores, determining the mean or average score, then converting the scores to letter grades based on an arbitrary scale: A = 95–100; B = 85–94; C = 75–84; D = 65–74; F = scores below 65
- A second teacher fitting grades to a modified normal curve with a few A's, a few F's, a larger number of D's, and the majority of grades B's and C's
- Third, a teacher who gave only A's and B's
- A fourth teacher who gave F's to two-thirds of the class
- Another teacher who gave every student an A
- The sixth and last teacher, who based grades exclusively on written tests

The inconsistencies in grading practices among teachers in the same department leads the department head to open a discussion with the teachers during one of their joint planning periods. The department head asks the teachers to consider two questions: What are the purposes of grading? On what guidelines can we as a group agree?

A group of elementary school teachers would be in agreement with this group of high school teachers if the high school group saw the reasons listed here as the purposes of a grading system:

- Reporting to pupils how well they have done during the marking period and at the end of the year
- Reporting to parents of the pupils how well their children have done in the subject
- A means for deciding on students' promotions to the next grade level
- A way of motivating students
- A means for deciding which students' names will be placed on the honor roll

A group of high school teachers might also state the purposes of marking as

- Reporting to employers and colleges (This purpose is often paramount with high school teachers.)
- Deciding on graduation and awards at graduation

Grading is a serious business with both teachers and students. Learners are conditioned from the day they set foot in the school to know that grades—regardless of the symbols used, be they pass–fail, satisfactory–unsatisfactory, 0 to 100 percent, or A–F—are important. Both teachers and parents have pushed students to bring home grades as high as possible. Parents often pay their children for each A they bring home. And it is far too common that marks produce conflict between parents and their children, particularly when parents lack patience and understanding of their children's difficulties. Teachers, students, and parents alike see tangible and intangible rewards stemming from high grades. For this reason marks do serve as motivators for many children, and conversely they serve as sources of frustration and despair for those students who do not or cannot achieve at least passing standards.

The responsibility for grading is a real form of power that teachers exert over learners. Conscientious teachers spend many anguished moments during their teaching careers over the grades assigned to students. They recognize the pressure marks put on students and seek by every means possible to make each grade a fair and just approximation of achievement. But no matter how scientific the process of grading may appear, grades are at best approximations of achievement. Every mark given by a teacher calls for a judgment, which is sometimes based on very limited evidence. Unfortunately, given the premium on marks, the symbols themselves have become for many students more important than the achievement that the marks are supposed to represent.

All marking systems have certain innate problems, some of which are seeds for controversy among teachers and between teachers and the public. It would be a most rewarding in-service activity if the supervisor could lead the teachers to consensus on certain practices they will follow in implementing the marking system of their school. There needs to be resolution and common agreement on such issues as these:

- Shall grades be based on mastery of content (criterion-referenced) or on comparative achievement of learners (norm-referenced)?
- How much evidence is needed for determining a grade?
- What factors should be considered in arriving at a grade in subject matter achievement?
- Should grading practices in homogeneous classes differ from grading practices in heterogeneous classes?
- Should achievement in the affective domain be evaluated and reported? If so, how?
- What do letter grades mean?
- What score constitutes passing a test? A marking period? A course? A grade level?
- Should a student's ability be considered in assigning a mark?
- Should a student's effort be considered in assigning a grade?
- Should a student's deportment be considered in assigning a grade?

Should affective behaviors (positive and negative) outside of class affect marks in a discipline?

Is it justifiable for some teachers to be "easy graders" and others "hard graders"?

A heated argument can be started among teachers on any of the foregoing questions. Teachers customarily base their practices not only on empirical data but also on philosophical premises they hold concerning the learner, the learning process, and society. By sharing their beliefs, teachers may come to modify their views and reach some common understandings. The supervisor should strive to obtain consensus among teachers on a few basic principles of marking:

1. *Marks should reflect as nearly as possible mastery of content.* As Bloom, Hastings, and Madaus pointed out, most learners in school can learn most of the content if they are properly placed in school to begin with and if instruction is skillfully implemented.[12]

2. *A multitude of evidence is necessary for determining a grade.* Success at any level or in any program should not rest on a single examination or a couple of tests. A variety of evaluation techniques should be employed, and repeated opportunities should be provided for the learners to demonstrate achievement.

3. *The meaning of each letter symbol should be defined in behavioral terms and those meanings communicated to students and parents.* Whatever factors teachers consider in assigning grades should be made known, and no factors that are not communicated should be considered.

4. *Marks in a discipline should reflect subject matter achievement. Extraneous behaviors in class or out should be recognized by means other than marks in the subject.* A frequent and often subliminal abuse of this principle is found in situations in which teachers consider a student's conduct in class and penalize him or her for misbehaving by reducing the mark in subject matter achievement. Sometimes teachers engage in the dubious practice of offering "extra credit" for good deeds such as contributing food to a charitable organization or even attendance at school functions.

5. *In schools that have set up a competency-based education program the faculty must decide what letter grade represents satisfactory attainment of minimal competencies at each grade level and in each course.* Whether students are grouped heterogeneously or, with decreasing frequency, homogeneously for learning, the minimal grade for satisfactory achievement of the prescribed minimal competencies should be, in our estimation, equivalent to a B. We are really dealing here with two conflicting systems when competency-based education is superimposed on an A–F letter-grade system. Competency-based education is really binary in nature. You master the competencies or you don't. Thus, we are dealing with a situation that begets satisfactory–unsatisfactory, pass–fail, or A–B. Because many students, teachers, and parents regard a C grade, supposedly average, as unsatisfactory work, C will not suffice as the grade for achievement of the minimal competencies. If B is the grade for acceptable performance on minimal competencies, there is still latitude for brighter or more industrious or more motivated students to perform at a higher level and attain A grades.

6. *Symbols for marking and reporting conduct, attitudes, personal habits, and other affective outcomes should be different from the symbols for reporting achievement in the cognitive and psychomotor domains.* We make no brief for any particular set of symbols. In practice, secondary schools have tended to stick with the A–F system for marking cognitive and psychomotor achievement, whereas elementary schools have frequently used two- or three-point systems such as satisfactory (S), unsatisfactory (U), or S,U, and N (needs improvement). If affective objectives are evaluated and reported—and we believe some of them should be—other letters or numbers should be used for this purpose. A three-point scale such as 1, 2, 3, or H (high), M (moderate), L (low) is a feasible alternative.

7. *Whatever measures teachers can take to reduce or remove the threatening nature of marks should be taken.* They can reduce the stress placed on tests and marks and report cards and help learners to adjust to them more easily. Teachers sometimes contribute to students' low marks by the manner in which they emphasize tests. A little positive set induction when administering a test can reduce students' anxiety and help them develop a sense of confidence.

Marking practices can serve the purposes for which they were intended if a careful set of guidelines is developed and put into practice. Improper marking practices can serve as a continuing source of conflict between students and teachers and between parents and teachers. Supervisors need to assist faculties in developing sound marking systems.

REPORTING STUDENT ACHIEVEMENT

Sooner or later the inevitable happens. Each student receives a piece of paper with the symbols that announce how well or how poorly he or she has done in school for that particular marking period. In theory, the report card is meant to communicate to parents the progress and achievement made by the learners. In practice, a report card by itself tells parents very little. It tells nothing about the process by which the teacher decided on the grade. If a student brings home low grades, the report card does not reveal why the student's grades are low or what the student must do to bring the grades up.

Over the years, schools have experimented with a variety of report cards and varying procedures for handling them. Some schools mail cards directly to the home instead of sending them with the pupils. Some secondary schools use single cards for reporting all subjects whereas other schools use individual report forms for each subject. Some reporting forms consist of only a single card; others are made of multiple copies. Some are handwritten by the teacher and some are machine processed. Some provide space for teachers' comments, and others add space for parents' comments. Some cards must be returned to the school, and other report forms are kept at home. If report cards have any common characteristic, it is the inadequacy of information supplied and of the interpretation of the meaning of the symbols used. True, there are often words or phrases that seek to interpret the grades, such as "A means excellent work," "C is average work," and so on. But these words tell little more than the letter grade itself.

Unfortunately, teachers are locked into the reporting system, and it requires lengthy and concerted action on the part of a total faculty in conjunction with the community to make a change. There are, however, ways to make the reporting system more meaningful and informative: First, teachers might supplement the limited information on the report card with a narrative report of student progress. In the narrative the teacher can point out areas in which the student does well and areas in which the student needs improvement. The narrative form of reporting has been popular with elementary school teachers and has, in fact, supplanted other types of reporting in some elementary schools. With the large number of students taught by secondary school teachers, a narrative for every student, though ideal, would be impractical. The secondary school teacher might reserve the narrative for students who have done something exceptionally well and for those students who are having particular difficulty. The secondary school teacher may take advantage of space on those reporting forms that provide for teacher's comments. Elementary, middle, and secondary school teachers should be willing, and in many instances are required, to supplement the reporting system with parent conferences.

Second, the school might, as many schools have done, adopt the practice of sending home interim or progress reports during the marking period instead of waiting until the end of the period to report to parents. If parents know in enough time that their children are doing poor work in school, they may be able to work with them and help them to improve. If the numbers of students preclude progress reports for each student, interim reports could be sent out only when students are having difficulty, their grade in the course has dropped, or they appear in danger of failing the course or grade.

Third, the teacher should regularly counsel students on their work, make suggestions for improving, and listen to difficulties students are having.

These supplements to the report card can go a long way toward enabling both students and parents to understand what the symbols on the cards mean, where the learners are having problems, and what the students must do to achieve mastery of the content. Supervisors need to help faculties analyze and improve their reporting systems.

SUMMARY

Evaluation is conceived as an integral part of the instructional system. The main purpose of evaluation is to determine whether students have met the prespecified objectives.

The process of evaluation begins with preassessment of entry skills students must exhibit to pursue the subject successfully. Formative evaluation should be conducted to check learners' progress during a unit, and summative evaluation should assess terminal behaviors.

Testing is one of the tools for assessing cognitive and psychomotor objectives. The teacher customarily makes use of two types of tests: essay and objective. Care must be exercised in the construction of test items so that they accurately measure attainment of the objectives.

In addition to testing, teachers may employ observation, oral and written reports, creative assignments, group evaluation, and self-evaluation. The accomplishment of affective objectives may be evaluated through techniques other than testing such as observation, surveys, inventories, essays, opinionnaires, and self-evaluation techniques.

Marks, or grades, should be accurate reflections of the objectives of instruction. Efforts should be made to define marks and make them as meaningful as possible. In the case of affective objectives, symbols used should be different from those used for reporting achievement of cognitive and psychomotor objectives.

Reporting systems are designed to let students, parents, and others know how well the learner is performing in school. The reporting system can be improved through the use of narrative reports, progress reports, and evaluation conferences.

The supervisor is urged to develop a number of in-service activities to help teachers with the improvement of skills of evaluation, measurement, testing, marking, and reporting.

QUESTIONS FOR DISCUSSION

1. What differences would you share with teachers about norm-referenced and criterion-referenced measurement?
2. How would you explain these terms to teachers?
   a. formative evaluation
   b. summative evaluation
3. Should teachers use only standardized tests or only teacher-made tests? Why?
4. Which is the better way to assess students' progress: through the use of essay tests or objective tests? Why?
5. What ways and methods would a supervisor employ to help teachers improve observation techniques?

ACTIVITIES FOR FURTHER STUDY

1. Define
   evaluation
   assessment
   measurement
   testing
   formative evaluation
   summative evaluation
   criterion-referenced measurement
   norm-referenced measurement
2. Select a topic for a unit in a subject you know well and specify the entry skills necessary for initiating study of that unit. Specify the means you would use to assess those skills.
3. Select a unit you have prepared in the past and describe in written form the total evaluation plan for that unit, including formal and informal evaluations, continuing and terminal evaluations.
4. Describe how you would calculate marks for a student at the end of the year and how you would determine whether a student passes the course or level.
5. *For those who are currently teaching:* Examine a unit test you have given to a group of students and on which they have not done well. Describe in what way results of the test have a bearing on the objectives of the unit, preassessment, and instructional procedures. *For those who are not currently teaching:* Secure a unit and test data from a teacher you know and make a similar analysis.
6. Prepare an instrument or a set of criteria for evaluating a group oral report and administer it either to your own or another teacher's students when a group oral report is being given.
7. Suggest entry skills pupils should possess to begin study of
   a. First grade
   b. Beginning typing
   c. World history
   d. Eighth-grade algebra
8. Confer with at least two teachers and discover whether they are using a norm-referenced or a criterion-referenced approach to measurement, and (tactfully) whether they know the distinctions between the two approaches.
9. Specify a usable set of criteria for evaluating

   a. A four-legged wooden stool made in ninth-grade industrial arts
   b. A fifth-grader's oral report on the Grand Canyon
   c. A sixth-grade committee report (oral) on "History of the American Flag"
   d. The American crawl (eleventh-grade physical education)
   e. A pair of earrings made of black coral (eighth-grade arts and crafts)
   f. A senior's term paper on the "The Uses of Computers"

10. State whether each of the following test items is well or poorly constructed. If you decide an item is poorly constructed, state your reason(s) and tell how the item can be improved.

   T F Television is the most important source of news today.
   T F Popes have always had their residence at the Vatican.

   A Native American tribe that inhabited the continental United States was
   a. The Aztecs
   b. The Mayans
   c. The Sioux

   A Communist country is
   a. Peru
   b. China
   c. Mali
   d. Iraq

   List four products France exports for sale.

   The American Revolution ended in _____.

   Discuss the Federal Reserve System.

11. State the ways you believe the attainment of affective objectives should be evaluated and reported.
12. Confer with at least two teachers and determine whether any attempt has been made by them to preassess entry skills for the units they are presently teaching. Summarize your findings.
13. Create an instrument for evaluating students' participation in class.
14. Attend a teacher's class for thirty minutes and, using the instrument you have designed for activity 13, evaluate the class participation of the students.
15. Create an instrument by which the teacher and/or the group members may evaluate the *group's* performance.
16. Obtain a report card of a friend's or relative's child and, with permission, bring it to class and try to interpret to the class the meaning of the grades.
17. Create test items that you consider to be well constructed. Develop two essay-test items and two each of the following objective-test items: recall, multiple choice, alternative response, matching, and rearrangement.
18. Confer with at least two teachers and gather their reactions to the use of essay and objective tests.
19. Write a position paper on the Bloom, Hastings, and Madaus thesis that more than 90 percent of the students could learn most of what we have to teach them.
20. Find out the passing grade in the high school you attended as a student. Compare passing grades of your high school with those of other high schools and account for the differences, if any.
21. State your position on the following: A grade of 70 should be considered passing in every subject in every school of your state. Give the reasons for your position.

22. Interview at least two teachers to find out how they determined the marks they gave to their students at the end of the last marking period. Summarize your findings in a written report.
23. Obtain a teacher-made objective test (it can be your own) and classify the test items on it according to the six major categories of the Bloom taxonomy of the cognitive domain. Decide at which level most of the test items fall.
24. Create two sample multiple-choice items to measure achievement at the following levels of cognition: application, analysis, synthesis, and evaluation.
25. Obtain an essay test (it can be your own) and evaluate it on the basis of the criteria in the following checklist.

CHECKLIST FOR EVALUATING ESSAY TESTS

	Yes	No
a. The questions relate to the objectives.	____	____
b. The purpose of the test items is clear.	____	____
c. The wording of the items is unambiguous.	____	____
d. There is more than one essay item.	____	____
e. The questions are focused so students know what will constitute a complete answer.	____	____
f. Students are told what factors will be evaluated in scoring.	____	____
g. Students are told weights assigned to each question.	____	____
h. A scoring key has been prepared showing key points students must cover to receive full credit for each answer.	____	____
i. There is sufficient time for students to respond fully.	____	____
j. English usage is correct.	____	____

26. Obtain an objective test (it can be your own) and evaluate it on the basis of the criteria in the following checklist.

CHECKLIST FOR EVALUATING OBJECTIVE TESTS

General	Yes	No
a. The test items relate to the objectives.	____	____
b. There is a variety of types of test items.	____	____
c. The items sample the content.	____	____
d. The items are clearly written.	____	____
e. The items avoid clues that give away the answers.	____	____
f. The items avoid the language of the text materials.	____	____
g. A key has been prepared.	____	____
h. The items can be scored objectively.	____	____
i. English usage is correct.	____	____

In addition to the general criteria, the following specific criteria apply to the various types of objective test items.

Completion Items

a. The items allow for only one correct answer.	____	____
b. Each item when completed will make a sentence.	____	____
c. Each item has only one blank to be filled in.	____	____
d. All blanks to be filled in are of equal length.	____	____

Multiple-Choice Items

a. There are at least four responses for each item.	____	____
b. The test avoids a consistent pattern of response.	____	____
c. The responses to each item are plausible.	____	____
d. The responses to each item are of approximately the same length.	____	____
e. Unless students are directed otherwise, the items call for only one answer.	____	____

Alternative-Response Items

a. The items avoid qualifiers that give away the answers.	____	____
b. The items avoid double negatives.	____	____
c. Cognitive items avoid opinions and judgments.	____	____
d. The test avoids a consistent pattern of response.	____	____

Matching Items

a. For each item there is at least one more response than stimuli.	____	____
b. Stimuli and matching responses are on different lines.	____	____
c. Each item is complete on one page.	____	____
d. The test avoids patterns of response.	____	____

Rearrangement Items

a. The responses are approximately the same length, where possible.	____	____
b. The responses for each item are scrambled so that correct responses do not follow each other.	____	____
c. The test avoids patterns of response.	____	____

NOTES

1. Jim Patterson and Peter Kim, *The Day America Told the Truth: What People Really Think about Everything That Really Matters* (New York: Prentice-Hall, 1991).
2. Michael Scriven, "The Methodology of Evaluation," *AERA Monograph Series on Evaluation: Perspectives of Curriculum Evaluation*, no. 1 (Chicago: Rand McNally, 1967), pp. 56–57. Made available from Xerox University Microfilms, 300 North Zeeb Road, Ann Arbor, Mich. 48106.
3. Ibid., p. 57.
4. Bloom, Hastings, and Madaus, *Handbook*, p. 53.
5. Ibid., p. 54.
6. Ibid.
7. Ibid.

8. Ibid.

9. Ibid., p. 46.

10. See "The National Goals—Putting Education Back on the Road," *Phi Delta Kappan* 72, no. 4 (December 1990): 259–314.

11. Oscar K. Buros, ed., *The Mental Measurements Yearbook* (Highland Park, N.Y.: Gryphon Press), revised periodically.

12. Bloom, Hastings, and Madaus, *Handbook*, p. 46.

BIBLIOGRAPHY

"Authentic Learning." *Educational Learning* 50 (April 1993): 4–82.

Becker, Wesley C., Siegfried Engelmann, and Don R. Thomas. *Teaching 3: Evaluation*. Chicago: Science Research Associates, 1975.

Beggs, Donald L., and Ernest L. Lewis. *Measurement and Evaluation in the School*. Boston: Houghton Mifflin, 1975.

Bloom, Benjamin S., J. Thomas Hastings, and George F. Madaus. *Handbook on Formative and Summative Evaluation of Student Learning*. New York: McGraw-Hill, 1971.

Bloom, Benjamin S., George F. Madaus, and J. Thomas Hastings. *Evaluation to Improve Learning*. New York: McGraw-Hill, 1981.

Buros, Oscar K., ed. *The Mental Measurements Yearbook*. Highland Park, N.Y.: Gryphon Press.

Curwin, Richard, and Allen Mendlen. *Discipline with Dignity*. Alexandria, Va.: Association for Supervision and Curriculum Development, 1988.

De Cecco, John P., and William R. Crawford. *Psychology of Learning and Instruction*, 2nd ed. Englewood Cliffs, N.J.: Prentice-Hall, 1968.

Dembo, Myron H. *Teaching for Learning: Applied Educational Psychology in the Classroom*. Santa Monica, Calif.: Goodyear, 1977.

Ebel, Robert L., and David A. Frisbie. *Essentials of Educational Measurement*, 4th ed. Englewood Cliffs, N.J.: Prentice-Hall, 1986.

Gay, L. R. *Educational Evaluation and Measurement: Competencies for Analysis and Application*, 2nd ed. Columbus, Ohio: Merrill, 1985.

Graves, Donald H., and Bonnie S. Sunstein, eds., *Portfolio Portraits*. Portsmouth, N.H.: Heinemann, 1992.

Greene, L. E., ed., "Standards and Assessments: Measuring What Students Should Know." *Principal* 73 (January 1994), 6–48.

Gronlund, Norman E. *Constructing Achievement Tests*, 3rd ed. Englewood Cliffs, N.J.: Prentice-Hall, 1982.

———. *Measurement and Evaluation in Teaching*, 3rd ed. New York: Macmillan, 1976.

———. *Preparing Criterion-Referenced Tests for Classroom Instruction*. New York: Macmillan, 1973.

Henson, Kenneth T. *Secondary Teaching Methods*. Lexington, Mass.: D. C. Heath, 1981.

Hill, John R. *Measurement and Evaluation in the Classroom*, 2nd ed. Columbus, Ohio: Merrill, 1981.

Lyman, Howard B. *Test Scores and What They Mean*, 2nd ed. Englewood Cliffs, N.J.: Prentice-Hall, 1971.

Mills, Richard. "Portfolios: An Exciting Angle on Student Performance." *The School Administrator* 46 (December 1989): 8–11.

"The National Goals—Putting Education Back on the Road." *Phi Delta Kappan* 72 (December 1990): 259–314.

Oliva, Peter F. *The Secondary School Today*, 2nd ed. New York: Harper & Row, 1972.

Patterson, Jim, and Peter Kim. *The Day America Told the Truth: What People Really Think about Everything That Really Matters*. New York: Prentice-Hall, 1991.

Payne, David A. *The Assessment of Learning: Cognitive and Affective*. Lexington, Mass.: D. C. Heath, 1974.

Popham, W. James. *Educational Evaluation*. Englewood Cliffs, N.J.: Prentice-Hall, 1975.

———. *Evaluating Instruction*. Englewood Cliffs, N.J.: Prentice-Hall, 1973.

———, ed. *Evaluation in Education: Current Applications*. Berkeley, Calif.: McCutchan, 1974.

Popham, W. James, and Eva L. Baker. *Systematic Instruction*. Englewood Cliffs, N.J.: Prentice-Hall, 1970.

"Reporting What Students Are Learning." *Educational Leadership* 52 (October 1994): 4–58.

Scriven, Michael. "The Methodology of Evaluation." *AERA Monograph Series on Evaluation: Perspectives of Curriculum Evaluation*, no. 1. Chicago: Rand McNally, 1967.

Simon, Sidney B., and James A. Bellanca, eds. *Degrading the Grading Myths: A Primer of Alternatives to Grades and Marks*. Alexandria, Va.: Association for Supervision and Curriculum Development, 1976.

"Standards and Assessments." *Principal* 73 (January 1994): 6–32.

Strenio, Andrew J., Jr. *The Testing Trap*. New York: Rawson, Wade, 1981.

TenBrink, Terry. "Evaluation." In *Classroom Teaching Skills: A Handbook*, 4th ed., ed. James Cooper, pp. 337–76. Lexington, Mass.: D. C. Heath, 1990.

"Testing and Evaluation." *Contemporary Education* 62 (Summer 1991): 237–326.

Tyler, Ralph W., Robert M. Gagné, and Michael Scriven. "Perspectives of Curriculum Evaluation," *AERA Monograph Series on Curriculum Evaluation*, no. 1. Chicago: Rand McNally, 1967.

"Using Performance Assessment. Using Portfolios." *Educational Leadership* 49 (May 1992): 8–78.

PART III

Leadership in Curriculum Development

7

Helping Teachers Plan and Implement Curricula

Objectives

After studying Chapter 7 you should be able to accomplish the following objectives:

1. Draw or describe your preferred model for curriculum development.
2. Draft a statement of philosophy and aims suitable for submission to a faculty committee for its consideration and revision.
3. Distinguish between aims, curriculum goals, and curriculum objectives.
4. Write curriculum goals and curriculum objectives.
5. Describe and apply the Tyler Rationale.
6. Distinguish between a comprehensive approach to curriculum development and a problem-centered approach.
7. Construct an outline for a curriculum guide.
8. Construct an outline for a course of study.
9. Construct an outline for a resource unit.
10. Explain what is meant by scope of the curriculum and how scope is determined.
11. Explain what is meant by sequence of the curriculum and how sequence is determined.
12. Explain what is meant by balance in the curriculum and how balance is achieved.
13. Distinguish between curriculum goals and objectives and instructional goals and objectives.
14. Describe how to organize a school and/or school system for curriculum development.

A MODEL FOR CURRICULUM DEVELOPMENT

The first chapter of this book described the responsibilities of the supervisor as falling in three domains: instructional development, curriculum development, and staff development. Chapters 7 and 8 explore the responsibilities of the supervisor in assisting teachers with the complex undertaking called curriculum development.[1] Part of the complexity is semantic: The word *curriculum* has different meanings to different people. To some people, the curriculum consists of all the experiences undergone by children wherever they may be: in school, at home, or on the street. To others, the curriculum is a set of subjects that children "take."

To compound the semantic problem further, some educators call a written curriculum plan a curriculum. When they write curriculum guides, they say they are "writing a curriculum." Part of the complexity of curriculum development is substantive: Although we can read and design curriculum plans and guides, what we see are in reality manifestations of the curriculum, not the curriculum itself. The curriculum itself is a concept—a planned concept—and observing a curriculum in action, as opposed to examining a curriculum plan that is to be put into action, reveals not curriculum but instruction.

Instruction—whether in the classroom or in extra-class activity, whether in the guidance office or the library—is the means of putting the curriculum into action. Further, attempting to observe a curriculum reveals only parts of the whole—those parts within a particular classroom or department or subject or level—not the grand design. Curriculum goes beyond immediate space and time, making it a difficult concept with which to work.

Working with the curriculum is difficult also because it usually involves more than one teacher. A successful curriculum requires an interdependent, working relationship among all school personnel and cooperative planning for that relationship.

The word *development* tacked onto *curriculum* compounds the pedagogical problem. What is curriculum development? How do you develop a curriculum? Who develops a curriculum? What does a curriculum look like after it is developed? When is a curriculum fully developed? Is there such a thing as an underdeveloped curriculum? Although these questions are pertinent ones, they are not easy to answer if we wish to go beyond superficiality. The answers to these problems in the literature may offer semantic difficulties, which stand as barriers to clear communication. Specialists in the field of curriculum talk and write about *curriculum development, curriculum planning, curriculum improvement, curriculum construction, curriculum reform, curriculum change,* and *curriculum evaluation.* All the terms are, of course, interrelated but not necessarily synonymous.

Before examining the theme of curriculum development and the respective roles of the supervisor and teachers in the task of curriculum development, let us define the terms *curriculum* and *curriculum development* to provide a frame of reference for subsequent discussion. By *curriculum* we mean those experiences of a child that come under the supervision of the school. Included in the concept of curriculum as described in this textbook are (1) all in-school experiences, including classroom learning experiences, student activities, use of the media center or library, use of learning resource centers, assemblies, use of the cafeteria, and social functions, and (2) out-of-school learning experiences directed by the school, including homework, field trips, and use of community resources.

The *Dictionary of Education* defines *curriculum development* as follows:

> Curriculum Development: a task of supervision directed toward designing or redesigning the guidelines for instruction; includes development of specifications indicating what is to be taught, by whom, when, where, and in what sequence or pattern.*

This definition might be modified in one very important respect: Curriculum development is not the task of supervision alone. It is a joint endeavor of all school personnel but primarily a cooperative activity of supervisors and teachers. *Curriculum development* is used in this text interchangeably with *curriculum improvement*. To make a slight distinction between the two, development might be conceptualized as planning at the initial stages; then, once a curricular plan is instituted, continuous development is curriculum improvement. However, in the literature, *curriculum development* and *curriculum improvement* are used synonymously and they are so used in this book.

You will note in the foregoing definition of *curriculum development* that the manner in which portions of the curriculum will be taught is not included. The question of "how" takes us into curriculum's companion field—instruction. Curriculum and instruction cannot really be separated in practice. Your text gives separate attention to curriculum and instruction, but this can be done for purposes of analysis only. Without a curriculum there can be no instruction; without instruction a curriculum is lifeless. The intimate relationship between curriculum and instruction underscores the necessity of the supervisor's working in both the instructional and curriculum development domains. Neither curriculum nor instruction is subordinate to the other. Both are equally important, and the supervisor has the responsibility of helping teachers with the improvement of both.

Curriculum development involves an almost continuous process of decision making. Teachers are engaged in this process when they attempt to answer questions such as these.

- When do we introduce fractions?
- At what grade level should we start a program in use of computers?
- Which exploratory experiences should we provide in the middle school?
- Is vocational agriculture needed in this community?
- Should geometry precede intermediate algebra?
- Should we offer French or should we offer Spanish?
- Where should we begin study of foreign languages?
- How much time should we devote to study of the American Revolution?
- How many years of science should we require for graduation from our high school?

---

*Carter V. Good, ed., *Dictionary of Education*, 3rd ed. (New York: McGraw-Hill, 1973), p. 158. Reproduced with permission of The McGraw-Hill Companies.

- What experiences essential to young people are omitted from our curriculum?
- Should our curriculum be subject centered or child centered?
- Are we providing experiences for development of self-discipline on the part of the learner?
- Shall we add sex education to the curriculum?
- Are there enough carryover sports in the physical education program?
- For what jobs in the community should our vocational program prepare young people?
- What program should we offer for children whose native language is other than English?
- Does our curriculum incorporate multicultural education?
- Should boys take a course in homemaking?
- Do elementary school pupils need the services of a guidance counselor?
- Do we have a balance between general education and specialized education in the curriculum?
- Should middle school pupils take typing?
- Are we identifying the health needs of our pupils?
- Should we separate exceptional children and put them into special classes?
- Should we adopt a continuous progress or nongraded plan?
- What kinds of musical experiences are appropriate for elementary school children?
- Are we providing opportunities for creative expression by pupils?

The foregoing questions are illustrative of the hundreds of kinds of questions that must be answered by a school system if its curriculum is not to remain dormant. Some of the questions must be asked repeatedly, for curriculum development is a continuous, nonending process. The answer to a curriculum question at one time may not suffice at another time. Circumstances change and the curriculum must change to reflect the new circumstances.

Most of the illustrative questions involve decision making by groups of teachers, sometimes the total faculty of a school, and often the faculties of all schools in a particular school system. Many of the questions are interdisciplinary in nature and call for input from many grades and fields of study.

The kinds of questions raised require prolonged study before decisions can be reached. Whereas instructional methods can be altered on short notice, curriculum changes take time—to examine, to make decisions, to implement, and to evaluate. Consequently, curriculum development is futuristically oriented. Improvements desired for next year or the year after should be studied this year. Some of the curriculum problems that schools have encountered arose because faculties rushed into curriculum change before adequately studying all its ramifications.

Curriculum development is normally a group undertaking. This does not mean that the individual teacher does not become involved in curriculum improvement within his or her own grade level or subject. The individual teacher must make many curriculum decisions. He or she must decide what limitations will be placed on the content chosen and in what order to present units. He or she must make sure that the content not only interrelates with previous study and future study by the pupils but also is relevant.

When curriculum decisions cross discipline lines, as they often do, a group of teachers under the leadership of a supervisor must conduct a study of the curriculum problems and make recommendations to the faculty and administration for changes they deem desirable. Teachers group and regroup depending on the nature of the curriculum problem under study. The problem of choosing a reading program for the elementary school will certainly involve all elementary school teachers in a particular school and will probably involve all elementary school teachers in the entire school system. The formation of a group that represents all teachers concerned with a problem is usually the means by which curriculum development is initiated.

Depending on the nature of the problem and the extent of its effect, curriculum development may be carried on by a building supervisor or a central office supervisor with the faculty or segments of the faculty of a particular school, or by a central office supervisor with the faculties of all schools of a particular level or levels throughout a school district. If a problem is localized in one particular school, curriculum development may be confined to that school. On the other hand, if a problem and its solution will affect teachers and pupils in more than one school, curriculum development must proceed on a districtwide rather than on a schoolwide basis. In practice, both schoolwide and districtwide curriculum development are frequently and continuously engaged in by teachers and supervisors.

The questions of what language arts experiences should be taught in a secondary school language arts program, for example, and the sequence in which the experiences should be programmed are appropriately the domain of the language arts faculty of that school and other schools in the district. Decisions on these matters may be made in consultation with the appropriate supervisors, such as the team leader, grade coordinator, department head, assistant principal for curriculum, supervisor of language arts, director of instruction, assistant superintendent for curriculum and instruction, and appropriate administrators. A decision on whether to require an additional year of language arts for graduation from high school is appropriately the concern of the total secondary school faculty of a school system. Any addition of a course to the curriculum or a course deletion has an effect on all teachers.

The supervisor has several responsibilities in the process of curriculum development. As one approach, he or she may initiate a broad study of the curriculum by enlisting teachers in the preparation or revision of the school's philosophy. The supervisor may stimulate teachers to identify curriculum problems of concern to them or may even suggest problems that might be of interest to them. He or she helps set up the groups and subgroups needed for study of a problem. It is the supervisor's responsibility to provide time, facilities, and resources teachers must have to perform their task of curriculum development. Unless these ingredients are made available to teachers, curriculum development is doomed to failure. The lack of these resources is a major reason the curriculum of many schools remains static. Teachers must be granted school time to work on curriculum revision. They should not be expected to tackle the strategic problems of curriculum improvement on their own time and not be compensated.

Curriculum development will cost a school system a certain amount for released time for teachers, provision of substitutes as needed, and purchase of materials that are essential for adequate study. School administrators must make a value judgment concerning whether a school system can afford not to continuously revitalize its curriculum and as a result deliver an outmoded, irrelevant curriculum to its learners.

THE SUPERVISOR IN CURRICULUM DEVELOPMENT

Some supervisors mistakenly concentrate most or all of their energies on curriculum development to the exclusion of leadership in the other two domains: instructional and staff development. They emphasize locating and disseminating curriculum materials, writing curriculum guides, and the like.

Some supervisors feel more comfortable in the curriculum domain, where much of the work takes place outside the classroom. By concentrating on curricula, they feel they can effect changes more readily than by working with individual teachers in improving their methods of instruction. As if journeying in the fourth dimension, some supervisors enter the domain of curriculum development and rarely exit. Unless a supervisory staff is large enough to differentiate leadership responsibilities in each of the three domains, a perpetual sojourn in the territory of curriculum development is as inappropriate as a detour past the domain, as if it were the Slough of Despond out of *The Pilgrim's Progress.*

It is often said that the supervisor acts as a catalyst, or change agent. In the job of curriculum development, it is the supervisor who helps teachers identify curriculum problems and helps facilitate the study and search for solutions. Supervisors stimulate teachers to look at the curriculum and come up with recommendations for improvements. It is the leader who sparks a dissatisfaction with the status quo and causes teachers to want to make revisions. The supervisor is a curriculum worker, a participant in a cooperative process of which he or she is only one member—a respected member, one hopes. The supervisor's authority and claim to respect should result not just from status but also from the level of credibility that he or she can induce in fellow workers. The supervisor is not the developer and should not behave in such a manner. It takes two or more to develop a curriculum.

To achieve credibility, the supervisor must have specialized skills. He or she must be grounded in curriculum theory, know what solutions have been tried in the past and how they have fared, and be cognizant of current developments in curriculum, nationally and internationally. Supervisors should be aware of, for example, the results of the National Assessment of Educational Progress.[2] The curriculum supervisor who is unaware of developments in foreign schools and the math supervisor who is not familiar with the international studies of achievement in mathematics[3] are lacking valuable input that they should be able to share with teachers who are studying related problems.

The supervisor must possess research skills, know how to help teachers develop curriculum proposals, be able to analyze research, be able to spot biases in research, and know how to interpret findings to teachers. The supervisor's role calls for a knowledge of learning theory and a sensitivity to problems of society. Among necessary skills of the supervisor is the ability to manage work groups and to facilitate their endeavors.

APPROACHES TO CURRICULUM DEVELOPMENT

Planning

Where does a supervisor begin this task of curriculum development? Two approaches may be followed, both of which are effective and viable. The first, the comprehensive approach, permits a total view of the curriculum. The second, the problem-centered approach, is confined to study of specific curriculum problems identified by teachers. Each approach has its own purposes. The comprehensive approach requires a global look at the curriculum and uncovers heretofore unidentified problem, whereas the problem-centered approach is a response to problems already identified by faculty members. A supervisor will take both approaches, often concurrently, conducting a problem-centered study while a comprehensive study is going on. The supervisor may plan for and initiate a comprehensive study while at the same time responding to the need for study of particular problems.

The Comprehensive Approach

The comprehensive approach to curriculum development may be conceptualized in the form of the simplified model in Figure 7.1.[4] You will note that this model with its three components is the same as the simplest model of instruction discussed in Chapter 3, except that the feedback lines have been added and the word *implementation* is used instead of *presentation*. Whereas the simplified model of instruction advises us to plan, implement, and evaluate *instruction*, the simplified model of curriculum improvement guides us to plan, implement, and evaluate *curriculum*. In both cases, we are following the same process but in each case we are working with a different entity. We could readily follow the simplified model for curriculum development but the expanded model in Figure 7.2 (page 286) gives us greater insights into the process.

Both the models of instruction found in Chapter 3 and the two models of curriculum development discussed in this chapter follow a systematic approach. Using the expanded, six-part model for curriculum development, we begin by specifying where we are going and what we wish to achieve (philosophy and aims, goals, and objectives); we design a curriculum plan (plan design); we put a plan into operation to attempt to achieve the objectives (implementation); we evaluate the success of the plan (evaluation); and we provide feedback so we can revise the components of the model (feedback lines). The process is cyclical and unending.

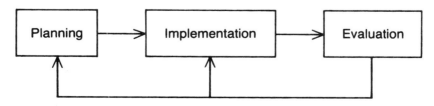

Figure 7.1. A Simplified Model for Curriculum Development.

Figure 7.2. Expanded Model for Curriculum Development. (For a more detailed, expanded model, which integrates an instructional model with a curriculum model, see Peter F. Oliva, *Developing the Curriculum*, 3rd ed. (New York: HarperCollins, 1992) chap. 5.)

Evaluation of the curriculum is shown as the last stage of the model. In effect, evaluation proceeds concurrently with the planning and implementing stages. During the earlier stages, curriculum workers design and faculty review the evaluation plans. Ultimately, data are collected and analyzed for the purpose of affirming, modifying, or rejecting the curriculum plans and practices.

Faculties embarking on curriculum development ordinarily work on one of three levels: class, grade, or subject level; schoolwide level; and systemwide level. When the supervisor engages teachers in a comprehensive approach to the total curriculum, study groups are formed that are representative of the entire school or of the entire school system. The supervisor must take responsibility for setting up the machinery for the curriculum study and help identify the groupings of teachers necessary for pursuing the study. Study committees must be established that are representative of the total faculty or faculties concerned, but at each stage of curriculum study the total faculty or faculties must be informed, consider committee reports, and react to proposals for curriculum change before they are put into operation.

To look comprehensively at the total curriculum, groups of teachers must be formed across grade levels and across disciplines. The initial formation of these groups is exceedingly important for they should be representative of the broad spectrum of interests of teachers. What the supervisor is seeking is commitment from teachers, and to achieve that commitment, teachers must feel that they are adequately represented on groups working in their name.

The model for curriculum development implies a fixed sequence of tasks. A study of the curriculum begins with writing a statement of the philosophy and aims espoused by the school or school system, which is followed by stating curricular goals and then by specifying curricular objectives. Each of the statements—philosophy and aims, goals, and objectives, which may be drawn up by a representative committee or committees—should meet with faculty approval.

Following approval of the objectives, curriculum proposals are developed by the representative committees and considered by the faculty; those that are endorsed by the faculty are then implemented. In the last stage of the model, evaluation plans are designed, reviewed by the faculty, and then carried out.

One committee that represents the faculty may provide the leadership for all phases of the study, or two or three committees may divide the responsibilities. Because there is a logical flow from philosophy and aims to goals to objectives, it is desirable to establish a Committee on Philosophy, Aims, Goals, and Objectives, which would be the task force for the first three components of the model. In addition to teachers who would constitute the majority, representatives of the nonprofessional staff, the community, and the student body (given appropriate maturity level) should serve on this committee so views of constituencies other than teachers can be made known. When the Committee on Philosophy, Aims, Goals, and Objectives finishes its task, the same or other groups will draft specific curricular plans and will design and conduct the evaluation of those plans.

The first five components of the model for curriculum development—philosophy and aims, curriculum goals, curriculum objectives, design of the plan, and implementation—are considered in this chapter. Evaluation of the curriculum is examined in the next chapter. To establish a frame of reference for the discussion in this chapter, we look at the preparation of statements of philosophy and aims, curriculum goals, and curriculum objectives that are schoolwide or systemwide and not specific to a particular grade or discipline.

Statements of philosophy and aims for an individual school should evolve as sets of beliefs and purposes espoused by the entire school faculty regardless of discipline or grade level. Sets of schoolwide curriculum goals and objectives should be adopted by the faculty before a committee begins writing curriculum goals and objectives for a particular discipline or grade level. Committees within the discipline or grade level should be established at a later time for writing curriculum goals and objectives that are in keeping with the broader goals and objectives agreed on by the total faculty. Leadership in the development of the curriculum of the particular teaching fields is a function of the specialist supervisor, whereas leadership in the development of overall curriculum rests with the generalist supervisor. The extent and degree of involvement of faculties as a whole in the process of curriculum development is a function of size. The larger the school or school system, the greater will be the responsibilities placed on representatives of the faculty or faculties.

Writing a School's Philosophy and Aims

Statement of Philosophy. Writing a school philosophy is primarily an affective exercise. Teachers who develop a statement of philosophy must verbalize their beliefs and express their feelings about education. Whether teachers realize it or not, the way they behave in the classroom is a direct reflection of beliefs they hold about the learner, about education, and about society. If they believe that learning should be a pleasant experience, they behave differently from the way they do when they believe that learning must be a distasteful experience—like taking medicine—for it to do the learner any good. They also order their curriculum and methods accordingly. If they believe in the worth of each individual, they construct a curriculum and employ methods that aim to foster individual development. When they write a philosophy, they are forced to look within themselves and to clarify, perhaps for the first time, what they truly believe about education.

Frankly speaking, the exercise of writing a statement of philosophical beliefs is not one that is terribly popular with teachers. One reason for this is cultural. The United States is not known as a nation of philosophers but as a country of pragmatists; thus, our people express a penchant for action, not thought; for practice, not theory. It is this penchant that causes students in teacher education institutions to express impatience with courses that they label "theory." The most popular courses in teacher education are the "nuts and bolts" courses and the practice courses such as student teaching. It is this deprecation of theory that has caused many students in teacher education to rank so-called foundations of education courses at the low end of the totem pole. The illustrious former president of Harvard University, James B. Conant, a scientist, joined the critics of foundational courses in his study of the education of teachers.[5] Teacher educators have long been considered impractical idealists, too immersed in theory, and too remote from the firing line ("those who can, do; those who can't, teach; those who can't teach, teach teachers"). The professional educator has his or her work cut out to convince the teacher trainee that foundations such as philosophy of education indeed have a place in both preservice and in-service education. The professional educator must do what he or she advocates that the teacher do with students—demonstrate that a field such as philosophy is relevant. Two ways may be attempted to achieve the goal of demonstrating relevance of philosophy. First, the preservice trainees or the in-service teachers should at some point approach philosophy from their own personal perspectives and clarify what they believe. Second, they should analyze the ways in which their philosophies are applied in the classroom and the ways in which the teaching practices they use devolve from their philosophical beliefs.

Teachers often balk at writing statements of philosophy not only because they are impatient for practical solutions to problems as opposed to theoretical statements but also because writing a philosophy is an introspective exercise. The pragmatic, even materialistic outlook on life precludes time for searching minds and hearts. Nor is it just a question of the time it takes for thinking through one's beliefs. People would much rather expose their actions than their thoughts.

Teachers express impatience with writing philosophical statements because they realize that philosophical beliefs cannot be labeled right or wrong in the same way factual statements can. They know that teachers will hold differing views about the rightness or wrongness of a philosophical statement and that such differences will produce a time-consuming argument, which they would just as soon avoid. Yet the arguing is the most significant part of the exercise of writing a philosophy. Discussion of profound ideas helps individuals to shape their own beliefs. The individual's beliefs are placed in the crucible of public opinion, a test some teachers would prefer to bypass.

Teachers sometimes object to writing a statement of philosophy because they feel the end result will be a set of clichés devoid of meaning and impossible to translate into practice. When they begin the task of writing a philosophy with this attitude, the outcome is a self-fulfilled prophecy—a philosophical statement that is empty and dead.

Most commonly, teachers are confronted with the necessity for producing a statement of philosophy in connection with regional accreditation of their school, a process discussed in the next chapter. Because accreditation acts as a pressure on teachers to develop a philosophical statement, there is danger that the task can become an academic exercise for the accreditation process and not for its own intrinsic value. The supervisor should not wait until some pressure such as an accreditation process pushes a group of teachers to setting down in writing their philosophical beliefs. Nor should a supervisor or principal ever make writing a philosophy more academic and more empty by rushing into the void and writing the philosophy himself or herself. Though teachers may resist writing a philosophy, they literally deride a school philosophy that has been written by a supervisor or administrator and rightfully reject it as an expression of a faculty philosophy.

The resistance of teachers to the task of writing a philosophy should not be magnified as the resistance is usually a gentle one. Teachers can and do intellectualize the need for some sort of philosophical statement. The job of the supervisor is to get teachers to internalize the task, to see a real need for the exercise, and to give them hope that the effort to produce the statement will be rewarded by visible results in practice.

We do not imply that all or even most schools are lacking in a statement of philosophy and that these statements must always be developed from scratch. Where a statement of philosophy exists, the task of the Committee on Philosophy, Aims, Goals, and Objectives is to review the existing statement, reaffirm it, modify it, or toss it out and begin anew, as they deem most appropriate.

Assume for purposes of illustration that a committee is charged with the task of drafting a statement of philosophy for a school that has never engaged in this exercise before. What should be included in such a statement? Several ideas immediately come to mind. The statement of philosophy should include the group's beliefs about the four elements listed.

- Purposes of education
- Nature of learning
- Nature of the learner
- Nature of society

The National Study of School Evaluation recommended twelve items that elementary school faculties should consider for possible inclusion in a statement of philosophy.[6] The items serve as guiding principles for faculties drafting a philosophical statement.

1. Relevance of the statement of philosophy to the larger purposes of the American democratic commitment.
2. Attention to intellectual, democratic, moral, and social values basic to satisfying the needs of the individual and his culture.
3. Recognition of individual differences.
4. The special characteristics and unique needs of elementary school pupils.
5. Concern for the nature of knowledge and for the nature of the learning process as they apply to learners and their total development.
6. Consistency of philosophy with actual practice.
7. Identification of the roles and relationships expected of the community, the pupil, the teacher, and the administration in the educational process of the school.
8. The role of the elementary school program of the school district and the importance of articulation with the other elements of the overall educational program.

9. The responsibility for making a determination as to a desirable balance among activities designed to develop the cognitive, affective, and psychomotor domains.
10. The relationship of the school to all other educational learning centers.
11. The responsibility of the school toward social and economic change.
12. The accountability of the school to the community it serves.

After the statement is drafted, it should be ratified by the total school faculty, and it then becomes the statement of principles from which the goals and objectives of the school are derived and a set of principles against which practice must be tested. Following is an illustration of a statement of philosophy developed by the faculty of the Carbondale, Illinois, Community High School.

Carbondale Community High School, District 165, Carbondale, Illinois

A Philosophy of Education

We believe it is the responsibility of School District 165 to provide:

An educational program which will aid the children of this community to grow physically, intellectually, morally, and emotionally, that they may live happily as children and that they may become adult citizens of a democracy, realizing the most complete life possible within the limits of their individual needs, interests, and abilities. Complete citizenship embodies the dignity of the individual and his/her responsibility to the group, both of which can be nurtured best through democratic living in a democratic situation.

As a basis for building this educational program:

We believe education is a growth process by which people learn to think and act more effectively.

We believe in the individual's worth and dignity as a person.

We believe the individual's welfare is dependent upon the welfare of others and all must have an understanding of the mutual rights and problems of all people.

We believe that a respect for and an understanding of the policies of democratic government must be held by all.

We believe that the privileges of the democratic way of life enjoyed by the individual imply a responsibility to help maintain this democracy.

We believe that complete citizenship can be realized only through the development of a personality, characterized by intellectual, emotional, and social maturity.

We believe that we must provide ways and means for the individual to discover and develop his/her ability and personality, in the classroom and in extracurricular activities.

We believe that in our democratic society, an opportunity for the development and mastery of fundamental attitudes, habits and skills must be offered to all the people according to their abilities.

We believe each person should acquire an understanding of and a respect for the traditions, customs and heritages of this country which have contributed to its development and which will affect its future progress.

We believe the home, the church, the community and the school must cooperate to assist young people in developing spiritually and morally.

We believe in providing for a wise use of leisure time that there may be increased pleasure in living, as well as increased efficiency.[7]

The inevitable question is raised concerning statements of philosophy: What if the philosophical beliefs of a school faculty are divergent, as is often the case? What if there are some teachers who subscribe to essentialistic doctrines and believe that subject matter should take precedence over the learner whereas others adhere to the pragmatic tenet that places the needs of the learner before subject matter? What if some teachers endorse the role of the school as a passive transmitter of knowledge and cultural heritage whereas other teachers champion the role of the school as a leader in reconstructing society? Differences in philosophical beliefs go to the heart of the exercise of writing a statement of philosophy and cause teachers to reveal their beliefs.

The differences in beliefs among teachers can make the task of writing a philosophy an exciting one. The process of resolving differences of philosophy is the same as with any issue where viewpoints collide: the search for consensus. The supervisor should strive to help a group of teachers reach consensus. Because human beings differ and will continue to differ, 100 percent consensus may be an impossible goal, but the supervisor should try to bring about as wide an agreement as possible. Only those items on which there is consensus of at least a majority of the faculty should be incorporated in the finished statement. Those items on which consensus is lacking should be the subjects for continuing study and discussion and may come up for consideration when the statement of philosophy is reviewed in the future. Once consensus is achieved, however, and a statement of philosophy is accepted by the faculty as a whole, each teacher is bound by that philosophy and should behave in accordance with it. There is nothing unusual in expecting teachers to act in accordance with a group-adopted philosophical statement; that is the essence of the democratic process. Although every person is assured of input in the formative stages, once adopted, the statement is binding on all the participants. Neither a nation nor a school can function if every individual is at complete liberty to go his or her own way and to reject consensus that has been democratically achieved. Those who disagree with majority consensus may still work within the context of the democratic process to bring about changes more to their liking.

Statement of Aims. A statement of aims can be considered an extension of the statement of philosophy. Faculties often produce documents entitled "Philosophy and Aims." The philosophy itself is cast into statements of belief. An accompanying statement of aims, derived from the philosophy, is a set of broad purposes of education. Curriculum goals and objectives refine the aims. The aims themselves are value-laden and, therefore, reveal philosophical positions.

Aims are often inseparable from the philosophy, nor is it necessary to separate them. The Carbondale High School example wrapped up aims in the first paragraph, where the faculty said:

> We believe it is the responsibility of School District 165 to provide: An educational program which will aid the children of this community to grow physically, intellectually, morally, and emotionally, that they may live happily as children and that they may become adult citizens of a democracy . . . through democratic living in a democratic situation.

Examples of philosophical statements in this same illustration are

- We believe education is a growth process by which people learn to think and act more effectively.

- We believe in the individual's worth and dignity as a person.

Typically, school philosophies begin with a statement of beliefs and then draw the aims of education from those beliefs. Instead of or in addition to writing its own aims, a faculty may wish to borrow well-known statements of aims such as the Seven Cardinal Principles, for example. The Commission on the Reorganization of Secondary Education proposed the following principles, that is, aims for secondary education: "health, command of the fundamental processes, worthy home membership, vocation, citizenship, worthy use of leisure, ethical character."[8]

Curriculum workers, in fact, should be aware of significant state and national proclamations of aims and goals for schools. Not only should they be familiar with statements of the past which may still have relevance for the schools, such as the principles of the Commission on the Reorganization of Secondary Education mentioned above, various statements of the Educational Policies Commission,[9] *Goals for Americans: Programs for Action in the Sixties*,[10] and *A Nation at Risk*.[11] They should also be conversant with the most recent pronouncements such as America 2000, in which former President George Bush and the National Governors' Association in 1989 set forth six national goals for achievement by the year 2000.

- All children will start school ready to learn.
- The high school graduation rate will increase to at least 90 percent.
- Students in the 4th, 8th, and 12th grades will demonstrate proficiency in English, mathematics, science, history, and geography.
- American students will rank first in math and science.
- Every adult American will be literate.
- Every school will be free of drugs and violence.[12]

Under President Bill Clinton's administration, two goals were added:

- Teachers will have access to training programs to improve their skills.
- Every school will strive to increase parental involvement and participation in their children's education.[13]

Statements of aims and general goals are meant to be universal, applying to all schools within a state in the case of statewide proclamations and to all schools in the country in the case of nationwide pronouncements. Certainly, statements of aims and goals on the local level should, as a rule, be compatible with state and national goals. In making statements of aims or general goals, local school faculties are saying that they believe schools in general should foster these purposes, that the broad aims they subscribe to for their schools and their communities are desirable for schools and communities throughout the country. Curriculum goals and objectives turn the general aims and goals of education into school-specific purposes.

Writing Curriculum Goals. After the faculty has established the philosophical premises and aims to which it claims allegiance, it should turn its attention to a statement of curriculum goals. In some cases faculties may specify curriculum goals by taking statements of aims and making them applicable to the local school.

The same confusion exists between goals and objectives that pertain to the curriculum as exists between goals and objectives in respect to instruction. The direction of curriculum development is sharpened if goals are distinguished from objectives. Both goals and objectives should be stated in terms of expectations of the learner rather than expectations of the school. Curriculum *goals* are expectations of the learners as they encounter the curriculum and are stated in more general, nonbehavioral terms. Curriculum *objectives* are expectations of the learners as they encounter the curriculum and are stated in more limited, measurable, and behavioral terms.

The task of distinguishing goals from objectives is seen in the following examples:

The *Elementary School Evaluative Criteria* contains a section on Guiding Principles for a Statement of Objectives.[14] These criteria ask for a report on philosophy, objectives, and commitments. Some people would call these objectives goals, or even aims.

The *Evaluative Criteria for Middle Level Schools* requires completion of a section on philosophy and goals.[15] An earlier version of criteria for middle and junior high schools offered several guiding principles for stating a philosophy and distinguished between goals and objectives.

> The statement of philosophy expresses ideals and beliefs. Goals are more precise delineations of those ideals and beliefs. Objectives are carefully specified statements of intended learner outcomes which contribute to the attainment of program goals and give direction to the school program.[16]

It is the goals that accompany the statement of philosophy for these criteria. Objectives are stated in the sections of the criteria on learning areas.

Like the *Evaluative Criteria for Middle Level Schools*, the *Evaluative Criteria* (for secondary schools) asks for a statement of philosophy and goals.[17]

The Educational Policies Commission, a body of the National Education Association, years ago developed a classic statement spelling out what it considered to be the needs of youths in secondary schools.[18] This statement of needs, which are, in reality, aims for secondary education, is widely known as the "Ten Imperative Needs of Youth" and consists of several declarations.

1. All youth need to develop salable skills.
2. All youth need to develop and maintain good health and physical fitness.
3. All youth need to understand the rights and duties of the citizen of a democratic society.
4. All youth need to understand the significance of the family.
5. All youth need to know how to purchase and use goods and services intelligently.
6. All youth need to understand the methods of science.
7. All youth need opportunities to develop their capacities to appreciate beauty in literature, art, music, and nature.
8. All youth need to be able to use their leisure time well.
9. All youth need to develop respect for other persons, to grow in their insight into ethical values and principles, to be able to live and work cooperatively with others.

10. All youth need to grow in their ability to think rationally, to express their thoughts clearly, and to read and listen with understanding.

If a secondary school faculty substituted *our* for *all*, it would have a statement of curricular goals, not that it is recommended that a statement of philosophy, aims, goals, or objectives be taken bodily from some source external to the school's faculty. The process of developing these statements is as important as—and may even be more important than—the products themselves.

The statement of the curricular goals is the first step in applying the school's statement of philosophy and aims. A number of years ago the Dade County (Florida) Public Schools developed a statement of goals they refer to as "Goals for Student Development." This statement is reproduced as an illustration of a systemwide effort to spell out the curricular goals of that system.[19] It furnishes an excellent illustration of the way in which a local school system takes a statement of goals developed by the state and modifies that statement to fit its own needs.[20] This statement has been incorporated into the school board's policies.

Goals for Student Development

Goal Area I:

Communication and Learning Skills. Students shall acquire, to the extent of their individual physical, mental, and emotional capacities, a mastery of the basic skills required in obtaining and expressing ideas through the effective use of words, numerals and other symbols.

a) Students shall achieve a working knowledge of reading, writing, speaking and arithmetic during the elementary school years, accompanied by gradual progress into the broader fields of mathematics, natural science, language arts and the humanities.

b) Students shall develop and use skills in the logical processes of search, analysis, evaluation and problem-solving, in critical thinking, and in the use of symbolism.

c) Students shall develop competence and motivation for continuing self-evaluation, self-instruction and adaptation to a changing environment.

d) Students shall have the opportunity during the elementary school years to develop and use the skills of speaking and understanding a foreign language in order to communicate effectively in the language for future personal or vocational achievements.

Goal Area II:

Citizenship Education. Students shall acquire and continually improve the habits and attitudes necessary for responsible citizenship.

a) Students shall acquire knowledge of various political systems with emphasis on democratic institutions, the heritage of the United States, the contributions of our diverse cultural backgrounds, and the responsibilities and privileges of citizenship.

b) Students shall develop the skills required for participation in the political processes of our country and for influencing decisions made by political organizations.

c) Students shall develop the competence and desire to become informed and critical participants in the electoral process of this country.

d) Students shall acquire those attributes necessary for functioning, on a daily basis, as good citizens in their own school and community settings.

Goal Area III:

Career and Occupational Education. Students shall acquire a knowledge and understanding of the opportunities open to them for preparing for a productive life, and shall develop those skills and abilities which will enable them to take full advantage of those opportunities—including a positive attitude toward work and respect for the dignity of all honorable occupations.

a) Students shall acquire knowledge of and develop an understanding of the fundamental structure and processes of America's economic system, together with an understanding of the opportunities and requirements for individual participation and success in this changing system.
b) Students shall develop occupational competencies, consistent with their interests, aptitudes and abilities, which are necessary for entry and advancement in the economic system; they shall develop those academic competencies necessary for the acquisition of technical or professional skills through post-high school training.
c) Students shall develop competence in the application of economic knowledge to practical economic functions: such as, planning and budgeting for the investment of personal income, calculating tax obligations, financing major purchases, and obtaining desirable employment.
d) Students shall develop an awareness of the relevance of the curriculum to the world of work and our social existence.

Goal Area IV:

Mental and Physical Health. Students shall acquire good health habits and an understanding of the conditions necessary for the maintenance of physical, emotional, and social well-being.

a) Students shall develop an understanding of the requirements of personal hygiene, adequate nutrition and leisure time activities essential to the maintenance of physical health, and a knowledge of the dangers to mental and physical health from addiction and other aversive practices.
b) Students shall develop skills in sports and other forms of recreation which will provide for life-long enjoyment of participation according to their own preferences and abilities.
c) Students shall develop competence in recognizing and preventing environmental health problems.
d) Students shall acquire a knowledge of basic psychological and sociological factors affecting human behavior and mental health, and shall develop competence for adjusting to changes in personal status and social patterns.

Goal Area V:

Home and Family Relationships. Students shall develop an appreciation of the family as a social institution.

a) Students shall develop an understanding of their roles and the roles of others as members of a family, together with a knowledge of the requirements for successful participation in family living.
b) Students shall develop an understanding of the role of the family as a basic unit in the society.
c) Students shall develop an awareness of the diversity of family patterns and the value of the contributions of the individuals to family and community living.

Goal Area VI:

Aesthetic and Cultural Appreciations. Students shall develop understanding and appreciation of human achievement in the natural sciences, the humanities and the arts.

a) Students shall acquire a knowledge of and an appreciation for major arts, music, literary and drama forms, and their place in the cultural heritage.

b) Students shall acquire a knowledge of the natural, physical and social sciences and their relationships to human and social development.
c) Students shall develop skills for creative use of leisure time and shall develop an interest in becoming active in one or more areas of creative endeavor.
d) Students shall develop discrimination skills in the critical evaluation of cultural offerings and opportunities.

Goal Area VII:
Human Relations. Students shall develop a concern for moral, ethical and spiritual values and for the application of such values to life situations.

a) Students shall acquire the greatest possible understanding and appreciation of themselves as well as of persons belonging to social, cultural and ethnic groups different from their own, and of the worthiness of all persons as members of society.
b) Students shall develop those skills and attitudes necessary for positive interpersonal and group relationships and shall recognize the importance of and need for ethical and moral standards of behavior.
c) Students shall recognize the value of that level of group discipline and self-discipline that promotes a sense of worth of the individual while contributing to the collective benefit of all involved.

Writing Curriculum Objectives. To this point the first two phases of the curriculum development process have been completed—the faculty has threshed out its statement of philosophy and aims and has adopted a statement of curriculum goals. The supervisor then takes them into the task of specifying curriculum objectives. Statements of curriculum objectives must ultimately be drafted and accepted on two levels: first, schoolwide (or systemwide), cutting across disciplines and grade levels, and second, within a particular discipline or grade level. The Committee on Philosophy, Aims, Goals, and Objectives may be charged with the task of developing the set of schoolwide objectives, and special committees from the disciplines or grade levels may undertake the job of specifying curriculum objectives peculiar to their special fields.

The progression from the statement of philosophy and aims to the statement of goals and finally to the statement of objectives is increasingly more specific. As was observed in writing the statements of goals, the statements of objectives should focus on what the learner does as opposed to what the school does. Well-defined curriculum objectives meet the same standards as well-defined instructional objectives. They state what learners are expected to achieve, under what conditions they must demonstrate the behavior, and what level of performance they must attain. A distinction may be made between these criteria as they apply to instructional objectives and as they apply to curriculum objectives. The latter is concerned with the achievement of groups of students; the former is concerned with the achievement of individual students in a class or subject.

As a general rule, it seems best when writing both goals and objectives in whatever area—instruction, curriculum, administration, supervision, or other area—to focus on the person or persons who must perform the desired behavior. This is particularly important in the case of objectives. The subsequent process of evaluation is simplified when the evaluator knows who does what under what conditions and to what degree of mastery. If the objectives do not show these elements, the evaluator needs first to revise the objectives so that these elements are clearly shown.

Some faculties write their curriculum goals and objectives in terms of what the school—and by inference the school's program or curriculum—will do rather than what the learners will do. Let's contrast the two ways of writing statements of goals and objectives by hypothesizing a junior-senior high school, grades seven to twelve, composed predominantly of a white, English-speaking student body, whose faculty believes the students should have some exposure to another language and culture. The faculty might write a curriculum goal statement—typical of many that can be found—that emphasizes the school's role: "The school should promote an understanding of another culture through the medium of foreign language study." Contrast that statement with the following statement, which starts off by mentioning the learners: "Students should gain an understanding of another culture through the medium of foreign language study." Admittedly, there is not a great deal of difference between these two goal statements, and the differences are not crucial in goal statements, for in practice we do not measure achievement of goals; we measure achievement of objectives.

Let us assume this same faculty attempts to write an objective for achieving the aforementioned goal. It might state: "The school will extend the study of Spanish downward from the high school to include grades seven and eight, making a six-year sequence." This statement omits mention of the learners, does specify the action ("extend the study . . . sequence"), does not mention conditions under which the action will take place, and offers no level of performance that would be helpful in subsequent curriculum evaluation.

The supervisor might suggest a revised version of the objective, such as "In keeping with a three-year developmental plan, by the end of next year every student in the ninth grade will have the opportunity to elect Spanish, and one-third of the ninth graders will have enrolled in Spanish; by the end of the second year every student in the eighth grade will have the opportunity to elect Spanish, and one-third of the eighth graders will have enrolled in the study of Spanish; by the end of the third year every student in the seventh grade will have completed a one-semester exploratory course in Spanish."

Does this illustration of a curriculum objective meet the criteria for a well-defined objective? Yes, it does. First, it focuses on the students. Second, it specifies the action (the students will have the opportunity and will enroll, enrolling actually being the action). Third, it spells out the conditions under which the action takes place (in keeping with a three-year development plan, by the end of the next year, by the end of the second year, by the end of the third year, and a one-semester exploratory course). Finally, it establishes a level of performance (every student in the ninth grade, one-third of the ninth graders; every student in the eighth grade, one-third of the eighth graders; and every student in the seventh grade). These levels of performance illustrate the distinction made earlier between level of performance in the case of curriculum objectives and level of performance in respect to instructional objectives. The level of performance in the case of a curriculum objective is measured in reference to the achievement of groups of learners, whereas the level of performance in the case of an instructional objective is measured for each individual.

A few years ago, the Dade County (Florida) Public Schools developed an extensive set of curriculum objectives. Following is a sampling of objectives from a

Dade County comprehensive plan.[21] Please note that the Dade County Schools used the words *objective* and *indicators*. We would call these *curriculum goals* and *curriculum objectives*.

> *Objective One*: Improve the academic performance of the above average student.
> INDICATORS OF ACCOMPLISHMENT:
>
> 1.a The number of students scoring above 550 out of 800 in either the verbal or math portions of the Scholastic Aptitude Test (SAT) and above 24 on the American College Test Examination (ACT) will increase by 5% for the school year 1985–86, 3% for 1986–87, and 2% for 1987–88.
> 1.b The number of students participating in the gifted program will increase by 10% in 1985–86 and 1986–87, 3% in 1987–88, and 2% in 1988–89.
>
> *Objective Two*: Decrease the dropout rate of all students with emphasis on minorities.
> INDICATORS OF ACCOMPLISHMENT:
>
> 2.a The dropout rate will decrease for each of the school years 1985–86 to 1988–89 from the current longitudinal rate of 29.5% to less than 20%.
> 2.b The decrease in the dropout rate among minorities will be proportional to the decrease in the overall dropout rate of the District.
>
> *Objective Three*: Improve student performance in the basic skills.
> INDICATORS OF ACCOMPLISHMENT:
>
> 3.a There will be a decrease in the percentage of Dade County Public School students scoring within the below average range (stanines 1–3) on the Stanford Achievement Test in the basic skills areas of reading comprehension, language, mathematical concepts, and mathematics application for each of the years 1985–86 to 1988–89.
> 3.b The percentile differences between males and females on the mathematics applications sub-test of the Stanford Achievement Test will decrease in those schools where the program has been implemented for each of the years 1985–86 through 1989–90 or until the scores of female students are equivalent to the scores of male students.
>
> *Objective Nine*: Increase the number of students who demonstrate computer competence.
> INDICATORS OF ACCOMPLISHMENT:
>
> 9.a The number of students completing computer courses will increase for each of the school years 1985–86 to 1989–90.
> 9.b By 1989–90, students in grades 3, 5, 8, and 10/11 will achieve at or above the average level for the state on the tests of minimum performance standards in computer education.

The curriculum goals ("objectives") in this example address needs of groups of students. The curriculum objectives ("indicators") state what the learners as a group will accomplish, specify or imply conditions under which the performance will be carried out, and indicate a general or specific level of group performance.

Periodically, the faculty of a school should subject its curriculum to comprehensive study. It gives the faculty an opportunity to look at the curriculum in toto and to avoid the common error in curriculum development, a patchwork approach of adding and dropping courses and units.

If there are specialist supervisors available in the school system that is conducting a curriculum study, these supervisors may enter into the process when the comprehensive study has been completed and initiate the development of goals and objectives pertinent to the particular specialties or grade levels. The goals and objectives of the special fields or grade levels must be compatible with the general goals and objectives of the school.

Writing Curriculum Guides. The specialist can help teachers take a comprehensive look at an entire discipline, field, or grade level. For example, the supervisor may work with the social studies teachers of a secondary school with the object of improving the entire social studies program. Writing a curriculum guide that covers the entire sequence of a field—in this case social studies—is a common way in which teachers become involved in systematic study of a particular field or across fields.[22]

A curriculum guide is a general plan for a particular sequence of courses within a discipline, for a particular sequence of grade levels, or for interdisciplinary programs. A curriculum guide may also be written for a particular grade level or course within a discipline. Curriculum guides are created in a number of formats, one of which includes these elements.

1. Introduction, which should include (a) some reference to the school's statement of philosophy and aims; (b) some reference to schoolwide curriculum goals and objectives that pertain to the field, for example, citizenship; and (c) curriculum goals and objectives for all students in the particular field or grade levels
2. Instructional goals
3. Instructional objectives
4. Learning activities
5. Evaluation techniques
6. Resources, both human and material

We find guides, for examples, on Language Arts K–4, Career Education in the Senior High School, and Mathematics Grades 4–6. Teachers develop a variety of curriculum materials or products. When a curriculum product is limited, as it may be, to a detailed plan for an individual course, as for example twelfth-grade American History, it becomes a course of study (see below). When a curriculum product is limited, as it may be, to a general plan for teaching a particular topic, it becomes a resource unit (see below).

One of the advantages of curriculum projects exemplified by the creation of curriculum guides, courses of study, and resource units lies in the fact that teachers not only go through the process—a valuable outcome in and of itself—but also come out with a useful product.

The task of writing curriculum materials clearly demonstrates again the inseparability of curriculum and instruction. When we include instructional goals and objectives, activities, resources, and evaluation techniques in the materials, we are moving from programmatic concerns (curriculum) into methods (instruction). In practice, when teachers write curriculum guides, courses of study, and resource units, they go beyond the curriculum questions of what? when? where? and by whom? and into the instructional question of how?

As curriculum development narrows from study of the entire curriculum of the school to study of the curriculum of an entire sequence within the total curriculum to study of the curriculum of a course or grade level to study of a particular topic, curriculum goals and objectives actually change into instructional goals and objectives. The emphasis shifts from levels of performance of groups of students, which would serve as an indicator of the success of the curriculum, to levels of mastery expected of individuals, which would serve as an indicator of the success of instruction.

Following are illustrations of curriculum and instructional goals and objectives. We will take one example of a goal and one example of an objective from each of four kinds of curriculum materials.

1. From a *comprehensive study* of an elementary school mathematics sequence that specified curriculum goals and objectives:
   Curriculum goal: Students should complete the mathematics sequence with competencies in mathematics that will enable them to function in their daily personal transactions.
   Curriculum objective: On completion of the mathematics sequence at least 90 percent of the sixth graders will score a grade of 75 percent or better on the terminal mathematics test developed by the elementary school teachers in cooperation with the mathematics supervisor.
2. From an early childhood *curriculum guide* on health education:
   Instructional goal: The student will understand the necessity for developing sanitary personal habits.
   Instructional objective: The student will wash his or her hands after using the lavatory.
3. From an eighth-grade English *course of study*:
   Instructional goal: The student will understand the differences between linking verbs, transitive verbs, and intransitive verbs.
   Instructional objective: On completion of a learning package on types of verbs the student will be able to identify linking verbs, transitive verbs, and intransitive verbs in a literary passage supplied by the teacher with 90 percent accuracy.
4. From a *resource unit* on common home repairs for a ninth-grade course in industrial arts:
   Instructional goal: The student will realize how much money can be saved by doing his or her own home repairs.
   Instructional objective: The student will repair a leaking kitchen faucet.

Curriculum guides are a type of product that can come out of a comprehensive curriculum study.

The Problem-Centered Approach

Although teachers do not always see the advantage or necessity of carrying out a complete and comprehensive review of the curriculum, they can become highly motivated to pursue study of curriculum problems that they themselves have identified. One or more teachers may wish, for example, to study ways of improving the reading program of the elementary school. A group of teachers might desire to find better ways of caring for the needs of the exceptional children in the school. A number of teachers might be interested in developing a multicultural education program.

The science teachers might express dissatisfaction with the school biology program and wish to overhaul it. A couple of teachers in English might be motivated to try out a team-teaching approach in their classes. The teachers of the primary grades might like to experiment with a whole language approach in their grades. The mathematics teachers in a middle school as a result of studying the achievement of their students in mathematics might begin to raise the question of whether their mathematics program is suitable for the learners in their classes. A middle school teacher of social studies might wish to implement cooperative learning in his or her classroom. The problems that teachers identify and the revisions of programs or innovations that they suggest may be within a particular field or grade level or may cut across fields and grade levels. In either case, the problems or programs are specific pieces of the curriculum and not the total curriculum of the school nor even the total sequence of a particular field. For that reason, we refer here to the study of specific problems and programs as the *problem-centered approach*.

Following the problem-centered approach, the supervisor responds to needs identified by the teachers. This does not mean that the supervisor must act only as a responder to teachers' needs but should also serve as a galvanizer, an idea person who assists teachers in identifying curriculum problems and innovative programs. In this capacity, the supervisor suggests ideas to teachers and attempts to stimulate their interest by raising questions such as "What would you think of . . . ?" "Have you thought about this kind of program?" "Do you think such a plan would work in our school?" "I just came across a report of a successful program at a school in New Mexico. Would you care to read about it?" The supervisor and the teachers jointly share the responsibility for uncovering problems as well as working toward their solution.

The problem-centered approach has a great deal of psychological merit, for teachers view this as an approach that will help them with problems or programs with which they are intimately involved. As an alternative to identifying a special problem or a particular program, the supervisor might suggest that the teachers work with him or her on the development of a year's course of study or syllabus for a particular subject or grade or on the construction of a resource unit on a particular topic to be presented during the year.

Courses of Study. A course of study is a curriculum document that covers only one subject or one year's work. Some people refer to a course of study as a *syllabus*. Typically, a syllabus is an outline of topics of a course, whereas a course of study includes several features in addition to the topics. Below is a minimal list of elements that should be included in a course of study.

1. Instructional goals
2. Instructional objectives
3. Entry skills necessary for successful pursuit of the subject
4. Sequence of topics or units
5. Suggested learning activities
6. Suggested evaluation techniques
7. Suggested resources

Some courses of study include all text materials and tests in addition to the preceding elements, making the course of study highly prescriptive.

Resource Units. The creation of a resource unit is a still narrower curriculum planning exercise in which a group of teachers prepares a curriculum document that focuses on a particular topic. For example, a group of elementary school teachers might develop a resource unit on Our National Parks. A group of secondary school teachers of history might construct a resource unit on World War I. The resource unit provides suggestions that teachers can use in developing unit plans for study of the topic in their own courses or grades. Minimal components of a resource unit are these:

1. Instructional goals
2. Instructional objectives
3. Suggested learning activities
4. Suggested evaluation techniques
5. Suggested resources

Thus, we can trace the production of curriculum documents or products from curriculum guide to course of study, to resource unit, to teaching/learning unit, to finally, the daily lesson plan.

The process by which teachers study the curriculum and create materials is a phase of curriculum development, whereas the process by which teachers carry out the curriculum is instruction.

The problem-centered approach should be followed in addition to but not in place of the comprehensive approach. The problem-centered approach permits the teachers to take a close look at the trees but without the comprehensive approach they may not see the forest. Both the comprehensive approach and the problem-centered approach have the same point of departure: specification of goals and objectives. Teachers should define where they are leading the learners before they jump into their vehicles and take off.

DESIGN OF THE PLAN. Between the completion of the statement of objectives and the implementation stage, curriculum plans must be drawn up. A curriculum plan that impacts more than one classroom will ordinarily be written by a committee of teachers. It should be presented in the form of a proposal to the entire faculty of which the committee is representative. When the curriculum change to be recommended is small, requiring no new resources and involving no great changes in staffing patterns or assignments, the plan may be a very simple one. When teachers decide to recommend a major innovative program, which will involve new distributions of resources and staff, a detailed proposal is necessary. A good deal of study, research, and thought must go into the development of a proposed plan. A full-blown proposal consists of the following parts.

1. Description of the proposed plan, including a time schedule for its implementation
2. Rationale and justification for the plan or program

3. Summary of the research related to the plan or program, with information on the success or failure of similar plans or programs elsewhere, if any
4. Human and material resources needed, including facilities necessary
5. Estimated costs of the plan or program
6. Plan for evaluating the success of the innovation

The development of a curriculum proposal is not a job that can be entered into lightly. It requires serious study and intelligent consideration of the many factors involved. It is all well and good for a group of middle school teachers, for example, to propose a program of computer literacy. But what are the implications in such a proposal? What would be the goals and objectives of the program? What would be the justification for offering such a program? What resources would be needed? How many new staff would be required? Where would staff be obtained? What equipment and materials would be required? Where would classes be held? What might have to be removed from the curriculum to find time for the new study proposed? What would the new program cost the school district? How will the success of the program be determined? The supervisor plays a vital role in helping teachers find answers to these questions so that a reasonable and possible proposal can be drafted.

A school or school system must establish the machinery for review and ratification of curriculum proposals, for an active faculty can generate numerous proposals and obviously not all proposals can be endorsed and implemented. A common route for curriculum proposals is from a group of teachers to the principal. If the change proposed is within the jurisdiction of the school alone and the school has the resources necessary, the principal can, if he or she wishes, endorse the proposal and it can be implemented. If aspects of the proposal go beyond the school and particularly if they necessitate new funds and staffing, the principal will have to refer the proposal to the superintendent and the superintendent may then need to seek support from the school board. This route, however, bypasses a good many teachers who might have an interest in the proposed program or who might be affected directly or indirectly. When the reallocation of resources becomes a factor, every teacher is concerned. Consequently, some systematic procedure should be set up for faculty review, evaluation, and endorsement of curriculum proposals.

Universities typically follow a model that some public schools use and that has much to commend it. A proposal must first gain departmental approval. It must then be approved by the Curriculum Committee and the faculty of the particular school of the university and by its dean. After these steps, a standing Curriculum Committee of the university receives the proposal, reviews it, holds hearings if necessary, and ultimately approves or disapproves the proposal. If the committee approves, the proposal is placed before the faculty of the university, either the faculty as a whole or an elected senate, for its approval or disapproval. Only after the faculty has given its endorsement does the proposal go on to the university administrators for final approval or disapproval. The Curriculum Committee is elected by the university faculty and its term of office is stipulated in the governance document of the institution.

The Curriculum Committee acts as a gatekeeper, screening out proposals, studying the implications in each, and assuring a level of quality. Each public school should create its Curriculum Committee to which curriculum proposals emanating from its teachers should be directed. This process is slower than the route from a group of teachers directly to the administrator, but it subjects proposals to a thorough and public analysis, prevents rash actions, and assures a broader basis of support from the faculty. Certainly, if empowerment of teachers means anything at all, it means teacher participation and responsibility in shaping the curriculum. A vehicle like the Curriculum Committee is a means of involving teachers in the fundamental professional activity of curriculum development.

One of the major responsibilities of the Curriculum Committee and subsequently the entire faculty as it evaluates curriculum proposals is some consideration about how the specific proposals fit into the grand scheme of the curriculum. All the bits and pieces of the curriculum should fit together and relate to each other. Reference should be made to the school's or school system's statements of philosophy, aims, goals, and objectives when action is being taken on specific proposals.

Up to this point, the roles of teachers, supervisors, and administrators in the process of curriculum development have been stressed, but not to be omitted is input from students, the public, and other school personnel. Although the faculty may carry the responsibility for curriculum development, efforts must be made from the stage of writing the philosophy through the endorsement of the curriculum proposal to obtain input from students, the nonprofessional staff, and the public. One way of achieving this input is through participation of these groups on school committees such as the Committee on Philosophy, Aims, Goals, and Objectives and the Curriculum Committee.

The concept of empowerment has extended not only to the professionals but also to laypeople and students. Reflecting the demand to involve patrons of the school and, to some extent, students, schools often look to advisory councils, some of which have been established by state mandate, for help in making decisions about the operation of the school, including the basic question of what shall be taught, how it will be translated into action, and how it will be evaluated. A manifestation in empowering laypersons, albeit outside the school system, is the movement in the late 1990s toward so-called charter schools, which enable private citizens to establish and operate schools with a minimum of state and district regulation, clearly a challenge to the public school system.[23]

Schools have met with varying success at involving students and the public on professional committees. The maturity of the student and the availability of laypersons are factors that must be weighed when school committees are established.

Input from groups other than the faculty is vitally necessary. In the following chapter, the technique of needs assessment is discussed as an alternative or supplement to student and public participation on school committees.

CONTINUING PROBLEMS OF CURRICULUM DEVELOPMENT

As teachers involve themselves in curriculum development they will encounter four recurrent and major problems: scope, sequence, balance, and organization. Each of the four problems must be resolved during the planning stage, requiring some very difficult decisions on the part of the faculty.

Scope of the Curriculum

The scope of the curriculum consists of the experiences or subject matter or content to which the learners are exposed. The content of every field of learning is so vast and is expanding at such a rate that covering any field in its entirety is impossible, although many teachers strive to do so. Some hard decisions must be made concerning what content should be selected for inclusion in the curriculum and what limitations will be placed on that content. The delineation of the scope of the curriculum entails a search for answers to two basic questions: Who should make the decisions about what content should be included in the curriculum? What content should be included?

Who Should Decide on Content? The question "Who should decide on content?" is simpler to answer than "What content should be included in the curriculum?" The professional faculty should make the decisions on the scope of the curriculum—and on sequence and balance as well—after obtaining as much input as possible from as many sources as possible, including students and the public.

A faculty, working as a total faculty, as a portion of the faculty, or as individual teachers, must decide what experiences, what courses, and what topics will become a part of the curriculum. Whether the entire faculty, a portion of the faculty, or individual teachers make the decisions on content depends on the aspect of the curriculum under consideration. The scope of the content would appear in a curriculum proposal and in a curriculum guide. As indicated earlier in this chapter, major decisions on curriculum that affect more than one teacher and involve the allocation of resources and staff should be put through the approval process with review by the Curriculum Committee and by the entire faculty. Curriculum decisions involving minor changes within fields or subjects and not involving questions of resource allocation and staffing are appropriately the prerogative of the particular teachers involved and need not go through the entire review process. The supervisor should help teachers determine whether a curricular revision should be taken to the Curriculum Committee and/or the entire faculty. It would not be necessary, for example, for a group of Algebra I teachers to submit a revised course of study in Algebra I to the Curriculum Committee and then to the faculty as a whole. On the other hand, if the algebra teachers wished to lengthen the study of algebra from two years to three years, that decision would be the province of the Curriculum Committee and the entire faculty. It is not necessary to involve the Curriculum Committee or the faculty in a review of resource units that fit into the scope of a particular grade or course or field unless a proposed unit embodies content of a controversial nature that might reflect on the entire faculty. Teachers in health or science, for example, who wish to offer a unit or course or sequenced program on sex education would be well advised to seek faculty approval as a great deal of controversy surrounds this area of study.

Broad decisions on content fall within the jurisdiction of the entire faculty of the school or, in many cases, the faculties of the school system as a whole. For example, if a group of elementary school teachers proposes that the elementary school adopt a new reading program, its proposal must be considered by all teachers. On the other hand, if a group of modern language teachers decides to shift the program from a grammar-translation method to an audio-lingual method, the modern language teachers need not clear this through the total approval process. In the latter case, the total faculty has made its input through endorsement of modern language study and need not concern itself with the specifics of content (for example, which authors are read) and the methods to be employed. A group of English teachers who draft a resource unit on contemporary British novelists need not take its resource unit to the Curriculum Committee and entire faculty but may make the decisions on this content itself. The individual teacher also has freedom to choose content, for example, within the resource unit. The teacher may choose to have students read a novel by William Golding instead of a novel by Alec Waugh, which was suggested in the resource unit, or may substitute Golding's *Lord of the Flies* for *The Spire*. In short, teachers make decisions on content, sometimes in large groups, sometimes in small groups, and sometimes individually.

Teachers are compelled to make curriculum decisions within certain restrictions. Some decisions on content have already been made for the teacher. Decisions that have been made for the teacher tend to be broader in scope than those that individual teachers or groups of teachers will make. Some decisions are of long standing. The curriculum of a school has been fleshed out by a group of planners before that school opens its doors. The existent curriculum of a school is one limit on the individual teacher's freedom to select content. A fifth-grade teacher, for example, whose elementary school offers a program in Spanish cannot elect to toss out Spanish and substitute German on the personal belief that German is a more important language. If the teacher believes strongly that German should be taught instead of Spanish, other teachers must be involved in consideration of the idea and must present a plan through the established channels for faculty approval.

The locality, through the school board, and the state, through its board of education, department of education, and legislature, place some restrictions on teachers' freedom to choose content. The tendency is for the locality and state to mandate certain offerings. A locality may stipulate, for example, that it will exceed the state's minimum requirements in certain subjects. Where a state might demand a minimum of three years of social studies for graduation, a locality might require four years. Where a state might require forty-five minutes of instruction in reading per day in the elementary school, the locality might require one hour. The local school board, elected by the people of the district and serving as agents of the state, has the power to make these kinds of decisions for the schools that it administers.

The state board of education, acting for the state in educational matters, makes curriculum decisions affecting all schools of the state. It sets minimal standards that all schools must meet. It often puts forth a statement of goals of education in the state, which must be considered by local faculties in the curriculum planning process. The state department of education administers policies set by the state board and establishes regulations that all school systems in the state must follow.

The state legislature occasionally makes a foray into the curriculum arena. When state legislators translate their curricular beliefs into law, their decisions are binding on the schools. Thus, found in the curriculum are legislatively mandated courses on the effects of alcohol, tobacco, and drugs on the human body; on the election process; and on sex education.

Throughout the 1980s, intent on reform of their educational systems, states became more prescriptive in what they required of local school systems. Not only did they stipulate instructional objectives to be achieved by students in various disciplines but they also mandated the processes for assessing students' mastery of the objectives. The movement toward state mandating has diminished while at the same time movements to empower teachers and parents at individual schools have grown in strength. Increasingly in the 1990s, with the growth of site-based management, both administrative and curricular decisions are being made at the local school level.

One other impingement on the teacher's power to select content is the textbook. The textbooks used within a school act not only as a resource but also as a limitation on the teacher's choice of content. The teacher who is new to a school will find that textbooks have already been chosen. Teachers who are already on the scene may have some input into the process of selecting textbooks. The process normally calls for faculty recommendations, but textbooks are usually purchased in quantities as a result of either local or state procedures. Frequently, certain series of textbooks are adopted and these must be used at various grade levels. Consequently, the individual teacher is bound by the final choices, which have been made as a consequence of group deliberations. The individual teacher may or may not be pleased by the choices made but must live with those choices for the school life of those textbooks, which is often five or more years. In some states, multiple adoptions of textbooks are made and the teacher may select from a number of options, a procedure that expands his or her freedom to choose content.

The textbook is less of an infringement on the teacher's freedom to choose content if supplementary materials are available. Some schools and communities are richer in this respect than others. Supplementary materials permit the teacher to go beyond the textbook for additional information and other points of view. It should be added, however, that in some cases where supplementary materials are available, some teachers elect not to go beyond the adopted textbook. They find that reliance on a single textbook is an easier path to follow. The search for suitable supplementary materials and their incorporation into teaching plans require more time and more decisions by the teacher. The supervisor has the continuing responsibility of helping in the search for useful materials and in making them known to teachers.

These limitations on the process of selecting content—by the locality, by the state, and by the adopted textbook—do place some restrictions on teachers. The locality or state may require a particular field of study and may even supply a curriculum guide—usually developed by a group of teachers—that specifies minimal competencies to be achieved by students. Yet many decisions on content remain to be made by the teacher. Within each discipline, the teacher must select topics that go beyond the minimal competencies and must choose the methods for presenting the subject matter.

What Content Should Be Included? More difficult to answer than "Who should select the content?" is the question "What content should be selected?" Once the curriculum decision has been made that the school will offer a particular program, whether that decision has been made by the existent curriculum, by the school's faculty, by faculties of the school district, by the school board, or by the state, the teacher who is designated to present that content has a multitude of decisions to make.

Every field covers an enormous territory of facts, skills, and attitudes from which selection has to be made. It should be more obvious than it seems to be that not all knowledge is of equal worth.[24] Although we are not likely to encounter much controversy in establishing that principle, the curricula of the schools often seem structured in such a way as to imply that all knowledge is equally valuable. The most conspicuous example of this implication is the typical high school, which allocates the same amount of time for every course in the curriculum, following the concept of the Carnegie unit, which goes back to the first decade of the twentieth century. In attempting to decide on the scope of the curriculum, teachers must keep in mind one overriding criterion: They should include in the curriculum that knowledge, those skills, and those affective learnings that are of most worth to the individual throughout life.

The teacher (or teachers working together) is the final judge concerning which cognitive, affective, and psychomotor learnings will be taught to the students. After having made the difficult decisions of which learnings will be taught, he or she must organize the content into coherent form and follow that organization by presenting the content to the students.

The teacher may choose simply to follow the selected learnings, the organization, and the methods of the adopted textbook. He or she may take the number of chapters or topics in the textbook, divide it by the number of weeks in the school year, and thereby calculate the number of weeks to be spent on each chapter or topic. Or the teacher may adhere strictly to a suggested or mandated curriculum guide and not go beyond its minimal competencies. In using these mechanical approaches to content selection the teacher is deferring all content decisions to the authors of the textbook or curriculum guide.

Teachers should inject themselves into the selection process and not be passive agents. They must make the decisions concerning which content is of most worth and not permit decisions over which they have jurisdiction to be made by others. Because all knowledge is not of equal value, effort must be made by teachers to set priorities on content. The supervisor must assist teachers in developing the skills of choosing or rejecting content and establishing criteria for priority of content.

This text discusses selection of content in a broad context, meaning the selection of subject matter, courses, or topics, that must subsequently be broken down into instructional goals and objectives from which content within a field may be said to derive.

One way to make curriculum decisions, derived from the work of Ralph W. Tyler, is known as the Tyler Rationale, which has proved to be a popular means of thinking about the curriculum and selecting content.[25]

The Tyler Rationale proposes that the curriculum worker consider three sources of content—student, society, and subject—and two screens—philosophy of education and psychology of learning. From the three sources are derived tentative general objectives (which might be either curriculum or instructional goals). The general objectives are passed through the two screens to yield precise instructional objectives. The rationale has been widely depicted as shown in Figure 7.3.

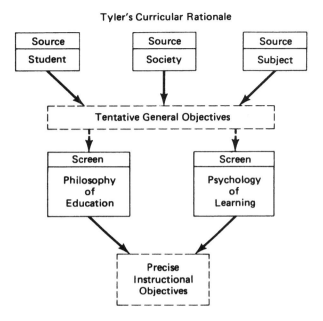

Figure 7.3. The Tyler Rationale. *Source: W. James Popham and Eva L. Baker,* Establishing Instructional Goals *(Englewood Cliffs, N.J.: Prentice-Hall, 1970), p. 87. Based on Ralph W. Tyler,* Basic Principles of Curriculum and Instruction *(Chicago: University of Chicago Press, 1949). Copyright 1949 by the University of Chicago. All rights reserved. Reprinted with permission from the University of Chicago.*

Content is derived from the three sources: student, society, and subject. The rationale implies that each of the three sources is important and has a bearing on the curriculum decisions being made. Content being considered for inclusion in the curriculum should be weighed against the three sources and answers should be found to these questions: Does the content meet the needs of students? Does the content satisfy a societal need? Does the content fit into the internal logic of the subject matter and is it recommended by persons who are regarded as specialists in the field?

When the content has been determined to meet these tests, some tentative general objectives can be formulated. The teacher or teachers would then decide whether the content is compatible with their stated philosophy and whether the content is psychologically feasible. If the content meets these last two tests, it may be considered for inclusion in the curriculum.

Using Tyler's terminology, we can illustrate the application of the rationale with a situation in which a group of physical education teachers wish to introduce a unit on volleyball into the curriculum. First, we relate the unit on volleyball to the three sources.

- SOURCE: STUDENT. Does the unit meet needs of students? Yes, it does. Students have need for active sports. Volleyball develops a team spirit and provides an outlet for group competition. It is a sport that students themselves have requested. It is also a sport they can carry over into adult life.

- SOURCE: SOCIETY. Does the unit meet any societal need? Yes, it does. Adults have the need for wholesome recreation, and volleyball is one way of satisfying this need. People of all ages can play volleyball and gain enjoyment from it.
- SOURCE: SUBJECT. Is volleyball an integral part of the field of physical education? Yes, it is. It is a sport recommended by many experts in the field of physical education as an excellent form of physical exercise and as a source of pleasure.

Because volleyball has met these three tests, we can draw up some tentative general objectives—for example, "Students should develop skills in carryover sports like volleyball," "Students not engaged in interscholastic sports should demonstrate physical fitness," "All students should learn to participate in team efforts such as those provided by volleyball."

After the tentative general objectives are determined, the teachers should ask themselves whether the unit on volleyball is compatible with their philosophical beliefs. They should decide whether this unit makes operational any philosophical statement on which the faculty has agreed. It should not be difficult to establish the position that volleyball is one way of appealing to individual differences and interests. As faculties are usually in agreement that the school should contribute to the student's physical as well as mental and intellectual development, volleyball would be compatible with the philosophy of education espoused by our hypothetical group of teachers.

The tentative general objectives must also be passed through the psychology of learning screen. The skills of volleyball are within the range of the learners at their stage of growth and development. Learners would be positively motivated to play volleyball, and this activity would help them to satisfy basic psychological needs of success, approval, and movement.

The unit on volleyball has been demonstrated to have been derived from all three sources and to have successfully passed through the two screens. It is now the teacher's task to specify the precise instructional objectives—for example, "The student will demonstrate the proper way of serving," "On a paper-and-pencil test on the rules of the game of volleyball the student will achieve a score of 90 percent."

Daniel Tanner and Laurel N. Tanner saw as one of the problems of the Tyler Rationale the apparent lack of interdependence of the various functions of curriculum development.[26] In spite of seeming deficiencies the Tyler Rationale has provided a way of thinking about curriculum development and has withstood the test of time as a useful tool in this process.

Some systematic way of thinking is necessary in determining the scope of the curriculum. The supervisor should guide the teachers not only in the process of identifying content but also in the process of thinking about the curriculum.

Sequence of the Curriculum
The scope of the curriculum tells what subject matter will be presented. The sequence of the curriculum tells in what order the subject matter will be presented. Faculties must sequence experiences, courses, series of courses (sequences of a discipline), and

topics within courses. By custom, pupils may not study fourth-grade mathematics until they have mastered third-grade mathematics. But what is there about the content of fourth-grade mathematics? Some teachers never raise this kind of question. They have taken for granted grade placement of content—and placement of content within a grade level—and have assumed that placement has been arrived at by deliberate thought, whereas placement of content has often been arbitrary. A common defense for grade placement of content is tradition: We have always done it this way. Surely, there must be more valid reasons for the content of fourth-grade mathematics to follow the content of third-grade mathematics than that tradition has dictated the placement or that the number three precedes the number four in a sequence. The ostensible reason the content of fourth-grade mathematics follows the content of third-grade mathematics is that the content of the two levels is sequential—success in fourth-grade mathematics depends on success in third-grade mathematics.

There must be some reason teachers in the elementary school present addition first, then subtraction, follow with multiplication, and end with division. There must be a reason algebra follows arithmetic and does not precede it. There must be a reason calculus is delayed until the last year of high school or until college.

How do we account for the fact that World History precedes twelfth-grade Problems of Democracy in many high schools? Why are the civilizations of 2,000 years ago studied before those of the twentieth century? What makes the history of a state a seventh-grade subject rather than a tenth-grade subject? Why does geometry precede second-year algebra in some secondary schools? Why do students read Shakespeare's *Julius Caesar* before they read *Hamlet*?

These questions are problems of sequencing. Jerome S. Bruner caused us to think about the problem of sequencing when he hypothesized that "any subject can be taught effectively in some intellectually honest form to any child at any stage of development."[27] One inference from this hypothesis is that children are often capable of more than they have been given credit for. Must first-year algebra, for example, be reserved for eighth grade or ninth grade or can algebra be taught "in some intellectually honest form" to children as young as kindergarteners? This latter question suggests that two inquiries must be made when sequencing content. One is empirical: Can content be placed at a particular grade level or at a particular point within a grade level? The other is philosophical: Should content be placed at a particular grade level or at a particular point within a grade level? Because algebra *can* be taught to kindergarteners, *should* it be taught to kindergarteners? Over the years, we have witnessed the shift of subject matter downward from college to the secondary school and from the secondary school to the middle and elementary school. Has the shift been made after due consideration of the purposes for such a move, or has the shift been made because of ill-defined reasons like "it seems the best thing to do"?

On what bases then may we determine the sequence of content? First, and rather obviously, simple content should precede complex content. Each step in complexity requires certain prerequisite knowledge and skills. This principle implies an analysis of the structure of the discipline and examination of the internal logic of the subject matter. We teach the building blocks of language, the sounds, before we teach words. Mastery of the sounds helps the learner in developing word-attack skills. We teach nouns before we teach pronouns—words that substitute for nouns. We teach concepts before we teach principles because we must have mastered the concepts before we can make use of them in rules.

Second, instruction must be developmentally appropriate. Content must match the maturation level of the learners. Kindergarteners as a rule are not ready for cursive writing, and this content must be delayed until children have developed enough coordination to write in cursive form. Lengthy content requiring a long span of attention must be placed appropriately, for we know that the attention span of learners increases with age and acculturation. Work involving the use of hazardous tools and materials must be delayed until children are old enough to observe fundamental safety precautions.

Third, content that satisfies the immediate needs of learners usually precedes content aimed at long-term needs. The social studies curriculum of the elementary school is often organized according to this principle. Children study the world closest to them—their school, their home, their neighborhood, their community—before they look beyond to the state, then the nation, and finally the world at large. They learn to write personal letters before they learn to write essays, which meets not only the third principle—satisfaction of immediate needs of learners—but also the first— simple content precedes complex.

Fourth, sequences are determined often from the faculty's statements of philosophy, aims, goals, and objectives. Although these statements are more guides to scope, they may also provide direction for sequence. For example, the sequence of modern language instruction today is derived from the philosophy, aims, goals, and objectives of the faculty. The goals of modern language instruction are, in order of priority, (1) understanding the language, (2) speaking the language, (3) reading the language, and (4) writing the language. Years ago reading and writing were the major goals, with little emphasis on understanding the spoken tongue and speaking it. As the goals changed, the content changed and the sequence of that content was altered.

Fifth, chronological order serves as a guide to sequencing some content. History is normally taught in chronological order, as is the literature of certain epochs. This principle allows for a very logical sequence pattern, but unfortunately it is not always the most motivating to the learner psychologically. Why, for example, couldn't the order of the history curriculum be reversed, starting with the most recent events—which would meet the criterion of immediate needs of learners—and working backward? Or why is a more complicated pattern not possible: the study of a recent historical event coupled with the search for its antecedents in the past? What is there about nineteenth-century literature that would necessitate its study before twentieth-century literature?

Sequences must be established, and sometimes these sequences will be arbitrary. When two units of content are of equal complexity and when the study of one is not dependent on the prior study of the other, an arbitrary judgment must be made by the teacher about which unit will come first. When each succeeding unit is progressively more complex and the series of units involves a hierarchy of knowledge and skills, the units must be placed in proper order.

The task of sequencing content recalls the necessity of specifying and testing for entry skills. If there is a hierarchy of skills in a particular sequence and if success at each succeeding level is dependent on success at a previous level, the teacher must preassess the presence of the necessary prerequisite skills.

When working with a group of teachers on the problem of sequencing of content, the supervisor should keep before the group the necessity of their answering this question: On what basis has the content been placed where it is?

Balance in the Curriculum

When teachers work together to outline the scope of the curriculum, they must give attention not only to what content will be included in the curriculum but also to the relationship between the various segments of the curriculum. They must strive to implement the principle of balance. The concept of balance implies that no portion of the curriculum will exert an overwhelming pressure on another portion.

The school's curriculum is out of balance when the school is known only for its razzle-dazzle marching band or its powerhouse of a football team. The curriculum is out of balance when children are made to study outmoded content that will be obsolete by the time they graduate from high school. The curriculum is out of balance when it revolves completely around content of the learners' choice.

Although some of the decisions on balance are internal to a particular subject or discipline, many of the decisions are interdisciplinary in nature and must be resolved by the total faculty. Vested interests play a part in making decisions on balance, and it takes a larger group beyond the vested interests to assure a balanced curriculum. Among the aspects of a curriculum that require balancing are these.

1. *There must be a balance between general education and specialized education.* Because general education is a main function of the elementary school, imbalance between general education—courses or experiences required of all students—and specialized education is more common to the secondary school. General education equips the student to cope with problems of daily living, to develop certain basic knowledge and skills, to become familiar with our culture, and to develop attitudes and competencies of good citizenship. Specialized education seeks to develop knowledge and skills within a discipline and is often preparatory to advanced study of the discipline.

   When there is imbalance we find specialized education stressed over general education or vice versa. As most teachers have a strong commitment to their own teaching fields, they naturally become strong partisans for study of their disciplines and there can be a tug-of-war for the loyalties and interests of the students. Both general education and specialized education are important, and one should not eclipse the other.

2. *There must be a balance between the academic and the vocational aspects of the curriculum.* The college prep sequence of a comprehensive high school should not consume all the attention and resources of the school. In vocational schools a sizable portion of the curriculum should be allocated to general education. Programs of career education have resulted in the inclusion of vocationally oriented experiences in the curriculum from the elementary grades through high school.

3. *There must be a balance between content aimed at the immediate and the long-range needs of learners.* Though it is advisable to begin with studies that satisfy the immediate needs of learners, a faculty is negligent if it builds its curriculum exclusively on children's immediate needs. Children are not mature enough to recognize some of the needs they will have later in life. Teachers must help them attempt to recognize the value of certain content that is required to satisfy future needs. On the other hand, the appeal to future needs alone is a common defense teachers use to get pupils to pursue studies in which they have little interest. Education is both preparation for life and training in the here and now. The content of the curriculum should reflect balance between satisfaction of present and future needs.

4. *There must be a balance between the child-centered approach and the subject-centered approach to curriculum.* These two approaches have historically locked horns, the subject-centered curriculum coming out on top in most cases, with the possible exception of the heyday of progressive education in the 1930s. A rapprochement took place after World War II. The subject matter curriculum had a brief and intense revival in the late 1950s as a reaction to Russian progress in science and technology and has once again surged to the forefront with the renewed emphasis on basic skills and the academics. What is needed is an effort to balance the best features of the child-centered curriculum with the best features of the subject-centered curriculum, with the realization by teachers that you cannot divorce the learner from what is being learned.

The foregoing aspects of the concept of balance require study and decisions by teachers in all disciplines and at all grade levels. The principle of balance must be applied as well within disciplines and within courses. A common imbalance in the English curriculum, for example, at the secondary school level and almost universally on the college level, is the heavy concentration on the study of literature to the detriment of the study of the language. The curriculum of a discipline is out of balance when students encounter the content through rote memorization to the exclusion of problem solving. The curriculum is out of balance when teachers consume an inordinate amount of time on special interests of their own and ignore other vital content. The supervisor should continuously examine the curriculum for imbalance and should lead teachers in finding ways to correct the imbalance.

Organization of the Curriculum

During the planning stage, decisions must be made about the organization of the curriculum. We must decide how the curriculum will be set up and delivered. Shall we change existing patterns for engaging the learners in the planned curricular experiences?

Ostensibly, curriculum planners begin with certain organizational parameters: a fixed number of days in the school year and a predetermined schedule—products of decisions made in prior years. What planners must decide is whether to make changes in the present organizational structure.

Some organizational practices will in all likelihood remain constant and probably should remain constant—for example, the use of interdisciplinary teams at the middle school level. Some practices will in all likelihood remain constant when they should be changed—for example, overreliance on the Carnegie unit at the high school level.

That changes in the delivery system can be made and are being made is seen in the examination, experimentation, and incorporation of a variety of innovations throughout the country. School systems in the past decade have, for example, increased the number of credits required for high-school graduation. Some of the innovations under consideration are relatively new, such as single-track and multi-track year-round schools. More frequently than in the past, plans for extending the school year from the traditional 180 days to as many as 210, emulating countries like Japan, are under study in some school systems.

Some of the newer organizational practices look to the past for direction, such as the use of double periods or block schedules at the high school level, the use of rotating schedules at the middle and senior high levels, the renewed interest in integrating curriculum content at all levels, and the advocacy of performance-based education.

In some cases, instead of creating new organizational practices, curriculum planners will make decisions to abandon existing organizational structures in keeping with the results of past implementation, such as the move away from open-space learning areas in the elementary school.

When schools are considering organizational change, supervisors have the heavy responsibility of reviewing the success or failure of similar changes in other school systems throughout the country. They need to refrain and restrain teachers from "hyping" innovations until there is reliable evidence that the innovative practices are more effective in student achievement than previous practices. The inclination to jump on the bandwagon of the latest "innovation" should be resisted. "Withitness," while a virtue in maintaining classroom control, is not necessarily a virtue in organizing the curriculum. Some innovations may be incompatible with the school's culture, the community, the philosophy of the school, and the students' needs.

Supervisors charged with examining the school's structure for curriculum delivery should avoid both extremes of accepting the status quo as perfection and seizing each new practice that comes along. Supervisors should lead teachers in deliberate but cautious change.

Curricular Reform. Supervisors need to stay current with curricular developments. Change in curriculum content and organization are proceeding at a frantic pace as educators grasp for solutions to underachieving public schools. Reform and restructuring are buzzwords of the 1980s and 1990s.

During the 1980s, reform of the public schools took the path of state mandates that prescribed instructional objectives and assessment of student achievement. In spite of all the efforts of the many states engaged in massive reform movements, the decade of the 1980s saw little improvement in pupil achievement. SAT scores, for example, remained depressingly low.

Showcased in the 1990s are plans to permit parental choice of school, public or private, with some form of governmental aid—subsidies or tax credits or vouchers. Proponents of government support reason that deficient schools will be forced to improve in order to meet competition from other public and private schools. On the scene are also public schools operated by contracting private organizations.[28]

Demands for empowerment of teachers and parents have reached state and national levels. States are relaxing their prescriptive behavior and are granting local schools some autonomy in developing their own programs, thus placing accountability squarely on the shoulders of the school districts. Sentiment for decentralizing authority and responsibility and for involving both teachers and patrons and, to a lesser extent, students in the operation of the local schools is spreading across the nation. In fact, downsizing of state departments of education is a trend in the late 1990s.

Whereas reform movements of the 1980s centered around curriculum content and instruction, the efforts of the 1990s have focused on restructuring administration and control as the means of raising the quality of the schools. Though not all school administrators are happy with the thrust of restructuring that dilutes their authority and necessitates changes in administrative style, the supervisor, as a helper to teachers, should be the first to encourage more meaningful involvement of teachers whose opinions historically have been undervalued.

Controversial Problems

During the planning stage the supervisor should engage teachers in examining some of the controversial curriculum issues of the day. Among the problems that many schools encounter are these.

- Providing for children with exceptionalities—providing the least restrictive environment, writing individualized educational plans, and including children with exceptionalities in the regular classroom.
- Confronting the necessity for providing health education to combat use of alcohol, drugs, and tobacco; the appropriate form of sex education, including AIDS education; and the highly controversial establishment of health clinics in the secondary schools, which may distribute both information about contraception and condoms.
- Achieving racial and ethnic integration, a problem still unresolved in some localities in spite of *Brown v. Board of Education of Topeka, Kansas* and subsequent court rulings.[29]
- Creating a curriculum to reflect cultural diversity.
- Deciding the place of bilingual education in the curriculum of schools hosting native speakers of languages other than English.
- Balancing diversity of values as represented by various ethnic and national groups with generalized, overarching American values.
- Determining the role of religion in the schools
- Dealing with the problem of censorship of books, materials, and content.
- Eliminating gender discrimination.

The supervisor should involve teachers in pursuing solutions to controversies that are apparent in their school systems; in formulating their own positions on the issues; in devising professional means of coping with the issues; and, most important, in demonstrating enough vision and initiative to prevent curriculum controversies from arising.[30]

Implementation and Evaluation

When all the endorsements to a curriculum proposal have been obtained and the administrator and school board have given the green light, the plan can be implemented. The proposal has indicated who would carry out the program and under what conditions. A time schedule has been established, showing when the program will begin, at what points it will be evaluated, and when a decision will be made on whether to continue it.

The design of the plan spells out what will be covered in the program and the curriculum organization pattern necessary for carrying out the plan. Further, the plan will detail costs and means of providing funds for its successful operation.

At this stage, detailed instructional goals and objectives must be set forth by the teachers delivering the content and appropriate strategies and resources selected. From this point on, the success of the curriculum plan is in the hands of the instructors. The supervisor continues to assist the teachers through the implementation stage. He or she works with them to put into effect the evaluation plan that is outlined in the curriculum proposal and helps them with both formative evaluation during the course of the program and summative evaluation at the end.

Nothing in the group process for curriculum development, however, should impede the initiative of a teacher or teachers who wish to try out new approaches and techniques in their own classrooms—providing those approaches and techniques do not impinge on other members of the faculty and their classes. An elementary school teacher who wishes to experiment with cooperative learning, for example, should feel free to do so. Pragmatic experimentation of both a curricular and instructional nature in the individual classrooms, sometimes referred to as action research, should be encouraged.

Plans for curriculum development should incorporate an evaluation plan. Once the plan is implemented, efforts must be made to evaluate its progress and results, a topic we discuss in the following chapter.

SUMMARY

Curriculum is conceived as all the experiences the learner engages in under the supervision of the school. Curriculum development or improvement is a continuous process carried out by faculties under the leadership of the supervisor.

Curriculum development begins with a statement of philosophy and aims agreed on by consensus of the faculty. The school's statement of philosophy and aims is translated first into broad curriculum goals, then into specific curricular objectives. The curriculum goals and objectives have a direct bearing on the instructional goals and objectives in each course or grade level.

Two approaches to curriculum development are suggested: the comprehensive approach, which provides for an overall study of the curriculum, and the problem-centered approach, which focuses on problems identified by teachers and on segments of the curriculum.

A six-part model for curriculum development is presented in the text. The components of this model are statement of philosophy and aims, statement of curriculum goals, statement of curriculum objectives, design of the plan, implementation of the curriculum, and evaluation of the curriculum. Both the comprehensive approach and the problem-centered approach have a place in curriculum study and are sometimes carried on concurrently.

Four continuing problems of curriculum development demand the attention of the supervisor and teachers: scope, sequence, balance, and organization. Guidelines for coping with these problems are suggested.

Curriculum development requires supervisors to be familiar with efforts to change, reform, and restructure the schools. Curriculum leaders work with faculties in finding ways to solve controversial curriculum issues and prevent controversies from arising.

The supervisor plays an instrumental role in promoting curriculum development. Nonprofessional school personnel, laypersons, and students should be brought into the process.

QUESTIONS FOR DISCUSSION

1. What knowledge is of most worth?
2. What effect does the movement toward empowerment of teachers and parents have on the curriculum?
3. What do you see as the major goals of the curriculum?
4. What effect should the presence of diverse ethnic groups have on the curriculum?
5. How should teachers deal with controversial content?

ACTIVITIES FOR FURTHER STUDY

1. Write a paper stating your opinions of deficiencies in curriculum leadership today and how you as a supervisor will attempt to overcome those deficiencies.
2. Outline basic philosophical beliefs you hold about education.
3. Describe responsibilities of supervisors who consider themselves "curriculum workers."
4. Select an elementary school subject at one grade level or a middle or secondary school subject, break a year's work into units, and place the units in sequence. Justify your sequence.
5. Locate a statement of philosophy and aims of a school you know well, examine it, and report practices in the school that are in keeping with the stated philosophy and aims and those that are not furthering the philosophy and aims.
6. Repeat exercise 5 with the school's statement of curriculum goals.
7. Repeat exercise 5 with the school's statement of curriculum objectives.
8. Find evidences of imbalance in a school's curriculum and suggest ways to correct the imbalance.
9. Give your own definition of curriculum.
10. Take a position on the premise that curriculum and instruction are interrelated but separate entities.
11. Write an illustration of a curriculum goal and two curriculum objectives derived from the goal.
12. Illustrate the difference between a curriculum goal and an instructional goal by writing an example of each.

13. Illustrate the difference between an instructional goal and an instructional objective by writing an example of each.

14. Explain the differences between a comprehensive approach to curriculum development and a problem-centered approach.

15. Locate a curriculum guide and evaluate it on the basis of criteria discussed in this chapter.

16. Locate a course of study and evaluate it on the basis of criteria discussed in this chapter.

17. Describe the components of the Tyler Rationale.

18. *Those who are teaching*: List several curriculum problems you believe are in need of study in your school. *Those who are not teaching*: Interview a teacher in a school and report curricular problems identified by that teacher.

19. *Those who are teaching*: Explain the process by which curriculum proposals are adopted in your schools. *Those who are not teaching*: Explain your belief on how curriculum proposals should be adopted.

20. Check on the process of curriculum development in any school of your choosing and report whether students and laypersons are involved in the process and, if so, how.

21. Examine a curriculum sequence in operation in any elementary, middle, or secondary school and report the bases on which the sequencing decisions were made.

22. Search the literature and report on any continuing problems of curriculum development other than scope, sequence, balance, and organization. (Suggested reference: Peter F. Oliva, *Developing the Curriculum*, 4th ed., chap. 13.)

23. Suggest curriculum elements that need balancing in addition to those described in this chapter. (Suggested reference: Peter F. Oliva, *Developing the Curriculum*, 4th ed., chap. 13.)

24. Analyze a curriculum guide or course of study in your field or grade level and conjecture on how decisions on scope were made.

25. State your position on the following controversial issues that impact the curriculum:

   a. Parents should be free to choose their children's schools, including home schooling, if they wish.

   b. Secondary school health clinics should distribute condoms to their students.

   c. Scientific creationism should be a part of the curriculum.

   d. Schools should promote the melting pot concept of values.

26. Identify a controversial issue in a school system you know well. Describe what, if anything, has been done about the issue and what your views are on solving the problem.

27. Outline a staff development workshop that you, as a supervisor, could conduct on any one of the following current instructional and curricular developments/practices:

   a. constructivist psychology

   b. cooperative learning

   c. cultural literacy (core knowledge)

   d. multicultural education

   e. outcomes-based education

   f. sexuality education

   g. whole language

28. Outline a staff development workshop that you, as a supervisor, could conduct on ethnic and gender discrimination in the curriculum.
29. Outline a staff development workshop that you, as a supervisor, could conduct on handling efforts to censor curriculum content, books, and other materials.

NOTES

1. For a full treatment of curriculum development see Peter F. Oliva, *Developing the Curriculum*, 4th ed. (New York: HarperCollins, 1997).
2. *National Assessment of Educational Progress*, Educational Testing Service Periodic Reports, Princeton, N.J. See also Chapter 8 of this book and Lawrence C. Stedman, "The New Mythology about the Status of U.S. Schools," *Educational Leadership* 52 (February 1995): 80–85.
3. See the *Comparative Education Review*, journal of the Comparative and International Education Society, published by the University of Chicago Press. See T. Husén, ed., *International Study of Achievement in Mathematics*, 2 vols. (New York: John Wiley, 1967); Curtis C. McKnight et al., *The Underachieving Curriculum: Assessing U.S. School Mathematics from an International Point of View* (Champaign, Ill.: Stipes Publishing, 1987); Archie E. Lapointe, Nancy A. Mead, and Gary W. Phillips, *A World of Differences: An International Assessment of Mathematics and Science* (Princeton, N.J.: Center for the Assessment of Educational Progress, Educational Testing Service, 1989). See also Stedman, "The New Mythology."
4. For discussion of models for curriculum development, see Oliva, *Developing the Curriculum*, chap. 5.
5. James B. Conant, *The Education of American Teachers* (New York: McGraw-Hill, 1963).
6. National Study of School Evaluation, *Elementary School Evaluative Criteria*, 2nd ed. (Falls Church, Va.: National Study of School Evaluation, 1981), p. 39. See also *Middle School/Junior High School Evaluative Criteria*, rev. ed., 1979, p. 39; *Secondary School Evaluative Criteria: Narrative Edition: A Guide for School Improvement*, 1975, pp. 39–40; *Evaluative Criteria*, 6th ed. (for secondary schools), 1987, pp. 52–53; and *Evaluative Criteria for Middle Level Schools*, 1990, p. 34, from the same source. See also Note 11, chap. 8 of this text regarding newer criteria from this source.
7. Carbondale Community High School District 165, Carbondale, Ill.
8. Commission on the Reorganization of Secondary Education, *Cardinal Principles of Secondary Education*, Bulletin no. 35 (Washington, D.C.: U.S. Office of Education, 1918).
9. Educational Policies Commission, *The Purposes of Education in American Democracy*, 1938; *Education for All American Youth*, 1944; *The Central Purpose of American Education*, 1961 (Washington, D.C.: National Education Association).
10. John W. Gardner, "National Goals in Education," *Goals for Americans: Programs for Action in the Sixties. The Report of the President's Commission on National Goals*, Henry M. Wriston, chairman (New York: American Assembly, Columbia University, 1960), pp. 81, 100.
11. National Commission on Excellence in Education, *A Nation at Risk: The Imperative for Educational Reform* (Washington, D.C.: U.S. Government Printing Office, 1983).
12. National Governors' Association, *America 2000* (Washington, D.C.: National Governors' Association, 1990). The governors began discussion of national education goals at their meeting with President Bush in Charlottesville, Virginia, in September 1989. See also Lamar Alexander, chairman, *Time for Results: The Governors' 1991 Report on Education* (Washington, D.C.: National Governors Association, 1991).
13. *Goals 2000 Educate America Act*, March 31, 1994.
14. *Elementary School Evaluative Criteria*, p. 40.

15. *Evaluative Criteria for Middle Level Schools*, pp. 17–37.
16. *Middle School/Junior High School Evaluative Criteria*, p. 39.
17. *Evaluative Criteria*, 6th ed., p. 51.
18. Educational Policies Commission, *Education for All American Youth* (Washington, D.C.: National Education Association, 1944), p. 216.
19. Dade County Public Schools, "Goals for Student Development," *District Comprehensive Educational Plan, Fiscal Years 1974–79* (Miami, Fla.: Dade County Public Schools, 1974), pp. 8–11. This statement has been reprinted also in Oliva, *Developing the Curriculum*, 4th ed., chap. 8.
20. See *Goals for Education in Florida* (Tallahassee: Florida Department of Education, n.d.).
21. Dade County Public Schools, *District Comprehensive Plan, 1985–86 to 1989–90* (Miami, Fla.: Dade County Public Schools, 1985), D-6, D-9, D-10, D-22.
22. For helpful script and transparencies on writing curriculum guides see Marilyn Winters, *Preparing Your Curriculum Guide* (Alexandria, Va.: Association for Supervision and Curriculum Development, 1980).
23. See Donna Harrington-Lueker, "Charter Schools," *American School Board Journal* 181 (September 1994): 22–26.
24. See Arno Bellack, "What Knowledge Is of Most Worth?" *The High School Journal* 48 (February 1965): 318–32. See also Herbert Spencer, "What Knowledge Is of Most Worth?" In *Education: Intellectual, Moral, and Spiritual* (New York: John B. Alden, 1885), p. 32. Reprinted in 1963 by Littlefield, Adams, Paterson, N.J.
25. Ralph W. Tyler, *Basic Principles of Curriculum and Instruction* (Chicago: University of Chicago Press, 1949).
26. Daniel Tanner and Laurel N. Tanner, *Curriculum Development: Theory into Practice*, 3rd ed. (New York: Merrill, 1995), p. 236.
27. Jerome S. Bruner, *The Process of Education* (Cambridge, Mass.: Harvard University Press, 1960), p. 33.
28. See, for example, "In Dade County [Florida], Company Gears Up to Help District Run a Public School," *Education Week* 9 (June 6, 1990): 1.
29. *Brown v. Board of Education of Topeka, Kansas*, 347 U.S. 483, 74 Sup. Ct. 686 (1954).
30. For fuller treatment of reform, restructuring, continuing, and controversial curriculum problems, see Oliva, *Developing the Curriculum*, 4th ed., chaps. 9 and 14.

BIBLIOGRAPHY

Alexander, Lamar, chairman. *Time for Results: The Governors' 1991 Report on Education.* Washington, D.C.: National Governors' Association, 1991.

Balance in the Curriculum, 1961 Yearbook. Alexandria, Va.: Association for Supervision and Curriculum Development, 1961.

Banathy, Bela H. *Instructional Systems*. Belmont, Calif.: Fearon, 1968.

Bellack, Arno. "What Knowledge Is of Most Worth?" *The High School Journal* 48 (February 1965): 318–32.

Bruner, Jerome S. *The Process of Education*. Cambridge, Mass.: Harvard University Press, 1960; rev. 1977.

Carbondale Community High School. *Statement of Philosophy*. Carbondale, Ill.: Carbondale Community High School District 165, n.d.

Commission on the Reorganization of Secondary Education. *Cardinal Principles of Secondary Education*. Bulletin no. 35. Washington, D.C.: U.S. Office of Education, 1918.

Conant, James B. *The Education of American Teachers*. New York: McGraw-Hill, 1963.

"Curriculum Implementation," *Educational Leadership* 37 (December 1979): 204–67.

"The Curriculum Planning Process." *Educational Leadership* 38 (May 1981): 598–632.

Dade County Public Schools. *District Comprehensive Plan, 1985–86 to 1989–90.* Miami, Fla.: Dade County Public Schools, 1985.

———. "Goals for Student Development.: *District Comprehensive Educational Plan, Fiscal Years 1974–79.* Miami, Fla.: Dade County Public Schools, 1974.

Davis, O. L., Jr., ed. *Perspectives on Curriculum Development, 1776–1976.* 1976 Yearbook. Alexandria, Va.: Association for Supervision and Curriculum Development, 1976.

Doll, Ronald C. *Curriculum Improvement: Decision Making and Process*, 9th ed. Boston: Allyn & Bacon, 1996.

Educational Policies Commission. *The Central Purpose of American Education.* Washington, D.C.: National Education Association, 1961.

———. *Education for All American Youth.* Washington, D.C.: National Education Association, 1944.

———. *The Purposes of Education in American Democracy.* Washington, D.C.: National Education Association, 1938.

English, Fenwick W., ed. *Fundamental Curriculum Decisions.* 1983 Yearbook. Alexandria, Va.: Association for Supervision and Curriculum Development, 1983.

Foshay, Arthur W., ed. *Considered Action for Curriculum Improvement.* 1980 Yearbook. Alexandria, Va.: Association for Supervision and Curriculum Development, 1980.

Frymeier, Jack R., and Horace C. Hawn. *Curriculum Improvement for Better Schools.* Worthington, Ohio: Charles A. Jones, 1970.

Gagné, Robert M. "Curriculum Research and the Promotion of Learning." *AERA Monograph Series on Evaluation: Perspectives of Curriculum Evaluation*, no. 1. Chicago: Rand McNally, 1967.

Gardner, John W. "National Goals in Education." *Goals for Americans: Programs for Action in the Sixties. The Report of the President's Commission on National Goals*, chairman, Henry M. Wriston. New York: American Assembly, Columbia University, 1960.

Glatthorn, Allan A. *Curriculum Leadership.* Glenview, Ill.: Scott, Foresman, 1987.

———. *Curriculum Renewal.* Alexandria, Va.: Association for Supervision and Curriculum Development, 1987.

Goals for Education in Florida. Tallahassee: Florida Department of Education, n.d.

Good, Carter V., ed. *Dictionary of Education*, 3rd ed. New York: McGraw-Hill, 1973.

Harrington-Lueker, Donna. "Charter Schools." *American School Board Journal* 181 (September 1994): 22–26.

Henson, Kenneth T. *Curriculum Development in an Age of Reform.* New York: HarperCollins, 1995.

Husén, T., ed. *International Study of Achievement in Mathematics*, 2 vols. New York: John Wiley, 1967.

"In Dade County [Florida], Company Gears Up to Help District Run a Public School." *Education Week* 9, no. 37 (June 6, 1990): 1.

LaPointe, Archie E., Nancy A. Mead, and Gary W. Phillips. *A World of Differences: An International Assessment of Mathematics and Science.* Princeton, N.J.: Center for the Assessment of Educational Progress, Educational Testing Service, 1989.

Leeper, Robert R., ed. *Role of the Supervisor and Curriculum Director in a Climate of Change.* 1965 Yearbook. Alexandria, Va.: Association for Supervision and Curriculum Development, 1965.

McKnight, Curtis C., et al. *The Underachieving Curriculum: Assessing U.S. School Mathematics from an International Point of View.* Champaign, Ill.: Stipes Publishing, 1987.

McNeil, John D. *Curriculum: A Comprehensive Introduction*, 5th ed. New York: HarperCollins, 1996.

Miller, John P., and Wayne Seller. *Curriculum: Perspectives and Practice.* White Plains, N.Y.: Longman, 1985.

Molnar, Alex, ed. *Current Thought on Curriculum.* 1985 Yearbook. Alexandria, Va.: Association for Supervision and Curriculum Development, 1985.

National Commission on Excellence. *A Nation at Risk: The Imperative for Educational Reform.* Washington, D.C.: U.S. Government Printing Office, 1983.

"The National Goals—Putting Education Back on the Road," *Phi Delta Kappan* 72 (December 1990): 259–314.

National Governors' Association. *America 2000.* Washington, D.C.: National Governors' Association, 1990.

National Study of School Evaluation. *Elementary School Evaluative Criteria,* 2nd ed. Falls Church, Va.: National Study of School Evaluation, 1981.

———. *Evaluative Criteria,* 6th ed. Falls Church, Va.: National Study of School Evaluation, 1987.

———. *Evaluative Criteria for Middle Level Schools.* Falls Church, Va.: National Study of School Evaluation, 1990.

———. *Middle School/Junior High School Evaluative Criteria,* rev. ed. Falls Church, Va.: National Study of School Evaluation, 1979.

———. *Secondary School Evaluative Criteria: Narrative Edition.* Falls Church, Va.: National Study of School Evaluation, 1975.

Nelson, Annabelle. *Curriculum Design Techniques.* Dubuque, Iowa: William C. Brown, 1990.

Noll, James W. *Taking Sides: Clashing Views on Controversial Educational Issues,* 6th ed. Guilford, Conn.: Dushkin Publishing Group, 1991.

Oliva, Peter F. *Developing the Curriculum,* 4th ed. New York: HarperCollins, 1997.

Oliver, Albert I. *Curriculum Improvement: A Guide to Problems, Principles, and Process,* 2nd ed. New York: Harper & Row, 1977.

Popham, W. James, and Eva L. Baker. *Establishing Instructional Goals.* Englewood Cliffs, N.J.: Prentice-Hall, 1970.

Pratt, David. *Curriculum: Design and Development.* New York: Harcourt Brace Jovanovich, 1980.

Saylor, J. Galen, William M. Alexander, and Arthur J. Lewis. *Curriculum Planning for Better Teaching and Learning,* 4th ed. New York: Holt, Rinehart and Winston, 1981.

Schubert, William H. *Curriculum: Perspective, Paradigm, and Possibility.* New York: Macmillan, 1986.

Spencer, Herbert. "What Knowledge Is of Most Worth?" In *Education: Intellectual, Moral, and Spiritual.* New York: John B. Alden, 1995. Reprinted, Paterson, N.J.: Littlefield, Adams, 1963.

Stedman, Lawrence C. "The New Mythology about the Status of U.S. Schools," *Educational Leadership* 52 (February 1995): 80–85.

Taba, Hilda. *Curriculum Development: Theory and Practice.* New York: Harcourt Brace Jovanovich, 1962.

Tanner, Daniel, and Laurel N. Tanner. *Curriculum Development: Theory into Practice,* 3rd ed. New York: Merrill, 1995.

Tyler, Ralph W. *Basic Principles of Curriculum and Instruction.* Chicago: University of Chicago Press, 1949.

Walker, Decker. *Fundamentals of Curriculum.* Orlando, Fla.: Harcourt Brace Jovanovich, 1990.

Wiles, Jon, and Joseph C. Bondi. *Curriculum Development: A Guide to Practice,* 4th ed. New York: Merrill, 1993..

Zais, Robert S. *Curriculum: Principles and Foundations.* New York: Harper & Row, 1976.

Multimedia

Winters, Marilyn, *Preparing Your Curriculum Guide*. 1980. An illustrated script and set of transparency masters that leaders can use to explain the process of developing curriculum guides to teachers, parents, and others. Association for Supervision and Curriculum Development, 1250 North Pitt St., Alexandria, Va. 22314.

8

Helping Teachers Evaluate Curricula

Objectives

After studying Chapter 8 you should be able to accomplish the following objectives:

1. Describe a model of curriculum evaluation.
2. Choose and defend your preferred model of curriculum evaluation.
3. Describe the supervisor's role in curriculum evaluation.
4. Explain the nine basic research concepts presented in this chapter.
5. Describe the four types of research presented in this chapter.
6. Explain what is meant by (1) context, (2) input, (3) process, and (4) product evaluation.
7. Outline a plan for a curriculum needs assessment.
8. Explain the nature and purposes of evaluative criteria.
9. Explain what is meant by curriculum mapping and state its uses.
10. Cite several general references useful in researching a topic.
11. Identify the National Assessment of Educational Progress.

CURRICULUM EVALUATION: ESSENTIAL AND DIFFICULT

The distraught teacher sat across from the supervisor and began to tell her story. "Last night after our evaluation workshop I went home exhausted and flopped on the bed. I fell into a restless sleep and had a terrible nightmare." In his best nondirective manner the supervisor said, "Tell me about your nightmare."

The teacher, reinforced by the supervisor's interest, continued: "I dreamed that

I was picked up by a tornado and set down in the middle of a conference of educational researchers. They were speaking a language I was convinced was not of this world and for some strange reason I wanted to associate it with ancient astronauts. Their discussions were animated and from what I could gather there were differences of opinion among the conference participants. I tuned in as attentively as I could, which wasn't difficult, for the voices were rather loud, and I heard in rapid-fire succession:

input	context
product	t-test
CIPP	Q-sort
process	validity
CSE	reliability
norm	model
formative	inferential
summative	noninferential

"When someone yelled 'null hypothesis,' I suddenly woke up, sat bolt upright in bed, sweating." The teacher looked at the supervisor and asked plaintively, "What does this dream mean? Is there something the matter with me?"

The supervisor smiled, reassured her that nothing was wrong, and then, departing from his nondirective manner, said, "I see four possible interpretations of your dream," hesitating to use the word *hypotheses*. "First, we served stale doughnuts at the evaluation workshop last night. Second, we threw too much at the group at one time. Third, you have a guilt feeling—you'd like to be doing more research but for one reason or another you don't do it. Fourth, the researchers are not communicating to you, the teacher. Since I picked up the doughnuts myself fresh from the bakery, we can discount the first interpretation. I suspect we can attribute your nightmare a little bit to each of the other three possibilities. In fact, your nightmare brings home to me the necessity for the supervisor to clarify the role of the teacher in evaluation and research. This is a task to which I must give priority."

This fictitious exchange between a teacher and supervisor expresses a feeling many teachers have when confronted with the tasks of evaluation and research. We have seen that evaluation is an integral component of models of both instruction and curriculum development. Of all components, evaluation is the one that is frequently neglected or often conducted poorly. Evaluation is such an essential phase of both instructional and curricular design that the profession cannot afford to slight it or ignore it. Chapter 6 introduced concepts of evaluation as they applied to the instructional process. This chapter extends some of the basic evaluation concepts and applies them to the process of curriculum development. It is concerned primarily with evaluation of the curriculum in whole or in part rather than with evaluation of instructional techniques per se. Making a rigid distinction between instruction and curriculum is inadvisable, however, for the two are inseparable.

When we speak of curriculum evaluation, the first thing that occurs to some educators is testing students' achievement in specific areas of the curriculum, such as reading, math, and so on. In fact, we need to evaluate much more than just the success of the learners. We need to account for the learners' success or failure. We need to know whether a program is working. We need to evaluate the following in addition to subject matter achievement of students in each discipline and grade:

- Curriculum goals and objectives
- Instructional goals and objectives
- Specific programs, both in the formative stage and at the end of a trial period
- Parents' and other laypersons' reactions to the curriculum
- Teachers' reactions to the curriculum
- General effectiveness of the school's program
- Quality and effectiveness of curriculum materials
- Organization of the curriculum
- Process for curriculum development and its effectiveness
- Projections for the future
- The evaluation program itself

Evaluation seeks to provide answers on which decisions can be based for change and future action. Teachers employ evaluation techniques when they attempt to answer such questions as these:

- Is homogeneous grouping more effective than heterogeneous grouping?
- Does an open-space program yield better results than the self-contained classroom?
- Do students learn mathematics better by means of LAPs (Learning Activity Packets) than through more traditional methods?
- Do students improve in behavior if they are sent to centers for special instruction?
- Does a career education program make any difference in students' knowledge of the world of work?
- Does geometry teach students to think?
- Does Latin help improve students' English?
- Is the scholastic achievement of students affected by the extra-class activity program, and if so, in what way is it affected?
- Does homemaking develop skills of worthy home membership?

Many of the answers given to curriculum questions such as these have been based on judgment without hard evidence. Teachers and others have assumed, for example, that the more years a learner is exposed to a discipline, the higher will be his or her level of attainment in that discipline. Another belief is that certain courses in the curriculum develop students' ability to think better than other courses. These assumptions are based on very flimsy evidence. James A. Beane offers a definition of a curriculum that all schools should strive to offer: "That curriculum is a 'coherent' curriculum—one that holds together, that makes sense as a whole; and its parts, whatever they are, are unified and connected by that sense of the whole."[1]

Each of the curriculum questions raised suggests additional questions that must be answered. When we ask, "Is homogeneous grouping more effective than heterogeneous grouping?" we must also ask, "What do you mean by homogeneous grouping?" "What kind of homogeneous grouping are we talking about?" "What do you mean by more effective—more effective in what respects?" The ramifications of questions about a curriculum show the complexity of evaluation, which may account for one of the reasons evaluation is omitted or handled poorly.

Curriculum, like education, of which it is a part, is a complex system comprising people, places, and things. Because of this complexity, isolating variables is extremely difficult. It is very difficult for a teacher to know that a particular program, a particular unit of content, or a particular teaching strategy has made a difference in the end result. For this reason, much educational research reaches conclusions such as "There was no significant difference in the two approaches" or "The results were inconclusive" or "An experimental approach achieved a result as good as the original approach." Though such conclusions may actually be significant in themselves, their indecisiveness has created impatience among teachers with educational research in general.

Preservice teacher education generally devotes little time to training in evaluation and research, an omission that must be addressed by graduate or in-service education. The supervisor must determine how great the need is and what particular training is called for.

One reason for the difficulty teachers have with evaluation and research is the esoteric language of evaluation, a method of communication that requires special training to understand. The experts in evaluation have the same problem in communicating evaluation concepts to teachers that teachers have in communicating pedagogical problems to the public. Making the process of evaluation even more difficult are the conflicting opinions of experts in the field on how evaluation and research are to be conducted.

A beneficial first step to improved communication could be a summit conference of experts in evaluation at which they would standardize the language of evaluation and research. The classroom teacher might then know whether formative evaluation is process research, whether process research is the same as process evaluation, and whether terminal evaluation is summative evaluation. Unlike the profession of writing, which requires a wide vocabulary and many synonyms, the specializations of evaluation and research demand a limited, precise vocabulary. Mathematics is sometimes called the "queen of the sciences" because its terminology is precise and its concepts clear. A hypotenuse cannot be called a diagonal or a slant-line. In deference to Gertrude Stein, a hypotenuse is a hypotenuse is a hypotenuse. It is one of the anomalies of the profession that the fields of evaluation and research, which draw heavily on mathematics and statistics, permit on occasion a looseness of language. This looseness makes it difficult for the teacher, who is expected to be an applier and consumer, to put sound evaluation principles into operation in the school.

A major reason that the evaluation component of curriculum design is slighted in school systems is the lack of qualified people to assume responsibility for leadership in this field. Some school systems are large enough and fortunate enough to be able to employ evaluators or research directors, but those categories of personnel are not common in most school systems. In fact, although it may seem at times that schools employ an army of supervisors, even supervisory assistance is lacking or limited in many school systems, let alone the assistance of trained evaluators.

THE SUPERVISOR'S ROLE IN EVALUATION

Evaluation of both the curriculum and instruction has taken on an increasing importance in the past few years. The impetus has come from two related movements: (1) empowering parents to choose the schools their children will attend, and (2) granting families governmental financial aid of one type or another to make that choice possible. Looming on the educational horizon and currently being created are new national examinations that will certainly reflect on the success of schools in effecting student achievement. Though not universally practiced throughout the country at the moment, parental choice and such devices as vouchers and tax credits have proved popular with the public, if not with all public school educators. They will continue to be discussed and in some states will be adopted.

The desirability of allowing parents to select schools gained national support in the spring of 1991 with then-President George Bush's education proposals, labeled *America 2000*. The proposals were presented by Lamar Alexander, at that time secretary of education, whose education agenda as former governor of Tennessee had gained favorable attention nationwide. These federal proposals not only called for parental choice of school but also for 535 model demonstration schools; awards to high-achieving students; and national examinations in English, mathematics, science, history, and geography at the fourth, eighth, and twelfth grade levels.[2]

Competition, then, has been injected into the picture, forcing schools to examine and in many cases to improve the curriculum and instruction in order to attract and hold a clientele driven by parental choice. As never before, schools must demonstrate their effectiveness. Evaluation is the means of such demonstration.

In the absence of fully qualified specialists in evaluation, the supervisor must provide the necessary leadership in curriculum evaluation and research. Supervisors must possess or achieve a level of competence in the skills of evaluation and research at a much more sophisticated level than that of most teachers. For research to be conducted, the supervisor must have the teachers' cooperation and support. He or she can help teachers design proposals and collect and interpret data, and can serve as the resource person to whom teachers turn for specialized help. Later in this chapter we examine ways in which the supervisor can help teachers with evaluation.

As a rule, teachers are generally participants rather than researchers in the evaluation process. The terms *applier*, *consumer*, and *interpreter* of research are often used in describing the evaluative role of teachers. The teacher should be able to analyze completed research to discover the implications it has for his or her school. With the help of a specialist, the teacher should be able to design simple proposals and conduct what we describe later as "action research." But for the most part, the teacher should not be expected to be a researcher.

Considering the necessity of evaluation for keeping the curriculum alive and given the shortage of specialized assistance in evaluation, the supervisor must fulfill the role of leader in curriculum evaluation. In this capacity, the supervisor should be able to help teachers in a number of ways.

Research Orientation

The supervisor should help teachers develop an inquiring point of view—a research orientation. A supervisor should raise questions with teachers and encourage them to raise questions about the curriculum, such as "Does the program work?" "How do I know if a program is successful?" "What kinds of data do I need to determine the effectiveness of a program?" "Is this program better than other programs?" "What effect does an innovation have on students?" "Aside from being new, does an innovation have any other merits?" "How can I improve a program?" "What do test results mean?" "How can I measure the success of a program?" "What are the objectives of a program and how can I assess the attainment of those objectives?"

The supervisor should encourage teachers to try new instructional strategies and new programs and to learn whether these are more effective than the old approaches and programs. The supervisor should encourage teachers to develop an evaluation mentality and not to remain content with the curriculum as it is. No school has reached utopia in curriculum development nor will it ever, for the curriculum must change to reflect new needs of learners and society. Continuous evaluation is at the heart of change. Although schools can and do make changes in their curricula without evaluation through a trial-and-error process, systematic evaluation can show the direction of changes that need to be made and reduce the time spent on wasteful trials. The supervisor should set an example for teachers by having a positive attitude toward evaluation and research and by demonstrating a disposition to seek more than empirical answers to curriculum problems.

BASIC RESEARCH CONCEPTS

The supervisor should tactfully verify the teacher's understanding of basic research concepts. If the supervisor finds a teacher's understanding of the concepts to be inadequate, he or she should consider some in-service training to correct this deficiency. With more decisions about a school's instructional program being made at the local school level, teachers may look to school administrators who have competency in educational research to help them in their training. For advanced research concepts, they may call on the services of the research or supervisor specialist.

Though experts in measurement may disagree, most teachers can function at a minimal level of research competency with an understanding of only nine basic concepts. This text cannot serve as a course in research methods, but it can describe these minimal nine concepts. The supervisor may wish to review them with groups of teachers.

1. *The normal curve.* The normal, or bell-shaped, curve is a statistical representation of the distribution of a trait such as intelligence, which is presumed to be distributed "normally" throughout the human population. Built into the concept of the normal curve is the understanding that the population it represents is a reasonably large group that has been chosen at random. This attribute is extremely important when test scores are being interpreted. With a large random sample of the population the test maker can assume that the performance of the population that took the test approximates the performance of the population in general in respect to the trait measured by the test.

Figure 8.1 is a graphic representation of a normal curve. The tallest line represents the mean of whatever is being measured. Fifty percent of the scores fall to the right of the mean and 50 percent to the left. By convention, the scores to the right are higher than the mean score and the scores to the left are lower than the mean score. In a normal distribution of scores, the mean score (arithmetic average) and the median score (mid-score) coincide.

The vertical lines to the right and left of the mean, which indicate standard deviations from the mean and are represented by the symbol σ (sigma), show the percentages of scores that are likely to fall within one, two, or three standard deviations from the mean. (*Standard deviation* is the seventh of the nine concepts teachers need; it is discussed later in this section.) Thus, we can say that 68.26 percent of the scores will fall within one standard deviation on either side of the mean; 95.44 percent will fall within two standard deviations from the mean; and 99.74 percent will come within three standard deviations from the mean.

The normal curve is a useful concept in interpreting scores made on standardized tests that have been normed on large, random samples of the population. It can help teachers see how their students compare with a "normal" population of students on the same test. The normal curve concept should never be used as some teachers employ it—to calculate the distribution of marks they will give to students in their classes. It is a misuse of the concept for teachers to decide that 2 percent of their students must earn A's and F's, 14 percent B's and D's, and 68 percent C's. The supervisor should help teachers detect abuses of the concept of the normal curve.

2. *Mean.* The mean is one of the measures of central tendency. It is the arithmetic average of a group of scores: the sum of the scores divided by the number of

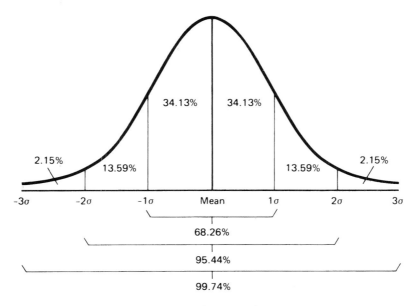

Figure 8.1. The Normal Curve.

scores. It is this concept that the layperson ordinarily refers to as the "average." The mean is the measure of central tendency most commonly used by statisticians.

3. *Median.* The median, another measure of central tendency, is the midpoint in a set of scores. In other terminology it is known as the *fiftieth percentile*. Fifty percent of the scores in a given distribution fall at or below the median, and 50 percent fall at or above the median. Because the median is the middle score, it is less affected by extreme scores than the mean. Of the two measures of central tendency, the mean and the median, the mean is much more widely used for it serves as a basis for other statistical calculations.

4. *Reliability.* The term *reliability* is equated with the term *consistency*, an essential characteristic of a test. A reliable test should consistently yield similar results under repeated administrations. Chapter 6 pointed out that essay tests tend to have low reliability. A test is unreliable not only when it yields different results on subsequent testings but also when it yields different results if scored by different scorers—a common fault of essay tests. As previously noted, scoring of essay tests can be made more reliable by creating a key in advance of the scoring.

No test is 100 percent reliable in the sense that identical results can be assured on repeated administrations. When teachers want to select a standardized test, they will want to know whether that test is reliable. To learn this, they consult the test maker's manual, which reports reliability in terms of a coefficient of correlation. The closer the coefficient of correlation, which is expressed in hundredths, comes to +1.00, the higher is the reliability of a test. Thus, for example, a coefficient of .90 would indicate that the test is reliable.

5. *Validity.* Besides being consistent or reliable, a test should be valid; that is, it should measure what it is supposed to measure. Reliability and validity are both essential characteristics of testing instruments. There is no virtue in using a test that consistently fails to measure what it is supposed to measure, or measures it inconsistently. At best, however, no test is a perfect instrument; no test is 100 percent valid. Like the reliability coefficient, the validity coefficient is reported in the test manual that accompanies a standardized test. The validity coefficient is likewise expressed in hundredths, and the closer the coefficient comes to +1.00, the more valid is the test. A validity coefficient of .55, for example, would indicate that the test had only moderate validity.

6. *Coefficient of correlation.* The concept of the correlation coefficient was introduced in the definitions of the terms *reliability* and *validity*. A coefficient of correlation is a mathematical measure for showing relationships between two variables— for example, between two different types of tests, between two administrations of the same test, and between scores made on a test and some external criterion.

Coefficients are expressed from +1.00, which is indicative of a perfect positive correlation between two variables, to −1.00, which is indicative of a perfect negative correlation between two variables. The midpoint of this range, .00, implies that there is no relationship between the two variables. Coefficients of correlation are expressed by the mathematical symbol r.

Generally speaking, a negative coefficient of correlation can be as useful to the statistician as a positive coefficient of correlation. It is of help to know, for example, that one test correlates negatively with another test. In the cases of reliability and validity, however, an inconsistent or invalid test is of little use to a prospective test purchaser, and the test maker is not likely to market tests that produce a negative coefficient of reliability or of validity.

7. *Standard deviation.* The standard deviation is a measure of variability that indicates the spread of a set of scores. Any standard textbook on research will show how the standard deviation is calculated. The teacher will have occasion to use the standard deviation in interpreting scores made by students on a standardized test. What the teacher needs to know is that the higher the value of the standard deviation, the wider the spread of the scores. The value of the standard deviation will be found in the test manual. As already noted, 68.26 percent, or approximately two-thirds, of the scores in a normal distribution are found within one standard deviation of the mean. Thus, for a test whose mean is 100 and whose standard deviation is 10, 68.26 percent of the scores may be expected to fall between 90 and 110. By the same token 95.44 percent of the scores will range from 80 to 120, and 99.74 percent will come between 70 and 130.

8. *Standard scores.* A standard score, known as the *sigma score* and designated with the symbol *z*, results when a raw score is converted to a figure that represents a value in terms of the standard deviation. Use of standard scores allows comparisons to be made of a student's scores on different tests on which the total number of points is not the same. If raw scores are used to calculate means, a distorted picture may emerge and make it difficult to compare scores. For example, what inferences could be drawn in comparing two scores made by a student on two different tests whose means are 50 and 46? The means are affected by extremes and the comparison is difficult. But suppose we could start from a common mean, say 0, as we do with standard scores; we can then decide whether a student has done better on one test than on another.

Take a case of a student who has scored 60 on a standardized test of business English and 40 on a standardized test of business arithmetic. The mean on the test of business English is 50 and the standard deviation is 5. The mean of the business arithmetic test is 46 and the standard deviation is 6. The statistician employs a simple formula to convert the raw score to a standard score:

$$z \text{ (standard score)} = \frac{X \text{ (raw score)} - m \text{ (mean)}}{S \text{ (standard deviation)}}$$

Applying the formula to the test of business English ($[60 - 50]/5$) gives us a standard score of $+2$. The business arithmetic test gives $(40 - 46)/6 = -1$. In the case of the student's score of 60 on the business English test, the sigma score $+2$ indicates that the score of 60 is two standard deviations above the mean. The score of 46 on the business arithmetic test shows up as a sigma score of -1, which is one standard deviation below the mean. A quick reference to Figure 8.1 shows us that with a score in business English that is two standard deviations above the mean, the student has scored better than 97 percent of the students in the sample that set the norms. In business arithmetic, however, the student scored lower than 84 percent of the norming sample. This information is much more meaningful than the raw scores of 50 and 46. The sigma score is a procedure for weighting scores equally so that more accurate comparisons can be made than with raw scores.

9. *Norms.* Norms are scores made by the group or groups on which a test was standardized and as such these scores become standards against which individual test scores are compared, hence the terms *standardized test* and *norm-referenced measurement.* Test makers report the norms of tests in their test manuals. The norms reported are based on test scores made by a large, random sample of the population and are generally interpreted as having national significance.

Test makers report norms most frequently in terms of (1) age norms, (2) grade norms, and (3) percentile rank. Age norms are expressed in years and months—for example, 10–5, which indicates a level of achievement in the trait measured by the test at an age level of ten years, five months. This level of achievement must be compared with the pupil's actual chronological age. For example, a child of eight years, five months chronological age who achieves a score on a standardized arithmetic test that puts the child at an age norm of ten years, five months, is two whole years advanced for his or her chronological age.

The grade norm fulfills a function similar to the age norm, but its point of reference is the year and month of school. A grade norm of 7.8 represents the eighth month of the seventh grade. Grade norms are written with decimals and are based on a ten-month school year. By way of illustration, a child in the fourth month of the eighth grade (8.4) who achieves a score on a standardized test that places him or her at the eighth month of the seventh grade (7.8) is reading below grade level.

The percentile rank is another means of expressing the relative position of scores made by those who take a standardized test. The middle, or median, score is said to be at the fiftieth percentile. Fifty percent of the scores fall at or above the fiftieth percentile and 50 percent fall at or below the fiftieth percentile. The student who achieves the middle score is considered to be equal to or surpassed by 50 percent of the student population and to have equaled or surpassed 50 percent. In layperson's language the student is average in the trait measured by the test. The student who ranks at the ninety-eighth percentile has done very well on the particular trait measured by that test. That student has equaled or surpassed 98 percent of the population and is equaled or surpassed by only 2 percent.

The norm data give the interpreter of results of a standardized test some indication of how students to whom they may administer a test fare in relation to those persons who were in the sample of the population on whom the test was standardized.

A mastery of these nine concepts should enable teachers to fulfill their roles as interpreters of research at a minimal level of competency. These nine concepts can provide a beginning point for in-service training under the guidance of the supervisor.

TYPES OF RESEARCH

The supervisor should help teachers distinguish between different types of research with the view toward identifying types in which teachers may be customarily engaged and kinds that are more likely to be the responsibility of research teams. There are essentially four types of research.

1. *Basic research.* Otherwise known as *fundamental* or *pure research,* basic research is normally carried on in the laboratory or in laboratory-like situations with animals or human subjects for the purpose of testing theoretical principles of behavior and with no particular application in mind. Studies of the ways in which animals and human beings learn are basic research. As a rule, the classroom teacher does not conduct basic research studies.

2. *Applied research.* Much of the research in education is applied research, the study of the applicability of instructional principles and learning theory in the classroom. Teachers are frequently involved in applied research studies under the direction of a supervisor or research specialist. Applied research follows generally accepted principles of research methodology, and its purpose is to find means of improving the curriculum and the instructional process.

3. *Action research.* Many teachers are engaged in this form of research and should be encouraged to pursue it by their supervisors. Action research consists of less controlled studies of specific applications of learning theory and methodology in a particular classroom. The teacher who tries out a new method of instruction and attempts to compare the success of that method with the success of previous methods is engaging in action research. We may think of action research as a type of applied research and as a study of the applicability of a principle or method in a specific situation. Action research is one means of fostering the research orientation of teachers. This type of research has been popular with curriculum workers but has not always been acceptable to specialists in measurement and research. The specialist in evaluation prefers to obtain results from research studies that can be generalized beyond the immediate classroom. He or she also likes to be assured that the variables in a study are more stringently controlled than they are in much action research. L. R. Gay addressed the value of action research when she said,

> The value of action research is confined primarily to those conducting it. Despite its shortcomings, it does represent a scientific approach to problem solving that is considerably better than changes based on alleged effectiveness of untried procedures, and infinitely better than no change at all.[3]

4. *Descriptive research.* Descriptive research is an accurate accounting of general or selected aspects of a given situation. This particular category of research includes a variety of types of studies in which teachers participate. What is commonly referred to as a *status study*, for example, a study of the extent to which schools in a state have remedial reading laboratories, is a form of descriptive research. Surveys of current practices and of opinions of groups that are conducted as a part of a needs assessment are descriptive research. A descriptive report of what goes on at a particular time in a classroom is a type of descriptive research that some evaluators call *process research*. Unfortunately, the term *process research* is used to connote formative evaluation, the testing of the prototype model and the periodic check of progress of a program, as well as a noninferential type of study of classroom activities.

Basic, applied, and action research are types of *experimental research*. Teachers frequently engage in action and descriptive research with minimal supervision, and they occasionally participate in applied research with closer supervision.

TYPES OF EVALUATION

The supervisor should help teachers distinguish between different types of evaluation and select and use an evaluation model. For purposes of analysis, types of evaluation are distinguished from types of research. This is a somewhat arbitrary classification as evaluation and research are so closely related. The terms that describe evaluation and research are sometimes used in the literature interchangeably. *Formative evaluation*, for example, may be referred to as *process research* but process research is not just formative evaluation. Other types of studies are subsumed under the rubric of process research. In very brief form, some of the more frequently encountered terms are described. The various terms and the models of evaluation discussed are worthwhile topics to be explored at length in in-service programs.

First, we review two terms introduced in the earlier chapter on the evaluation of instruction: *formative evaluation* and *summative evaluation*. Formative evaluation is essentially an analysis of a program at its early stages, the testing of a prototype program so that changes can be made during the course of the program before it has gone too far. Summative evaluation is terminal evaluation; it is conducted at the end of the program and allows the teacher or evaluator to decide whether the program has been successful, that is, whether the objectives have been reached.

Evaluation Models

Next, we examine evaluation models. These can serve not only to extend the teacher's understanding of evaluation concepts but also to be guides for carrying out a curriculum study. We have selected two well-known models to examine. The CIPP (Context, Input, Process, and Product) Evaluation Model, shown in Figure 8.2, contains four evaluation components: context evaluation, input evaluation, process evaluation, and product evaluation (see rectangles in Figure 8.2).[4] The CSE (Center for the Study of Evaluation) Evaluation Model, shown in Figure 8.3, comprises five evaluation phases: needs assessment, program planning, implementation evaluation, progress evaluation, and outcome evaluation.[5] Let's briefly review the evaluation components of each of these two evaluation models.

1. *Context evaluation.* Context evaluation is the first component of the CIPP Evaluation Model. According to this model, the evaluation process begins with an analysis of the context or environment in which a curriculum study is to be conducted. It continues with a description of the conditions, both actual and hoped for, of that environment. It includes an assessment of the needs of the system and a determination of the unmet needs of the system. It also accounts for the reasons the continuing needs are not being met.

2. *Input evaluation.* This second phase of the CIPP Evaluation Model consists of making decisions on procedures that will be followed in pursuit of the objectives. The evaluators at this stage must choose from alternative routes to the realization of the objectives. In making these decisions, the evaluators must keep in mind the limitations of resources, including available time and funds.

3. *Process evaluation.* The third element of the CIPP Evaluation Model, process evaluation, is monitoring of the curriculum plan as it unfolds. The evaluators look for deficiencies in the system and attempt to correct them. They maintain a continuing record of what is happening during the implementation process.

4. *Product evaluation.* The fourth and final component of the CIPP Evaluation

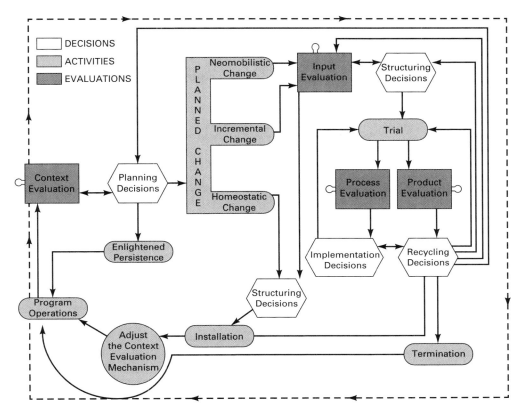

Figure 8.2. The CIPP Evaluation Model. *Source: Daniel L. Stufflebeam et al.,* Educational Evaluation and Decision Making *(Itasca, Ill.: F. E. Peacock, 1971), p. 236. Reprinted with permission of Phi Delta Kappa.*

Model is product evaluation. This type of evaluation is both formative and summative, as it seeks to measure both during the curriculum study and at the end of the study whether the objectives have been reached.

Now compare the terminology of the CSE Evaluation Model:

1. *Needs assessment.* The CSE Evaluation Model begins with needs assessment as its first component. Generally, a needs assessment, discussed more fully later in this chapter, is the process of identifying unmet needs of a school system by comparing the achievement levels of that school system with its stated objectives. The discrepancies between achievement levels and objectives are needs that are not being met by that school system. An assessment of needs and the consequent determination of unmet needs necessitate the development of new objectives for the realization of those needs. Note the element of needs assessment within context evaluation of the CIPP Evaluation Model.

2. *Program planning.* The CSE Evaluation Model prescribes program planning as its second stage. At this stage, performance objectives are specified and a program

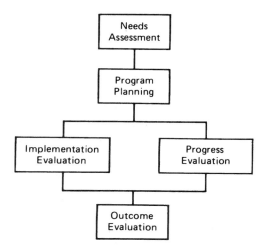

Figure 8.3. The CSE Evaluation Model. *Source: Center for the Study of Evaluation,* Evaluation Workshop I: An Orientation, Participants' Notebook *(Del Monte Research Park, Monterey, Calif.: CTB/McGraw-Hill, 1971), p. A–2. Reprinted with permission from McGraw-Hill, Inc.*

is selected and prepared. Also at this stage, input evaluation, as in the CIPP Model, comes into play with an analysis of various strategies for accomplishing the objectives and of the resources that can be made available.

3. *Implementation evaluation.* The third component of the CSE Evaluation Model, implementation evaluation, is a check of the various parts of the program design to determine whether the design has been implemented properly. This stage of evaluation is an effort to spot difficulties, to learn whether the personnel involved, the materials and equipment needs, and the facilities to be used are all in order, and to discover whether the program is meeting its time and budgetary commitments. Implementation evaluation is related to process evaluation of the CIPP Model.

4. *Progress evaluation.* During the course of a program, the evaluator arranges to obtain continuous feedback on whether the program objectives are being met so that adjustments can be made in the program. Progress evaluation is the fourth element of the CSE Evaluation Model and is formative in nature.

5. *Outcome evaluation.* The fifth and final stage of the CSE Evaluation Model is outcome evaluation, which is a terminal assessment of the accomplishments of the program. At this stage, decisions are reached concerning whether the objectives have been realized and whether the program should continue. Outcome evaluation is essentially the same as product evaluation of the CIPP Evaluation Model when conducted at the end of the program. In more general terms, outcome evaluation is equivalent to summative evaluation.

The terms in the preceding section are some of the most frequently encountered evaluation terms but are by no means an exhaustive listing of the concepts in this complex field. The models and descriptions have been selected to give the prospective supervisor a flavor of the thinking that goes on in the field of evaluation. The supervisor should explore more detailed sources for help in working with teachers in evaluating the curriculum. Together, they may select from the models described or from other models as guides to the process of evaluation.[6]

At some point, teachers and supervisors should examine the evaluation plan itself. They should ask questions such as "Are we following a model for curriculum evaluation?" "Do we have a comprehensive evaluation plan?" "Have we collected both formative and summative data?" "Have we used proper means of gathering data?" "Have we involved the right people?" "Do we need to use outside evaluators?" "Have we validated the curriculum goals and objectives?"

When fulfilling the role of curriculum evaluators, supervisors and teachers would be well advised to familiarize themselves with the standards developed by the Joint Committee on Standards for Educational Evaluation.[7] This committee proposed thirty standards centered around four concerns: the utility, feasibility, propriety, and accuracy of an evaluation. The utility standards address questions such as the identification of the audience, the credibility of the evaluators, and the clarity and timeliness of the evaluation report. The feasibility standards include consideration of the practicality of the evaluation procedures and cost effectiveness. Propriety standards relate to such concerns as conflicts of interest, the public's right to know, and the rights of human subjects. The accuracy standards direct evaluators' attention to such items as the validity and reliability of measurement, the analysis of quantitative and qualitative information, and the objectivity of reporting. The supervisor should exercise leadership in curriculum evaluation by directing those charged with evaluation of a program in application of the thirty standards.

CONDUCTING A CURRICULUM NEEDS ASSESSMENT

The supervisor should assist a faculty in planning, conducting, and analyzing an assessment of curriculum needs. As the name implies, a curriculum needs assessment is an evaluation of program needs. It is a process for deciding whether the objectives of the school are being reached and whether there are existing needs of learners that are not being met. A needs assessment conducted by a faculty is significant not only for the data it generates but also for the excellent in-service training it provides teachers in one aspect of evaluation.

A needs assessment should not be viewed as a specific evaluation program with a fixed set of procedures that can be applied anywhere but rather as a general procedure that varies from school to school or school system to school system. Although the general process is similar from locality to locality, the choice of instruments for collecting data, the steps followed, and the detailed procedures differ considerably.

Fenwick W. English and Roger A. Kaufman defined needs assessment as a multifaceted process:

> Needs assessment is a process of defining the desired end (or outcome, product, or result) of a given sequence of curriculum development. . . .
>
> Needs assessment is a process of making specific, in some intelligible manner, what schooling should be about and how it can be assessed. . . .
>
> Needs assessment is an empirical process for defining the outcomes of education, and as such it is then a set of criteria by which curricula may be developed and compared. . . .

Needs assessment is a process for determining the validity of behavioral objectives and if standardized tests and/or criterion-referenced tests are appropriate and under what conditions.

Needs assessment is a logical problem solving tool by which a variety of means may be selected and related to each other in the development of curriculum.

Needs assessment is a tool which formally harvests the gaps between current results (or outcomes, products) and required or desired results, places these gaps in priority order, and selects those gaps (needs) of the highest priority for action, usually through the implementation of a new or existing curriculum or management process.[8]

A needs assessment has two basic purposes: (1) to determine whether stated objectives have been accomplished and (2) to identify needs that have not been met and for which objectives have not been stated. A faculty may approach a needs assessment on a broad scale, studying academic, physical health, mental health, and social needs of learners. Or a faculty may delimit a study to a particular set of needs that it will survey at one time.

As it has done so many times before, a faculty must go back to its statement of curriculum objectives. If it has not developed a statement of objectives, this task must be a first item of business. The objectives serve as the take-off point for a needs assessment. Although a faculty will specify many curricular objectives, it may wish to assess needs in respect to those objectives it believes to be most important or urgent. To accomplish this task, the faculty will rank the curricular objectives in order of relative importance and will assess those at the top of its ranking. Although the high-priority objectives will be assessed first, it should be understood that a faculty will ultimately survey all objectives.

Once the curriculum objectives have been specified, the faculty must then plan ways by which the objectives are being or will be measured. Many data are already available in the school—in teachers' records, principal's office, guidance office, school nurse's files. Additional data will need to be collected to supplement existing data. The faculty must decide on the means it will employ to collect the necessary data. Normally it will make use of standardized test data, teacher-test data, questionnaires, health records, rating scales, and checklists.

Because the faculty is taking a broad look at the school's program, an adequate needs assessment attempts to gather data from the widest possible number of sources. Students, teachers, administrators, other school personnel, and the lay public should make input into a needs assessment.

The faculty should indicate specifically what evaluative data it will need to decide whether each of the stated objectives is being met. Once it has gathered the evaluative data, it must then decide on the basis of those data whether the learners are reaching the objectives. For each objective that is being realized, the faculty can congratulate itself. For each objective that is not being accomplished, the faculty must answer these questions: (1) Is the objective that is not being met still valid and worth pursuing? (2) What should be done about this situation? If the objective is deemed no longer valid, it can be dropped from the school's statement of objectives. However, if the objective is judged still worthwhile and is not being reached, some strategy for reaching it must be devised—this unattained objective is an unmet need.

But a needs assessment should go further than determining whether the currently stated objectives are being met. The assessment should serve as a means of validating the goals and objectives themselves. Unstated objectives that teachers, administrators, other school personnel, students, and patrons of the school identify may also be unmet needs if enough persons believe they are. A common technique for getting at the question of unstated objectives (or, conversely, stated objectives that many people feel are not needed) is the questionnaire or opinion survey. The opinions of students and former students (graduates and dropouts), of all school personnel, and of a representative sample of the community should be sought. In sampling lay opinion, we do not hold with the technique employed by some schools—sampling only the community leaders or the power structure of the community. Nor do we recommend that sampling be confined to parents of children in the schools. Education in a community is everybody's business and not simply the domain of an elite or parents of school-age children. One of the subsets of the community easiest to ignore is the disadvantaged or poor segment; special effort should be taken to make sure faculties have gathered data from this source as well.

On questionnaires of this type, the recipients are asked to identify goals and objectives of the school, problems they believe exist in the school, subject matter they feel to be lacking, programs they would like to see incorporated into the school's program, instructional approaches they would like to see attempted, pupil services they would like to see added, ways in which they feel school funds should be expended, and qualifications they believe teachers exhibit or should possess. The advent of parental choice of school makes the survey of public opinions more crucial than ever.

A final step in the needs assessment is the ranking of unmet needs. From this point, the faculty begins to devise strategies and programs for meeting the identified needs.

Objections have been raised to the needs assessment process. Some maintain that it is too time-consuming. They feel that teachers already know what the school needs. They claim the needs assessment focuses on lacks instead of strengths and assert that the results will repeat those of previous assessments.

On the other hand, the proponents of needs assessments, with whom we agree, see the process as an opportunity to involve all the constituencies of the school. The process makes teachers, students, and laypersons feel that their opinions are important. A needs assessment offers a systematic process for identifying gaps in the curriculum.

When a school system opts to conduct a needs assessment, the alert supervisor in charge might secure in advance descriptions of needs assessment processes carried out elsewhere. A number of years ago, the Research and Development Utilization Project of the Georgia Department of Education, by way of illustration, developed a needs assessment process that provided a checklist of six steps,[9] each of which is subdivided into certain tasks to be accomplished.

Step 1   Initiate the needs assessment process
- ☐ Task 1 Establish a Needs Assessment Committee
- ☐ Task 2 Orient the Committee to the Overall Needs Assessment Process
- ☐ Task 3 Make Tentative Plans

Step 2   Conduct perceived needs assessment
    ☐ Task 1 Review/Finalize the Perceived Needs Assessment Process
    ☐ Task 2 Conduct the Perceived Needs Assessments
    ☐ Task 3 Identify Sets of Top Needs
Step 3   Verify perceived needs by objective means
    ☐ Task 1 Plan for Verification
    ☐ Task 2 Validate the Perceived Needs
Step 4   Determine systemwide need priorities
    ☐ Task 1 Organize for a Systemwide Ranking of Needs
    ☐ Task 2 Conduct the Assessment
    ☐ Task 3 Place Cross-system Needs in Priority Order
Step 5   Choose need to be addressed by improvement efforts
    ☐ Task 1 Determine Which Need Is to Be Improved
    ☐ Task 2 Obtain School System Approval
    ☐ Task 3 Communicate Findings/Undertaking to Public
Step 6   Conduct a causal analysis of the need to be improved
    ☐ Task 1 Organize to Conduct the Causal Analysis
    ☐ Task 2 Analyze the Need in Relation to Six Causal Areas
    ☐ Task 3 Place Causal Factors in Priority Order
    ☐ Task 4 Evaluate Your Needs Assessment Process Using "Needs Assessment: Checklist of Steps"
    ☐ Task 5 Develop a Report of Causal Factors

A set of procedures like this one is an effective evaluation process that reveals to curriculum planners where the curriculum is not meeting the needs of the learners. The process causes the planners to set priorities and develop plans for meeting student needs. As has been observed, procedures for a needs assessment vary from community to community depending on the desires of those charged with the task.

The Delphi Technique

School systems can no longer afford to focus only on the here and now. Like business and industry they must anticipate future needs of the products of our schools. A promising procedure for predicting future educational needs, the Delphi Technique, has enjoyed popularity in the social sciences and education.[10] When a researcher—for example, the supervisor—wishes to employ the Delphi Technique, he or she prepares a set of statements that is sent out in written form to respondents who are considered experts in the field.

The statements, which may be developed by the supervisor in collaboration with the teachers and others, consist of possible goals, values, and programs. The respondents to the instrument that contains the statements independently predict dates, in the fashion of the Delphic oracle, by which they believe the goals, values, or programs will occur. A number of experts in education, for example, might be polled for the dates (years) by which they believe certain programs, such as universal parental choice of school or open enrollments in public schools, administration of national tests of achievement throughout the country, instruction in use of computers required for all students, sex education for all pupils, and proficiency of all students in writing skills will become reality.

The Delphi Technique involves repeated administering and refinement of the instrument and permits revisions of the answers by individual respondents, who do not collaborate or consult with each other while the technique is being carried out. The technique should not be thought of as a controlled research study or identification of specific unmet needs of a particular school. One strength of the Delphi Technique is to encourage futuristic thinking and to identify the beginnings of possible trends. Another strength is to bring about consensus among experts without direct collaboration.

The purpose of the Delphi Technique is to attempt to forecast trends by relying on informed guesses of experts. The best judgments of experts are gathered, their predictions are summarized, and the results are made known to those who may be concerned. The results of a Delphi study in education may cause school personnel to focus on modifications of aspects of education. If, for example, a number of educators believe that all children will not have mastered the basic number facts until twenty years from now (if ever), curriculum planners should stop and ponder the significance of these predictions. By finding the consensus of experts, curriculum planners can shed some light on needs for program planning and curriculum development. If the goal is worth seeking (which respondents may indicate) and if the accomplishment of the goal will require many years, the Delphi study says that, in effect, we had better get moving now on plans to reach that goal, perhaps starting even sooner than we had intended.

A Delphi study can also reinforce or negate beliefs held by the supervisor and other school personnel. If the experts who respond to a study reveal their belief that cooperative learning will be common practice within the next ten years, they may be identifying the beginning of a trend. School systems that have already planned for and put into operation cooperative learning plans would surmise that they are at least in keeping with a developing trend. They may even make the assumption that the trend is occurring as a response to certain needs. If, on the other hand, the experts feel that cooperative learning would not become commonplace for another twenty-five years, school systems that do not adopt this practice would need to decide whether they should do so or whether approaches other than cooperative learning should take higher priority.

The supervisor who wishes to try out the Delphi Technique might assemble a group of interested teachers and other school personnel and brainstorm with them some possible goals, values, and programs that could be included on an instrument to be sent out to a number of experts. When the items for the instrument have been selected, the supervisor duplicates the instrument and sends it out to the experts— for example, college professors of education, administrators, other supervisors, or state department of education specialists.

When the respondents return their instruments, the supervisor tabulates them and sends a revised instrument back to them along with a summary of the results, including the range of predicted dates by which they anticipate items would be realized. The respondents are encouraged to revise their predictions and to state reasons if their predictions fall at extremes of the range created by the responses. The supervisor repeats the process, again furnishing a summary of the results to the respondents and reporting the reasons given by respondents for extreme answers. The supervisor may repeat the process as many times as it appears fruitful and as the respondents are willing to participate. As a general rule, after three or four times the responses tend to converge into consensus. This process may take several months to complete.

The supervisor summarizes the final results of the study and distributes them to both respondents and others, including teachers. Following distribution of the results, the supervisor meets with groups of teachers to discuss implications of the findings and to set strategies for tackling some of the problems revealed by the study.

EVALUATIVE CRITERIA

The supervisor will find it profitable to direct the faculty in a total school evaluation periodically, using a national set of standards called *Evaluative Criteria*.[11] Sets of criteria have been developed by educators under the direction of the National Study of School Evaluation for evaluating three levels of schooling: elementary, middle school/junior high, and secondary. The secondary school standards were originally developed in 1940 and have been revised about every ten years. The middle school/junior high and elementary school standards are newer, the first criteria for middle school/junior high appearing in 1963 and the first for elementary school in 1973.

These criteria grew out of efforts of the six regional accrediting associations to specify standards that the secondary schools are expected to meet if they are to be accredited, that is, to earn the stamp of approval of the accrediting association. The purpose of the criteria is to assure fulfillment of a set of minimal standards and to provide a systematic procedure for studying and improving all phases of a school's program.

The standards contained in the *Evaluation Criteria* are used most often in conjunction with a school's efforts to achieve accreditation by its respective regional association, mostly by secondary schools. When junior high schools, middle schools, and elementary schools also seek regional accreditation, they use the particular criteria for their levels. Regardless of whether the criteria are used as a part of the accreditation process, they offer a valuable set of standards for any faculty and they set forth an effective self-study procedure, which faculties might consider following.

When using the criteria, the total faculty subjects its program to continuing study over a period of time, ordinarily a year. To conduct a self-study, the building supervisor (the principal or someone designated by the principal) should provide for the following steps:

1. Appoint or elect a steering committee of the faculty to spearhead the study.
2. Assign each member of the faculty to one or more subcommittees.
3. Provide time for reports of the subcommittees to the entire faculty, with subsequent discussion of each report.
4. Modify the school's program as the study moves along.
5. Arrange for the visit of a visiting committee of the regional accrediting association if the study is tied into the accreditation process. This step would be omitted if the school is not seeking new or continuing accreditation.

6. Follow up and modify the school's program during and at the conclusion of the study. If the study has been conducted as part of the accreditation process, the visiting committee will have made recommendations for the school's consideration and these recommendations should be studied for possible implementation.

A look at the sections of the *Evaluative Criteria* will help a faculty understand the comprehensiveness of these criteria. The criteria go beyond the curriculum itself and into other phases of the school's operation. Sections that appear in the current editions of the criteria are listed here.

SECONDARY

School and Community
Philosophy and Goals
Curriculum
  Agriculture
  Business Education
  Distributive Education
  Driver and Traffic Safety
    Education
  English
  Foreign Languages
  Health Education
  Home Economics
  Marketing Education
  Mathematics
  Music
  Physical Education
  Religion
  Science
  Social Studies
  Special Education
  Technology Education (Industrial
    Arts)
  Trade, Technical, and Industrial
    Education
  Visual Arts
Auxiliary Services
Guidance Services
Learning Media Services
School Facilities
School Staff and Administration
Student Activities Program
  Other Programs
Individual Faculty Member

MIDDLE LEVEL SCHOOLS

Educational Setting
  Philosophy and Goals
  School and Community
  School Climate
Curriculum
Fine Arts
  Music
  Visual Arts
Foreign Languages
Language Arts
Mathematics
Physical Education and Health
  Education
Practical Arts
  Business
  Home Economics
  Technology Education (Industrial
    Arts)
Religion
Science
Social Studies
Special Education
Other Program Areas
Co-Curricular Program
Learning Media Services
Student Personnel Services
School Facilities
School Staff and Administration
Individual Faculty Data

ELEMENTARY SCHOOL

School and Community
Philosophy and Objectives

Design for Learning

Pupil Services

Areas of Learning (same format for each area of the curriculum)

School Plant

Plans and Priorities

School Staff and Administration

Independent, Church-Related, and Other Non-Public Schools

Individual Faculty Data

Learning Media Services

The steering committee for a self-study will ordinarily assign teachers to two committees: a subject-area committee and a general committee. Each subject-area committee makes a detailed evaluation of the offerings in its own area following a prescribed format. For some faculties, a self-study of this kind is the first opportunity they will have to exchange views and to acquaint each other with what is happening in their fields. The section on school and community for each of the three sets of criteria pulls together demographic data about a community and is of particular help in orienting members of the faculty who are new to a community. As noted in the previous chapter on curriculum development, these criteria require the faculty to state its philosophy, aims, goals, and objectives as a prelude to evaluating the curriculum itself.

When schools couple the self-study with a bid for accreditation, these criteria must be applied in addition to separate sets of standards of the regional accrediting associations themselves. The regional standards add one further dimension to the process of evaluating the school's total program. Those schools that achieve accreditation are required to renew their accreditation annually, conduct an abbreviated interim evaluation of their program every five years, and conduct a full-scale self-study every ten years. Some schools work out arrangements for obtaining the services of a consultant during a self-study; often they reach an agreement with a university to provide a professor as the consultant and to award academic credit for participation in the study. The academic credit serves as a motivator to many teachers and is a device the supervisor would do well to explore.

Some time ago, Vynce A. Hines and William M. Alexander conducted a study to determine the scope and extent of curriculum change in high schools as a result of self-evaluation for purposes of regional accreditation and to learn the impact of self-studies on the attitudes and practices of the teachers involved. Based on our experience serving on visiting accreditation committees, we believe these findings still hold true.

> Curriculum change occurs from 25 to 75 percent more often during the year of the self-study and the year immediately following in schools making the self-study than in their controls (schools not doing the self-study). Schools working on their own make 25 percent more changes; schools with consultant help make about 50 percent more curriculum changes; schools with university courses, 75 percent.
>
> Curriculum changes are most likely to be course changes, to be faculty initiated, to have a positive influence on the attainment of the school objectives, and to be judged as minor changes by the research staff. Most changes are modifications of existing courses, services, or activities. Courses, services, and activities are rarely dropped.
>
> About 50 percent of the Visiting Committee recommendations are rejected or just not implemented because of faculty and administrative disagreement, cost, lack of space and facilities, and unavailability of suitable personnel.

Outstanding outcomes of the self-study and Visiting Committee recommendations, according to teachers, were increased library materials, increased audiovisual aids, and an increase in the number of teachers trying innovations. . . .

Teachers felt that the most important changes influencing them were a better understanding of the school philosophy and an enhanced appreciation of the work of other departments. Negatively, about 10 percent reported worsened attitudes toward the evaluative process and smaller percents reported worsened attitudes toward pupils and toward the community. . . .

To maximize the impact of school evaluations on curriculum change (a) the interval (between self-studies) should probably be not greater than five or six years; (b) schools should arrange for a field laboratory course with access to university consultants; (c) faculty and community should be involved in developing the school philosophy and studying the school and community prior to the beginning of other subcommittee work . . . (f) annual follow-up reports should be made on action taken on recommendations of the Visiting Committee.[12]

Though a similar study today would be informative, observation of the process of regional accreditation of schools reveals basically the same results as reported in Hines's and Alexander's early study. The self-study technique recommended by the *Evaluative Criteria* offers a fruitful way in which a faculty may evaluate its total program.

CURRICULUM MAPPING

Fenwick W. English has advocated a useful evaluation technique known as *curriculum mapping*. In essence, a curriculum map is an analysis of what a teacher has actually taught and the amount of time spent on the tasks. As English explained,

Curriculum mapping is a content analysis of the classroom curriculum as the teacher teaches it. It is an analysis of the *real* curriculum. . . .

There are many kinds of curriculum maps (keep in mind that a map is not a lesson plan). What do the maps tell us? They tell us the level of repetition that does or does not exist, how teachers spend time on task. They help us to know what the real curriculum is in order to adjust the test and the curriculum guide.[13]

English pointed out the difference between a lesson plan and a curriculum map as follows:

The difference between curriculum mapping and a lesson plan is that a lesson plan is in the future tense and a curriculum map is in the past tense, i.e., what was taught, last week, last semester, last year, and a representation of time on task of the teacher involved.[14]

English also described the characteristics of curriculum maps.

While mapping formats may vary, most maps have at least two constants: content taught and time spent. Content may include not only conventional subject matter but anything children are expected to learn: processes, activities, or methods. The intent is to portray time devoted to each major learning task within each classroom or other functional unit. . . .

Mapping provides the curriculum developer with a glimpse of how much time teachers spend on each major topic.[15]

The values of curriculum mapping were summed up by English when he observed,

Curriculum mapping reveals to a staff, principal, or supervisor what is actually being taught, how long it is being taught, and the match between what is being taught and the district's testing program. Curriculum mapping invents or creates no "new" curriculum. Rather it attempts to describe the curriculum that currently exists. The curriculum developer can use the results to gradually make the written curriculum and the real curriculum more congruent with one another.[16]

The comparison of curriculum maps of teachers of all sections of the same grade level or subject can reveal great variations in topics taught and amount of time spent on each. When school districts administer a systemwide test to students in all sections of a grade or subject, the variations in content and time can create problems for the learners. The supervisor can help teachers examine what they have actually taught through the technique of curriculum mapping.

TEACHER PARTICIPATION IN RESEARCH

The supervisor will help teachers develop curriculum proposals and participate in research studies. The nature of the proposal and the degree of teacher participation will depend on the magnitude of the studies. If a proposed study is to be a rigorous piece of applied research, it will ordinarily be drafted by the supervisor or research specialist and will conform to a detailed set of guidelines such as those required by the U.S. Department of Education for proposals submitted to it for funding. If it is a modest piece of applied research affecting a large portion of the faculty or the entire faculty of a school, a proposal may be developed along the lines suggested for plan design in the previous chapter. If a teacher or couple of teachers wish to carry out a piece of action research that will affect only their own classes, a streamlined, simplified proposal may be all that is needed, consisting of a statement of the proposal, hypotheses to be tested, and procedures to be followed, including means of evaluating.

Proposals for action research will ordinarily originate from the teachers themselves, though the supervisor may plant the seed that flowers into an action research study. Proposals for more sophisticated research may originate with teachers but more likely will originate with supervisors or research specialists. Wherever they originate, if teachers will be asked to participate, the proposals should be talked out before the first word is set down. The cooperation of the teachers must be assured and their continuous participation must be a certainty. The teachers will need to develop a sense of identity with the study. They may be called on to assist under guidance in formulating hypotheses, validating the objectives and the instruments, carrying out procedures, collecting data, analyzing data, and certainly in the decision making that takes place as a result of the data analysis.

Even with action research, teachers should seek to validate the goals and objectives of the proposed program and the instruments they will use. The instruments can be validated by subjecting them to review by other specialists in the field in which the research study falls. The goals and objectives may be validated by this same review process by experts or by reference to published findings of others who have studied the problem.

The supervisor should be as concerned with teachers' development of the skills of creating curriculum proposals as with the end product—the curriculum proposal itself. Writing curriculum proposals is one method of promoting a research orientation among teachers.

EVALUATION OF MATERIALS AND STUDIES

The supervisor should assist teachers in evaluating both curriculum materials and research studies conducted elsewhere that may have significance for them. A major responsibility of the supervisor is to be on the lookout for new curriculum materials and channel them to teachers who might make use of them. The supervisor should help teachers decide whether the new materials would be useful in their situation. Together with the teachers, the supervisor should examine the purposes of the materials, the uses to which they could be put, the limitations of the materials, and of course, the costs.

The supervisor also has the responsibility of alerting teachers to reports of research studies that may be significant to them. It is usually much easier for the supervisor to fulfill the task of locating and disseminating curriculum materials than it is to search out and distribute reports of research. Many curriculum materials come across the supervisor's desk without any solicitation. Manufacturers and publishers of curriculum materials have a product they wish to sell and they are quick to make their products known. Supervisors encounter curriculum materials in their travels about the country and at state, regional, and national meetings as well as through catalogs and announcements of new materials they receive in the mail.

Supervisors do not, as a rule, have too much difficulty bringing new curricular materials to the attention of teachers. This is one task of supervision in which some supervisors overcompensate for lacks in other areas. Where supervisors are almost universally weak is in the location and dissemination of research that is going on or has been conducted that may help teachers in their school system. It is also difficult to decide whether a research study once located is important enough to be made available to teachers in the system. The sources of reports of research are often difficult to determine and frequently unavailable to supervisors. The identification of research studies has become easier with the accessibility of ERIC documents and other research sources through computer networks.

Fortunately, there are helpful tools available to assist the supervisor in finding research studies. In some cases, these tools may already be available in the school system somewhere. In other cases, certain resources can be purchased by the school system for the specific purpose of helping school personnel keep up with research. In still other cases, the supervisor may have to spend several hours at the closest public and university libraries periodically poring over research reference materials.

Where can the supervisor turn to locate research studies? The sources are many and are usually available in most college and university libraries, in some large public libraries, and sometimes in the professional libraries of school systems. A few of the more significant sources are listed here.

1. *Education Index* (New York: H. W. Wilson Company). This is a standard reference to articles in education journals. The supervisor may locate what appears to be a pertinent article reporting a piece of research and would then need to go to the issue of the journal itself to read the article. The journal is published monthly. Most libraries bind all the issues for one year into a single volume.

2. *Reader's Guide to Periodical Literature.* (New York: H. W. Wilson Company). This standard reference fulfills the same function as the *Education Index* except that it indexes articles from journals of general interest. The journal is published monthly. Most libraries bind all the issues for one year into a single volume.

3. *ERIC materials.* The most elaborate and comprehensive source of research information was established in 1964 by the former U.S. Office of Education, the system known in the profession as ERIC (Educational Resources Information Center), a system comprising some sixteen clearinghouses, each of which is devoted to gathering, evaluating, abstracting, and disseminating information in a particular field of specialization.

Many college libraries receive ERIC documents, and some of these libraries have arranged to receive automatically all documents made available through ERIC. Though documents may be obtained in hard (paper) copy or on microfiche, the tendency for libraries today is to obtain the documents in microfiche form, which is cheaper and far easier to store.

The supervisor may wish to invest in the *Thesaurus of ERIC Descriptors* (Phoenix: Oryx Press) to help locate studies in particular fields of specialization. The *Thesaurus* provides a classification system for indexing ERIC documents and greatly simplifies the search process.

The supervisor should make use of two periodicals: *Resources in Education* (Washington, D.C.: U.S. Government Printing Office) and the *Current Index to Journals in Education* (Phoenix: Oryx Press). *Resources in Education* is a monthly abstract journal made up of résumés of studies and reports and of indexes to these materials. The *Current Index to Journals in Education* is a monthly publication that follows the classification scheme of the *Thesaurus of ERIC Descriptors* and lists references to studies reported in education journals.

Access to ERIC materials is necessary for anyone who is making a search of the literature on a particular topic. ERIC clearinghouses will provide copies of bibliographies that they may have developed for their particular fields of specialization. Some colleges and universities offer various computerized data banks, including ERIC, that can greatly expedite searches.

4. *The Encyclopedia of Educational Research* (New York: Macmillan). This reference summarizes many educational research studies. It is revised every ten years and is sponsored by the American Educational Research Association.

5. *Dissertation Abstracts International* (Ann Arbor, Mich.: University Microfilms). This monthly publication contains abstracts of doctoral dissertations written in the United States and Canada. The user of this publication can order a copy of a dissertation on microfilm from University Microfilms. Users may also subscribe to University Microfilms' DATRIX service for locating abstracts of dissertations on particular fields of specialization.

6. *Publications of the American Educational Research Association* (Washington, D.C.). These publications contain reviews and reports of research studies on a wide variety of topics. Among the AERA publications are *American Educational Research Journal* (quarterly), *Educational Researcher* (monthly), *Monograph Series on Evaluation: Perspectives of Curriculum Evaluation* (six monographs), *Review of Educational Research* (quarterly), and *Review of Research in Education* (annually).

7. *The National Assessment of Educational Progress.* Supervisors, particularly specialist-supervisors in selected fields, should keep themselves and their teachers abreast of findings of the National Assessment of Educational Progress (NAEP), funded by the Office for Educational Research and Improvement of the U.S. Department of Education and one of the most extensive testing projects undertaken in the United States. Originally based in Denver under the egis of the Education Commission of the States, NAEP began collecting data on the achievement of four age groups throughout the country in ten subject areas and on their attitudes toward the subjects.

The NAEP program dates from the efforts of Ralph Tyler and the Committee on Assessing the Progress of Education, which under the instigation of the Carnegie Corporation in 1964 began development of a nationwide program to assess educational progress of learners. At the onset of NAEP, the program came under heavy attack from professional educators who feared this assessment could lead to a national standardized curriculum, a step that has been anathema to most educators but quite appealing to a sizable segment of the public. The educators were concerned that comparisons of schools and even individuals might be made from the data, which might destroy the images of schools that showed up poorly and might cause harm to individuals. In spite of objections, the NAEP moved ahead by identifying objectives in ten subject areas: science, writing, citizenship, reading, literature, social studies, music, mathematics, career and occupational development, and art. Following specification of the objectives, criterion-referenced assessment instruments were developed.

Assessment began in 1969–1970, and the first results were reported in 1970. In the 1980s, NAEP engaged in the assessment of student achievement in computer competence, geography, and history. Over the years, NAEP has conducted periodic assessments and reassessments in the various subject areas.

NAEP has been able to allay the fears of professional educators by its refusal to establish norms on the various tests or to make individual scores known. The program collects group data and reports them for the nation, by geographical region, by size of community, by type of community, by sex, by black or white ethnic group, by educational level of parents, and by age groups. The target age groups are nine-year-olds, thirteen-year-olds, seventeen-year-olds (in school and out), and young adults twenty-six to thirty-five.

NAEP leaves the interpretation of the results to the local communities. The results give supervisors and teachers a useful set of data for comparative purposes and may aid in curriculum development. One of the advantages of the national assessment program is that results in certain areas may throw out clues to school districts for conducting their own local assessments. The national assessment program has also established a model that states are using in their own assessment programs.

The Education Commission of the States administered NAEP during its first fourteen years. Effective July 1, 1983, administration of NAEP transferred to the Educational Testing Service in Princeton, New Jersey. Supervisors seeking information on the National Assessment of Educational Progress may obtain assessment reports and a newsletter from the National Assessment of Educational Progress, Educational Testing Service, Princeton, New Jersey.

8. *International assessments.* Assessments of achievement in subject areas by learners in various countries are difficult to come by, but where they do exist and are available, they may have at least an academic interest for supervisors and teachers and may have implications for curriculum planning. The problems of testing across cultures and making comparisons of performance are large indeed. Educational philosophies, goals, and objectives vary from country to country and affect both the curriculum and instructional methods. Student populations and socioeconomic factors as well as teacher training are variables that make comparisons tricky. Nevertheless, the supervisor who is on top of what is happening in curriculum evaluation should at least be familiar with significant studies that have been widely disseminated. Mention was made in the previous chapter of international studies of achievement in mathematics. Two studies conducted by the International Association for the Evaluation of Educational Achievement (IEA) have reported data on the achievement of students in a number of countries. The First International Study of Achievement in Mathematics gathered data on the achievement of some 130,000 students in mathematics taught by some 13,000 teachers in over 5,000 schools of twelve countries.[17] IEA has conducted other cross-national studies of student achievement in civic education, English, French, literature, reading comprehension, and science. All in all, IEA surveyed some 250,000 students taught by some 50,000 teachers in twenty-two countries.[18] More recently, the Second International Mathematics Study assessed achievement of 12,000 eighth- and twelfth-grade students in college preparatory mathematics classes in twenty countries.[19] In 1988, the Center for Assessment of Educational Progress of the Educational Testing Service conducted the First International Assessment of Educational Progress (IAEP). IAEP assessed proficiency of thirteen-year-olds in science and mathematics in five countries. This assessment reaffirmed the relatively low ranking of American students in these two disciplines.[20] Though we may have some reservations about these studies, we might all wish that American pupils had performed better in the comparisons than they did. In 1991, then-President Bush expressed this desire by presenting the *America 2000* education package. Together, he and the nation's governors, in a move reaffirmed by the U.S. Congress and President Clinton, proposed to the country a lofty and formidable goal: to raise the ranking of American students, in mathematics and science achievement, to first in the world by the year 2000.[21] Two additional goals—expectations for professional development for educators and increased parental involvement in learning—have been added to the national program under the Clinton administration.[22]

STATE ASSESSMENT PROGRAMS

The supervisor should assume responsibility for directing teachers in state assessment programs and in evaluation of the school's program for purposes of state accreditation. States have moved heavily into statewide assessment of pupil achievement in various subject areas. Some of the states are capitalizing on the model of the National Assessment of Educational Progress, using their own criterion-referenced tests. Other states have called for both criterion-referenced and norm-referenced testing at various levels of the educational ladder. Results obtained from state assessments have particular significance for communities within the state. The supervisor should discuss with teachers the results of state assessments and together they should interpret the data and plan for curriculum changes that seem warranted.

State departments of education are charged with the responsibility of evaluating and/or accrediting schools within their states. States vary in the procedures they use to evaluate individual schools and to decide whether they meet state standards. The purpose of state evaluation and accreditation is the maintenance of minimal standards by the schools of the state, not only in respect to the curriculum but in all aspects of the schools' operations. States ordinarily carry out periodic assessments of schools for purposes of state accreditation, sometimes in conjunction with regional accrediting association visits.

LOCAL ASSESSMENT PROGRAMS

The supervisor will work with teachers to plan and carry out local assessments of achievement of students in various subject areas. Whether or not the state requires participation in its assessment program, local school districts will find it helpful to develop their own assessment programs. Local assessment programs may supplement state and national assessments, may fill in the gaps not tested by the state and national programs, and may provide experiences that prepare students for state and national assessments. Local school systems may use input from state, national, and even international studies in developing their own assessment programs. Such programs are a part of the needs assessment referred to earlier. As well as serving to identify unmet needs, local assessment programs facilitate comparisons among schools within the school district. The selection or creation of appropriate testing instruments will be a major problem in local assessment, and for this problem the supervisor may need to seek assistance from research specialists either inside or outside the school system. The supervisor will be called on to display a wide repertoire of knowledge and skills in working with teachers on the critical task of curriculum evaluation.

SUMMARY

Evaluation is a fundamental part of the curriculum development process. Through evaluation, teachers learn whether stated objectives have been reached. Only through evaluation can intelligent curriculum decisions be made.

The supervisor plays a major role as leader and resource person in the evaluation phase of curriculum development. Though a research director or evaluation specialist might possess a higher degree of skill in evaluation and research than the supervisor, the positions of research director and evaluator are not universally found in the school systems and the supervisor must fulfill the role of leader in evaluation.

In carrying out this role, the supervisor should seek to help teachers develop an evaluative frame of mind, an inquiring attitude, and a research orientation. The supervisor should help teachers state curricular objectives in performance terms to simplify the task of evaluation.

The understanding of nine basic research concepts will help teachers in their role as consumers and appliers of research. A knowledge of these concepts will enable teachers to utilize standardized test data more effectively and to interpret research studies that have been conducted inside and outside the school system.

The supervisor should acquaint teachers with various types of evaluation and research. The purpose of acquainting teachers with the kinds of studies that are conducted is to show them the range of possibilities and to indicate types of studies in which they are most likely to be involved. Generally, teachers engage in descriptive research, action research, and some applied research.

The supervisor should help teachers develop skill in conducting needs assessments to discover unmet needs. Thorough needs assessments obtain input from students, teachers, administrators, other school personnel, and the community. A special caution is suggested—those conducting needs assessments should be concerned that data are sought from all segments of the community and not just selected segments.

Teachers should be instructed in the use of evaluation materials developed for both state and regional accreditation. Although regional accreditation is voluntary, state evaluation and accreditation are required. A self-study by a faculty utilizing the *Evaluative Criteria* for its particular school level is a comprehensive way of evaluating a total school program.

The supervisor should keep teachers abreast of information on state, national, and international assessment of achievement of learners. Regardless of whether a school district participates in a state or national assessment program, it should under the leadership of the supervisor develop its own local assessment program. The purposes of local assessment are (1) to identify unmet needs, (2) to make comparisons of schools within a district, and (3) to make decisions about the curriculum.

The supervisor in the role of an evaluative resource person should be knowledgeable about sources of research information and should program time in such a way that he or she can review recent research and disseminate research information to the teachers being supervised.

QUESTIONS FOR DISCUSSION

1. How could a supervisor help a teacher determine whether the curriculum being used meets the needs of all the students?
2. How could a supervisor help a teacher do an action research project?
3. Why should a needs assessment be the first step in curriculum development?
4. What are reasons a supervisor should have teachers use curriculum mapping?
5. What is the role of the National Assessment of Educational Progress (NAEP) in improving education? Do you approve or disapprove of the role?

ACTIVITIES FOR FURTHER STUDY

1. Search the literature and report on a model of curriculum evaluation other than those described in this chapter.
2. Find a report of a curriculum study carried on in a school outside your own district and prepare a critique of the study concerning research design, validation of the goals and objectives, validation of the instruments, procedures used, treatment of the data, conclusions, and applicability to your school district.
3. Draft a plan for an introductory in-service program on curriculum evaluation.

4. Design an instrument to assess student academic needs. Administer this instrument to a random sample of twenty to twenty-five students and summarize your findings.

5. Design an instrument to assess attitudes of the public toward the school's curriculum. Administer this instrument to a random sample of twenty to twenty-five laypersons and summarize your findings.

6. Choose a curriculum problem and design a plan to study that problem.

7. Construct and analyze a curriculum map for your grade or subject for a period of one semester.

8. Define *mean, median, reliability, validity, norm, percentile, correlation coefficient, standard score,* and *standard deviation.*

9. Choose a curriculum topic and conduct a search for information about it in ERIC.

10. Choose a curriculum topic and locate abstracts on it in *Resources in Education.*

11. Choose a curriculum topic and locate studies on it in the *Current Index to Journals in Education.*

12. Examine and write a brief report on the nature and use of the *Thesaurus of ERIC Descriptors.*

13. Examine the regional accreditation report of a school that has obtained accreditation by its regional accrediting association and decide which recommendations of the visiting committee have been implemented since the report was issued and which have not been implemented. If a recommendation has not been implemented, formulate hypotheses about why the recommendation has not been put into practice.

14. Distinguish between hard copy, microfilm, and microfiche. Explain the advantages and disadvantages of each of these media.

15. Examine and fill out a 3 × 5-inch card reporting characteristics of each of the following sources of research information:
    a. *The Encyclopedia of Educational Research*
    b. *The Review of Educational Research*
    c. *Dissertation Abstracts International*

16. Write a position paper on "The Role of the Supervisor in Conducting Local Research."

17. Write a paper utilizing selected references accounting for objections researchers make to action research and propose some ways to overcome these objections.

18. List at least five curriculum problems in a field of specialization you know well that call for rigorous applied research studies.

19. List at least three curriculum problems or instructional problems in a field of specialization you know well that would be suitable for action research.

20. Apply one subject area section of the *Evaluative Criteria* for your particular school level in the school whose program you know best.

21. Sample and report opinions of at least five teachers concerning the forces they believe have the greatest impact on curriculum change. Ask them to identify any curriculum change that has come about as a result of local research.

22. Choose a field of your interest or expertise in which assessments have been made by the National Assessment of Educational Progress and report findings and implications of the results.

23. Interview at least six teachers to learn whether they have participated in any type of evaluative study of the curriculum in the last five years. If they have, report the type of study and determine whether the study was required (as, for example, a study in connection with state or regional accreditation).

24. Talk with the principal of a school and ascertain his or her views on the necessity of curriculum evaluation and what he or she believes is going on in the school in the way of curriculum evaluation. Raise the same question with (a) the assistant principal for curriculum, if there is one; (b) a generalist supervisor; and (c) a specialist supervisor (the specialist could be a grade coordinator, team leader, or department head) at the same school.

25. Conduct a brief study employing the Delphi Technique.

26. Write a paper describing the roles of each of the following in curriculum evaluation:
    a. Principal
    b. Supervisor
    c. Teacher
    d. Students
    e. Public

27. Identify in your school system a curriculum innovation that in its initial proposal contained a plan for evaluating its success. List criteria on which to analyze the evaluation plan and make a critique of the plan on the basis of these criteria.

28. *Those who are teaching* will design and carry out a piece of action research and report either progress or final results. *Those who are not teaching* will interview a teacher who is conducting a piece of action research and report on its design, procedures, and results.

29. Find out and report whether your state has in effect a statewide plan for assessing pupil achievement in the subject areas.

30. Locate and report on the standards required of all public schools in your state.

31. Describe how your state monitors the accomplishment of state-mandated standards by the public schools.

32. If your state has an accreditation process, compare the criteria required for state accreditation with criteria required for regional accreditation.

NOTES

1. James A. Beane, ed., *Toward a Coherent Curriculum—1995 Yearbook of the Association for Supervision and Curriculum Development* (Alexandria, Va.: Association for Supervision and Curriculum Development, 1995), p. 3.

2. See releases in the press April 19 and 20, 1991.

3. L. R. Gay, *Educational Research: Competencies for Analysis and Application*, 4th ed. (New York: Macmillan, 1992), p. 11.

4. Daniel L. Stufflebeam et al., *Educational Evaluation and Decision Making* (Itasca, Ill.: F. E. Peacock, 1971).

5. The Center for the Study of Evaluation, *Evaluation Workshop I: An Orientation* (Del Monte Research Park, Monterey, Calif.: CTB/McGraw-Hill, 1971). See also Stephen Klein, Gary Fenstermacher, and Marvin C. Alkin, "The Center's Changing Evaluation Model," *Evaluation Comment* 4 (1971): 9–12.

6. For other models of curriculum evaluation, see J. Galen Saylor, William M. Alexander, and Arthur J. Lewis, *Curriculum Planning for Better Teaching and Learning*, 4th ed. (New York: Holt, Rinehart and Winston, 1981), chap. 7; and Peter F. Oliva, *Developing the Curriculum*, 4th ed. (New York: HarperCollins, 1997), chap. 13.

7. The Joint Committee on Standards for Educational Evaluation, *The Program Standards: How to Assess Evaluations of Educational Programs*, 2nd ed. (Thousand Oaks, Calif.: Sage, 1994).

8. Fenwick W. English and Roger A. Kaufman, *Needs Assessment: A Focus for Curriculum Development* (Alexandria, Va.: Association for Supervision and Curriculum Development, 1975), pp. 3–4.

9. Willard Crouthamel and Stephen M. Preston, *Needs Assessment: User's Manual; Needs Assessment: Resource Guide; Needs Assessment: Checklist of Steps* (Atlanta: Research and Development Utilization Project, Georgia Department of Education, 1979).

10. See Olaf Helmer, "Analysis of the Future: The Delphi Method," in *Technological Forecasting for Industry and Government Methods and Applications*, ed. James R. Bright (Englewood Cliffs, N.J.: Prentice-Hall, 1968), pp. 116–22; Olaf Helmer, "The Delphi Method—An Illustration," in *Technological Forecasting for Industry and Government Methods and Applications*, ed. James R. Bright (Englewood Cliffs, N.J.: Prentice-Hall, 1968), pp. 123–33; T. J. Gordon, "New Approaches to Delphi," in *Technological Forecasting for Industry and Government Methods and Applications*, ed. James R. Bright (Englewood Cliffs, N.J.: Prentice-Hall, 1968), pp. 134–43. See also W. Timothy Weaver, "The Delphi Forecasting Method," *Phi Delta Kappan* 52 (January 1971): 267–71; bibliography on the Delphi Technique, W. Timothy Weaver, "The Delphi Forecasting Methods," *Phi Delta Kappan* 52 (January 1971): 271; Frederick R. Cyphert and Walter L. Gant, "The Delphi Technique: A Case Study," *Phi Delta Kappan* 52 (January 1971): 267–71.

11. National Study of School Evaluation, *Evaluative Criteria*, 6th ed., 1987 (secondary); *Middle School/Junior High School Evaluative Criteria*, rev. ed., 1979; *Elementary School Evaluative Criteria*, 2nd ed., 1981; *Secondary School Evaluation Criteria: Narrative Edition*, 1975; *Evaluative Criteria for Middle Level Schools*, 1990 (Falls Church, Va.: National Study of School Evaluation). Some schools are now using newer criteria: *Middle Level School Improvement, Focusing on Desired Learner Outcomes*, 1993; *High School Improvement, Focusing on Desired Learner Outcomes*, 1993 (Falls Church, Va.: National Study of School Evaluation).

12. Vynce A. Hines and William M. Alexander, *High School Self-Evaluation and Curriculum Change*, Final Report, Project 3120, Contract No. OE 6–10–154, Bureau of Research, Office of Education (Washington, D.C.: U.S. Department of Health, Education, and Welfare, 1967), pp. 64–65.

13. Fenwick W. English, "Curriculum Mapping," *The Professional Educator* 3 (Spring 1980): 11–12.

14. Ibid., p. 11.

15. Fenwick W. English, "Curriculum Mapping," *Educational Leadership* 37 (April 1980): 559.

16. Ibid.

17. T. Husén, ed., *International Study of Achievement in Mathematics*, 2 vols. (New York: Wiley, 1967).

18. See Joseph Featherstone, "Measuring What Schools Achieve: Learning and Testing," *The New Republic* 169 (December 15, 1973): 19–21; and T. Neville Posthlethwaite, "International Educational Surveys," *Contemporary Education* 42 (November 1970): 61–68.

19. See Second International Mathematics Study, *The Underachieving Curriculum: Assessing U.S. School Mathematics from an International Point of View* (Champaign, Ill.: Stipes Publishing, 1987). See also Sue Harris, "The Third International Mathematics and Science Study (TIMSS)," *Mathematics in School* 23 (November 1994): 34–35.

20. See Archie E. Lapointe, Nancy A. Mead, and Gary W. Phillips, *A World of Differences: An International Assessment of Mathematics and Science* (Princeton, N.J.: Educational Testing Service, Center for Assessment of Educational Progress, 1989).

21. *National Goals for Education* (Washington, D.C.: U.S. Department of Education, July 1990).

22. *Goals 2000 Educate America Act* (Washington, D.C.: U.S. Department of Education, 1994).

BIBLIOGRAPHY

Alkin, Marvin C., ed. *The Encyclopedia of Educational Research*, 6th ed. New York: Macmillan, 1992.

American Educational Research Association. *American Educational Research Journal.* Washington, D.C.: American Educational Research Association, quarterly.

————. *Educational Researcher.* Washington, D.C.: American Educational Research Association, monthly.

————. *Monograph Series on Evaluation: Perspectives of Curriculum Evaluation 1–6.* Ann Arbor, Mich.: Xerox University Microfilms.

————. *Review of Educational Research.* Washington, D.C.: American Educational Research Association, quarterly.

————. *Review of Research in Education.* Itasca, Ill.: F. E. Peacock, annually.

Armstrong, David G. *Developing and Documenting the Curriculum.* Boston: Allyn & Bacon, 1989.

Beane, James A. *Toward a Coherent Curriculum—1995 Yearbook of the Association for Supervision and Curriculum Development.* Alexandria, Va.: Association for Supervision and Curriculum Development.

Beggs, Donald, and Ernest Lewis. *Measurement and Evaluation in the Schools.* Boston: Houghton Mifflin, 1975.

Borg, Walter R. *Applying Educational Research: A Practical Guide for Teachers.* White Plains, N.Y.: Longman, 1981.

Bright, James R., ed. *Technological Forecasting for Industry and Government Methods and Applications.* Englewood Cliffs, N.J.: Prentice-Hall, 1968.

Calhoun, Emily. *How to Use Action Research in the Self-Renewing School.* Alexandria, Va.: Association for Supervision and Curriculum Development, 1994.

California Evaluation Improvement Project. *Program Evaluator's Guide*, 2nd ed. Princeton, N.J.: Evaluation Improvement Program, Educational Testing Service, 1979.

The Center for the Study of Evaluation. *Evaluation Workshop I: An Orientation.* Monterey, Calif.: CTB/McGraw-Hill, 1971. Participant's Notebook and Leadership Manual.

Corey, Stephen M. *Action Research to Improve School Practices.* New York: Teachers College, Columbia University, 1953.

Crouthamel, Willard, and Stephen M. Preston. *Needs Assessment: Checklist of Steps; Needs Assessment: Resource Guide; Needs Assessment: User's Manual.* Atlanta: Research and Development Utilization Project, Georgia Department of Education, 1979.

"Curriculum Evaluation: Uses, Misuses, and Nonuses." *Educational Leadership* 35 (January 1978): 243–97.

Cyphert, Frederick R., and Walter L. Gant. "The Delphi Technique: A Case Study." In *Technological Forecasting for Industry and Government Methods and Applications*, edited by James R. Bright. Englewood Cliffs, N.J.: Prentice-Hall, 1968.

De Cecco, John P., and William R. Crawford. *The Psychology of Learning and Instruction*, 2nd ed. Englewood Cliffs, N.J.: Prentice-Hall, 1974.

Dissertation Abstracts International. Ann Arbor, Mich.: University Microfilms.

Drake, Susan. *Planning Integrated Curriculum: The Call to Adventure.* Alexandria, Va.: Association for Supervision and Curriculum Development, 1993.

Education Index. New York: H. W. Wilson Company.

Eisner, Elliot W. "Educational Connoisseurship and Criticism: Their Form and Functions in Educational Evaluation." *The Journal of Aesthetic Education* 10 (July–October 1976): 135–50.

————. *The Educational Imagination: On the Design and Evaluation of School Programs*, 2nd ed. New York: Macmillan, 1985.

Elmore, Richard, and Susan Fuhrman, ed. *The Governance of Curriculum: The 1994 ASCD*

Yearbook. Alexandria, Va.: The Association for Supervision and Curriculum Development, 1994.

English, Fenwick W. "Curriculum Mapping." *Educational Leadership* 37 (April 1980): 558–59.

———. "Curriculum Mapping." *The Professional Educator* 3 (Spring 1980): 8–12.

———. *Deciding What to Teach and Test*. Thousand Oaks, Ca.: Corwin Press, 1992.

———, ed. *Fundamental Curriculum Decisions*. 1983 Yearbook. Alexandria, Va.: Association for Supervision and Curriculum Development, 1983.

English, Fenwick W., and Roger A. Kaufman. *Needs Assessment: A Focus for Curriculum Development*. Alexandria, Va.: Association for Supervision and Curriculum Development, 1975.

Featherstone, Joseph. "Measuring What Schools Achieve: Learning and Testing." *The New Republic* 169 (December 15, 1973): 19–21.

Foshay, Arthur W., ed. *Considered Action for Curriculum Improvement*. 1980 Yearbook. Alexandria, Va.: Association for Supervision and Curriculum Development, 1980.

Gay, L. R. *Educational Evaluation and Measurement: Competencies for Analysis and Application*, 2nd ed. Columbus, Ohio: Merrill, 1985.

———. *Educational Research: Competencies for Analysis and Application*, 4th ed. New York: Macmillan, 1992. (5th ed. Englewood Cliffs, N.J.: Merrill, 1996.)

Goals 2000 Education America Act. Washington, D.C.: U.S. Department of Education, 1994.

Gordon, T. J. "New Approaches to Delphi." In *Technological Forecasting for Industry and Government Methods and Applications*, edited by James R. Bright. Englewood Cliffs, N.J.: Prentice-Hall, 1968.

Gronlund, Norman E. *Measurement and Evaluation in Teaching*, 6th ed. New York: Macmillan, 1990.

Harris, Sue. "The Third International Mathematics and Science Study (TIMSS)," *Mathematics in School* 23 (November 1994): 34–35.

Hawkins, Mary Louise, and M. Dolores Graham. *Curriculum Architecture: Creating a Place of Our Own*. Columbus, Ohio: National Middle School Association, 1994.

Helmer, Olaf. "Analysis of the Future: The Delphi Method." In *Technological Forecasting for Industry and Government Methods and Applications*, edited by James R. Bright. Englewood Cliffs, N.J.: Prentice-Hall, 1968.

Herman, Joan L., and Lynn Winters. *Tracking Your School's Success: A Guide to Sensible Evaluation*. Newbury Park, Calif.: Corwin Press, 1992.

Hines, Vynce A., and William M. Alexander. *High School Self-Evaluation and Curriculum Change*. Final Report, Project 3120, Contract No. OE 6–10–154, Bureau of Research, Office of Education. Washington, D.C.: U.S. Department of Health, Education, and Welfare, 1967.

Husén, Torsten, ed. *International Study of Achievement in Mathematics*, 2 vols. New York: Wiley, 1967.

Jacobs, Heidi H., ed. *Interdisciplinary Curriculum: Design and Implementation*. Alexandria, Va.: Association for Supervision and Curriculum Development, 1989.

Johnson, Mauritz, Jr. *Intentionality in Education: A Conceptual Model of Curricular and Instructional Planning and Evaluation*. New York: Center for Curriculum Research and Services, 1977.

Joint Committee on Standards for Educational Evaluation. *The Program Standards: How to Assess Evaluations of Educational Programs*, 2nd ed. Thousand Oaks, Calif.: Sage, 1994.

Kaufman, Roger A. *Educational System Planning*. Englewood Cliffs, N.J.: Prentice-Hall, 1972.

Klein, Stephen, Gary Fenstermacher, and Marvin C. Alkin. "The Center's Changing Evaluation Model." *Evaluation Comment* 4 (1971): 9–12.

Lapointe, Archie E., Nancy A. Mead, and Gary W. Phillips. *A World of Differences: An International Assessment of Mathematics and Science*. Princeton, N.J.: Educational Testing Service, Center for Assessment of Educational Progress, 1989.

Lewy, Arieh, ed. *Handbook of Curriculum Evaluation*. White Plains, N.Y.: Longman, 1977.

Lindvall, C. M., and Richard C. Cox, with John O. Bolvin. "Evaluation as a Tool in Curriculum Development: The IPI Evaluation Program." *AERA Monograph Series on Curriculum Evaluation*, no. 5. Chicago: Rand McNally, 1970.

Linn, Robert L., and Norman E. Gronlund. *Measurement and Assessment in Teaching*, 7th ed. Englewood Cliffs, N.J.: Merrill, 1995.

Marzano, Robert, Debra Pickering, and Jay McTighe. *Assessing Student Outcomes: Performance Assessment Using the Dimensions of Learning Model*. Alexandria, Va.: Association for Supervision and Curriculum Development, 1993.

McKnight, Curtis C., et al. *The Underachieving Curriculum: Assessing U.S. School Mathematics from an International Point of View*. Champaign, Ill.: Stipes, 1987.

National Study of School Evaluation. *Elementary School Evaluative Criteria*, 2nd ed. Falls Church, Va.: National Study of School Evaluation, 1981.

———. *Evaluative Criteria* (secondary), 6th ed. Falls Church, Va.: National Study of School Evaluation, 1987.

———. *Evaluative Criteria for Middle Level Schools*. Falls Church, Va.: National Study of School Evaluation, 1990.

———. *High School Improvement, Focusing on Desired Learner Outcomes*. Falls Church, Va.: National Study of School Evaluation, 1993.

———. *Middle Level School Improvement, Focusing on Desired Learner Outcomes*. Falls Church, Va.: National Study of School Evaluation, 1993.

———. *Middle School/Junior High School Evaluative Criteria*, rev. ed. Falls Church, Va.: National Study of School Evaluation, 1979.

———. *Secondary School Evaluation Criteria: Narrative Edition*. Falls Church, Va.: National Study of School Evaluation, 1975.

Oliva, Peter F. *Developing the Curriculum*, 4th ed. New York: HarperCollins, 1997.

Payne, David A., ed. *Curriculum Evaluation*. Lexington, Mass.: D. C. Heath, 1974.

Plakos, Marie, John Plakos, and Robert Babcock. *Workbook on Program Evaluation*, 2nd ed. Princeton, N.J.: Educational Testing Service, 1978.

Popham, W. James. *Educational Evaluation*. Englewood Cliffs, N.J.: Prentice-Hall, 1975.

Posthlethwaite, T. Neville. "International Educational Surveys." *Contemporary Education* 42 (November 1970): 61–68.

Provus, Malcolm. *Discrepancy Evaluation for Educational Program Improvement and Assessment*. Berkeley, Calif.: McCutchan, 1971.

Reader's Guide to Periodical Literature. New York: H. W. Wilson Company.

Sagor, Richard. *How to Conduct Collaborative Action Research*. Alexandria, Va.: Association for Supervision and Curriculum Development, 1993.

Saylor, J. Galen, William M. Alexander, and Arthur J. Lewis. *Curriculum Planning for Better Teaching and Learning*, 4th ed. New York: Holt, Rinehart and Winston, 1981.

Scriven, Michael. "The Methodology of Evaluation." *Perspectives of Curriculum Evaluation*, AERA Monograph Series on Curriculum Evaluation, No. 1. Chicago: Rand McNally, 1967.

Second International Mathematics Study. *The Underachieving Curriculum: Assessing U.S. School Mathematics from an International Point of View*. Champaign, Ill.: Stipes Publishing, 1987.

Stake, Robert E. "Language, Rationality, and Assessment." In *Improving Educational Assessment and an Inventory of Measures of Affective Behavior*, ed. Walcott H. Beatty. Alexandria, Va.: Commission on Assessment of Educational Outcomes, Association for Supervision and Curriculum Development, 1969.

Stufflebeam, Daniel L., Walter J. Foley, William J. Gephart, Egon G. Guba, Robert J. Hammond, Howard O. Merriman, and Malcolm M. Provus. *Educational Evaluation and Decision Making*. Itasca, Ill.: F. E. Peacock, 1971.

Tuckman, Bruce W. *Conducting Educational Research*, 4th ed. New York: Harcourt Brace Jovanovich, 1984.

Tyler, Ralph W. *Basic Principles of Curriculum and Instruction*. Chicago: University of Chicago Press, 1949.

————, ed. *Educational Evaluation: New Roles, New Means*. 68th Yearbook of the National Society for the Study of Education. Chicago: University of Chicago Press, 1969.

Tyler, Ralph W., Robert M. Gagné, and Michael Scriven. *Perspectives of Curriculum Evaluation*. AERA Monograph Series on Curriculum Evaluation, no. 1. Chicago: Rand McNally, 1967.

U.S. Department of Education. *National Goals for Education*. Washington, D.C.: U.S. Department of Education, July 1990.

Weaver, W. Timothy. "The Delphi Forecasting Method." *Phi Delta Kappan* 52 (January 1971): 267–71.

Worthen, Blaine R., and James R. Sanders. *Educational Evaluation: Alternative Approaches and Practical Guidelines*. White Plains, N.Y.: Longman, 1987.

Multimedia

Morris, Lyon Lyons. *Program Evaluation Kit*. Beverly Hills, Calif.: Sage, 1978. The kit consists of the following volumes: *Evaluator's Handbook, How to Deal with Goals and Objectives, How to Design a Program Evaluation, How to Measure Program Implementation, How to Measure Attitudes, How to Measure Achievement, How to Calculate Statistics, How to Present an Evaluation Report*.

Reports of the IAEP

Reports of the International Assessment of Educational Progress are obtained from the Center for Assessment of Educational Progress, Educational Testing Service, Princeton, NJ 08541.

Reports of the NAEP

Reports of the National Assessment of Educational Progress are obtained from the National Assessment of Educational Progress, Educational Testing Service, Princeton, NJ 08541.

Audiotapes

The Curriculum/Assessment Connection. 1994. Three 40- to 60-minute audiotapes feature Richard Strong, Bena Kallick, and Grant Wiggins on developing performance outcomes, designing and scoring outcomes, and implementing a performance-based curriculum. Association for Supervision and Curriculum Development, 1250 North Pitt Street, Alexandria, VA 22314.

Videotapes

Action Research: Inquiry, Reflection, and Decision Making. 1994. The four-videotape program developed by Emily Calhoun contains a twenty-five minute overview tape and three case studies. Includes a Facilitator's Guide, the book *How to Use Action Research in the Self-Renewing School*, and participants' packets. Association for Supervision and Curriculum Development, 1250 North Pitt Street, Alexandria, VA 22314.

Curriculum Mapping. 1981. 20 min. Fenwick English explains techniques for improving the curriculum by determining what is actually being taught. Association for Supervision and Curriculum Development, 1250 North Pitt Street, Alexandria, VA 22314.

Integrating the Curriculum. 1994. 1 hour on two videotapes. The program shows practical ways to link content from various disciplines and shows integrated curricula being implemented in elementary, middle, and high school classes. Association for Supervision and Curriculum Development, 1250 North Pitt Street, Alexandria, VA 22314.

Planning Curriculum with a Futures Perspective. 1982. 21 min. Willis Harman, Arthur Lewis, Don Glines, Robert Bundy, and Sherry Schiller analyze trends and ways schools can help students prepare for the future. Association for Supervision and Curriculum Development, 1250 North Pitt Street, Alexandria, VA 22314.

The Teacher's Responsibility in Implementing and Monitoring the Curriculum. 1994. 22 min. Richard Dufour, an Illinois high school principal, emphasizes the importance of each teacher's responsibility in implementing and monitoring the curriculum. National Association of Secondary School Principals, 1904 Association Drive, Reston, VA 22091-1537.

ERIC Materials

Current Index to Journals in Education. Monthly. Oryx Press, 2214 North Central at Encanto, Phoenix, AZ 85004.

Resources in Education. Monthly. Washington, D.C., Superintendent of Documents, U.S. Government Printing Office, Washington, DC 20402. Semiannual indexes available from the U.S. Government Printing Office. Annual cumulations: abstracts (2 volumes) and index (1 volume) available from Oryx Press. *Resources in Education* replaced *Research in Education* in January 1975.

Thesaurus of ERIC Descriptors, 9th ed. Oryx Press, 1982.

PART IV

Leadership in Staff Development

9

Helping Teachers through In-service Programs

Objectives

After studying Chapter 9 you should be able to accomplish the following objectives:

1. Define staff development and in-service education.
2. State characteristics of an effective in-service program.
3. Describe your preferred model of in-service education
4. Conduct an in-service needs assessment.
5. Describe features of a school district master plan for staff development.
6. Describe features of an individual school plan for staff development.
7. Propose an outline for writing in-service training components.
8. Suggest several types of in-service activities.
9. Suggest defensible incentives for teacher participation in in-service activities.
10. Explain whether and when outside consultants should be used.
11. Conduct an evaluation of an in-service activity.
12. Propose criteria for evaluating a master plan for staff development.

SUPERVISION AND STAFF DEVELOPMENT

Our peregrination into the world of supervision brings us now to the domain of staff development. It would be a rare specialist in supervision who would advise us not to enter and work in this domain. Where specialists differ, as we have seen in Chapter 2, is on the following questions:

- Is supervision only staff development?
- Is staff development the same as in-service education?
- Do we provide in-service education for groups or individuals or both?

Let's recall the model of supervision presented in Chapter 1. This model depicts three domains, side by side, with no barriers to block off interaction among them. Following this model, we saw distinctions among the domains of instructional development, curriculum development, and staff development as one of emphasis rather than discreteness. We pointed out that supervision flows from one domain to the other and supervisors may work in two or more domains simultaneously. Nevertheless, the model does depict three domains, not one.

Some specialists in supervision would limit the task of supervision to a single domain. Sometimes, however, supervisors focus on the improvement of *instruction* or of *curriculum* rather than improvement of the *staff member*. Staff development connotes the idea of *training*, the goal of which is improvement of the persons who make up the organization and the organization itself.

Teachers may undergo staff development within the instructional and curriculum domains as they do when they perfect skills in instructional and curriculum development, learn new pedagogical skills, and become familiar with new programs. They may also undergo training that does not fall within the realms of instructional development and curriculum development—for example, developing pride in their organization, enhancing their self-concepts, developing leadership skills, participating in quality circles for solving management problems, and coping with stress.

Not every activity engaged in by teachers must have as its purpose the training of personnel. Some activities of teachers focus on carrying out instructional and curriculum tasks, solving instructional and curriculum problems, and creating materials. There comes a time when professional teachers would reject the notion that every activity is a training experience for them. Although we agree that in one sense every professional experience is developmental, we do not limit our conception of supervision to staff development alone.

Purposes of Staff Development

Here we consider the purposes of staff development, but before doing so, we recap and expand on the definitions of staff development introduced in Chapter 2. Most specialists in supervision agree that staff development is a function of supervision. Most also agree that in-service education is a function of supervision. There is considerable disagreement, however, about whether staff development is the same as in-service education. We have used the terms *staff development* and *in-service education* synonymously in this text, as did Lloyd W. Dull,[1] as this is how these terms are often used in present practice.

Not all specialists in supervision, however, would agree with that usage. Some would maintain that *staff development* is the broader term, which includes working with individuals and groups in both formal and informal situations, whereas *in-service education* is limited to working with groups in formal training programs.

Others view in-service education as training that helps teachers do their present jobs better whereas staff development is training for the purpose of developing new knowledge and skills beyond their current assignments. Still others hold that staff development is an organized program to help teachers feel better about themselves and their jobs and to develop personal skills whereas in-service education is training for new curricula and the improvement of pedagogical skills.

Ben M. Harris conceptualized in-service education as a part of staff development.[2] He divided staff development into two categories: staffing and training. Included in the concept of staffing were selecting, assigning, evaluating, retiring, and dismissing staff. The training aspect included in-service education and advanced preparation, which were defined in Chapter 2.

E. Lawrence Dale held in-service education to be one of several functions of staff development. Dale defined staff development as "the totality of educational and personal experiences that contribute toward an individual's being more competent and satisfied in an assigned professional role."[3]

Thomas J. Sergiovanni and Robert J. Starratt saw the term *in-service education* as implying a deficiency that the teacher must overcome whereas staff development and *renewal* are terms focusing on teacher growth.[4] Donald C. Orlich, like Harris, identified *staff development* as broader than *in-service education*, with the former including the latter. In this case, in-service education satisfies immediate training needs whereas staff development is more comprehensive, including personal development.[5] Bruce Joyce and Beverly Showers offer the proposition that staff development is a service organization within the educational system.[6]

We could make further semantic distinctions by injecting the terms *professional development* and *personal development* into our discussion. In its purest sense, professional development encompasses training activities aimed at improving the teacher's skills in his or her present position or at developing the teacher for service within the profession outside classroom teaching. Personal development embraces activities directed toward enhancing the teacher's general knowledge, attitudes, interpersonal skills, values, and the like.

In this chapter, we use the term *staff development* as we defined it in Chapter 2 when we equated it to in-service education: "a program of organized activities of both a group and individual nature planned and carried out to promote the personal and professional growth of staff members, in this case, teachers." Staff development is in-service education, or put another way, the staff is developed through in-service education. In-service education may be either remedial or developmental, corrective or enriching. Further, *staff development* as used in this text subsumes *professional* and *personal development*, which are particular types of staff development or in-service education.

To learn why staff development is necessary, let's examine what happens in our profession. Every June, on the campuses of hundreds of colleges and universities, several thousand young people receive the long-awaited degree that certifies they have completed their teacher-training program. With degree and state credentials in hand, they join the competition for teaching jobs. In four years of training—the most common period throughout the country—they have accumulated perhaps 180 quarter-hours of credit, have completed forty to fifty courses in a wide range of fields, and may have achieved a minimal level in a certain number of professional competencies.

Because approximately one-half of a college program consists of general education—a necessary and desirable feature—only about half of a college education for teachers consists of work in the teaching field and pedagogy. The preservice trainees' program usually culminates in a brief student-teaching experience of eight to fifteen weeks, and the amount of actual "hands-on" experience during that time differs from school to school and from supervising teacher to supervising teacher. Given all the knowledge and skills necessary for successful teaching, the college training program is only a beginning. Hence the need for a continuing in-service program.

Programs for teachers in the field provide the instructional staff with opportunities to expand their knowledge and improve skills that have been developed in a rudimentary fashion in the college training program and to achieve new knowledge and develop new skills called for in their teaching assignments. In-service education combats complacency and satisfaction with the status quo, which set in as new teachers adjust to the routines of their positions.

The Supervisor's Role in In-service Education

The supervisor as in-service leader attempts to jar teachers' complacency and create dissatisfactions with the status quo. It is the supervisor's job to stimulate teachers to want to find new and better ways of accomplishing their instructional duties and improving the curriculum. The supervisor has the responsibility for identifying teachers' in-service needs through surveys, requests from teachers, and observation. The supervisor plans, sets into operation, and evaluates in-service programs. The supervisor directs the development of the master plan for staff development, makes its components known, and facilitates its use. The supervisor records the teachers' participation and success in in-service activities.

The supervisor's role is made more difficult by lack of agreement and uncertainties about the scope and nature of in-service education. Swirling around in-service education are the following issues, some of which we touched on in Chapter 2.

1. There is no agreement that in-service education is really necessary. One school of thought holds that teachers are trained, professional people; once they are employed, they have little need for continuing education. This group thinks that teachers will learn as they teach and that they can take care of what little updating they need by self-study.

2. There is no agreement on whether in-service education is effective. Summarizing several research studies, John T. Lovell commented,

> It was . . . found that teachers do not perceive that they are getting the services they need and often perceive supervisors as spending much of their time in the central offices working on administrative tasks not directly related to the needs of teachers. There was also evidence that the direct services that teachers were receiving were ineffective according to certain criteria of effectiveness.[7]

Fred H. Wood and Steven R. Thompson averred that "most staff development programs are irrelevant and ineffective, a waste of time and money."[8] The effectiveness of in-service education is extremely difficult to pinpoint especially in terms of its ultimate purpose: the improvement of student achievement. Much of the research focuses on teachers' perceptions of the effectiveness or ineffectiveness of in-service programs. Harris mentioned several studies, some of which supported and some of which were critical of in-service education.[9]

David W. Champagne attributed students' improvement in basic skills, increases in SAT scores, improved student attitudes toward school, improved school attendance, and decreases in vandalism and teacher absenteeism (in a Pennsylvania study in the mid-1970s) to a staff-development program that instructed teachers on how to offer high-interest projects in their classes.[10] Champagne pointed to the success of the Newington (Connecticut) Public Schools in turning around teacher attitudes toward supervision from highly negative to highly positive through a well-planned staff-development program.[11] He called attention to the improvement David N. Aspy achieved in interpersonal skills through a teacher-training program in which he used procedures of Robert R. Carkhuff.[12]

> These pieces of evidence taken together add up to a persuasive argument for continuing staff development, supervision, and evaluation. Successful programs will have visible, tangible results at all levels and justify the energy used to create them and the money used to sustain them.[13]

3. There is disagreement on what kinds of in-service education are best. Some specialists advocate group study; others propose clinical approaches; some want peer supervision; still others recommend self-study by the teacher. These differing opinions make it difficult for practitioners to decide where to focus their efforts.

4. There is uncertainty about the thrust of in-service education. Should we, for example, spend our time correcting deficiencies or providing enriching, developmental activities? Should in-service education be reactive to such forces as increased knowledge in all fields, increased use of technology, changes in students served, and changed attitudes of the public on the emphases they wish the schools to take? Or should we be proactive and develop in-service programs that anticipate changes and take teachers to the forefront of new developments? Should supervisors wait and watch or should they move out and expand?

5. There is disagreement on the role of theory in in-service education. Teachers tend to want practical helps with the day-to-day problems of instruction. They see little value in theory, which they believe—often erroneously—does not aid them in the classroom. Lovell confirmed that most research studies "indicated that teachers and supervisors desired service directly related to the improvement of classroom instruction."[14]

Teachers, by and large, express the same negative attitudes toward theory as they do toward theory's companion, philosophy. They do not agree with John Dewey that

> theory is in the end, as has been well said, the most practical of all things, because this widening of the range of attention beyond nearby purpose and desire eventually results in the creation of wider and farther-reaching purposes and enables us to use a much wider and deeper range of conditions and means than were expressed in the observation of primitive practical purposes.[15]

Supervisors must take care how they introduce theory into in-service education.

6. There are uncertainties about which teachers in-service education should assist. Should supervisors provide programs for beginning teachers, experienced ones, or both? Should they serve effective teachers, ineffective ones, or both? Are the beginning teachers the most ineffective, the most in need of help? There are those who believe that supervisors should not waste their time on the poorest teachers, as they cannot be salvaged anyway. On the other hand, both moral and legal considerations prevent ignoring teachers who need help. Administrators must attempt remedial measures before seeking dismissal of an incompetent teacher.

7. There is uncertainty about the proper focus of in-service education. How should in-service education seek to develop teachers?

- As instructors? If so, in-service programs must concentrate on methods.
- As curriculum developers? If so, teachers must be trained to plan, implement, and evaluate programs.
- As people? If so, this focus calls for training in human-relations skills.
- As subject matter specialists? If so, content of the discipline is the name of the game.
- As experts in the ecology of the classroom? If so, supervisors need to assist teachers in becoming more sensitive to linguistic nuances, nonverbal communication, and social and cultural differences.
- As educated citizens? If so, supervisors would plan programs in liberal studies that enhance the teachers' general knowledge or cultural literacy. Rarely do we find in-service education programs of this nature. Except for training programs in such areas as group dynamics and interpersonal skills, in-service education usually concentrates on professional development of the teacher rather than personal development.

8. There is uncertainty about whether it is best to respond to teachers' needs through a comprehensive, long-range plan or through separate, discrete plans that are designed to satisfy particular needs. Programs more often respond to specific needs and are thus reactive in nature rather than anticipate needs and thus become proactive. Single training sessions commonly require no follow-up sessions during which teachers may demonstrate mastery of the skills and knowledge presented in the sessions. Roy A. Edelfelt commented,

> In most cases needs have been translated into programs piecemeal. Programs are often oneshot sessions on a single topic (e.g., discipline techniques, management of stress and conflict, economic education) or courses that address a particular need (e.g., personal writing, conversational French, or learning activities for the gifted and talented).[16]

9. There is a question of whether staff-development activities should be planned and coordinated at the individual school level or at the school district level. Decisions must be made about the amount of time and funding allotted for staff development on a school-by-school basis and on a systemwide basis.

10. There is uncertainty in how to entice teachers to participate in in-service education. It would be the best of all possible worlds if teachers were intrinsically motivated to demand training for self-improvement. To a certain extent teachers will seek training to resolve immediate needs. Beyond that purpose, staff development has an uphill fight for teacher acceptance.

With the influx of technology into the schools, added emphasis has been placed on the need to provide appropriate staff development opportunities for classroom teachers. One such school district, the Concord, North Carolina, School District, located twenty minutes northeast of Charlotte, has developed an extensive staff development program that includes 95 courses offered on a district level. Technology specialists (teachers who have been trained in the use of technology and who hold a state license) work in nearly all the district's twenty schools. The school system spends close to two million dollars, or 45 percent of the district's technology budget, on staff development.[17]

We can conclude without a doubt that *after-school, required* in-service programs are both deadening and certain to arouse teacher hostility. We must admit that teaching is exhausting work. We need to remember that a significant number of teachers leave the profession. We must recognize the phenomenon of teacher burnout. This recognition often takes the form of in-service seminars on the maladies of stress and burnout. Yet, these seminars usually focus on what the *teacher* can do to minimize stress and avoid burnout. Additionally, we need more in-service programs for administrators and supervisors on what *they* may do to reduce or eliminate both the teachers' and their own stress and burnout. If in-service education is to be successful, we must look to extrinsic motivation and provide incentives. We will examine some of these incentives later in this chapter.

11. There is disagreement on who should control in-service education. Should the chief administrator or his or her director of staff development make the decisions on what will be offered through in-service education and how? Should the teachers themselves control their in-service education either through their associations and unions or through teacher education centers? Teachers are increasingly insisting on being involved in the planning of in-service education. Ninety-three percent of 646 teachers, for example, in a Tennessee survey of attitudes toward in-service education responded positively to the notion of teacher involvement in planning.[18]

Toni Sharma, a fourth-grade teacher, in an amusing but pointed article, satirized in-service education by likening it to the plight of Flossie, the cow, which Grandpop penned in a stanchion and Zeke, the inseminator, artificially inseminated.

> Too often, those in charge of inservice training make decisions for teachers just like the ones Zeke and Grandpop made for Flossie. They decide when to bring us together. They assume that injections of information they select will be helpful to all teachers, regardless of their individual needs. They assume that teachers have too narrow a perspective and that teachers' opinions are not valid. And finally, they assume that a direct and measurable outcome must result from inservice training.
>
> Unfortunately, it's all too easy to subscribe to those assumptions. . . . I have allowed my head to be penned in the stanchion.
>
> Now I want to take charge. . . . I want to determine my own needs, set my own goals, decide when and how and with whom I'll work toward those goals. I am going to control my own learning.[19]

As the movement toward empowerment of teachers gains in strength and intensity, we may expect to find teachers exerting more say over their professional destinies. Empowerment of teachers will not happen overnight, however; this is evident from results of the 1990 survey of some 21,000 elementary and secondary school teachers conducted by the Carnegie Foundation for the Advancement of Teaching.

In response to a question on the extent of involvement of teachers in various tasks and in comparing the involvement in 1990 with results from a similar study in 1987, the Carnegie Foundation discovered a sizable percentage of teachers only slightly or not at all involved in areas where teachers should be involved if the concept of empowerment is to mean anything, as shown in Table 9.1.[20]

The forces of empowerment do, indeed, march slowly. They must overcome tradition, administrator and supervisor resistance, and teachers' own apathy.

ASSUMPTIONS ABOUT IN-SERVICE EDUCATION

Whatever model of in-service education a school or school system follows, it is based on certain assumptions. Fred H. Wood, Steven R. Thompson, and Sister Frances Russell outlined a model of in-service education based on a set of assumptions that we believe hold true for any model.

1. All personnel in schools, to stay current and effective, need and should be involved in inservice throughout their careers. . . .
2. Significant improvement in educational practice takes considerable time and is the result of systematic, long-range staff development. . . .
3. Inservice education should have an impact on the quality of the school program and focus on helping staff improve their abilities to perform their professional responsibilities. . . .
4. Adult learners are motivated to risk learning new behaviors when they believe they have control over the learning situation and are free from threat of failure. . . .
5. Educators vary widely in their professional competencies, readiness, and approaches to learning. . . .
6. Professional growth requires personal and group commitment to new performance norms. . . .
7. Organizational health including factors such as social climate, trust, open communication, and peer support for change in practice influences the success of professional development programs. . . .
8. The school is the primary unit of change; not the district or the individual. . . .

TABLE 9.1. TEACHER INVOLVEMENT IN DECISION MAKING

Area	Percentage of Teachers Who Stated Only Slightly Involved or Not at All in 1990	Percentage of Teachers Who Stated Only Slightly Involved or Not at All in 1987
Shaping the Curriculum	35	37
Designing Staff Development/ In-Service Programs	57	57
Deciding on How the School Budget Is Spent	80	81
Selecting New Teachers	90	93
Evaluating Teacher Performance	92	90

Source: Adapted from Carnegie Foundation for the Advancement of Teaching, *The Condition of Teaching, 1990* (Princeton, N.J.: Carnegie Foundation for the Advancement of Teaching, 1990), pp. 55–56. Reprinted with permission of the Carnegie Foundation for the Advancement of Teaching.

9. School districts have the primary responsibility for providing the resources and training necessary for a school staff to implement new programs and improve instruction. . . .
10. The school principal is the gatekeeper for adoption and continued use of new practices and programs in a school. . . .
11. Effective in-service programs must be based upon research, theory, and the best education practice.[21]

As a case in point, the following eight key elements developed for technology staff development activities by the advisory boards of *Electronic Learning, Instructor,* and *Middle Years,* in conjunction with industry experts in technology staff development, apply to **all** staff development activities.

1. Even if outside consultants are used for workshops, local staff is available for follow-up.
2. Following workshops, teachers have easy access to the same technology they were trained on.
3. Teachers are the primary trainers of teachers.
4. Training is tied directly to classroom/curriculum/school reform objectives.
5. A minimum of 25 percent of the technology budget is set aside for staff development.
6. Learning to use technology is required, not voluntary.
7. Principals, superintendents, and other administrators take technology staff development courses along with their teachers.
8. Time for technology staff development is integrated into teachers' work schedules.[22]

Three themes come through repeatedly, loudly, and clearly in discussions of in-service education: In-service programs should be a continuing operation, they should be comprehensive in nature, and they should be cooperatively planned.

CHARACTERISTICS OF EFFECTIVE IN-SERVICE PROGRAMS

School systems vary widely in respect to both the quantity and quality of their in-service programs. Some in-service programs operate on a casual, informal, troubleshooting basis whereas others offer highly structured, planned programs in addition to the informal, unstructured type. Factors that appear to make a difference in quantity and quality of in-service opportunities are (1) motivational level of the teachers, (2) leadership from administrators and supervisors, and (3) financial resources.

Where teachers accept the need and desirability of continuing their professional education, in-service programs thrive. Where administrators and supervisors take an active role in promoting and planning in-service opportunities, and where funds are available, teacher participation in in-service training is high.

Citing studies made by Patricia Kells et al., Patricia J. Jamison, and Leonard C. Burrello and Tim Orbaugh listed the following six major observations about what constitutes effective in-service education.[23]

1. *In-service education should be designed so that programs are integrated into and supported by the organization within which they function.* A comprehensive plan for in-service education in the school and/or district should be drawn up and funding should be made available.

2. *In-service education programs should be designed to result in collaborative programs.* The plan should include ways to involve all the constituencies of the school: teachers, administrators, supervisors, nonteaching staff, students, and laypersons.

3. *In-service education programs should be grounded in the needs of the participants.* The plan should be developed from an assessment of the needs and interests of the persons to be served.

4. *In-service education programs should be responsive to changing needs.* The plan should allow for changes as conditions change and as research brings forth new knowledge.

5. *In-service education programs should be accessible.* The location, the physical facilities, and the timing are all important factors to be considered in an in-service education plan.

6. *In-service education activities should be evaluated over time and be compatible with the underlying philosophy and approach of the district.* Evaluative data are needed in order to carry out future planning and implementation.

In-service programs are designed to bring about improvements, innovation, and change. Researchers at the University of Texas, among others, observed that personal dimension was a key factor in instituting innovations. To facilitate the process of effecting innovations, the University of Texas Research and Development Center developed the Concerns-Based Adoption Model (CBAM) by which staff development leaders can determine stages of concerns of each teacher about an innovation and levels of their use of innovations. Gene E. Hall et al. categorized teacher concerns in six stages of development—from simple awareness to refocusing of their thinking toward adaptation that may improve the innovation. Hall et al. outlined eight levels of use teachers make of an innovation—from nonuse to renewal during which the teacher strives to improve on the innovation.[24]

The supervisor of staff development should lead both school and nonschool personnel in examining the assumptions and principles on which in-service education will be designed. A profitable activity would be to measure stages of development of teachers' concerns about an innovation and their levels of using an innovation. Supervisors can be more effective in bringing about innovations when they can identify stages of teachers' concerns and their level of use of an innovative practice or program.

A MODEL FOR IN-SERVICE EDUCATION

To learn the steps the supervisor should take in establishing an in-service education program, we can turn to the general utility model, which you have seen twice before—once as a simple model of instruction and once as a basic model of curriculum development. We have added two components and converted the general model into a sequence of steps for managing an in-service education program. The model for in-service education appears in Figure 9.1.

The diagram in this figure shows us that the training phases of in-service education consist of planning the training, carrying it out, and evaluating it. Because the

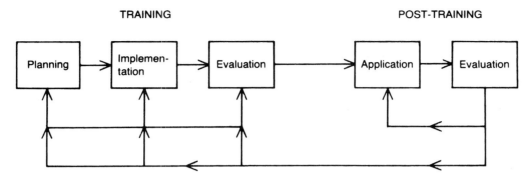

Figure 9.1. A Model for In-service Education.

purpose of training is to bring about changes in the classroom and/or in the person, we must look beyond the training programs themselves. We could actually repeat the general model and indicate that we plan for the after-training period, get the training program into operation in the classroom (or in our personal behavior), and evaluate our success in the classroom or in our personal lives. To reduce redundancy, we have labeled the phases of the posttraining period *Application* and *Evaluation*. Thus, we have a model with two submodels. The feedback lines cycle within the training model, within the posttraining model, and between the two submodels. Let's examine each of the five phases of the model. First, consider the three components of the training submodel: Planning, Implementation, and Evaluation. We then look at the two components of the posttraining submodel: Application and Evaluation.

Planning

Most of the literature on in-service education recommends a survey of the in-service needs of the clientele to be served as a first step in the process, which is called a *needs assessment*. Peter A. Williamson and Julia A. Elfman stated the steps of the in-service needs assessment succinctly as follows:

- The first step is the creation of a staff development committee for the building. . . .
- Next, the committee should identify the needs of the school. . . .
- Third, rank the needs. . . .
- Then, design a plan of action.[25]

The professional staff should have the opportunity to identify training needs. Those needs deemed to be the most critical and most pervasive should be placed at the top of the list for in-service training. Teachers are sometimes in disagreement with administrators and supervisors over which needs are most pressing in a school system. Occasionally, some administrators and supervisors seek to promote a pet idea or program. Unless a program is mandated by the state or by the local school board, administrators or supervisors would be well advised to defer to the judgment of the teachers when there are differing opinions over training programs for teachers. Unless teachers see the value of a training program, no lasting results may be expected from it.

State Assessments. One approach to identifying needs of teachers is the statewide survey. A survey conducted in the mid-1970s by Jay Lutz and Garrett Foster highlighted differences between perceived needs of beginning teachers and those of experienced teachers.[26] Were we to conduct a similar study in any state today, we would undoubtedly find the same needs. A survey of this nature yields a type of information that provides clues to areas worth exploring for in-service training.

District Assessments. A recent survey conducted in one large Florida school district on an annual basis furnishes an illustration of a district needs assessment. By means of a Training Needs Assessment Survey for Staff Development Inservice Program, the Brevard County, Florida, School District determined the in-service course preferences of more than 2,801 teachers in forty-eight elementary and twenty-three secondary schools of the school district.[27] From a list of fifty-four courses on the survey response form, teachers identified their choices for study. Significantly, the use of technology was identified twice among the top six priorities. Following are the course titles selected by the teachers, ranked from one to six, and the percentage of teachers who chose them.

1	Multiple Means of Assessment	73%
2	Technology in Teaching and Learning	72%
3	Technology in School Processes	70%
4	Updating Content Knowledge	67%
5	Motivation	66%
6	Critical and Creative Thinking	66%

The results are shared with the improvement team of every school, to be used as in-service plans for the next school year are determined. In some cases, the items at top priority receive the focus of the school district's staff development division so that the resources of the district can be pooled for broader effectiveness during identified staff development days and times.

Local School Assessments. More and more educators are coming to believe that the most effective instructional, curricular, and staff-development plans are those based at the individual school. The concept of school-based management generally construed as applying to budgeting is being extended to all areas of leadership, not just the managerial aspects of school operation. John I. Goodlad spoke to this point when he said, *"The optimal unit for educational change is the single school with its pupils, teachers, principal—those who live there every day—as primary participants."*[28] Several years later he reaffirmed this position.[29]

The principal should exercise leadership in assessing in-service needs of teachers in his or her school, analyzing data that may reflect in-service needs, and preparing a staff-development plan for that school.

Of needs assessments in general Linda L. Jones and Andrew E. Hayes cautioned,

The literature on inservice education almost always recommends a thorough assessment of teacher needs before staff development efforts. The need for doing this has been well established, but planners of staff development programs and persons conducting research on staff development may wrongly assume that statements of needs made by teachers *are* their needs rather than symptoms of needs that must be diagnosed more completely.[30]

These authors are pointing to the problem inherent in any survey of felt or perceived needs. The respondents must know what they know and what they do not know. They may perceive themselves to have knowledge or skills that they do not actually possess or may even ask for repetition of topics of which they can already demonstrate mastery. Jones and Hayes commented, "Needs perceptions are an inadequate indicator of staff development needs."[31]

Yet we would not want to eliminate surveys of perceived needs. Teachers want, even demand, involvement in planning and opportunities to select the programs in which they will participate. Like curriculum needs assessments, in-service needs assessments should be verified by additional means such as data on student achievement, parental feedback, and supervisors' observations of classroom performance. In the event of discrepancy between perceived needs and actual needs, unless teachers can be persuaded otherwise, we believe we must take the path counseled by the perceptual psychologists and deal with *perceptions* before we can deal with *reality*.

By whatever means, supervisors and those who work with them must obtain from the prospective participants their preferences for in-service activities. Once the teachers' choices are made known, these must be ranked in order of preferred priorities. From that point, a plan must be drawn up that will indicate which of the top needs will be addressed, how, and at what cost.

Master Plans. Supervisors of staff development typically draw up master plans for their school districts. These plans are based on feedback obtained from surveys of in-service needs. Some school systems prepare new plans annually. Some develop plans to cover a longer period, sometimes up to five years, with updating annually. Master plans describe each course, workshop, and other activity, which are referred to as *components* and often read like a college catalog.

Components are made available to the teachers. Some components are delivered in the form of group study; some may be completed either in a group or independently; others are individualized components by their very nature—for example, educational travel and supervision of student teachers.

Components are written and delivered by teachers, supervisors, and college instructors. Components are designed to develop basic teaching skills, to update the teachers' knowledge and skills, and/or to provide exploratory experiences. Some states require their school systems to submit comprehensive master plans for approval. Brevard County (Florida) offers a wide variety of staff-development courses.[32] An example is shown here.

Science for Tomorrow

COURSE NO. MIS #19–316–317
INSTRUCTOR: Bill Stalk
CREDIT: 50 Clock Hours/5SDUs

DAY OF WEEK: Tuesday/Thursday
TIME: 6:30–9:30 P.M.
FIRST DAY: May 23
LAST DAY: July 13
LOCATION: Florida Tech
OPEN TO: K–12 Science Teachers
Participants will have the opportunity to learn about and experience cutting-edge research in various science areas.

School systems usually keep meticulous records of approvals of courses, completion of courses by individuals, types of offerings, statistics, and evaluations of programs and instructors.

Individual School Plans. Staff-development plans of the individual school and the district supplement each other. The district's master plan reaches beyond the needs of the teachers of the individual school. Studies of in-service needs of teachers in the individual school must be followed up with some kind of plan. A typical school's staff-development plan for a year would include:

- Dates on which activities take place
- Hours devoted to each activity
- Activities
- Resource persons
- Participants' tasks
- Completion dates

Writing Components. At some point, supervisors, teachers, or outside consultants face the task of writing training programs. Though formats may differ, an outline that has proved satisfactory for writing in-service components is the following:

- Title page
- General description
- Objectives
- Pretest
- Training activities
- Training materials
- Posttest

When teachers are asked to write components for a district master plan or individual school plan, they should be given released time and/or extra pay for this additional service, which is over and above their normal assigned teaching duties. Further, a cost accounting must be made for each in-service activity to ensure that the school and district stay within their staff-development budgets.

Implementation

The in-service activities should be varied in respect to both type of activity and time devoted to each. Newer and more complex activities will likely require that longer periods of time be set aside for their study and practice. As discussed below, a number of possibilities for providing a varied in-service program are open to the supervisor:

1. *Formal college or university courses.* Perhaps the most common of all in-service activities and sometimes the only organized activity is the college or university course, which may be taught on the campus of a nearby college or university or off campus in the local schools. Thousands of teachers are studying at night, on weekends, and during the summers to obtain advanced degrees and new areas of certification or to update certificates. Teacher education institutions have traditionally responded to in-service needs by offering courses on campus in the evening, on weekends, in intensive periods of time, and by taking the courses to teachers in the field.

One of the supervisors of a school system should be charged with summarizing needs of teachers and requests for courses and transmitting that information to the teacher education institutions in the area. By the same token, the institutions should continuously seek feedback from the public school systems they serve about the needs of the teachers and the ways the institutions can address these needs.

2. *Locally developed or sponsored staff development courses or modules.* Many school systems have set supervisors and teachers to work, with or without the aid of outside consultants, at writing in-service programs, which are then made available to other teachers wishing to improve their knowledge and skills in certain areas. Teachers and supervisors often participate in developing components (sometimes called "teacher-training modules") such as these:

- Selecting standardized tests
- Writing behavioral objectives
- Lesson planning
- Nonverbal behavior
- Conducting a class discussion
- Using the resources of the Internet in the classroom
- Classroom management
- Conflict resolution and peer mediation
- Cooperating with parents
- Inclusive classrooms
- Questioning techniques
- Developing a culturally diverse classroom
- Behavior modification
- Alternative assessment techniques
- Writing classroom tests
- Year-round education
- Assessing affective objectives
- Updates on specific curriculum areas

The development of teacher-training components is valuable not only in terms of product—the completed component, which may be used in in-service education— but also in terms of process—the professional growth of the teachers who do the writing. Many components have been developed in various parts of the country by local school systems and by state and federally funded projects.

3. *Workshops and institutes.* Though it is often difficult or impossible to distinguish a workshop from an institute, generally, workshops provide participants with opportunities to work together to find solutions to problems they themselves have identified, whereas institutes bring information and suggested solutions to problems to participants and may or may not offer opportunities for the participants to work together. Workshops typically focus on "hands-on" activities with much teacher participation. Most workshops and institutes run from one to three days, though some, like more formal "courses," may last a couple of weeks or longer.

Workshops and institutes may be staffed by local personnel or by outside consultants and may or may not be tied in with a college or university for awarding academic credit for participation. In organizing workshops or institutes the supervisor has the responsibility for making sure that the participants understand the objectives, for working out logistical arrangements, and for conducting an evaluation that will provide feedback for subsequent workshops and institutes. Unless a workshop or institute offers the participants academic credit there are customarily no examinations required.

4. *Conferences.* The conference is a group meeting in which a variety of developmental activities, such as lectures, panels, symposia, and so on, takes place. It is a technique for imparting information and ideas to a large group of people in the shortest possible time. The supervisor may find it expedient to call a conference of teachers to hear a specialist on a particular topic or to clarify certain issues or problems. Whenever possible, conference presentations should be followed with small group discussions. Because the majority of participants at most conferences play a passive role, conferences as an in-service device are more limited than workshops, institutes, or courses.

Locally sponsored conferences take precedence over distant conferences as a typical in-service activity. Attendance of teachers at state, regional, and national conferences and conventions of the professional associations is a worthy developmental activity, but most school systems find it cost prohibitive to send many teachers to out-of-town conferences, pay their expenses, and provide substitutes for their classes during the time they are gone. As a result, attendance at distant meetings, if permitted at all, is ordinarily limited to the few teachers who serve as officers of the associations whose expenses are often paid by the associations, who have some important role on the program of the association's convention, or who are willing to cover their own travel and convention costs.

Very few schools have fully tapped the potential of state, regional, and national conferences and conventions as an in-service technique, for rarely does a participant share the knowledge gained with his or her colleagues. School systems could further the use of conferences as an in-service technique by encouraging the use of professional leave days for attendance at conferences and by requiring those whose expenses are paid by the school system to prepare written (or oral) reports of what they learned from the conference and to share the reports with their peers.

5. *Supervision of student teachers and interns.* Directing a student teacher can be a valuable learning experience for both the student teacher and the supervisor. Unfortunately, some teachers see the supervision of a student teacher as a chore to be tolerated rather than as an in-service educational experience. Student teachers, if properly used, can be a tremendous help to a teacher, for they bring with them not only a pair of willing hands but also some of the latest ideas, strategies, and techniques from which the observant supervising teacher can profit.

The supervisor of staff development should present having a student teacher as a privilege and a help rather than a burden. In cooperation with the teacher education institution from which the student teacher comes, the supervisor should help to identify those teachers who will make effective student-teacher supervisors. As word gets out that student teachers are being placed with the "better" teachers, more teachers will want to earn that label, will request student teachers, and will try to provide a worthwhile experience for these teachers-to-be.

Although student teaching is ordinarily the culmination of the preservice training program for the student teacher, it should be considered a two-way street. Not only may the supervising teacher learn from the student teacher but also the acts of explaining, interpreting, and providing counsel to the student teacher serve to improve the supervising teacher's effectiveness. Several states now have year-long internships, particularly for those who have not gone through a teacher education program.

6. *Visiting days.* An in-service technique used by some school systems is release of a teacher for a day to go to another class or school to observe fellow teachers and to discuss mutual teaching problems. By visiting other teachers, the individual is able to broaden his or her horizon and perhaps find solutions to troubling problems. By observing other instructors, visiting teachers may learn new approaches and techniques and may discover materials that are unfamiliar and may prove helpful in their classes. At the very least they may take comfort from seeing that others encounter concerns or problems or have difficulties similar to their own.

7. *Approved travel.* Some school systems permit teachers to engage in educational travel, which can be directly helpful in their classrooms. To gain supervisory approval for travel as an in-service activity, teachers frequently must submit a plan with a rationale and must report on their travel after they return.

The foregoing techniques are seven of the most common forms of organized in-service education programs. Dynamic school systems do not limit themselves to one or two types of programs but engage in many. Supervisors of in-service education would do well to keep in mind guidelines for effective staff development programs such as the following, proposed by Wood and Thompson.

- Include more participant control over the "what" and "how" of learning;
- Focus on job related tasks that the participants consider real and important;
- Provide choices and alternatives that accommodate the differences among participants;
- Include opportunities for participants in inservice training to practice what they are to learn in simulated and real work settings as part of their training;
- Encourage the learners to work in small groups and to learn from each other; and
- Reduce the use and threat of external judgments from one's superior by allowing peer-participants to give each other feedback concerning performance and areas of needed improvement.[33]

Incentives for Participation. The school system must establish incentives for teachers to participate in organized in-service activities. Personal satisfaction and professional improvement are not sufficient incentives by themselves. Today's school systems are encountering increasing resistance from organized teachers to demands on their time without compensation. In-service programs are going to cost a school system some money, and funds for training programs must be incorporated into the total budget. School systems offer several types of incentives to teachers, such as those discussed below, to secure their participation in in-service programs.

1. *Released time.* Typically, teachers may be expected to remain after school for short periods of time and to attend faculty meetings. Contractual arrangements between a school board and an organized group of teachers often specify the exact number of hours and number of meetings that are considered a part of the teachers' obligations. Though the periods of time may often be used for in-service training, they are often too short and too few for any sustained group study. Beyond the stipulated obligations of teachers, released time during the school day (and/or other incentives acceptable to the teachers) must be provided if any meaningful in-service programs are to be conducted. Some school systems use the mechanism of "teacher days," certain days during the year when teachers are on duty but children are not in attendance. Some systems allot a concentrated period of days at the end of the school year or before school opens in the late summer or fall during which teachers are paid and in-service activities may take place. Other systems release teachers for in-service projects and hire substitutes to take their places while they are participating. Jones High School in Orlando, Florida, seeks to meet some of its staff-development needs through voluntary weekly (Tuesday) forums. Teachers attend during their planning periods. The activity is repeated every period throughout the day. Although repetition may be burdensome to the presenters, this format gives priority to the teachers' schedules. It does not require them to come earlier (school starts at 7:30 A.M.) nor to stay late, tired after teaching their full schedule.

We can gain some idea of how staff development is actually being conducted by reviewing the results of a national survey. The first national survey of technology staff development conducted by an independent research company, Willard and Shullman, for *Electronic Learning, Instructor,* and *Middle Years,* indicated that 37 percent of the respondents participated in staff development activities during the school day. Thirty-one percent participated after school, 14 percent on official district release days, six percent during the summer, and three percent over a weekend.[34]

Activities requiring extended blocks of time and considerable hands-on practice must follow other scheduling formats. Unless there are incentives to induce teachers to study on their own time, a fundamental principle for in-service activities sponsored by the local school system is the provision of time for the teachers at the expense of the school system.

2. *In-service credits for salary increments.* Some school systems with well-organized in-service programs allot credit for participation in each activity. Credits are known variously as staff-development units (SDUs), continuing education units (CEUs), master plan points (MPPs), and professional incentive points (PIPs). In cases where the district's plan for staff development is approved by the state department of education, SDUs, CEUs, and MPPs may be applied, like college credits, to extending or renewing a certificate; this is an attractive inducement to many teachers.

Certain school systems, on their own, require teachers to undertake some in-service work to renew their tenure.

Teachers earn credits on a formula basis. Five SDUs, for example, commonly require fifty hours of class time (or equivalent in self-study), which make them roughly comparable to five quarter hours of college academic credit. With these incentives, teachers may be expected to participate on their own time.

3. *Financial support for college study.* To encourage teachers to take courses at nearby colleges and universities, some school systems pay teachers for a given number of college credits earned during the year. Ordinarily, these credits must be directly related to the teacher's field of specialization.

Reimbursement for college study makes formal study appealing to many teachers. Because school systems pay higher salaries to teachers with advanced degrees, academic credit from a college or university is often a sufficient incentive in itself. However, after the teacher has achieved that degree (or a given number of college credits beyond the bachelor's degree), some device such as reimbursement for college study is desirable to encourage the teacher to continue self-improvement.

Supervisors should work with colleges and universities in the area to secure, if possible, favorable tuition rates for school personnel. They frequently negotiate with colleges and universities for tuition certificates for teachers who serve the higher education institutions as supervisors of student teachers or interns.

The state may enter the picture with plans for encouraging teachers to enroll in college courses, as did Georgia with its Quality Basic Education Act of 1985. Under this act, the state appropriated funds not only for typical staff-development activities on site but also for professional development funds to support teachers in summer school. Certainly, annual support of staff development by the states would go a long way toward raising the level of teacher performance. The supervisor should actively promote whatever means are possible to motivate teachers to participate in in-service training.

Funding. Successful in-service education cannot be provided without an investment of time and money. Staff-development programs are funded from a variety of sources: the local district, the state, and teachers themselves. With continuing emphasis on achieving high-quality education, staff-development needs should be given priority in funding. Local school systems often build staff-development monies into their budgets. As states are mandating evaluations of teacher performance, a natural concomitant is state funding for staff development for both remedial and developmental purposes.

To supplement their resources, some school systems charge a small fee to those who participate in in-service activities. A laudable goal would be to provide all staff-development activities without cost to the participants. The availability of in-service components without fee would be one further incentive for teachers to participate. In-service education should be perceived as a major responsibility to be supported by local and state funds. Education might well emulate practice in the business world, where companies commit a significant portion of their budgets to continuing development of their employees.

Use of Consultants. Staff-development plans rely heavily on persons within the school system to serve as instructors. In some cases, faculty members who have demonstrated proficiency in knowledge of curriculum or in the use of effective strategies may serve as consultants to their colleagues. On the other hand, the services of consultants from outside the school system are often sought for workshops, institutes, and conferences. The use of outside consultants is a stock response to the provision of in-service training, and though the employment of outside consultants is often necessary and may result in changes in teacher behavior through exposure to the consultant's views, care must be exercised in the employment of consultants and the uses that are made of their services.

In an early study entitled *High School Self-Evaluation and Curriculum Change*, Vynce A. Hines and William M. Alexander found that the use of consultants from outside the school system is judged by teachers as one of the least important factors in curriculum change.[35] According to this study, the factors teachers rated as more influential in curriculum change were the administrative staff of their own school, the administrative staff of the school system, the regional accrediting association, the faculty of the school, and the state department of education. A similar study today would almost certainly reaffirm these findings.

When planning for the use of outside consultants, the supervisor may gain the maximum productivity from their visits by following a few simple rules:

1. The supervisor should seek faculty input in the selection of consultants. This participation will make the faculty more receptive to the message the consultants may bring them.
2. The consultants chosen should be qualified beyond question for the roles asked of them. The supervisor should do some advance checking, preferably with school systems that have called on the consultants' services in the past, to be sure that the consultants chosen are the best-qualified persons to be obtained.
3. The consultants should be oriented well in advance to the task expected of them. Far too much valuable consultant time is lost while a consultant orients himself or herself to the task after arriving on the scene.
4. The consultants should be available for questions and discussion following their presentations. The consultant who hurries in, makes a presentation, and exits often leaves a group at the very point when the participants could benefit from interaction with him or her. Some consultants have important things to say. Some share research they have conducted or new techniques they have found helpful. Others give a good pep talk and some are effective at entertaining teacher groups. Keynote speakers at conferences often fill this last bill very well. Some of the more charismatic keynote speakers have the ability to maintain the rapt attention of audiences of a thousand or more.

For workshops and institutes, however, where teachers settle down to find specific answers to immediate problems or to learn new techniques for accomplishing their instructional duties, the purely informational or the inspirational types of consultants will usually not suffice. Teachers need the services of experts who will lead them through the study they are undertaking and remain with them long enough (*at the very least* for an extended and unhurried question-and-answer session) to permit them to begin discovering answers to their many questions and problems.

Evaluation

To assess the effectiveness of in-service education and to strengthen subsequent programs, continuing evaluation is essential. The achievement of participants, each in-service activity, and school and master plans for staff development should be evaluated.

The evaluation of participants' achievement in in-service programs conducted by the school systems tends to be less formal than assessment in college courses. Teachers are unwilling to sit still for formal examinations at workshops, institutes, and conferences. More often than not, the nature of an in-service activity does not lend itself to terminal examinations. Evaluation is necessary, of course, but evaluation of in-service programs can consist of the supervisor's observation of the participants' performance during the activity and after, of oral and written reports during the in-service program, and of short quizzes—for example, pretests and posttests.

Each in-service activity must be evaluated as to efficacy of the content, the delivery system, and the instructor (or consultant). It has become standard operating procedure for the staff-development coordinator or the in-service activity instructor to distribute an end-of-activity evaluation form, which participants fill out anonymously. Two illustrations will give us an idea of the types of information gathered from in-service education participants.

For several years, the Association for Supervision and Curriculum Development has administered evaluation forms at the conclusion of sessions at its professional development programs and annual conferences. These brief evaluation forms are seen in Figures 9.2 (pp. 386–387) and 9.3 (p. 388). Members of the Human Resources Division of the School District of Brevard County, Florida, request participants to complete the form shown in Figure 9.4 (p. 389).

Posttraining Application and Evaluation

Perhaps even more important than end-of-activity evaluations is follow-up evaluation of participants' performance after the activity. The ultimate test of an in-service activity is translation of the knowledge and skills learned into the participant's personal and/or professional behavior. Too many evaluations stop when participants fill out reaction forms on conclusion of an in-service program. What a school system really needs to know is whether the activity made any difference in teacher performance, that is, whether the teachers applied in the classroom the knowledge and skills they learned in training. Consequently, some plan needs to be developed to evaluate attainment of an activity's objectives over a period of time.

The success or failure of in-service programs rests heavily on the shoulders of those supervisors who are charged by the administrators with the direction of staff-development activities. Success of staff-development programs correlates directly with the leadership skills of the supervisor.

≤SCD **Professional Development Program Evaluation Form**

Program Title:

We would appreciate knowing how you rate this program in comparison to similar professional development sessions you have attended. For each of the items below, please provide a 1 to 5 rating by filling in the SCANTRON form in pencil or ink pen.

Example:

CORRECT
INCORRECT

1=strongly disagree   2=disagree   3=undecided   4=agree   5=strongly agree

Overall Program

1. The total program was of high quality.   ⊏1⊐ ⊏2⊐ ⊏3⊐ ⊏4⊐ ⊏5⊐

    Comments:_____
_____
_____
_____

2. The objectives of the program were met:

    A.   ⊏1⊐ ⊏2⊐ ⊏3⊐ ⊏4⊐ ⊏5⊐

    B.   ⊏1⊐ ⊏2⊐ ⊏3⊐ ⊏4⊐ ⊏5⊐

3. The program content will be useful to me.   ⊏1⊐ ⊏2⊐ ⊏3⊐ ⊏4⊐ ⊏5⊐

    Comments:_____
_____

Presenter: _____

4. The speaker's overall effectiveness was high.   ⊏1⊐ ⊏2⊐ ⊏3⊐ ⊏4⊐ ⊏5⊐

5. The content of the speaker's presentation was useful.   ⊏1⊐ ⊏2⊐ ⊏3⊐ ⊏4⊐ ⊏5⊐

6. The speaker used effective instructional techniques.   ⊏1⊐ ⊏2⊐ ⊏3⊐ ⊏4⊐ ⊏5⊐

7. The speaker used high quality materials.   ⊏1⊐ ⊏2⊐ ⊏3⊐ ⊏4⊐ ⊏5⊐

    Comments:_____
_____
_____

Presenter: _____

8. The speaker's overall effectiveness was high.   ⊏1⊐ ⊏2⊐ ⊏3⊐ ⊏4⊐ ⊏5⊐

9. The content of the speaker's presentation was useful.   ⊏1⊐ ⊏2⊐ ⊏3⊐ ⊏4⊐ ⊏5⊐

10. The speaker used effective instructional techniques.   ⊏1⊐ ⊏2⊐ ⊏3⊐ ⊏4⊐ ⊏5⊐

11. The speaker used high quality materials.   ⊏1⊐ ⊏2⊐ ⊏3⊐ ⊏4⊐ ⊏5⊐

    Comments:_____
_____
_____

Figure 9.2. Professional Development Program Evaluation Form. *Source: Association for Supervision and Curriculum Development (Alexandria, Va.: Association for Supervision and Curriculum Development). Reprinted with permission of the Association for Supervision and Curriculum Development.*

Presenter: _____

	👎				👍

12. The speaker's overall effectiveness was high. ⊏1⊐ ⊏2⊐ ⊏3⊐ ⊏4⊐ ⊏5⊐

13. The content of the speaker's presentation was useful. ⊏1⊐ ⊏2⊐ ⊏3⊐ ⊏4⊐ ⊏5⊐

14. The speaker used effective instructional techniques. ⊏1⊐ ⊏2⊐ ⊏3⊐ ⊏4⊐ ⊏5⊐

15. The speaker used high quality materials. ⊏1⊐ ⊏2⊐ ⊏3⊐ ⊏4⊐ ⊏5⊐

Comments: _____

_____

_____

Meeting Facilities

16. The accommodations were of high quality (i.e., guest rooms, restaurants, public areas, etc.) ⊏1⊐ ⊏2⊐ ⊏3⊐ ⊏4⊐ ⊏5⊐

17. The hotel guest services were of high quality (i.e., check-in, restaurants, room service, cleanliness, etc.) ⊏1⊐ ⊏2⊐ ⊏3⊐ ⊏4⊐ ⊏5⊐

18. I liked the hotel location. ⊏1⊐ ⊏2⊐ ⊏3⊐ ⊏4⊐ ⊏5⊐

Comments: _____

_____

_____

ASCD's Registration Process: (Optional)

19. Responses to requests for information are courteous and timely. ⊏1⊐ ⊏2⊐ ⊏3⊐ ⊏4⊐ ⊏5⊐

20. ASCD's registration process is well organized and efficient. ⊏1⊐ ⊏2⊐ ⊏3⊐ ⊏4⊐ ⊏5⊐

Comments: _____

_____

I would recommend this program to a colleague. YES ☐ NO ☐

My job title is: _____

Please fill in if ASCD member ☐
Please fill in if HRDP member ☐

Please list other topics, issues and speakers which you would like to see offered as future ASCD Professional Development programs:

_____

_____

Comments:

_____

_____

_____

ANNUAL CONFERENCE EVALUATION FORM ASCD CH

	EXCELLENT	GOOD	FAIR	POOR	NOT APPLICABLE

TOPIC

1. Applicability to my work
2. Quality of information
3. Quality of handouts/materials shared
4. Presentation accurately described in Program book

PROCESS

1. Overall use of effective teaching strategies
2. Opportunity for interaction and discussion
3. I met colleagues with whom I will be able to network
4. Because of attending this session, I am interested in learning more about the topic presented

OVERALL RATING OF ACTIVITY PRESENTER(S)

NAME:
  1. Organized/Prepared
  2. Overall rating as presenter

NAME:
  1. Organized/Prepared
  2. Overall rating as presenter

NAME:
  1. Organized/Prepared
  2. Overall rating as presenter

NAME:
  1. Organized/Prepared
  2. Overall rating as presenter

- MAKE HEAVY **DARK** MARKS THAT COMPLETELY FILL EACH BLOCK
- **EXAMPLE:** ▬ BLOCK IS FILLED **COMPLETELY**
- ERASE **COMPLETELY** TO CHANGE
- DO NOT USE A RED PEN

★★

PLEASE MAKE FURTHER COMMENTS HERE:

_____
_____
_____
_____
_____
_____
_____
_____

★★

ABOUT ME My job title is:

☐ Principal – Elementary	☐ Teacher – Elementary	☐ Superintendent	☐ Curriculum Specialist
☐ Principal – Middle/Jr. High	☐ Teacher – Middle/Jr. High	☐ Central Office	☐ Supervisor
☐ Principal – High School	☐ Teacher – High School	☐ Professor	
	☐ Other_____		

★★

PLEASE CONTINUE THE EVALUATION ON THE BACK OF THIS FORM. THANK YOU.   **ASCD COPY**

Figure 9.3. ASCD Session Evaluation Form. *Source: Association for Supervision and Curriculum Development, Session Evaluation Form (Alexandria, Va.: Association for Supervision and Curriculum Development). Reprinted with permission of the Association for Supervision and Curriculum Development.*

388

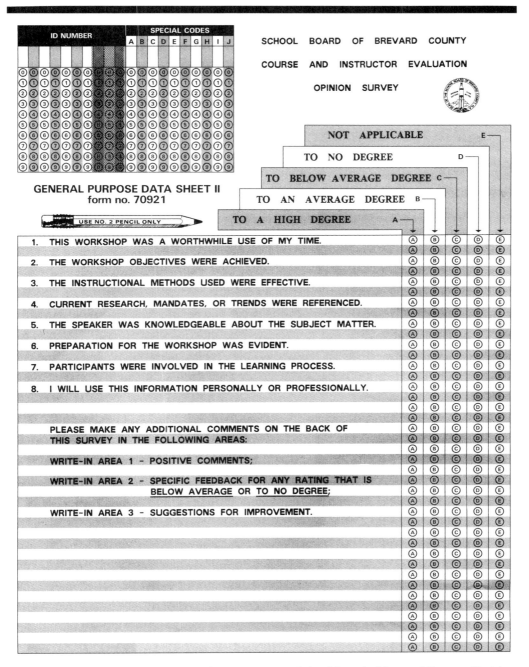

Figure 9.4. Course and Instructor Evaluation. *Source: School Board of Brevard County, Florida. Reprinted with permission of the School Board of Brevard County, Florida.*

CONTROL OF IN-SERVICE EDUCATION

The locus of control of in-service education is a subject of controversy. Disagreements center on questions like, Who shall make the policies pertaining to in-service education? How shall decisions be made about in-service offerings? How shall in-service budgets be expended? The school board, the superintendent, and the director of staff development are too simplistic as answers to the first question. True, the school board sets all school policies, the top executive administers them, and the administrator's aides carry out responsibilities delegated to them. But within the larger context of school management are varying opinions and practices related to the provision of in-service education.

Administration of in-service education in the public schools rests with four offices: (1) the principal of the individual school, (2) the central office director of staff development, (3) the intermediate unit, and (4) the teacher education center. The first two offices come within the jurisdiction of the local school superintendent. The third falls beyond the purview of the local superintendent. The fourth center may or may not lie within the authority of the superintendent.

Historically, in-service education has been the responsibility of the normal schools and colleges of education. From the mid-twentieth century school, districts have assumed a large role in establishing and operating in-service programs. Increasingly, school district administrators are delegating responsibilities for staff-development programs to the principals of the individual schools within the system. Of this trend Dull said, "During the past decade the focus of control over staff development has moved rapidly from institutions of higher education to local school districts, and even from the school district to the local school where principals are providing more and more leadership in staff development."[36]

Some states have established intermediate units known as regional or cooperative educational service agencies. These agencies, headed by a superintendent or director, serve a number of school districts. In some areas of the country, particularly the sparsely settled rural regions, the regional educational service agencies offer the lion's share of staff-development activities. Some of the urban areas have chosen to participate in the support of the regional educational service agencies and use the services of the supervisors on the agencies' staffs. Other urban districts have remained aloof from the regional educational service agencies and manage their own staff-development programs. Still others call on the regional educational service agencies as needed while at the same time conducting their own staff-development programs.

Teacher Education Centers

The rise of teacher education centers in the 1970s has had a significant impact on the administration and operation of staff-development programs. The teacher education center in America can be traced to the teacher centers that started to spring up in Great Britain in the mid-1960s. We should, however, at the onset, distinguish between the *teacher center* and the *teacher education center*. Although both types of centers have a bearing on staff development, they are not identical.

Teacher centers are physical plants that house all kinds of instructional, curriculum, and professional materials for teachers' use. They serve as meeting places for workshops, conferences, and the like. They are sites where teachers can come together professionally and socially. In some respects, they are staffed curriculum laboratories or curriculum materials centers. Illustrative of this type of center are not only the British teacher centers but also the Centres Régionaux de Documentation Pédagogique, which have been in existence in France for many years. Some school districts in the United States have established British and French types of teacher centers. These centers belong to the school district and are entirely under the authority of the superintendent and school board.

The teacher education center is "a horse of a different color," or perhaps we should say "a concept of a different genre." Patterns of organization of teacher education centers throughout the country differ considerably. Teacher education centers may possess a single building, several buildings, or no building at all. They may or may not provide the helpful facilities and resources to be found in a teacher center. In other words, the teacher education center may or may not incorporate a teacher center within its plan.

The teacher education center is a concept based on certain assumptions, among which are the following:

- Greater control over staff-development programs should be placed in the hands of those most directly affected—the teachers.
- To an ever-increasing extent, in-service programs offered by the schools of education should be taken off the campus and placed in the real world of the teacher.
- Teachers, administrators, and college professors, sometimes in collaboration with students and laypersons, should cooperatively plan and carry out in-service activities.

With ten teacher education centers created through state funding under the Teacher Education Center Act of 1973, the state of Florida became an early leader in the teacher education center (TEC) movement. In 1991, all sixty-seven of the county districts were affiliated, as a result of state mandate, with one of the state's forty-eight teacher education centers. Florida defined a teacher education center as

> an organized arrangement to promote collaboration in teacher education, both pre-service and in-service. It involves teachers, school districts, and teacher education institutions. A teacher education center draws resources from existing teacher education programs. It does not replace these institutions. It is especially concerned with those aspects of teacher education requiring mutual involvement of concerned institutions.[37]

A common pattern of organization of TECs places administrative control of the center under a local school board and its superintendent. Some centers serve a single school system; others serve a number of school systems. A center director, commonly a person experienced in staff development, administers the operation of the center. The director is advised by a council composed of teachers (who constitute the majority of the council), representatives of teacher education institutions in the area, representatives of the nonteaching staff, and representatives of the community. The council sets policies and oversees the operation of the center in keeping with

local and state regulations and laws. Sometimes the teacher education center director is also the director of staff development of his or her school system. Teacher education centers are operated with local and/or state funds and, at one time in some
cases, were assisted with federal funding.

The program of a teacher education center includes, among other activities, those
designed to do the following:

- To assess in-service training needs as perceived by classroom teachers, school
  district personnel, college or university personnel, and other concerned agencies.
- To provide adequate joint planning by school districts and colleges or universities, public or private, and to develop programs, including long-term
  training activities based on those identified in-service needs.
- To provide human and material resources for in-service training by whichever
  agents are best prepared to deliver them.
- To assess needs and provide the resources and experiences for clinical preservice teacher training, thus relating theoretical and practical study.
- To facilitate the entry or reentry of educational personnel into the teaching
  profession.
- To facilitate training processes which are based on assessment of needs, the
  development of experiences to meet those needs, and evaluation of the extent to which the needs were met.
- To facilitate internal and external evaluation which would include, but not
  be limited to, data gathering, process evaluation, product evaluation, and validation of teaching competency.[38]

Philosophically and operationally teacher education centers are committed to

- Career-long teacher education to help teachers keep pace with the changing
  and diversified systems of instruction (continuity between preservice and in-
  service).
- Cooperation and collaboration among teachers, school districts, and colleges
  or universities which allow for the emergence of new training strategies and
  procedures.
- Commitment to shared power among involved agencies to encourage new
  kinds of collaborative models.
- Pooling of resources in an organized effort to promote widespread use of new
  educational material and equipment for greater benefits for each agency in
  the teacher education center.
- Field-based preservice teacher education to provide greater involvement in
  actual on-going classroom experiences.
- Broader focus on inservice training to maintain skills for present roles and
  prepare for new roles and responsibilities.[39]

Where teacher education centers are operational, more of the in-service education
heretofore conducted on the campuses of the teacher education institutions moves
off the campuses and into the regions served by the centers. The centers provide experiences in real schools with real children. Teacher education centers can inject re-

alism into the preparation of prospective teachers and into in-service training pro-grams.

The federal government in 1976, during President Gerald Ford's administration, demonstrated interest in teacher education centers. Unfortunately, federal support was short-lived. Although the nationwide movement toward teacher education centers has leveled off, where they do exist administrators and supervisors are required to share prerogatives with the teachers, a practice that fits in well with the empowerment movement of the 1990s.

SUMMARY

Staff development and *in-service education* are used interchangeably in this chapter and text. Supervisors spend considerable time in planning, implementing, and evaluating staff-development programs. In fact, no task looms larger on the supervisor's agenda than staff development.

In-service education programs should be planned and carried out in cooperation with those for whom the programs are designed. Several issues and assumptions were examined and a model of in-service education was presented, consisting of three training components and two posttraining components.

Planning for in-service education begins with an assessment of needs as perceived by the teachers. After needs are surveyed, they are ranked and top needs filled.

Active school systems make available to teachers a wide variety of opportunities for improving themselves both personally and professionally. The goal of in-service education is the continuous professional development of the teachers, which in turn will enhance the achievement of the learners. Among the types of organized in-service programs are college and university courses, workshops and institutes, conferences, supervision of student teachers and interns, visiting days, and approved travel.

Directors of staff development are often charged with the task of preparing a comprehensive master plan for their school districts. Principals are frequently assigned the job of creating a staff-development plan for their schools.

To gain teachers' participation in organized in-service training some incentives are essential. Among the incentives found successful in school systems are released time, salary increments based on the accumulation of in-service credits, financial support for college and university study, reduced tuition rates for teachers attending colleges and universities, certificates for supervisors of student teachers and interns entitling them to register for college or university courses, pay differentials for advanced degrees or accumulated college and university credits, and in-service activities without cost to teachers.

Supervisors should plan for the evaluation of in-service activities. Participants should evaluate the contributions of the staff, the instruction, the facilities, and their own accomplishments. They should be given the opportunity to express their satisfaction or dissatisfaction with the activities, materials, procedures, and personnel. An evaluation form tailored to the particular in-service activity should be developed by the supervisor and staff of the in-service activity and distributed to the participants to fill out at the end of the program. Supervisors should conduct follow-up evaluations to learn whether teachers are using what they have learned in in-service programs.

Control of in-service education is an issue. Staff-development activities are sponsored by individual schools, the central office, intermediate units, schools and departments of education, and teacher education centers.

Some school districts have established teacher centers, which house resources for teachers and serve as meeting places. Some school systems alone or in cooperation with other systems have created teacher education centers, which assume a major role in planning and administering in-service education. Providing various options for in-service education can lead to a staff better prepared to face the challenges of teaching. Effective presentations, cost-effective delivery systems, and a staff willing to participate make for more effective instruction. The true measures of success of professional development programs are improvement in student achievement and enhancement of teacher effectiveness, motivation, and satisfaction.

QUESTIONS FOR DISCUSSION

1. Why do some people refer to the supervisor as the ultimate team leader?
2. Why does the nature of the relationships among the adults who inhabit a school have more to do with the school's quality and character and with the accomplishments of its pupils than any other factor?
3. What is the importance of each of the five components of an in-service education model: planning, implementation, evaluation, application, and reevaluation?
4. What should be included in a staff development course announcement for your level or subject of teaching?
5. What would you include in a needs assessment focused on in-service needs of teachers?

ACTIVITIES FOR FURTHER STUDY

1. Define *staff development, in-service education*, and *professional development*.
2. Poll a group of teachers and summarize their views on the following:
   a. What types of in-service activities do they prefer?
   b. Do they feel they have input into the organization of in-service training programs?
   c. What incentives do they believe are needed to secure teacher participation in in-service programs?
   d. Are they aware of in-service opportunities in their school system?
   e. Do they feel satisfied with the range and type of in-service opportunities?
3. Distinguish between a *workshop, institute, seminar*, and *course* as applied to in-service education.
4. Consult with administrators and supervisors in a school system and/or search the literature for types of organized in-service education opportunities not mentioned in this chapter.
5. Find out and report the annual cost of in-service activities of a school system you know well. Tell what percentage of funding comes from state sources, what per-

centage from local sources, and what percentage, if any, from federal sources. Calculate what the cost of in-service education is per pupil. Decide whether the total expenditure for in-service education is too much, too little, or about right.

6. Develop an instrument for evaluating a specific workshop, institute, conference, or other in-service activity; attend that activity; apply the instrument you have developed; summarize the data; and draw conclusions.

7. Develop a set of guidelines to help teachers achieve the maximum benefits from supervising student teachers or interns.

8. Gather and report data from several school systems elsewhere in the state or nation on prevailing practices concerning incentives provided for teachers to secure their participation in in-service training.

9. If there is a teacher education center in the area, obtain information about the center by interviewing center officials or by examining literature of the center about its in-service programs. Describe the composition of the teacher education center advisory council or committee and tell to whom the center director reports. Prepare a report that summarizes the in-service programs, shows the roles of the center and the teacher education institutions with which the center works, and contrasts in-service programs as conducted by the center with in-service programs as they exist without a center. Determine whether there is any change in the role of supervisors of a school system when a teacher education center exists in the system.

10. Analyze a master plan for staff development; using a set of criteria that you have located or developed, point out its adequacies and weaknesses.

11. Analyze a staff-development plan for an individual school; using a set of criteria you have located or developed, point out its adequacies and weaknesses.

12. Conduct an in-service needs assessment in your school. Verify teachers' perceived needs against empirical data.

13. Survey the attitudes of teachers in a school about in-service education. If you discover negative attitudes, account for the negativism and suggest ways to overcome it.

14. Summarize the in-service education model proposed by Fred H. Wood, Steven R. Thompson, and Sister Frances Russell (see bibliography at the end of the chapter).

15. Learn whether an intermediate unit (regional educational service agency) serves your school district. If so, find what services it provides and how many consultants it has and in what areas.

16. Draft a plan for a workshop or institute on a topic you believe is needed by a school system you know well. Include in your plan objectives, activities, materials, personnel, and means of evaluation.

17. Draft a plan for a conference on a topic you believe is needed by a school system you know well. Include in your plan objectives, activities, materials, personnel, and means of evaluation.

18. Write a report on the development and status of teacher education centers in the United States.

19. List characteristics of an effective in-service activity.

20. Report on follow-up evaluation of any in-service activity conducted in your school or school district within the last five years.

21. Prepare a report on the Concerns-Based Adoption Model (CBAM) for determining stages of teacher concerns about an innovation and their levels of use of the innovation. (See chapter bibliography for references by Gene E. Hall and Susan

Loucks and by Gene E. Hall, Susan F. Loucks, William L. Rutherford, and Beaulah W. Newlove.)

NOTES

1. Lloyd W. Dull, *Supervision: School Leadership Handbook* (Columbus, Ohio: Merrill, 1981), p. 110.
2. Ben M. Harris, *In-service Education for Staff Development* (Boston: Allyn & Bacon, 1989), pp. 18–21.
3. E. Lawrence Dale, "What Is Staff Development?" *Educational Leadership* 40 (October 1982): 31.
4. Thomas J. Sergiovanni and Robert J. Starratt, *Supervision: A Redefinition*, 5th ed. (New York: McGraw-Hill, 1993), p. 267.
5. Donald C. Orlich, *Staff Development: Enhancing Human Potential* (Boston: Allyn & Bacon, 1989), pp. 4–6.
6. Bruce Joyce and Beverly Showers, *Student Achievement through Staff Development* (White Plains, N.Y.: Longman, 1995), p. 25.
7. John T. Lovell, "Instructional Supervision: Emerging Perspective," in *The Role and Responsibilities of Instructional Supervisors*, Report of the ASCD Working Group on the Roles and Responsibilities of Supervisors, A. W. Sturges, chairman (Alexandria, Va.: Association for Supervision and Curriculum Development, October 1, 1978), p. 43.
8. Fred H. Wood and Steven R. Thompson, "Guidelines for Better Staff Development," *Educational Leadership* 37 (February 1980): 374.
9. Ben M. Harris, *Improving Staff Performance through In-Service Education* (Boston: Allyn & Bacon, 1980), pp. 33–37.
10. David W. Champagne, "Does Staff Development Do Any Good?" *Educational Leadership* 37 (February 1980): 401–2. See "An Exercise in Freedom: A Place Where Test Scores Appear to Be Rising," in *The Test Score Decline*, ed. L. Lipsitz (Englewood Cliffs, N.J.: Educational Technology Publications, 1977).
11. Champagne, "Does Staff Development Do Any Good?" pp. 402–3. See ERIC report by William P. Ward, ERIC ED 119 387 EA 008 045.
12. Champagne, "Does Staff Development Do Any Good?" p. 403. See David N. Aspy and Flora N. Roebuck, "From Humane Ideas to Human Technology and Back Again Many Times," *Education* 95 (Winter 1974): 163–71.
13. Champagne, "Does Staff Development Do Any Good?" p. 403.
14. Lovell, "Instructional Supervision," p. 35.
15. John Dewey, *The Sources of a Science of Education* (New York: Liveright, 1929), p. 17.
16. Roy A. Edelfelt, "Critical Issues in Developing Teacher Centers," *Phi Delta Kappan* 63 (February 1982): 403.
17. Jessica Siegel, "The State of Teacher Training," *Electronic Learning* 14 (May/June 1995): 51.
18. Harris, *Improving Staff Performance*, p. 37.
19. Toni Sharma, "Inservicing the Teachers," *Phi Delta Kappan* 63 (February 1982): 403.
20. Carnegie Foundation for the Advancement of Teaching, *The Condition of Teaching, 1990* (Princeton, N.J.: Carnegie Foundation for the Advancement of Teaching, 1990), pp. 55–56.
21. Fred H. Wood, Steven R. Thompson, and Sister Frances Russell, "Designing Effective Staff Development Programs," in *Staff Development/Organization Development*, 1981 Yearbook (Alexandria, Va.: Association for Supervision and Curriculum Development, 1981), pp. 61–63. See also slightly revised version in Fred H. Wood, Frank O. McQuarrie, Jr., and Steven R. Thompson, "Practitioners and Professors Agree on Effective Staff Development Practices," *Educational Leadership* 40 (October 1982): 28–29.

22. Siegel, "The State of Teacher Training," p. 50.
23. Leonard C. Burrello and Tim Orbaugh, "Reducing the Discrepancy between the Known and the Unknown in Inservice Education," *Phi Delta Kappan* 63 (February 1982): 385–86. See Patricia P. Kells et al., *Quality Practice Task Force Final Report* (Bloomington, Ind.: National Inservice Network, 1980); and Patricia J. Jamison, "The Development and Validation of a Conceptual Model and Quality Practices Designed to Guide the Planning, Implementation, and Evaluation of Inservice Education Programs," doctoral dissertation, College Park, University of Maryland, 1981.
24. See Gene E. Hall and Susan Loucks, "Teacher Concerns as a Basis for Facilitating and Personalizing Staff Development," *Teachers College Record* 80 (September 1978): 36–53. See also Gene E. Hall, Susan F. Loucks, William L. Rutherford, and Beaulah W. Newlove, "Levels of Use of the Innovation: A Framework for Analyzing Innovation Adoption," *Journal of Teacher Education* 26 (Spring 1975): 52–56; and John P. Miller and Wayne Seller, *Curriculum: Perspectives and Practice* (White Plains, N.Y.: Longman, 1985), pp. 249–63.
25. Peter A. Williamson and Julia A. Elfman, "A Commonsense Approach to Teacher Inservice Training," *Phi Delta Kappan* 63 (February 1982): 401.
26. Jay Lutz and Garrett Foster, "Greater Involvement Urged," *Florida Schools* 37 (February 1975): 20–21.
27. Brevard County Department of Human Resources, *Training Needs Survey* (Melbourne, Fla.: Brevard County Department of Human Resources, March 1995).
28. John I. Goodlad, *The Dynamics of Educational Change: Toward Responsive Schools* (New York: McGraw-Hill, 1975), p. 175.
29. John I. Goodlad, *A Place Called School: Prospects for the Future* (New York: McGraw-Hill, 1984), pp. 318–19.
30. Linda L. Jones and Andrew E. Hayes, "How Valid Are Surveys of Teacher Needs?" *Educational Leadership* 37 (February 1980): 390.
31. Ibid., p. 391.
32. Brevard County Public Schools, *Memorandum about the Comprehensive Overview of Summer Training Opportunities*, May 15, 1995.
33. Wood and Thompson, "Guidelines for Better Staff Development," p. 377.
34. Siegel, "The State of Teacher Training," p. 48.
35. Vynce A. Hines and William M. Alexander, *High School Self-Evaluation and Curriculum Change*, Final Report, Project 3120, Contract no. OE 6-10-54, Bureau of Research, Office of Education (Washington, D.C.: U.S. Department of Health, Education, and Welfare, August 1967), p. 64.
36. Dull, *Supervision*, p. 111.
37. Florida Department of Education, *State Council for Teacher Education Centers Annual Report* (Tallahassee: Florida Department of Education, 1975), p. 2.
38. State Legislature of Florida, *Florida Statutes*, 1974 Supplement, Section 231.603, "Establishing Teacher Education Centers," Subsections 2(a) through (g), as amended by the 1975 session of the legislature. From *State Council for Teacher Education Centers Annual Report*, 1975, p. 27.
39. Florida Department of Education, *State Council for Teacher Education Centers Annual Report*, p. 2.

BIBLIOGRAPHY

Beegle, Charles W., and Roy A. Edelfelt, eds. *Staff Development: Staff Liberation*. Alexandria, Va.: Association for Supervision and Curriculum Development, 1977.

Bishop, Leslee J. *Staff Development and Instructional Improvement: Plans and Procedures*. Boston: Allyn & Bacon, 1976.

Burrello, Leonard C., and Tim Orbaugh. "Reducing the Discrepancy between the Known and the Unknown in Inservice Education." *Phi Delta Kappan* 63 (February 1982): 385–88.

Brandt, Ron, Betty Dillon-Peterson, Bruce Joyce, Emily Calhoun, Fred Wood, Thomas R. Guskey, Michael Fullan, Richard Schmuck, Susan Loucks-Horsley. "Reflection on 25 Years of Staff Development." *Journal of Staff Development* (Fall 1994): 2–8.

Brevard County Department of Human Resources. *Training Needs Survey*. Melbourne, Fla.: Brevard County Department of Human Resources, March 1995.

Brevard County Public Schools. *Memorandum about the Comprehensive Overview of Summer Training Opportunities*. Melbourne, Fla.: Brevard County Public Schools, May 15, 1995.

Caldwell, Sarah J. *Staff Development: A Handbook of Effective Practices*. Oxford, Ohio: National Staff Development Council, 1989.

Carnegie Foundation for the Advancement of Teaching. *The Condition of Teaching, 1990*. Princeton, N.J.: Carnegie Foundation for the Advancement of Teaching, 1990.

Center on Evaluation, Development, and Research. *Staff Development*. Bloomington, Ind.: Center on Evaluation, Development, and Research, Phi Delta Kappa, 1985/86.

Champagne, David W. "Does Staff Development Do Any Good?" *Educational Leadership* 37 (February 1980): 400–403.

Dale, E. Lawrence. "What Is Staff Development?" *Educational Leadership* 40 (October 1982):31.

Dewey, John. *The Sources of a Science of Education*. New York: Liveright, 1929.

Dillon-Peterson, Betty, ed. *Staff Development/Organization Development*, 1981 Yearbook. Alexandria, Va.: Association for Supervision and Curriculum Development, 1981.

Doll, Ronald C. *Supervision for Staff Development: Ideas and Application*. Boston: Allyn & Bacon, 1983.

Duke, Daniel L. "How a Staff Development Plan Can Rescue At-Risk Students." *Educational Leadership* 50 (December 1992/January 1993): 28–33.

Dull, Lloyd W. *Supervision: School Leadership Handbook*. Columbus, Ohio: Merrill, 1981.

Dumser, Patricia M. "Mini-Sabbaticals Widen a Teacher's World." *Educational Leadership* 49 (November 1991): 77–78.

Edelfelt, Roy A. "Critical Issues in Developing Teacher Centers." *Phi Delta Kappan* 63 (February 1982): 390–93.

Ellis, Susan S. "Principals as Staff Developers—We Better Know What We're Asking Teachers to Do: An Interview with Larry Dixon." *Journal of Staff Development* 16 (Spring 1995): 56–58.

"An Exercise in Freedom: A Place Where Test Scores Appear to Be Rising." In *The Test Score Decline*, edited by L. Lipsitz. Englewood Cliffs, N.J.: Educational Technology Publications, 1977.

Firth, Gerald R. "Ten Issues on Staff Development." *Educational Leadership* 35 (December 1977): 215–20.

Florida Department of Education. *Guidelines for Developing a Competency-Based Inservice Program*. Chipley: Panhandle Area Educational Cooperative, 1974.

Florida Department of Education. *State Council for Teacher Education Centers Annual Report*. Tallahassee: Florida Department of Education, 1975.

Goodlad, John I. *A Place Called School: Prospects for the Future*. New York: McGraw-Hill, 1984.

Guskey, Thomas R. "Results-Oriented Professional Development: In Search of an Optimal Mix of Effective Practices." *Journal of Staff Development* 15 (Fall 1994): 42–50.

Guskey, Thomas R., and Dennis Sparks. "What to Consider When Evaluating Staff Development." *Educational Leadership* 49 (November 1991): 73–76.

Hall, Gene E., and Susan Loucks. "Teacher Concerns as a Basis for Facilitating and Personalizing Staff Development." *Teachers College Record* 80 (September 1978): 36–53.

Hall, Gene E., Susan F. Loucks, William L. Rutherford, and Beaulah W. Newlove. "Levels of

Use of the Innovation: A Framework for Analyzing Innovation Adoption." *Journal of Teacher Education* 26 (Spring 1975): 52–56.

Harris, Ben M. *Improving Staff Performance through In-Service Education.* Boston: Allyn & Bacon, 1980.

———. *In-Service Education for Staff Development.* Boston: Allyn & Bacon, 1989.

———. *Supervisory Behavior in Education,* 3rd ed. Englewood Cliffs, N.J.: Prentice-Hall, 1985.

Harrison, Raymond H. *Supervisory Leadership in Education.* New York: Van Nostrand Reinhold, 1968.

Hines, Vynce A., and William M. Alexander. *High School Self-Evaluation and Curriculum Change.* Final Report, Project 3120, Contract No. OE 6-10-54, Bureau of Research, Office of Education. Washington, D.C.: U.S. Department of Health, Education, and Welfare, August 1967.

Huge, James. *The Role of the Building Principal as a Staff Development Leader.* Alexandria, Va.: Association for Supervision and Curriculum Development, 1977.

"Inservice Education in Practice." *Phi Delta Kappan* 63 (February 1982): 385–403.

Jamison, Patricia J. "The Development and Validation of a Conceptual Model and Quality Practices Designed to Guide the Planning, Implementation, and Evaluation of Inservice Education Programs." Doctoral dissertation, College Park, University of Maryland, 1981.

Jones, Linda L., and Andrew E. Hayes. "How Valid Are Surveys of Teacher Needs?" *Educational Leadership* 37 (February 1980): 390–92.

Joyce, Bruce, ed. *Changing School Culture through Staff Development.* 1990 Yearbook. Alexandria, Va.: Association for Supervision and Curriculum Development, 1990.

———. *Staff Development.* White Plains, N.Y.: Longman, 1987.

Joyce, Bruce, and Beverly Showers. *Student Achievement through Staff Development.* White Plains, N.Y.: Longman, 1995.

Kells, Patricia P., et al. *Quality Practice Task Force: Final Report.* Bloomington, Ind.: National Inservice Network, 1980.

Knoll, Marcia K. *Supervision for Better Instruction: Practical Techniques for Improving Staff Performance.* Englewood Cliffs, N.J.: Prentice-Hall, 1987.

Lewis, Arthur J., and Alice Miel. *Supervision for Improved Instruction: New Challenges and New Responses.* Belmont, Calif.: Wadsworth, 1972.

Lieberman, Ann, and Lynne Miller, eds. *Staff Development for Education in the '90s,* 2nd ed. New York: Teachers College Press, 1991.

Loucks-Horsley, Susan, Catherine K. Harding, Margaret A. Arbuckle, Lynn B. Murray, Cynthia Dubea, and Martha K. Williams. *Continuing to Learn—A Guidebook for Teacher Development.* Oxford, Ohio: National Staff Development Council, 1987.

Lovell, John T. "Instructional Supervision: Emerging Perspective." In *The Role and Responsibilities of Instructional Supervisors.* Report of the ASCD Working Group on the Roles and Responsibilities of Supervisors. Chairman, A. W. Sturges. Alexandria, Va.: Association for Supervision and Curriculum Development, October 1, 1978.

Lutz, Jay, and Garrett Foster. "Greater Involvement Urged." *Florida Schools* 37 (February 1975): 20–21.

Mann, Dale. "The Politics of Inservice." *Theory into Practice* 17 (June 1978): 212–17.

Miller, John P., and Wayne Seller. *Curriculum: Perspectives and Practice.* White Plains, N.Y.: Longman, 1985.

Novelli, Joan. "A New Look at Teacher Centers." *Instructor* 100 (November 1990): 28, 33–35.

Orlich, Donald C. *Staff Development: Enhancing Human Potential.* Boston: Allyn & Bacon, 1989.

Readings from Educational Leadership: Coaching and Staff Development. Alexandria, Va.: Association for Supervision and Curriculum Development, 1989.

Rubin, Louis J., ed. *Improving In-service Education: Proposals and Procedures for Change.* Boston: Allyn & Bacon, 1971.

————. *The In-service Education of Teachers*. Boston: Allyn & Bacon, 1978.

Sergiovanni, Thomas J., ed. *Professional Supervision for Professional Teachers*. Alexandria, Va.: Association for Supervision and Curriculum Development, 1975.

Sergiovanni, Thomas J., and Robert J. Starratt. *Supervision: A Redefinition,* 5th ed. New York: McGraw-Hill, 1993.

Sharma, Toni. "Inservicing the Teachers," *Phi Delta Kappan* 63 (February 1982): 403.

Showers, Beverly, Bruce Joyce, and Barrie Bennett. "Synthesis of Research on Staff Development: A Framework for Future Study and a State-of-the-Art Analysis." *Educational Leadership* 45 (November 1987): 77–87.

Siegel, Jessica. "The State of Teacher Training." *Electronic Learning* 14 (May/June 1995): 43–53.

Sparks, Dennis C. "A Comprehensive Teacher Education Program." *Phi Delta Kappan* 63 (February 1982): 395–97.

————. "A Paradigm Shift in Staff Development." *Journal of Staff Development* 15 (Winter 1994): 26–29.

Sparks, Dennis, and Susan Loucks-Horsley. *Five Models of Staff Development for Teachers*. Oxford, Ohio: National Staff Development Council, 1990.

Sparks, Georgea Mohlman. "Synthesis of Research on Staff Development for Effective Teaching." *Educational Leadership* 41 (November 1983): 65–72.

"Staff Development." *Educational Leadership* 40 (October 1982): 4–59.

"Staff Development: An Important Part of Leadership." *NASSP Bulletin* (September 1991).

"Staff Development in Small and Rural School Districts." American Association of School Administrators, 31 pages.

"Staff Development/New Directions." *Theory into Practice* 17 (June 1978): 195–278.

Steig, Lester R., and E. Kemp Frederick. *School Personnel and In-service Training Practices*. West Nyack, N.Y.: Parker, 1969.

Stone, Fulton, Geraline Heard, Ann L. Ishler, Sandee Crowther, Kathy Boyer, Sue Schiff, and Joan Solomon. "Staff Development Policy Making in the States." *Journal of Staff Development* 16 (Spring 1995): 8–15.

"Supervision as Staff Development." *Educational Leadership* 37 (February 1980): 374–423.

Todnem, Guy R., and Michael P. Warner. "Assessment While Initiating a SIP Process." *Journal of Staff Development* 16 (Winter 1995): 54–56.

————. "Demonstrating the Benefits of Staff Development: Using Assessment Data in SIP Decision-Making." *Journal of Staff Development* 16 (Spring 1995): 62–64.

Unruh, Adolph, and Harold E. Turner. *Supervision for Change and Innovation*. Boston: Houghton Mifflin, 1970.

Wiles, Jon, and Joseph Bondi. *Supervision: A Guide to Practice,* 4th ed. Englewood Cliffs, N.J.: Merrill, 1995.

Wilhelms, Fred T. *Supervision in a New Key*. Alexandria, Va.: Association for Supervision and Curriculum Development, 1973.

Williamson, Peter A., and Julia A. Elfman. "A Commonsense Approach to Teacher Inservice Training." *Phi Delta Kappan* 63 (February 1982): 401.

Wood, Fred H., Frank O. McQuarrie, and Steven R. Thompson. "Practitioners and Professors Agree on Effective Staff Development Practices." *Educational Leadership* 40 (October 1982): 28–31.

Wood, Fred H., and Steven R. Thompson. "Guidelines for Better Staff Development." *Educational Leadership* 37 (February 1980): 374–78.

Wood, Fred H., Steven R. Thompson, and Sister Frances Russell. "Designing Effective Staff Development Programs." In *Staff Development/Organization Development*. 1981 Yearbook, ed. Betty Dillon-Peterson, pp. 59–91. Alexandria, Va.: Association for Supervision and Curriculum Development, 1981.

Yarger, Sam J. "The Legacy of the Teacher Center." In *Changing School Culture through Staff*

Development. 1990 Yearbook, ed. Bruce Joyce, pp. 104–16. Alexandria, Va: Association for Supervision and Curriculum Development, 1990.

Multimedia

Northwest Regional Educational Laboratory, 710 S. W. Second Ave., Portland, OR 97204. Instructional system on the topic, *Research Utilizing Problem Solving.* Classroom Version. Participant materials, audiotape, text (Diagnosing Classroom Learning Environments by Fox, Luszki, and Schmuck), and leader's guide. Thirty hours of instruction on (1) identifying the problem, (2) diagnosing the problem situation, (3) considering alternative actions, (4) trying out a plan of action, and (5) adapting the plan. Available from Commercial-Educational Distributing Services, P.O. Box 3711, Portland, OR 97208.

Audiotapes

Orlich, Donald C. *Staff Development and Teacher Behavioral Changes.* 1993. National Staff Development Council, P.O. Box 240, Oxford, OH 45056.

Satles, Beth D., Sandra R. Orletsky, Jackie Walsh, and Jack Barnette. *Unsolved Mysteries: How Effective Is Staff Development in Promoting Long-Term Change?* 2 cassettes. National Staff Development Council, P.O. Box 240, Oxford, OH 45056.

Warner, Michael P., and Guy Todnem. *The Many Hats of Staff Development.* 1994. 1 cassette. National Staff Development Council, P.O. Box 240, Oxford, OH 45056.

Westbrook, Jody M., and Ward English. *Capture the Talent: Campus-Based Staff Developers.* 1994. 2 cassettes. National Staff Development Council, P.O. Box 240, Oxford, OH 45056.

Journals and Other Periodicals

The Journal of Staff Development (quarterly). *The Developer* (ten per year), and *School Team Innovator* (eight per year). All are available as part of membership in the National Staff Development Council, 5198 Westgate Drive, P.O. Box 240, Oxford, OH 45056.

Questionnaire

Teacher Skill-Interest Questionnaire: A District Needs Assessment. Instrument for assessing in-service needs of teachers. Evaluative Research Associates, 8444 Florissant Road, Suite 207, St. Louis, MO 63121. Developed for use as a district needs assessment by Ferguson-Florissant Reorganized School District.

Videotapes

School Improvement through Staff Development. 1985. 30 min. Dennis Sparks, Executive Secretary for the National Staff Development Council, and Georgea Sparks-Langer talk with teachers and principals about the importance of systematic school improvement and procedures for implementing. *Leader's Guide.* Association for Supervision and Curriculum Development, 1250 North Pitt Street, Alexandria, VA 22314.

Best of Wavelength. 1991. A three-volume video library of humorous sketches suitable for group or individual viewing. Some of the topics covered include attitudes, behaving and competencies, issues, images, diversity, and assessment. *Leader's Guide.* National Staff Development Council, P.O. Box 240, Oxford, OH 45056.

ASCD Network

Staff Development. For the name of the current facilitator of the staff development network, contact Susan K. Nicklas, Director, Field Services, ASCD, 1250 North Pitt Street, Alexandria, VA 22314; phone (703) 549-9110, extension 500, fax (703) 548-8725.

10

Helping Teachers on a One-to-one Basis

Objectives

After studying Chapter 10 you should be able to accomplish the following objectives:

1. Define formative evaluation as applied to teacher performance.
2. Distinguish between clinical supervision and general supervision.
3. Describe one or more models of clinical supervision.
4. Describe skills needed by the supervisor for clinical supervision.
5. Select or create and apply appropriate classroom observation instruments.
6. Demonstrate selected techniques of classroom observation.
7. Assess your own readiness to render clinical supervision.
8. Plan for the use of teacher colleagues in supervision.

FORMATIVE EVALUATION

Recall for a moment two of the three components of a teacher evaluation system: formative evaluation and summative evaluation. Formative evaluation, discussed in this chapter, is assessment of teacher performance by an instructional supervisor during the year for the purpose of improving instruction. Summative evaluation, the topic of Chapter 13, is assessment of teacher performance by an administrator for the purpose of making decisions about such matters as tenure, retention, career ladder, and merit increments.

If the school system is large enough, an instructional supervisor will probably be the formative evaluator and the administrator will be the summative evaluator.

Formative evaluators may be central office or individual school personnel. From the central office come curriculum coordinators or consultants and other instructional supervisors. In the elementary schools, there are lead teachers, curriculum resource teachers, team leaders, grade coordinators, and peers. In secondary schools, in addition to peers, department heads may serve as formative evaluators. In the middle schools, we may encounter formative evaluators in positions similar to those in both elementary and secondary schools. However, the summative evaluator may also be the formative evaluator, as in the case of a principal in a small school that has no other supervisory personnel. The principal's summative evaluations will be based on formative evaluations. The formative evaluations in this case fulfill a double purpose: They provide information that can be used for improving instruction and for making personnel decisions.

If a school system is large enough, it should have two kinds of formative evaluation: one by the instructional supervisor with no summative evaluation and one by the administrator, culminating in a summative evaluation.

When two different formative evaluations are possible, the evaluation done by the instructional supervisor should not be reported to the administrator unless the teacher requests it or agrees to it. In this chapter, our attention is on the formative evaluation carried out by the instructional supervisor. We examine in particular the structured approach to formative evaluation known as clinical supervision.

CLINICAL SUPERVISION

In Chapter 2, we considered whether supervisors should work primarily with groups or with individuals. Many specialists in supervision believe that supervisors should concentrate their energies on individual teachers in their classrooms. These specialists recommend that supervisors take what is called a clinical approach.

The term *clinical supervision* came into vogue in 1961 when Morris Cogan used it in a proposal he made at Harvard University entitled *Case Studies and Research in Clinical Supervision*. As Cogan himself pointed out, the term met with a great deal of resistance.[1] The words invoke images of doctors and laboratory technicians analyzing and diagnosing a patient's ailments. No one looks forward with delight to a trip to the clinic.

Yet the concepts of analysis, diagnosis, and remediation can apply as well in professional education as in medicine or dentistry or athletics. When Cogan spoke of supervision, he meant clinical supervision unless he specified otherwise. Cogan defined clinical supervision in the following way:

> Clinical supervision may therefore be defined as the rationale and practice designed to improve the teacher's classroom performance. It takes its principal data from the events of the classroom. The analysis of these data and the relationship between teacher and supervisor form the basis of the program, procedures, and strategies designed to improve the students' learning by improving the teacher's classroom behavior.[2]

Cogan offered a simple test for distinguishing between general and clinical supervision.

> . . . *general supervision* subsumes supervisory operations that take place principally outside the classroom. . . . *General supervision*, therefore, denotes activities like the writing and revision of curriculums, the preparation of units and materials of instruction, the development of processes and instruments for reporting to parents, and such broad concerns as the evaluation of the total educational program.[3]

Clearly, Cogan felt that clinical supervision should be stressed over general supervision.

Although clinical supervision as a concept appears to be a rather recent development, we can find in the early history of this field a type—although a quite different type—of clinical supervision. The earliest supervisors served as inspectors. They visited classrooms, observed the teacher's performance, and checked on the condition of the classroom. They did analyze; they did diagnose; and if they proposed remediation, it was more in line with the concept of a medical prescription. Supervision in the individual teacher's classroom preceded organized in-service education of groups of teachers. The supervising principal, headmaster, or superintendent felt it was his or her obligation to discover what was happening in the various classrooms. The intent was more to ensure that the teacher was carrying out approved policies, procedures, and programs than to provide assistance to the teacher for the improvement of instruction. Under an aura of investigation, early "snoopervisors" were decidedly clinical in the purest sense of the word: detached, aloof, critical, and judgmental. They wanted to see that rooms were kept clean, bulletin boards neat, property protected, shades properly drawn, children well disciplined, and lessons heard and repeated by the learners.

The purposes and practices of clinical supervision today differ radically from historic approaches to supervision of individual teachers. One factor, however, remains constant. Clinical supervision takes place in the classroom where there is only one teacher. Thus, it is an individualized approach to supervision.

Robert H. Anderson and Robert J. Krajewski, in revising the work of Robert Goldhammer, defined clinical supervision as "that aspect of supervision which draws upon data from first-hand observation of actual teaching, or other professional events, and involves face-to-face and other associated interactions between the observer(s) and person(s) observed in the course of analyzing the observed professional behaviors and activities and seeking to define and/or develop next steps toward improved performance."[4] They attributed the nine characteristics listed below to clinical supervision.

1. It is a technology for improving instruction.
2. It is a deliberate intervention into the instructional process.
3. It is goal-oriented, combining school needs with the personal growth needs of those who work within the school.
4. It assumes a working relationship between teacher(s) and supervisor(s).
5. It requires a high degree of mutual trust, as reflected in understanding, support, and commitment for growth.
6. It is systematic, although it requires a flexible and continuously changing methodology.
7. It creates productive (i.e., healthy) tension for bridging the gap between the real and the ideal.

8. It assumes that the supervisor knows a great deal about the analysis of instruction and learning and also about productive human interaction.
9. It requires both pre-service training, especially in observation techniques, and continuous in-service reflection on effective approaches.[5]

Clinical supervision should be perceived as a concept, not a single, fixed set of procedures. Practices may vary—though as we see when we examine models of clinical supervision, they do not vary as widely as might be supposed. As Goldhammer said, however, "a face-to-face relationship between supervisors and teachers" is fundamental to clinical supervision.[6] In this chapter, we explore the basic model of clinical supervision—the one-to-one relationship between supervisor and teacher.

Goldhammer took note of "variations of the basic model that include group supervision, that is, supervision of individual teachers by groups of supervisors, groups of teachers by groups of supervisors, and groups of teachers by an individual supervisor."[7] Though supervision of a teacher's classroom performance by a group of supervisors may be possible, we feel the group variations of the model to be limited in usefulness, feasibility, and practicality. A one-to-one basis appears to us to be the most effective approach to clinical supervision. One possible exception may occur with well-knit teaching teams in which peers collaborate to provide guidance to their own members. Another viable group approach to supervision is use of intensive assistance teams whose purpose is to help marginal teachers (see Chapter 13).

Clinical supervision is today well accepted in the field of instructional supervision. Barbara Nelson Pavan noted:

> With the advent of the 1980s, clinical supervision has almost become an educational fad, at least in word, if not in practice. For the first time since the seeds were sown, cultivated, and fertilized by groups of faculty members, students, and classroom teachers interacting in various training projects at Harvard beginning in the 1960s, mentioning clinical supervision to a group of educators does not result in blank stares . . . clinical supervision has come of age.[8]

THE SUPERVISOR'S ROLE IN CLINICAL SUPERVISION

Whether supervision is evaluation is one of the perennial issues of this field. Some experts reject the term *evaluation* when applied to instructional supervision. They prefer terms like *facilitating, collaborating, consulting, helping, coaching,* or *mentoring.* Our position is that any time a person makes a judgment about another person, place, or thing, that person is engaging in *evaluation,* or, if you prefer, *assessment.* The heart of the evaluation issue is what we do with the evaluation data. Evaluation can be positive and helpful. It does not have to be negative and destructive.

Keith A. Acheson and Meredith Damien Gall pictured the supervisor as primarily a facilitator.[9] They took note, however, of the continuing dilemma supervisors face when they must fulfill the dual roles of facilitator and evaluator.

> This book is strongly oriented toward the role of clinical supervisor as facilitator, but we acknowledge that most supervisors must also evaluate teachers. . . .
> The conflict between facilitation and evaluation is not unique to teacher supervision; supervisors in all occupations and professions face the same problem. Even teachers must play the dual role of evaluator and facilitator.[10]

When the same person is charged with the responsibility for both formative and summative evaluation, the dilemma may be minimized when the supervisors have a high degree of competence and interpersonal skills. Teachers will accept evaluation of the rating type (summative) and evaluation of the helping variety (formative) from the same person if they have confidence in that person. The dilemma, of course, is eliminated when formative evaluation is carried out by a staff supervisor and summative by a line administrator-supervisor.

The role of the supervisor as facilitator is compatible with the role of the supervisor as teacher. In fact, facilitating behavior is both a generic skill in one sense and a model of teacher behavior in another sense.

Like this textbook, most of the literature on clinical supervision emphasizes the analysis of teaching for the purpose of improving instruction. Acheson and Gall, for example, viewed clinical supervision as "supervision to help the teacher improve his or her instructional performance."[11]

Ralph L. Mosher and David E. Purpel called for clinical supervisors skilled not only in analyzing teaching but also in curriculum development:

> Clinical supervision has, since its inception, been based on specialized, expert knowledge of the content of instruction. A current and related development, largely attributable to Purpel, is emphasis on supervision as instruction in curriculum. Specialized knowledge of curriculum theory and development is therefore a prerequisite to a comprehensive analysis of teaching.[12]

They further stated:

> Clinical supervision is one means by which teachers can confront and modify both the content and the practice of teaching. Indeed, it is virtually inseparable from curriculum development activity, both in its theoretical principles and as a strategy for involving teachers in analysis of their instruction. The most productive way to get teachers to analyze and change how they teach, in the writer's experience, is to involve them in analysis of what they teach.[13]

Noreen Garman saw the role of the supervisor in clinical supervision as being friend, confidante, and respected colleague.[14] She described clinical supervision as embracing four concepts:

- Collegiality: an internal state embodying a spirit of "connectedness," that is, identification with another person for whom one holds respect and affection.
- Collaboration: teacher and supervisor sharing a common language so that they may share each other's perceptions.
- Skilled service: the supervisor's special competence based on training and experience from which teachers can benefit.
- Ethical conduct: exercising judgment and maintaining trust.[15]

Said Garman, "In clinical supervision one doesn't have ethics, one does ethics."[16] Replying to the question, "When are we really clinical supervisors?" Garman painted the following word picture:

> A person becomes a clinical supervisor when he/she begins to think and act as if the "cycle of supervision" were a metaphor as well as a method; when observation and analysis are not only procedural phases for actions in classrooms, but also represent the empirical approach inherent in a skilled service; when the notion of conference not only means two people meeting before and after classroom visits, but also suggests dynamic forms of collaboration in education alliances; when the im-

age of "cycle" not only guarantees repeated performance, but also refers to high levels of involvement and commitment that press participants toward the "connectedness" of collegiality; when the teacher-supervisor relationship stands for ethical conduct as it is lived out in important choices.[17]

There is considerable disagreement among specialists in supervision over the question of whether the supervisor-teacher relationship should be a superior-subordinate relationship or a relationship between equals. Some experts feel that the superior-subordinate relationship is necessary to nudge teachers to make changes. These people believe that since the superior-subordinate relationship does exist, we should make the best of it. Others feel that although the superior-subordinate relationship exists, the inequality of the partners should be deemphasized or ignored. Still others feel that a superior-subordinate relationship has no place in the modern-day supervision of professionals and can be dispensed with, at least in the case of staff supervisors who do not possess line authority.

Robert J. Alfonso and Lee Goldsberry made clear the existence of the supervisor's authority:

> Supervision is a formal organizational act; moreover, supervision always implies a superordinate-subordinate relationship. The terms "peer supervision" and "colleague supervision" may be contradictions, for one cannot be both a peer/colleague and a supervisor at the same time. Clearly, teachers can and should help each other in a variety of ways, but a supervisor is vested with organizational authority for decision making about others.[18]

In another context Alfonso with coauthors Firth and Neville examined the dimensions of leadership and included among a number of propositions the following: "The probability of successful leadership will be increased if the leader maintains some degree of psychological distance from subordinates."[19] They developed this point in the following passage:

> Supervisors are likely to be more effective if they do not become an integral part of the teacher group. While obviously joined to them and responsible for them, a sense of psychological distance is necessary. This is not to suggest that supervisors need to be aloof, undemocratic, or "company people," but rather that their relationships to teachers must permit psychological freedom and objectivity. While writing in supervision has often suggested a close relationship, research indicates that maintaining some degree of psychological distance enhances a supervisor's ability to make discriminations between teachers and to assess their ability and effectiveness more clearly and objectively. Supervisors need to maintain the delicate balance that enables one to operate freely as a member of a group while still retaining a recognized degree of psychological detachment.[20]

On the other hand, Garman advocated a close relationship when she said, "A heightened sense of collegiality is possible when I can imagine myself as a member of an organic unit, when the distinction between supervisor and teacher is less discernible and I can transcend my conventional role status."[21]

Differing interpretations of the supervisor's role highlight once again the problem of the dual roles of many supervisors: helper and evaluator. The helper has little or no need of psychological distance whereas the evaluator finds maintaining distance useful and, perhaps, necessary. The clinical supervisor, who works in a helping, face-to-face relationship with teachers, has less need to maintain a superior-subordinate relationship than the administrative supervisor, who must make the hard decisions about retention and dismissal.

The supervisor enters the process of clinical supervision as a knowledgeable helper. He or she brings to the process skills in pedagogy and personal relations. He or she knows how to analyze teaching, diagnose difficulties, confer with teachers, and make recommendations to the teacher for improvement. The supervisor knows sources of information and materials, is able to help with assessment of student performance, and can assist in interpreting applicable research. In addition, the supervisor possesses skills to help teachers with curriculum development.

Describing clinical supervision as a "personalized-consultative approach," Daniel Tanner and Laurel Tanner noted cooperative planning, collegial working relationships, and focus on actual classroom practice as its appealing features.[22]

MODELS OF CLINICAL SUPERVISION

The literature offers us a number of models of clinical supervision that recommend certain steps or stages to be followed. As early as 1930, George C. Kyte proposed such a model. Though he did not use the label "clinical," he suggested a pattern that anticipated the clinical approach thirty years later. Referring to supervisory observation—the heart of clinical supervision—Kyte outlined a three-phase process:

1. planning for the observation of teaching.
2. getting the most out of the observation period.
3. analyzing the teaching observed.[23]

In discussing the first phase, Kyte emphasized the plans the supervisor would make for the forthcoming observation as well as for preobservation conferencing, a key feature of clinical supervision models. He noted the desirability of conferences with the teacher both before and after observing, and Kyte described the two kinds of conferences:

> Two kinds of individual conferences are conducted in supervision. The less common one in practice, though markedly important, is that which is preparatory to work projected. The series of first conferences with a new teacher, the consultations planned in response to a teacher's request for help on a new undertaking, and the interviews for the purpose of planning classroom experimentation frequently are of this nature. The more common type of conference, however, is that which occurs after a supervisory visit has been made to the classroom, or the products of pupils' efforts have been submitted to a supervisory officer.[24]

By putting these elements together, we create the following four-stage model:

1. Preobservation conference and planning for the observation
2. Observation
3. Analysis of the data
4. Postobservation conference

Some of Kyte's recommendations are remarkably contemporary, as shown here.

a. Regarding planning and preparation for observation:
   Purposeful planning includes (a) the selection of sound objectives, (b) the analysis of teacher personnel, (c) the survey of learning conditions, (d) the di-

agnosis of teaching difficulties, (e) the determining of teacher needs, and (f) the choice of supervisory aid.[25] . . . When the supervisor has made adequate preparation for the visit to a classroom, he will enter the room with a clear understanding of what he expects to stress in his observation, why he should so place his emphasis, and how he will make use of the results to aid the teacher.[26]

b. Regarding observation:

[The author] has observed teaching, taking personal notes, and using a trained secretary to obtain stenographic notes. . . . The reaction of the teachers to their first experience of this nature was somewhat unfavorable. . . . When copies of the notes were given to them and they were told that the stenographic records would be used as the basis of the conference, they frankly admitted that the notes proved helpful to them before they came to the conference, and very helpful as a basis for getting help through the conference. . . . After the third experience, they were unanimous in their recommendation that detailed records be made during the supervisory observation, because of the greater aid resulting.[27] . . . Frequently the supervisors utilize published forms, or ones that they have improvised for their own use in recording their observations.[28] . . .

c. Regarding analysis of the observation data:

Just as soon after the observation as possible, the supervisor should set aside time to go over his notes in order to add items which may recur to him while the observed lesson is still freshly impressed upon him. He should give careful thought to the lesson as a whole, and to the points which he noted with a view to preparing for the conference. . . . A careful analysis of the lesson should be made by the supervisor before conferring with the teacher. If the supervisor is to be a super-teacher, he must make the same sort of preparation for his "recitation" with the teacher, the conference, as the teacher is expected to make for his classroom recitation.[29]

Kyte found twenty-five "teacher-rating devices," which we would now call observation instruments, published between 1920 and 1930. He summarized the items assessed by these devices, as shown in Table 10.1. Note that many of the items are skills that present-day observation systems seek to assess.

Kyte suggested ways of recording classroom observations in the following passage:

In addition to long-hand and stenographic accounts of observations, other means of attempting to gather objective data are used. Many printed forms exist which suggest various ways of collecting the desired information. Check-lists, word- or phrase-responses, and complete sentences are typical methods of recording the supervisor's reactions. Still another and a more recent type is exemplified by the chart of the classroom used, with a legend for recording child-participation.[30]

Kyte made reference to a recording system suggested by Roswell C. Puckett in 1928. The seating chart and detailed legend, shown in Figure 10.1 (p. 411), are similar in nature to some of the observational techniques in use today.

Kyte dealt with the continuing questions of whether to make announced or unannounced visits (both have their place)[31] and how long a visit to make (elementary: thirty minutes; secondary: one period).[32] Kyte's work was very much in line with present clinical supervision practice.

TABLE 10.1. DISTRIBUTION OF ITEMS REGARDING THE TECHNIQUE OF TEACHING LISTED FREQUENTLY IN TWENTY-FIVE TEACHER-RATING DEVICES

Nature of Items Listed	Rating Devices	
	Number	*Percent*
Making the assignment	19	76
Discipline of the pupils	19	76
Training pupils to study	17	68
Attention to individual needs	17	68
Participation of pupils	16	64
Skill in questioning	16	64
Care of hygienic conditions	16	64
Skill in stimulating thought	15	60
Selection of subject matter	15	60
Organization of subject matter	15	60
Definiteness of instructions	14	56
Skill in motivating work	13	52
Skill in habit formation	13	52
Securing and holding interest	12	48
Definite and clear aims	12	48
Careful preparation of teacher	12	48
Care of routine	12	48
Economic use of school time	11	44
Use of instructional materials	10	40
Neatness of room	10	40
Orderliness of room	10	40
Evidence of growth of pupils	10	40

Source: George C. Kyte, How to Supervise: A Guide to Educational Principles and Practices of Educational Supervision *(Boston: Houghton Mifflin, 1930), p. 151. Reprinted with permission of Houghton Mifflin, Inc.*

Five Models

Understanding the concept of clinical supervision is easier if we, like Cogan, perceive it as a cycle with a number of recurring stages or phases.[33] Several authorities have suggested models to guide the practice of teachers and supervisors as they engage in the cycle of supervision. Table 10.2 (p. 412) shows the stages or phases recommended by the models of Goldhammer,[34] Mosher and Purpel,[35] Cogan,[36] Acheson and Gall,[37] and Jerry J. Bellon and Elner C. Bellon.[38]

Although models differ in number of stages or phases, they all possess three essential ingredients: (1) There is some kind of contact or communication with the teacher prior to an observation; (2) there is some type of classroom observation; and (3) there is some kind of follow-up of the observation. For some of the proponents of clinical supervision the process involves two—and only two—players: one supervisor and one teacher. To others, a teacher-peer may substitute for the supervisor. In still more complex versions of the process, a number of peers—as in the case of teaching teams—may substitute for the supervisor. We examine the concept and use of colleagues in the supervisory process later in this chapter when we discuss peer supervision, coaching, and mentoring.

Whether the helper's role in clinical supervision is performed by a supervisor from the central office or from the individual school or by a teacher's peer(s), three phases appear to be essential to the process: (1) preobservation conference, (2) observation, and (3) postobservation conference.

Preobservation Conference

The word *conference* as used in the cycle of clinical supervision is, we believe, almost too formal a term. It implies an atmosphere, structure, and length that can arouse a teacher's negative feelings. Add the term *clinical* and we have a potential for setting

Pupil responses in a IX B civics class

- Pupil raised hand.
- ⊙ Pupil raised hand and was called on by teacher.
- ⊚ Pupil raised hand, was called on by teacher, and made a single-word response.
- ⊙- Pupil raised hand, was called on by teacher, and made a fair response.
- ⊚ Pupil raised hand, was called on by teacher, and made a good response.
- -⊙ Pupil raised hand, was called on by teacher, and made a very good response.
- □ Pupil called on when he did not have hand raised.
- ⊓ Pupil called on when he did not have hand raised; made a single-word response.
- □- Pupil called on when he did not have hand raised; made a fair response.
- ⊔ Pupil called on when he did not have hand raised; made a good response.
- -□ Pupil called on when he did not have hand raised; made a very good response.
- ⊠ Pupil called on when he did not have hand raised; made no response.
- > Pupil asked a question.

Figure 10.1. Record of Pupil Participation in a Recitation. *Source: Roswell C. Puckett, "Making Supervision Objective," School Review 36, no. 3 (March 1928): 210–11. Reprinted with permission of The University of Chicago, Chicago, Illinois, publisher.*

TABLE 10.2. FIVE MODELS OF CLINICAL SUPERVISION

Goldhammer (1969) Goldhammer, Anderson, and Krajewski (1980) Five Stages	Mosher and Purpel (1972) Three Stages	Cogan (1973) Eight Phases	Acheson and Gall (1980) Three Phases	Bellon and Bellon (1982) Three Phases
1. Preobservation conference	1. Planning	1. Establishing the teacher-supervisor relationship	1. Planning conference	1. Pre Observation Conference
		2. Planning with the teacher		
		3. Planning the strategy of observation		
2. Observation	2. Observation	4. Observing instruction	2. Classroom observation	2. Classroom Observation
3. Analysis and strategy	3. Evaluation or analysis	5. Analyzing the teaching-learning processes		
		6. Planning the strategy of the conference		
4. Supervision conference		7. The conference	3. Feedback conference	3. Post Observation Conference
5. Postconference analysis		8. Renewed planning		

Source: Columns 1–4 are a modification of Table 1: The Process of Clinical Supervision, in Barbara Nelson Pavan, "Clinical Supervision: Some Signs of Progress," Texas Tech Journal of Education 7, no. 3 (Fall 1980): 248. Reprinted with permission of Texas Tech Journal of Education. Column 5 from Jerry I. Bellon and Elner C. Bellon, Classroom Supervision and Instructional Improvement: A Synergetic Process, 2nd ed. (Dubuque, Iowa: Kendall/Hunt Publishing Company, 1982), pp. 29–32. Reprinted with permission of Kendall/Hunt Publishing Company.

up an avoidance behavior on the part of the teacher. Teachers might be more accepting and solicitous of help if in their presence we used words like chat, talk, or dialog instead of conference, and individualized, personal, or classroom instead of clinical. Among supervisors, however, we could continue to use the technical language that has already been invented.

A preobservation conference is a face-to-face talk between teacher and supervisor prior to the supervisor's visit to the teacher's classroom. The purpose of the preobservation conference is to settle on necessary preliminaries. The two participants to the conference have already agreed or assumed that the supervisor will visit the teacher and observe the teacher's performance. Ideally, the teacher is as desirous of having the supervisor visit as the supervisor is of making the visit. Whether the teacher looks forward to help of this nature from the supervisor will depend on whether a feeling of mutual respect has been developed between the two. Conceivably, clinical supervision can be carried on without the existence of mutual respect but in that event the cycle is perfunctory, resented by the teacher, and doomed to failure. Though we would limit the concept of peer supervision to assistance given by one teacher to another, the clinical supervisor should be a peer in the best sense of the term.

Sometimes it seems as if clinical supervision—or any type of supervision—is the supervisor's show. In all stages of the cycle of clinical supervision, the teacher and supervisor should perceive each other as working together for the ultimate benefit of the learners.

At the preobservation conference, the teacher and supervisor together should decide what class the supervisor will visit and when. Thus, the supervisor's schedule is set in advance. The evaluator of teacher performance may feel the need for unannounced visits, but these are not necessary for the clinical supervisor. The clinical supervisor is not seeking to check on teachers, to keep them "on the ball," or to assess their competence or professionalism for administrative purposes. The clinical supervisor is coming to visit, observe, and help as a trained, skilled colleague.

Once the teacher and supervisor have decided on a specific class, the teacher will provide background to help the supervisor understand the composition of the group. The teacher will inform the supervisor about the background of the learners and will discuss special problems he or she is encountering with the group.

In the preobservation conference the teacher will identify special teaching problems he or she is encountering and with which he or she would like some help. Thus, the two participants focus on specific teacher and student behaviors that the supervisor will observe. The teacher may feel the need for someone to observe and provide feedback about such specific behaviors as these:

- Verbal interaction between students and teacher
- The teacher's use of oral questioning
- The teacher's methods of subgrouping
- Students' verbal and nonverbal interaction with one another
- The teacher's presentation of a particular item of content
- The teacher's use of simple control techniques
- The teacher's voice patterns

- The teacher's nonverbal behavior
- The teacher's use of classroom management techniques
- The teacher's individualized help to learners
- The teacher's awareness of what's happening in the classroom
- The teacher's use of media in presenting a lesson
- The clarity with which the teacher gives directions
- The teacher's use of language
- The teacher's sensitivity to cultural diversity in the classroom.
- The teacher's awareness of equity and equality when dealing with students of each gender.
- The teacher's ability to deal with students who have special needs.

The teacher will acquaint the supervisor with the unit and lesson plans that will be taught when the supervisor visits. The teacher will explain the objectives of the lesson, the methods of presentation, and techniques of evaluating student performance. The teacher and supervisor will agree on the supervisor's role during the visit. Although some educators think it is permissible for the supervisor to play an active role during the visit—for example, to talk with students—most consider the appropriate role of the supervisor to be that of unobtrusive observer. Also, if the supervisor is to make an accurate record of what is taking place during an observation, he or she cannot be distracted from this task nor should he or she distract the teacher with interjections into the proceedings. We agree with Goldhammer, who said, "As a rule, Supervisor should not intervene in the teaching in any manner during Observation. . . . Supervisor should only intervene by explicit prior agreement with Teacher, and in a manner seeming mutually agreeable and appropriate to both except, of course, in physical emergencies."[39]

The supervisor and teacher should agree on procedures the supervisor will follow to record data. Thus, the teacher will not be upset when the supervisor makes marks on an observation instrument or sits busily writing a verbatim account of the events.

The teacher and supervisor should decide whether the use of audio- or videotaping is desirable and, if so, must work out details of their use. The participants need to agree on how long the supervisor will remain in the classroom and where the supervisor will be seated.

Regarding the time needed, Acheson and Gall advised, "Planning conferences need not be long. As a supervisor, you might allow twenty to thirty minutes for the first planning conference unless the teacher has a particularly difficult problem to discuss. Later planning conferences might require only five to ten minutes."[40]

The supervisor should seek to calm the anxieties the teacher may have about the visit. Assuring the teacher of the confidentiality of the data will help. Specialists suggest that conferences be conducted either in the teacher's classroom or office or at another mutually agreed-on location, not in the supervisor's office. Holding the follow-up conference in the teacher's classroom allows for easy access to the setting in which the teaching occurred. References then can be made to teacher's location, student access to materials, chalkboard, and group activities. Conferencing in the supervisor's office perpetuates the notion of a superordinate-subordinate relationship, which the supervisor should attempt to deemphasize. The supervisor should let the teacher know when he or she will be able to provide feedback about the observation. The supervisor will explain to the teacher that he or she will need some time after the conference to analyze the data and prepare for a postobservation conference. In the preobservation conference, the groundwork is laid for the observation.

Although we are in agreement with supervision specialists who see merit in conducting preobservation conferences, we would be remiss if we did not advise the reader that, as with so many educational practices, we do not have unanimous agreement in the value of preobservation conferencing. Madeline Hunter, for example, let her objections be known, advocating elimination of the preobservation conference. Hunter cited time constraints and other reasons.[41]

Observation

If we were to draw up a list of supervisory tasks that require specialized skills, classroom observation would head the list. On the surface, observation would seem simple. The supervisor enters the classroom, preferably at the start of a lesson, sits down at the back of the room, watches for a half-hour to an hour, makes notes, gets up, and leaves. Yet classroom observation demands a high level of technical and analytical skills. The supervisor must know what to look for; how to look; how to collect, analyze, and interpret the data. Garman noted the complexity of the task of the supervisor who works with teachers in a clinical setting. She identified five modes of inquiry to be practiced by the supervisor: discovery, verification, explanation, interpretation, and evaluation. Each mode fulfills a different purpose, uses different methods of collecting data—some quantitative and some qualitative—and requires different treatments.[42]

Every observation is a new situation; classroom transactions are never the same. The supervisor must draw on all his or her training and experience to turn in a creditable performance at observing the teacher and students in action.

What to Observe. Two basic approaches to observation are possible, the choice of which is dependent on the purpose of the supervisor's visit. For want of better terms, we call the two approaches *global* and *specific*.

GLOBAL APPROACH. The global approach to teacher evaluation is a generalized assessment of teacher performance on a wide variety of teaching skills, usually generic in nature. The global approach appears to be the more common approach of both staff and line supervisors. The supervisor often uses an instrument of some type to guide the assessment of teacher performance, although he or she may record the classroom events without resorting to an instrument. Whatever instrument or system is to be used, the teacher must be made familiar with it.

A global approach is a useful technique for the staff supervisor when the teacher and supervisor wish to make a general appraisal of the teacher's performance. As the global approach is essentially an assessment of the teacher's total performance, it is particularly suitable for the use of line supervisors—that is, administrator-supervisors—as a basis for summative evaluation. The administrator-supervisor, by observing a teacher several times and assessing the teacher's overall performance, can compile sufficient data to make an annual, summative appraisal of performance.

As mentioned in the previous chapter, efforts have been made over the past two decades to identify the generic skills or competencies that make up the teaching act. The profession has moved closer to the concept of teaching as a science. Thus, supervisors have adopted what we might call a scientific approach, diagnosing teacher performance in respect to specific, identifiable behaviors.

ARTISTIC APPROACH. Some of the experts would have us look more closely at teaching as an art rather than a science and, thus, supervision as an art rather than a science. Elliot W. Eisner listed several of the fallacies he saw in scientific supervision as follows:

- the *fallacy of additivity* which is committed by attempting to study or supervise teaching using a procedure that implies or assumes that the incidence of particular teaching behaviors—structuring, giving examples, positive and negative reinforcement, and so forth—all have equal pedagogical weight and can be added together to secure an index of the quality of teaching. . . .
- the *fallacy of composition*, that the whole is equal to the sum of its parts. This is committed when the quality of teaching is determined by counting the incidence of teacher behaviors in a variable or category and then adding to this sum the scores produced in other variables. . . .
- the *fallacy of concreteness*. This fallacy is an offshoot of behaviorism which holds that the exclusive referent for observation is the manifest behavior of the student. . . . When we observe pupils or teachers we do not merely look at the behavior they display, but also at its meaning and the quality of their experience. . . .
- the *fallacy of the act* . . . the tendency to neglect the process of educational life as it unfolds in classrooms and schools. . . .
- the *fallacy of method*: neglecting those aspects of teaching that are immune to the criteria and instruments that the researcher employs.[43]

Eisner advocated an artistic approach to supervision by which he meant

an approach to supervision that relies on the sensitivity, perceptivity, and knowledge of the supervisor as a way of appreciating the significant subtleties occurring in the classroom, and that exploits the expressive, poetic, and often metaphorical potential of language to convey to teachers or to others whose decisions affect what goes on in schools, what has been observed.[44]

Instead of focusing on just the readily observable specific teaching skills, Eisner would have the supervisor attempt "to improve the quality of educational life in the school."[45] Eisner believed that the supervisor must "hear the music" as well as observe the action; he or she must judge the character and quality of the teacher's performance, not just the quantitative aspects.

... teachers, too, are differentiated by their style and by their particular strengths. Artistically oriented supervision would recognize this style and try to help the teacher exploit it by strengthening the positive directions already taken. . . . The connoisseur of teaching, like the connoisseur of the violin or cello, would appreciate these characteristic traits of the performer in addition to the general overall quality of the performance. In other words, both the general level of teaching competence and the unique characteristics of the performance would be perceived and appraised.[46]

Eisner did not believe that artistic supervision could be accomplished with rating instruments. The artistic supervisor, according to Eisner, must possess the ability to appreciate what is happening in the classroom, which he labeled "educational connoisseurship," and to interpret the quality of performance to the teacher, which he called "educational criticism."[47]

Practically, such artistic supervision would require a virtuoso performance beyond the range of many persons who hold supervisory positions. The preparation of specialists who can tune into the varied nuances of teaching also poses a problem.

INTERPRETIVE AND ECOLOGICAL APPROACHES. Like an artistic approach, other current bodies of thought reject or deemphasize some of the present processes and practices in analyzing teacher competencies.[48] They would abandon or minimize the scientific approach to supervision, which seeks to collect objective data on the teacher's demonstration of generic competencies. In its place they advocate interpretive or hermeneutic and ecological approaches to classroom supervision.

Proponents of an interpretive approach would replace the scientific approach, which draws on the methodology of the natural sciences, with an approach from the social sciences. The interpretive school holds that supervisors must go beyond the collection and analysis of generic teaching skills and raise questions with the teacher about why teachers and students performed as they did in a given class. They maintain that teaching is context specific and differs from teacher to teacher and from class to class.

Neither usual preobservation conferencing nor customary data collection nor typical postobservation conferencing is essential to the interpretive or ecological approaches. Some feel that the preobservation conference should be primarily an occasion for gathering information about the teacher's intentions. Some perceive the postobservation conference—a widely advocated and practiced procedure—as often ritualistic in nature, focusing on the diagnosis of teacher behaviors.[49]

The ecological approach features analysis of the linguistic and cultural patterns of the classroom, an awareness of the metaphors in the teaching and supervisory process, and a sensitivity to the use of both verbal and nonverbal language. The ecological agenda comprises not a clinical diagnosis of generic teaching skills but analysis of the social and cultural implications of the teacher's and students' language and actions in the classroom. Said C. A. Bowers and David J. Flinders, "It is the ability to recognize the classroom as a language/culture medium that most clearly shapes and defines the appropriate role of the supervisor."[50] They recommended that supervisors look for the structure of the lesson; the presence or absence of cultural and gender biases in language, actions, and content; culturally appropriate participation patterns; assumptions on which language used by the teacher is based; nonverbal communication; and student involvement.[51]

Generally, the thrust of instructional supervision at the present time emphasizes the diagnosis of specific, observable teaching behaviors and the collection of objective data that can be discussed with the teacher. Though some people aver—and rightly so—that data can never be completely objective and that most data are but an approximation of what is happening in the classroom, supervisors who are aware of their own biases and values can seek to be as objective as possible. Probably no observation, regardless of the approach followed by the supervisor, can ever be completely objective. Yet the effort to strive toward objectivity has long been sanctioned by administrators, supervisors, and teachers themselves who have often decried the lack of objectivity on the part of persons evaluating their performance.

The artistic, interpretive, and ecological approaches to supervision would replace or decrease emphasis on generic teaching behaviors, structured evaluation instruments, and supervisor-teacher distance with collegial interpretation of the classroom environment and events that took place in the classroom during observation. Present practices and training programs remain somewhat more geared to the scientific approach to supervision.

How to Record. Depending on what the teacher and supervisor have agreed should be observed, they have the choice of recording the events of the classroom by electronic means, written means, or a combination of the two. If they elect to use the first, a decision must be made, assuming the necessary equipment is available, between audio- and videotaping. An audiotape is a helpful supplement to the supervisor's observation and provides an oral verbatim record of what has occurred. An audio record is deficient in that it does not reveal movement and nonverbal behavior of both teachers and students. For this reason the supervisor's presence is necessary even if an audiotape is made of the lesson. Videotaping holds much promise as a supervisory tool. If the group is small, the videotape can reveal most or all the class transaction. Conceivably, with videotaping the supervisor might not need to be present to analyze the classroom events. Analysis could be done from the tapes. Attempts have been made to apply this technique to the supervision of student teachers. Videotaping can augment the supervisor's help by providing additional data beyond what the supervisor has garnered from classroom visits.

Regardless of the means of recording, the teacher and supervisor must be in agreement on their use. The presence of electronic equipment can cause teachers and students to be distracted; however, a practice run or two will take the edge off the novelty. After the taping loses its newness, the teacher and students shed their self-consciousness at being before the camera.

In order for the supervisor to concentrate on the lesson, a technician should be available for the actual taping. This could be done by a trained cadre of older students if media technicians are not available. Because the camcorder is so prevalent today, it is surprising that more supervisors and teachers do not make greater use of this technological aid in the improvement of instruction.

Even if electronic equipment is used in observing, the supervisor must become proficient in recording classroom events by written means. Among the available techniques are (1) verbatim recording, (2) note taking, (3) use of instruments, and (4) charting.

VERBATIM RECORDING. Goldhammer strongly recommended that the supervisor make verbatim records of the classroom events.[52] He argued logically that verbatim records provide an accurate account of what has taken place and permit the supervisor to recall with the teacher exactly what occurred. Verbatim records are the written counterpart of electronic records. The supervisor has taken down what has been said word for word, creating an exact transcript of the lesson.

To record a lesson verbatim, the supervisor must be adept at recording either by longhand or shorthand. We are not advocates of verbatim recording. We feel this technique keeps supervisors so busy that they do not have time to discern the nuances of what is happening in the classroom. Unless the supervisor is isolated at the back of the room, the recording of the lesson word for word can in itself be distracting to the teacher and students.

NOTE TAKING. The supervisor may discreetly take notes on everything and anything observed. Remember that the majority of observations conducted by clinical supervisors will focus on specific behaviors. It does not seem necessary to record behaviors beyond those that the supervisor has agreed to observe, as would be necessary in verbatim recording. A verbatim record is not necessary if the lesson is taped by either audio or video means. Making notes is less conspicuous and therefore less distracting than verbatim recording. Judicious notes made by a keen observer can provide an adequate recording of the classroom activities. The supervisor may find it helpful to record the time (hour and minutes) at which each note was written.

Acheson and Gall suggested note taking which they called an "anecdotal record"—a technique that could be used when the teacher and supervisor have not identified specific behaviors to observe.[53] The anecdotal record, composed of "short," "objective," and "nonevaluative" handwritten notes, forms the basis of a "protocol,"[54] i.e., a description of the events. Acheson and Gall recommended that the handwritten notes be typed so they may be more easily studied by the teacher.[55]

SELECTIVE VERBATIM. Somewhat less than a complete verbatim transcript and somewhat more than simple notes is *selective verbatim*, a word-for-word recording of *selected* rather than *total* verbal events. Perhaps a fair analogy to selective verbatim is the recording of "sound bites."

The supervisor may selectively sample a variety of verbal events during the observation period, may choose to record specific behaviors that he or she feels significant, or may limit recording to specific behaviors previously agreed-on by the supervisor and teacher. The supervisor may wish to use a combination of verbatim recording and note taking. Recording of observation data can be a very personal undertaking and, like handwriting, may not be decipherable from one supervisor to the other.

SPECIFIC APPROACH. When verbatim recording, note taking, and selective verbatim recording address behaviors specified in advance by the teacher and supervisor, the supervisor is following what we can term a *specific approach*. Acheson and Gall included prior selection of verbal events in their definition of selective verbatim.

> As the term implies, the supervisor makes a written record of exactly what is said, that is, a verbatim transcript. Not all verbal events are recorded, however. Supervisor and teacher select beforehand certain kinds of verbal events to be written down; in this sense, the verbatim record is intended to be "selective."[56]

The teacher and supervisor in the preobservation conference may decide on the specific behaviors of teachers and students that the supervisor will observe. The supervisor then concentrates on the evidence of the presence or absence of the specific behaviors. Thus, if the teacher and supervisor have agreed, for example, that the supervisor will diagnose the teacher's skill in providing reinforcement to the learner, the supervisor will confine the observation and analysis to that particular skill.

Karolyn J. Snyder has developed an observation training program centering around variables identified by Benjamin S. Bloom.[57] Mosher and Purpel listed the following noteworthy factors in teaching:

- The teacher's ability to communicate.
- The logic of the teaching strategy or method employed.
- The teacher's performance of "instrumental tasks."
- The motivational effect of the teaching.
- The quality of the personal relationship established between the teacher and his pupils.
- Content.[58]

A number of specific, observable behaviors are subsumed under each factor. Some teachers may wish supervisors to look at one or more steps in the Madeline Hunter model (mentioned in Chapter 4) or with the supervisor may identify other generic skills.

In the preobservation conference the teacher and supervisor specify the particular behaviors to be observed at the observation to follow. It is the analysis of these behaviors that the teacher and supervisor discuss in the postobservation conference.

Instruments. Many supervisors prefer to use an instrument of some kind to guide their observations. Which instrument they use will depend on the decision made by the teacher and supervisor about whether the supervisor will make a comprehensive—that is, global—analysis of the teacher's performance or whether he or she will limit the observation to specific behaviors. Next we examine the nature of two types of instruments: one to make a comprehensive or global assessment and one to evaluate specific behaviors.

GLOBAL. We do not have to look far to find examples of instruments designed to survey teaching behaviors rather broadly. The movement toward the specification of generic competencies stimulated school systems to create instruments for assessing those competencies. The checklist shown at the end of Chapter 4 is an illustration of an instrument that could be—and subsequently has been—used to assess the generic competencies discussed in the early chapters of this book.[59]

An additional illustration of a formative, global instrument is one currently used in the Richmond County (Georgia) Public Schools (see Figure 10.2). This observation instrument is based on generic competencies specified by the state of Georgia.[60] We take a closer look at Georgia's observation system in Chapter 13.

As you examine recent instruments from various school systems, note the tendency to reduce the number of competencies and to make provision for comments. Comprehensive observation instruments of the type shown are widely used by both staff supervisors and line administrators.

SPECIFIC. When it comes to the use of instruments for evaluating specific behaviors, the range of possibilities is both expanded and narrowed. It is expanded because the specific behaviors are so varied; it is narrowed because the number of instruments

STANDARD PROCESS
CONFIDENTIAL GTOI OBSERVATION RECORD: STANDARD FORM
(Refer to back for instructions)

Teacher's Name _____ System _____ School _____

Teacher's System State Code	Teacher's School State Code	Last 4 Digits Teacher SSN	Last 4 Digits Observer SSN	Date			Observation Number	Beginning Time: _____	Total Minutes	Lesson Segment (Circle One)
				MO	DAY	YR		Ending Time: _____		B M E O

Focus of Lesson: _____

_____

MARK SCORES FOR EACH DIMENSION

TEACHING TASK I: PROVIDES INSTRUCTION

Comments: _____

_____

_____

_____

_____

_____

_____

A. Instructional Level   (N) (S)

B. Content Development

   1. Teacher-Focused   (N) (S)

     and/or   and/or

   2. Student-Focused   (N) (S)

C. Building for Transfer   (N) (S) (NA)

TEACHING TASK II: ASSESSES AND ENCOURAGES STUDENT PROGRESS

Comments: _____

_____

_____

_____

_____

_____

A. Promoting Engagement   (N) (S)

B. Monitoring Progress   (N) (S)

C. Responding to Student Performance   (N) (S)

D. Supporting Students   (N) (S)

TEACHING TASK III: MANAGES THE LEARNING ENVIRONMENT

Comments: _____

_____

_____

_____

_____

_____

A. Use of Time   (N) (S)

B. Physical Setting   (N) (S)

C. Appropriate Behavior   (N) (S)

(SIGNATURES)

OBSERVER: _____ DATE _____ POSITION: _____

TEACHER: _____ DATE _____

Sign and return copy to principal's office. Signature acknowledges receipt of form, not necessarily concurrence. Written comments may be provided and/or attached. Initial and date here if comments are attached. _____

Teacher's Comments: _____

_____

Figure 10.2. Observation Record: Standard Form. Richmond County (Georgia) Public Schools. Reprinted with permission.

for evaluating particular behaviors is so small. For some specific behaviors there are no existing instruments, in which case the supervisor will either have to create one or use another means for gathering the data.

The supervisor may be fortunate enough to find a ready-made instrument. The Flanders Interaction Analysis Categories instrument discussed in Chapter 12 is an example of an instrument created to evaluate one specific set of behaviors: verbal interaction.[61] Charles M. Galloway designed a system for evaluating nonverbal behavior, primarily the teacher's.[62] Jacob S. Kounin developed a system for evaluating classroom management and discipline.[63] A search of the literature will reveal a number of instruments that may be useful to the supervisor. As a starting point you may wish to consult the bibliographies at the end of this chapter and Chapter 13 of this text.

If the supervisor is unable to find or create an instrument to evaluate specific behaviors agreed on by the teacher and supervisor, selective verbatim recording or making notes of classroom events may be the solution. If using an instrument, recording selective verbatim responses, or taking notes does not appear feasible, charting specific behaviors may be a way to record observation of certain classroom behaviors. In addressing the practice of coaching (discussed later in this chapter), Karolyn J. Snyder predicted a move from the global to the specific when she commented, "The focus of coaching is likely to shift in the future away from predictable teaching behaviors for all situations, toward situational patterns with variable student populations and contexts."[64]

Techniques Other than Instrumentation. Supervisors may employ techniques other than use of instruments when observing a teacher. They may record events globally through verbatim and selective verbatim techniques. They may collect data on many behaviors by using what Acheson and Gall have labeled a "wide lens" approach: anecdotal records, audiotaping, and videotaping.[65]

Supervisors may record specific behaviors through charting techniques. You have already seen an example of charting earlier in this chapter—Puckett's system for recording pupil participation in a recitation. Starting with a class seating chart and a devised key, the supervisor can record a wide variety of data, determining which pupils are on task and which off task, observing and recording the flow of communication between teacher and pupils and among students, and sketching the movement of the teacher and students about the room.[66]

By the careful use of symbols of his or her own choosing the supervisor can record on a class seating chart a great deal of information about what is taking place. Observation is the stage in clinical supervision during which data are collected. The supervisor must master skills of observing and recording classroom events.

Postobservation Conference

Soon after the observation, the teacher and supervisor meet once again at a mutually satisfactory location for the phase most specialists believe to be the most difficult and most important in the entire cycle: the postobservation or follow-up conference. The major purpose of the postobservation conference is to give feedback to the teacher about the teacher's performance. Certainly, perceptive teachers can think through and make an analysis of their own performance. With a videotape of their performance, teachers should be able to diagnose their teaching almost as well as the supervisor can. But feedback from an interested helper enables teachers to see their performance as others see it.

The discussion at the follow-up conference should focus on the data collected by the supervisor, not on the supervisor's experiences, biases, and feelings. The supervisor must take every precaution to keep the conference from being a threatening situation to the teacher. Therefore, the proper subject of the conference is the teaching observed by the supervisor, not the teacher.

Experts generally agree that a short period of time should elapse before the supervisor and teacher get together to discuss the data. This allows the supervisor time to organize and analyze the data and to prepare for the conference. Thus, at the preobservation conference, the supervisor will have advised the teacher that he or she will need a day or more to transcribe notes; listen to or look at tapes; search for evidence of the behaviors that were to be observed; organize notes in some coherent form; and decide what approach to take in the conference. The supervisor may make some nonjudgmental comments at the end of the observation, assuring the teacher that he or she will be back in touch in a day or two to set a time for the conference. At this point, they might tentatively select the day and time convenient to both.

Madeline Hunter identified six types of supervisory conferences: five instructional (i.e., postobservation) and one evaluative ("the summation of what has occurred in and resulted from a series of instructional conferences").[67] Hunter set forth purposes and objectives for each of the five types of instructional conferences as follows:

1. Type A Instructional Conference—*Purpose*: To identify, label, and explain the teacher's effective instructional behaviors giving research-based reasons for their effectiveness so the teacher knows what he or she has done and why it worked, and in the future can do it on purpose. *Objective*: At the end of the conference (not in some nebulous future) the teacher will identify teaching decisions and behaviors that promoted learning and state why they were effective. . . .
2. Type B Instructional Conference—*Purpose*: To stimulate the development of a repertoire of effective teaching responses so the teacher is not limited to those most frequently used. *Objective*: Teacher and observer will generate alternatives to behaviors which were effective in the observed lesson in case they should be less effective in a different situation. . . .
3. Type C Instructional Conference—*Purpose*: To encourage teachers to identify those parts of a teaching episode with which they were not satisfied so that, in collaboration with the observer, strategies for reducing or eliminating future unsatisfactory outcomes will be developed. *Objective*: The teacher will identify solutions with potential for changing unsatisfying aspects of the lesson. . . .
4. Type D Instructional Conference—*Purpose*: To identify and label those less effective aspects of teaching that were not evident to the teacher and to develop alternative procedures that have potential for effectiveness. *Objective*: The teacher will select alternative behaviors he or she might substitute for behaviors perceived by the observer (and hopefully by the teacher) as not so effective. . . .
5. Type E Instructional Conference—*Purpose*: To promote continuing growth of excellent teachers. *Objective*: The teacher will select next steps in expanding his or her own professional growth.[68]

Participants should not perceive the postobservation conference as an assessment of the teacher's performance comparable to the principal's summative evaluation but rather as an opportunity for the supervisor to provide valuable feedback for the teacher's consideration. To conduct an effective conference, the supervisor must know how to give helpful, and sometimes negative, feedback without injuring the teacher's ego or arousing defensive behaviors. Kyte suggested a three-point outline for the conference that remains good procedure:

1. strong points of the lesson
2. weak points in the lesson
3. doubtful points not clearly understood[69]

Mosher and Purpel recommended that the supervisor avoid making two types of analysis with the teacher: the simple inventory of events and recounting of critical incidents that took place during the observation. Instead they advised that the supervisor help the teacher to discern *"recurring patterns* in content, teaching or student behavior and of their *possible interrelations."*[70]

The supervisor's manner and attitudes are as important as the technical analysis made for the teacher. In Chapter 2 you read of contrasts between directive and nondirective behavior. A nondirective posture can put the teacher at ease. For example, a few processing-type comments at the beginning of the conference can go a long way toward establishing rapport. A question to the teacher such as "How did you feel about the lesson?" can be useful in breaking the ice. Surely, the supervisor should not come to the conference with a rigid analysis on the basis of which he or she proceeds to lecture the teacher. The supervisor needs to avoid sermonizing and conveying a loftier-than-thou superiority. Supervisors should remember that it is far easier to tell a person, especially after the fact, how to do something than to do it themselves.

Supervisors should remember that teachers want specific help, specific suggestions. They want supervisors to talk to specific points that can help them to improve. The supervisor needs to appear friendly and professional, avoiding extended chattiness and effusive behavior.

A nondirective approach that probes for the teacher's feelings and an analysis of his or her own performance is generally appropriate, but directive behavior at times may be necessary. For example, the supervisor may need to focus on a point with an expression such as "Here's the way I see it. I believe it would have been more effective if. . . ." The degree of directiveness and nondirectiveness needs to be tailored to the individual teacher and to the relationship between the teacher and the supervisor. When nondirective measures fail with an uncommunicative and inarticulate teacher, the supervisor may need to resort to more directive means.

Carl D. Glickman has introduced a collaborative orientation between directive and nondirective behavior.[71] Glickman described a supervisory behavior continuum from directive to collaborative to nondirective orientation. For each of these dominant behaviors, Glickman outlined a pattern of specific behaviors.

The supervisor must detect which dominant behavior will be most effective with a particular teacher and adjust his or her style accordingly. Thus, the supervisor's behavior is not a monolithic, unchanging, machinelike process with a single orientation that will be unfailingly successful in all situations; rather, it is a flexible, changing, human process. Much as teachers must take students from where they are, supervisors must adjust their approach to the individual teachers with whom they work.

The postobservation conference has maximum chance for success if both the teacher and supervisor manifest a sense of confidence in their own roles. A successful conference cannot occur without a feeling of rapport, which the supervisor should have established with the teacher long before initiating the cycle of clinical supervision.

PROBLEMS IN CLINICAL SUPERVISION

Clinical supervision is not without its critics, who raise the following questions:

- Who will do the supervising?
- Do we have the necessary resources?
- For whom should clinical supervision be provided?
- Are there other models for assisting teachers that are as effective as or more effective than clinical supervision?

Each of these issues is examined in the next sections.

Who Will Do the Supervising?

Two of the issues explored in Chapter 2 pose the questions of whether the administrator can be the supervisor and whether supervision is evaluation. Much of the literature on instructional supervision, including this textbook, urges consultative, developmental supervision to distance itself as much as possible from administration. Joseph Scime, expressing an opposing view, felt that costs in time, money, and personnel make it impossible to implement clinical supervision models that exclude evaluation.[72] Therefore, both clinical supervision and administrative evaluation, according to Scime, must fall to the building administrator. In studying the relationship of building administrators who perform both clinical and evaluative supervisory tasks, Scime discovered that a majority of the teachers in the study (about 64 percent) believed that the building administrator, through classroom observation, almost always or frequently supported their efforts to improve instruction. On the other hand, Scime found that a majority of the teachers (about 62 percent) perceived that only sometimes or never did clinical supervision given by the building administrator help them improve instruction.[73]

Speaking of the principal serving as instructional leader, Goldhammer, Anderson, and Krajewski noted, "Unfortunately, principals are often as beleaguered and time-pressed as their central office colleagues; and while it is increasingly fashionable to talk about the instructional-leadership role of the principal, often that person is hard pressed to do the job well."[74] It is worth reiterating that in some schools where the principal serves as both administrator and instructional supervisor help in supervising is often available and unused in the form of department heads, grade coordinators, team leaders, and school-based resource people.

Another question, considered in Chapter 2, is raised in reference to supervision in general: Should the clinical supervisor be a generalist or a specialist? Both prevailing practice and present-day preservice and in-service training programs appear to be slanted toward the use of generalists who can appraise generic teaching skills. Much of the literature, including this textbook, aims at the development of skills in supervising across disciplines and levels.

Mosher and Purpel stressed the importance of the supervisor's specialization in the teaching field: "The supervisor is, first, a content specialist, because it is not considered feasible to analyze teaching effectiveness independently of the content of what is being taught. This may appear to labor the obvious. Nonetheless, the question of whether people can supervise across subject-matter areas is very much an issue in supervision."[75]

Given the choice, we would incline toward using the services of instructional supervisors who are trained and experienced in their fields of specialization as well as general methods of instruction. But as Voltaire made us realize, the quest for the best of all possible worlds can be both ludicrous and not very productive. Wealthier school systems can probably afford to deploy a cadre of specialists who are at the same time generalists. The less-well-to-do school districts may have to work with one or more generalists who are not familiar with specialties outside their own field(s) of specialization. In any case, whether a school system uses generalists or specialists as supervisors, effective supervision is still possible in either case with appropriate in-service training.

Colleagueship in Supervision

Dissatisfaction with supervisory help (or the lack of it), an absence of designated supervisors, lack of time for those supervisors who are designated to serve all teachers, and a natural inclination to look to one's immediate colleagues for assistance have resulted in variations on the typical designated supervisor-teacher clinical model. More frequently, teachers are assuming responsibilities for helping each other in the improvement of instruction. Goldhammer, Anderson, and Krajewski espoused the concept of collegiality, stating that "now, more than ever, we stress the dimension of *collegiality*, and urge that CS [clinical supervision] be seen as a tool for use in not only the usual superordinate-subordinate relationship but also peer relationships as well."[76] Three variations of a collegial approach to supervision are *peer supervision*, *coaching*, and *mentoring*.

Peer Supervision. The principle of peer or collegial supervision is introduced when classroom teachers call on their department heads, grade coordinators, team leaders, lead teachers, and other classroom teachers for assistance. That help may be rendered on a casual, informal basis or, increasingly, on a planned, structured basis. The practice of peer supervision is growing even though some educators feel that the concept itself is an anomaly—as the very word *supervision* implies a superordinate-subordinate relationship.

In her study of 240 beginning teachers in Florida and Georgia, Joyce B. Coleman found that peer teachers provided more supervisory assistance to first-year teachers than did administrators or designated supervisors and that beginning teachers valued and preferred supervisory help from peers over administrators or other supervisors.[77] Alfonso and Goldsberry found that "teachers report other colleagues to be their first source of professional help, even when supervisory assistance is available."[78] Glickman et al., observing that "teachers naturally turn to each other for help more often than to a supervisor," concluded, "since supervision is concerned primarily with improving instruction rather than with summative evaluation (renewal of contracts), teachers helping teachers has become a formalized and well-received way of assuring direct assistance to every staff member."[79] Training peers in observation and conferencing techniques as well as providing time for them to carry out their supervisory tasks are essential to an effective, structured program of peer supervision. Where mutual respect and trust exist, peer or collegial supervision can be an effective process.[80]

Coaching. Schools may institute coaching models in which teachers help each other develop new teaching strategies and resolve instructional problems. Goldhammer, Anderson, and Krajewski labeled the period from 1985 to the 1990s as the era of coaching/instructional supervision.[81] Bruce Joyce and Beverly Showers pioneered the application of the sports term *coaching* to the development of classroom instructional strategies.[82] Snyder viewed coaching as "a data-based technique that enables staff members to learn new skills, to modify practices, to solve problems together, and to develop basic skills."[83] As a structured adaptation of collegial supervision, coaching provides a means for teacher teams of two or more to work together and help each other.

Robert J. Garmston described three coaching models: technical, collegial, and challenge.[84] With technical coaching, two teachers or consultants with teachers are paired to practice a specific skill taught in a staff development program. Collegial coaching offers a model in which pairs of teachers observe and critique each other on strategies designated by the teacher to be observed. Conducted in small groups rather than in pairs, challenge grouping begins with identification of an instructional problem and proceeds through group deliberation to attempt to solve the problem. Joyce pointed out in an interview with Ronald S. Brandt that successful coaching requires considerable training of the participants.[85]

Mentoring. As a broad concept, mentoring implies the assistance of a knowledgeable, more experienced person to a less knowledgeable, less experienced person. Thus, we find schools with mentors who work with students and others who work with new teachers. Mentors are often motivated to serve because of their identification as superior or master teachers and by a desire to help newcomers in the profession. Provision of released time and a stipend serve as additional incentives. Mentoring of novice teachers or protégés is now found in many school districts across the country, including school systems in California,[86] Connecticut,[87] Georgia,[88] Kentucky,[89] Minnesota,[90] New York,[91] North Carolina,[92] Pennsylvania,[93] and Texas.[94]

Collegial supervision and its variants, coaching and mentoring, extend supervisory resources by enlisting teachers themselves in the process. Extensions of the more common supervisory-teacher model of clinical supervision may very well result in drastic changes in the role of the supervisor. For example, Garman discussed the formation of an "organic team" of six teaching colleagues who directed their own activities.[95] A supervisor who works with a group of this nature would serve as a facilitator and resource person.

Colleagueship in supervision can supplement or conceivably even replace more customary modes of instructional supervision. Recognizing the need for instructional supervision and the shortage of instructional supervisors, Alfonso and Goldsberry suggested "a new role for supervisors. They might become 'orchestrators' of instructional supervision, persons who serve a broker role in the school system, identifying needs and then selecting and recruiting from throughout the school or school system those persons who can contribute to specific tasks of instructional improvement."[96] These authors recommended that instructional supervisors take on the responsibility for developing colleagueship in supervision.

Teacher colleagues—peer coaches, mentors, master teachers, and lead teachers—often take on responsibilities other than helping teachers on a one-to-one basis. Recognition and incentives are customarily provided for these collegial supervisors in the form of differentiated staffing, career ladder, and merit pay plans, a topic to which we return in Chapter 14.

Do We Have the Necessary Resources?

Time, money, and personnel—all interrelated—pose problems when a school system is deciding whether to launch a program of clinical supervision. We can calculate a large amount of time per teacher if we tally the hours for each phase of clinical supervision. A bare minimum of time to be spent for each teacher is shown here.

Preobservation conference	20 minutes
Observation	30 minutes
Analysis of data	30 minutes
Postobservation conference	30 minutes
	110 minutes

Thus, the supervisor needs at the very least approximately two hours per teacher per cycle of clinical supervision; this figure is somewhat unrealistically on the low side. You can see the enormity of the time problem if you multiply this estimate by the number of times the teacher and supervisor repeat the cycle, allow time for the supervisor to make a record of the preobservation and postobservation conferences, allocate time for typing transcripts or notes of observation, increase the time of observation from thirty minutes to fifty, and set aside time for what Goldhammer called a "postmortem" or "postconference analysis."[97] The time factor is enlarged if arrangements must be made for electronic media; time is doubled if the supervisor is to review an audio- or videotape of the lesson. If teachers are to become an integral part of the supervisory process as in peer supervision, time and money must be found for releasing them from some classroom duties and for their training. Funds must also be provided, as in the case of mentors, for stipends. School system administrators will need to decide how to allocate their dollars for personnel, equipment, and materials between clinical supervision and general supervision, including curriculum and staff development.

For Whom Should Clinical Supervision Be Provided?

Ideally, clinical supervision should be available to all teachers—experienced, inexperienced, effective, ineffective, pedestrian, and talented. Given the paucity of resources and the demands of the job, it is doubtful that an adequate program of clinical supervision can be made available to every teacher. Consequently, those teachers who are having problems are more likely to need and call for assistance of this nature.

Some supervisors feel it best to ignore those teachers who are doing high-quality work. Hunter, however, argued against neglecting excellent teachers. She commented, "We have learned to challenge gifted students to encourage continuing growth, but often our gifted teachers are left to provide their own stimulation or to become bored and atrophied."[98]

If adequate material and human resources are, indeed, available, clinical supervision should be provided for all teachers who wish to secure this type of aid. The instructional supervisor, as contrasted with the administrative supervisor, cannot and should not thrust himself or herself on the teacher. Thus, a number of teachers may opt out of the opportunity to receive help from the supervisory consultant. To some degree, supervisors can judge their own success by the demand of teachers for their services.

If a school system is not able to cater to the supervisory needs of all teachers, it must do what school systems have always done—set priorities and/or put out fires. Those that are most in need must be assured of help if for no other reason than the well-being of their students. A better solution, of course, would be sufficient funding for our schools so that adequate supervision can be made available to all who need and want it.

Are There Models Other Than the Clinical?

Allan A. Glatthorn proposed that supervision be differentiated, that teachers "should have some choice about the kind of supervision they receive."[99] Clinical supervision would be one of the choices available.

> In the differentiated system, teachers can choose, within limits, whether they wish to receive clinical supervision, work with a colleague in a program of cooperative development, direct their own professional growth, or have their teaching monitored by an administrator.[100]

The clinical model calls for diagnosis of teaching behaviors and prescriptions to change. Theresa Reilkoff took note of problems with the clinical supervision model when she said, ". . . principals, researchers, and theoreticians seem to view clinical supervision as it is currently conceived to be of limited practical value in the classroom because of its formalism, its time constraints, its drain on the personal and professional resources of teachers and supervisors, and its paternalism."[101]

To overcome these difficulties she advocated instead what she called "supportive supervision," defined here.

> Supportive supervision is that system in which supervisor and teacher collaborate to assess and maximize student performance. Unlike clinical supervision, which focuses on teaching behavior, supportive supervision focuses on the student. Student attitudes, behaviors, and learning outcomes are analyzed for the purpose of their improvement. At no time during this action-oriented process is the teacher evaluated or negatively criticized.[102]

Yet the clinical model has taken root. It is reinforced by the practice of specifying teacher competencies. It offers a system that has had a lengthy period of development. There is even some degree of evidence that clinical supervision may be helpful, as Reilkoff duly noted:

> Although outcomes of clinical supervision have not as yet been subject to rigorous statistical analysis, emergent work does suggest that the practice of clinical supervision contributes to statistically significant changes in teachers' verbal interactions, teaching strategies, and teaching behavior, at least in carefully controlled laboratory conditions.[103]

Cheryl Granade Sullivan's earlier observation that the research on clinical supervision has not reached a point where we can safely make generalizations about the clinical model to some extent still holds true.[104] Mosher and Purpel took note of some of the difficulties with clinical supervision but saw value in the process:

> Clinical supervision is full of gaps. It is a fact—an extremely sobering one—that we don't know, either theoretically or empirically, who the effective teacher is or what effective teaching is. It is a fact that there is evidence of very low validity and reliability in the analyses, inferences and evaluations supervisors make about teaching behavior. It is a fact that there is no conclusive empirical evidence that clinical supervision changes what teachers do. We do, however, have significant clinical opinion and experience on these questions. A decade of practice, some attempt to conceptualize clinical supervision and considerable experience suggest that this method of instructing teachers does make a difference.[105]

We can argue about process and procedures, but logic supports a one-to-one, face-to-face relationship between a teacher and an able supervisor as an incomparable means of helping the teacher grow. In fact, it is a way of helping both the teacher and supervisor to grow. When personal and professional growth takes place, the entire school system and its clientele benefit. Clinical supervision provides a setting for such growth to occur. We concur with Saundra J. Tracy and Robert H. MacNaughton when they said, "Perhaps the greatest legacy of clinical supervision reflected in current supervisory practice is its emphasis on working directly with teachers to improve instruction."[106]

SUMMARY

Clinical supervision is the provision of supervisory help to the individual teacher. It is formative in nature, designed to assist the teacher to improve instruction. The typical clinical model calls for a one-to-one, face-to-face relationship between the teacher and supervisor. Clinical supervision focuses on the events that take place in the classroom.

Models of clinical supervision posit a cycle that consists of a number of stages or phases. Minimally, a model would encompass three stages: preobservation conference, observation, and postobservation conference.

In the preobservation conference the teacher and supervisor make plans for the supervisor's forthcoming visit to the classroom. They decide on specific behaviors or events to be observed. During the observation, the supervisor looks for evidence of the behaviors or events and makes a record of what occurred.

Two types of observations can be made: global and specific. In the global observation, the supervisor records all teacher behaviors; in the specific observation, he or she notes selected behaviors that have usually been agreed on in advance. Among the means for recording classroom events are (1) electronic media, (2) verbatim and selective verbatim transcripts, (3) note taking, (4) instruments, and (5) charting.

A postobservation conference should take place after the supervisor has had time to analyze and organize the data. Both pre- and postobservation conferences should occur in a mutually acceptable location. In the cycle of clinical supervision the supervisor plays the role of knowledgeable, trained, and experienced peer of the teacher. He or she should demonstrate skill in following nondirective, collaborative, and directive approaches and know when to use each.

Clinical supervision requires the supervisor to possess skills in observing, diagnosing, prescribing, and conferencing. In addition, the supervisor must manifest attitudes of a helping relationship and interest in the teacher.

The aim of clinical supervision is improvement of instruction and thereby improvement in student achievement. It is not designed for evaluating teachers for administrative purposes.

Peer supervision, coaching, and mentoring offer viable models for delivering clinical supervision. The provision of adequate time, personnel, equipment, and materials poses a problem for school systems that want to conduct a program of clinical supervision.

Alternatives to the clinical model have been suggested, such as differentiated and supportive supervision. Although more research is needed, there is some indication that clinical supervision can be effective.

QUESTIONS FOR DISCUSSION

1. What should supervisors look for when observing a teacher?
2. Should supervisors use observation instruments when observing a teacher? If so, what type would you suggest?
3. Under what circumstances would peer supervision be most feasible?
4. When could mentors replace other designated supervisors?
5. Is adequate clinical supervision possible?

ACTIVITIES FOR FURTHER STUDY

1. Describe each of the following.
   a. Clinical supervision
   b. Peer supervision
   c. Developmental supervision
   d. Differentiated supervision
   e. Supportive supervision
2. Prepare a report on one or more of the following models of clinical supervision (see bibliography at end of chapter):
   a. Acheson and Gall
   b. Bellon and Bellon

    c. Cogan

    d. Goldhammer, Anderson, and Krajewski

    e. Mosher and Purpel

3. Prepare a report on Goldhammer's model of clinical supervision (see chapter bibliography).

4. Contrast the first edition of Goldhammer's book with the third edition, revised by Anderson and Krajewski (see chapter bibliography).

5. Report on any existing programs of clinical supervision that you can locate.

6. Role-play a preobservation conference.

7. Observe a class in action and make a written verbatim record of the events for twenty minutes.

8. Observe a class in action and record the events by using selective verbatim recording for thirty minutes.

9. Observe a class in action and record the events by means of notes for thirty minutes.

10. Report on the kinds of data that can be recorded by means of a class seating chart.

11. Using the book by Keith A. Acheson and Meredith Damien Gall as a guide, select a seating chart exercise, try it out on a class, and report on your experience in using the technique (see chapter bibliography).

12. Videotape a class and analyze the tape. If the teacher of the class wishes, conduct a second analysis with him or her.

13. Prepare a review of Elliot W. Eisner's views on artistic supervision (see chapter bibliography).

14. Review the literature on interpretive or hermeneutic and ecological approaches to supervision. Describe their assumptions and recommended practices. See references by Noreen B. Garman and C. A. Bowers and David J. Flinders, for example.

15. Critique Allan A. Glatthorn's proposals for differentiated supervision (see chapter bibliography).

16. Critique Theresa Reilkoff's proposal for supportive supervision (see chapter bibliography).

17. Prepare a report on Carl D. Glickman's descriptions of nondirective, collaborative, and directive supervisory behaviors (see chapter bibliography).

18. Report on recommendations for observing made by writers on the subject prior to 1950.

19. Collect and analyze samples of classroom observation instruments.

20. Respond to this question: Under what conditions should clinical supervisors conduct global assessments of the teacher's performance?

21. Defend or challenge the concept of peer supervision, stating reasons.

22. Locate, in the literature or in practice, models of clinical supervision that are not on a one-teacher-to-one-supervisor basis. Discuss the pros and cons of group models.

23. Select one of the following specific behaviors and choose or create an instrument by which you would assess it. If you use an existing instrument, cite the specific instrument and source:

    a. Verbal interaction

    b. Nonverbal behavior

    c. Providing feedback to the students

    d. Stimulus variation

    e. Individualization of instruction

24. Design, conduct, and report on a simple study to determine the following:
    a. Whether principals feel they can be effective as instructional supervisors
    b. Whether teachers feel the principal can be effective as an instructional supervisor

25. Design, conduct, and report on a simple study to determine the following:
    a. Whether supervisors feel they can assist teachers effectively in a field of specialization for which they have not been trained
    b. Whether teachers feel supervisors can assist them effectively in a field of specialization for which the supervisors have not been trained.

26. Design your own classroom observation instrument for global evaluation of teacher performance.

27. Apply the observation instruments you created for activities 23 and 26 in a live situation or with a videotape of an actual classroom situation and interpret the data.

28. Select or create and apply in a live situation an observation instrument designed to assess overall performance of a teacher on specific rather than generic teaching skills in a particular subject area, such as the evaluation of teaching third-grade reading, the teaching of sixth-grade science, the teaching of beginning algebra, and the teaching of tenth-grade physical education.

29. Prepare a report on any programs of peer supervision, coaching, or mentoring found in the literature or in a school with which you are personally familiar.

30. Critique the article by Thomas J. Sergiovanni (see chapter bibliography) in which he distinguishes science from scientism.

31. Describe basic tenets of the following approaches to supervision and identify one or more advocates of each approach:
    a. scientific
    b. artistic
    c. human relations
    d. human resources
    e. interpretive (hermeneutic)
    f. ecological

32. Describe the three models of assisting and assessing educational personnel discussed by Saundra J. Tracy and Robert H. MacNaughton (see chapter bibliography):
    a. means-oriented model
    b. ends-oriented model
    c. teacher concern-oriented model

NOTES

1. Morris L. Cogan, *Clinical Supervision* (Boston: Houghton Mifflin, 1973), p. 8.
2. Ibid., p. 9.
3. Ibid.
4. Robert Goldhammer, Robert H. Anderson, and Robert J. Krajewski, *Clinical Supervision: Special Methods for the Supervision of Teachers*, 3rd ed. (Orlando, Fla.: Harcourt Brace Jovanovich, 1993), p. 34.
5. Ibid., pp. 52–53.
6. Robert Goldhammer, *Clinical Supervision: Special Methods for the Supervision of Teachers* (New York: Holt, Rinehart and Winston, 1969), p. 54.

7. Ibid.

8. Barbara Nelson Pavan, "Clinical Supervision: Some Signs of Progress," *Texas Tech Journal of Education* 7 (Fall 1980): 241, 250.

9. Keith A. Acheson and Meredith Damien Gall, *Techniques in the Clinical Supervision of Teachers: Preservice and Inservice Applications*, 2nd ed. (White Plains, N.Y.: Longman, 1987), p. 18.

10. Ibid.

11. Ibid., p. 11.

12. Ralph L. Mosher and David E. Purpel, *Supervision: The Reluctant Profession* (Boston: Houghton Mifflin, 1972), p. 84.

13. Ibid., pp. 110–11.

14. Noreen Garman, "The Clinical Approach to Supervision," in *Supervision of Teaching*, 1982 Yearbook, ed. Thomas J. Sergiovanni (Alexandria, Va.: Association for Supervision and Curriculum Development, 1982), pp. 35–52.

15. Ibid., p. 38.

16. Ibid., p. 52.

17. Ibid.

18. Robert J. Alfonso and Lee Goldsberry, "Colleagueship in Supervision," in *Supervision of Teaching*, p. 94.

19. Robert J. Alfonso, Gerald R. Firth, and Richard F. Neville, *Instructional Supervision: A Behavior System*, 2nd ed. (Boston: Allyn & Bacon, 1981), p. 121.

20. Ibid.

21. Garman, "Clinical Approach to Supervision," p. 42.

22. Daniel Tanner and Laurel Tanner, *Supervision in Education: Problems and Practices* (New York: Macmillan, 1987), p. 183.

23. George C. Kyte, *How to Supervise: A Guide to Educational Principles and Progressive Practices of Educational Supervision* (Boston: Houghton Mifflin, 1930), p. 138.

24. Ibid., p. 171.

25. Ibid., p. 142.

26. Ibid., p. 147.

27. Ibid., pp. 149–50.

28. Ibid., p. 150.

29. Ibid., pp. 156–57.

30. Ibid., p. 160.

31. Ibid., p. 139.

32. Ibid., p. 158.

33. Cogan, *Clinical Supervision*, p. 10.

34. Goldhammer, *Clinical Supervision*, pp. 56–72; Goldhammer, Anderson, and Krajewski, *Clinical Supervision*, Chapter 3.

35. Mosher and Purpel, *Supervision*, p. 81.

36. Cogan, *Clinical Supervision*, pp. 10–13.

37. Acheson and Gall, *Techniques in Clinical Supervision*, pp. 10–15.

38. Jerry J. Bellon and Elner C. Bellon, *Classroom Supervision and Instructional Improvement: A Synergetic Process*, 2nd ed. (Dubuque, Iowa: Kendall/Hunt Publishing Company, 1982), chaps. 4, 5, and 6.

39. Goldhammer, *Clinical Supervision*, p. 89.

40. Acheson and Gall, *Techniques in Clinical Supervision*, p. 72.

41. See Madeline Hunter, "Let's Eliminate the Preobservation Conference," *Educational Leadership* 43, no. 6 (March 1986): 69–70.

42. Garman, "The Clinical Approach to Supervision," pp. 50–52. See also Noreen B. Garman,

"Theories Embedded in the Events of Clinical Supervision," *Journal of Curriculum and Supervision* 5 (Spring 1990): 209–10.

43. Elliot W. Eisner, "An Artistic Approach to Supervision," in *Supervision of Teaching*, 1982 Yearbook, ed. Thomas J. Sergiovanni (Alexandria, Va.: Association for Supervision and Curriculum Development, 1982), pp. 55–57.

44. Ibid., p. 59.

45. Ibid., p. 60.

46. Ibid., pp. 60–61.

47. Ibid., p. 62.

48. See, for example, Garman, "Theories Embedded."

49. Ibid., p. 211.

50. C. A. Bowers and David J. Flinders, *Culturally Responsive Teaching and Supervision: A Handbook for Staff Development* (New York: Teachers College Press, 1991), p. 5.

51. Ibid., pp. 30–51.

52. Goldhammer, *Clinical Supervision*, pp. 88–89.

53. Acheson and Gall, *Techniques in Clinical Supervision*, p. 120.

54. Ibid., pp. 119–20.

55. Ibid., p. 121.

56. Ibid., p. 81.

57. Karolyn J. Snyder, *ACT: Administrator-for-Change Training, Module Six* (Lubbock, Tex.: Pedamorphosis, 1978). Pedamorphosis, Inc., is located in Tampa, Florida (P.O. Box 271699, ZIP 33688-1669).

58. Mosher and Purpel, *Supervision*, pp. 92–95.

59. This checklist has been used in a form slightly modified at the suggestion of Dr. Sarah W. J. Pell of Florida International University. The modified form omits the sections on selection of resources and selection of strategies; provides a space for comments to the right of the Yes and No columns; and adds at the bottom places for data on duration of time in minutes, names of teacher and school, grade, and date.

60. The Georgia instruments for on-the-job assessment of beginning teachers known as the Teacher Performance Assessment Instruments in use from 1979 to 1984 specified fourteen generic competencies. A revision in 1984 reduced the number to eight. These instruments have also been employed in school systems outside Georgia. In 1990 the state of Georgia stopped using these instruments.

61. Ned A. Flanders, *Analyzing Teacher Behavior* (Reading, Mass.: Addison-Wesley, 1970).

62. Charles M. Galloway, "An Exploratory Study of Observational Procedures for Determining Teacher Nonverbal Communication," doctoral dissertation, University of Florida, 1962. *Dissertation Abstracts International*, 1962, p. 2310.

63. Jacob S. Kounin, *Discipline and Group Management in Classrooms* (New York: Holt, Rinehart and Winston, 1970).

64. Karolyn J. Snyder, "School Transformation: The Context for Professional Coaching and Problem Solving," in *Clinical Supervision: Coaching for Higher Performance*, ed. Robert H. Anderson and Karolyn J. Snyder (Lancaster, Pa.: Technomic, 1993), p. 33.

65. Acheson and Gall, *Techniques in Clinical Supervision*, chap. 8.

66. See ibid., chap. 7, for helpful discussion of techniques of this type.

67. Madeline Hunter, "Six Types of Supervisory Conferences," *Educational Leadership* 37 (February 1980): 412.

68. Ibid., pp. 409–12.

69. Kyte, *How to Supervise*, pp. 187–88.

70. Mosher and Purpel, *Supervision*, pp. 97–98.

71. See Carl D. Glickman, *Developmental Supervision: Alternative Practices for Helping Teachers Improve Instruction* (Alexandria, Va.: Association for Supervision and Curriculum Developrnent, 1981), pp. 17–37. See also Carl D. Glickman, Stephen P. Gordon, and Jovita M. Ross-Gordon, *Supervision of Instruction: A Developmental Approach*, 3rd ed. (Boston, Allyn & Bacon, 1995), Part III.

72. Joseph Scime, "The Conflict between Evaluation and Supervision: A Study of a Clinical Supervision Program Designed to Link Instruction, Supervision, and Evaluation to Staff Development," doctoral dissertation, George Peabody College for Teachers, Vanderbilt University, 1984.

73. Ibid., pp. 64, 104, 126.

74. Goldhammer, Anderson, and Krajewski, *Clinical Supervision*, p. 33.

75. Mosher and Purpel, *Supervision*, p. 83.

76. Goldhammer, Anderson, and Krajewski, *Clinical Supervision*, p. 34.

77. Joyce Bowman Coleman, "The Perceived Quantities and Qualities of Supervisory Assistance Provided to Beginning Teachers in Florida and Georgia," doctoral dissertation, Athens, University of Georgia, 1986.

78. Alfonso and Goldsberry, "Colleagueship in Supervision," p. 91.

79. Glickman, Gordon, and Ross-Gordon, *Supervision of Instruction*, p. 293.

80. Richard D. Hawthorne distinguished between a peer model and a collegial model. With a peer model, according to Hawthorne, one teacher evaluates another whereas with a collegial model, a small group of teachers evaluates another teacher. See Richard D. Hawthorne, "Teacher Evaluation," in *Supervision: School Leadership Handbook*, ed. Lloyd W. Dull (Columbus, Ohio: Merrill, 1981), p. 270.

81. Goldhammer, Anderson, and Krajewski, *Clinical Supervision*, p. 23.

82. See Bruce Joyce and Beverly Showers, "The Coaching of Teaching," *Educational Leadership* 40 (October 1982): 4–10.

83. Snyder, "Schooling Transformation," p. 32.

84. Robert J. Garmston, "How Administrators Support Peer Coaching," *Educational Leadership* 44 (February 1987): 18–26.

85. Ronald S. Brandt, "On Teachers Coaching Teachers: A Conversation with Bruce Joyce," *Educational Leadership* 44 (February 1987): 13.

86. See Laura A. Wagner, "Ambiguities and Possibilities in California's Mentor Teacher Program," *Educational Leadership* 43 (November 1985): 23–29. See also Judith Warren Little and Linda Nelson, eds., *Mentor Teacher: A Leader's Guide to Mentor Training* (San Francisco, Calif.: Far West Laboratory for Educational Research and Development, 1990), ERIC Document ED 328 940 EA 021 515.

87. Joseph J. Caruso, "Supervisory Roles and Responsibilities of Principals to Teacher Leaders and Novice Teachers in Four Connecticut Schools: A Close-Up Look," paper presented at the annual meeting of the American Educational Research Association, Boston, 1990. ERIC Document ED 321 389 EA 022 041.

88. Theresa M. Bey and Anne Hightower, *Teacher Education and Mentoring Program: Program Design and Research Results* (Athens: University of Georgia, 1990), ERIC Document ED 328 540 SP 032 888.

89. Chuck Hulick and Bobby G. Malone, "The Kentucky Beginning Teacher Internship Program: A Preliminary Evaluation," paper presented at the annual conference of the National Council on Inservice Education, New Orleans, 1988, ERIC Document ED 313 327 SP 031 613.

90. Minnesota State Department of Education, *Mentoring Is Networking: A Guide to Program Planning* (St. Paul, Minn.: Instructional Design Section, Minnesota State Department of Education, 1989), ERIC Document ED 327 503 SP 032 812.

91. Gerald M. Mager et al. *A Follow-Up on the Experiences of Intern Teachers: A Report to the State Education Department on the New York State Mentor Teacher-Internship Program for 1986–87 and 1987–88* (Syracuse, N.Y.: Syracuse University, 1990), ERIC Document ED 328 528 SP 032 840.

92. Alan J. Reiman and Roy A. Edelfelt, *School-Based Mentoring Programs: Untangling the Tensions between Theory and Practice* (Raleigh: Department of Curriculum and Instruction, North Carolina State University, 1990), ERIC Document ED 329 520 SP 032 904.

93. Charles R. Duke and Robin Gates, *The Status of Teacher Induction Programs in Rural Pennsylvania School Districts* (Harrisburg: Pennsylvania Academy for the Profession of Teaching, 1990), ERIC Document ED 329 414 RC 018 030.

94. Teddy A. McDavid, "Supporting First-Year Teachers with Professional Development Specialists," *Teacher Education and Practice* 6, no. 2 (Fall–Winter, 1990–1991): 83–85.

95. Garman, "Clinical Approach to Supervision," pp. 48–49.

96. Alfonso and Goldsberry, "Colleagueship in Supervision," p. 107.

97. Goldhammer, *Clinical Supervision*, p. 273.

98. Hunter, "Supervisory Conference," p. 412.

99. Allan A. Glatthorn, *Differentiated Supervision* (Alexandria, Va.: Association for Supervision and Curriculum Development, 1984), p. 1.

100. Ibid.

101. Theresa Reilkoff, "Advantages of Supportive Supervision over Clinical Supervision of Teachers," *NASSP Bulletin* 65 (November 1981): 30.

102. Ibid., p. 31.

103. Ibid., p. 29.

104. Cheryl Granade Sullivan, *Clinical Supervision: A State of the Art Review* (Alexandria, Va.: Association for Supervision and Curriculum Development, 1980), pp. 22–23.

105. Mosher and Purpel, *Supervision*, p. 111.

106. Saundra J. Tracy and Robert H. MacNaughton, *Assisting and Assessing Educational Personnel: The Impact of Clinical Supervision* (Boston: Allyn & Bacon, 1993), p. 323.

BIBLIOGRAPHY

Acheson, Keith A., and Meredith Damien Gall. *Techniques in the Clinical Supervision of Teachers: Preservice and Inservice Applications,* 2nd ed. White Plains, N.Y.: Longman, 1987.

Alfonso, Robert J. "Will Peer Supervision Work?" *Educational Leadership* 34 (May 1977): 594–601.

Alfonso, Robert J., Gerald R. Firth, and Richard F. Neville. *Instructional Supervision: A Behavior System,* 2nd ed. Boston: Allyn & Bacon, 1981.

Alfonso, Robert J., and Lee Goldsberry. "Colleagueship in Supervision." In *Supervision of Teaching.* 1982 Yearbook, ed. Thomas J. Sergiovanni. Alexandria, Va.: Association for Supervision and Curriculum Development, 1982.

Anderson, Robert H., and Karolyn J. Snyder, eds. *Clinical Supervision: Coaching for Higher Performance.* Lancaster, Pa.: Technomic, 1993.

Barber, Larry W. *Improving Teacher Performance: Formative Evaluation.* Bloomington, Ind.: Phi Delta Kappa, 1985.

Beach, Don M., and Judy Reinhartz. *Supervision: A Focus on Instruction.* New York: Harper & Row, 1989.

Beegle, Charles W., and Richard M. Brandt, eds. *Observational Methods in the Classroom.* Alexandria, Va.: Association for Supervision and Curriculum Development, 1973.

Bellon, Jerry J., and Elner C. Bellon. *Classroom Supervision and Instructional Improvement: A Synergetic Process*, 2nd ed. Dubuque, Iowa: Kendall/Hunt Publishing Company, 1982.

Berry, Barnett, and Rick Ginsberg. "Creating Lead Teachers: From Policy to Implementation." *Phi Delta Kappan* 71 (April 1990): 616–21.

Bey, Theresa M., and Anne Hightower. *Teacher Education and Mentoring Program: Program Design and Research Results*. Athens: University of Georgia, 1990. ERIC Document ED 328 540 SP 032 888.

Bey, Theresa M., and C. Thomas Holmes, eds. *Mentoring, Developing Successful New Teachers*. Reston, Va.: Association of Teacher Educators, 1990. ERIC Document ED 322 118 SP 032 484.

Borich, Gary D. *Observation Skills for Effective Teaching*. Columbus, Ohio: Merrill, 1990.

Bowers, C. A., and David J. Flinders. *Culturally Responsive Teaching and Supervision: A Handbook for Staff Development*. New York: Teachers College Press, 1991.

———. *Responsive Teaching: An Ecological Approach to Classroom Patterns of Language, Culture, and Thought*. New York: Teachers College Press, 1990.

Brandt, Ronald S. "On Teachers Coaching Teachers: A Conversation with Bruce Joyce." *Educational Leadership* 44 (February 1987): 12–17.

Caruso, Joseph J. "Supervisory Roles and Responsibilities of Principals to Teacher Leaders and Novice Teachers in Four Connecticut Schools: A Close-Up Look." Paper presented at the annual meeting of the American Educational Research Association, Boston, 1990. ERIC Document ED 321 389 EA 022 041.

Champagne, David W., and R. Craig Hogen. *Consultant Supervision: Theory and Skill Development*. Wheaton, Ill.: CH Publications, 1981.

"The Coaching of Teaching." *Educational Leadership* 40 (October 1982): 3–59.

Cogan, Morris L. *Clinical Supervision*. Boston: Houghton Mifflin, 1973.

———. "Rationale for Clinical Supervision." *Journal of Research and Development in Education* 9 (Winter 1976): 3–19.

Coleman, Joyce Bowman. "The Perceived Quantities and Qualities of Supervisory Assistance Provided to Beginning Teachers in Florida and Georgia." Doctoral dissertation, Athens, University of Georgia, 1986.

Cooper, James M., ed. *Developing Skills for Instructional Supervision*. White Plains, N.Y.: Longman, 1984.

Costa, Arthur J., and Robert J. Garmston. *Cognitive Coaching: A Foundation for Renaissance Schools*. Norwood, Mass.: Christopher Gordon Publishers, 1994.

Cox, Diane. "Mentor Teachers: An Important School Reform Component." *Thrust for Educational Leadership* 19 (November/December 1989): 56–58.

Daresh, John C., and Marsha A. Playko. *Supervision as a Proactive Process*, 2nd ed. Prospect Heights, Ill.: Waveland Press, 1995.

Doll, Ronald C. *Supervision for Staff Development: Ideas and Application*. Boston: Allyn & Bacon, 1983.

Duke, Daniel L., and Richard J. Stiggins. *Teacher Evaluation: Five Keys to Growth*. Washington, D.C.: National Education Association, 1986.

Dukes, Charles R., and Robin Gates. *The Status of Teacher Induction Programs in Rural Pennsylvania School Districts*. Harrisburg: Pennsylvania Academy for the Profession of Teaching, 1990. ERIC Document ED 329 414 RC 018 030.

Dull, Lloyd W. *Supervision: School Leadership Handbook*. Columbus, Ohio: Merrill, 1981.

Eisner, Elliot W. "An Artistic Approach to Supervision." In *Supervision of Teaching*. 1982 Yearbook, ed. Thomas J. Sergiovanni. Alexandria, Va.: Association for Supervision and Curriculum Development, 1982.

Flanders, Ned. A. *Analyzing Teacher Behavior*. Reading, Mass.: Addison-Wesley, 1970.

———. "Interaction Analysis and Clinical Supervision." *Journal of Research and Development in Education* 9 (Winter 1976): 47–57.

Flinders, David J. "Supervision as Cultural Inquiry." *Journal of Curriculum and Supervision* 6 (Winter 1991): 87–106.

Galloway, Charles M. "An Exploratory Study of Observational Procedures for Determining Teacher Nonverbal Communication." Doctoral dissertation, University of Florida, 1962. *Dissertation Abstracts International*, 1962, p. 2310.

———. *Silent Language in the Classroom.* Bloomington, Ind.: Phi Delta Kappa Educational Foundation, 1976.

Garman, Noreen B. "The Clinical Approach to Supervision." In *Supervision of Teaching.* 1982 Yearbook, ed. Thomas J. Sergiovanni. Alexandria, Va.: Association for Supervision and Curriculum Development, 1982.

———. "Clinical Supervision: Quackery or Remedy for Professional Development?" *Journal of Curriculum and Supervision* 1 (Winter 1986): 148–57.

———. "Theories Embedded in the Events of Clinical Supervision: A Hermeneutic Approach." *Journal of Curriculum and Supervision* 5 (Spring 1990): 201–13.

Garman, Noreen B., Carl D. Glickman, Madeline Hunter, and Nelson L. Haggerson. "Conflicting Conceptions of Clinical Supervision and the Enhancement of Professional Growth and Renewal: Point and Counterpoint." *Journal of Curriculum and Supervision* 2 (Winter 1987): 152–77.

Garmston, Robert J. "How Administrators Support Peer Coaching." *Educational Leadership* 44 (February 1987): 18–26.

Glatthorn, Allan A. *Differentiated Supervision.* Alexandria, Va.: Association for Supervision and Curriculum Development, 1984.

———. *Supervisory Leadership: Introduction to Instructional Supervision.* Glenview, Ill.: Scott, Foresman/Little, Brown, 1990.

Glickman, Carl D. *Developmental Supervision: Alternative Practices for Helping Teachers Improve Instruction.* Alexandria, Va.: Association for Supervision and Curriculum Development, 1981.

———, ed. *Supervision in Transition.* 1992 Yearbook. Alexandria, Va.: Association for Supervision and Curriculum Development, 1992.

Glickman, Carl D., Stephen P. Gordon, and Jovita M. Ross-Gordon. *Supervision of Instruction: A Developmental Approach*, 3rd ed. Boston: Allyn & Bacon, 1995.

Goldhammer, Robert. *Clinical Supervision: Special Methods for the Supervision of Teachers.* New York: Holt, Rinehart and Winston, 1969.

Goldhammer, Robert, Robert H. Anderson, and Robert J. Krajewski. *Clinical Supervision: Special Methods for the Supervision of Teachers*, 3rd ed. Orlando, Fla.: Harcourt Brace Jovanovich, 1993.

Gottesman, Barbara L., and James O. Jennings. *Peer Coaching for Educators.* Lancaster, Penn.: Technomic, 1994.

Gray, William A., and Marilynee M. Gray. "Synthesis of Research on Mentoring Beginning Teachers." *Educational Leadership* 43 (November 1985): 37–45.

Harris, Ben M. *Developmental Teacher Evaluation.* Boston: Allyn & Bacon, 1986.

———. *In-Service Education for Staff Development.* Boston: Allyn & Bacon, 1989.

———. "Limits and Supplements to Formal Clinical Procedures." *Journal of Research and Development in Education* 9 (Winter 1976): 3–19.

Hawthorne, Richard D. "Teacher Evaluation." In *Supervision: School Leadership Handbook*, ed. Lloyd W. Dull. Columbus, Ohio: Merrill, 1981.

Hills, Jean. "Issues in Research on Instructional Supervision: A Contribution to the Discussion." *Journal of Curriculum and Supervision* 7 (Fall 1991): 1–12.

Holland, Patricia E. "Implicit Assumptions about the Supervisory Conference: A Review and Analysis of Literature." *Journal of Curriculum and Supervision* 4 (Summer 1989): 362–79.

————. "Keeping Faith with Cogan: Current Theorizing in a Maturing Practice of Clinical Supervision." *Journal of Curriculum and Supervision* 3 (Winter 1988): 97–108.

Hosford, Philip, and John Neuenfeldt. "Teacher Evaluation via Videotape: Hope or Heresy?" *Educational Leadership* 36 (March 1979): 418–22.

Hulick, Chuck, and Bobby G. Malone. "The Kentucky Beginning Teacher Internship Program: A Preliminary Evaluation." Paper presented at the annual conference of the National Council on Inservice Education, New Orleans, 1988. ERIC Document ED 313 327 SP 031 613.

Hunter, Madeline. "Let's Eliminate the Preobservation Conference." *Educational Leadership* 43 (March 1986): 69–70.

————. "Six Types of Supervisory Conferences." *Educational Leadership* 37 (February 1980): 408–12.

Hyman, Ronald T. "Peer Coaching: Premises, Problems, Potential." *The Education Digest* 56 (September 1990): 52–56.

————. *School Administrator's Faculty Supervision Handbook.* Englewood Cliffs, N.J.: Prentice-Hall, 1986.

Joyce, Bruce, and Beverly Showers. "The Coaching of Teaching." *Educational Leadership* 44 (October 1982): 4–10.

Kindsvatter, Richard, and William W. Wilen. "A Systematic Approach to Improving Conference Skills." *Educational Leadership* 38 (April 1981): 525–29.

Knoll, Marcia Kalb. *Supervision for Better Instruction: Practical Techniques for Improving Staff Performance.* Englewood Cliffs, N.J.: Prentice-Hall, 1987.

Kounin, Jacob S. *Discipline and Group Management in Classrooms.* New York: Holt, Rinehart and Winston, 1970.

Krajewski, Robert J. "Clinical Supervision to Facilitate Teacher Self-Improvement." *Journal of Research and Development in Education* 9 (Winter 1976): 58–66.

Krey, Robert D., Lanore A. Netzer, and Glen G. Eye. "Assumptions Supporting Structure in Clinical Supervision." *Contemporary Education* 49 (Fall 1977): 16–23.

Kyte, George C. *How to Supervise: A Guide to Educational Principles and Progressive Practices of Educational Supervision.* Boston: Houghton Mifflin, 1930.

Lerch, Robert D. "The Clinical Model: The Optimum Approach to Supervision." *The Clearing House* 53 (January 1980): 238–40.

Little, Judith Warren, and Linda Nelson, eds. *Mentor Teacher: A Leader's Guide to Mentor Training.* San Francisco, Calif.: Far West Laboratory for Educational Research and Development, 1990. ERIC Document ED 328 940 EA 021 515.

Lovell, John T., and Kimball Wiles. *Supervision for Better Schools*, 5th ed. Englewood Cliffs, N.J.: Prentice-Hall, 1983.

Mager, Gerald M., et al. *A Follow-Up on the Experiences of Intern Teachers: A Report to the State Education Department on the New York State Mentor Teacher-Internship Program for 1986–87 and 1987–88.* Syracuse, N.Y.: Syracuse University, 1990. ERIC Document ED 328 528 SP 032 840.

McDavid, Teddy A. "Supporting First-Year Teachers with Professional Development Specialists." *Teacher Education and Practice* 6, no. 2 (Fall–Winter, 1990–1991): 83–85.

McGreal, Thomas L. *Successful Teacher Evaluation.* Alexandria, Va.: Association for Supervision and Curriculum Development, 1983.

McLeary, Lloyd E. "Competencies in Clinical Supervision." *Journal of Research and Development in Education* 9 (Winter 1976): 30–35.

McNeil, John D. "A Scientific Approach to Supervision." In *Supervision of Teaching.* 1982 Yearbook, ed. Thomas J. Sergiovanni. Alexandria, Va.: Association for Supervision and Curriculum Development, 1982.

McNergney, Robert F., and Carol A. Carrier. *Teacher Development.* New York: Macmillan, 1981.

Marks, James R., Emery Stoops, and Joyce King-Stoops. *Handbook of Educational Supervision,* 2nd ed. Boston: Allyn & Bacon, 1978.

Mattaliano, Anthony. "Clinical Supervision: The Key Competencies Required for Effective Practice." Doctoral dissertation, Amherst, University of Massachusetts, 1977.

Maxwell, C. R. *The Observation of Teaching.* Boston: Houghton Mifflin, 1917.

Medley, Donald M., Homer Coker, and Robert S. Soar. *Measurement-Based Evaluation of Teacher Performance: An Empirical Approach.* White Plains, N.Y.: Longman, 1984.

Minnesota State Department of Education. *Mentoring Is Networking: A Guide to Program Planning.* St. Paul, Minn.: Instructional Design Section, Minnesota State Department of Education, 1989. ERIC Document ED 327 503 SP 032 812.

Mosher, Ralph L., and David E. Purpel. *Supervision: The Reluctant Profession.* Boston: Houghton Mifflin, 1972.

Odell, Sandra J. *Mentor Teacher Programs.* Washington, D.C.: National Education Association, 1990.

Olsen, Karen D. *The Mentor Teacher Role: Owner's Manual,* 5th ed. Oak Creek, Ariz.: Books for Educators, 1989. ERIC Document ED 319 722 SP 032 356.

Pavan, Barbara Nelson. "Clinical Supervision: Some Signs of Progress." *Texas Tech Journal of Education* 7 (Fall 1980): 241–51.

Playko, Marsha. "What It Means to Be Mentored." *NASSP Bulletin* 74 (May 1990): 29–32.

Quisenberry, Nancy L., et al. *Teacher Induction: An Annotated Bibliography, 1985–1989.* ERIC Document ED 317 517 SP 032 129.

Reavis, Charles A. *Teacher Improvement through Clinical Supervision.* Bloomington, Ind.: Phi Delta Kappa Educational Foundation, 1978.

Reilkoff, Theresa. "Advantages of Supportive Supervision over Clinical Supervision of Teachers." *NASSP Bulletin* 65 (November 1981): 28–34.

Reiman, Alan J., and Roy A. Edelfelt. *School-Based Mentoring Programs: Untangling the Tensions between Theory and Practice.* Raleigh: Department of Curriculum and Instruction, North Carolina State University, 1990. ERIC Document ED 329 520 SP 032 904.

Scime, Joseph. "The Conflict between Evaluation and Supervision: A Study of a Clinical Supervision Program Designed to Link Instruction, Supervision, and Evaluation to Staff Development." Doctoral dissertation, George Peabody College for Teachers, Vanderbilt University, 1984.

Sergiovanni, Thomas J. "The Metaphorical Use of Theory and Models in Supervision." *Journal of Curriculum and Supervision* 2 (Spring 1987): 221–32.

———. "Science and Scientism in Supervision and Teaching." *Journal of Curriculum and Supervision* 4 (Winter 1989): 93–105.

———. "Toward a Theory of Clinical Supervision." *Journal of Research and Development in Education* 9 (Winter 1976): 3–19.

———, ed. *Supervision of Teaching.* 1982 Yearbook. Alexandria, Va.: Association for Supervision and Curriculum Development, 1982.

Shalaway, Linda. "Sharpening Supervision Skills." *Educational Leadership* 38 (April 1981).

———. "Studying Mentor Teaching." *Instructor* 100 (October 1990): 92.

Showers, Beverly. "Teachers Coaching Teachers." *Educational Leadership* 42 (April 1985): 43–48.

Smyth, John. "A 'Critical' Perspective for Clinical Supervision." *Journal of Curriculum and Supervision* 3 (Winter 1988): 136–56.

———. "Instructional Supervision and the Redefinition of Who Does It in Schools." *Journal of Curriculum and Supervision* 7 (Fall 1991): 90–99.

———. "Teachers as Collaborative Learners in Clinical Supervision: A State of the Art Review." *Journal of Education for Teaching* 10 (1984): 24–28.

————, ed. *Learning about Teaching through Clinical Supervision*. London: Croom Helm, 1986.

Snyder, Karolyn J. *ACT: Administrator-for-Change Training, Module Six*. Lubbock, Tex.: Pedamorphosis, 1978.

————. "School Transformation: The Context for Professional Coaching and Problem Solving." In *Clinical Supervision: Coaching for Higher Performance*, ed. Robert H. Anderson and Karolyn J. Snyder. Lancaster, Pa.: Technomic, 1993.

"Staff Development through Coaching." *Educational Leadership* 44 (February 1987): 3–36.

Stallings, Jane. *Learning to Look*. Berkeley, Calif.: Wadsworth, 1977.

Strother, Deborah Burnett. "Peer Coaching for Teachers: Opening Classroom Doors." *Phi Delta Kappan* 70 (June 1989): 824–27.

Sullivan, Cheryl Granade. *Clinical Supervision: A State of the Art Review*. Alexandria, Va.: Association for Supervision and Curriculum Development, 1980.

Tanner, Daniel, and Laurel Tanner. *Supervision in Education: Problems and Practices*. New York: Macmillan, 1987.

Tennessee Education Association. *Bridges to Strength: Establishing a Mentoring Program for Beginning Teachers: An Administrator's Guide*. Charleston, W.Va.: Appalachia Educational Laboratory, 1988.

Tracy, Saundra J., and Robert H. MacNaughton. *Assisting and Assessing Educational Personnel: The Impact of Clinical Supervision*. Boston: Allyn & Bacon, 1993.

U.S. Department of Education. *One on One: A Guide for Establishing Mentor Programs*. Washington, D.C.: U.S. Department of Education, 1990.

Wagner, Laura A. "Ambiguities and Possibilities in California's Mentor Teacher Program." *Educational Leadership* 43 (November 1985): 23–29.

Wingspan: The Pedamorphosis Communique 1 (1981): issue on clinical supervision; 3 (December 1986): issue on the future preparation of supervisors.

Zumwalt, Karen K., ed. *Improving Teaching*. 1986 Yearbook. Alexandria, Va.: Association for Supervision and Curriculum Development, 1986.

Audiotapes

Carl D. Glickman. *Developmental Supervision: Alternative Approaches for Helping Teachers*. 90 min. Alexandria, Va.: Association for Supervision and Curriculum Development, 1981.

Madeline Hunter. *Improving the Quality of Instruction through Professional Development*. 50 min. Alexandria, Va.: Association for Supervision and Curriculum Development, 1977.

————. *Supervisory Conferences with Teachers*. 55 min. Alexandria, Va.: Association for Supervision and Curriculum Development, 1980.

New Directions in Teacher Supervision and Evaluation. Four 60-min. tapes. Presenters: Tom McGreal, Rosemary Tripi Wong, Harry Wong, Pam Robbins, and Judy-Arin Krupp. Alexandria, Va.: Association for Supervision and Curriculm Development, 1992.

Alan E. Simon. *Peer Supervision: An Alternative*. 40 min. Alexandria, Va.: Association for Supervision and Curriculum Development, 1979.

Kit

Ben M. Harris and Jane Hill. *DeTek: The Developmental Teacher Evaluation Kit*. Austin, Tex.: Southwest Educational Development Laboratory.

Videotapes

Another Set of Eyes: Conferencing Skills. 1989. Three tapes, over two hours on conferencing skills, featuring Arthur Costa and Robert Garmston. Demonstrates trust-building, questioning, responding, and empowering skills. *Trainer's Manual*. Association for Supervision and Curriculum Development, 1250 North Pitt Street, Alexandria, VA 22314.

Another Set of Eyes: Techniques for Classroom Observation. 1988. Two tapes, one and a half hours, featuring Keith Acheson. Demonstrates selective verbatim recording, verbal flow, at task observation, class traffic, interaction analysis, and global scan. *Trainer's Manual.* Association for Supervision and Curriculum Development, 1250 North Pitt Street, Alexandria, VA 22314.

Instructional Conference (Series 2). 1987. Six tapes: *Designing the Conference, Communicating Effectively, Third Grade Lesson & Conference, Ninth Grade Lesson & Conference, High School Lesson & Conference, Two Lessons for Group Practice.* These tapes are part of *Clinical Supervision: A Videotape Series for Instructional Leadership.* For Series 1, *Effective Instruction,* see Bibliography, Videotapes, chap. 4 of this text. Orange County Department of Education, P.O. Box 9050, Costa Mesa, CA 92628-9050.

Mentoring the New Teacher. 1994. 8 case-study videotapes, each 17–20 min. One 6-min. overview tape. *Facilitator's Guide.* 2 books: *How to Mentor in the Midst of Change* by Cheryl Sullivan and *How to Help Beginning Teachers Succeed* by Stephen Gordon. Directed by Eric L. Johnson. Produced by James B. Rowley and Patricia M. Hart, University of Dayton School of Education.

Opening Doors: An Introduction to Peer Coaching. 1988. 2 tapes. Over one hour. Demonstrates the peer coaching process. Gives examples of mirroring, collaborative coaching, and expert coaching. *Facilitator's Manual.* Pat Wolfe and Pam Robbins, program consultants. Association for Supervision and Curriculum Development, 1250 North Pitt Street, Alexandria, VA 22314.

The Supervisory Process: Helping Teachers to Improve Instruction. 1978. 30 min. Demonstrates steps in clinical supervision process. Narration by Ron Stodghill. Association for Supervision and Curriculum Development, 1250 North Pitt Street, Alexandria, VA 22314.

Video Library of Teaching Episodes. Episodes 1–20. 1988–89. 20 tapes. 15–20 min. Lessons on each tape with background information, analysis, and discussion. Association for Supervision and Curriculum Development, 1250 North Pitt Street, Alexandria, VA 22314.

Video Library of Teaching Episodes. Episodes 21–30. Urban Schools. 1991. 10 tapes. 15–20 min. Lessons on each tape with interviews with teachers, background information, analysis, and discussion. Taped in Baltimore, Kansas City, and Washington, D.C. Association for Supervision and Curriculum Development, 1250 North Pitt Street, Alexandria, VA 22314.

Helping Teachers Work Together

Objectives

After studying Chapter 11 you should be able to accomplish the following objectives:

1. Describe leadership skills needed by the supervisor.
2. Describe types of leadership styles and decide which style you prefer to follow.
3. Explain the supervisor's role as change agent.
4. Explain key concepts in organizational development and tell how they apply to the role of the supervisor.
5. Identify problems and suggest improvements in the use of oral, written, and nonverbal language.
6. Demonstrate skills as a group leader.
7. Describe impediments to successful group work and the supervisor's role in reducing them.
8. Design a training program in group interaction.

LIVING IN GROUPS

Unless a person lives in the middle of the Gobi Desert, much of that person's life from the cradle to the grave will be spent in groups of some kind or other. Each person is a member of a primary group—the family—and he or she goes to school in groups and plays in groups. As giant urban concentrations or megalopolises continue to sprawl up, down, and across America, and as the beehive high-rise condominium becomes commonplace, individuals will be thrown closer and closer together. The era of the "rugged individualist" has just about disappeared if indeed it has not already, and group living has become not only a way of life but also a way of survival. Even in the Gobi Desert, patterns of group behavior arise when the camel trains stop at the caravansary; and when two or more camel herders meet, a group is born. If the citizens of the Gobi do not discover each other, sooner or later a group of touring American educators will discover them, and by their example of group organization, reveal to them the group process in action.

The phenomenon of group endeavor is not new in the United States. As early as the nineteenth century, the Frenchman Alexis de Tocqueville observed:

> Americans of all ages, all conditions, and all dispositions constantly form associations. They have not only commercial and manufacturing companies, in which all take part, but associations of a thousand other kinds, religious, moral, serious, futile, general or restricted, enormous or diminutive. The Americans make associations to give entertainments, to found seminaries, to build inns, to construct churches, to diffuse books, to send missionaries to the antipodes; in this manner they found hospitals, prisons, and schools. If it is proposed to inculcate some truth or to foster some feeling by the encouragement of a great example, they form a society. Wherever at the head of some new undertaking you see the government in France, or a man of rank in England, in the United States, you will be sure to find an association.[1]

Most of the nation's work is conducted through group interaction. This is also true of the school; most of the work of the school is carried on through the interaction of the school personnel. Though the teacher in the self-contained elementary, middle school, or high school classroom may face students alone (and with them form a separate teacher-student grouping), much planning, policymaking, curriculum development, and decision making that affect the individual teacher take place in group situations.

A teacher today can no longer work completely independently of other teachers as he or she may have done in the days of the little red schoolhouse. Every decision a teacher makes has the potential of affecting other teachers. If a teacher independently, for example, decides to remove a set of adopted textbooks and put in those more compatible with his or her objectives, a sequence may be destroyed. If a teacher decides to make the standards of his or her grade or course so high that all pupils fail, repercussions may fall not only on him or her but on other teachers and administrators in the school. Certainly there is need for some degree of consistency among faculty in their interpretations of policies and procedures, which they should have had a hand in drafting. A faculty must function as a group, and the success of a school is to large measure determined by the success with which teachers are able to work together. A corollary to this statement is the proposition that the success of a supervisor is to a considerable degree determined by his or her success in helping teachers work together.

To some teachers, it seems as if their lives are one grouping and regrouping after another, with each group requiring a new set of relationships. Teachers may be members of a host of school committees and groups—the faculty as a whole, ad hoc committees, standing committees, departments, teaching teams, in-service study groups, school advisory councils, curriculum councils, parent-teacher associations, teacher-student organizations, school district committees, professional organizations, associations of special fields, state committees, and national groups.

Presumably, all the groups to which a teacher belongs have certain objectives. Whether a group's objectives are realized depends on a number of variables: the quality of leadership in the group, the quality of followership in the group, and the skills of interaction among all members of the group. Groups fail to achieve their objectives when any one of these variables is deficient.

Suppose an anthropologist were to study a group of teachers at their national convention. He spends the three days of the conference dropping in on various meetings and group sessions and takes copious notes. After observing the work sessions—and incidentally participating in the social agenda—he studies his notations, among which are the following:

- General assembly—keynote address on "Teaching: Its Joys and Tribulations"—the first persons to arrive fill up the last two rows in the auditorium. They are asked to move forward.
- Panel discussion on cooperative learning—last half hour is dialogue between two of the panelists.
- Seminar on computer-assisted instruction—"resource person" doesn't show, calls in his regrets.
- Seminar on alternative schools—guest speaker—continuous coming and going of the audience.
- Discussion group on parental choice of school—discussion digresses to disciplinary problems in the schools.
- Seminar on reading problems—one participant cuts off others in the group, dominates the discussion.
- Seminar on merit pay—group becomes polarized, half pro, half con.
- Panel discussion on restructuring schools—two hours allotted, half an hour for each of four discussants; first speaker talks fifty minutes; last speaker winds up with ten minutes.
- Roundtable on whole language—everyone attempts to talk at the same time.

Our anthropologist wonders what the participants in these groups brought away from the conference. Admittedly, these were pro tempore groups composed of persons who were relative strangers. But he wonders nevertheless if the groups should not have been more productive. As he compares them with some of the groups that gave evidence of productivity, he tries to sort out some of the threads. He detects in the groups that had problems a lack of interest among the participants, a lack of commitment to the group's activity, a lack of organization and planning, a lack of sensitivity among the group participants for the concerns of others, a lack of ability or willingness to listen to each other, a lack of communication skills, a lack of a feeling of achievement as a result of group deliberation, and often, perhaps most serious of all, a lack of purpose.

It might be conjectured that groups at a conference do not give a true picture of groups in action. Teachers are away from home; the groups are transient and temporary; most of the participants have little control over the organization, content, and conduct of the deliberations. Our anthropologist would like to test the premise that when teachers know each other intimately and work side by side daily their group sessions are more productive. He learns of a senior high school that has just begun a self-study in preparation for a year-end visit by a committee from the regional accrediting association. He is given carte blanche to attend any of the sessions of faculty and committees he wishes, an invitation of which he takes full advantage. He is not surprised when he finds the following situations:

- The Committee on Philosophy, Aims, Goals and Objectives is about evenly divided among those who might be labeled "child-centered" and those who might be called "subject-centered." They seem unable to resolve their differences. One of the child-centered faction by default writes the committee's "report," which they will submit to the total faculty.
- The Committee on School and Community has a difficult time apportioning the work. Data have to be collected and put into tabular and graphic form. Several teachers protest a lack of time to do this job. As few volunteer for specific tasks, the chairperson has to assign responsibilities arbitrarily.
- When the Committee on Philosophy, Aims, Goals, and Objectives reports to the total faculty, several teachers sit in the back of the room talking, another is reading a newspaper, several arrive late, and two have scheduled other appointments. Time runs out before the faculty can reach consensus.
- The language arts group spends an entire session airing their concerns about pupils' deficiencies in reading and writing.
- The mathematics group whips through its set of *Evaluative Criteria* without thought or discussion in forty-five minutes.
- The foreign language teachers engage in a prolonged, heated discussion of who should take foreign languages—require of everybody or restrict to the academically talented?
- The Guidance Committee wanders into the subject of the administrator's failings.

Are these groups productive? Some would say yes; others would say no, depending on their orientation to the group process itself. Each of these groups appears to have problems.

Supervisors will spend a great part of their professional lives meeting with groups of teachers—total faculties, departments, teams, task forces, study groups, and committees. They will work with groups of teachers from single schools and with groups representing many or all schools of a district. They will have many meetings that are unproductive. On the other hand, there will be times when the supervisors will feel that a group's effort couldn't have been more productive, and they will feel gratified at having participated in situations like the following:

1. An early childhood teaching team becomes aware of problems in handling children of minorities in its classes, proposes analysis of the problem, studies the problem thoroughly, works diligently to formulate proposals for better meeting the needs of these children, and energetically attempts to implement its proposals.

2. A committee of elementary school teachers becomes concerned with the school's grading system, looks at alternate ways of grading, and drafts a proposal to take to the faculty for its consideration.

3. A middle school faculty, which feels its preadolescents as a group are lacking in motivation and are disinterested in school, engages in a free-wheeling discussion of why the pupils act as they do and ends its discussion with a motion to analyze the relevance of the curriculum. A task force is created under the leadership of the supervisor to examine the curriculum and report back to the faculty with recommendations for making the curriculum more relevant.

4. The department of English in a high school undertakes an analysis of the reading achievement level of the students in its school. Finding many students with reading deficiencies, the teachers agree on a proposal, which instead of blaming the elementary school, middle school, and junior high school faculties for the students' deficiencies, outlines ways for the total faculty to implement remedial and developmental programs and to institute techniques of teaching reading in the content areas.

In each of these four situations, the teachers have felt an obligation and responsibility to participate fully and to give of their energies and ideas. Not only has each teacher taken responsibility for participating but also everyone has sensed that his or her ideas and concerns were valued by both the group leader and other group members and that all members have had the opportunity to express their ideas and concerns. The members of these groups felt that their missions were worthwhile.

THE SUPERVISOR AS GROUP LEADER

The successful supervisor must demonstrate the capacity to lead others. The effective instructional supervisor must not only possess leadership skills but also be able to nurture leadership in others. Carl D. Glickman, Stephen P. Gordon, and Jovita M. Ross-Gordon noted that "learning the skills of working with groups to solve instructional problems is a critical task of supervision."[2]

Definition of Leadership

Many studies have sought to discover the nature of leaders and leadership.[3] Unfortunately, because leadership is a human quality, like most human qualities it defies precise description, quantification, generalization, and predictability. We can find almost as many definitions of *leadership* as there are of *supervision*. Several of them are given here.

> The leader is the individual in the group given the task of directing and coordinating task-relevant group activities.[4]
>
> Leadership may be considered as the process (act) of influencing the activities of an organized group in its efforts toward goal setting and goal achievement.[5]
>
> . . . we define leadership as that behavior of an individual which initiates a new structure in interaction within a social system; it initiates change in the goals, objectives, configurations, procedures, inputs, processes, and ultimately the outputs of social systems.[6]

Although most administrators feel they are leaders and bristle when it is suggested otherwise, James M. Lipham distinguished between an administrator and a leader:

> . . . the leader is concerned with initiating changes in established structures, proce-dures, or goals; he is disruptive of the existing state of affairs. The administrator . . . may be identified as the individual who utilizes existing structures or procedures to achieve an organizational goal or objectives . . . the administrator is concerned primarily with maintaining, rather than changing established structures, proce-dures, or goals. Thus, the administrator may be viewed as a stabilizing force.[7]

Unfortunately, some school systems do not want their administrators and su-pervisors to be leaders. The school boards and the communities in these cases are happy with things just as they are. They want administrators and supervisors who will conserve, not disrupt, maintain rather than change. They lack dynamism and are satisfied with the status quo. What is unfortunate is that those administrators and supervisors who enter systems of this kind imbued with a zeal to exert leader-ship and effect change soon discover that if they wish to remain in the system they must conform to local expectations.

W. H. Cowley (1928) and Robert L. De Bruyn (1976) defined *leader* and *leader-ship* in simple terms. Cowley saw a leader as "an individual who is moving in a par-ticular direction and inducing others to follow after him."[8] De Bruyn's definition of *leadership* was "causing others to want what you are doing to accomplish the work of the school."[9] *Leadership* can be conceptualized as the ability to cause people to make improvements in the institution.

Traits of Leaders

Society and all its institutions would benefit greatly if someone could draw up a foolproof list of traits that leaders should possess. On everyone's list would proba-bly be

- Initiative
- Forcefulness
- Decisiveness
- Expertise
- Enthusiasm

Yet studies of leadership have shown no consistent pattern of traits that all lead-ers possess.[10] The studies have revealed that in respect to their followers, leaders generally are

- More self-confident
- Slightly more intelligent
- More motivated to succeed
- More mature emotionally
- More gregarious
- More goal-oriented
- Taller

Some would add that leaders are more disposed than others to take risks and to accept the consequences of their actions. Others would say that a leader must be assertive or aggressive. If we may assume that there are more leaders among administrators than among other school personnel, then it also pays to be male, white, Anglo-Saxon, Protestant (WASP), for more administrators in the United States possess these characteristics than do not. With the exception of gender, we might write off these characteristics as the effect of sheer numbers. Because there are more WASPs in the country, it appears logical that a higher percentage of administrators would fall into that category. The phenomenon of male dominance of school leadership positions may be explained by cultural conditioning and plain old chauvinism. But how do we explain that the majority of superintendents and principals of secondary schools are social studies and physical education majors? Art, foreign language, and music majors in top positions of leadership are quite rare. Is it a matter of numbers again? Social studies and physical education are popular fields and in some parts of the country a surplus of these degree holders is evident. Then why is the English major not at the top in leadership positions? English is also a heavily subscribed field. Do those that have it (leadership, that is) gravitate instinctively to social studies and physical education? Is it because these disciplines are people-oriented whereas other fields are more subject-oriented? Or do the disciplines make the leader?

Ralph M. Stogdill conducted an extensive review of leadership studies and concluded, on the basis of ten or fifteen of these studies, that the average leader exceeds the average member of a group in a number of respects including intelligence, dependability, sociability, initiative, and verbal facility. Several traits—originality, judgment, aggressiveness, and humor—showed the highest correlation with leadership. Certain factors, however—age, height, and weight—evidenced low positive correlation.[11]

Even if a supervisor possesses every desirable trait on everyone's shopping list, there is still no certainty that once in the position, he or she would evidence successful leadership skills. Successful leadership is as much a matter of the situation as of the personal skills and characteristics of the person designated to lead. Persons who may fail in one setting may very well succeed in another. Paul Hersey and Kenneth H. Blanchard described a model of Situational Leadership consisting of four leadership styles differing in the degree to which they combine relationship (supportive) and task (guiding) behavior in the managerial setting.[12]

One trait that has not shown up as common to all leaders but which is worthy of further research is the elusive characteristic of charisma, the personal magnetism of a leader. What is surprising is how little attention has been given by the experts in administration to the phenomenon of charisma. Should we therefore deduce that charisma is unimportant to the success of leaders?

Certainly we can recall charismatic leaders out of the past. Moses and Christ must have possessed charisma. John F. Kennedy is almost always mentioned as a president who had charisma. George S. Patton and Douglas MacArthur of World War II fame were charismatic generals; most professional entertainers demonstrate charisma. We could speculate whether Adolf Hitler would have risen to a position of power if he had not been so charismatic.

Charisma is a power that enables leaders to attract people to follow them, sometimes to the ends of the earth. Some indefinable something in the individual's personality, whether a product of the genes or the environment or both, enables the charismatic individual to assemble a following. What little literature there is on this subject suggests that leaders who possess charisma are fortunate; this trait adds a dimension to their leadership that is not possessed by noncharismatic individuals. On the other hand, charisma is not an essential characteristic of leadership, which is fortunate as charismatic leaders are in short supply.

Much of the literature on supervision treats leadership behavior as if it were generic, applicable to both administration and supervision. That is, the literature assumes that principles and skills of leadership are common to both administrators and supervisors. Generally, this is true. However, distinctions should be drawn in degree if not in substance between skills needed by instructional supervisors and those needed by administrators. With that differentiation in mind, we can consider skills of leadership that logically and empirically appear to apply to both supervisors, who are leaders in staff positions, and administrators, who are leaders in line positions.

Styles of Leadership

A more profitable avenue of study than traits of leaders is examination of styles or approaches to leadership. Two of these—three, if we include the more common mix of the basic two—have been described. Table 11.1 shows the terminology that four often-cited sources have applied to the two styles.[13] Though the terminologies differ, style 1 incorporates principles of directive behavior, focus on the needs of the institution, and concern for status. Style 2 emphasizes nondirective behavior, focus on the person, and openness of the system. The supervisor who embraces approach 1 is directive (ordering, prescribing, telling) in behavior, task- rather than people-oriented, and concerned about administrative efficiency. The supervisor who employs approach 2 is nondirective (helping, facilitating, counseling), conscious of interpersonal relations, and concerned about the human dimension of supervision. In practice, supervisors must learn to adapt the two styles to their situations. As there is a time to reap and a time to sow, there is a time to exhibit authoritarian behavior and a time to stress human relations skills.

The instructional supervisor who occupies a staff or advisory rather than a line or power position should be an exemplar of approach 2, using approach 1 only in rare instances when teacher behavior runs counter to the best interests of the students and the institution. In truth, staff personnel cannot follow approach 1 in their

TABLE 11.1. TWO BASIC STYLES OF LEADERSHIP

	Lewis, Lippitt, and White	McGregor	Fiedler	Morphet, Johns, and Reller
Style 1	Authoritarian	Theory X	Task-oriented	Traditional, monocratic, bureaucratic
Style 2	Democratic	Theory Y	Relations-oriented	Emerging, pluralistic, collegial

own right for they are not armed with line authority and must either be recipients of authority delegated by the administrator or refer troublesome problems to the administrator. Human relations must be the strong suit of the supervisory leader.

Human-relations-oriented supervisors work in a cooperative mode with the teacher. They offer assistance; they serve as resource persons and advisers. They are concerned with building rapport and mutual trust. They create a nonthreatening climate where teachers' weaknesses can be revealed without punishment and where remediation can be undertaken without embarrassment. They are colleagues and friends whose purpose is helping the teachers improve instruction so that together they may enhance student learning.

Thomas J. Sergiovanni and Robert J. Starratt would have supervisors move beyond a human-relations approach to what they called human-resources supervision.[14] The human relations supervisor, like the task-oriented supervisor, has an increase in school effectiveness as the goal, with teacher satisfaction as a means to the goal. The human resources supervisor has teacher satisfaction as the goal, with increased school effectiveness as the means to that goal.

The human resources supervisor pays close attention to teachers' satisfaction with their jobs, their commitment and loyalty to the organization, the presence or absence of mutual trust among members of the organization, the mechanisms for teachers' input into the system's operation, and the frequency and quality of communication among members of the organization. (At present, it appears that the term and concept of human-relations supervision are encountered more frequently than human-resources supervision.)

Sergiovanni drew a thoughtful distinction between "value dimensions" and "value-added dimensions" of leadership. He viewed the more traditional aspects of leadership as value dimensions designed to ensure functioning of the schools, such as directive managerial behavior and use of extrinsic motivators. Advocating a move toward "value-added leadership," he included among value-added dimensions collegiality and use of intrinsic motivators. Sergiovanni contrasted "calculated leadership" (a value dimension) with "leadership by outrage" (a value-added dimension). Calm and detached administrative behavior is characteristic of "calculated leadership"; passion, personal involvement, deep commitment, and risk taking are characteristics of "leadership by outrage." Sergiovanni observed that principles of value-added leadership are just now making their appearance in the business and educational literature.[15]

Though consensus is lacking on which skills are essential to the group leader, authorities on leadership seem to agree that in addition to the human orientation, supervisors should be skilled in (1) decision making, (2) effecting change, (3) organizational development, (4) communicating, and (5) group process. Let's look briefly at some of the salient points of each of these interrelated skills as they relate to the role of the supervisor.

Decision Making

President Harry S Truman summed up the heart of the administrative process in the famous slogan he kept on his desk in the Oval Office: "The buck stops here." Ultimately, the administrator must make and be responsible for decisions. Though school administrators and supervisors will not be called on to make earth-shattering decisions like Truman's decision to drop the atomic bomb on Japan, nevertheless the ability to make decisions is the most important single ingredient of administrative and supervisory behavior. Numerous authorities have emphasized the importance of decision-making skills for the successful administrator or manager.[16]

Some would certainly add *decisiveness* to a list of traits that administrators and supervisors should possess. Unfortunately, teachers and others often interpret decisiveness as the ability to make on-the-spot judgments and decisions. Administrators and supervisors must be able to sense when they can fulfill the desires of their followers for immediate decisions and when they should suspend judgment until more facts are available. Discretion is not only the better part of valor; it is also the better part of decision making. Administrators and supervisors who render snap judgments and call them correctly will certainly gain status. On the other hand, once they start to make wrong decisions and suffer unpleasant consequences as a result, they can plummet in the eyes of their followers. Administrators and supervisors need to develop a companion skill known as *tolerance for ambiguity*. Not all decisions can, must, or should be made on the spot. Sometimes no decision is the wiser decision. The astute administrator or supervisor knows when to make a snap judgment, when to delay for further facts and then come to a decision, and when to make no decision, allowing time for the situation to correct itself.

Administrators and supervisors are called on daily to render many small or large decisions. They must make decisions about planning, implementing, evaluating, and recycling. Supervisors' decisions fall within the three domains discussed in Chapter 1: instructional, curriculum, and staff development.

In Chapter 8, on curriculum evaluation, you became familiar with the CIPP model, which is a systematic process for making educational decisions. The model shows clearly the pervasiveness of the task of decision making. It shows the kinds of changes that may take place, the kinds of evaluations that are carried out, and the types of decisions that must be made. This model features planning, structuring, implementing, and recycling decisions as tasks of educational evaluation. Though focusing on educational evaluation, the model serves as an overview of decision making generally. Evaluation is the rendering of judgments, and in that respect evaluation is decision making. Every time an administrator or supervisor makes a decision he or she evaluates the situation prior to rendering a judgment; then the judgment itself must be evaluated and sometimes revised.

Decision making is so habitual to competent administrators and supervisors that they do not perceive themselves as going through a process. Yet each time we make a decision we do go through a series of steps or stages. In many instances, the human brain runs through the stages so rapidly that we are not aware we are analyzing the problem before making a decision. What we are doing is actually problem solving.

We can find in the literature a number of models of the decision-making process that consist of steps to be taken by the administrator or supervisor.[17] For guidance in decision making, we might fall back on the old reliable generic model for problem solving, referred to as the *scientific method*. In conducting research we follow certain steps of an orderly process:

- Identify the problem.
- Formulate a hypothesis.

- Collect data.
- Analyze data.
- Draw conclusions.
- Verify or reject the hypothesis.

In one sense, decision making is research. To reach some decisions, we must conduct thorough research. Everyday routine decisions do not require a great deal in the way of bona fide research, but the elements of collection of data, analysis, and so on are there, perhaps only in embryo form. We can adapt the research model and make it more operational in nature as shown here.

- Identify the problem.
- Select the solution from alternatives.
- Put the solution into operation.
- Evaluate the solution.
- Recycle the decision, if needed.

We should not confuse immediate decisions with off-the-top-of-the-head decisions. Administrators and supervisors make immediate decisions many times. Even then, however, they should base them on the best data, which in many cases administrators and supervisors have at their fingertips. Spontaneous decisions are intuitive, hasty, ill-considered decisions that ignore data. In choosing a solution to a problem, it is essential to use all available data, to avoid off-the-top-of-the-head judgments. Only in crises or emergencies when there is no time to gather data—the data must come out of the administrator's or supervisor's experience—can spontaneous decisions be justified.

Robert J. Alfonso, Gerald R. Firth, and Richard F. Neville have drawn twenty-three implications for decision theory for instructional supervisory behavior.[18] Among these are the following four propositions:

> Proposition 1: Conscious decision making provides the opportunity for organizational growth and refinement.
> Proposition 13: Decision making can be made more responsive and effective when it is recognized that decisions are seldom optimal, but are typically the selection of the best choice among those available.
> Proposition 14: Decision making is swayed by the dynamic interaction between internal and external environments, and by the psychological makeup of the decision maker.
> Proposition 16: Although executive decisions are important in establishing goals, decisions made at the operational level are still more important, since they directly affect personal commitment and, thereby, production and effectiveness.[19]

Supervisors make decisions both unilaterally and in cooperation with others in the course of their daily work. The supervisor may have to decide by himself or herself, for example, which competing demands to meet and needs to fill. "To which classroom will I go today?" is a supervisory decision. Of course, the decision should not be purely arbitrary but should be based on the best available data.

Supervisors should, however, seek to expand the scope of cooperative decision making. The supervisor should not, for example, decide by himself or herself to initiate a curricular innovation, to select a certain series of textbooks, to devise a system of classroom observation, or to institute a staff-development program. These are matters for cooperative decision making.

Supervisors should not only be concerned with their own decision making but should also seek to help teachers make decisions. Teachers want assistance with such problems as these: What is the best way to handle certain types of pupils? Did I handle a particular pupil correctly? Should I introduce more inquiry learning? Supervisors' success is gauged at least in part on how successfully they make decisions and how effective they are at helping others to reach decisions.

Effecting Change

In the span of years since the end of World War II, our schools have flirted with team teaching, nongraded schools, programmed instruction, instructional television, open-space education, individualized guided education, computer-assisted instruction, mainstreaming, and a host of other innovations. Some of these innovations have remained; others have disappeared. Change, however, continues to be the order of the day.

The behavioral scientists tell us that institutions must change if they are to grow and develop. Can you imagine the Latin Grammar School (with its heavy emphasis on Latin and Greek and its absence of modern foreign languages, industrial arts, business education, interscholastic athletics, a marching band, and guidance) as the model secondary institution of the twenty-first century? Can you imagine public education restricted to males, as in the days of the Latin Grammar School and early academies?

Change has been exceedingly rapid in contemporary society, toppling old mores and values, as Alvin Toffler described so vividly in *Future Shock* and *The Third Wave*.[20] Whereas change used to come slowly, modern technology, communication, and transportation catapult us into making changes often before we are emotionally ready to change.

What school systems need is planned change—not haphazard, not impulsive change. Nor can a school system afford to maintain the status quo, no matter where the system is located. The students who are the products of the system suffer as much from no change as from unplanned change. Were students to spend their whole lives in a single community and in one career, the school might have a ready excuse for maintaining the status quo. Perhaps what was good enough for our grandparents would, under those conditions, be good enough for our grandchildren. But our country is large; our people are mobile; our industries are far flung. Technology has the bad habit of making careers obsolete so that more training and retraining become necessary throughout life. Recommending "a single curriculum for all students that is both rigorous and relevant," Willard Daggett proposed making the content of the curriculum "more relevant to our technological information-based society."[21]

The school system "on the cutting edge" will not only plan and effect change but also anticipate change. It will use such procedures as the Delphi Technique, which was mentioned in Chapter 8, consulting the experts who are willing to gaze into their crystal balls and predict where schools are going five, ten, fifteen, twenty-five years hence. The march of the computer, the diminishing of fossil fuels, the high cost of housing, the decrease in farming population, the growth of megalopolises all have their role in producing changes in our society, which, in turn, impact schools, learning, and education.

The instructional supervisor is in the forefront of the change process in education. The supervisor is in a strategic position to influence the largest professional group, the teachers, to make changes in the system. In this process the supervisor is often referred to as a *change agent*. In the language of the behavioral scientist, a change agent helps a client system to bring about change. The change agent works with individuals and groups to effect improvements. In the case of the instructional supervisor, changes are sought in instruction, in the curriculum, and in the staff. A change agent is concerned with changes in the behavior of the people who belong to the organization, the goals of the organization, the structure of the organization itself, and the technical processes the organization employs.

The change agent recognizes that if an institution is to maintain its vitality, it must grow and develop just as individuals grow and develop. The change agent strives to plan for change, to control and eliminate unplanned change. The change agent would be the first to reject the notion of change for the sake of change. Change must be purposeful. It must come about because it produces results better than what preceded it.

Change may mean instituting a completely new practice. It may also mean supplanting a practice already in operation. Thus the change agent has entrenched attitudes to overcome if teachers feel commitment to the old practice. The status quo is far more comfortable and certainly requires less work than moving in new directions. The change agent must take teachers with him or her each step in the process, helping them to convince themselves that the new practice is superior to the old. Demonstrations of effectiveness elsewhere can help secure teacher acceptance. Piloting and gradual phasing in of an innovation can be helpful techniques for assuring commitment.

We encounter disagreement over the question of whether a change agent should come from inside or from outside the system. Although there are cogent arguments for the employment of change agents from the outside, there are practical arguments for choosing change agents from within the system. School systems may not be able to afford the services of people from the outside. They already have employees in supervisory roles who can serve as agents of change. Capable supervisors have already established a sense of trust with other school personnel; *trust* is an ingredient essential to the change process.

The behavioral scientists call the procedures they use to effect change *intervention techniques* or *strategies*. Change-agent supervisors work with teachers to improve their teaching skills by providing in-service education opportunities. They seek solutions to system problems through the group process, which necessitates the formation of committees, task forces, and councils. A change to a new reading program in the elementary school, for example, will require study and commitment of those who will be expected to plan, execute, and evaluate it.

Change agents work with teachers to improve the curriculum. Cooperatively, teachers and supervisors conduct needs assessments and decide on ways to fill gaps in the curriculum. A change from separate disciplines to an integrated curriculum or from a traditional to a magnet school, for examples, will require deliberation and approval of all the constituencies of the school.

Change agents work with teachers and administrators to revise school policies and procedures that have become outmoded and nonfunctional. They help teachers perfect interpersonal skills through self-instruction and training sessions.

Some changes are minor; others are major. Some changes affect only a single teacher; others touch all school personnel and the community as well. The goal of many changes is adoption throughout the system. In fact, farsighted change agents hope that an innovation tested and found successful in their schools will be diffused and adopted by school systems throughout the country. The behavioral objectives movement, for example, which began to develop in the late 1950s with the work of such educators as Ralph W. Tyler at the University of Chicago, has been widely accepted across the nation. This change was not perceived as a modification of instructional practice for a particular school but rather a change that had universality.

On a system-wide level a central office supervisor or administrator can act as change agent. In the individual school, the principal fulfilling his or her role as instructional leader can be and should be the primary change agent. Shirley M. Hord and others saw leadership in change often brought about not by one leader—a principal, for example—but by a facilitating team composed of principal, central office supervisor or administrator, and teachers from whom peers sought help.[22]

The change process is essentially an exercise in human relations skills. A curriculum change, for example, can only result when people are changed. An administrator can command change, can even bring about surface conformity. What an administrator cannot command is a commitment to a mandated change. People accept change when they feel they have a personal stake in it and when they believe change will improve the lives of those affected by it.

Supervisors must be open individuals who are receptive to change themselves. Since the impetus for change must often come from the leader, a closed personality who sees little value in change ("if it works, don't fix it") can block a school's progress. Schools need self-starting, energetic, future-looking persons in supervisory positions.

Alfonso, Firth, and Neville set forth thirty-seven propositions about change theory that are of importance to instructional supervisors.[23] From this list, we might note the following, which seem of particular significance:

> Proposition 1: Planning and initiating change will be more effective when the objectives and policies of the organization are clear, realistic, and understood.
> Proposition 11: The effectiveness of a change effort will be increased when one sees the nature of the change as enhancing one's own personal relationships and status in the organization.
> Proposition 19: Change will be more effective if it does not appear to disturb the existing organizational structure of status, relationship, and recognition.
> Proposition 29: Change agents will be more effective when the change agent, as perceived by other group members, has prestige and acceptance within the group.[24]

The supervisor is a key change agent. Effecting change is what the supervisor's job is all about. Whether as group leader or as individual counselor, the supervisor helps the people in the system and the system itself to be better than they would have been without his or her intervention.

Although modern theories of administration and supervision advocate participation of subordinates in the management of institutions, we would err if we implied that change always occurs through extensive involvement of the persons affected by it. State mandates, for example, have produced significant changes in curriculum and management of school systems, with varying degrees of involvement of school persons at the local level and with varying degrees of commitment to the changes. Even states, however, ordinarily involve representatives of school systems when planning for change. Legislators, state board of education members, and employees of the state department of education can often be influenced before putting a change into place.

On the local level, where all school persons are readily accessible and under supervision of a central administrator, we see little need for locally mandated innovations without extensive involvement of teachers and others from the time the idea is suggested through planning, implementing, and evaluating the change. As the current movement for empowerment of teachers gains strength, meaningful involvement of teachers in school governance must become standard practice.

Organizational Development

Leaders help not only people but also their organizations to grow and develop. In one sense, organizational development is a type of change process. Richard Beckhard defined organizational development as "an effort (1) planned, (2) organization-wide, and (3) managed from the top, to (4) increase organization effectiveness and health through (5) planned interventions in the organization's 'process,' using behavioral science knowledge."[25]

Key terms in organizational development are

- Interaction of groups
- Team building
- Conflict resolution
- In-service education
- Systems planning
- Communication
- Collaboration
- Change agents
- Role clarification
- Leadership behavior

Wendell L. French and Cecil H. Bell, Jr., wove together some of the basic concepts of organizational development in the following definition:

a long-range effort to improve an organization's problem-solving and renewal processes, particularly through a more effective and collaborative management of organization culture—with special emphasis on the culture of formal work teams— with the assistance of a change agent, or catalyst, and the use of the theory and technology of applied behavioral science, including action research.[26]

The administrator or supervisor who seeks to develop the organization would help a group to gather data about its current situation, to analyze the data, to detect places where improvements in its functioning could be made, and to recommend ways to improve. Central to the process are the group's endeavors to understand itself, to become more cohesive, and cooperatively to find solutions to its problems.

Group difficulties may stem from (1) poor interpersonal relationships among groups and individuals and (2) poor management (leadership). Interpersonal relationships may be improved through group deliberation/group process and through group encounter techniques like sensitivity training (T-groups). Particularly important in the development of healthy interpersonal relationships is the reduction or elimination of conflicts.

Fred Luthans identified four types of conflict that develop in organizations: "(1) hierarchical conflict (between the various levels of the organization . . .); (2) functional conflict (between the various functional departments of the organization . . .); (3) line-staff conflict (between line personnel and staff personnel . . .); and (4) formal-informal conflict (between the formal and informal organizations . . .)."[27]

A widely cited model of educational administration developed by Jacob W. Getzels and Egon Guba depicted the interrelationships of institutional roles and individual needs in creating the particular behavior of the social institution. Their model, which appears in Figure 11.1, posited a nomothetic (institutional, sociological) dimension and an idiographic (personal, psychological) dimension.

Getzels and Herbert A. Thelen developed an even more complex model by adding anthropological (cultural), group, and biological dimensions, which further affect the observed behavior of the institution.[28]

From the Getzels-Guba model we can deduce that

1. The school is a social system.
2. Social systems evidence two classes of phenomena (dimensions): the nomothetic, by which an institution prescribes certain roles for its employees with certain expectations for each role, and the idiographic, by which individuals with their own peculiar personalities try to satisfy their own needs-dispositions.

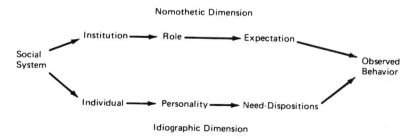

Figure 11.1. Getzels-Guba Model of Educational Administration as a Social Process. *Source: Jacob W. Getzels, "Administration as a Social Process," in* Administration Theory in Education, *Andrew W. Halpin, ed. (New York: Macmillan, 1958), pp. 152–53. Reprinted with permission of Jacob W. Getzels.*

3. The behavior of people within the system and the uniqueness of the system are functions of the interaction of both dimensions.

4. Leaders of a social system may be any one of three types: They may lean to the nomothetic or normative dimension, emphasizing the goals of the institution; they may lean to the idiographic or human dimension, emphasizing the goals of the individuals who make up the system; or they may shift from one dimension to the other as required by the needs of the institution and the persons employed by the institution. In the last case such leadership has been referred to as transactional.

5. Three types of conflicts may arise in a social system: intrarole, intrapersonality, and role personality. Intrarole conflicts occur when (1) the person who holds a particular role is subjected to disagreement among groups about the expectations of the role. Teachers, for example, may view the principal's role somewhat differently from the way students or parents view the role. (2) The person who holds the role is subjected to disagreement from within a given group about the expectations of the role. Some teachers, for example, may hold a view of the principal's role that is different from that of other teachers. (3) The person who holds a role is called on to fill more than one role at the same time. Administrators, for example, may have to perform at the same time as instructional supervisors.

Intrapersonality conflicts come about as a result of conflicting personality needs of the holder of a role. A principal, for example, may be torn between a desire to please teachers and a desire to please the superintendent. Because the superintendent is "the boss," the decision is often easy to make.

Role-personality conflicts result from differing expectations written into the role and the needs-dispositions of the holder of the role. A principal may be expected by terms of the job description to be a strong disciplinarian but at the same time may not believe in corporal punishment.

Conflicts are resolved in a variety of ways. Some of the means for resolving and managing conflict are more effective and longer lasting than others. Some of the ways of settling conflicts are discussed here.

- *Administrative order*. This is a far from satisfactory solution. It may result in temporary conformity but leaves the conflict to fester and erupt again.
- *Consensus*. Achieving agreement from most or, if possible, all participants in a conflict is the ideal way to resolve conflicts.
- *Compromise*. Some people feel that compromise is unsatisfactory as each side has to give up something. On the other hand, compromise takes place every day in our society and is especially apparent in the governmental structures of our republic.
- *Changing the structure of the organization to eliminate sources of conflict*. Persons can be moved around, down, up, or even out. Procedures can be changed so that the organization may function more smoothly.
- *Policy formulation*. Conflicts arise in the absence of policies to guide action. They can be reduced by the group's creation of policies to which all can subscribe.

- *New solutions.* Creative solutions may be found; these may be a departure from the existing practices, which provoked conflict.

Harmony and team spirit are paramount goals in organizational development.

The organization may be developed through improved management techniques. Management training, therefore, is an important feature of organizational development. Key concerns of managers interested in developing the organization are (1) involvement of personnel, (2) planning, (3) time, and (4) stress.

Involvement of Personnel. The best way to ensure positive change in an organization is to involve the personnel of the organization in its operation. Subordinates need to feel some stake in the organization. They want a chance to express their ideas. Japanese industry provides such channels through their "quality-control circles," often called simply "quality circles." In this approach, which William G. Ouchi has labeled *Theory Z*,[29] Japanese employees meet regularly with their supervisors in groups whose mission is to identify problems of the organization and recommend solutions. Through involvement in running the organization, workers develop loyalty and commitment to its goals.

Observers of the industrial scene credit organizational principles referred to as *Total Quality Management*, advocated by W. Edwards Deming, an American, with helping the Japanese revitalize their economy after World War II. Deming proposed that workers and managers share responsibilities for managing the enterprise and jointly seek solutions to their organization's problems.[30] It is interesting that principles of shared management originated in the United States, migrated to Japan where they were adopted, and only recently have been put into practice in some American corporations.

Planning. A planning technique that has grown in popularity is known as MBO or MBO/R, management by objectives/results. Those who manage or supervise by objectives follow an orderly process, which comprises the following steps:

1. Specify the goals of the institution.
2. Specify the objectives of the institution and standards of performance of the target group(s).
3. Select strategies to accomplish the objectives.
4. Identify resources needed: human and material.
5. Establish timelines for achieving objectives.
6. Implement the strategies.
7. Evaluate success in accomplishing objectives.
8. Recycle.

Some supervisors project objectives and timelines over a five-year period, for example, and then prepare full and detailed plans annually. Management or supervision by objectives for results is a logical and systematic way of planning, implementing, and evaluating the work of the organization.

TIME AND STRESS. If organizations are to thrive, the human beings who make the systems go must remain physically and emotionally healthy. If the human beings are to maintain vitality, they must learn to manage the bothersome and companion elements of time and stress.

For many administrators and supervisors, there is never enough time to "get it all done." Work, as we know, is infinitely expandable. Compulsive, perfectionist individuals find themselves running hard just to keep up. The relentless computers and their human programmers keep grinding out paperwork, so that the harder we run, the farther behind we seem to get. At some point someone—a thoughtful administrator, a perceptive supervisor, or a facilitator from the outside—needs to blow the whistle and ask individuals to analyze what they are doing, how they are doing it, what is really necessary, how time is being utilized, and what factors are provoking stress.

Time can be managed from two perspectives. First, we can all examine whether the organizational tasks that we now feel to be necessary are really essential. Do we need all the committee meetings, for example? Are we, perhaps, closet meeting-lovers, which is almost as bad as being overt meeting-haters? Does every administrator have to grind out requests for reports from subordinates to satisfy his or her own administrative needs and to justify his or her own position? Why, for example, must different "shops" within the same system demand the same factual data from subordinates, each in a slightly different format?

We need "human engineers" in our social systems who are empowered to confront each generator of paperwork and require that person to justify the existence of each item. Why must the standard response to even the simplest requests for action be "write me a memo" when a phone call or face-to-face dialog would be sufficient? We will without a doubt discover that half the organization's paperwork could be eliminated without causing the organization any harm. Imagine the savings in time and money from such a reduction!

Second, employees must make decisions on how to set priorities for demands on their time. All of us are prone sometimes to spend time on trivial matters and to neglect the significant ones. All of us sometimes let others control our time instead of seizing the moment ourselves. Gilbert R. Weldy suggested sixteen guidelines for managing time wisely:

1. Analyze how time is used and misused.
2. Establish priorities.
3. Budget time by appointing a time.
4. Delegate with discretion.
5. Set a deadline.
6. Develop enthusiasm.
7. Concentrate totally.
8. Be courteous.
9. Control "other imposed" time.
10. Recognize and respond to fatigue.
11. Save time in meetings.
12. Read with discrimination.
13. Help your memory.

   14. Use clerical services judiciously.
   15. Plan work to save time.
   16. Use time to improve skills.[31]

Stress arises from a number of pressures, some of which are self-imposed and some of which come from the outside. We may not be able to prevent pressures from without but we can learn to respond to them. We can certainly, at least to some degree, control self-imposed stress. If we manage our time wisely, for example, we can cut down on occasions for stress. If we take ourselves a bit less seriously, we can reduce stress. If we try to get our priorities straight, we can decrease stress. If we learn to say no on occasion, we can both reduce stress and save time. If we are a stressful type to begin with, we should not gravitate to stressful positions. It is amazing to see how many teachers who have difficulty managing stress in the classroom aspire to positions as administrators and supervisors! Each prospective administrator and supervisor must ask himself or herself these questions: Do I have the personality to assume a leadership position? Do I work well under pressure? Do I have a tolerance for ambiguity?

Michael C. Giammatteo and Dolores M. Giammatteo offered several suggestions for managing stress.[32] They proposed that executives develop an awareness of their own reaction to stressful conditions, a tolerance level, and techniques for reducing stress. Executives should determine whether they are Type A individuals, who are prone to stress and even heart attack. Giammatteo and Giammatteo provided a checklist (see Table 11.2) for executives (equally applicable in our opinion to leaders of all types, including instructional supervisors) to determine whether they are Type A personalities.

Those whose answers are predominantly yes are Type A personalities: hard-driving, pushing shakers and movers; those whose answers are predominantly no are Type B personalities, relaxed, easy-going, laid back, and less subject to stress. Obviously, what is needed is an administrator or supervisor who is a combination of the two types, an A/B Type, who knows when to work hard and when to relax.

Executives should develop an ability to anticipate and avoid stressful conditions. They need to ignore minor stressful events and they need to be more trusting that their subordinates will perform as they should. Executives should learn to allocate time for personal and family interests, delegate responsibilities, and even on occasion reduce standards or expectations. We all need to remind ourselves now and then that the world can run very well without us.

Stress is a major, perhaps *the*, factor in teacher, administrator, and supervisor burnout. The supervisor as change agent needs to help both teachers and himself or herself to use time wisely and to reduce stress.

Communication

Supervisors must be able to communicate effectively with both groups and individuals. The ability to project and understand messages is a fundamental skill of administrators and supervisors. Supervisors must give attention to (1) oral language, (2) written language, (3) nonverbal language, and (4) silent language.

TABLE 11.2. TYPE A BEHAVIOR: AWARENESS EXERCISE. ARE YOU A TYPE A? DO YOU CHARACTERISTICALLY EXHIBIT TYPE A BEHAVIOR? QUICKLY FILL OUT THE FOLLOWING QUESTIONNAIRE TO SEE.

Yes	No	Don't Know	
——	——	——	1. I'm frequently in a hurry.
——	——	——	2. I'm typically doing several projects at the same time.
——	——	——	3. I'm always pushed by deadlines.
——	——	——	4. I usually take on as many (or a few more) projects as I can handle.
——	——	——	5. I really seek recognition from my boss and/or peers.
——	——	——	6. I believe it's important for a person to push herself or himself for success, and I seek out opportunities for promotions and advancements.
——	——	——	7. I enjoy competition in all areas.
——	——	——	8. I really enjoy winning, and hate to lose.
——	——	——	9. My job is the most important thing in my life.
——	——	——	10. I sometimes feel I neglect my family by putting my job first.
——	——	——	11. I'm usually too busy with my job to have time for many hobbies or outside activities.
——	——	——	12. When I'm given a job I really feel personally responsible for its success—i.e., even though others may be involved, I feel that it just won't come out as well unless I'm personally involved from start to finish.
——	——	——	13. I have trouble trusting people easily.
——	——	——	14. I tend to talk fast.
——	——	——	15. When speaking I believe in giving special emphasis to my meaning with strong vocal inflection and gestures.
——	——	——	16. I feel some impatience in most meetings and conversations—I just wish they would speed up and get on with it.
——	——	——	17. I tend to get irritable and lose my cool easily when obviously simple things don't go right.
——	——	——	18. I make a list of things I must get done each day.
——	——	——	19. I generally have strong opinions on most things.
——	——	——	20. I don't seem to get much time to keep up with my reading.

If you answered yes to 15 of these questions, you may be falling into the "Type A" behavior pattern.

Source: Michael C. Giammatteo and Dolores M. Giammatteo, Executive Well Being: Stress and Administrators *(Reston, Va.: National Association of Secondary School Principals, 1980), pp. 20–21. Reprinted with permission of the National Association of Secondary School Principals.*

Oral Language. To some people, professionals and laypersons alike, effectiveness in communication is equated with the ability to articulate, to express oneself orally, to deliver ripostes on the spot, and to answer questions, if not with lucidity, at least with verbal dexterity. Articulateness is a skill much prized by the public, who often settle for glibness over substance, for style over content.

President Jimmy Carter put his finger on this problem when he commented on his own difficulty in communicating:

> I am not a great speaker and am sometimes not at ease with large groups. I acknowledge those characteristics freely. They have been pointed out to me often enough to convince me. I can think on my feet. A poll of oldtime White House correspondents ranked me first in handling press conferences. It is hard to express effectively all sides of a complicated issue, and I tend to do that. It is much easier to take one simplistic side of an issue and express it clearly.[33]

Whether the politician says anything of substance or not, the public are impressed by the William Jennings Bryans who bestir them not to "crucify mankind on a cross of gold." Like charisma, articulateness is a trait much to be desired. It puts its possessor one rung up on the status ladder. The ability to speak and respond clearly is essential. That ability, however, should be accompanied by forthrightness, candor, and substance.

Supervisors must know how to communicate with people at various levels. They do not address adults as they do children. They do not fire a rapid barrage of idiomatic English at members of minorities who barely speak the language. They do not use the "refined" language of "high society" with the less educated. They do not use "ten-dollar" words where "half-dollar" words are needed to cement communication. They don't use football language in addressing the ladies' sewing circle. They do not use barroom language at a church wedding. They do not use education jargon in talking to the parents' advisory committee. They do not talk to teachers as if they were untrustworthy, lazy, disloyal, or uncooperative. They do not name-drop, throw in obtuse and incomplete references, and relate in-house jokes if they hope to communicate.

Supervisors who are aware of the power of language not only choose their words carefully but also watch their tone. The tone often speaks louder than the words, revealing meaning just the opposite of the words. Although the lyrics may say one thing, the melody may put forth a different motif.

In our society, quite contrary to some, speakers are expected to be animated and cheerful. They are expected to maintain eye contact with the recipient of their messages. Americans tend to go to the heart of the problem whereas other cultures are less direct, indulging in small talk and social pleasantries like having tea or coffee before getting down to serious communication. It must have been an American who invented the business lunch, a custom designed to make use of every working moment and to relegate the joys of eating to a secondary role.

Sometime in their preparation, supervisors should take linguistics and speech courses and, if necessary, speech therapy. They should also study basic principles of communication. Alfonso, Firth, and Neville have listed twenty-eight propositions pertaining to communication skills.[34] Among these are the following:

- Proposition 10: Communication will be more effective when the views of the sender and the receiver(s) are in harmony.
- Proposition 14: Communication will be more effective in influencing group behavior and attitudes when it utilizes discussion and decision making.
- Proposition 15: Communication will be more effective when the sender and receiver are dealing with situations in which both have obtained previous experience.

- Proposition 18: Communication will be more effective if the style and techniques selected by the sender are consistent with the expectations of the receivers.

- Proposition 19: Communication will be more effective if senders take into account social and educational similarities and differences between themselves and receivers, as well as those among receivers.

- Proposition 20: Communication will be more effective if senders take into account their own personality characteristics and those of receivers.[35]

The ability to communicate orally with one's clientele is not only the stock of the salesperson but also the primary tool of the supervisor.

Written Communication. Only slightly behind oral communication in importance is the ability of supervisors to express themselves in written form. In their daily work they write letters, memos, curriculum guides, evaluations of materials and teachers, newsletters, research reports, and other documents. Recipients of written materials make judgments about the source and the materials on the basis of their style, accuracy, clarity, necessity, and proper use of English. As with oral communication, tone is also important. We have all been recipients of imperious memoranda, and you know how we reacted.

Administrators and supervisors get themselves in trouble with correspondence in which a careless phrase or word creates animosity on the part of the receiver. Senders should not write messages when they are angry or at a low ebb. Messages should always be reread for accuracy, tone, and language usage.

The sender should consider the purpose of each message. If the sender must write a negative communication, it is wise to hold the message for a day or two while he or she reconsiders the problem. Writing may well be the wrong way of delivering negative messages, especially if we are talking about messages destined for people in the system; oral communication may be much fairer, more effective, and even courageous. Too many people in status positions hide behind memos, fearing to confront a person in a face-to-face situation in which the recipient can respond.

Many times it is effective practice to accompany oral communication with written; the two reinforce each other. They attend to the difference in people's learning styles. Some people learn more effectively through their ears; others through their eyes. As Alfonso, Firth, and Neville posited, "Proposition 5: Communication will be more effective in promoting change if the sender utilizes many communication channels rather than a few."[36]

One final caution is in order: The supervisor should decide whether a written message is absolutely necessary. Time is required to write it, office supplies are consumed, someone has to deliver it, the receiver has to read it, the receiver may be required or desire to respond, and the cycle starts all over. Supervisors who often complain about being swamped with paperwork must ask themselves whether they are contributors to the paper trail.

Nonverbal Language. More attention should be given to the study of nonverbal language. Teachers are expected to be animated and convey enthusiasm. This is done as much through gestures, eye movements, interjections, smiles, frowns, posture, meaningful sounds, and laughter as through words. In fact, nonverbal language can say more than words. A guilty look on a person's face can shout that he or she is lying. We know it and are convinced that the person is lying in spite of any verbal protestations to the contrary.

C. A. Bowers and David J. Flinders identified three channels of nonverbal communication and pointed out that these channels may have cultural implications: *proxemics* or the way the teacher uses classroom space; *kinesics* or body language; and *prosody* or patterns of the teacher's voice.[37] Charles Galloway commented, "Nonverbal behaviors are the primary vehicles for expressing emotion. Behaviors, better than words, convey hate, fear, anger, and anxiety."[38]

BODY LANGUAGE. Human beings send messages through body movements and gestures. Describing body language Julius Fast said:

> . . . we all, in one way or another, send our little messages out to the world. We say, "Help me, I'm lonely. Take me, I'm available. Leave me alone, I'm depressed." And rarely do we send our messages consciously. We act out our state of being with nonverbal body language. We lift one eyebrow for disbelief. We rub our noses for puzzlement. We clasp our arms to isolate ourselves or to protect ourselves. We shrug our shoulders for indifference, wink one eye for intimacy, tap our fingers for impatience, slap our forehead for forgetfulness.[39]

Fast reinforced the theme of his book on body language with a delightful dedication:

> This book is gratefully dedicated to all the passengers of the second car in the Independent Subway's F train, eastbound from Fifth Avenue at 5:22 P.M.[40]

Desmond Morris and his colleagues traced the origins and distribution of common gestures used in many parts of the world. Complete with illustrations, their book interprets the meaning of numerous gestures, including some of the most insulting, used by a sizable portion of the human race.[41]

The supervisor needs to study the meaning of gestures in our society and in other cultures. America is, after all, a multicultural nation. Our schools today reflect this diversity creating the need for multicultural awareness and education. We have only to walk down the streets of San Francisco's Chinatown, New York's Little Italy, or Miami's Little Havana to become aware of subcultures on the American scene. The adults of the subculture (and the children to a lesser extent) perpetuate the traditions, rituals, and customs of the old country.

Different cultures communicate by using different gestures. In some cultures, it is not insulting to point a finger at a person; in others, it is. In some cultures, you can touch a person when you speak; in others, you must not. Some cultures believe in eye contact; others believe eye contact is rude. Some say no by raising their chins and giving a little click of the tongue; others shake the head from side to side. An acceptable gesture in one culture can be an obscenity in another.

Supervisors need to develop a sensitivity to nonverbal language of the persons with whom they work. They should help teachers read the nonverbal language of pupils. Regarding nonverbal communication Alfonso, Firth, and Neville advised:

> Proposition 21: Communication will be more effective if verbal messages and nonverbal cues from the sender reinforce each other.[42]

Supervisors should be skillful in using and reading nonverbal language and must help teachers to use and understand it as well.

The Silent Language. Edward T. Hall wrote a well-known little book called *The Silent Language,* in which he explained the pitfalls people of one culture stumble into when they find themselves in another culture without an understanding of existing but silent cultural characteristics.[43] Although Hall included elements of nonverbal language, his concept of the silent language goes beyond nonverbal language. Hall listed ten kinds of human activities that vary from culture to culture and which he called the Primary Message Systems:

1. *Interaction*: ways we interact with our environment, as through speech and writing. This is the only Primary Message System which involves language.
2. *Association*: ways in which human beings associate with each other, including rank and status.
3. *Subsistence*: ways in which cultures feed themselves and go about earning subsistence; attitudes toward manual labor; characteristic economy.
4. *Bisexuality*: behavior of the sexes toward each other and toward the opposite sex; behavior expected or permitted of each sex by the culture.
5. *Territoriality*: ways human beings defend their turf.
6. *Temporality*: differing conceptions of time, including punctuality or the lack of it.
7. *Learning*: differences in ways of learning to learn.
8. *Play*: recreation and leisure.
9. *Defense*: ways in which cultures protect themselves from enemies, potential and real, and from adversities of nature.
10. *Exploitation* (use of materials): ways of exploiting the environment, as through technology, for example.[44]

Hall's target audience was Americans going abroad. He believed that by understanding the Primary Message Systems of other cultures, Americans could avoid cultural dissonance and conflict. His concept of a silent language, however, is useful to supervisors who are in school systems with a multicultural population. The Primary Message Systems, though perhaps muted by the (North) American culture, can still be operant, and may be more pronounced in some school personnel and students than in others. We would single out attitudes about feminine and masculine behavior, protectiveness of one's vested interests and space, attitudes toward time and its use, and attitudes toward curricula and methods as having special significance to the supervisor in our pluralistic society.

If a supervisor is to be an effective group leader, he or she must demonstrate skills in communication. The supervisor must be both a practitioner and a student of language. The supervisor needs to be able to help teachers understand and cope with cultural diversity.

Group Process
For this analysis, let's discuss the process supervisors follow when they accept the role of group leader. Of course, the supervisor will not always serve as leader of a group; teachers may and should fill leadership positions as the situations demand.

In fact, leadership from the group should be encouraged by the supervisor, and he or she should continuously provide opportunities for developing leadership. It is unfortunate, perhaps, that discussing group process involves the terms *leaders* and *followers*, for the term *follower* implies an unthinking docility that is undesirable here. The *leader-follower* terminology also plants the idea that the leader is never a follower and that followers are never leaders. In professional groups such as teacher committees, teams, and faculties, that is not the case at all, for leadership and followership are roles that are constantly rotated as the occasion demands and as certain kinds of expertise are called for. Some teachers who consistently play the role of follower and never seek to exert leadership do so because they have been conditioned by status leaders to believe that followership is their only role, and therefore, they have never tested their own leadership skills.

The development of leadership skills from within the group should be a goal the supervisor places high on the agenda, making the supervisor, in effect, the leader of leaders. The term *follower*, as used here, connotes no demeaning status but simply means a person who is not serving as a leader at that time. Let's look at how the supervisor's skills in group process can help teachers work together. The following guidelines are applicable to the deliberations of a task-oriented work group.

1. *A good deal of what is called processing can take place at the initial meeting of a faculty group.* It is then that members of the group are introduced to one another and housekeeping chores are dispensed with. Coffee-and-donuts—or, in this health-conscious age, fruit and other nonfattening foods—are served at this time, a commendable way to loosen up a group and set a pleasant working atmosphere. In the introductory remarks, the supervisor will help the group feel that their task is important and that they are the ideal ones to carry it out. Relevance of their task is just as important to a group as relevance of content is to a learner. If the task is trivial and unimportant, professional people should not be asked to waste their time on it.

2. *The goals and objectives of the group's work should be set at the initial or next meeting.* Commonly, the goal has already been determined prior to the group's formation. Indeed, it is the reason the group was established. The goal may come in the form of a charge from the administrator or from the faculty. The group's task is to refine the goal and from it derive the specific objectives of its work. It must decide not only on its objectives but also on how to pursue them—who will do what, on what kind of time schedule it will operate, and how it will evaluate its work. The time schedule is an important feature some groups overlook; consequently, they put off a significant portion of their work until the last minute. A task force would do well to specify completion dates for segments of its work. This procedure not only helps keep the work on schedule but also reassures the group periodically that it is making progress. Feedback showing continuous progress is a strong motivator to keep a group working on a task.

3. *The supervisor has the responsibility for keeping the group on task, which is often no easy job.* The word *taskmaster* is too strong as it implies a despotism that is not advocated; but it is the supervisor's duty to try to prevent groups from digressing and to remind them of the topic at hand when they do go off on tangents.

Some supervisors make the mistake of interpreting their leadership role as one that is nondirective or laissez-faire. With such an approach, however, groups can flounder, procrastinate, and fail to achieve their objectives. Someone must serve as the "gatekeeper," the work conscience of the group, and the supervisor is in a strategic position to fulfill that role.

The role of group leader requires more than merely presiding at group meetings; it necessitates planning and continuous facilitation. The leader must make sure ahead of time that those who are scheduled to present data for the group's deliberation will be ready and present. He or she must be certain that all resources needed by the group will be available at the time the group needs access to them. Equipment, materials, and resource people must be arranged for well in advance of a meeting and be ready for use if the group is to be kept on task. Once the group is in session, the leader continues to serve as a facilitator who attempts to secure maximum participation of all members of the group.

4. *The supervisor must demonstrate skill in the group process.* It is up to the supervisor to recognize types of behavior of group members that impede the group's progress and to know when individuals are performing what some call "self-serving functions." For example, he or she should be able to detect individuals who exhibit aggressive behavior, dominate the discussion and cut off their colleagues, make a play for attention, thwart the efforts of the group, and have their own special axes to grind. At the same time, the supervisor should be perceptive enough to realize that some members have withdrawn from participation, some appear disinterested, and some are fearful of expressing themselves.

As a responsible chairperson, the supervisor can reduce some of the problems that may occur because the members are not themselves skilled in the group process. Although parliamentary procedure with all its refinements is neither necessary nor desirable in most work groups, reliance on some of its more overt manifestations may prove helpful to the group leader. As a parliamentary leader, the supervisor can insist that people speak one at a time. He or she can fail to recognize the attention getter and the individual who wishes to monopolize the discussion.

Ideally, the supervisor should try to bring about the participation of every member of the group. Every member should be made to feel that his or her contributions are significant enough to be considered and discussed. In almost every group, however, we find people who are "quick starters," those who are more verbal and more vocal than others and are always ready to voice their opinions. The quick starter can be a boon to the group leader by helping to get discussion under way with minimal prodding. On the other hand, the quick starters should not be permitted to run away with the discussion. Frequently, a few vocal participants in a group carry on a discussion as if they were the only persons present. The group leader can neither permit nor afford to permit a few verbal individuals to usurp the discussion. The leader must seek input from the slow starters, ask for their opinions, turn to them for reactions, and pose questions to them. For both the quick starters and slow starters the development of discussion skills may be a byproduct of a task-oriented group process.

The supervisor involves group members not only in the discussion phases of the group's work but also in carrying out specific responsibilities designed to accomplish their mission. When the task is complex, subtasks must be assigned and distributed among the entire group so that as many members as possible will feel a close identity with the group's work. The easiest solution to the division of labor is to leave it to volunteers, but that is not always best for the growth of both the individuals and the group. A volunteer may not be the most qualified person in the group to perform a particular task. Besides, others who participate, not vocally but silently, should be drawn into the task. The supervisor resolves this problem by requesting those who are most qualified to accept specific subtasks regardless of their verbal skills and by encouraging distribution of assignments as broadly as possible among the members.

5. *At the end of each session the supervisor should summarize what the group has agreed on and decisions should be made about what steps will be taken next.* Each person's assignments and responsibilities should be clearly understood before the group adjourns. Whenever possible, the group should reach closure on issues under discussion and not leave them hanging. The supervisor has to take care not to force closure prematurely nor prevent closure by dragging out a discussion.

6. *Periodically, the group should take stock of its progress, evaluate its accomplishments, and determine whether it is on schedule.* Every member of the group should know exactly where the group is at any time. If there are subgroups working, they should keep the parent group continuously advised of their progress. The supervisor helps to pace the group's progress by calling to its attention, when it has completed phases of the task, what remains to be done and when the objectives have been realized.

7. *The group must be made to feel that its efforts have been worthwhile.* When a group is working on a particular problem for which it offers a solution, the ultimate hope is that the group's recommendation will be put into practice. Nothing is more motivating to a group than to see its recommendations carried out. Teachers will realize that not every recommendation of every group can be put into operation. Barring actual adoption of a group's recommendations, however, its proposals should be granted a full hearing, and if the recommendations cannot be accepted, the group should be told why. Far too many times service on a committee has left teachers with the hopeless feeling that nothing will come of all the time and effort they put into the committee's work. It is understandable that teachers are often reluctant to commit to some committee projects when their past experience tells them the effort will have no result.

The group leader is a key factor in a group's success or failure in achieving its purposes. The leader sets the stage for the group's deliberations and oversees the operation. But the success of a group does not depend on the leader's skills alone. Each member must possess sufficient skills in interaction to further the interests of all. When a group is involved in a task-oriented situation, it may learn interaction skills incidentally as byproducts of its work. In an ongoing task-oriented situation, the supervisor should be aware that the members of the group are functioning at two levels. They are or should be working to accomplish the objectives of the group as well as to develop their own interaction skills. Although training in skills is tangential to the endeavor of a task-oriented group, special training in the functioning of groups and group interaction is a worthwhile in-service project.

Task versus Process. Groups are made up of two kinds of participants: those who are task-oriented and those who are process-oriented. Task-oriented people want to have the objectives clearly defined. They want to proceed with the job, get it done, and feel a sense of achievement. They are conscious of the time press and impatient with digressions that prevent the group from realizing its goals.

Process-oriented individuals believe that the goals of the group are of secondary importance. In their minds, it is the interaction among people that really counts. As a result of interaction, the goals themselves may change. The interaction is the true goal and not the task imposed by a superior or by the group itself. Process-oriented people believe that everyone should have the opportunity to express himself or herself to the fullest, not only about cognitive matters but also about how he or she feels toward the topic under discussion.

It is a rare faculty group that does not have members of both persuasions. Surely a task orientation without process can lead to sterile and perfunctory decisions, but process without task orientation can lead to frustration and stagnation of a group. As a group leader, the supervisor must achieve a healthy balance between the two orientations, enough that the task-oriented will feel the job is being accomplished and the process-oriented will feel they have had sufficient opportunity to express their views.

If you have attended group sessions you probably have seen that when group deliberations fail, they do so more often because of a lack of task orientation than because of a lack of process orientation. An overemphasis on processing has caused many groups to give up on their tasks. Given their workloads and the many demands on their time and energies, teachers simply cannot tolerate unlimited processing. Teachers as a group are predisposed to a task-oriented approach, according to Ben M. Harris and William R. Hartgraves, who made the following observations:

> *Are supervisors accepted by teachers as valuable members of the instructional staff?*
> Yes, supervisors are highly valued, when teachers have close contact with them in project or other task-oriented situations . . .
> *Are supervisors effective in improving instruction when they serve in a counseling or consultative capacity to individual teachers?*
> Yes, if these consultations are task-oriented and are part of a larger program of activities for change.[45]

A certain amount of processing must occur before a group can get deeply into its task, but the leader must help the group complete its processing so it can move toward achievement of its goals.

GROUP PROCESS VERSUS GROUP COUNSELING

There is a world of difference between the type of group processing—verbal interaction—that is related to a group's pursuit of a goal and the type of group processing that is a goal in itself. In the profession there is a saying that educational change results from a change in people. Although this position is praiseworthy, you can take issue with some of the efforts made to implement the saying. Some supervisors foster a type of group process that is designed not to accomplish a specific task but to help teachers solve their personal problems—in effect, group counseling. When helping teachers with personal problems is the focus of group activity, the group process *is* the task rather than the vehicle for accomplishing the task.

We do not discount the necessity for helping some teachers with personal problems, but we do not see this as a substitute for educational decision making. It should not be bootlegged in under the guise of decision making, or presented as a compulsory or near-compulsory type of activity, or conducted by the typical supervisor. A therapy program should be attempted only by those who are fully qualified to provide that type of help. Far too many supervisors have dabbled in group counseling without sufficient training. Attendance as a participant or trainee at a group therapy institute or workshop does not qualify supervisors to engage in group counseling, which is an effort to help teachers solve their personal problems. Perhaps this is an example of the "physician-heal-thyself" syndrome, in which some supervisors attempt to solve their own personal problems by trying to help others solve theirs.

Group process as interaction among members of a group in quest of a particular task should be distinguished from group process with the goal of solving personal problems of the members. Ideally, the supervisor, in the role of group leader, guides a group toward accomplishment of its task but also helps the group to develop its interaction skills. In-service training in how groups operate, problems in group deliberation, and roles of leaders and followers are decidedly in order. As a matter of fact, personality modification—the goal of group counseling—may come about through training in group interaction skills. As an example, those experienced with groups know that hostility in a member can impede the work of a group. For the group to advance, the hostility roadblock must be overcome. To begin, the group may first attempt to examine the process of group deliberation. By referring to some of the many studies of human groups, the members of the group learn about barriers to group endeavors, including the phenomenon of hostility. This is an intellectualized, conceptual approach. The aim is not to identify the hostility with a particular member of the group, but the hope is that the person will internalize the problem and change his or her behavior. The supervisor as leader is not concerned with the roots of the member's hostility—whether the member hates his or her father or mother or this school, or whether he or she feels unfulfilled or is in the throes of a divorce or is short of money or the countless sources of this type of behavior. The reasons for a person's hostility are external to the group's concerns.

Although a member's hostility is important to that individual, the endeavors of the group supersede his or her personal problems. If the supervisor is to retain the other members of the group, who are experiencing frustration as a result of interaction with the hostile member, the supervisor must, as leader, move the work of the group forward. In a group-counseling situation, members of the group would have every opportunity to release their aggressions, frustrations, and hostilities, but the typical faculty work group is not a counseling situation; it is a task-oriented workforce with limits of time and energy. Because the supervisor works with faculty groups on problems of curriculum and instruction, their time and energy must be dedicated to the solution of those problems. If the supervisor attempts to keep a group on target, the hostile member may be able to intellectualize a problem to the point of being able to shelve his or her hostility and permit the group to achieve its mission. This does not mean that all hostility disappears nor that the member is even a step closer to solving a personal problem. It does mean that the individual has learned to sublimate a personal problem at least long enough for the group to complete its task.

Nothing in these comments should be interpreted to imply that counseling of whatever persuasion—individual or group—is not important. Indeed, it is. A teacher's personality has a tremendous impact on the learners. An enlightened school system will provide opportunities for teachers to obtain individual or group counseling if they wish to so avail themselves. But group counseling in whatever form—T-groups, encounter groups, therapy groups, sensitivity groups—should not be mixed with a task-oriented group process, nor should it be a required part of an in-service training program, a point elaborated toward the end of this chapter.

In this light, the supervisor who is concerned about helping teachers work together should consider a three-part plan consisting of the following elements:

1. The supervisor's development of his or her own leadership skills in conducting task-oriented group sessions
2. Provision of an in-service program on the development of group interaction, human relations, and communications skills—a voluntary, elective program, preferably with tangible incentives for participation
3. Provision of group-therapy-type sessions on a completely voluntary basis and under the direction of trained counselors.

TRAINING IN GROUP INTERACTION

When the supervisor discovers that groups he or she is working with are experiencing difficulty and members of the groups are unable to communicate with each other, it may be expeditious to set up a program designed to help teachers develop interaction skills. Training in interaction skills has application not only for teachers' relationships with each other but also for their relationships with students, other school personnel, and parents. Because training in interpersonal and human-relations skills skirts the fringes of awareness and sensitivity training, this type of training ought to be elective. In fact, participation in any type of training that is primarily for personal development should be voluntary. To make participation appealing to teachers, however, some sort of incentive system should be in operation, as noted in the preceding chapter.

Unless supervisors have had the necessary training, and very commonly they have not, they will need to ask specialists in communication skills or human-relations skills to conduct the training. Consultant monies are often available for staff-development programs, and supervisors might well consider bringing in consultants for this purpose.

In-service education for the development of interaction skills may take a variety of forms. Two promising routes, which may be viewed as companion techniques rather than separate procedures, are (1) formal study and discussion of some of the literature on the sociology and social psychology of human groups, and (2) practice in demonstrating interpersonal skills in a group setting. Although either of these techniques can be implemented without the other, the training program is much stronger if it includes both components. Consultants for the formal study may be found among university specialists in sociology, psychology, education, or management. Consultants for the practice or laboratory training may come from universities' and other agencies' specialists in human-relations skills, social psychology, and communications.

In the first phase of an in-service program on group interaction, the consultant may take the group through some of the classic literature on group formation and functioning. The participants might read and discuss, for example, George C. Homans's *The Human Group*, which provides an excellent introduction to this topic.[46] The consultant might have the participants read and discuss some of the literature on the famed Western Electric research, which provided evidence that when workers are involved in planning, research, and profit sharing their productivity rises.[47] These researchers speak also to the well-known Hawthorne Effect, a rise in productivity as a result of workers' feelings of involvement rather than from a change of technique.

Worthy of teachers' attention are Toffler's books mentioned earlier in this chapter. These works describe well the necessity for human beings to work together to solve social problems that become more acute with each passing year. Teachers might be made familiar with material such as Stuart Chase's popular book, *Roads to Agreement*, which interprets the purpose and functioning of groups in lay language and suggests ways to resolve group conflicts.[48]

No study of group behavior can omit the research of Kurt Lewin, Ronald Lippitt, and Ralph K. White on experimentally created social climates.[49] In studying the effects of three types of adult leadership—authoritarian, democratic, and laissez-faire—on four groups of eleven-year-old children, Lewin, Lippitt, and White made these discoveries:

> Under the authoritarian leadership, the children were more dependent upon the leader, more discontent, made more demands for attention, were less friendly, produced less work-minded conversation than under the democratic leadership. There was no group initiative in the authoritarian group climate.
>
> The laissez-faire atmosphere produced more dependence on the leader, more discontent, less friendliness, fewer group-minded suggestions, less work-minded conversation than under the democratic climate. In the absence of the laissez-faire leader, work was unproductive. The laissez-faire group was extremely dependent upon the leader for information.
>
> . . . relationships among the individuals in the democratic leadership atmosphere were friendlier. Those under the democratic leadership sought more attention and approval from fellow club members. They depended upon each other for recognition as opposed to recognition by the leader under the authoritarian and laissez-faire systems . . . in the absence of the leader the democratic groups proceeded at their work in productive fashion.[50]

The Lewin, Lippitt, and White studies have implications for the types of group climate leaders foster, and they suggest that leaders should examine the social climate of the groups with which they work.

Consultants frequently engage trainees in a study of roles played by individuals in group settings, such as "information giver," "harmonizer," "gatekeeper," and "blocker," terms of great currency in studies of the inner workings of a group. Kenneth D. Benne and Paul Sheats have used these terms and others for their classification of roles played by members of a group.[51] By studying a set of descriptive terms such as the well-known Benne-Sheats classification scheme, teachers who are investigating the functioning of groups may begin to become aware of some of the maintenance tasks required of groups and some of the positive and negative roles played by group members. In the case of negative roles, a teacher may begin to realize some of the impediments to the group process, may attempt to learn whether any of the negative descriptors could apply to him or her, and may change behavior if it appears that a negative descriptor does, indeed, fit.

PRACTICE IN INTERACTION SKILLS

Following the more formal study of group behavior and the functioning of individuals in group settings, laboratory experiences can be created that provide participants with opportunities to demonstrate interaction skills. Training in interaction, communication, and human-relations skills can supplement training in generic instructional skills and study of subject matter. As training in interaction or interpersonal skills runs the risk of some psychological discomfort for some participants, only those trained in the use of group interaction laboratory techniques should attempt to conduct this type of training.

Although training in group interaction comes close to group counseling and awareness training, it stops short of in-depth counseling on personal problems. Its aim is to improve the dynamics of the group and not to provide therapy for individuals' personal problems. Although leaders of training programs in interaction skills must possess special training, they need not necessarily be trained psychologists.

Record of Behavior of Individuals in Groups

A fruitful approach to training in interaction skills is an adaptation and application of the Benne-Sheats classification system just mentioned. An instrument can be created, such as the record of behavior of individuals in groups (Figure 11.2), which can be used to analyze roles played by members of a group as they work together. The roles played by individuals in groups are shown in Table 11.3. The record of behavior converts the Benne-Sheats classification into an instrument by which an observer can record the number of times each individual plays a particular role.[52] The record of behavior lists at the left the task, maintenance, and individual roles played by members of a group. Spaces are provided so an impartial observer can tally instances of specific role performances by individual members of the group. The purpose of such a procedure is to make members of a group more aware of the roles they play.

Using the record of how individuals behave in groups, faculties can devise procedures for studying their own behavior. By digesting the feedback that comes out of each study, they can improve their group's functioning.

	Members								
	A	B	C	D	E	F	G	H	I
Task roles									
Initiator–contributor									
Information seeker									
Opinion seeker									
Information giver									
Opinion giver									
Elaborator									
Coordinator									
Orienter									
Evaluator–critic									
Energizer									
Procedural technician									
Recorder									
Building/maintenance roles									
Encourager									
Harmonizer									
Compromiser									
Gate keeper									
Standard setter									
Group observer									
Follower									
Individual roles									
Aggressor									
Blocker									
Recognition seeker									
Self-confessor									
Playboy									
Dominator									
Help seeker									
Special interest pleader									

Figure 11.2. Record of Behavior of Individuals in Groups. *Source: Kenneth D. Benne and Paul Sheats, "Functional Roles of Group Members,"* Journal of Social Issues *4, no. 2 (Spring 1948): 43–46, as adapted by Peter F. Oliva,* Developing the Curriculum, *2nd ed. (Glenview, Ill.: Scott, Foresman, 1988), ch. 4. Reprinted with permission of the Society for the Psychological Study of Social Issues and Kenneth D. Benne.*

TABLE 11.3. ROLES OF INDIVIDUALS IN GROUPS

Group Task Roles

a. Initiator-contributor: Suggests ideas, ways of solving problems, or procedures.
b. Information seeker: Seeks facts.
c. Opinion seeker: Asks for opinions about the values of suggestions made by members of the group.
d. Information giver: Supplies facts or facts as he/she sees them.
e. Opinion giver: Presents his/her own opinions about the subject under discussion.
f. Elaborator: States implications of suggestions and describes how suggestions might work out if adopted.
g. Coordinator: Tries to synthesize suggestions.
h. Orienter: Lets group know when it is off task.
i. Evaluator-critic: Evaluates suggestions made by group members as to criteria which he/she feels important.
j. Energizer: Spurs the group to activity.
k. Procedural technician: Performs the routine tasks which have to be done such as distributing materials.
l. Recorder: Keeps the group's record.

Group Building and Maintenance Roles

a. Encourager: Praises people for their suggestions.
b. Harmonizer: Settles disagreements among members.
c. Compromiser: Modifies his/her position in the interests of group progress.
d. Gatekeeper: Tries to assure that everybody has a chance to contribute to the discussion.
e. Standard setter or ego ideal: Urges the group to live up to high standards.
f. Group-observer and commentator: Records and reports on the functioning of the group.
g. Follower: Accepts suggestions of others.

Individual Roles

a. Aggressor: Attacks others or their ideas.
b. Blocker: Opposes suggestions and group decisions.
c. Recognition-seeker: Seeks personal attention.
d. Self-confessor: Expresses personal feelings not applicable to the group's efforts.
e. Playboy: Refrains from getting involved in the group's work with sometimes disturbing behavior.
f. Dominator: Interrupts others and tries to assert own superiority.
g. Help-seeker: Tries to elicit sympathy for himself/herself.
h. Special interest pleader: Reinforces his/her position by claiming to speak for others not represented in the group.

Source: From Kenneth D. Benne and Paul Sheats, "Functional Roles of Group Members," The Journal of Social Issues 4, no. 2 (Spring 1948): 43–46; as reproduced in Peter F. Oliva, Developing the Curriculum, 2nd ed. (Glenview, Ill.: Scott, Foresman, 1988), ch. 4. Reprinted with permission of the Society for the Psychological Study of Social Issues and Kenneth D. Benne.

PROVISION OF GROUP THERAPY-TYPE SESSIONS

An observer of the schools does not need much time to conclude that some teachers "need help," as the euphemism goes. The critics of education have pointed out enough horrifying examples to underscore the need of some teachers for help with their personal problems. However, because some teachers need help does not mean that all teachers do; and those who do may not profit from the "help" that may be given them.

Undoubtedly, as a part of a school system's program for the personal and professional development of teachers, opportunities should be made available for therapy, awareness, or sensitivity training in one or more of its many varieties. Under no circumstances, however, should this type of training be required.

Although school systems may provide incentives for participation in group counseling sessions, teachers should clearly understand the nature of the training program they are getting into and should have the right to refuse to participate. Sometimes sensitivity training is brought surreptitiously into task-oriented groups without the advance knowledge and consent of the participants. Other unacceptable techniques for garnering attendance at awareness sessions are the use of peer pressure to gain participation and, worst of all, administrative fiat.

Sensitivity sessions can be recommended for those participants who volunteer for the program and who recognize a need for the training. Without the individual's willing participation, results will be minimal or even harmful. If teachers are coerced or pressured to participate in awareness sessions, they start the program with a level of hostility, can actively sabotage the sessions, or can shrewdly play games with the trainer and other members of the group.

The supervisor's role in sensitivity training is to help facilitate voluntary sessions, preferably systemwide (or on a broader scale yet) rather than limited to the faculty of one school who must face each other day in, day out. The supervisor should help make arrangements for the sessions, help secure thoroughly trained staff, notify faculty of the sessions, and then step out of the trainer's way. The supervisor should not serve either as a member of the trainer's staff or as a participant in the program. The presence of a person who in any way is viewed by the trainees as a superior and in a position to penalize them for "opening up" will only impede the group and may, in fact, destroy its effectiveness.

These recommendations on sensitivity training are meant to be a middle ground between extravagant claims by some advocates of sensitivity training and unreasonable objections of some opponents of all forms of awareness training. The extreme advocates see sensitivity training as the greatest tonic since cod liver oil and the extreme nay-sayers view awareness training as witch's brew. Sensitivity training is one way by which some teachers can learn to work together.

National Staff Development Council

Supervisors will find the National Staff Development Council a valuable source of help and support. Founded in 1980, the Council promotes staff-development practices and programs, sponsors workshops, and holds annual national conferences on staff development. The association disseminates information and shares ideas through its publications: *The Developer* and the *Journal of Staff Development*.[53] Unlike the much larger and much older organization, the Association for Supervision and Curriculum Development, whose interests encompass curriculum, instruction, and supervision at all levels of the educational ladder, the National Staff Development Council focuses on the needs of local school district supervisors in their roles as staff developers.

SUMMARY

Supervisors spend a considerable portion of their time with teachers in groups of varying sizes and composition. To accomplish much of the school's work teachers must learn to function together in groups, and one of the goals of supervision is the enhancement of teachers' skills in working cooperatively. Groups are composed of both task-oriented and process-oriented people. The task-oriented seek to get the job done, and the process-oriented are concerned with individual expression and self-fulfillment. Although a certain amount of processing is necessary in any group endeavor, most faculty groups should be task-oriented.

Supervisors must possess leadership skills. They should generally follow a democratic, human-relations-oriented approach but must know when to use an authoritarian, task-oriented approach. To be effective leaders, supervisors must be skilled in decision making, effecting change, organizational development, communication, and group process.

Decision making is at the heart of administrative and supervisory behavior. The supervisor can expect to be called on to serve as a change agent, contributing to the development of both staff members and the organization.

Organizations possess both an institutional and a personal dimension. The behavior of the members of the institution and the uniqueness of the institution itself result from the interaction of the two dimensions.

Supervisors must be able to manage their own time, stress, and conflicts and at the same time help staff members to do likewise. Supervisors must be skillful in the use of oral, written, and nonverbal language. They should help staff members develop awareness of the importance of their own oral, written, and nonverbal communication skills. Supervisors must also help teachers understand the cultural phenomenon of the silent language.

A supervisor should exert democratic group leadership and should help teachers develop skills in the group process. Goals and objectives should be established at the beginning of the group's work, and after the group has begun its work it should try to keep on task. Groups should evaluate their progress and should be assured that their efforts will be recognized. The most effective type of recognition is full consideration or adoption of group decisions.

The supervisor works to develop skills in group interaction in two ways: (1) by example and direction in the performance of a task and (2) by instituting special voluntary training in group interaction skills. Training in interaction skills should include study of group behavior and functioning and provision of opportunities for individuals to demonstrate interaction skills.

Sensitivity training should be made available to teachers on a voluntary basis and should be under the direction of specialists trained in group therapy.

QUESTIONS FOR DISCUSSION

1. How do qualifications needed by supervisors differ from those of administrators?
2. How can you handle teachers who disrupt the work of a task force of which they are members?
3. Are the school's internal politics detrimental to the school's goals?
4. How do you go about team building?
5. How can you nurture leadership among the faculty?

ACTIVITIES FOR FURTHER STUDY

1. Distinguish among leader, administrator, and manager.
2. Describe the characteristics of Theory X and Theory Y leaders (see Douglas M. McGregor in chapter bibliography).
3. Identify three styles of leadership and tell which style you prefer and why.
4. Write a paper contrasting human-relations supervision and human-resources supervision.
5. Contrast Value-Added Dimensions with Value Dimensions of leadership as perceived by Thomas J. Sergiovanni (see chapter bibliography).
6. Make a list of your own propositions regarding (a) decision making, (b) change theory, and (c) communication skills. Also, consult Robert J. Alfonso, Gerald R. Firth, and Richard F. Neville (see chapter bibliography) for additional propositions.
7. Tell how the supervisor works in the capacity of change agent.
8. Define the term *organizational development* and explain how this term differs from *staff development*.
9. List several sources of conflict in an organization and tell what the supervisor can do to reduce each.
10. Explain the terms *nomothetic* and *idiographic* and what their significance is.
11. Describe Theory Z and draw implications for school supervisors (see William G. Ouchi in chapter bibliography).
12. Prepare a report on American companies that use a Japanese-style approach of group participation in management.
13. Suggest ways to improve the management of your time.
14. Identify several sources of stress and tell how you would manage these.
15. Study the literature on management by objectives/results and write a critique of the process.
16. Suggest several ways of improving communications between (a) supervisor and administrator, (b) supervisor and teachers, (c) among teachers.
17. Read and write a report on Charles Galloway's *Silent Language in the Classroom* (see chapter bibliography). Draw implications for the supervisor and teacher.
18. Read and write a report on Julius Fast's *Body Language* (see chapter bibliography). Draw implications for the supervisor and teacher.

19. Read and write a report on Desmond Morris et al., *Gestures: Their Origins and Distribution* (see chapter bibliography). Draw implications for the supervisor and teacher.
20. Read and write a report on Edward T. Hall's *The Silent Language* (see chapter bibliography). Draw implications for the supervisor and teacher.
21. Explain and give examples of (a) nonverbal language, (b) body language, and (c) silent language.
22. Describe the three channels of nonverbal communication—proxemics, kinesics, and prosody as used by C. A. Bowers and David J. Flinders (see chapter bibliography)—and draw implications for the supervisor and teacher.
23. Describe skills needed to lead (a) a faculty meeting, (b) a faculty study committee, and (c) an encounter group.
24. Distinguish between task-oriented and process-oriented groups. Draw implications for the instructional supervisor.
25. Explain the place of group therapy or sensitivity sessions in in-service education.
26. Describe the Getzels-Guba model of educational administration as a social process and draw implications for the supervisor (see chapter bibliography).
27. Describe the Getzels-Thelen model of the classroom group as a social system and draw implications for the supervisor (see chapter bibliography).
28. Plan a series of study sessions on group behavior to include types of consultants needed, resources to be used, and media to be employed.
29. Plan an in-service program for training in interpersonal skills.
30. Serve as a member of a task-oriented faculty group and write a report diagnosing problems in the group process. (Individuals should not be named in the report.)
31. Serve as a leader of a task-oriented faculty group and write a self-evaluation of your performance as the group's leader.
32. Write a position paper on one of these topics: (a) Supervision Must Be Primarily Task-Oriented, or (b) Supervision Must Be Primarily Process-Oriented. Support your position with quotations from at least two references not mentioned in this chapter.
33. Report the specified goals and objectives of any faculty work group of which you are now a member or of which you have recently been a member. Comment on the adequacy of the statement of goals and objectives of this group.
34. Observe (with permission) a faculty group in action and apply an instrument such as one based on the Benne-Sheats classification of roles; provide the group with feedback from your observation.
35. Observe chairpersons of at least two faculty groups in action and without identifying the chairpersons classify their leadership as democratic, authoritarian, or laissez-faire.
36. Compile a bibliography of at least six references you would recommend to teachers on group behavior. (Omit references cited in this chapter.)
37. Read and write a report on Alvin Toffler's *Future Shock* and/or *The Third Wave* (see chapter bibliography). Draw implications for the supervisor and teacher.
38. View the film *Future Shock*, if available, and write a critique of its implications for your school.
39. Examine the curriculum development program of a school you know well and list opportunities teachers have had to work together on that program in the last five months. (Do not list routine administrative faculty meetings.)
40. Poll several teachers and ask the following questions: In your experience, are most faculty committees productive or not productive? If you believe they are not

productive, what are the reasons for their lack of productivity? Summarize the teachers' comments in a short paper.

41. Discover and report to class what opportunities for group leadership have been made available to teachers in a school you know well in the last six months.

42. Determine and report to class the attitudes of at least three teachers toward a program of sensitivity training for teachers.

43. Ask at least four teachers to suggest ways in which a supervisor can help teachers to work together. Summarize the teachers' suggestions and report them to your class.

44. List a set of interaction, human-relations, and communications skills that you believe are essential to the teacher in your role as group leader of your classes.

45. Write a paper using selected references on the topic Techniques for Developing Human-Relations Skills of Teachers.

46. Prepare a report on the contributions of W. Edwards Deming to the field of management.

47. Summarize, citing several text and/or periodical references, principles of Total Quality Management.

NOTES

1. Alexis de Tocqueville, *Democracy in America, Part the Second: The Social Influence of Democracy*, trans. Henry Reeve (New York: J. & H. G. Langley, 1840), rev. Francis Bowen (New York: Alfred A. Knopf, 1945), p. 106.

2. Carl D. Glickman, Stephen P. Gordon, and Jovita M. Ross-Gordon, *Supervision of Instruction: A Developmental Approach* (Boston: Allyn & Bacon, 1995), p. 311.

3. See John K. Hemphill and Alvin E. Coons, *Leader Behavior Description* (Columbus: Personnel Research Board, Ohio State University, 1950). See also Ralph M. Stogdill, *Handbook of Leadership: A Survey of Theory and Research* (New York: Free Press, 1974); Rensis Likert, *The Human Organization: Its Management* (New York: McGraw-Hill, 1967).

4. Fred E. Fiedler, *A Theory of Leadership Effectiveness* (New York: McGraw-Hill, 1967), p. 8.

5. Ralph M. Stogdill, "Leadership, Membership, and Organization," *Psychological Bulletin* 47 (1950): 4. See also Stogdill, *Handbook of Leadership*, p. 10.

6. James M. Lipham and James A. Hoeh, Jr., *The Principalship: Foundations and Functions* (New York: Harper & Row, 1974), p. 182.

7. James M. Lipham, "Leadership and Administration," *Behavioral Science and Educational Administration*, 63d Yearbook, Part II, ed. Daniel E. Griffiths (Chicago: National Society for the Study of Education, 1964), p. 122.

8. W. H. Cowley, "Three Distinctions in the Study of Leaders," *Journal of Abnormal and Social Psychology* 23 (July–September 1928): 145.

9. Robert L. De Bruyn, *Causing Others to Want Your Leadership* (Manhattan, Kan.: R. L. De Bruyn & Associates, 1976), p. 14.

10. See Ralph M. Stogdill, "Personal Factors Associated with Leadership: A Study of the Literature," *Journal of Psychology* 25 (January 1948): 35–71. Reprinted in Stogdill, *Handbook of Leadership*, chap. 5. See also Ralph B. Kimbrough and Michael Y. Nunnery, *Educational Administration: An Introduction*, 3rd ed. (New York: Macmillan, 1988), pp. 346–48.

11. Stogdill, *Handbook of Leadership*, pp. 62–63.

12. Paul Hersey and Kenneth H. Blanchard, *Management of Organizational Behavior: Utilizing Human Resources*, 5th ed. (Englewood Cliffs, N.J.: Prentice-Hall, 1988), pp. 169–201.

13. Kurt Lewin, Ronald Lippitt, and Ralph K. White, "Patterns of Aggressive Behavior in Experimentally Created 'Social Climates,'" *Journal of Social Psychology* 10 (May 1939):

271–99; Douglas M. McGregor, *The Human Side of Enterprise* (New York: McGraw-Hill, 1960); Fred E. Fiedler, A *Theory of Leadership Effectiveness*; Edgar L. Morphet, Roe L. Johns, and Theodore L. Reller, *Educational Organization and Administration*: *Concepts, Practices, and Issues*, 4th ed. (Englewood Cliffs, N.J.: Prentice-Hall, 1982).

14. Thomas J. Sergiovanni and Robert J. Starratt, *Supervision: A Redefinition*, 5th ed. (New York: McGraw-Hill, 1993). See also Raymond Miles, "Human Relations or Human Resources?" *Harvard Business Review* 43 (July–August 1965): 148–63; Mason Haire, Edwin Ghiselli, and Lyman Porter, *Management Thinking: An International Study* (New York: Wiley, 1966).

15. Thomas J. Sergiovanni, *Value-Added Leadership: How to Get Extraordinary Performance in Schools* (Orlando, Fla.: Harcourt Brace Jovanovich, 1990).

16. See Chester I. Barnard, *The Functions of the Executive* (Cambridge, Mass.: Harvard University Press, 1938); Daniel E. Griffiths, *Administrative Theory* (New York: Appleton-Century-Crofts, 1959); Herbert A. Simon, *The New Science of Management Decision* (New York: Harper & Row, 1960).

17. See Griffiths, *Administrative Theory*, pp. 92–113. See also Alvar Elbing, *Behavior Decisions in Organizations*, 2nd ed. (Glenview, Ill.: Scott, Foresman, 1978); Roger A. Kaufman, "Systems Approaches to Education: Discussion and Attempted Integration," in *Social and Technological Change: Implications for Education*, Philip K. Piele, Terry L. Eidell, and Stuart C. Smith, eds. (Eugene: Center for the Advanced Study of Educational Administration, University of Oregon, 1970), p. 160.

18. Robert J. Alfonso, Gerald R. Firth, and Richard F. Neville, *Instructional Supervision: A Behavior System*, 2nd ed. (Boston: Allyn & Bacon, 1981), chap. 7.

19. Ibid., pp. 228, 233, 234, 235.

20. Alvin Toffler, *Future Shock* (New York: Random House, 1970); *The Third Wave* (New York: William Morrow, 1980).

21. John O'Neil, "On Preparing Students for the World of Work: A Conversation with Willard Daggett," *Educational Leadership* 52, no. 8 (May 1995): 46–48.

22. Shirley M. Hord, William L. Rutherford, Leslie Huling-Austin, and Gene E. Hall, *Taking Charge of Change* (Alexandria, Va.: Association for Supervision and Curriculum Development, 1987), pp. 84–85.

23. Alfonso, Firth, and Neville, *Instructional Supervision*, ch. 8.

24. Ibid., pp. 273, 276, 278, 282.

25. Richard Beckhard, *Organization Development: Strategies and Models* (Reading, Mass.: Addison-Wesley, 1969), p. 9.

26. Wendell L. French and Cecil H. Bell, Jr., *Organization Development* (Englewood Cliffs, N.J.: Prentice-Hall, 1973), p. 15.

27. Fred Luthans, *Organizational Behavior*, 6th ed. (New York: McGraw-Hill, 1992), p. 391.

28. See Jacob W. Getzels and Herbert A. Thelen, "The Classroom Group as a Unique Social System," in *The Dynamics of Instructional Groups: Sociological Aspects of Teaching and Learning*, 59th Yearbook, Part II, ed. Nelson B. Henry (Chicago: National Society for the Study of Education, 1960), p. 80.

29. See William G. Ouchi, *Theory Z: How American Business Can Meet the Japanese Challenge* (Reading, Mass.: Addison-Wesley, 1981). See also Joel Kotkin and Yoriko Kishimoto, "Theory F," *Inc.* 8 (April 1986): 53–60. The F in Theory F stands for Fear.

30. W. Edwards Deming, *Out of the Crisis: Productivity and Competitive Position* (Cambridge, Mass.: Massachusetts Institute of Technology, 1986).

31. Gilbert R. Weldy, *Time: A Resource for the School Administrator* (Reston, Va.: National Association of Secondary School Principals, 1974).

32. Michael C. Giammatteo and Dolores M. Giammatteo, *Executive Well-Being: Stress and Administrators* (Reston, Va.: National Association of Secondary School Principals, 1980).

33. "The Man from Plains Sums It Up," *Time* (October 11, 1982): 63.
34. Alfonso, Firth, and Neville, *Instructional Supervision*, pp. 174–86.
35. Ibid., pp. 178–82.
36. Ibid., p. 176.
37. C. A. Bowers and David J. Flinders, *Culturally Responsive Teaching and Supervision: A Handbook for Staff Development* (New York: Teachers College Press, 1991), pp. 16–18, 44–48. See also David J. Flinders, "Supervision as Cultural Inquiry," *Journal of Curriculum and Supervision* 6 (Winter 1991): 87–106.
38. Charles Galloway, *Silent Language in the Classroom* (Bloomington, Ind.: Phi Delta Kappa Educational Foundation, 1976), p. 10. See also Charles W. Beegle and Richard H. Brandt, *Observational Methods in the Classroom* (Alexandria, Va.: Association for Supervision and Curriculum Development, 1973), pp. 45–55.
39. Julius Fast, *Body Language* (New York: M. Evans and Company, 1970), pp. 15–16.
40. Ibid., p. 4.
41. Desmond Morris et al., *Gestures: Their Origins and Distribution* (New York: Stein and Day, 1979).
42. Alfonso, Firth, and Neville, *Instructional Supervision*, p. 182.
43. Edward T. Hall, *The Silent Language* (New York: Doubleday, 1959).
44. Ibid., pp. 45–46.
45. Ben M. Harris and William R. Hartgraves, "Supervisor Effectiveness: A Research Résumé," *Educational Leadership* 30 (October 1972): 78.
46. George C. Homans, *The Human Group* (New York: Harcourt Brace Jovanovich, 1950).
47. F. J. Roethlisberger and William J. Dickson, *Management and the Worker* (Cambridge, Mass.: Harvard University Press, 1939). For a critical view of the Western Electric researches see Berkeley Rice, "The Hawthorne Defect: Persistence of a Flawed Theory," *Psychology Today* 16 (February 1982): 70–74.
48. Stuart Chase, *Roads to Agreement* (New York: Harper & Row, 1951).
49. Lewin, Lippitt, and White, "Patterns of Aggressive Behavior."
50. Lewin, Lippitt, and White research as summarized by Peter F. Oliva, "High School Discipline in American Society," *The National Association of Secondary School Principals Bulletin* 40 (January 1956): 7–8.
51. Kenneth D. Benne and Paul Sheats, "Functional Roles of Group Members." *Journal of Social Issues* 4 (Spring 1948): 43–46, a discussion of roles as developed by the First National Training Laboratory in Group Development, 1947.
52. See also Thomas J. Sergiovanni and Robert J. Starratt, *Emerging Patterns of Supervision: Human Perspectives* (New York: McGraw-Hill, 1971), pp. 194–99.
53. National Staff Development Council, P.O. Box 240, Oxford, OH 45056.

BIBLIOGRAPHY

Alfonso, Robert J., Gerald R. Firth, and Richard F. Neville. *Instructional Supervision: A Behavior System.* Boston: Allyn & Bacon, 1981.

Barnard, Chester I. *The Functions of the Executive.* Cambridge, Mass.: Harvard University Press, 1938.

Bartky, John A. *Supervision as Human Relations.* Boston: D. C. Heath, 1953.

Beckhard, Richard. *Organizational Development: Strategies and Models.* Reading, Mass.: Addison-Wesley, 1969.

Beegle, Charles W., and Richard H. Brandt. *Observational Methods in the Classroom.* Alexandria, Va.: Association for Supervision and Curriculum Development, 1973.

Benne, Kenneth D., and Paul Sheats. "Functional Roles of Group Members." *Journal of Social Issues* 4 (Spring 1948): 41–49.

Bennis, Warren G., Kenneth D. Benne, and Robert Chin, eds. *The Planning of Change*, 4th ed. Orlando, Fla.: Holt, Rinehart and Winston, 1984.

Bowers, C. A., and David J. Flinders. *Culturally Responsive Teaching and Supervision: A Handbook for Staff Development.* New York: Teachers College Press, 1991.

——. *Responsive Teaching: An Ecological Approach to Classroom Patterns of Language, Culture, and Thought.* New York: Teachers College Press, 1990.

Bradford, Leland P., and John R. P. French, eds. "The Dynamics of the Discussion Group." *Journal of Social Issues* 4 (Spring 1948): entire issue.

Carkhuff, Robert R., David H. Berenson, and Richard M. Pierce. *The Skills of Teaching: Interpersonal Skills.* Amherst, Mass.: Human Resource Development Press, 1977.

Chase, Stuart. *Roads to Agreement.* New York: Harper & Row, 1951.

Crosby, Muriel. *Supervision as Co-operative Action.* New York: Appleton-Century-Crofts, 1957.

Daresh, John C., and Marsha A. Playko. *Supervision as a Proactive Process: Concepts and Cases.* Prospect Heights, Ill.: Waveland Press, 1995.

De Bruyn, Robert L. *Causing Others to Want Your Leadership.* Manhattan, Kan.: R. L. De Bruyn & Associates, 1976.

Deming, W. Edwards. *Out of the Crisis: Productivity and Competitive Position.* Cambridge, Mass.: Massachusetts Institute of Technology, 1986.

Dillon-Peterson, Betty, ed. *Staff Development/Organization Development.* 1981 Yearbook. Alexandria, Va.: Association for Supervision and Curriculum Development, 1981.

Drucker, Peter F. *Management: Tasks, Responsibilities, Practices.* New York: Harper & Row, 1974.

Duke, Daniel L. *School Leadership and Instructional Improvement.* New York: Random House, 1987.

Fast, Julius. *Body Language.* New York: M. Evans and Company, 1970.

——. *The Body Language of Sex, Power, and Aggression.* New York: M. Evans and Company, 1977.

Fiedler, Fred E. *A Theory of Leadership Effectiveness.* New York: McGraw-Hill, 1967.

Flinders, David J. "Supervision as Cultural Inquiry." *Journal of Curriculum and Supervision* 6 (Winter 1991): 87–106.

French, Wendell L., and Cecil H. Bell, Jr. *Organization Development.* Englewood Cliffs, N.J.: Prentice-Hall, 1973.

Galloway, Charles. "The Nonverbal Realities of Classroom Life." In *Observational Methods in the Classroom.* Charles Beegle and Richard H. Brandt, eds. Alexandria, Va.: Association for Supervision and Curriculum Development, 1973.

——. *Silent Language in the Classroom.* Bloomington, Ind.: Phi Delta Kappa Educational Foundation, 1976.

Getzels, Jacob W. "Administration as a Social Process." In *Administrative Theory in Education.* Andrew W. Halpin, ed. New York: Macmillan, 1958.

Getzels, Jacob W., and Herbert A. Thelen. "The Classroom Group as a Unique Social System." In *The Dynamics of Instructional Groups: Sociological Aspects of Teaching and Learning.* 59th Yearbook, Part II. Nelson B. Henry, ed. Chicago: National Society for the Study of Education, 1960.

Giammatteo, Michael C., and Dolores M. Giammatteo. *Executive Well-Being: Stress and Administrators.* Reston, Va.: National Association of Secondary School Principals, 1980.

Glickman, Carl D., Stephen P. Gordon, and Jovita M. Ross-Gordon. *Supervision of Instruction: A Developmental Approach.* Boston: Allyn & Bacon, 1995.

Greenfield, William. *Instructional Leadership: Concepts, Issues, and Controversies.* Boston: Allyn & Bacon, 1987.

Griffiths, Daniel E. *Administrative Theory*. New York: Appleton-Century-Crofts, 1959.

Haire, Mason, Edwin Ghiselli, and Lyman Porter. *Management Thinking: An International Study*. New York: Wiley, 1966.

Hall, Edward T. *The Silent Language*. New York: Doubleday, 1959.

Harris, Ben M., and William R. Hartgraves. "Supervisor Effectiveness: A Research Résumé." *Educational Leadership* 30 (October 1972): 73–79.

Hemphill, John K., and Alvin E. Coons. *Leader Behavior Description*. Columbus: Ohio State University, 1950.

Hersey, Paul, and Kenneth H. Blanchard. *Management of Organizational Behavior: Utilizing Human Resources*, 5th ed. Englewood Cliffs, N.J.: Prentice-Hall, 1988.

Homans, George C. *The Human Group*. New York: Harcourt Brace Jovanovich, 1950.

Hord, Shirley M., William L. Rutherford, Leslie Huling-Austin, and Gene E. Hall. *Taking Charge of Change*. Alexandria, Va.: Association for Supervision and Curriculum Development, 1987.

Kaufman, Roger A. *Educational System Planning*. Englewood Cliffs, N.J.: Prentice-Hall, 1972.

Kimbrough, Ralph B., and Michael Y. Nunnery. *Educational Administration: An Introduction*, 3rd ed. New York: Macmillan, 1988.

Knezevich, Stephen J. *Administration of Public Education*, 4th ed. New York: HarperCollins, 1984.

Landsberger, Henry A. *Hawthorne Revisited: Management and the Worker: Its Critics and Developments in Human Relations in Industry*. Ithaca, N.Y.: Cornell University, 1958.

Lewin, Kurt, Ronald Lippitt, and Ralph K. White. "Patterns of Aggressive Behavior in Experimentally Created 'Social Climates.'" *Journal of Social Psychology* 10 (May 1939): 271–99.

Likert, Rensis. *The Human Organization: Its Management*. New York: McGraw-Hill, 1967.

Lipham, James M. "Leadership and Administration." *Behavioral Science and Educational Administration*. 63rd Yearbook, Part II, edited by Daniel E. Griffiths. Chicago: National Society for the Study of Education.

Lipham, James M., and James A. Hoeh, Jr. *The Principalship: Foundations and Functions*. New York: Harper & Row, 1974.

Luthans, Fred. *Organizational Behavior*, 6th ed. New York: McGraw-Hill, 1992.

McGregor, Douglas M. *The Human Side of Enterprise*. New York: McGraw-Hill, 1960.

Miles, Raymond. "Human Relations or Human Resources?" *Harvard Business Review* 43 (July–August 1965): 148–63.

Morphet, Edgar L., Roe L. Johns, and Theodore L. Reller. *Educational Organization and Administration: Concepts, Practices, and Issues*, 4th ed. Englewood Cliffs, N.J.: Prentice-Hall, 1982.

Morris, Desmond, Peter Collett, Peter Marsh, and Marie O'Shaughnessey. *Gestures: Their Origins and Distribution*. New York: Stein and Day, 1979.

O'Neil, John. "On Preparing Students for the World of Work: A Conversation with Willard Daggett." *Educational Leadership* 52, no. 8 (May 1995): 46–48.

Ouchi, William G. *Theory Z: How American Business Can Meet the Japanese Challenge*. Reading, Mass.: Addison-Wesley, 1981.

Owens, Robert G. *Organizational Behavior in Schools*, 5th ed. Englewood Cliffs, N.J.: Prentice-Hall, 1995.

Rice, Berkeley. "The Hawthorne Defect: Persistence of a Flawed Theory." *Psychology Today* 16 (February 1982): 70–74.

Roethlisberger, F. J., and William J. Dickson. *Management and the Worker*. Cambridge, Mass.: Harvard University Press, 1939.

Sergiovanni, Thomas J. *Moral Leadership: Getting to the Heart of School Improvement*. San Francisco: Jossey-Bass, 1992.

———. *The Principalship: A Reflective Practice Prospective*, 3rd ed. Needham Heights, Mass.: Allyn & Bacon, 1995.

———. *Value-Added Leadership: How to Get Extraordinary Performance in Schools.* Orlando, Fla.: Harcourt Brace Jovanovich, 1990.

———, ed. *Professional Supervision for Professional Teachers.* Alexandria, Va.: Association for Supervision and Curriculum Development, 1975.

Sergiovanni, Thomas J., and Robert J. Starratt. *Supervision: A Redefinition*, 5th ed. New York: McGraw-Hill, 1993.

Simon, Herbert A. *The New Science of Management Decision.* New York: Harper & Row, 1960.

Steffy, Betty. *Career Stages of Classroom Teachers.* Lancaster, Pa.: Technomic, 1989.

Stogdill, Ralph M. *Handbook of Leadership: A Survey of Theory and Research.* New York: Free Press, 1974.

———. "Leadership, Membership, and Organization." *Psychological Bulletin* 47 (January 1950): 1–14.

———. "Personal Factors Associated with Leadership: A Study of the Literature." *Journal of Psychology* 25 (January 1948): 35–71.

Tanner, Daniel, and Laurel N. Tanner. *Curriculum Development: Theory into Practice*, 3rd ed. New York: Merrill, 1995.

Toffler, Alvin. *Future Shock.* New York: Random House, 1970.

———. *The Third Wave.* New York: William Morrow, 1980.

Tocqueville, Alexis de. *Democracy in America, Part the Second: The Social Influence of Democracy.* Translated by Henry Reeve. New York: J. & H. G. Langley, 1840. Reprint New York: Alfred A. Knopf, 1945.

Weldy, Gilbert R. *Time: A Resource for the School Administrator.* Reston, Va.: National Association of Secondary School Principals, 1974.

Weller, Richard H. *Verbal Communication in Instructional Supervision: An Observational System for and Research Study of Clinical Supervision in Groups.* New York: Teachers College Press, 1971.

Wiles, Jon, and Joseph C. Bondi. *Curriculum Development: A Guide to Practice*, 4th ed. New York: Merrill, 1993.

Zumwalt, Karen K. *Improving Teaching.* 1986 Yearbook. Alexandria, Va.: Association for Supervision and Curriculum Development, 1986.

Films

Future Shock. 42 minutes. 16 mm. Sound, color. Metromedia Producers Corporation. Released by McGraw-Hill, 1972.

Gung Ho. 111 min. Sound, color. Paramount Pictures. Entertaining comedy directed by Ron Howard, starring Michael Keaton. Depicts cultural tensions between Japanese owners and American workers when a Japanese automobile manufacturing company takes over a defunct American automobile factory. 1986.

Multimedia

Northwest Regional Educational Laboratory, 101 S.W. Main Street, Suite 500, Portland, OR 97204-3212.

Instructional system in *Interpersonal Communication.* Participant materials, nine 16 mm. sound films, one audiotape, leader's manual. 30 hours.

Instructional system in *Interpersonal Influence.* Participant materials, four 16 mm. sound films, two audiotapes, leader's manual. Thirty-three hours of instruction on introduction of basic concepts and tools for understanding interpersonal influence, characteristic individual patterns of response to influence situations, and analysis and interpretation of interpersonal influence in small group settings.

Instructional system in *Research Utilizing Problem Solving*, Administrators' Version. Participant materials, audiotape, text (*Diagnosing Professional Climates of Schools* by Fox, Jung, Schmuck, et al.), and leader's guide. Thirty hours of instruction on (1) identifying the problem, (2) diagnosing the problem situation, (3) considering alternative actions, (4) trying out a plan of action, and (5) adapting the plan.

Videotapes

Adult Conflict Resolution. 1994. 40 min. *Facilitator's Guide.* Association for Supervision and Curriculum Development, 1250 North Pitt St., Alexandria, VA 22314.

Bellanca, Jim. *Quality Circles: Problem-Solving Tool for Educators.* 1984. 30 min. Association for Supervision and Curriculum Development, 1250 North Pitt Street, Alexandria, VA 22314.

Cawelti, Gordon. *Selecting Appropriate Leadership Styles for Instructional Improvement.* 1978. 33 min. Association for Supervision and Curriculum Development, 1250 North Pitt Street, Alexandria, VA 22314.

Shared Decision Making. 1994. 2 tapes, 30 min. ea. *Facilitator's Guide.* Association for Supervision and Curriculum Development, 1250 North Pitt St., Alexandria, VA 22314.

12

Helping Teachers Evaluate Their Own Performance

Objectives

After studying Chapter 12 you should be able to accomplish the following objectives:

1. Identify and describe three components of teacher evaluation systems.
2. Develop and use a teacher self-appraisal instrument.
3. Explain the meaning of external and internal analysis as applied to teacher performance.
4. Describe several models of teaching.
5. Analyze your own model of teaching.
6. Produce and classify protocol materials.
7. Use teacher-training packages in assisting teachers to improve instruction.
8. Develop and use an instrument for student evaluation of teacher performance.
9. Develop and use an instrument for parent evaluation of teacher performance.

THREE FACES OF EVALUATION OF TEACHER PERFORMANCE

Teachers sometimes feel that they are the most scrutinized professionals in the world. They live in the public eye. They are subject to more restrictions on their behavior than most professionals, excluding the clergy. Their performance in class and their behavior out of class are evaluated by the public, students, other teachers, and administrators.

Preservice teachers should be advised to expect continuous evaluation of their performance as a way of life. The profession has come to admit that there are wide variations in knowledge, energy, dedication, and skill among the more than two million teachers throughout this land. The profession has also acknowledged that developments in all subject fields and in pedagogy have been rapid, necessitating continual assessment and in-service study on the part of school personnel.

At the same time, there is awareness among teachers, administrators, and supervisors that the evaluation of human performance in any field is a difficult, sensitive matter subject to gross mistakes and misjudgments. No aspect of teaching can be more threatening to teachers than evaluation of their performance. No aspect of administration can be more agonizing for a conscientious administrator than evaluation of teachers. The administrator who asserts that the evaluation of teacher performance is easy, nonthreatening, and routine seriously underestimates the complexities and effects of teacher assessment. The administrator who has this attitude is probably one who has forgotten his or her reactions to evaluation as a teacher and who is not subjected to systematic, formal evaluation as an administrator.

Although teachers need to be receptive to evaluation as a means of improving themselves and the profession, school systems need to devise ways to evaluate teachers that are feasible, fair, humane, and as objective as possible. Currently, over 15,000 systems of teacher evaluation exist, one for each of the more than 15,000 school districts that make up the enterprise of American public education. Of course, we exaggerate a bit. Some states require a specific, uniform assessment program for certain purposes—for example, state certification. Even in those cases, however, many school districts within the state may follow their own systems of evaluation for their own purpose in addition to the state required program.

In this chapter and the next, we examine the complex problem of evaluating teacher performance. As we discuss teacher evaluation, we talk about both evaluation of instruction (and to some extent, of the course or subject) and evaluation of the instructor. These two aspects are, of course, interrelated. By evaluation of instruction we mean appraisal of the effectiveness of the instructional skills and strategies chosen by the teacher. By evaluation of the instructor we mean assessment of the teacher's classroom performance (behavior), his or her effectiveness in employing the skills and strategies selected, and certain personal and professional attributes. In these three chapters we use the words *evaluation*, *assessment*, and *appraisal* interchangeably.

A fully developed program of teacher appraisal consists of three components: *self-evaluation*, *formative evaluation*, and *summative evaluation*. The last term, *summative evaluation*, is the annual assessment done by the administrator, not only for the purpose of improving instruction but also and primarily for asssessing personnel. The latter use involves making decisions about offering a teacher another teaching contract and eventually a long-term teaching contract with tenure; advancement to a leadership position; and in those situations that have it, merit pay or entry and advancement on the career ladder. Summative evaluation is discussed in Chapter 13.

The second term, *formative evaluation*, is ongoing assessment of teacher performance. Administrators and supervisors visit teachers periodically, observe their classes, and confer with the teachers to help them to improve their instruction. We looked at this component in Chapter 10.

The focuses of this chapter are ways in which teachers may appraise their own performance and means by which supervisors can help them do so. All school systems have instituted some sort of summative evaluation of teacher performance. Most school systems have implemented a formative evaluation system of one type or another. Fewer school systems have developed a systematic process for teacher self-appraisal. We believe that a systematic, structured way of encouraging teachers to evaluate themselves is essential and should be an integral part of the evaluation process.

A refrain from Robert Burns may run through the mind of the supervisor pondering the task of helping teachers to evaluate themselves:

> Oh wad some power the giftie gie us
> To see oursels as ithers see us!
> It wad frae monie a blunder free us
> An' foolish notion.

The thoughtful supervisor knows that to contribute to improving the curriculum and instruction, he or she must possess the power to help teachers see themselves "as ithers see us." Perhaps *power* is too strong a word in reference to the supervisor's role—*ability* might be better. The supervisor must possess the ability or skills necessary to encourage teachers to look at their own behavior with a view to improving themselves. More, the supervisor should be able to look at his or her own supervisory behavior, a topic discussed in Chapter 14.

The skill of introspection is difficult to develop. When seeking ways to help teachers evaluate themselves, the supervisor is up against some formidable antagonistic attitudes. Among the notions teachers hold about evaluation of their behaviors are these:

- It is the student alone who should be evaluated; the teacher occupies a position beyond evaluation.
- Apart from the teacher, no one is capable of making an evaluation of that teacher's behavior.
- Every teacher has reached such a high state of professional competence that evaluation is not necessary.
- Teachers already know how to teach twice as well as they have the time or energy to teach or are permitted to teach.
- No other profession makes the assumption that a professional person must be regularly evaluated.
- Teaching is such a highly personalized and individualized art that emphasis on evaluating generic teaching behaviors is misplaced.

When contemplating the problem of helping teachers evaluate themselves, the supervisor also runs into some real and often unexpressed fears of teachers, who have such worries as these:

- They will be exposed and their shortcomings made known to the world.
- They will be subjected to ridicule if they make mistakes.

- Anything less than perfection will penalize them in terms of salary, tenure, or promotion.

Consequently, the teaching profession has built into itself some potent avoidance behaviors. The profession has resisted merit increment plans by raising such questions as Who will do the evaluating? How do you allow for individuality? How can you identify merit in teaching? Some teachers view their own classrooms as their own territorial domains, into which the entrance of administrators, supervisors, and the public is considered an unwarranted intrusion. The flag of academic freedom is frequently hoisted to justify the teacher's performance. Some teachers hold to the viewpoint that if they pass the initial test of an interview, have the appropriate teaching credentials, and are hired by the administrator, they have demonstrated all the competence they need to demonstrate. If it turns out that their professional skills are less than might be desired, they view that situation as the administrator's problem, not theirs.

Because of the antagonistic attitudes and fears of teachers toward evaluation, the supervisor's primary role in the evaluation of teacher competence should be one of helping teachers to evaluate themselves rather than one of evaluating teachers. This subtle distinction is crucial to the problem of evaluation. The role of the supervisor as teacher evaluator can set up barriers between the teacher and the supervisor and perpetuate the fears of teachers. In this evaluative role, the supervisor can be seen as a threat to the teacher rather than a help, and rapport between the supervisor and the teacher may be difficult to achieve.

The supervisor's role in evaluating teachers reveals the school system's concept of supervision—that is, whether supervision is conceived as a function of administration or as a service support to teachers. A central theme of this text has been that supervision for today's schools is first of all a service and only secondarily an administrative function.

Many school systems require supervisors to evaluate teachers, rate them on certain competencies, and fill out annual reports of performance that are submitted to the administrator. It would be preferable, however, for the administrator to assume the role of teacher-rater, removing this task from the shoulders of the supervisor and allowing the supervisor to concentrate on the role he or she should fulfill—helping teachers improve their teaching skills. If a supervisor must rate a teacher and report the ratings to the administrator—and this must be done in many school systems— the ratings themselves should be played down, teachers themselves should enter fully into the process of rating, ratings should be liberally interpreted, and emphasis throughout the process should be on helping teachers to evaluate their own performances. Further, the confidentiality of such evaluations must be preserved and restricted to only those who have the right to see them.

Supervisors who must rate teachers are walking a tightrope. They must have built a solid base of trust and confidence and a reputation for fairness if their relationship with teachers is to withstand the trauma of rating. It would be preferable if the service-oriented supervisor never had to rate a teacher, but such an expectation would be unrealistic in the light of many administrators' expectations of supervisors. The challenge to the supervisor, therefore, is to make the system work to achieve the major goal being sought—improved achievement of learners through improved teacher competence.

Of course, ratings of teachers are necessary. Personnel decisions must be made on the basis of competence. Whenever possible, however, the administrator, not the supervisor, should bear the primary responsibility for making judgments about the competence or incompetence of teachers. Thus, the burden of formative evaluation would fall on staff persons identified as instructional supervisors and summative evaluation on the shoulders of the administrator. We know that in some of the smallest school systems there are no instructional supervisors at either the district or individual school level. In those cases, both administrative and supervisory responsibilities will of necessity fall on the principal. Although some principals are adept at fulfilling what can be conflicting roles, the result is often an emphasis on summative evaluation for the purpose of making personnel decisions and deemphasis of formative evaluation for the purpose of improving instruction.

The principles of evaluation discussed in Chapters 10 and 12 are aimed at those persons who function as supervisors and as administrators when they are fulfilling the role of instructional supervisor. Chapter 13 is aimed at administrators when they are fulfilling their role as personnel managers.

The instructional supervisor should use every technique that can be mustered to help teachers evaluate their own competencies with as little stress on rating as possible. If it is the supervisor's duty to make an annual report on a teacher, the supervisor should make evaluation an exercise in teacher self-evaluation under his or her guidance. The evaluation should be a process of discussion between the teacher and supervisor and a means for the teacher to set his or her own goals for the future. During the rating process the supervisor must present a demeanor of helping and not convey the impression that the teacher is being graded.

COMPETENCIES TO BE EVALUATED

Before considering techniques the supervisor can employ to help teachers evaluate themselves, let us look at some of the competencies school systems believe are important enough to be evaluated. If teachers are to be evaluated, they should know well in advance the criteria on which assessments will be made.

School systems vary on the teacher behaviors they consider important. Among the categories of behavior that appear on instruments for assessing teacher performance are (1) instructional skills, (2) personal traits, and (3) professional attributes. The Teacher Service Report of the Webster Groves, Missouri, School District, shown in Figure 12.1, illustrates the categories of performance often evaluated by school systems. This instrument is used to assess teacher performance and professional responsibilities. Several behaviors, with indicators, are rated under each of the two major categories. The evaluator decides whether the teacher meets Webster Groves expectations, should work on certain goals, or should undergo intensive assistance.

The form in Figure 12.1 serves the purpose of summative or annual evaluation, which we discuss in Chapter 13. Summative evaluations often include assessment of professional and personal attributes as well as instructional skills. Without per-

	Meets W. G. Exp.		Could Be	Must Be	Intensive Assistance
	Yes	No	A Goal	A Goal	Required

I. TEACHING PERFORMANCE
A.   INSTRUCTING (as observed in the classroom)

	Yes	No	Could Be A Goal	Must Be A Goal	Intensive Assistance Required
1. Motivates Students to Learn	___	___	(If "no," check sub-topics)		
a. Stimulates learning through planned student activities	___	___	___	___	___
b. Encourages class discussion and students' questions and expressions	___	___	___	___	___
c. Uses teaching aids	___	___	___	___	___
d. Displays enthusiasm	___	___	___	___	___
e. Possesses adequate knowledge of subject matter and uses it effectively	___	___	___	___	___
2. Communicates with Clarity and Effectiveness	___	___			
a. Gives clear explanations	___	___	___	___	___
b. Writes clearly and correctly	___	___	___	___	___
c. Speaks clearly and correctly	___	___	___	___	___
d. Adapts vocabulary to audience being addressed	___	___	___	___	___
3. Meets Individual Differences and Needs	___	___			
a. Adapts plans in response to individual needs	___	___	___	___	___
b. Knows and interacts with students as individuals	___	___	___	___	___
c. Instructs at a pace which stimulates understanding	___	___	___	___	___
d. Instructs at a pace which maximizes achievement	___	___	___	___	___
e. Asks questions which require varying levels of thinking, consistent with student readiness	___	___	___	___	___
f. Uses a variety of appropriate methods	___	___	___	___	___
4. Assesses Student Progress	___	___			
a. Reinforces student learning to insure maximum retention	___	___	___	___	___
b. Acknowledges students' successes as well as failures	___	___	___	___	___
c. Uses evaluation of student work as a positive and integral part of instruction	___	___	___	___	___
d. Documents student progress with sufficient and objective data	___	___	___	___	___
5. Maintains Orderly Environment Conducive to Learning	___	___			
a. Defines reasonable conduct to students and requires conformity to this standard	___	___	___	___	___
b. Shows consistency and fairness in dealing with students	___	___	___	___	___

(continued)

Figure 12.1. Teacher Service Report. *Source: School District of Webster Groves, Webster Groves, Missouri. Reprinted with permission of Webster Groves School District.*

    c. Makes appropriate effort to solve problems
before making referrals

    d. Emphasizes importance of self-respect
and respect for others

    e. Communicates with, seeks support of and
constructively involves parents when problems
develop

    f. Takes diagnostic and remedial approach
to discipline

B. **PLANNING (as evidenced by artifacts and interview)**

    1. Plans and Organizes to Promote Learning

        a. Pursues objectives which are consistent
with District philosophy and goals and
courses of study

        b. Assesses the achievement and ability
levels of students

        c. Develops written plans

        d. Plans student activities based on the needs
of each student

        e. Plans clear, specific and purposeful
assignments

        f. Provides information and lesson
plans for substitutes

        g. Recognizes and encourages development
of students' strengths and special interests

II. PROFESSIONAL RESPONSIBILITIES

A. **Maintains High Level of Personal and
Organizational Professionalism**

    1. Suggests ideas for changes and improvements

    2. Is willing to try new methods and materials

    3. Seeks and uses the help of specialists,
support personnel and appropriate
available resources

    4. Accepts constructive criticism

    5. Engages in appropriate studies and
experiences to improve competence

    6. Participates in professional activities

    7. Contributes to building and District planning
and committee efforts

    8. Maintains professional relationship with students

    9. Discusses students in a professional manner

B. **Contributes to the Total Team Effort**

    1. Recognizes and performs extra classroom
responsibilities

    2. Supports staff members who perform extra
classroom responsibilities

    3. Contributes to maintaining schoolwide discipline

    4. Acts responsibly when emergencies arise

C. **Embodies Positive Role Model**

    1. Maintains positive relations with parents
and patrons

    2. Contributes to positive image of
school district in community

Figure 12.1. (continued)

3. Represents School District in professional
   manner   ___   ___   _____   _____   _____
4. Maintains poise, composure and dignity   ___   ___   _____   _____   _____
5. Meets responsibilities as scheduled   ___   ___   _____   _____   _____
6. Sustains a satisfactory attendance record   ___   ___   _____   _____   _____
7. Possess and appreciates a sense of humor   ___   ___   _____   _____   _____
8. Possesses physical fitness and mental and
   emotional stability at a level which does not
   restrict performance of duties   ___   ___   _____   _____   _____
9. Grooms and dresses appropriately
   for assignments and circumstances   ___   ___   _____   _____   _____

The evaluator recommends the following items as possible and most appropriate topics for goals:

_____   _____
_____   _____
_____   _____

The evaluator is encouraged to comment below on outstanding or commendable service.

RECOMMENDATION OF EVALUATOR (Use attachments if necessary.)

The interests of the school and the staff member will be well served by the staff member's
remaining in this school next year.
Yes ___ No ___ If no, why not?

Should this staff member be placed on special probation for next year? (To be answered only
after the probationary period.)
Yes ___ No ___ If yes, why?

Signed _____

Teacher's Statement (Optional)

The teacher may comment on any part of this evaluation.

Signed _____

The signatures below indicate that the teacher and evaluator have discussed this report, and the staff
member has received a copy.

Date _____   Evaluator's Signature _____

Date _____   Teacher's Signature _____

sonal and professional behaviors, you would have an instrument for classroom observation, which we discussed in Chapter 10.

When administrators and supervisors initiate the process of identifying teacher competencies and attributes and the means of evaluating these competencies and attributes, teachers must be brought into the developmental process. Participation in the development of evaluation plans from the beginning is the best means of securing the commitment of teachers to the evaluation process.

Among the numerous evaluation systems, two general categories of teacher behavior predominate: instructional skills, which lie more in the cognitive and performance areas, and personal-professional attributes, which lie more in the affective area. The assumption is made that these two major categories of teacher behavior are worthy of appraisal, and ways will be suggested by which the supervisor can help teachers evaluate themselves in these broad areas.

Evaluation of Instructional Skills

Previous chapters of this text have sought to describe instructional skills that are desirable for teachers to master while focusing the evaluative spotlight on learners and their performance. Now the spotlight is trained on the teachers' performance. The supervisor mulls the question, "How can I best go about helping teachers to see and analyze their own performance?" Several avenues are possible, one or more of which may run into a dead end:

- The supervisor may enter the teacher's classroom unannounced and unexpected, sit down at the back of the room, observe the teacher's performance, take notes while the teacher is teaching, write up a summary, and hand it to the teacher.
- The supervisor may appear periodically, evaluate the teacher's performances by using a rating instrument, and deliver the instrument to the administrator.
- The supervisor may drop in informally several times to get acquainted and to learn whether the teacher needs help of any kind before turning to procedures for a more structured type of evaluation.
- The supervisor may set up some in-service training programs designed to help teachers evaluate their own performance before entering into a more structured type of evaluation.

The supervisor must gain the teacher's confidence before the two of them can together talk about evaluating the teacher's performance. Of the four approaches just described, the last two are acceptable. The first two approaches are not acceptable, for they are grading approaches that place the teacher under threat. Provision must be made for discussion and analysis in a trusting, threat-free environment as nearly as can be accomplished.

To institute teachers' examination of their own competence, the supervisor may take an approach that consists of the following three stages:

1. Examination of teacher performance in general terms—that is, analysis of the teaching act in a theoretical context. This is accomplished by study of the literature and other selected media on teaching.

2. Examination of the performance of other teachers both inside and outside the school system. This is accomplished by the use of audio and visual media and by teachers visiting each other's classrooms.
3. Examination of the teacher's own performance. This is accomplished through the use of both written materials and other selected media.

We elaborate on these three stages further in the chapter. We have chosen to call the first two stages *external analysis*. At these points, teachers look at teaching in general and at the performance of other teachers. They are looking beyond themselves. As they make external analyses of teaching, they begin to internalize, drawing implications for their own teaching. They begin to develop certain understandings about teaching and start to see how they can improve themselves.

The third stage is *internal analysis*, at which time the teacher focuses on his or her own behaviors. As this point the teacher comes to center stage and, instead of concentrating on the teaching act impersonally, in a general way, or on the performance of other teachers, is brought around to evaluating his or her own performance.

The purpose of this three-stage sequence from external to internal analysis is to allow time for the supervisor to help teachers build a positive mind-set toward evaluation, equip them with skills for evaluating themselves, and develop a feeling of self-confidence in their own abilities.

The literature on teacher behavior is vast and still growing. Many studies of teacher performance have been conducted, and numerous training programs have been developed that permit teachers to look at teaching and at their own performance. The next section offers the prospective supervisor several strategies for developing skills of self-evaluation, briefly describes the nature of these strategies, and directs the supervisor to a number of sources and programs.

Models of Teaching. Although there is no single best point of departure for the evaluation of teacher competence, one that can be a productive route, a form of external analysis (a look at the teaching act), is the study and recognition of models of teaching. An examination of various models of teaching provides the teacher with an opportunity to identify the model or models he or she either makes use of or can make use of. Bruce Joyce, Marsha Weil, and Beverly Showers defined a model of teaching as "a plan or pattern that we can use to design face-to-face teaching in classrooms or tutorial settings and to shape instructional materials—including books, films, tapes, computer-mediated programs, and curricula (long-term courses of studies)."[1]

In the fourth edition of their book, Joyce, Weil, and Showers described sixteen models of teaching grouped into four families: social families, information-processing families, personal families, and behavioral systems families.[2] Some models of teaching are more evident than others. The following models can be identified among many that are followed by teachers.

1. *The teacher as lecturer.* This historic model conceives of the teacher as a conveyor of information from his or her mind to the minds of the learners through the medium of primarily oral language.

2. *The teacher as expert resource person.* The teacher who follows this model is available to share information about content and sources whenever learners have need for help.

3. *The teacher as facilitator.* Following this model the teacher does everything possible to provide resources and direction to the learners so they may go about their studies and continuously guides their learning in the process of study.

4. *The teacher as counselor.* The teacher who adopts this model sees the personal development of the learner as more important than the content, advises students, encourages them, and more important, listens to the learners' problems.

5. *The teacher as a leader of group meetings.* This teacher is the master of ceremonies, the group's chairperson, who promotes the work of the group, directs its activities, and encourages participation from all the group's members.

6. *The teacher as tutor.* The teacher following this model engages in instruction on a one-to-one basis, and in so doing may employ a variety of techniques, including contractual-type arrangements that provide for independent study.

7. *The teacher as manager of mediated instruction.* Various media play a primary role in the presentation of instruction via this model. The teacher selects the necessary media, arranges for their use, and follows up the mediated presentations with discussion and evaluation.

8. *The teacher as laboratory supervisor.* This model requires the establishing of a laboratory approach to instruction—experimenting, constructing, researching activities, which the learners carry out under the supervision of the teacher.

9. *The teacher as programmer.* From the fields of programmed instruction and computer-assisted instruction this model directs the teacher to write specific programs, which the learners then work through either individually or in groups.

10. *The teacher as manipulator of the learning environment.* This behavioristic model calls for the teacher to manipulate the stimuli in the classroom environment. The teacher gives and withholds reinforcement for specific kinds of learning that the students are attempting.

Research does not identify any single model as preferable to all other models. We cannot say that there is a single, superior model of teaching. The study of models of teaching serves the worthwhile function of causing supervisors and teachers to realize that a number of models of teacher behavior are possible—how many can only be conjectured.

In some respects a model of teaching resembles a style of teaching. Style injects a very personal, individualized dimension, for the concept of style of teaching includes elements of the teacher's personality—facial expressions, gesturing, kinesthetic movements, choice of vocabulary, dramatic flare, wit—the total personal delivery system.

As research into learning and teacher behavior continues, new models and adaptations of old models may be expected. A productive in-service program would lie in the identification and analysis of various models of teaching. The purpose of such an in-service program would not be to cause teachers to select from one of the models and to adopt it for exclusive use but to give them some basis for identifying their own pattern or patterns and adding new models to their repertoire. The choice of a model or models is a function of the nature of the grade level, discipline, instructional objectives, and the teacher's own personality. Some of the models have general applicability at all grade levels and in all disciplines; others are more suited to particular grade levels and disciplines. Effective teachers demonstrate competence in several models of teaching. After a study of models of teaching, the supervisor may turn the external analysis of models into an internal analysis by asking teachers to describe and classify their own models.

Protocol Materials. Protocol materials are brief taped or filmed incidents of actual classroom situations. They have been described as

> vignettes of behavior which illustrate key concepts that enable the teacher to better interpret behavior in the classroom and the school. The main purpose of Protocol Materials is to develop conceptual knowledge through concept analysis and to link specific behavior to a conceptual basis.[3]

By capturing classroom behavior on tape or film, teachers can study and restudy the behavior. Protocol materials differ from ordinary taping and filming of classroom situations in that the producers of protocol materials zero in on the concepts they wish to illustrate. They may be looking for examples of focusing, probing questions, verbal interaction, behavior modification, teacher enthusiasm, or other teaching skills. They capture the performance of a particular skill on tape or film so it can be studied at a future time.

Supervisors may seek protocol materials from other school systems or educational agencies. However, with today's portable videotaping equipment, the supervisor can, with the help of media support personnel, produce a library of local protocol materials—taped situations in the local schools. Locally produced protocol materials will have heightened meaning for teachers in the system who make use of the materials. The full cooperation and permission of classroom teachers would have to be assured in advance for taping to take place in their classrooms. It is most probable that only the most confident teachers would be willing—at least at first—for themselves and their classes to be taped and for the protocols to be studied by other teachers in the system.

B. Othanel Smith, Saul B. Cohen, and Arthur Pearl spoke to the purpose of protocol materials, which they called "samples of behavior to be studied":

> The study of protocol materials will not only result in the prospective teacher's ability to understand and to interpret situations he will face in the classroom, school, and community; it will also increase the teacher's interest in theory, for he will see clearly for the first time that it is useful.[4]

We would add that not only the prospective teacher can profit from the use of protocol materials but the in-service teacher as well. Smith, Cohen, and Pearl give examples of types of situations that protocols can point up: interference of concepts, conflict situations, self-image, self-fulfillment, differential reinforcement, and vicarious reinforcement.

Smith, Cohen, and Pearl advised the use of protocol materials for the purpose of expanding the teacher's theoretical knowledge.

> Apart from situational instruction, theoretical knowledge is apt to remain pedagogically useless. Protocol materials should not be used merely to illustrate points

in education courses. The whole procedure should be turned about so that the principles of the psychological, sociological, and philosophical studies, as well as those of pedagogy, are brought to the analysis of protocol materials, not the other way around. These materials suggest the knowledge that is relevant to the teacher's work.[5]

To make effective use of protocol materials a school system that contemplates the purchase or production of protocols will need to develop a system for classifying and cataloging behaviors. Smith, Cohen, and Pearl suggested a simple classification system:

1. Classroom situations
   a. Instructional situations
   b. Situations of classroom management and control
2. Extraclassroom situations
   a. Situations that arise in planning school programs, working with peers and the administration
   b. Situations that occur in working with parents and other members of the community
   c. Situations that occur in working in professional organizations[6]

Note that protocol materials do not have to be confined exclusively to classroom behaviors. Because we are concerned at this time with the evaluation of instructional skills, we are interested primarily in classroom situations. To aid in the establishment of a bank of protocol materials, the supervisor might well appoint a protocols development committee composed of teachers and other specialists in the school system. Although interest in the development of protocol materials was more pronounced in the 1970s, the technique has much to recommend it to supervisors seeking ways to help teachers improve instruction.

Taped Lessons. Teachers may examine other teachers' performance through videotape. In this respect, videotapes of teacher performance resemble protocol materials. However, protocol tapes and films depict brief episodes of key concepts whereas the videotapes addressed here capture a complete lesson, running anywhere from thirty minutes to an hour or more.

Thus, teachers can follow a lesson as it unfolds and witness skillful teachers in action. Supervisors and teachers can watch taped lessons together and discuss what they have seen.

Possible sources of taped lessons are educational associations and teacher-training institutions. Rather than depend on locating tapes from outside sources, however, the supervisor could easily build a library of videotapes of effective teaching within the system. As in the case of the protocol materials, the teachers to be taped would need to give their consent and feel comfortable with having their colleagues view and discuss their performance.

Teacher-Training Modules. Over the years, teacher-training institutions, state departments of education, and other educational agencies have produced training packages known in the profession as *teacher-training modules*. A large number were developed in past years for use in preservice and in-service teacher training. Each module focuses on the development of a particular competency. In format, a module consists of printed materials often accompanied by other media. The modular approach is an individualized process of training, and though modules may be used in a group setting, each individual teacher must work through his or her own module.

At one time or another the following organizations were engaged in the development of teacher-training modules: Brigham Young University, Dade County (Florida) Public Schools, Florida Department of Education, Florida State University, the University of Georgia, Northwest Regional Laboratory, Southwest Minnesota State College, State University College of Buffalo, Thiokol Chemical Corporation, University of Toledo, University of Houston, Weber State College (Utah), and Western Washington State College. The development of teacher-training modules was a reflection of the interest of institutions and states in a competency-based approach to teacher education.

Two of the better-known sets of teacher-training modules were the Weber State College *WILKITS*[7] and the *Florida B-2 Modules*.[8] The *WILKITS* (Weber State College, Utah, *Individualized Learning Kits*) were produced for Weber State College's preservice training program. Weber State, one of the early developers of competency-based teacher education programs, deviated from the traditional approach to teacher education and confronted students with a series of eighty-five modules, each of which trained them in some phase of professional education. Here are titles of some of these modules:

- Classroom Management and Discipline
- Self-concept
- Motivation and Learning
- Professional Relationships
- Purposes and Methods of Classroom Evaluation
- Reading Study Techniques
- Classroom Strategies Inquiry

The *Florida B-2 Modules* were developed through a grant from the U.S. Office of Education to the Florida State Department of Education under Part B, Subpart 2, of the Education Professions Development Act. Modules were prepared and grouped into ten clusters: I. *Teacher Aide Training*, II. *Planning Skills for Teachers*, III. *Presentation Skills for Teachers*, IV. *Classroom Procedures*, V. *Questioning Skills*, VI. *Assessment*, VII. *Special Skills*, VIII. *Assessing Educational Personnel*, IX. *School Volunteer Training*, and X. *Occupational Specialist Program*. A variety of films, filmstrips, and audiotapes accompanied the printed materials.

Although interest in the competency-based approach to teacher education and activity in developing teacher-training modules has declined in recent years, the use of teacher-training modules is an approach to staff development still worthy of consideration. Teacher-training modules provide one way for teachers to examine some of the dimensions of teaching. The supervisor may wish to select teachers to work with him or her to develop modules for their own school system. ASCD training materials, such as *Opening Doors: An Introduction to Peer Coaching* and *Another Set of*

Eyes: Techniques for Classroom Observation and Conferencing Skills, emulate a training-module approach.

Laboratory Approaches. Several approaches to the evaluation of teacher behavior followed to a large extent in preservice programs are equally suitable to in-service training programs, although in the latter case they pose special operational and motivational problems. Referred to as *laboratory* or *clinical approaches*, they include peer teaching and microteaching, both with and without videotaping.

Central to the laboratory approach is microteaching, in which a teacher or prospective teacher demonstrates in a clinical setting a particular teaching skill before a small group of students (preferably not his or her own) or peers. The purpose of microteaching is to enable the teachers to gain feedback about their teaching so they may make improvements. When the microteaching session is conducted with colleagues serving as students, it is called *peer teaching*. Although microteaching and peer teaching can be carried out in a clinic that is not equipped with videotaping facilities, they gain added impact when videotaped. Taping permits the teacher to view his or her own performance and allows repeated analysis.

The process of microteaching calls for a presentation of a very short (mini) lesson, after which the teacher's performance is critiqued on the basis of an instrument or prespecified set of criteria. After the critique, the teacher repeats the lesson and it is again analyzed. When the subjects are students, it is preferable for the repetition to be conducted with a different group of students. The critique of the lesson may be directed by the supervisor or other consultant, by a peer, or by the teacher if the lesson is videotaped.

The supervisor should take the initiative to establish a microteaching laboratory in the school or school system. Space and equipment needed are minimal. The laboratory, a small room reasonably free from external noise, is usually equipped with a desk, chalkboard, and technology for the teacher to use while teaching: camcorder, VCR, a television monitor, and other media.

The laboratory approach establishes an artificial, simulated, controlled situation, but it provides an opportunity for development or refinement of a particular technique or skill that the teacher may use in a real classroom. A motivational problem exists in stimulating the willingness of the teacher to be placed in a learner-type situation; to appear before colleagues and/or students; and to face criticism, albeit constructive, of his or her performance. An operational problem arises in finding suitable space, providing necessary equipment, and finding a convenient time for all personnel involved—teachers, students, peers, observers, and media personnel. None of these sets of problems is insurmountable if the laboratory is an accepted and voluntary part of a total in-service program. Beginning teachers who have not yet begun to develop all the defense mechanisms of experienced teachers are likely to make the most use of the laboratories or clinics. A special incentive such as released time, additional pay, or university credit will make the use of a laboratory approach more palatable to teachers.

Observation Systems. The intensive research into teaching performance has brought into being a number of systems for studying, analyzing, and recording teacher behavior in the classroom. These systems provide a means by which trained observers may record the actual performance of a teacher and by which teachers may evaluate their own performance through the use of videotaped recordings. The ultimate purpose of an observation system is to provide opportunities for teachers to analyze their own teaching systematically in order to make improvements. An observation system structures the teacher's evaluation by enabling him or her to look for pre-specified aspects of teaching.

Although a few systems of observation analysis are very well known to the profession, many exist that are not as well known. As long ago as 1974, Anita Simon and E. Gil Boyer compiled an anthology of ninety-nine observation instruments.[9] The present number of observation instruments is much larger as many school systems have now developed their own instruments.

The aspects of teacher performance that the numerous instruments choose for observation vary somewhat from system to system. Some focus on the teacher, some on the student, and others on teacher-student interaction. Some stress cognitive learning whereas others look at affective behavior. Some emphasize verbal behavior, others nonverbal behavior. Some instruments are refinements of previously created instruments, capitalizing on the research that has taken place.

"The question naturally arises," said Smith, Cohen, and Pearl, "as to which of the many observation systems should be used for the training of teachers. But a review of the literature indicates that the analyses differ more in the labels used than in the substance of the categories themselves. In other words, there is not as much variation among the analyses as the terminology seems to indicate."[10] A viable procedure for selecting an observation instrument is the supervisor's appointment of a committee of teachers to study various systems and choose an instrument they would be willing to use. If they were a particularly creative group, they might even wish to develop their own instrument, an activity that the supervisor might well encourage. The process of selecting or developing an instrument would be valuable in-service training for those participating on the committee.

It would be impossible and superfluous for this text to examine all the observation instruments now available. The Simon and Boyer reference analyzed instruments as to focus of the system, coding units used, uses to which the system can be put, and setting in which the systems have been used. The supervisor and the committee might begin their work by sending for copies of instruments and accompanying explanatory literature of systems in which they may have a particular interest.

To give an idea of what kinds of behavior the developers of observation instruments consider important enough to be observed and analyzed—and as a consequence, to be improved—we examine the categories of two instruments: Ned A. Flanders' pioneering Flanders Interaction Analysis Categories (FIAC) (Figure 12.2) and Bruce W. Tuckman's *Tuckman Teacher Feedback Form* (Figure 12.3).

Observation analysis has been introduced in this chapter with the Flanders and Tuckman instruments to point out that teachers can use a systematic form of observation in analyzing their own performance. Classroom observation by the supervisor will be discussed at greater length with additional examples of observation instruments in the next chapter.

Flanders's system concentrates on verbal interaction whereas Tuckman's in-

Teacher Talk	Response	1. *Accepts feeling.* Accepts and clarifies an attitude or the feeling tone of a student in a nonthreatening manner. Feelings may be positive or negative. Predicting and recalling feelings are included. 2. *Praises or encourages.* Praises or encourages students; says "um hum" or "go on"; makes jokes that release tension, but not at the expense of a student. 3. *Accepts or uses ideas of students.* Acknowledges student talk. Clarifies, builds on, or asks questions based on student ideas.
		4. *Asks questions.* Asks questions about content or procedure, based on teacher ideas, with the intent that a student will answer.
	Initiation	5. *Lectures.* Offers facts or opinions about content or procedures; expresses his or her own ideas, gives his or her own explanation, or cites an authority other than a student. 6. *Gives directions.* Gives directions, commands, or orders with which a student is expected to comply. 7. *Criticizes student or justifies authority.* Makes statements intended to change student behavior from nonacceptable to acceptable patterns; arbitrarily corrects student answers; bawls someone out. Or states why the teacher is doing what he or she is doing; uses extreme self-reference.
Student Talk	Response	8. *Student talk—response.* Student talk in response to a teacher contact that structures or limits the situation. Freedom to express own ideas is limited.
	Initiation	9. *Student talk—initiation.* Student initiates or expresses his or her own ideas, either spontaneously or in response to the teacher's solicitation. Freedom to develop opinions and a line of thought; going beyond existing structure.
Silence		10. *Silence or confusion.* Pauses, short periods of silence, and periods of confusion in which communication cannot be understood by the observer.

Figure 12.2. Flanders Interaction Analysis Categories (FIAC). Based on Ned A. Flanders, *Analyzing Teaching Behavior*, 1970. No scale is implied by these numbers. Each number is classificatory; it designates a particular kind of communication event. To write these numbers down during observation is to enumerate, not to judge, a position on a scale. *Source: Ned A. Flanders et al.,* Interaction Analysis: Teacher Handbook *(San Francisco: Far West Laboratory for Educational Research and Development, 1972), p. 5.*

strument assesses certain personal characteristics of teachers that can affect classroom climate and instruction. Flanders's system prescribes a tally every three seconds, and Tuckman's system uses a simple checklist. Both instruments may be used for either self-appraisal or appraisal to judge teachers' performance on items assessed by these instruments. When teachers apply the Flanders instrument to assess their own performance, they may do so by reviewing a transcript, audiotape, or videotape of the lessons. The Tuckman instrument may be converted from an appraisal form to a teacher preference or self-appraisal form by changing the data at the top of the instrument shown from "Person Observed," "Observer," and "Date" to "Name," "Date," and "My Preference for."

Observation analysis can be implemented in a number of ways. Proceeding from an external approach to an internal approach, let's examine several ways to use observation instruments.

- Following a technique employed in many teacher-training institutions, the teacher may view videotapes of classroom sessions showing other teachers in action and apply an instrument to these recordings of teacher performance. The Association for Supervision and Curriculum Development (ASCD) offers helpful videotapes of classroom episodes. The teacher may analyze the performance of teachers on these tapes and make recommendations *for that teacher*. At the same time, the teacher will also be making self-recommendations.

Person Observed _____   Observer _____

Date: _____

1.	Original	Conventional
2.	Patient	Impatient
3.	Cold	Warm
4.	Hostile	Amiable
5.	Creative	Routinized
6.	Inhibited	Uninhibited
7.	Iconoclastic	Ritualistic
8.	Gentle	Harsh
9.	Unfair	Fair
10.	Capricious	Purposeful
11.	Cautious	Experimenting
12.	Disorganized	Organized
13.	Unfriendly	Sociable
14.	Resourceful	Uncertain
15.	Reserved	Outspoken
16.	Imaginative	Exacting
17.	Erratic	Systematic
18.	Aggressive	Passive
19.	Accepting (People)	Critical
20.	Quiet	Bubbly
21.	Outgoing	Withdrawn
22.	In Control	On the Run
23.	Flighty	Conscientious
24.	Dominant	Submissive
25.	Observant	Preoccupied
26.	Introverted	Extraverted
27.	Assertive	Soft-Spoken
28.	Timid	Adventurous

Figure 12.3. Tuckman Teacher Feedback Form (Short Form). *Source: Bruce Wayne Tuckman, "New Instrument: The Tuckman Teacher Feedback Form (TTFF)," Journal of Educational Measurement 13, no. 3 (Fall 1976): 234. Reprinted with permission of Bruce W. Tuckman.*

- The teacher may permit an observation of his or her teaching to be made live in the classroom—without taping—by an outside, trained observer; by a colleague; or by the supervisor who will employ an observation instrument and review the observation with the teacher. This approach is, perhaps, the most threatening of all approaches and one some teachers find difficult to accept. It requires real confidence for a teacher to ask for and receive what amounts to criticism, even in the most positive terms, of his or her teaching, especially in the face-to-face arrangement of this approach.

- Some teachers may allow themselves to be taped and may ask a trained observer, colleague, or supervisor to apply an observation instrument to the taped session and then review the analysis with the individual teacher. The element of threat is still present, but it is softened by the relative remoteness of the videotape. It is less threatening because the teacher is not undergoing analytical observation while teaching; this comes afterward when the observer views the tape.

- The teacher may arrange to be taped and then personally use an observation instrument to critique his or her own performance. Except in the case of research studies when observations must be carried out by trained members of a research staff, this approach holds the most promise for lasting change and continuous improvement in teaching performance. This threat-free approach encourages teachers to look at their own teaching, knowing that no one is present to criticize them for poor performance.

To achieve reliable observation, the observer (who may actually be the teacher) must be thoroughly familiar with the categories of behavior to be observed and the procedures for recording and interpreting the data. The observer should undergo a training period and a number of practice sessions to gain skill in using the instrument. Because the supervisor will want each teacher to develop proficiency in analyzing his or her own behavior, in-service training in the observation system must precede actual use of the system.

Access to portable videotaping equipment is a must if teachers are ever going to see themselves in action and be able to study their own performance. No matter how helpful an observer may be to a teacher, there is nothing that can replace a teacher's viewing his or her own teaching performance.

In the late 1960s, Flanders's observation instrument and one designed by E. Wayne Roberson[11] were used in a research project that permitted teachers of the Tucson Public Schools to study their own behavior from videotape recordings made in their own classrooms.[12] This research study, known as the Teacher Self-Appraisal Program, stated its purpose as follows:

> The basic purpose of the program is to help teachers to be aware of their attitudes and classroom behavior in light of their behavioral objectives. Then, if they see that their classroom behavior is not in accord with their attitudes and behavioral objectives, they can initiate a change in their behavior.[13]

The study hypothesized, "if teachers could see themselves interacting with their students in the classroom, in the light of their behavioral objectives, they would be better able to appraise and analyze their behavior."[14] To test the hypothesis the project used these procedures.

1. Instruction in writing behavioral objectives.
2. Group situations so teachers could communicate their attitudes and ideas to each other.
3. Videotapes of their classroom behavior.
4. Instruction in analytically viewing their classroom behavior through the use of Flanders's and Roberson's codes.[15]

The Tucson study concluded that teachers who participated in the program were

- spending significantly less time giving information
- spending significantly more time calling for responses from students
- spending significantly less time on Demonstration
- using significantly more Receptive Verbal and Non-Verbal expressions
- using significantly less Routine Verbal and Non-Verbal expressions[16]

The study found no significant overall change in cognitive objectives or methods used by the teachers, but it did find overall significant changes in the affective objectives and verbal and nonverbal behavior.

Faculties considering the use of observation instruments might wish to create and try out a simplified, even rough or crude, instrument to become familiar with the concept of observation analysis. Their initial efforts at creating an instrument might result in a simple instrument, such as the one below, on which an observer would make tallies of each evidence of the specified behaviors of the teacher and students.

TEACHER BEHAVIOR	TALLY	STUDENT BEHAVIOR	TALLY
• Lecturing _____		• Responding to teacher's questions _____	
• Leading discussion _____		• Asking questions of the teacher _____	
• Questioning orally _____		• Participation in class discussion _____	
• Reinforcing pupil responses _____		• Participating in work activities _____	
• Directing class activities _____		• Performing leadership role _____	
• Moving about the class _____		• Misbehaving _____	

When using an instrument of this nature, the observer—who could be the teacher employing videotapes of his or her own classes—makes a tally mark every time the teacher shows any of the specified teacher behaviors and every time any pupil shows any of the behaviors in the student behavior column. Such a simplified instrument may be used as an introduction to more sophisticated and validated instruments. Observation analysis through the use of coding instruments offers a productive route for helping teachers evaluate themselves.

Teacher performance can be evaluated through the study of models of teaching, the use of selected media and training packages, the use of laboratories, and the application of observation systems. With videotaping equipment in the classroom and laboratory, teachers can be helped to appraise and improve their own teaching.

Evaluation of Personal-Professional Attributes

Moving from the evaluation of cognitive and instructional skills to the areas of personal and professional attributes presents different problems. Not only is it difficult to define the personal and professional attributes teachers ought to possess and on which there is universal agreement, but it is also difficult to assess these and, if they are found to be lacking, to effect a change in the teacher.

How does one judge relationships with administrators, for example? Should subservience be rewarded over outspokenness? How do you rate appearance? Are the teacher's memberships and participation in professional organizations of concern to administrators? If so, should the teacher be evaluated by number of memberships or by degree of participation? In the eyes of the administrator, is membership in a professional organization today a plus or a minus?

If teachers are to be evaluated by someone else—or by themselves—on personal-professional attributes, these traits must be clearly spelled out and instances of behavior wherein the attributes can be demonstrated must be described. The democratic approach to supervision would dictate that teachers be involved in deciding what personal-professional attributes will be evaluated and what evidences of these traits will be recorded. Beyond insubordination and criminal and moral offenses, personal and professional attributes are most difficult to document.

Certain personality characteristics and certain human-relations skills are essential to successful teacher performance:

- Sense of humor
- Ability to relate to students, other teachers, administrators, and the public
- Positive self-concept
- Open personality
- Use of appropriate verbal and nonverbal language
- Respect for the individual
- Respect for multicultural differences
- Absence of prejudice
- Expectation for excellence
- Respect for the confidentiality of school matters
- Well-modulated voice
- Cooperative attitude
- Appropriate clothing
- Industriousness; high energy level

These are only a few of the general personality traits necessary for success in any field or in life as a whole.

The problem for the supervisor when trying to help teachers evaluate their personal and professional attributes is to find ways in which teachers may reflect on their own traits, agree that there is need for improvement, and make changes accordingly. Personality traits are especially difficult to change, ingrained as they are in the individual's history, lifestyle, and philosophy of life.

Are there any techniques that may help teachers evaluate themselves on personal and professional attributes? There are, but as every member of the clergy realizes, no amount of sermonizing will succeed in moving a person to change behavior if the person does not wish to change.

The supervisor may once again begin with an external approach—an intellectualizing of traits that most educators feel teachers should possess. The process of identifying these traits and agreeing on ways they can be observed are the first hurdles to be cleared. The supervisor might direct teachers to some of the literature on the development of the self-concept and the meaning of the self-actualizing personality, such as found in the writings of Arthur W. Combs,[17] Earl C. Kelley,[18] and Abraham H. Maslow.[19] The popular 1962 Yearbook of the Association for Supervision and Curriculum Development is another helpful source of writings on these topics.[20]

It is in the area of personal development that consultants may be helpful to groups of teachers, if only for the purpose of bringing them inspirational messages. The use of certain personality inventories and attitude instruments, such as William C. Schutz's *FIRO-B* and Katherine C. Briggs's and Isabel Briggs Myers's *Myers-Briggs Type Indicator*, may lead teachers into greater awareness of certain personal traits.[21] Whereas *FIRO-B* explores ways in which individuals interact with other people, the *Myers-Briggs Type Indicator* focuses on the traits of extroversion versus introversion, sensation versus intuition, thinking versus feeling, and judgment versus perception.

There is a school of thought that warmly endorses encounter groups or sensitivity training—"touchy-feely," in the vernacular—as the answer to the search for ways for individuals to change their behavior. Yet, we have reservations about possible negative effects of sensitivity training on some participants. Caution is required that such training be on a voluntary basis, free of pressure to participate, and stringently controlled and conducted by trained leaders.

The issue of evaluating personal and professional attributes leads to two conclusions: (1) If a supervisor is called on to evaluate a teacher in respect to these traits, the attributes to be evaluated should cover a very limited, specifically defined, and observable set of characteristics agreed on in advance by teachers. (2) Lasting change can come about only as teachers evaluate their own behavior and internalize the necessity for change.

USING EVALUATION INSTRUMENTS

If the instructional supervisor is required, as happens in some school systems, to evaluate teachers annually or periodically for reporting purposes, teachers should enter fully into the evaluation process. What some people call "goal-oriented supervision" is a desirable approach. With this approach, the teacher and supervisor agree on the areas of performance the teacher will work on during the year. When it is time for an evaluation at the end of the year, the supervisor and teacher meet and evaluate whether and to what degree the teacher has improved in the performance areas.

This approach to evaluation fulfills the principle of bringing the teacher into the evaluation process. More and more school districts are adopting these procedures of teacher observation and evaluation. Further, it delimits the job targets, and the teacher is not required to demonstrate improvement across the board, which is a much more realistic approach than expecting improvement in many or all performance areas.[22]

The Cincinnati Public Schools have developed an in-depth teacher appraisal system that consists of evaluation by principals[23] and teacher self-evaluation.[24] The process of evaluation of the teacher (appraisee) by the administrator (appraiser) consists of the following steps:

I. Review appraisees' responsibilities as specified in the following documents:
    A. *Board Policies—Cincinnati Board of Education*
    B. The *Collective Bargaining Contract*
    C. Individual employee's contract
    D. Local school handbook/faculty manual
    E. Instructional guides provided by the school system and/or local school.
II. Conduct orientation sessions and respond to inquiries related to the appraisal process.
III. Conduct observations, on at least a monthly basis from the beginning of the school year, which should be followed by conferences when feasible during which appraisees are informed of their performance levels. Complete "Observation Report Forms" and distribute copies within one week of observations.
IV. Hold appraisal conference during which job targets will be finalized and the five major roles discussed in detail. Job targets should be demonstrable, observable, and measurable. They should relate to the teaching assignment. *The Manual for Self-Appraisal* contains performance standards which should be helpful in formulating job targets. In the event it is necessary for job targets to be specified by appraisers, this fact shall be indicated on the "Job Development Form." [Note: a sixth role, part of which applies to teachers, part to all school employees, has been added.]
V. Complete "Job Target Progress Report" and "Performance Evaluation Summary" and hold final appraisal conference.
VI. Submit copies of completed forms to participants and Certificated Personnel Branch in compliance with designated dates.[25]

The supervisor may participate as an appraiser if requested to do so by the principal or the teacher. Whether serving as an appraiser or not, the supervisor (called "instructional consultant") is kept informed of the teacher's performance and progress and receives copies of the completed evaluation forms.

To gather, report, and record the data required by the evaluation process the Cincinnati Public Schools have created five instruments or forms:

1. *Job Target Development Form.* On this form (Figure 12.4), which the principal fills out, the teacher and principal state agreed-on job targets for the year and means of achieving these targets. The role of the supervisor at this stage of the evaluation process is described in the following terms: "It is recommended that all supervisors be involved in the establishment of job targets even though they may not be identified as appraisers."[26]

2. *Observation Report Form.* The appraiser using this form (Figure 12.5) reports observations of teacher classroom performance relative to the job targets and major roles shown in Figure 12.8.

3. *Job Targets Progress Report.* The teacher and principal fill out a copy of this

JOB TARGET DEVELOPMENT FORM

This form is to be used by the appraisee and appraisers to develop tentative job targets and also to list the negotiated job targets established during the initial appraisal conference.

Appraisee _____ School _____ Grade/Subject _____
Appraisers _____ Date _____
_____

STATEMENT OF JOB TARGETS MUTUALLY AGREED UPON BY APPRAISEE AND APPRAISERS IN ORDER OF PRIORITY:

_____

STATEMENT OF SPECIFIC MEANS TO BE EMPHASIZED IN THE ATTAINMENT OF EACH JOB TARGET.

_____   _____
Appraisee's Signature   Appraisers' Signature(s)

Distribution: Copy 1—Principal   Copy 2—Supervisor
                     Copy 3—Appraisee

Figure 12.4. Job Target Development Form. *Source: Cincinnati Public Schools,* Teacher Appraisal Manual *(Cincinnati, Ohio: Certificated Personnel Branch, August 1984), p. 17. Reprinted with permission of the Cincinnati Public Schools.*

CINCINNATI PUBLIC SCHOOLS
Certificated Personnel Branch

OBSERVATION REPORT FORM

Appraisee _____ School _____ Grade/Subject _____
Appraiser _____ Date _____
Time of Arrival _____ Time of Departure _____
Type of Activity Observed _____
(Note: <u>Not</u> Carbonized—Use carbon paper)

Distribution: Copy 1—Personnel (to be submitted with final appraisal reports)
                     Copy 2—Observer; Copy 3—Other Appraiser; Copy 4—Appraisee

Figure 12.5. Observation Report Form. *Source: Cincinnati Public Schools,* Teacher Appraisal Manual *(Cincinnati, Ohio: Certificated Personnel Branch, August 1984), p. 18. Reprinted with permission of the Cincinnati Public Schools.*

JOB TARGETS PROGRESS REPORT

This form is to be completed during the final appraisal conference between the appraisee and appraisers.

Appraisee _____ School _____ Grade/Subject _____

Appraisers _____ Date _____

Job Target(s)	Appraisee's Comments on Progress	Appraisers' Comments on Progress

_____   _____
        Appraisee's Signature   Appraisers' Signature(s)

Distribution: Copy 1—Personnel   Copy 2—Supervisor
                    Copy 3—Principal   Copy 4—Appraisee

Figure 12.6. Job Targets Progress Report. *Source: Cincinnati Public Schools,* Teacher Appraisal Manual *(Cincinnati, Ohio: Certificated Personnel Branch, August 1984), p. 19. Reprinted with permission of the Cincinnati Public Schools.*

form (Figure 12.6) prior to the final appraisal conference between the teacher and principal. On this form the teacher and principal report in the respective comment sections how well they perceive the teacher to have done in relation to job targets. If the teacher or principal feels that certain job targets have not been reached, an explanation is provided. Copies of a completed form are attached to the summary of the final appraisal.

4. *Performance Evaluation Summary for Teachers.* The principal completes the form (Figure 12.7) prior to the final appraisal conference with the teacher, evaluating the teacher's progress in respect to the major roles. Although both the principal and teacher sign the completed summary form, the teacher's signature does not necessarily imply agreement with the principal's evaluation.

5. *Self-Appraisal Instrument.* The self-appraisal instrument, *Principles of the Self-Appraisal* (Figure 12.8), is an extensive personal inventory designed to permit the teacher to make a self-appraisal on six major roles considered important by the school system: instructional leader, social interaction leader, promoter of healthful emotional growth, communications facilitator, professional educator, and promoter of positive human relations. This is a personal exercise in which the teacher may decide to participate or not. The *Teacher Appraisal Manual* observes, "Appraisees are encouraged to administer the self-appraisal process which is voluntary."[27]

The self-appraisal instrument is divided into six sections, each section corresponding to one of the six roles previously mentioned. A description of one or more categories within each of the roles is given, and each description is followed by a

PERFORMANCE EVALUATION SUMMARY FOR TEACHERS

Appraisee _____ School _____ Grade/Subject _____
Appraiser(s) _____ Date _____

U-Unsatisfactory	S-Satisfactory	O-Outstanding					
M-Marginal	VG-Very Good		U	M	S	VG	O

I. *Instructional Leader*
Knowledge of and preparation for field of specialization; use of appropriate methods, techniques and resources.
COMMENTS: ☐ ☐ ☐ ☐ ☐

II. *Social Interaction Leader*
Teacher-pupil rapport; classroom interpersonal relationships; provision for appropriate success experiences for each student.
COMMENTS: ☐ ☐ ☐ ☐ ☐

III. *Promoter of Healthful Emotional Growth*
Use of appropriate techniques and school-community resources in resolving adjustment problems; maintains a positive learning environment.
COMMENTS: ☐ ☐ ☐ ☐ ☐

IV. *Communication Facilitator among school personnel, parents and community participants*
Presents positive image as an employee of Board of Education; provides adequate, accurate information about educational programs.
COMMENTS: ☐ ☐ ☐ ☐ ☐

V. *Professional Educator*
Behavioral characteristics and professional relationships related to successful job performance.
COMMENTS: ☐ ☐ ☐ ☐ ☐

VI. *Promoter of Positive Human Relations*
Role Definition: Contributes to and actively supports policies, practices, and programs that enhance positive human relations among students, parents, employees, and other community members. Develops and demonstrates personal and professional characteristics and skills that produce a quality, integrated educational program for all students.
COMMENTS: ☐ ☐ ☐ ☐ ☐

OVERALL PERFORMANCE EVALUATION
COMMENTS: ☐ ☐ ☐ ☐ ☐

_____   _____
Appraisee's Signature   Appraisers' Signature(s)

The appraisee's signature does not necessarily signify agreement with the evaluation.

Distribution: Copy 1—Personnel; Copy 2—Principal
                 Copy 3—Supervisor; Copy 4—Appraisee

Figure 12.7. Performance Evaluation Summary for Teachers. *Source: Cincinnati Public Schools, Teacher Appraisal Manual (Cincinnati, Ohio: Certificated Personnel Branch, August 1984), p. 20. Reprinted with permission of the Cincinnati Public Schools.*

ROLE I—INSTRUCTIONAL LEADER
CATEGORY A

The teacher understands and applies psychological readiness principles. Readiness for new learning is a state of mastery of simpler skills that permits a pupil to master more advanced skills. Readiness is a complex product of the interactions of physiological maturation, psychological abilities, prerequisite learning, and motivation. New experience presented too early or too late may be less effective and even damaging to pupil development.

CODE: FP—Frequently Practiced   IP—Infrequently Practiced
       NA—Non Applicable

		FP	IP	NA
A-1	The teacher ascertains each student's mastery of simpler tasks prerequisite to the task at hand.	☐	☐	☐
A-2	The teacher recognizes that there are often wide variations in psychological-readiness levels within each pupil, and adjusts instructional techniques accordingly or provides experiences designed to raise low levels of readiness.	☐	☐	☐

(7 principles)

CATEGORY B

The teacher provides a success-oriented learning environment for each student. Tasks that establish such an environment for a pupil tend to facilitate motivation, feelings of competence, adjustment, and achievement.

		FP	IP	NA
B-1	The teacher provides classroom challenges within the range of ability of the pupils in the class.	☐	☐	☐
B-2	The teacher demonstrates awareness that classroom challenges may make demands on social and motor-coordination skills as well as on academic skills.	☐	☐	☐

(9 principles)

CATEGORY C

The teacher plans skillfully for an effective teaching-learning situation.

		FP	IP	NA
C-1	The teacher endeavors to make the physical setting conducive to learning.	☐	☐	☐
C-2	The teacher, whenever possible or appropriate, involves his students in formulating educational objectives and in planning instructional activities.	☐	☐	☐

(6 principles)

CATEGORY D

The teacher individualizes instruction where appropriate. Pupils may vary in readiness for new learning due to a number of factors. A good teacher makes routine provision for readiness through effective assessment and through adjustment in the "range of challenge" presented to individual students.

		FP	IP	NA
D-1	The teacher uses recent standardized scores, available achievement test reresults, pupil-interest levels, etc., as possible predictors of readiness to learn.	☐	☐	☐
D-2	The teacher reclassifies, when possible, advanced or retarded pupils as recent evidence indicates that variation in the rate of intellectual growth has occurred.	☐	☐	☐

(8 principles)

Figure 12.8. Principles of the Self-appraisal. *Source: Cincinnati Public Schools,* Teacher Self-Appraisal Manual *(Cincinnati, Ohio: Certificated Personnel Branch, August 1984), pp. 8–30. Reprinted with permission of the Cincinnati Public Schools.*

CATEGORY E

The teacher facilitates student motivation toward academic and social achievement. Teachers who motivate pupils to learn contribute to pupil growth in cognitive abilities and academic and social-skill mastery.

	FP	IP	NA
E-1 The teacher helps pupils believe that achievement at a higher level is possible.	☐	☐	☐
E-2 The teacher helps pupils believe that they should try harder to achieve.	☐	☐	☐

(9 principles)

CATEGORY F

The teacher facilitates intellectual development as the pupil's cognitive abilities increase when there is deliberate attempt to (a) help the pupil perceive differences and arrive at generalizations, and (b) increase the pupil's ability to use words and deal with abstractions.

	FP	IP	NA
F-1 The teacher encourages logical reasoning.	☐	☐	☐
F-2 The teacher points out relevancy and provides organizational guidelines for pupils prior to learning new material.	☐	☐	☐

(11 principles)

CATEGORY G

The teacher facilitates motor-skill development through skill areas such as speaking, singing, playing games, and other physical activities.

	FP	IP	NA
G-1 The teacher helps pupils grow in articulation abilities.	☐	☐	☐
G-2 The teacher helps pupils grow in the ability to walk, run, skip, dance, climb, throw, catch, etc.	☐	☐	☐

(8 principles)

CATEGORY H

The teacher uses effective reinforcement techniques. Learning is more rapid and less apt to be lost if performance is accompanied or followed by reinforcement in general accordance with principles of effective reinforcement.

	FP	IP	NA
H-1 The teacher provides opportunities for pupils to experience intrinsic satisfaction from successful performance whenever possible.	☐	☐	☐
H-2 The teacher selects extrinsic satisfactions according to the unique needs of each individual pupil.	☐	☐	☐

(14 principles)

CATEGORY I

The teacher accurately interprets evaluation results and uses the information to improve the conditions of learning.

	FP	IP	NA
I-1 The teacher takes into account general characteristics affecting the testing situation, such as reading speed, vocabulary, comprehension, "clerical" test-taking skills, the chance factor, and test anxiety.	☐	☐	☐
I-2 The teacher takes into account temporary characteristics affecting the testing			

(continued)

517

situation, such as: health, motivation and set, environmental testing conditions, fatigue, and memory lapse.

☐ ☐ ☐

(11 principles)

CATEGORY J

The teacher understands and applies sound principles of learning.

	FP	IP	NA
J-1 The teacher understands that transfer of learning occurs whenever previous learning is related to later learning.	☐	☐	☐
J-2 The teacher teaches for the application of the principles underlying the content of his subject.	☐	☐	☐

(17 principles)

ROLE II—SOCIAL INTERACTION LEADER

CATEGORY A

The teacher establishes a democratic classroom atmosphere. The democratic classroom atmosphere as referred to here is defined as one containing elements of warmth and *effective limit-keeping*. Such an atmosphere has been shown to promote higher levels of creativity, peer interaction, motivation, sex-role identification, and acceptable public behavior.

	FP	IP	NA
A-1 The teacher provides a level of acceptance in the classroom that allows pupils to feel socially worthy.	☐	☐	☐
A-2 The teacher reacts sympathetically to pupil problems.	☐	☐	☐

(7 principles)

CATEGORY B

The teacher guides peer interactions effectively. Teachers who are knowledgeable about the principles of group dynamics can increase peer acceptance of isolates, guide peer groups into socially acceptable paths, encourage individual development of social skills.

	FP	IP	NA
B-1 The teacher serves as a constructive influence on the nature and direction of peer relationships by establishing rapport with students.	☐	☐	☐
B-2 The teacher attempts to determine the reasons a social isolate is not participating in peer activities.	☐	☐	☐

(13 principles)

CATEGORY C

The teacher adjusts social interaction activities to group norms. Since social readiness is determined by physiological maturation and various kinds of social experiences, the teacher must be aware of the general level of motivation and skill in peer interaction of the pupils in his classroom and be able to promote those activities within the "range of challenge" of the group.

	FP	IP	NA
C-1 The teacher takes into account that the student's ability to perceive intentions and motivations of others, to perform social roles, and to control aggressive impulses develops gradually throughout the school years.	☐	☐	☐
C-2 The teacher takes into account that adolescents must show more initiative in order to achieve peer acceptance than they did as children.	☐	☐	☐

(3 principles)

Figure 12.8. (continued)

CATEGORY D

The teacher adapts classroom activities to the pupil who is atypical in terms of social skills. A good teacher makes routine provision for immature and advanced pupils by adjusting social demands toward their "range of challenge."

		FP	IP	NA
D-1	The teacher gives support to pupils experiencing social stress due to late or early physical maturation.	☐	☐	☐
D-2	The teacher makes a special effort to discover isolates and to increase their social acceptability with classmates.	☐	☐	☐

(7 principles)

CATEGORY E

The teacher facilitates development of moral character and moral behavior. Teachers who help pupils develop favorable attitudes toward moral and social values, who encourage growth in the understanding of values, and who provide practice in moral behavior, contribute to the ability of the pupil to guide his own behavior in a mature manner.

		FP	IP	NA
E-1	The teacher takes into account that moral character and moral behavior are learned in part by the student's identification with an imitation of admired, respected models.	☐	☐	☐
E-2	The teacher takes into account that moral character and moral behavior are learned in part by experiencing repeated satisfaction from the possession of the expression of moral values.	☐	☐	☐

(5 principles)

ROLE III—PROMOTER OF HEALTHFUL EMOTIONAL GROWTH

CATEGORY A

The teacher recognizes symptoms of poor adjustment. Depending upon the adaptive habits of individual pupils, the teacher should be able to recognize the subtle symptoms of high emotional tension as well as the withdrawal and aggressive responses pupils resort to in an effort to reduce uncomfortable levels of emotional tension.

		FP	IP	NA
A-1	The teacher takes into account that thumb sucking, fingernail biting, tics, hyperactivity, overreacting, etc., function as tension-reduction behaviors, and may be symptomatic of high anxiety.	☐	☐	☐
A-2	The teacher takes into account that low self-esteem and inappropriate levels of aspiration are symptomatic of high anxiety.	☐	☐	☐

(6 principles)

CATEGORY B

The teacher reduces disabling levels of anxiety. Teachers should be aware of techniques useful in reducing anxiety and be able to skillfully apply the most appropriate techniques in the classroom situation.

		FP	IP	NA
B-1	The teacher absolutely avoids the use of psychotherapy techniques requiring a great deal of sophisticated training for safe, effective practice.	☐	☐	☐
B-2	The teacher gives extra emotional support to those pupils who are experiencing high-stress feelings.	☐	☐	☐

(11 principles)

(continued)

CATEGORY C

The teacher strengthens weak skill areas as an aid to adjustment. Pupils often exhibit high anxiety because of a lack of ability to adapt to the demands of their situation. Teachers should attempt to engage in academic and social skill remediation with these pupils.

	FP	IP	NA
C-1 The teacher takes into account that pupils are often anxious because of a chronic lack of ability to adapt and because of a lack of ability to achieve normal satisfactions through their own efforts.	☐	☐	☐
C-2 The teacher encourages independent pupil behavior, provides acceptance for the pupil in spite of mistakes and failures, and gives guidance appropriate to meeting the demands of the task.	☐	☐	☐

(8 principles)

CATEGORY D

The teacher uses effective case-study methods and employs necessary referral techniques. In order to provide the most supportive situation for an anxious pupil, the teacher must be able to gather and analyze background information bearing on the emotional disorder, and develop tentative plans for the amelioration of the problem.

	FP	IP	NA
D-1 The teacher takes into account the need for careful analysis of a pupil's situation when the usual trial-and-error approaches to reducing pupil anxiety have not been effective.	☐	☐	☐
D-2 The teacher asks for the help of and works with parents and school specialists when conducting an analysis of a pupil's situation.	☐	☐	☐

(7 principles)

ROLE IV—COMMUNICATIONS FACILITATOR

CATEGORY A

The teacher communicates information and suggestions to parents and colleagues about the intellectual, social, and emotional development of his students. Teachers should be aware of the effect of parental behavior and attitudes on children and should be able to interpret progress of students to parents or colleagues in a positive fashion and make suggestions for enhancing or remediating intellectual, social and emotional development.

	FP	IP	NA
A-1 The teacher takes into account that parents are given the prime responsibility for educating their child and that the teacher is acting as agent for the parents.	☐	☐	☐
A-2 The teacher takes into account that parental patterns of supervision lead to different patterns of performance in children.	☐	☐	☐

(10 principles)

ROLE V—PROFESSIONAL EDUCATOR

CATEGORY A

All staff members in the Cincinnati Public Schools are expected to contribute to the overall functioning of the school system by assuming responsibilities other than classroom teaching, conducting themselves appropriately and developing positive professional relationships.

Figure 12.8. (continued)

	FP	IP	NA
A-1 The staff member's attire and grooming is appropriate for the instructional setting in which he performs.	☐	☐	☐
A-2 The staff member completes all required records promptly, legibly and accurately.	☐	☐	☐

(6 principles)

ROLE VI—PROMOTER OF POSITIVE HUMAN RELATIONS

CATEGORY A
Applies to All Employees

Employees of the Cincinnati Board of Education are expected to conduct themselves in a manner which enhances human relations.

The employee:

	FP	IP	NA
A-1 TREATS all individuals with respect and dignity.	☐	☐	☐
A-2 AVOIDS use of oral and written vocabulary that is offensive to or makes generalizations about minority groups.	☐	☐	☐

(16 principles)

CATEGORY B
Applies to Classroom Teachers Directly
Responsible for Instructional Activities

Employees shall create a learning environment which provides opportunities for students to achieve and practice positive human relations.

The employee:

	FP	IP	NA
B-1 PROVIDES quality educational opportunities for all students.	☐	☐	☐
B-2 RECOGNIZES that there are often wide variations in the social and economic background of students and ADJUSTS instructional techniques accordingly.	☐	☐	☐

(17 principles)

number of teaching principles to which the teacher responds: frequently practiced, infrequently practiced, and nonapplicable.

The teacher can compute a performance index for each category of the instrument by (1) counting the number of principles in each category less those which do not apply, (2) counting the number of principles in each category to which he or she has responded "frequently practiced," and (3) consulting a Performance Index Calculation Chart to determine the performance index for each category. After calculating the performance index on each category, the teacher can plot the indices on a Profile Blank, which shows graphically the teacher's perceived strengths and weaknesses in relation to the six roles.

To show how the self-appraisal instrument is constructed, portions of the six roles with their respective categories are reproduced. Space precludes reproduction of the entire instrument as it contains 216 principles divided into twenty-three categories.

When the teacher has completed the self-appraisal inventory, the next steps are the calculation of performance indices for each category and the construction of a profile. Taking some purely arbitrary figures, a profile for a hypothetical teacher might look like the one in Figure 12.9.

The Profile Blank readily shows areas of teacher performance to which the teacher may wish to give consideration. The Cincinnati appraisal program, which was developed by a committee of teachers, administrators, and supervisors, uses not only appraisal of teachers by administrators and, in some cases, by supervisors but also teacher self-appraisal.

STUDENT EVALUATIONS

More frequently than in days gone by the recipients of instruction—the learners—are being asked to give their reactions to the teacher's performance. The learners can provide insights into the instruction that cannot be gained otherwise.

Conscientious teachers seek the counsel of their students about the effectiveness of their instruction. They want to know whether students perceive that they have learned. Student evaluations of the instructor and the instruction provide one more source of data about the effectiveness of teaching.

Teachers at all levels should be encouraged by their supervisors to solicit student reactions to their performance. Student evaluations should be gathered anonymously (or as anonymously as possible given the teacher's intimate knowledge of the students' handwriting). The use of forms that have students mark in their choices of responses from a list would keep the responses anonymous.

Supervisors should help teachers fashion student evaluation instruments if the teachers feel the need for such help. Instruments may be simple checklists or rating scales. A place for comments can allow for observations that students may wish to make. It is in the comments section, if handwritten, however, that the learners are most likely to reveal their identity by the distinctiveness of their handwriting. In some cases the handwritten responses are typed on a summary sheet to reduce the possibility of identifying remarks from individual students. Teachers must be professional enough not to retaliate for negative comments they are able to ascribe to a particular student. To reduce the potential threat implicit in student evaluations, the results should be available only to the teacher for his or her own guidance and should be revealed to others only if the teacher decides to do so.

The results should be given close attention, but at the same time teachers should realize that student evaluations represent the learners' perceptions of instruction and not their actual achievement. Perceptions, however, are extremely important and must be dealt with. Thus, if the majority of learners feel, for example, that the teacher's grading system is unfair, the teacher needs to decide whether there is merit to the criticisms. If the teacher agrees that the students have justification for their beliefs, he or she can modify the system. If the teacher finds that the criticisms are not accurate, he or she should spend some time explaining the rationale for the grading procedures.

Institutions of higher education have gathered student evaluations of faculty performance for years. In colleges and universities, the results of student evaluation

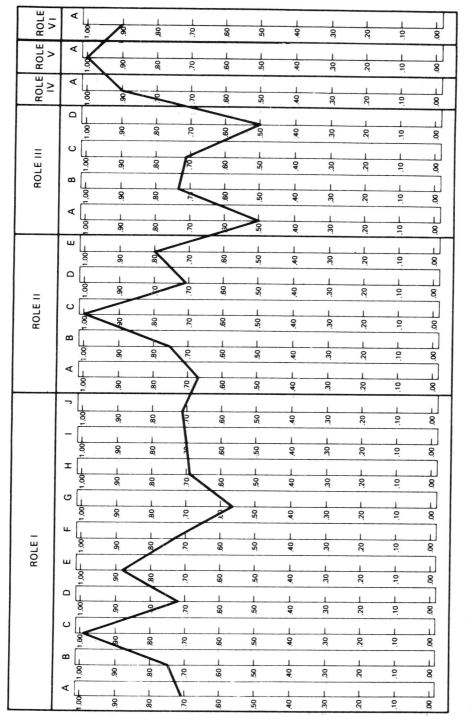

Figure 12.9. Profile Blank for Self-appraisal. *Source: Cincinnati Public Schools, Teacher Self-Appraisal Manual (Cincinnati, Ohio: Certificated Personnel Branch, August 1984), p. 29. Reprinted with permission of the Cincinnati Public Schools.*

are regularly shared with the faculty member and his or her administrative superiors and become a part of the documentation required for decisions on merit increases in salary, promotion, and tenure.

Following the movements for student rights, teacher accountability, and student participation in governance, the public schools have begun to establish procedures for collecting student reactions to instruction. Student input about the teacher's performance is being sought at all school levels.

Two samples of student evaluation forms follow. The first (Figure 12.10) is an instrument that could be used with students in grades three through five. It once was part of the state of Georgia's Teacher Performance Assessment Instruments. This same instrument can be used in grades six through adult level in a checklist form without the faces. The second (Figure 12.11) is a checklist currently used by senior high school students from Miami Southridge Senior High School, Miami, Florida.

Students can provide valuable insights about the course, the instruction, and the instructor. Though somewhat threatening to teachers at first, student evaluations come to be a valuable tool in the improvement of instruction.

PARENT EVALUATIONS

Although they involve parents in a variety of ways, such as serving on advisory committees and PTAs, working as volunteer aides, and expressing their views on curricular needs, schools rarely seek parental feedback about the teacher's performance in any systematized fashion. Schools poll parents on many things except what they think about the instructional skills of their children's teachers. Questionnaires to parents could be easily modeled on student questionnaires, with such items as

- My child's teacher enjoys teaching.
- My child's teacher is patient and understanding.
- My child's teacher is fair when students misbehave.
- My child's teacher gives clear directions and explanations.
- My child's teacher seeks my advice concerning my child.
- My child's teacher keeps me informed about my child's progress.

This dimension of evaluation is lacking in most school systems. The solicitation of anonymous parent evaluations about the teacher's performance is a path lightly trod in the evaluation of instruction. In seeking parental opinions, we must keep in mind, as in the case of student evaluations, that parent evaluations are perceptions that may or may not be accurate. Both student and parent evaluations can help teachers evaluate themselves.

SUMMARY

Supervisors effect changes in instruction as they help teachers evaluate themselves. The supervisor must master a variety of techniques for getting teachers to look at their own behavior. An external approach is recommended as a step to be taken prior to an internal approach—the provision of opportunities for teachers to analyze their own

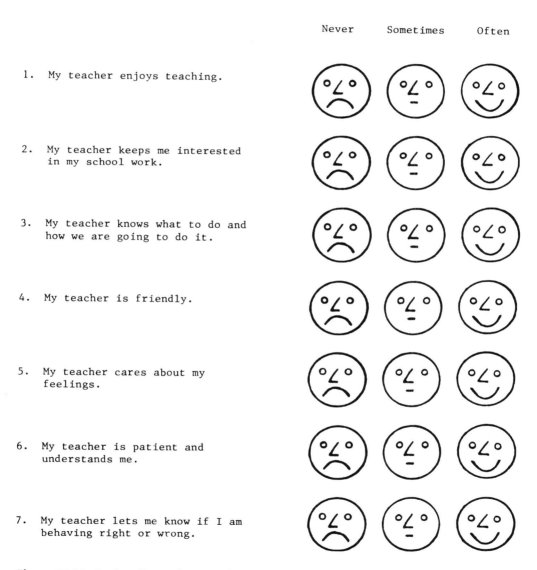

SCHOOL_____

DATE_____

TEACHER_____

Check the face that is most like your teacher.

	Never	Sometimes	Often
1. My teacher enjoys teaching.			
2. My teacher keeps me interested in my school work.			
3. My teacher knows what to do and how we are going to do it.			
4. My teacher is friendly.			
5. My teacher cares about my feelings.			
6. My teacher is patient and understands me.			
7. My teacher lets me know if I am behaving right or wrong.			

Figure 12.10. Student Perceptions (grades 3–5). *Source: Georgia Department of Education, Teacher Performance Assessment Instruments: A Handbook for Interpretation (Atlanta: Division of Staff Development, revised 1980), pp. 139–42. Reprinted with permission of the Georgia Department of Education.*

525

	Never	Sometimes	Often

8. My teacher is polite and nice.

9. My teacher does things that keep children well-behaved.

10. My teacher is fair when children misbehave.

11. My teacher teaches in ways that help me learn.

12. My teacher uses things like charts, movies, filmstrips, and records.

13. My teacher chooses books, workbooks, worksheets, and other things that help me learn.

14. My teacher gives clear explanations and directions about my class work.

15. My teacher explains things again if I don't understand.

16. My teacher listens to me and uses my ideas.

Figure 12.10. (continued)

	Never	Sometimes	Often

17. My teacher tells me when my
    answers are right or wrong.

18. My teacher talks and writes so that
    I can understand.

19. My teacher teaches things in an
    order that makes sense.

20. My teacher uses more than one way
    to teach.

21. My teacher works with large groups,
    small groups, and individual children.

22. My teacher gets me interested in new
    lessons.

23. My teacher gives me a chance to do
    things in this class.

24. I work or pay attention during a
    whole lesson.

25. My teacher does things to keep me
    working or paying attention during
    a lesson.

(continued)

	Never	Sometimes	Often
26. My teacher tells me why the things we learn in school are important.	☹	😐	🙂
27. My teacher knows a lot about what is taught in school.	☹	😐	🙂
28. My teacher does things like checking the roll and handing out papers quickly.	☹	😐	🙂
29. My teacher is ready to begin a new activity as soon as we finish one.	☹	😐	🙂
30. My teacher makes my classroom look like a nice place to be.	☹	😐	🙂

performances. Teacher evaluation systems should include three components: self-appraisal, formative evaluation during the year, and summative or annual evaluation.

Competencies that school systems consider important enough to be evaluated tend to fall within two major categories: instructional skills and personal-professional attributes. Techniques for evaluating instructional skills include an examination of models of teaching; the use of protocol materials, videotapes, and teacher-training packages; and the application of observation analysis systems.

Teacher self-appraisal should be the goal of efforts to evaluate teaching competency. Self-appraisal can be realized through videotaping in the classroom or clinic. Clinical approaches—peer teaching and microteaching—offer the opportunity to try out new techniques and skills in a controlled learning situation.

Personal and professional attributes are difficult to identify and evaluate. Agreement of the faculty on the personal and professional traits that should be evaluated and how they will be assessed is essential. Self-evaluation of personal and professional characteristics may be initiated by a review of the literature on personality development and by the use of selected personal attitude inventories.

MIAMI SOUTHRIDGE SENIOR HIGH SCHOOL

Student Evaluation of Classroom Instruction

PURPOSE: To provide your teachers with information that will be useful in improving classroom instruction.

Directions: Check the space that you feel best describes the classroom atmosphere. Be fair and honest. You do <u>not</u> have to sign your name. (This is a voluntary exercise.)

	Always	Often	Seldom	Never
1. The classroom atmosphere is free from bias and prejudice.	——	——	——	——
2. The lessons are clear and well organized.	——	——	——	——
3. The lessons and assignments have meaning and are purposeful.	——	——	——	——
4. Student participation in class discussions is encouraged.	——	——	——	——
5. Individual help is available when needed.	——	——	——	——
6. The students have the right to express their own opinions on controversial issues without jeopardizing relations with the teacher.	——	——	——	——
7. My personal rights as a student are respected.	——	——	——	——
8. All tests are graded and reviewed. Questions regarding the test are answered.	——	——	——	——
9. The classroom discipline is fair, consistent, and encourages learning.	——	——	——	——
10. The test schedule is announced and adhered to.	——	——	——	——
11. A variety of teaching methods is used in classroom instruction.	——	——	——	——

12. The attendance procedures and classroom policies are clearly explained at the beginning of the semester.   Yes _____   No _____

13. The grading policy is explained at the beginning of each semester.   Yes _____   No _____

14. The students are notified of unsatisfactory progress with sufficient time for corrective action.   Yes _____   No _____

COMMENTS: _____

_____

THANK YOU!

Figure 12.11. Student Evaluation of Classroom Instruction. *Source: Dade County Public Schools, Student Evaluation of Classroom Instruction, Miami, Fla., Miami Southridge Senior High School. Reprinted with permission of the Dade County Public Schools.*

In addition to the teachers' appraisal of their own performance, student and parental evaluations of instruction can aid teachers in analyzing their own behavior and making needed improvements.

Many school systems require supervisors to evaluate teachers periodically. The supervisor is advised to institute a goal-oriented evaluative process whereby the supervisor and teacher agree on the teacher's job targets for the year and also agree to monitor and evaluate these jointly. Though the supervisor may evaluate *teachers*, his or her primary role should be helping teachers to evaluate *themselves*. Changes in behavior, whether in instructional skills or in personal-professional attributes, can come about only if the teacher sees the need for change and agrees to try to improve.

QUESTIONS FOR DISCUSSION

1. How would you work with teachers to be sure there is a teacher in every classroom who cares that every student, every day, learns and grows and feels like a real human being?
2. Which of the ten models of teaching presented in this chapter do you utilize most frequently and also advocate?
3. Which of the observation systems presented in this chapter do you think would yield the most information for a supervisor and teachers? Why?
4. What would you include in a teacher self-appraisal form you would use with teachers?
5. What use can supervisors make of protocol materials?

ACTIVITIES FOR FURTHER STUDY

1. Choose one of the models of teaching found in Bruce Joyce, Marsha Weil, and Beverly Showers, *Models of Teaching*, 4th ed., and describe its characteristics and uses.
2. Write a paper analyzing your own model of teaching.
3. Create a classification system for retrieval of protocol materials.
4. Employ videotaping equipment and create a protocol, identifying the behavior shown in the protocol.
5. Preview a protocol material and write a brief evaluation of its effectiveness in bringing out the particular point it aims to portray.
6. Develop a plan for a clinical laboratory, with complete specifications for equipment, including costs.
7. Prepare a five-minute lesson to demonstrate one generic teaching skill, have it videotaped, watch the tape of your performance, select and apply an observation instrument, and present a critique of your own performance.
8. Select an observation instrument and train a teacher to use it to analyze (a) a film or videotape of another teacher teaching and (b) a videotape of the teacher himself or herself teaching.
9. Using appropriate visual materials prepare a presentation on Ned A. Flanders's Flanders Interaction Analysis Categories.
10. Draft a proposal describing personal-professional attributes that you feel should be evaluated and how they would be assessed.
11. Obtain samples of teacher-training packages and analyze their suitability as materials for studying the teaching act.
12. Create and, if you are teaching, use an instrument for student evaluation of your teaching performance.

13. Create and, if you are teaching, use an instrument for parent evaluation of your teaching performance.

NOTES

1. Bruce Joyce and Marsha Weil with Beverly Showers, *Models of Teaching*, 4th ed. (Boston: Allyn & Bacon, 1992).
2. Ibid.
3. National Resource and Dissemination Center, *Protocol Materials for Use in Preservice and Inservice Teacher Education*, Tampa, Fla., n.d., unnumbered page 1. Center is no longer operating.
4. B. Othanel Smith, Saul B. Cohen, and Arthur Pearl, *Teachers for the Real World* (Washington, D.C.: American Association of Colleges for Teacher Education, 1969), p. 63.
5. Ibid.
6. Ibid., pp. 51–52.
7. *WILKITS* (Ogden, Utah: Weber State College).
8. Florida Department of Education, *B-2 Teacher Education Modules* (Chipley, Fla.: Panhandle Area Educational Cooperative).
9. Anita Simon and E. Gil Boyer, *Mirrors for Behavior III: An Anthology of Observation Instruments* (Philadelphia: Research for Better Schools, 1974).
10. Smith, Cohen, and Pearl, *Teachers for the Real World*, p. 55.
11. See E. Wayne Roberson, "The Preparation of an Instrument for the Analysis of Classroom Behavior," doctoral dissertation, Tucson, University of Arizona, 1967.
12. Russell N. Jensen, Darleen Videen, and Charles F. Grubbs, *Teacher Self-Appraisal Program, 1967–68* (Tucson, Ariz.: Research and Development, Tucson Public Schools, July 1968).
13. Ibid., p. 3.
14. Ibid., p. 1.
15. Ibid., p. 4.
16. Ibid., p. 17.
17. Arthur W. Combs, *Individual Behavior: A Perceptual Approach*, rev. ed. (New York: Harper & Row, 1959).
18. Earl C. Kelley, *Education for What Is Real* (New York: Harper & Row, 1947).
19. Abraham H. Maslow, *Motivation and Personality*, 2nd ed. (New York: Harper & Row, 1970).
20. Arthur W. Combs, ed., *Perceiving, Behaving, Becoming*, 1962 Yearbook (Alexandria, Va.: Association for Supervision and Curriculum Development, 1962).
21. William C. Schutz, *FIRO-B* (Palo Alto, Calif.: Consulting Psychologists Press, 1957). See also William C. Schutz, *FIRO: A Three Dimensional Theory of Interpersonal Behavior* (New York: Holt, Rinehart and Winston, 1958); Katherine C. Briggs and Isabel Briggs Myers, *Myers-Briggs Type Indicator* (Palo Alto, Calif.: Consulting Psychologists Press, 1983).
22. For specification of the objectives of the individual within the framework of the objectives of the institution, see some of the literature on management by objectives such as John William Humble, ed., *Management by Objectives in Action* (New York: McGraw-Hill, 1970); George S. Odiorne, *Management by Objectives: A System of Managerial Leadership* (New York: Pitman, 1965); and Robert O. Riggs, "Management by Objectives: Its Utilization in the Management of Administrative Performance," *Contemporary Education* 63 (January 1972): 129–33. See also Robert E. Boston and David A. Spencer, *Management by Objectives* (Minneapolis, Minn.: Amidon & Associates, 1973).
23. Cincinnati Public Schools, *Teacher Appraisal Manual* (Cincinnati, Ohio: Certificated Personnel Branch, August 1984).

24. Cincinnati Public Schools, *Teacher Self-Appraisal Manual* (Cincinnati, Ohio: Certificated Personnel Branch, August 1984).
25. Cincinnati Public Schools, *Teacher Appraisal Manual*, pp. 7–8.
26. Ibid., p. 14.
27. Ibid., p. 5.

BIBLIOGRAPHY

Allen, Dwight, and Kevin Ryan, *Microteaching*. Reading, Mass.: Addison-Wesley, 1969.

Allen, Paul M., William D. Barnes, Jerald L. Reece, and E. Wayne Roberson. *Teacher Self-Appraisal: A Way of Looking over Your Own Shoulder*. Worthington, Ohio: Charles A. Jones, 1970.

Amidon, Edmund J., and Ned A. Flanders. *The Role of the Teacher in the Classroom: A Manual for Understanding and Improving Classroom Behavior*, rev. ed. Minneapolis: Association for Productive Teaching, 1971.

Amidon, Edmund J., and John B. Hough, eds. *Interaction Analysis: Theory, Research, and Application*. Reading, Mass.: Addison-Wesley, 1967.

Amidon, Edmund J., and Elizabeth Hunter. *Improved Teaching: The Analysis of Classroom Verbal Interaction*. New York: Holt, Rinehart and Winston, 1966.

Bellack, Arno A., H. M. Kliebard, R. T. Hyman, and F. L. Smith, Jr. *The Language of the Classroom*. New York: Teachers College Press, 1966.

Borg, Walter R., et al. *The Minicourse: A Microteaching Approach to Teacher Education*. Beverly Hills, Calif.: Macmillan, 1970.

Boston, Robert E., and David A. Spencer. *Management by Objectives*. Minneapolis, Minn.: Amidon, 1973.

Briggs, Katherine C., and Isabel Briggs Myers. *Myers-Briggs Type Indicator*. Palo Alto, Calif.: Consulting Psychologists Press, 1983.

Briggs, Leslie J. *The Use and Evaluation of "Protocol" Materials in Teacher Education Program*. Tallahassee, Fla.: State Department of Education, 1971.

Brighton, Stayner F. *Increasing Your Accuracy in Teacher Evaluation*. Englewood Cliffs, N.J.: Prentice-Hall, 1965.

Brophy, Jere E., and Thomas L. Good. *Teacher-Child Dyadic Interaction: A Manual for Coding Classroom Behavior*. Austin: University of Texas, 1969.

Brown, Bob Burton, Richard L. Ober, Robert S. Soar, and Jeannine N. Webb. *The Florida Taxonomy of Cognitive Behavior*. Gainesville, Fla.: Institute for Development of Human Resources, 1968. Manual and instrument.

Brown, George. *Microteaching: A Programme of Teaching Skills*. London: Methuen, 1975.

Burke, Caseel. *The Individualized, Competency-Based System of Teacher Education at Weber State College*. Washington, D.C.: American Association of Colleges for Teacher Education, 1972.

Cincinnati Public Schools. *Teacher Appraisal Manual*. Cincinnati, Ohio: Certificated Personnel Branch, 1984.

————. *Teacher Self-Appraisal Manual*. Cincinnati, Ohio: Certificated Personnel Branch, 1984.

Combs, Arthur W. *Individual Behavior: A Perceptual Approach*, rev. ed. New York: Harper & Row, 1959.

————. *The Professional Preparation of Teachers: A Perceptual View of Teacher Preparation*. Boston: Allyn & Bacon, 1965.

————, ed. *Perceiving, Behaving, Becoming.* 1962 Yearbook. Alexandria, Va.: Association for Supervision and Curriculum Development, 1962.

Dietz, Mary E. "Using Portfolios as a Framework for Professional Development." *Journal of Staff Development* 16 (Spring 1995): 40–43.

Flanders, Ned A. *Analyzing Teacher Behavior*. Reading, Mass.: Addison-Wesley, 1970.

———. *Interaction Analysis: Teacher Handbook*. San Francisco: Far West Laboratory for Educational Research and Development, 1972.

———, et al. *Interaction Analysis: A Minicourse from the Far West Laboratory: Handbook*. St. Paul, Minn.: Paul S. Amidon and Associates, 1974.

Florida Department of Education. *B-2 Teacher Education Modules*. Chipley, Fla.: Panhandle Area Educational Cooperative, n.d.

Hamachek, Don E. *Encounters with the Self*, 2nd ed. New York: Holt, Rinehart and Winston, 1978.

Hartzell, Gary N. "Helping Administrators Learn to Avoid Seven Common Employee Appraisal Errors." *Journal of Staff Development* 16 (Spring 1995): 32–37.

Houston, W. Robert, et al. *Resources for Performance-Based Education*. Albany. Division of Teacher Education and Certification, New York State Education Department, 1973.

Houston, W. Robert, Karen S. Nelson, and Elizabeth C. Houston. *Resources for Performance-Based Education, Supplement A*. Albany: Division of Teacher Education and Certification, New York State Education Department, 1973.

Humble, John William, ed. *Management by Objectives in Action*. New York: McGraw-Hill, 1970.

Hunter, Madeline. "Teacher Competency: Problem, Theory, and Practice." *Theory into Practice* 15 (April 1976): 162–71.

Hutchins, C. L., Barbara Dunning, Marilyn Madsen, and Sylvia I. Rainey. *Minicourses Work*. San Francisco: Far West Laboratory for Educational Research and Development, 1971.

Hyman, Ronald T. *School Administrator's Faculty Supervision Handbook*. Englewood Cliffs, N.J.: Prentice-Hall, 1986.

Jensen, Richard N. *Microteaching: Planning and Implementing a Competency-Based Training Program*. Springfield, Ill.: Charles C. Thomas, 1974.

Jensen, Russell N., Darleen Videen, and Charles F. Grubbs. *Teacher Self-Appraisal Program, 1967–68*. Tucson, Ariz.: Research and Development, Tucson Public Schools, July 1968.

Jourard, Sidney M. *The Transparent Self*. New York: Van Nostrand Reinhold, 1971.

Joyce, Bruce, and Marsha Weil with Beverly Showers. *Models of Teaching*, 4th ed. Boston: Allyn & Bacon, 1992.

Kelley, Earl C. *Education for What Is Real*. New York: Harper & Row, 1947.

McNergney, Robert F., and Carol A. Carrier. *Teacher Development*. New York: Macmillan, 1981.

Maslow, Abraham H. *Motivation and Personality*, 2nd ed. New York: Harper & Row, 1970.

———. *Toward a Psychology of Being*, 2nd ed. Princeton, N.J.: D. Van Nostrand, 1968.

National Resource and Dissemination Center. *Protocol Materials for Use in Preservice and Inservice Teacher Education*. Tampa, Fla.: National Resource and Dissemination Center, n.d. (Center is no longer operating.)

Nuthall, Graham, and Ivan Snook. "Contemporary Models of Teaching." In *Second Handbook of Research on Teaching*, ed. Robert M. W. Travers. Chicago: Rand McNally, 1973.

Ober, Richard L. "Theory and Practice through Systematic Observation." *Research Bulletin of the Florida Educational Research and Development Council* 4 (Spring 1968).

Odiorne, George S. *Management by Objectives: A System of Managerial Leadership*. New York: Pitman, 1965.

Peterson, Penelope L., and Herbert J. Walberg, eds. *Handbook on Teaching: Concepts, Findings, and Implications*. Berkeley, Calif.: McCutchan, 1979.

Riggs, Robert O. "Management by Objectives: Its Utilization in the Management of Administrative Performance." *Contemporary Education* 63 (January 1972): 129–33.

Robbins, Pam. *How to Plan and Implement a Peer Coaching Program*. Alexandria, Va.: ASCD, 1991.

Roberson, E. Wayne. *A Manual for Utilizing the Teacher Self-Appraisal Observation System*. Tucson, Ariz.: Educational Innovators Press, 1973.

————. *The Preparation of an Instrument for the Analysis of Teacher Classroom Behavior*. Tucson: University of Arizona, 1967.

Rogers, Carl R. *Being, Becoming, and Behavior*. Boston: Houghton Mifflin, 1961.

Schutz, William C. *FIRO-B*. Palo Alto, Calif.: Consulting Psychologists Press, 1957.

————. *FIRO: A Three Dimensional Theory of Interpersonal Behavior*. New York: Holt, Rinehart and Winston, 1958.

Simon, Anita, and E. Gil Boyer. *Mirrors for Behavior III: An Anthology of Observation Instruments*. Philadelphia: Research for Better Schools, 1974.

Smith, B. Othanel, Saul B. Cohen, and Arthur Pearl. *Teachers for the Real World*. Washington, D.C.: American Association of Colleges for Teacher Education, 1969.

Stanley, Sarah, and James Popham. *Teacher Evaluation: Six Prescriptions for Success*. Alexandria, Va.: ASCD, 1988.

The Teacher Self-Appraisal Program: An Inservice Program for Classroom Accountability: A Five-Year Overview. Tucson: Research Department, Tucson Public Schools, 1971.

Turner, Robert L., ed. *A General Catalog of Teaching Skills*. Bloomington: Indiana University, 1973.

Wittrock, Merlin C. *Handbook of Research on Teaching*, 3rd ed. New York: Macmillan, 1986.

Inventories

Katherine C. Briggs and Isabel Briggs Myers. *Myers-Briggs Type Indicator*. 1983. Inventory of traits of extroversion versus introversion, sensation versus intuition, thinking versus feeling, and judgment versus perception. Consulting Psychologists Press, Inc., 577 College Avenue, Palo Alto, CA 94306.

William C. Schutz, *FIRO-B*. 1957. Survey of interpersonal skills. Consulting Psychologists Press, Inc., 577 College Avenue, Palo Alto, CA 94306.

Videotapes

Another Set of Eyes: Conferencing Skills. 1989. Three tapes, over two hours on conferencing skills, featuring Arthur Costa and Robert Garmston. Demonstrates trust-building, questioning, responding, and empowering skills. *Trainer's Manual*. Association for Supervision and Curriculum Development, 1250 North Pitt Street, Alexandria, VA 22314.

Another Set of Eyes: Techniques for Classroom Observation. 1988. Two tapes, one and a half hours, featuring Keith Acheson. Demonstrates selective verbatim recording, verbal flow, at task observation, class traffic, interaction analysis, and global scan. *Trainer's Manual*. Association for Supervision and Curriculum Development, 1250 North Pitt Street, Alexandria, VA 22314.

Teacher Evaluation: Doing It Right, Parts 1 and 2. 1994. The two videotapes (Part 1: 23 minutes and Part 2: 22 minutes) feature Lawrence S. Finkel sharing information on improving evaluator skills in effective teaching, supervising the marginal teacher, conferencing techniques, and classroom observation methods. National Association of Secondary School Principals, 1904 Association Drive, Reston, VA 22091-1537.

Teaching Episodes. 1992. 100-minute videotape of 19 teaching episodes. National Staff Development Council, P.O. Box 240, Oxford, OH 45056.

Video Library of Teaching Episodes. Episodes 1–20. 1988–89. 20 tapes. 15–20 min. Lessons on each tape with background information, analysis, and discussion. Association for Supervision and Curriculum Development, 1250 North Pitt Street, Alexandria, VA 22314.

Video Library of Teaching Episodes. Episodes 21–30. Urban Schools. 1991. 10 tapes. 15–20 min. Lessons on each tape with interviews with teachers, background information, analysis, and discussion. Taped in Baltimore, Kansas City, and Washington, D.C. Association for Supervision and Curriculum Development, 1250 North Pitt Street, Alexandria, VA 22314.

PART V

The Summative Dimension of Teacher Evaluation

13

Summative Assessment of Teacher Performance

Objectives

After studying Chapter 13 you should be able to accomplish the following objectives:

1. Define *summative evaluation* as applied to teacher performance.
2. Distinguish between administrative assessment and clinical supervision.
3. Describe the principal's role in summative evaluation.
4. Describe the instructional supervisor's role, if any, in summative evaluation.
5. Describe how to collect data for purposes of summative evaluation.
6. State what teacher behaviors should be administratively assessed. Defend your choice of behaviors.
7. Describe how you would assess each behavior that you believe should be assessed.
8. Distinguish between and write competencies, indicators, and descriptors.
9. Select or create and apply, if required by the job, an instrument by which the administrator may assess teacher performance.

SUMMATIVE EVALUATION

Summative evaluation as the term is used in this chapter is the overall assessment of teacher performance made by the administrator (or the administrator and others) that culminates in a comprehensive appraisal either annually or as otherwise required by the state or locality. Included within the concept of summative evaluation are the periodic (some would say formative) evaluations made during the year for the purpose of collecting data with which to make the summative appraisal at the end of the year. Jerry J. Bellon and Elner C. Bellon, for example, postulated three formative observational phases of classroom supervision that were cited in the preceding chapter. They also called attention to a fourth phase of a supervisory process: the Evaluation Program, during which the data from periodic formative evaluations form the basis for the annual or summative evaluation.[1]

Tentatively, we had considered calling this chapter "Helping Teachers through Assessment of Performance." Yet in reality, there is some question about the degree to which teachers benefit from summative evaluations even though it is claimed by some that the purpose of summative assessment is the improvement of instruction. On receipt of their "report cards," a copy of the principal's written report of the periodic and summative appraisals, if they have earned "passing grades," many teachers simply file the reports away and wait for the next one.

Some educators attribute the lack of help in evaluation systems to misuse of the process. Arthur Shaw took this position when he said, "Evaluation is often dreaded by principals, feared by teachers, and seldom utilized by school districts for the purposes for which it was intended—the improvement of instruction and the subsequent facilitation of learning."[2]

Actually, the effective, conscientious, professional teachers will try out recommendations made by the administrator if they feel the recommendations are sound. Ineffective teachers who receive low ratings are forced to attempt to make improvements in their teaching if they wish to maintain their positions. Thus, summative or administrative assessment does have as a goal the improvement of instruction. It might be said that the system succeeds in this goal to some degree in spite of itself.

The major purpose of administrative assessment of teachers, however, lies in another direction. Summative evaluation is essentially an exercise, albeit a necessary one, in personnel, not instructional, management. Whereas the primary purpose of formative evaluation as carried out in clinical supervision, for example, is to improve the teacher's instructional skills, the main purpose of summative evaluation is the making of decisions about personnel. Both formative and summative evaluation have as their ultimate purpose improvement in student learning.

On the college level, annual evaluations of faculty are made for the purpose of deciding on tenure, promotion, and salary increments. On the public school level, the decisions to be made are primarily retention, including tenure or continuation of contract and dismissal or termination of contract. Occasionally, summative evaluations are used for making decisions about transfer of teachers to other schools or assignments or to other responsibilities—for example, team leader, grade coordinator, lead teacher, department head, teacher on special assignment, and workshop staff.

Although almost any evaluation system has to some degree the improvement of instruction as its purpose, summative evaluation aims ultimately to rid the profession of incompetent teachers. As such, summative evaluation is a necessary function of administration. True, effective (however defined) teachers may take to heart suggestions made in the evaluation for improving instruction. True, ineffective (however defined) teachers may be pressured by the administrator to undergo some remedial training to remedy deficiencies. But the bottom line—which gives summative evaluation an aura of threat—is the potential for dismissal. Even the mere existence of written evaluations that are good to excellent but less than perfect is cause for concern to teachers who know that personnel files can dog them the same way cumulative records can hound students. A careless, inaccurate, or biased comment of an evaluator can be a source of both professional and psychological harm to the teacher.

You may well ask why, if summative assessment is a personnel rather than an instructional matter, a chapter on the subject is included in this textbook. We offer the following reasons:

1. In some schools, particularly small ones, the principal *is* the instructional supervisor. He or she takes on responsibilities for both formative and summative evaluation, combining the functions.
2. In some school systems the instructional (staff) supervisor is either charged with the responsibility for both formative and summative evaluation, even though the administrator may actually sign the year-end assessment report, or called on to participate with the administrator and/or others in the summative evaluation process.
3. Instructional supervisors and administrators must be able to distinguish between the purposes and processes of formative and summative evaluation of teachers.
4. Both staff and line supervisors owe it to the profession, to teachers, to students, to the public, and to themselves to make the summative assessment of teachers as fair, meaningful, and constructive as possible, basing it on the evidence presented by the formative evaluations.
5. The summative evaluation process should be coordinated with the processes of teacher self-appraisal and formative evaluation.

In evaluating teachers for personnel purposes, school systems must provide answers to the following questions:

- Who should be evaluated?
- Who should do the evaluating?
- What should be evaluated?
- How should the evaluations be done?
- How should the data be used?

Answers to these questions appear at first deceptively simple. But they are not. Our decentralized system of education has produced a variety of answers; we provide our own later in the chapter when we examine each of these questions.

Perry A. Zirkel reported that as early as 1980, "fewer than half ($n = 23$) of the states have statutes or administrative regulations directly dealing with the evaluation of public school teachers."[3] It comes as a surprise to learn that some states have no established regulations to control a process so fundamental to education as the evaluation of teachers. Zirkel noted that even in the majority of states with teacher evaluation laws, the local level is "the primary locus for establishing the policies and procedures for teacher evaluation."[4] As a result, the responsibility for establishing policies about teacher evaluation falls on the local boards of education. In some states "the input of local teachers is provided for in the form of either advice (Arizona, California), consultation (Nevada, Oklahoma), or negotiation (Connecticut)."[5] On the other hand, the state of Georgia, for example, has mandated annual evaluation of performance of all school personnel and has developed model instruments, model processes, and technical assistance for local units of administration.[6] Thus, responsibility for establishing procedures for the evaluation of school personnel is shared by the state and local levels.

Zirkel pointed out that local regulations must conform to state minimum statutory standards and that both state and local regulations must abide by federal constitutional and statutory provisions. These include the First and Fourteenth Amendments, the Civil Rights Act of 1964, Section 504 of the Rehabilitation Act of 1973, and the Age Discrimination in Employment Amendments of 1978.[7]

Who Should Be Evaluated?

Teachers, of course, should be evaluated. But the answer is not that simple. A great diversity of practice exists in the assessment of school personnel. Some states require evaluation of all certificated personnel (Florida and Georgia, for example). Some states (Arizona, for example) limit evaluation to certificated *teachers*. Other states (Kansas and West Virginia) require that all employees be evaluated. Some states (Florida, Louisiana, and Nevada) list the personnel to be evaluated by category, as teachers, counselors, librarians, and so on. Some states (Massachusetts and Michigan) call for the evaluation of nontenured teachers only, whereas others (Florida, for example) stipulate that both tenured and nontenured teachers be evaluated.[8]

One might argue that after teachers have gone through their probationary period and have been accorded tenure, they are fully competent and need no further supervision or evaluating. The argument might be pushed back even further and a case made that if teachers were carefully selected, once on the job there'd be no need for continuing supervision and evaluation. Would that this were so! In that utopian world, instruction would be superb and school administration would be child's play. We all know, however, that the presence of ineffective teachers in our midst makes that argument specious and untenable. Though much can be said in defense of tenure, and we would not advocate giving it up, on the negative side is the presence of tenured teachers who perform poorly, lack motivation, barely meet minimum professional standards, or are actually incompetent. Tenure is no guarantee of the presence of able teachers. Consequently, evaluation of teacher performance is necessary. The evaluation of all teachers (although not necessarily every teacher every year nor even on the same cycle), tenured and nontenured, appears to be prevailing practice.

Who Should Evaluate Teachers?

You would probably answer the question "Who should evaluate teachers?" with "The principal." But this answer is not universal. Zirkel observed that Florida, Hawaii, New Jersey, New Mexico, and Wyoming specify that the evaluation of teachers be performed by the principal or immediate supervisor.[9] In most states that have addressed teacher evaluation, the choice of evaluator is left to the local board of education.[10] In some states (Connecticut and Pennsylvania, for example), the decision on who will do the evaluating is left to the superintendent.[11] A rather unique process is followed by Massachusetts. Here a committee of three people does the evaluating; one person is selected by the teacher to be evaluated, one by the local school board, and one by the two selected committee members.[12]

Generally, either by state mandate, local board regulations, or just tradition—or we might add, by reasonable administrative practice—responsibility for evaluating personnel of his or her school falls to the principal. Most principals regard this task as their responsibility, indeed, their prerogative. Whether they carry out that responsibility themselves is another matter. In some cases in which principals bear the responsibility, they delegate to their assistant principals the task of collecting data and reporting to them. The principal in these instances evaluates teachers on secondary rather than firsthand data.

Some persons hold that the principal should not perform the task of evaluating teachers. Shaw, for example, voiced this sentiment that applies equally well today:

> The answer to the problem lies not so much in changing the attitudes of the administrators who now do the bulk of the evaluation, but with teachers who must somehow wrest the privilege away from administrative personnel in order to come full cycle as a viable profession and emerge as the leaders of instruction. As the Texas Federation of Teachers proposes: "Control and entry into and egress from the teaching profession should be in the hands of the practicing professionals."
>
> As long as teachers allow themselves to be capriciously evaluated, the teaching profession will not assume its proper role in the educational world. A profession sets its own standards and requires members to adhere to these standards. Improved teacher evaluation techniques may be the key to realizing these standards.[13]

Shaw's proposal is not too likely to be implemented in the immediate future—though it would certainly take teachers a long way down the road to empowerment.

Who may do the evaluating is bound not only by state and local board regulations but also by contracts negotiated between school management and teachers' organizations. The contracts usually specify who may do the evaluating, how often, how the data will be used, and what records will be kept.

Controversy swirls around the issue of whether staff supervisors from the central office or individual school should be involved in the summative evaluation of teachers. In some school systems that have negotiated contracts, department chairpersons are forbidden to do any formal evaluating of teachers because the chairpersons are considered members of the bargaining unit—that is, teachers—and summative evaluations (and formative evaluations as well, which are for the purpose of making a summative evaluation) must be done by management—that is, administrators.

Many of us in supervision believe, as we have noted elsewhere in this book, that instructional supervisors should be as far removed from summative evaluation as possible. They should try to avoid summative assessments that require the data to be furnished to the administrator for personnel action. They should become involved only under the following conditions:

1. If such evaluations are standard practice agreed on by the teachers when the evaluation process was set up
2. If a teacher requests the supervisor to do his or her evaluation
3. If the principal requests the supervisor to do so *and the teacher consents*
4. If a teacher is facing dismissal for incompetence and an expert judgment is needed
5. If so ordered by the superintendent
6. If doing so does not violate the state law, school board policy, or terms of a negotiated contract

Generally, the principal is responsible for the summative evaluation of teachers; this, we believe, is as it should be. The principal should personally observe all teachers a sufficient number of times in their classrooms to form a judgment about their performance and provide a basis for a written annual assessment. In this process, the principal engages in both formative and summative evaluation. The principal may, if he or she chooses, seek additional evaluation by his or her assistant administrators as supplementary to but not in place of the principal's own evaluating. Although the principal is charged with many duties, it seems that if he or she must delegate certain tasks, the task of teacher evaluation cannot be one of them. It is the principal who should possess the highest degree of competence in evaluating personnel and should therefore feel it is incumbent to put those skills to use. We believe teachers have the right to expect an evaluation of their performance, if it is done at all, from their status leader—the principal. None of the principal's activity in formative or summative evaluation obviates the formative evaluation carried on by instructional supervisors.

What Should Be Evaluated?
Would that we could give a simple answer to the question "What should be evaluated?" Some would say teacher competence, which is both a simple answer and a simplistic one. The response made by some evaluators to how they know good teaching is like the response that is given to the question "How do you know a good painting?" The answer, "I know it when I see it," does not tell us very much. Teaching is often judged in the same way. To some extent we can all identify good teachers and good teaching. The problem is that we are often not in agreement on who the good teachers are and what good teaching is. John D. McNeil, referring to A. S. Barr's summary of studies of teaching effectiveness, observed that the problem is common.

> He [Barr] correctly saw that the problem that needs clarifying before all others is the criterion of teaching effectiveness. Different people employ different criteria and approaches to the evaluation of teachers. Some prefer to approach effectiveness from the point of view of personal prerequisites; some from teacher-pupil behaviors; some from basic knowledge, attitudes, and skill; and some from the point of view of results or products. These different approaches give different answers to the question, "Is this teacher an effective teacher?"[14]

Teaching effectiveness, like beauty, can be in the eye of the beholder. We need to come to grips with the basic problem: What is effectiveness in teaching? We may arrive at an answer to this question in a number of ways. First, we may accept what the experts—for example, professors of education—tell us is good or effective teaching. We find, however, that lacking hard data, the experts disagree. Some look for a heavy affective orientation in teaching; others advocate a heavy cognitive load. Some professors have a fondness for particular methods and feel other methods to be inferior. For example, some champion inquiry learning, cooperative learning, and small-group instruction. Others favor didactic teaching and the use of large groups.[15]

In spite of disagreements, however, there is considerable uniformity of thought about teaching effectiveness. We know that teachers who like children are more effective instructors than those who do not. We know that student achievement is higher when teachers reinforce correct responses. We know that as a rule, if students are to be motivated, the teacher must be motivated. We know that a teacher cannot teach what he or she does not know. Many educators follow what Allen R. Warner and Dora H. Scott referred to as "the contemporary conventional wisdom of teaching."[16] Both the experts and the not-so-expert rely heavily on conventional wisdom, which itself is derived from research, personal and vicarious experience, and common sense.

Second, we can base a definition of teacher effectiveness on description of what teachers actually do. We can observe what most teachers do and try to describe the teaching act from the data gleaned from those observations. We could sharpen our observation by first identifying good teachers and poor teachers and then studying what good teachers do. But that puts us in a catch-22 situation, for the good teachers must be identified, and we will certainly encounter differences among the identifiers as to what good teaching is. We might be fortunate enough, however, to achieve consensus among the identifiers.

Third, we can gather empirical data about teaching behaviors that are related to certain learner variables—for example, student achievement. We can try to find out which behaviors have a positive effect on student achievement so that teachers may repeat those behaviors. The research on effective teaching mentioned in Chapter 4 establishes some generally accepted principles to guide us.

Fourth, we can ask a group of teachers or a mixed group of professional educators to describe effective teaching behaviors. Many professional educators have been involved in identifying generic competencies in their states. Although the lists of competencies vary from state to state, which once again reveals the uncertainty in the profession concerning what good teaching is, nevertheless the competencies are uniform within those states that have undertaken the task and thus provide some direction for the evaluation of teachers.

In the absence of recommended or mandated systemwide or statewide processes, which have already specified the teaching competencies to be evaluated, or even as supplementary to state and local systems of evaluation, the faculty of each school should reach consensus on what it believes is good teaching. No exercise could be a more valuable in-service activity than the production of a description of what is effective teaching as perceived by local schoolteachers and administrators.

Richard P. Manatt's report on the School Improvement Model, a system of teacher and administrator evaluation in five school organizations in Iowa and Minnesota, furnishes an example of specification of competencies.[17] In describing the Model, Manatt listed a composite of performance criteria assessed by one or more of the five organizations as shown in Figure 13.1.

---

1. Maintains an effective relationship with students' families.
2. Provides instruction appropriate for capabilities, rates of learning styles of students.
3. Prepares appropriate evaluation activities.
4. Communicates effectively with students.
5. Monitors seatwork closely.
6. Demonstrates sensitivity in relating to students.
7. Promotes positive self-concept in students.
8. Promotes students' self-discipline and responsibility.
9. Uses a variety of teaching techniques.
10. Spends time at the beginning of the learning demonstrating processes to the student (cueing).
11. Uses controlled (guided) practice before assigning homework (independent practice).
12. Organizes students for effective instruction.
13. Provides students with specific evaluative feedback.
14. Selects and uses appropriate lesson content, learning activities, and materials.
15. Demonstrates ability to monitor student behavior.
16. Writes effective lesson plans.
17. Demonstrates a willingness to keep curriculum and instructional practices current.
18. Has high expectations.
19. Organizes resources and materials for effective instruction.
20. Models and gives concrete examples.

This list is a composite of discriminating criteria used by one or more of the five SIM school organizations.

Figure 13.1. Discriminating Teacher Performance Criteria in Rank Order. *Source: Richard P. Manatt, "Lessons from a Comprehensive Performance Appraisal Project," Educational Leadership 44, no. 7 (April 1987): 10. Reprinted with permission of the Association for Supervision and Curriculum Development and Richard P. Manatt. Copyright 1987 by the Association for Supervision and Curriculum Development. All rights reserved.*

Because the principal, who is a generalist, will ordinarily be the person doing the evaluating, he or she will evaluate teacher performance in relation to specified generic competencies. The principal's major purpose in observing and evaluating is to gather reliable data for annual assessment and making personnel decisions, so his or her observations will usually be of the global variety. The principal will evaluate teachers each time he or she observes them on all the specified competencies.

Ben M. Harris and his colleagues suggested that competencies possess the following characteristics:

1. There should be relatively few *important* competencies that are demonstrably related to effective teaching and learning.
2. The competencies should be sufficiently specific so that they are clearly definable.
3. The competencies should be amenable to reliable measurement.
4. For formative evaluation purposes, the performance manifestation of the competencies should be subject to change through school-sponsored, in-service programs and instructional supervision.[18]

We would amend the fourth characteristic to read "for both formative and summative evaluation purposes."

Any study of personnel evaluation as carried out in the schools reveals that administrators seek to evaluate more than teaching competencies. The process extends beyond the classroom into personal and professional attributes of teachers. Harris et al. observed that "basically, there are three approaches to the evaluation of personnel: (1) the characteristics of the individual, sometimes called 'presage criteria,' (2) the products attributed to the individual, and (3) the processes used by the individual."[19]

Let's take a quick look at these three approaches.

Characteristics of the Teacher. The personal characteristics of the teacher do make a difference to the learners, to the school, and to the community. In days gone by, administrators and school boards prescribed in detail, for example, how a teacher would dress. Male teachers have been required to wear suits; female teachers have been prohibited from wearing cosmetics; both male and female teachers have been required to teach Sunday school. And of course, neither could imbibe alcoholic beverages or use tobacco.

The number of restrictions on personal behavior has diminished in recent years. We now find general statements in school board policies about clean and appropriate dress and grooming and general decorum in behavior. In fact, some school district policies are written so loosely that the decision about what teachers can and should wear to school is left for the school principal to make. This is not to say that personal and professional characteristics are not important—they are; nor that they should not be evaluated—they should be. John C. Reynolds commented, "Four factors generally differentiate effective teachers from ineffective teachers—superior personality organization, good judgment/reasoning, capacity to relate to others, and a knowledge of basic content and instructional methods."[20]

The first three factors are largely personal in nature. Faculties can and should draw up their own list—if it is not already a part of the evaluation system—of personal and professional characteristics they deem essential to the teacher, such as warmth, enthusiasm, communication skills, concern for cultural differences, and so on. The rub comes, however, in the assessment of these traits.

Process and Product. Prevailing practice in teacher evaluation seeks to assess teacher performance in terms of process, personal characteristics, and professional attributes. For formative purposes, teachers are judged on process, the effectiveness with which they demonstrate generic teaching skills in the classroom. For summative purposes, personal characteristics and professional attributes are often assessed in addition to process skills. If you examine the typical classroom observation instrument, you will find teacher effectiveness described in terms of competencies that the teacher must possess. If you look at a typical summative evaluation instrument, you will see teacher performance judged in relation to classroom competencies and many times, in addition, personal and professional traits. In current practice the majority of items on evaluation instruments focus on process or methods used by the teacher. As a rule, processes are easier to observe and evaluate than personal and professional characteristics or products of teaching.

The belief is growing that teacher performance should be assessed, at least in part, on the school's products—that is, the performance of students. The accountability movement aims to discover what success teachers have had in promoting student achievement. National, state, and local assessments of student achievement have evolved to determine whether students have mastered the content with which they have been confronted. Test data reveal one dimension of product evaluation. They do not disclose, however, less observable behaviors, particularly those in the affective domain. An assessment of the product of teaching should be built into the teacher evaluation system. As Shaw said, "At least some of the evaluation should center on whether the teacher has changed any student behavior; has the teacher taught the student anything?"[21] Increasingly, we find school districts including in their systems of evaluation of both teachers and administrators the degree of success of the students as measured by criterion-referenced and norm-referenced tests.

Processes, personal and professional characteristics, and products are all applicable elements to be evaluated. Whether an element is to be evaluated, however, should be agreed on by both the evaluators and the evaluatees. Together the representatives of the administrators and teachers should create a system that meets with general consensus, that does not conflict with state or federal laws and constitutional provisions, and that, of course, the local school board endorses.

How Should the Evaluations Be Done?

Sampling of Behavior. The evaluator should make enough visits to a teacher's classroom and observe long enough each time to obtain a generous sampling of the teacher's performance. The principal or other evaluator must decide how many times he or she will visit, observe, and evaluate each teacher at the school. Practice varies widely; the states offer no uniform answer to this problem. Zirkel wrote, "A few states ($n = 3$) answer this question with a weasel word—'continuously' in Connecticut, 'on a regular basis' in West Virginia, and 'periodically' in Wyoming. What such continual evaluation means is left immediately to professional discretion and ultimately to judicial determination."[22]

Some states (Alaska, Florida, Michigan, Oregon, and Washington, for example) specify that evaluations be conducted yearly. Some states require more frequent evaluations for nontenured teachers than for tenured teachers. California and Louisiana, for example, require an evaluation every year for nontenured teachers but every two years for tenured teachers. In Oklahoma and South Dakota, nontenured teachers are evaluated twice a year; tenured teachers every three years. Nontenured teachers in New Jersey are evaluated three times a year; tenured teachers once.[23]

Hawaii takes into consideration the teacher's experience, requiring evaluations four times the first year, twice the second year, and annually each year thereafter. Kansas follows a different pattern, requiring evaluations twice during the first and second years, annually during the third and fourth years, and once every three years thereafter.[24]

Which pattern is best? Who can say? Some argue that the more frequently an administrator observes a teacher, the better he or she is able to judge that teacher's performance and the fairer will be any personnel decisions made as a result. There is some evidence that the more frequently administrators visit teachers, the more readily teachers accept the evaluation process.[25]

We have neglected to mention one of the purposes of administrative evaluation besides evaluation of the teacher—that is, to keep the administrator apprised of what is going on in the school. The principal who sits in his or her office behind the desk cannot know what is happening. He or she has no idea of what is being taught, what delivery methods are being used, whether lesson plans are being followed, whether students and teachers are using their time wisely.

The number of visits to observe the teacher must be tempered to the size of the staff and the number of evaluators. We know administrators who make classroom observation visits to each teacher once a month. We know others who visit all teachers five times a year; still others who visit teachers on annual contract (nontenured) four times a year and tenured teachers twice a year. There is no magic number.

Certainly, the administrator should observe a teacher often enough to gather sufficient data on which to make judgments about the teacher's performance. Gene Huddle concluded, "Teacher observation in any form occurs infrequently for most teachers."[26] Huddle supported this statement by citing a study of more than 400 secondary school administrators and 10,000 teachers conducted by the National Institute of Education. The study found that 26 percent of the teachers who responded reported that they had not been visited by an administrator at all during the previous year; 27 percent had been visited once; and 23 percent, twice.[27]

When the principal sums up his or her observations in an end-of-year report for each teacher, he or she should have observed each teacher a sufficient number of times to complete the report accurately and fairly. Further, if the principal begins to detect evidence of incompetence on the part of a teacher, he or she should very well visit that teacher often enough that if the time comes to build a case for dismissal, he or she will have the necessary documentation.

As far as length of each visit is concerned, the principal or other evaluator should remain in the classroom long enough to obtain a fair appraisal of the teacher's performance. If possible, the administrator, or evaluator, should plan to enter the classroom during the transition times between subjects. The teacher can be observed as the transition from one subject to another is made. Also, the time needed to begin the next subject can be observed. Unfortunately, that is rather vague advice. Like graduate students who invariably want to know how long a term paper should be, evaluators want more than the answer "long enough to do the job." Thus, we would fall back on a rule of thumb for formative clinical observations: at least thirty minutes at the elementary school level, one class period for the secondary school level.

Announced versus Unannounced Visits. We believe the clinical supervisor should always schedule visits in advance at a time agreeable to the teacher; the summative evaluator, however, may find it desirable to make a combination of announced and unannounced visits. Because entrapment is not the name of the game, a sufficient number of prearranged visits should be made. The teacher should be seen at his or her best. On the other hand, unannounced or drop-in visits can confirm whether the observations made at announced times revealed the teacher's typical performance. They can introduce an element of simple control, tacitly advising the teacher that he or she is expected to be prepared to teach all day, every day. They can let the teacher know that the principal is on the job and is interested in what is happening in the school.

Some administrators make daily casual, brief, frequent drop-in visits to each teacher. We should distinguish these brief appearances of the administrator, during which he or she makes only the most perfunctory observation, from actual classroom observation of the teacher's instruction. The short, quick drop-in visit, though useful, is more of a monitoring or even social procedure than instructional supervision. Tom Peters and Robert Waterman, Jr., in their book, *In Search of Excellence*, referred to this management style as "managing by wandering around" or "managing by walking about (MBWA)."[28]

Collecting and Recording the Data. If an evaluation system is not already in place, the faculty and administrators will need to decide what data they want collected and how the data will be gathered. They will need to select or create instruments for recording both the periodic observations and the final appraisal.

For the periodic observations in the teacher's classroom, a global instrument such as the ones described in the preceding chapter is desirable. These instruments, known generally as classroom observation forms, are designed to help the evaluator assess what is occurring in the classroom. Occasionally, these forms include items for which evidence must be found by means other than classroom observation.

The summative evaluation instrument, called by some the teacher appraisal form, must bear some relationship to both the classroom observation form and any teacher self-appraisal form in use. In some cases, the teacher appraisal form is identical to the classroom observation form. The classroom observation form should be limited to *only* those items that can be observed in the classroom. The teacher appraisal form then could include all the items on the classroom observation form plus items for which data must be obtained in other ways—for example, certain personal and professional characteristics, products, and processes in outside-of-class activities.

Some of the data to be collected will come from classroom observations. Other data will result from examination of the teacher's lesson and unit plans. Some data will be derived from conferences with the teacher. Student test data will furnish clues to teacher performance. Comments from students, parents, teachers, and even other administrators about a given teacher should be, as the cliché goes, treated with a grain of salt until firsthand evidence confirms or refutes the statement made either on behalf of or in criticism of the teacher.

Personnel evaluation calls for the rating of teachers. Of course, ratings of personnel should be made, for there are teachers in the profession who should not be teaching at all. The administrator, not the supervisor, should bear the primary responsibility for making judgments about the competence or incompetence of teachers. It appears appropriate and timely for the profession as well to set up some mechanism for monitoring itself. Other professions, notably medicine and law, have devised ways to warn or remove members of the profession deemed unsuitable. It is often rebutted that teaching is not a profession, that teachers' salaries are not comparable to those of the medical and legal professions, and therefore that such monitoring would be out of line. Perhaps one of the reasons teaching is not regarded by some of the public as a profession is the inability or unwillingness of the profession itself to spell out and monitor standards of performance. The lack of a monitoring system should not thrust the burden onto the shoulders of the helpless supervisor. The development of national standards is a move in the direction of identifying elements of teaching effectiveness.

Harris et al. underscored the care that must be taken in rating personnel: "It is crucial that the decisions concerning ratings be based on relevant, descriptive, and verifiable data."[29] Further, they cautioned, "Every effort should be made to reassure teachers through processes that are assistance-oriented and through instruments that are objective, descriptive, and diagnostic."[30] The evaluator must have firm evidence for each behavior rated or else he or she should not rate that behavior.

After each evaluation, periodic and final, the evaluator should confer with the teacher. The administrator does hope that the periodic evaluations will result in improvement in instruction during the year and that the summative appraisal will work the same way for instruction during the ensuing year. It is customary for both the administrator and the teacher to sign the summative evaluation report. The teacher's signature does not necessarily signify agreement with the administrator's rating but rather that the teacher has seen the evaluation, acknowledges it, and has received a copy. Some school districts have included a section where the teacher may add comments or reactions.

It is of interest to note the evolution of some evaluation systems on both a state and local/district level. The metamorphoses undergone by Georgia in the past decade provide an example of a state constantly seeking to perfect its personnel evaluation system. In the early 1980s, the state of Georgia mandated and conducted a statewide assessment system for permanent certification of beginning teachers by means of a process called the Teacher Performance Assessment Instruments (TPAI), a process, by the way, that has been exported to some school systems outside Georgia.[31] With the TPAI evaluations, agencies outside the school systems, known as Regional Assessment Centers (RAC), conducted assessments using three independent assessors: an RAC employee, an administrator, and a peer teacher, all of whom had been trained in the use of the instruments.

Teachers prepared for their assessments in advance by creating a set of lesson plans, known as a portfolio. During the period when the planned lessons were taught, assessors visited—observing at least 30 minutes and rating the teacher's performance. Follow-up visits were often necessary.

As you might guess, controversy swirled around such questions as interrater reliability and the validity of some of the items on the instrument. Nevertheless, determinations of eligibility for permanent state certification were made on the basis of scores assigned by the raters. As a rule, the RAC assessments were not conducted primarily for the purpose of improving instruction, which might be incidental to the assessments, but rather for certification purposes.

In 1989, after considerable investment, the state of Georgia abolished the TPAI process. For one reason, the state was awash in the development of evaluation systems for all types of school personnel. In the case of teacher evaluation, duplication of processes, assessor time, and costs were factors in the decision to cease using the TPAI. That same year, the state switched to the Georgia Teacher Evaluation Program to accomplish the dual purpose of permanent certification and summative evaluation.

Assessment in Georgia is now the responsibility of district-level and school-based administrators and supervisors. Until 1995, the state mandated use of four instruments: the Georgia Teacher Observation Instrument (GTOI), consisting of three forms, the Standard, the Formative, and the Extended, which follow the classroom teacher's job description; an instrument for assessing Georgia Teacher Duties and Responsibilities (GTDR); the Georgia Teacher Evaluation Program Annual Evaluation Summary Report, which summarizes both the observation and duties and responsibilities assessments; and the Professional Development Plan.[32]

The Standard form of the GTOI (see Figure 10.2) is initially used for all teachers. Administrators and supervisors using that form observe teachers three times a year, unannounced, for at least twenty minutes each observation. The Formative instrument is used in two subsequent years with one observation per year. If evaluations continue satisfactory, teachers are observed once a year using the Standard form. The Extended form is employed for teachers assessed as needing improvement and those who wish further feedback. Observations are announced when the Extended form is used.

The statement of dimensions on which the evaluation system is based and the GTDR, which allows for additions from the local school district, are reproduced in Figures 13.2 and 13.3. Georgia has, however, continued to modify its teacher assessment programs. In keeping with the movement to decentralize responsibilities and diminish state mandating, since 1995 Georgia has granted its school systems freedom to use the GTOI or another "validated" instrument of its choosing.

Like the states, school districts have engaged in studying and revising their evaluation systems. Monroe County (Florida) furnishes an excellent illustration of the evolution of district appraisal systems. Quite some time ago, Monroe County used a comprehensive teacher appraisal rating scale that measured personal qualifications, professional attitudes, and personal-professional relationships in addition to teaching effectiveness. Currently, the county employs, on an annual basis and for each teacher, a rating scale with spaces for comments about each competency (Figure 13.4, pp. 553–555). The school district utilizes an interim review process after an initial year of comprehensive assessment or every three years for a teacher who has had successful years of teaching. No observations are required; however, two objectives are determined by November 1 and evaluated during a conference by May 1. Details are recorded on a form shown in Figure 13.5 (p. 556).

Annual critiques of some forty teacher evaluation instruments every year since 1981 at Action Laboratories of the annual conferences of the Association for Supervision and Curriculum Development affirm that the early Monroe County model is typical of many evaluation instruments used throughout the country by school districts during the 1980s and on into the 1990s. Process remains the paramount feature of these evaluation systems.

Rating Scales versus Open-Ended Instruments. Both a rating scale and an open-ended instrument have their advantages and disadvantages. A rating scale is easier to fill out; it focuses on specific behaviors; the data can be treated quantitatively, if one prefers to do so. The open-ended instrument permits greater flexibility for the eval-

TEACHING TASK I: PROVIDES INSTRUCTIONS

Dimension A: Instructional Level—The amount and organization of the lesson content are appropriate for the students based on their abilities and the complexity and difficulty of the material.

Dimension B: Content Development—Content is developed through appropriate teacher-focused or student-focused activities.

Dimension C: Building for Transfer—Lesson includes initial focus, content emphasis or linking, and summaries which build for transfer of learning.

TEACHING TASK II: ASSESSES AND ENCOURAGES STUDENT PROGRESS

Dimension A: Promoting engagement—Instructional engagement is promoted through stimulating presentations, active participation, or techniques which promote overt or covert involvement.

Dimension B: Monitoring Progress—Progress, understanding, and bases of misunderstanding are assessed by interpreting relevant student responses, contributions, performances, or products.

Dimension C: Responding to Student Performance—Students are provided reinforcement for adequate performances when appropriate and specific feedback or correctives for inadequate performances.

Dimension D: Supporting Students—Support for students is conveyed by using techniques such as providing encouragement, lowering concern levels, dignifying academic responses, and using language free of sarcasm, ridicule, and humiliating references.

TEACHING TASK III: MANAGES THE LEARNING ENVIRONMENT

Dimension A: Use of Time—Use of instructional time is optimized by techniques such as providing clear directions and using efficient methods for transitions, materials distribution, and other routine matters and by techniques such as focusing on objectives and providing sufficient instructional activities.

Dimension B: Physical Setting—The physical setting allows the students to observe the focus of instruction, to work without disruption, to obtain materials, and to move about easily; and it allows the teacher to monitor the students and to move among them.

Dimension C: Appropriate Behavior—Appropriate behavior is maintained by monitoring the behavior of the entire class, providing feedback, and intervening when necessary.

Figure 13.2. GTOI Dimension Statements: Standard Form. *Source: Georgia Department of Education,* Georgia Teacher Evaluation Program: Evaluation Manual *(Atlanta, Ga.: Georgia Department of Education, May, 1989), p. 21. Reprinted with permission of the Georgia Department of Education.*

uator; it is a more personal, individualized approach, which avoids quantification of the data.

Some school systems use a teacher evaluation form that requires quantification of the data. Using a rating scale with, for example, a low of 1 and a high of 5, principals rate a set of generic competencies and average them. If the teacher's average score falls below 3.5, he or she is considered to be performing unsatisfactorily and might expect to suffer the consequences that follow unsatisfactory work.

With an evaluation system of this type, principals encounter the same type of difficulty as teachers who must decide whether a student has earned a 78 or an 82, a C+ or a B−. When a cutoff score signals the boundary between satisfactory and unsatisfactory performance, the sagacious principal, aware of his or her own fallibility in judgment, tends to inflate the "grades" and gives the benefit to the teacher.

I.   Teacher Duties and Responsibilities
     A. Follows professional practices consistent with school and system policies in working with
         students, students' records, parents, and colleagues
         1. Interacts in a professional manner with students and parents
         2. Is available to students and parents for conferences according to system policies
         3. Facilitates home-school communication by such means as holding conferences, telephoning,
             and sending written communications
         4. Maintains confidentiality of students and students' records
         5. Works cooperatively with school administrators, special support personnel, colleagues, and
             parents
     B. Complies with school, system, and state administrative regulations and board of education
         policies
         1. Conducts assigned classes at the times scheduled
         2. Enforces regulations concerning student conduct and discipline
         3. Is punctual
         4. Provides adequate information, plans, and materials for substitute teacher
         5. Maintains accurate, complete, and appropriate records and files reports promptly
         6. Attends and participates in faculty meetings and other assigned meetings and activities
             according to school policy
         7. Complies with conditions as stated in contract
     C. Demonstrates professional practices in teaching
         1. Models correct use of language, oral and written
         2. Demonstrates accurate and up-to-date knowledge of content
         3. Implements designated curriculum
         4. Maintains lesson plans as required by school policy
         5. Assigns reasonable tasks and homework to students
     D. Acts in a professional manner and assumes responsibility for the total school program, its safety
         and good order
         1. Takes precautions to protect records, equipment, materials, and facilities
         2. Assumes responsibility for supervising students in out-of-class settings
II. Duties and Responsibilities, Prescribed by Local School and System (Optional)
     A. _____
     B. _____
     C. _____
III. Professional Development Plan
     In cases where a Professional Development Plan is required for specific needs development, progress
     relative to completing the annual Professional Development Plan shall be one of the assessments
     during the annual evaluation process. For teachers in the unsatisfactory category, the ultimate
     evaluation of successful completion of a Professional Development Plan is significant improvement in
     targeted areas as measured by the next year's annual evaluation.

Figure 13.3. Georgia Teacher Duties and Responsibilities Instrument. *Source: Georgia
Department of Education, Georgia Teacher Evaluation Program: Evaluation Manual (Atlanta, Ga.:
Georgia Department of Education, May 1989), p. 60. Reprinted with permission of the Georgia
Department of Education.*

The open-ended system eliminates this problem but introduces other problems of
its own.

A binary rating system—a checklist, for example—reduces the necessity for
making fine numerical distinctions, but because behavior is reported with only two
symbols—for example, S (Satisfactory) and U (Unsatisfactory) or A (Acceptable) and
U (Unacceptable)—a wide range of behavior is encompassed within each of the two

THE SCHOOL BOARD OF MONROE COUNTY, FLORIDA
TEACHER ANNUAL ASSESSMENT PLAN
—COMPREHENSIVE ASSESSMENT FORM—

Name _____ SS # _____-____-_____ School _____

Code: C = Commendable   A = Acceptable   S = Satisfactory   NI = Needs Improvement
U = Unsatisfactory

A. MANAGEMENT OF STUDENT CONDUCT   C   A
   1. Classroom rules are clearly defined, posted and
       enforced (Comments) _____   S   NI   U
       _____

   2. Stops misconduct appropriately; does not delay
       (Comments) _____   S   NI   U
       _____

   3. Maintains instructional momentum; gives clear
       group directions, does not overdwell
       (Comments) _____   S   NI   U
       _____

   4. Consistently maintains effective learning environment
       (Comments) _____   S   NI   U
       _____

B. INSTRUCTION, ORGANIZATION AND DEVELOPMENT   C   A
   1. Daily lesson plans are appropriate and consistent
       with established curriculum
       (Comments) _____   S   NI   U
       _____

   2. Long-range planning is evident
       (Comments) _____   S   NI   U
       _____

   3. Demonstrates efficient use of instructional time
       (Comments) _____   S   NI   U
       _____

   4. Selects and uses instructional material/aids
       effectively (Comments) _____   S   NI   U
       _____

   5. Reviews subject matter
       (Comments) _____   S   NI   U
       _____

   6. Provides for lesson development
       (Comments) _____   S   NI   U
       _____

   7. Practice and home/seatwork management
       (Comments) _____   S   NI   U
       _____

   8. Effective classroom interaction
       (Comments) _____   S   NI   U
       _____

   9. Communicates effectively orally
       (Comments) _____   S   NI   U
       _____

(continued)

Figure 13.4. Teacher Annual Assessment Plan. *Source: Monroe County Public Schools, Teacher Annual Assessment Plan, Key West, Fla. Reprinted with permission of the Monroe County Public Schools.*

10. Shows enthusiasm and motivates students
    (Comments) _____   S   NI   U
    _____

C. KNOWLEDGE OF SUBJECT MATTER   C   A
    1. Academic comments are accurate, factually based
       and evidence a sound knowledge of the curriculum.
       (Comments) _____   S   NI   U
    2. Develops *concepts* effectively (all subjects)
       (Comments) _____   S   NI   U
       _____

    3. Explains *laws/principles* effectively (sciences)
       (Comments) _____   S   NI   U
       _____

    4. Presents *academic rules* effectively (all subjects)
       (Comments) _____   S   NI   U
       _____

    5. Teaches higher order thinking (all subjects)
       (Comments) _____   S   NI   U
       _____

D. EVALUATION OF INSTRUCTIONAL NEEDS   C   A
    1. Uses fair/appropriate methods of evaluation
       (Comments) _____   S   NI   U
       _____

    2. Regularly monitors student progress & uses test
       data to adjust instruction to student needs
       (Comments) _____   S   NI   U
       _____

    3. Provides guidance to students in analyzing,
       evaluating and reviewing their work
       (Comments) _____   S   NI   U
       _____

E. PROFESSIONAL RESPONSIBILITIES   C   A
    1. Participates in school's planning activities
       (Comments) _____   S   NI   U
       _____

    2. Communicates effectively with parents & others
       (Comments) _____   S   NI   U
       _____

    3. Follows requirements of State law, Board policies,
       Code of Ethics and building level procedures
       (Comments) _____   S   NI   U
       _____

    4. Completes reports/forms in a timely and accurate
       manner (Comments) _____   S   NI   U
       _____

    5. Continues professional growth via participation
       in inservices/college courses as appropriate
       (Comments) _____   S   NI   U
       _____

    6. (Optional) Contributions to the school/district
       (List) _____

Figure 13.4. (continued)

SUMMARY EVALUATION RATING: Commendable [ ]   Acceptable [ ]   Unacceptable [ ]
ADDITIONAL COMMENTS _____
_____
EVALUATOR SIGNATURE _____ DATE ___/___
TEACHER COMMENTS _____
_____
TEACHER SIGNATURE _____ DATE ___/___
Signature of Teacher does not necessarily imply agreement with evaluation, but acknowledges it was
discussed with Evaluator

symbols. The binary rating system takes a great deal of pressure off the adminis-trator because decisions about teachers' competencies do not have to be as carefully deliberated. Although many teachers prefer the broader symbols, some teachers feel that terms like *satisfactory* and *acceptable* do not do justice to those teachers who are performing at a high level. In this respect, teachers who reject the binary approach emulate those students who object to satisfactory-unsatisfactory, pass-fail, credit-no credit systems and demand A through F letter grades, which allow for distinctions in achievement along with commensurate rewards.

Competencies, Indicators, and Descriptors. If you incline to the use of instruments that detail specific competencies, as we do, you should collect data using instru-ments that break the competencies into more specific indicators and, if so desired, into descriptors of the indicators.

We may define a competency as a particular teaching behavior or skill. The Georgia State Department of Education defined a competency as follows: "A generic *teacher competency* is a conceptualization of a responsible and purposeful performance essential to the effective professional conduct of all teachers."[33] The Georgia Department notes, however, that "This definition results in statements which are too broad for assessment purposes."[34]

Planning for instruction, using student responses, and managing the classroom are examples of generic competencies. We make a mistake if we try to evaluate these competencies without detailing what they mean. We need some guidelines to help us gather evidence that the teacher possesses the competency. Indicators serve as those guideposts. The Georgia State Department of Education explained indicators in the following way: "Competency *indicators* . . . define behaviors representative of the competency. The more indicators a person demonstrates proficiently, the more likely it is that that person is demonstrating the target competency."[35]

Most of the evaluation instruments we have seen divide the competencies no further than the indicator level. The Georgia Teacher Assessment program broke in-dicators into *descriptors*. In defining descriptors, the Georgia Department said, "They are more specific than either competencies or indicators, and are used to describe the quality of a teacher's performance relevant to a competency indicator."[36]

An example of a competency with one of its indicators and descriptors for that indicator, taken from the *Teacher Performance Assessment Instruments* used in Georgia in the 1980s, follows on p. 557.

School Year: 19___–19___

THE SCHOOL BOARD OF MONROE COUNTY, FLORIDA
INTERIM REVIEW FORM
TEACHER ANNUAL ASSESSMENT PLAN

Name _____ SS # _____-____-_____ School _____

Code: S = Satisfactory   C = Commendable   (from 199__ "Comprehensive Assessment Form")

A. MANAGEMENT OF STUDENT CONDUCT	S	C
B. INSTRUCTION, ORGANIZATION AND DEVELOPMENT	S	C
C. KNOWLEDGE OF SUBJECT MATTER	S	C
D. EVALUATION OF INSTRUCTIONAL NEEDS	S	C
E. PROFESSIONAL RESPONSIBILITIES	S	C

GOALS FOCUSED EVALUATION PLAN

OBJECTIVES:

1.

2.

ACTIVITIES DESIGNED TO ACCOMPLISH EACH OBJECTIVE

Objective 1.

Objective 2.

EVIDENCE TO BE USED TO VERIFY ACCOMPLISHMENT OF OBJECTIVE(S)

Objective 1.

Objective 2.

Objective #1:   Fully Achieved [ ]   Partially Achieved [ ]   Not Achieved [ ]
Objective #2:   Fully Achieved [ ]   Partially Achieved [ ]   Not Achieved [ ]
SUMMARY EVALUATION RATING: Satisfactory [ ]   Commendable [ ]

EVALUATOR COMMENTS _____
EVALUATOR SIGNATURE_____ DATE ___/___/___
TEACHER COMMENTS _____

TEACHER SIGNATURE _____ DATE ___/___/___

Figure 13.5. Teacher Annual Assessment Plan—Interim Review Form. *Source: Monroe County Public Schools, Teacher's Annual Evaluation, Key West, Fla. Reprinted with permission of the Monroe County Public Schools.*

Competency VI: Uses Instructional Techniques, Methods, and Media Related to the Objectives

Indicator 12: Uses procedures which get learners initially involved in lessons. Descriptors:

a. Helps learners recall past experiences or knowledge.
b. Uses existing interests of learners as a link to new activities.
c. Stimulates new interests in activities with techniques such as discrepant events or thought-provoking questions.
d. Helps learners understand what they may achieve by participating in the activities.[37]

Indicators and descriptors are helpful in refining a competency. They serve as guides for the evaluator's observations and provide a basis for assessment. When a teacher asks, "What do you mean by this competency?" the evaluator can easily reply, "It means these indicators" or "It means these indicators and descriptors." Georgia itself has moved away from the use of the terms *indicators*, *descriptors*, and *competencies* and instead uses the terms *tasks*, *dimensions*, *subdimensions*, and *effective practices*.[38]

The terminology of competencies and indicators stems from the broader concept of competency-based education—particularly popular in the 1970s. Although the terminology may differ among school systems (for example, competency may be *objective* or *skill* and indicator may be *subobjective* or *subskill*), the practice of specifying competencies, objectives, and skills in performance terms remains strong and, we believe, essential.

Georgia's experience demonstrates well the power of state mandating because the Georgia Teacher Assessment Program was designed for purposes of certifying beginning teachers. However, many school districts of the state simply adapted the state's assessment model and established that model as its summative, and, in some cases, formative evaluation process.

How Should the Data Be Used?

The data collected about a teacher's performance are used by the administrator for (1) conferences with the teacher; (2) creation of a professional improvement plan; and (3) personnel decisions, including decisions about merit pay, career ladder, change of assignment or increased responsibilities, retention, and dismissal.

Conferences. Conferences should be held with the teacher after each observation and for the summative evaluation. When the administrator is making global assessments, preobservation conferences are less important and may be transacted in a few minutes to schedule a visit or to obtain any special information the administrator would need to know about the class.

Conferences between the teacher and administrator serve two purposes. First, they offer an opportunity for the administrator to gather data not witnessed during a classroom visit; they give the teacher an opportunity to describe or interpret some of the events the administrator viewed. Second, they are the setting for an evaluation. Although the administrator's periodic observations are or can be formative in nature, they are also evaluations. Each conference with the administrator, then, is evaluative in nature. As the leopard cannot shed its spots, the administrator cannot wash away his or her line authority. The administrator is simply not the same person, nor should he or she be, as the staff instructional supervisor. Consequently, the administrator should not and, because of legal responsiblities, cannot avoid the evaluative dimension of observations and conferences.

The rules of the game are different for the line administrator and the staff supervisor. The staff supervisor divulges to persons other than the teacher only what is necessary or required about a teacher's performance. The line administrator tells everything, in writing, and forwards it to the superintendent's office. In the case of teachers charged with incompetence, the data go beyond the superintendent's office. The staff supervisor does not have to make the hard personnel decisions; the line administrator does. The staff supervisor relies on the authority of persuasion and expertise, the line administrator on the authority of the office.

Administrators or supervisors who must be both evaluator and instructional supervisor at the same time have a difficult role. Their observations and conferences must be both formative and summative, the latter focusing on evaluative statements. Although they diagnose and prescribe, they must also rate. Although they may try to minimize the element of threat, they cannot erase all teacher anxiety.

Administrators cannot, and should not if they could, obliterate all traces of status. Though we believe protocol is overdone in many cases, a modicum of protocol is essential to the efficient operation of the program. Teachers want and expect their administrators to maintain some semblance of status. Thus, whereas we would argue that the clinical supervisor should confer with a teacher in the teacher's classroom or on neutral territory, we would take the position that it is proper for evaluative conferences to be held in the administrator's office or in the administrator's conference room. The administrator can ease the tension by coming out from behind the desk and conferring with the teacher while sitting at a round table or in comfortable chairs.

During each of the postobservation conferences the administrator should make and record suggestions for improvement that he or she feels it is necessary for the teacher to make. The Glynn County (Georgia) school administrators have recorded suggestions on a Conference Objectives and Action Plan, reproduced in Figure 13.6. At the summative conference, which is scheduled toward the end of the school year, the administrator brings together all the data he or she has gathered during the year pertaining to the various criteria on which teachers in that school are evaluated.

Madeline Hunter referred to the summative conference as the *evaluative conference* and made it clear that it should be based on previous conferences during the year, which she called instructional conferences. She described an evaluative conference as follows:

> The objective of an *evaluative conference* is that a teacher's placement on a continuum from "unsatisfactory" to "outstanding" will be established and the teacher will have the opportunity to examine the evidence used. . . . An evaluative conference should be the summation of what has occurred in and resulted from a series of instructional conferences. Information given and conclusions reached in an evaluative conference should come as no surprise to the teacher because the supporting evidence has been discussed in previous instructional conferences. As a result, the evaluative conference has high probability for being perceived as fair, just, and sup-

CONFERENCE OBJECTIVES AND ACTION PLAN

Teacher's Name _____ School _____

Conference Objective(s) (What is the focus of the post-observation conference?)

_____

1. Goal(s) (What will the teacher work on?)

_____

2. Specific Objective(s) (What will be the outcome?)

_____

3. Procedures and/or Resources   Time Line (When will it be done?)
   for Achieving Objectives
   (How will it be done?)

_____

4. Measurement of Progress on Objectives (How will it be checked?)

_____   _____   _____
Teacher   Principal/Assessor   Date

Figure 13.6. Conference Objectives and Action Plan. *Source: Glynn County Public Schools, Brunswick, Ga. Reprinted with permission of the Glynn County Public Schools.*

portable by objective evidence rather than based on subjective opinion. This conference is the culmination of a year's diagnostic, prescriptive, collaborative work with a teacher and supervisor who shared responsibility for the teacher's continuous professional growth.[39]

Though the teacher may offer opinions, it is incumbent on the administrator to make suggestions for improvement if he or she feels the teacher needs to improve certain behaviors. The general perception, and legal expectation, is that the administrator, not the teacher, has the responsibility to recommend remedial measures for a teacher who shows deficiencies. If the principal seeks to dismiss a teacher for incompetence, the first question that will be asked, under due process expectations, is "What did you do to help the teacher overcome the deficiencies?" Thus, rating a teacher is not enough. The principal must propose actions the teacher can take if deficiencies are noted. Further, the principal has the obligation to monitor the teacher's progress in overcoming the deficiencies.

Professional Improvement Plans. As a part of summative evaluation, administrators typically draw up a professional improvement plan for teachers showing areas that need improving or that could be enhanced. For those teachers demonstrating deficiencies, the administrator includes means of overcoming the deficiencies, states how evaluation of the improvement will be carried out, and establishes timeliness. The Oconee County (Georgia) Performance Improvement Plan, reproduced in Figure 13.7, is an example of a form the administrator would fill out and that both the teacher and administrator would sign. Tied in with the state's annual evaluation

OCONEE COUNTY SCHOOL SYSTEM
Performance Improvement Plan

I.   List areas to be improved

    A. _____

    B. _____

    C. _____

         Signature _____   Signature _____
         Position _____   Evaluator

II. Plan for self-improvement

    A. _____

    B. _____

    C. _____

III. Evaluator's plan to assist the staff member to improve performance

    A. _____

    B. _____

    C. _____

         Date Plan Initiated _____
         Date Outcome of Plans to Be Evaluated_____

IV. Outcomes of Improvement plan
    Staff Member's Comments _____

    Evaluator's Comments _____

V.   Evaluator's Recommendations _____

Figure 13.7. Performance Improvement Plan. *Source: Oconee County Public Schools, Watkinsville, Ga. Reprinted with permission of the Oconee County Public Schools.*

program is the Professional Development Plan shown in Figure 13.8, which permits administrators to recommend required and optional plans for professional development or enhancement.

Improvement activities commonly suggested for the teacher are a college course, a staff-development activity in the local system, visits to peers' classes, working with a colleague or mentor, and reading the professional literature. Manatt has advocated the use of a three-person intensive assistance team composed of administrators and supervisors to help a marginal teacher—that is, one who is not effective but might improve with help.[40]

When the summative conference is terminated and recommendations for improvement have been made, copies of the completed evaluation instrument and pro-

CONFIDENTIAL
PROFESSIONAL DEVELOPMENT PLAN
Annual Evaluation Program! GLEI ! GTOI ! GTDRI ! OTHER: _____

Evaluatee: _____ System: _____ School: _____ Date: _____

Check one of the following: ! Optional Plan for Enhancement
                              ! Optional Plan for Specific Needs Development
                              ! Required Plan for Specific Needs Development

---

Specific Objectives for Improvement:

Activities and Timeline:

Criteria for Measurement of Progress:

Record of Participation in Recommended Activities:

Record of Performance on Specified Criteria:

(Signatures) Evaluator: _____ Date: _____ (Evaluatee's signature acknowledges receipt of a copy. Written comments may be provided below and/or attached to the evaluator's copy. If additional comments are attached, initial and date here: ____)

                 Evaluatee: _____ Date: _____

Evaluatee's Comments: _____

89/90   EVALUATEE'S COPY

Figure 13.8. Professional Development Plan. *Source: Georgia Department of Education,* Georgia Teacher Evaluation Program: Evaluation Manual *(Atlanta, Ga.: Georgia Department of Education, 1989), p. 12. Reprinted with permission of the Georgia Department of Education.*

fessional development plan, duly signed by both the administrator and teacher, should be placed on file. Normally, the teacher would receive a copy, the principal would retain a copy, and a copy would be sent to the appropriate official at the central office.

Harris and others noted the importance of selection, formative evaluation, and summative evaluation in making personnel decisions:

> If formative evaluation is well done, most summative evaluation decisions should be routine (e.g., continuation on the job for the majority of the teachers) or non-threatening (e.g., transfer, change of function, or placement in a tenure status). Recommendations for termination of contract or other unpleasant eventualities are and should be relatively rare. They should be extremely rare if initial selection of personnel is carefully done and if formative evaluation and follow-up growth activities are carried out.[41]

Personnel Decisions. Administrators will have a number of decisions to make on the basis of their evaluation of the teacher's performance. If their district operates a merit pay system or career ladder, they will have to decide which teachers should receive these incentives. They will often have to make decisions about changes of assignment from one group of students to another, from one grade to another, from their school to another school, from present position to special assignment, and from a teaching position to an administrative position. They will also have to face questions of retention and dismissal.

The decision to retain a teacher is much easier to make than a decision for dismissal. The dismissal of a teacher is a stressful burden both for the administrator and, of course, for the teacher to be dismissed. It is particularly stressful if the administrator was the person who hired the teacher in the first place. The necessity for dismissing a teacher whom the administrator has hired can reflect on that administrator's judgment in initially selecting people.

Retention becomes acute at the point when a teacher is being considered for a continuing contract or tenure, usually at the end of three years of teaching in a school system. The administrator knows that a decision to retain will mean that the teacher will be with the school or in the school system for a long time, possibly a lifetime. The administrator knows also that it is far easier to dismiss a nontenured teacher than a tenured one. Although there may be moral and ethical reasons for informing a nontenured teacher of causes of nonretention, there are not usually legal reasons compelling an administrator to do so. The teacher on annual contract may simply be notified that the contract will not be renewed for the following year.

Dismissal of a teacher after the teacher has earned tenure is much more difficult. Teachers may be discharged if their positions are abolished. The major grounds for dismissal, however, are what some people call the three I's: insubordination, immorality, and incompetence. Proving insubordinate and immoral behavior is relatively easy, although immorality is becoming an increasingly difficult question as standards of behavior differ greatly from community to community. Incompetence is the bear for administrators. We all know that there are incompetent people in teaching positions. We know that there are teachers who are deficient in knowledge of subject matter, in use of English, in teaching skills, and in interpersonal skills. Yet it is difficult to prove incompetence. How incompetent does one have to be for removal from the teaching profession? Neither the teacher's organizations nor the profession in general has fully come to grips with this question. The major burden for removing an incompetent teacher is placed on the shoulders of the principal.

Dismissal for incompetence requires a great deal, some principals would say an excessive amount, of documentation. The principal must build a case carefully, citing chapter and verse, to remove a teacher who is tenured. State laws and local policies have set certain specific procedures concerning notices to be given to the teacher, hearings provided for, and appeals that may be taken before a teacher can be discharged. Many educators believe that if a state has a strong due process law, tenure is not an essential provision. Teachers, however, somewhat distrustful of administration in general, still incline to preservation of the principle of tenure.

To some degree, the profession regulates standards of professional competence through professional practices commissions established in some states. The Professional Practices Commission of Georgia, for example, "was established for the purpose of setting and enforcing standards of competent professional performance and ethical conduct for educators in Georgia."[42] The commission, composed of seventeen practicing members of the education profession, advises in matters of school law; counsels members of the profession; investigates complaints brought against educators; holds hearings to adjudicate matters brought before a local board of education; conducts professional, on-site reviews of the services of an educator whose performance has been questioned; and makes recommendations to the state board of education or the department of education in matters concerning denial, suspension, or revocation of teaching certificates.[43] A state professional practices commission can be of help to teachers, administrators, and the profession by setting standards of competence and assisting schools in maintaining those standards. Standards set by the National Board for Professional Teaching Standards (NBPTS) may lend guidance to states and administrators in determining the competence of a teacher.

PROBLEMS IN SUMMATIVE EVALUATION

We are sure you can name teachers who, having received their summative appraisal reports, declare, "How can the principal know how well I am doing? He (she) has spent hardly any time in my classroom." Even when they receive glowing reports from the administrators, the teachers resent this type of administrative behavior. A variation on this theme is the comment voiced by numerous teachers, "But he (she) has been to visit me only once this year and then he (she) stayed only ten minutes." One of the scandals of summative evaluation practices is the failure of the administrator to obtain an adequate sampling of a teacher's performance. The teacher should be visited, observed, and evaluated several times during the year. We can find examples of administrators who limit their visits to a few minutes once or twice during the year. We have even heard of cases of administrators who render summative judgments without a single visit to the teacher's classroom!

Many principals delegate teacher evaluation to their assistant principals. In fact, this is accepted practice in some school systems. There is nothing inherently wrong with such a process, but if we, as principals, are required to sign our names to evaluation reports, if we are the persons who must make personnel decisions or recommendations to the superintendent about personnel, and if we are the ones who must document teaching performance, we would want more than secondhand information. Otherwise, the process should be turned over completely to the assistant principal, who would not only do the observing, the conferencing, and the evaluating but also sign the appraisal reports and defend them if challenged.

Principals err in evaluating personnel when they skew their ratings to the high side of the scale. The easy rater may be compensating for failure to gather enough data to make accurate evaluations, may feel that the whole process is burdensome and unnecessary, may be striving to maintain rapport with teachers, or may simply feel that teachers need positive reinforcement for their efforts. Overrating of teacher performance is, therefore, a much more common error than is underrating. Permit us to generalize: If we were to analyze the administrative evaluations of both public school and college faculties, we would conclude that almost all our teachers have reached a state of perfection. Giving high ratings is an easy way out for the administrator who wishes to avoid the stress that comes from conflicts with teachers over low ratings. High, even satisfactory, ratings of less than competent teachers have come back to haunt administrators when they attempted to dismiss a teacher who had routinely received acceptable appraisals.

Ratings should be as objective as possible. We all have room for growth, so suggestions should be made that will lead to improvement. Teachers have reason to be concerned about the lack of reliability among evaluators. Teachers are confused and resentful when one evaluator rates a teacher's performance high whereas another rates the same teacher's performance low. Evaluators must take care not to let their own biases about teaching and about individual teachers affect their ratings.

Still another problem sometimes encountered is the lack of specific feedback to the teacher. If teachers are to profit from an assessment, they must know what they need to do to be more effective. Personal conferences between the teacher and evaluator are essential to the process. Sufficient time must be allocated for each conference so the teachers feel they have had adequate opportunities to express themselves and to understand what it is the administrator expects.

Many of the problems associated with summative evaluation can be alleviated through appropriate in-service training of the evaluators. Administrators are in as great a need of in-service education as are the teachers they supervise.

SUMMARY

Summative evaluation of teacher performance is the assessment administrators make toward the end of the year for purposes of arriving at personnel decisions. The summative appraisal is based on periodic or formative evaluations conducted during the year. All teachers should be evaluated periodically. The frequency and length of visits to the classroom vary greatly from school to school and from school system to school system. In practice, nontenured teachers are evaluated more frequently than are tenured teachers. The frequency of summative appraisals varies from state to state.

Principals are expected to and should evaluate the teachers of their school. They may call for help from assistants as needed. Administrators and teachers should be in agreement about what should be evaluated. Generally, administrators collect data concerning processes, personal and professional characteristics of teachers, and products and outcomes of teaching.

Administrators normally use a classroom observation instrument to make periodic or formative evaluations during the year. This type of instrument permits a comprehensive assessment of teacher competencies. Competencies are best evaluated if defined with indicators and, if desired, descriptors of the indicators. The year-end summative appraisal is based on the periodic evaluations made during the year and any additional data required by the instrument in use. The summative instrument is usually correlated with the classroom observation form and with any teacher self-appraisal instrument.

If teachers are expected to make improvements in their teaching, the administrator must give them specific feedback. This means at the very least a conference following each formative evaluation and at the summative appraisal conference. Administrators will develop or co-develop a professional improvement plan for teachers.

Copies of the written evaluations and improvement plans should be given to the teacher and placed on file in the principal's office and in the appropriate office of the central administration. Evaluative data are used for administrative decisions on merit pay, career ladder, change of assignment, increased responsibilities, retention, and dismissal. In presenting a case for dismissal of a teacher, the administrator must adhere to due process. Administrators must make their ratings of teachers as fair and objective as possible. If a teacher is found to be deficient in some way, it is the administrator's responsibility to recommend and monitor measures that may assist the teacher in overcoming the deficiencies.

QUESTIONS FOR DISCUSSION

1. What problems were identified with summative evaluations? How would you correct them?
2. Should instructional supervisors be engaged in preparing summative assessments of teachers? Why or why not?
3. How should administrators use summative assessments?
4. Should supervisors make announced or unannounced classroom visits?
5. What is the impact professional improvement plans (PIP) have on the assessment of teacher performance?

ACTIVITIES FOR FURTHER STUDY

1. Distinguish between summative evaluation and formative evaluation of teacher performance.
2. Create a set of correlated instruments for (a) teacher self-appraisal, (b) classroom observation, and (c) summative evaluation of teachers.
3. Interview and report on views of at least three teachers regarding administrative ratings of teacher competence concerning categories rated and procedures.

4. Locate samples of summative evaluation instruments used by school systems to evaluate teacher competencies and compare them in respect to similarities and differences. Choose the one you would prefer.

5. Report (if the data can be obtained) on the performance of a faculty as a group (not as individuals) on annual ratings of competence in one school by percentages of faculty on each category rated.

6. Report (if data are available) on the number of dismissals or terminations of contract in a particular school system for the past five years. Classify the data according to reasons for dismissal and whether each teacher was tenured or nontenured.

7. Interview several teachers and determine (a) whether recommendations for improving instruction are regularly made by evaluators, (b) whether the teachers try to follow the recommendations, and (c) whether the evaluator monitors their progress in implementing the recommendations.

8. Report on a principal's perceptions of teacher evaluation, describing processes, difficulties, and suggestions for prospective evaluators.

9. Write several indicators for each of the following competencies:
   a. The teacher demonstrates the ability to communicate clearly to learners.
   b. The teacher demonstrates the ability to motivate the learners.
   c. The teacher demonstrates skill in classroom management.
   d. The teacher demonstrates professional behavior.
   e. The teacher demonstrates enthusiasm.

10. For each of the following indicators suggest a competency of which it might be indicative:
   1. The teacher uses strategies appropriate to learners.
   2. The teacher uses evaluation techniques that relate to the objectives.
   3. The teacher varies the stimuli.
   4. The teacher uses English correctly.
   5. The teacher shows personal interest in the learners.

11. For each indicator in Activity 10 write two descriptors.

12. Of the following types of summative instruments, tell which you prefer and why:
   a. Rating scale with numbers, as 1 to 5
   b. Checklist with two categories, as satisfactory and unsatisfactory
   c. Open-ended, narrative
   d. Other (specify)

13. Show your position on the following:
   a. How often should a principal visit and observe each teacher?
   b. How long should a principal remain in the classroom when observing?
   c. Should the principal's visits be (1) all announced, (2) all unannounced, or (3) a combination of announced and unannounced? If (3), what percentage of each?

14. Reply to the following questions:
   a. Is annual evaluation of each teacher necessary?
   b. If you believe an annual evaluation of each teacher is not necessary, how often should a summative appraisal be made for each teacher?
   c. Should the frequency of summative evaluation be varied on the basis of tenured and nontenured status of the teachers?

15. Prepare a position statement on this question: Should the principal delegate responsibility for teacher evaluation to an assistant principal?

16. Show your position on this question: Can the principal serve as a clinical supervisor?

17. Describe some observable symptoms of teacher incompetence.
18. Report on the work of the professional practices commission or similar body if there is one in your state.
19. Prepare a statement on what you believe the profession should do to weed out incompetent teachers. Be specific about persons or groups within the profession who you believe should take responsibility for this task.
20. Suggest procedures for selection of teachers that would help to ensure the employment of competent teachers. Specify the school personnel you feel should be involved in the selection of teachers.
21. Show your position on the question, Should states mandate a uniform teacher evaluation process to be followed by all school systems of the state?
22. Report on the work of the National Board for Professional Teaching Standards (NBPTS).

NOTES

1. Jerry J. Bellon and Elner C. Bellon, *Classroom Supervision and Instructional Improvement: A Synergetic Process*, 2nd ed. (Dubuque, Iowa: Kendall/Hunt, 1982), p. 32.
2. Arthur Shaw, "Improving Instruction through Evaluation: One Teacher's View," *Action in Teacher Education* 2 (Winter 1979–80): 1.
3. Perry A. Zirkel, "Teacher Evaluation: An Overview," *Action in Teacher Education* 2 (Winter 1979–80): 19.
4. Ibid.
5. Ibid.
6. *Georgia's Quality Basic Education Act*, Part 6 Personnel, Subpart 2, 20–2–210, "Performance Evaluations," 1985 and Georgia Teacher Evaluation Program, 1989.
7. Zirkel, "Teacher Evaluation," pp. 17, 19.
8. Some of the data are from Zirkel, "Teacher Evaluation," p. 19.
9. Ibid.
10. Ibid.
11. Ibid.
12. Ibid.
13. Shaw, "Improving Instruction," p. 4.
14. John D. McNeil, "A Scientific Approach to Supervision," in *Supervision of Teaching*, 1982 Yearbook, ed. Thomas J. Sergiovanni (Alexandria, Va.: Association for Supervision and Curriculum Development, 1982), p. 23.
15. See Peter F. Oliva and Kenneth T. Henson, "The Expert Syndrome," *Contemporary Education* 53 (Winter 1982): 61–64.
16. Allen R. Warner and Dora H. Scott, "Evaluating Teacher Effectiveness: Professional Dimensions," *Action in Teacher Education* 2 (Winter 1979–80): 30.
17. Richard P. Manatt, "Lessons from a Comprehensive Performance Appraisal Project," *Educational Leadership* 44 (April 1987): 8–14.
18. Ben M. Harris et al., *Personnel Administration in Education: Leadership for Instructional Improvement*, 2nd ed. (Boston: Allyn & Bacon, 1985), p. 226.
19. Ibid., p. 234.
20. John C. Reynolds, "In Search of Mr. (Ms.) Goodteacher," *Action in Teacher Education* 2 (Winter 1979–80): 37.
21. Shaw, "Improving Instruction," p. 4.
22. Zirkel, "Teacher Evaluation," pp. 19–20.
23. Ibid., p. 20.
24. Ibid.

25. Gary Natriello, *Evaluation Frequency, Teacher Influence, and the Internalization of Evaluation Processes* (Eugene: Center for Educational Policy and Management, College of Education, University of Oregon, 1983).
26. Gene Huddle, "Teacher Evaluation—How Important for Effective Schools? Eight Messages from Research," *NASSP Bulletin* 69 (March 1985): 58.
27. Ibid., pp. 58–59.
28. Tom Peters and Robert Waterman, Jr., *In Search of Excellence* (New York: Warner Books, 1982), p. 122.
29. Harris et al., *Personnel Administration in Education*, p. 240.
30. Ibid., p. 241.
31. Georgia Department of Education, *Teacher Performance Assessment Instruments: A Handbook for Interpretation* (Atlanta: Georgia Department of Education, 1980). Formerly used for on-the-job assessment of beginning teachers for the purpose of certification, these instruments were revised in 1985 and discontinued in 1989.
32. Georgia Department of Education, *Georgia Teacher Evaluation Program: Evaluation Manual* (Atlanta, Ga.: Georgia Department of Education, 1989).
33. Georgia Department of Education, *Teacher Performance Assessment Instruments*, p. 3.
34. Ibid.
35. Ibid.
36. Ibid., p. 4.
37. Ibid., p. 87.
38. Georgia Department of Education, *Georgia Teacher Evaluation Program*.
39. Madeline Hunter, "Six Types of Supervisory Conferences," *Educational Leadership* 37 (February 1980): 408, 412.
40. See Richard P. Manatt, narrator of videotape, *Supervising the Marginal Teacher* (Alexandria, Va.: Association for Supervision and Curriculum Development, 1983).
41. Harris et al., *Personnel Administration in Education*, p. 240.
42. Professional Practices Commission, *Professional Practices Commission: Serving Education in Georgia* (brochure), Atlanta, Ga. For an illustration of the rules of a Professional Practices Council see Florida Administrative Code: Chapter 6B-1, *The Code of Ethics of the Education Profession in Florida*, and Chapter 6B-5, *Standards of Competent Professional Performance*.
43. Ibid.

BIBLIOGRAPHY

Allred, Malcolm, et al. *Teaching Skills: A Dimension of Professional Competence*. Salt Lake City: Utah State Board of Education, 1978.
Association of Teacher Educators. "Evaluating Teacher Effectiveness." *Action in Teacher Education* 2 (Winter 1979–80): 1–66.
Bartky, John A. *Administration as Educational Leadership*. Palo Alto, Calif.: Stanford University Press, 1956.
Bellon, Jerry J., and Elner C. Bellon. *Classroom Supervision and Instructional Improvement: A Synergetic Process*, 2nd ed. Dubuque, Iowa: Kendall/Hunt, 1982.
Berliner, David D., et al. *Phase III of the Beginning Teacher Effectiveness Study*. San Francisco: Far West Laboratory for Educational Research and Development, 1976.
Bolton, Dale L. *Selection and Evaluation of Teachers*. Berkeley, Calif.: McCutchan, 1973.
Borich, G. D., and S. K. Madden. *Evaluating Classroom Instruction: A Sourcebook of Instruments*. Reading, Mass.: Addison-Wesley, 1977.
Bridges, Edward M. *Managing the Incompetent Teacher*. Eugene, Ore.: ERIC Clearinghouse on Educational Management, 1984.

Brophy, Jere E., and C. M. Evertson. *Process-Product Correlation in the Texas Teacher Effectiveness Study*. Austin: University of Texas, 1974.

Cooper, James M., ed. *Developing Skills for Instructional Supervision*. White Plains, N.Y.: Longman, 1984.

Duke, Daniel L. *School Leadership and Instructional Improvement*. New York: Random House, 1987.

Duke, Daniel L., and Richard J. Stiggins. *Teacher Evaluation: Five Keys to Growth*. Washington, D.C.: National Education Association, 1986.

"Evaluating School Personnel." *National Elementary Principal* 52 (February 1973): 10–98.

Evertson, Carolyn, and Freda M. Holley. "Classroom Observation." In *Handbook of Teacher Evaluation*. Jason Millman, ed. Beverly Hills, Calif.: Sage, 1981.

Flanders, Ned A. *Analyzing Teacher Behavior*. Reading, Mass.: Addison-Wesley, 1970.

Gage, N. L. *The Scientific Basis of the Art of Teaching*. New York: Teachers College Press, 1978.

———. *Teacher Effectiveness and Teacher Education: The Search for a Scientific Basis*. Palo Alto, Calif.: Pacific Books, 1972.

———, ed. *Handbook of Research on Teaching*. Chicago: Rand McNally, 1963.

Georgia Department of Education. *Georgia Teacher Evaluation Program: Evaluation Manual*. Atlanta: Georgia Department of Education, 1989.

———. *Teacher Performance Assessment Instruments: A Handbook for Interpretation*. Atlanta: Georgia Department of Education, 1980.

Glass, Gene. "Teacher Effectiveness." In *Evaluating Educational Performance*. Herbert J. Walberg, ed. Berkeley, Calif.: McCutchan, 1974.

Glatthorn, Allan A. *Differentiated Supervision*. Alexandria, Va.: Association for Supervision and Curriculum Development, 1984.

Glickman, Carl D., Stephen P. Gordon, and Jovita M. Ross-Gordon. *Supervision of Instruction: A Developmental Approach*, 3rd ed. Boston: Allyn & Bacon, 1995.

Haefele, Donald L. "How to Evaluate Thee, Teacher—Let Me Count the Ways." *Phi Delta Kappan* 61 (January 1980): 349–52.

Harris, Ben M. *Developmental Teacher Evaluation*. Boston: Allyn & Bacon, 1986.

Harris, Ben M., Kenneth E. McIntyre, Vance C. Littleton, Jr., and Daniel F. Long. *Personnel Administration in Education: Leadership for Instructional Improvement*, 2nd ed. Boston: Allyn & Bacon, 1985.

Hawley, Robert C. *Assessing Teacher Performance: Task and Analysis*. Amherst, Mass.: Education Resources Associates, 1982.

Hunter, Madeline. "Appraising Teaching Performance: One Approach." *The National Elementary Principal* 52 (February 1973): 62–63.

———. "Six Types of Supervisory Conferences." *Educational Leadership* 37 (February 1980): 408–12.

Hyman, Ronald T. *School Administrator's Faculty Supervision Handbook*. Englewood Cliffs, N.J.: Prentice-Hall, 1986.

Kowalski, J. D. S. *Evaluating Teachers' Performance*. Arlington, Va.: Educational Research Services, 1978.

Kyte, George C. *The Principal at Work*. Boston: Ginn and Company, 1941.

Levin, Benjy. "Teacher Evaluation: A Review of the Research." *Educational Leadership* 37 (December 1979): 240–45. See bibliography at end of article.

Manatt, Richard P. "Lessons from a Comprehensive Performance Appraisal Project." *Educational Leadership* 44 (April 1987): 8–14.

McGreal, Thomas L. *Successful Teacher Evaluation*. Alexandria, Va.: Association for Supervision and Curriculum Development, 1983.

McLaughlin, Milbrey Wallin, and R. Scott Pfeifer. *Teacher Evaluation: Improvement, Accountability, and Effective Learning*. New York: Teachers College Press, 1988.

McNeil, John D. "A Scientific Approach to Supervision." In *Supervision of Teaching*, 1982 Yearbook. Thomas J. Sergiovanni, ed. Alexandria, Va.: Association for Supervision and Curriculum Development, 1982.

McNeil, John D., and W. James Popham. "The Assessment of Teacher Competence." In *Second Handbook of Research on Teaching*. Robert M. W. Travers, ed. Chicago: Rand McNally, 1973.

Marks, James R., Emery Stoops, and Joyce King-Stoops. *Handbook of Educational Supervision: A Guide for the Practitioner*, 3rd ed. Boston: Allyn & Bacon, 1985.

Medley, Donald M. "The Effectiveness of Teachers." In *Research on Teaching: Concepts, Findings, and Implications*. Penelope L. Peterson and Herbert J. Walberg, eds. Berkeley, Calif.: McCutchan, 1979.

Medley, Donald M., Homer Coker, and Robert S. Soar. *Measurement-Based Evaluation of Teacher Performance: An Empirical Approach*. White Plains, N.Y.: Longman, 1984.

Miller, R. I. *Evaluating Faculty Performance*. San Francisco: Jossey-Bass, 1972.

Millman, Jason. "Student Achievement as a Measure of Teacher Competence." In *Handbook of Teacher Evaluation*. Jason Millman, ed. Beverly Hills, Calif.: Sage, 1981.

———, ed. *Handbook of Teacher Evaluation*. Beverly Hills, Calif.: Sage, 1981.

Millman, Jason, and Linda Darling-Hammond. *The New Handbook of Teacher Evaluation: Assessing Elementary and Secondary School Teachers*. Newbury Park, Calif.: Sage, 1990.

Natriello, Gary. *Evaluation Frequency, Teacher Influence, and the Internalization of Evaluation Processes*. Eugene: Center for Educational Policy and Management, College of Education, University of Oregon, 1983.

Oliva, Peter F. "Evaluation of Teacher Performance: Identifying Effective Teachers." *American Middle School Education* 9 (Spring 1986): 30–37.

———. "What Are the Essential Generic Teaching Competencies?" *Theory into Practice* (Spring 1980): 117–21.

Oliva, Peter F., and Kenneth T. Henson. "The Expert Syndrome." *Contemporary Education* 53 (Winter 1982): 61–64.

Pajak, Edward. *Approaches to Clinical Supervision: Alternatives for Improving Instruction*. Norwood, Mass.: Christopher-Gordon, 1993.

Peters, Tom, and Robert Waterman, Jr. *In Search of Excellence*. New York: Warner Books, 1982.

Peterson, Donovan, and Kathryn Peterson. "A Research-Based Approach to Teacher Evaluation." *NASSP Bulletin* 68 (February 1984): 39–46.

Professional Practices Commission. *Professional Practices Commission: Serving Education in Georgia*. Atlanta: Georgia Department of Education, Professional Practices Commission, n.d.

"Progress in Evaluating Teaching." *Educational Leadership* 44 (April 1987): 3–80.

Reynolds, John C. "In Search of Mr. (Ms.) Goodteacher." *Action in Teacher Education* 2 (Winter 1979–80): 35–38.

Rosenshine, Barak V. "Academic Engaged Time, Content Covered, and Direct Instruction." *Journal of Education* 160 (August 1978): 38–66.

———. "Classroom Instruction." In *The Psychology of Teaching Methods*. N. L. Gage, ed. Chicago: National Society for the Study of Education, 1976.

———. "Content, Time, and Direct Instruction." In *Research on Teaching: Concepts, Findings, and Implications*. Penelope L. Peterson and Herbert J. Walberg, eds. Berkeley, Calif.: McCutchan, 1979.

Rosenshine, Barak V., and Norma Furst. "The Use of Direct Observation to Study Teaching." In *Second Handbook of Research on Teaching*. Robert M. W. Travers, ed. Chicago: Rand McNally, 1973.

Sergiovanni, Thomas J., and Robert J. Starratt. *Supervision: A Redefinition*, 5th ed. New York: McGraw-Hill, 1993.

Shavelson, Richard, and Nancy Dempsey-Atwood. "Generalizability of Measures of Teaching Behavior." *Review of Educational Research* 46 (Fall 1976): 553–611.

Shaw, Arthur. "Improving Instruction through Evaluation: One Teacher's View." *Action in Teacher Education* 2 (Winter 1979–80): 1–4.

Simon, Anita, and E. Gil Boyer. *Mirrors for Behavior III: An Anthology of Observation Instruments.* Philadelphia: Research for Better Schools, 1974.

Stallings, Jane. *Learning to Look.* Belmont, Calif.: Wadsworth, 1977.

Stanley, Sarah J., and W. James Popham, eds. *Teacher Evaluation: Six Prescriptions for Success.* Alexandria, Va.: Association for Supervision and Curriculum Development, 1988.

Strike, Kenneth A., and Barry Bull. "Fairness and the Legal Context of Teacher Evaluation." In *Handbook of Teacher Evaluation.* Jason Millman, ed. Beverly Hills, Calif.: Sage, 1981.

Sweeney, Jim, and Dick Manatt. "A Team Approach to Supervising the Marginal Teacher." *Educational Leadership* 41 (April 1984): 25–27.

"Teacher Evaluation." *NASSP Bulletin* 68 (February 1984): 1–60.

Teacher Performance Assessment Instruments: A Handbook for Interpretation. Atlanta: Georgia State Department of Education, 1980.

Thomas, M. Donald. *Performance Evaluation of Educational Personnel.* Bloomington, Ind.: Phi Delta Kappa Educational Foundation, 1979.

Walberg, Herbert J., ed. *Evaluating Educational Performance.* Berkeley, Calif.: McCutchan, 1974.

Warner, Allen R., and Dora H. Scott. "Evaluating Teacher Effectiveness: Professional Dimensions." *Action in Teacher Education* 2 (Winter 1979–80): 27–34.

Wise, Arthur, Linda Darling Hammond, Milbry McLaughlin, and Harriet Bernstein. *Teacher Evaluation: A Study of Effective Practices.* Santa Monica, Calif.: Rand Corporation, 1985.

Wittrock, Merlin C., ed. *Handbook of Research on Teaching,* 3rd ed. New York: Macmillan, 1986.

Zirkel, Perry A. "Teacher Evaluation: A Legal Overview." *Action in Teacher Education* 2 (Winter 1979–80): 17–25.

Audiotapes

Eisner, Elliot W. *Educational Connoisseurship and Educational Criticism: A New Evaluation Approach.* Alexandria, Va.: Association for Supervision and Curriculum Development, 1978. 55 min.

Holste, Don, and Richard J. Bodine. *Stimulating Professional Growth through Systematic Personnel Appraisal.* Alexandria, Va.: Association for Supervision and Curriculum Development, 1979.

McGreal, Thomas. *Alternative Models for Use in Designing Local Teacher Evaluation Systems.* Alexandria, Va.: Association for Supervision and Curriculum Development, 1980. 92 min.

Videotapes

Another Set of Eyes: Conferencing Skills. 1989. Three tapes, over two hours, on conferencing skills, featuring Arthur Costa and Robert Garmston. Demonstrates trust-building, questioning, responding, and empowering skills. *Trainer's Manual.* Association for Supervision and Curriculum Development, 1250 North Pitt Street, Alexandria, VA 22314.

Evaluating Teacher Performance: Part I. The Process. 1981. This 60-minute tape features Richard P. Manatt discussing the process of evaluating teacher performance. Association for Supervision and Curriculum Development, 1250 North Pitt Street, Alexandria, VA 22314.

Evaluating Teacher Performance: Part II. Teaching Episodes. 1981. This 60-minute tape features Richard P. Manatt discussing the evaluation of teacher performance based on several teaching episodes. Association for Supervision and Curriculum Development, 1250 North Pitt Street, Alexandria, VA 22314.

Instructional Supervision: Effective Practices for School Leaders. 1994. In this 29-minute video,

Lawrence S. Finkel discusses the important step-by-step approach in implementing effective processes of clinical supervision. National Association of Secondary School Principals (NASSP), 1904 Association Drive, Reston, VA 22091-1537.

Supervising the Marginal Teacher. 1983. Richard P. Manatt uses the 60 minutes of video to focus on approaches and techniques to use when supervising a marginal teacher. Association for Supervision and Curriculum Development, 1250 North Pitt Street, Alexandria, VA 22314.

Teacher Evaluation: Doing It Right, Parts 1 and 2. 1994. The two videotapes (Part 1: 23 minutes and Part 2: 22 minutes) feature Lawrence S. Finkel sharing information on improving evaluator skills in effective teaching, supervising the marginal teacher, conferencing techniques, and classroom observation methods. National Association of Secondary School Principals, 1904 Association Drive, Reston, VA 22091-1537.

Teacher Performance Evaluation Cycle. 1988. Richard P. Manatt is featured on the 6 videotapes discussing the effective implementation of a lesson plan and four 20- to 40-minute teaching episodes. Association for Supervision and Curriculum Development, 1250 North Pitt Street, Alexandria, VA 22314.

Kit

Harris, Ben M., and Jane Hill. *DeTek: The Developmental Teacher Evaluation Kit*. Southwest Educational Development Laboratory, 211 East Seventh Street, Austin, TX 78701.

PART VI

Instructional Supervision: Evaluation and Change

14

Improving Instructional Supervision

Objectives

After studying Chapter 14 you should be able to accomplish the following objectives:

1. Design an instrument by which administrators can evaluate supervisors.
2. Design an instrument for self-evaluation of the supervisor.
3. Design an instrument for evaluation of the supervisor by the teachers.
4. Design a plan for evaluating the supervisory program.
5. Predict likely developments in supervision in the future.

ROLE OF THE SUPERVISOR: A REPRISE

Throughout this text, the supervisor has been seen performing a variety of roles. This staff person has been conceptualized as an individual whose primary role is the improvement of instruction and the curriculum through individual and group assistance to teachers. The instructional supervisor is a service-oriented staff person who would be more effective if freed of administrative responsibilities.

As noted at the beginning of this text, there are many types of supervisors: generalists, specialists, supervisor-administrators, building supervisors, district supervisors, department heads, team leaders, grade coordinators, and state supervisors. The role and function of each of these supervisors differ to some extent though their primary roles are similar—the improvement of programs for young people through the professional development of teachers. Consequently, the principles of supervision that have been discussed in this text have relevance for all supervisors. Specific practices and procedures, however, will need to be modified to fit the various types of supervisor roles.

All supervisors have certain common interests, such as helping teachers with planning, selection of strategies and resources, and evaluation. Some supervisors—for example, those on the state level—are more remote from the firing line than local supervisors, but they still follow similar principles of supervision in somewhat modified ways. The supervisors at each higher level of the educational hierarchy may aid supervisors below them as well as the teachers; therefore, they must be thoroughly conversant with duties and responsibilities of supervisors at lower levels of the echelon.

The responsibilities of the supervisor imply a number of roles, four of which were conceptualized in the model of supervision in Chapter 1. The supervisor is

- A *coordinator*, who seeks to achieve articulation between programs and levels and helps teachers become aware of each other's problems
- A *consultant*, on call to individual teachers and groups who wish to take advantage of his or her expertise
- A *group leader*, who knows how to work with groups and get the most out of them
- An *evaluator*, who helps teachers evaluate instruction, the curriculum, and themselves

Additionally, the supervisor is

- An *expert on instruction*, knowledgeable about the latest and best methods
- A *curriculum expert*, knowledgeable about the curriculum and ways to improve it
- A *communicator*, who can relate information and ideas to teachers and is a good listener
- An *organizer*, skillful in establishing various kinds of programs of value to teachers
- A *stimulator*, who suggests ideas for teachers to consider
- An *orienter*, who takes responsibility for helping teachers who are new to the system and community to become acquainted
- A *public relations person*, who may be invited to interpret the school's curriculum to the public, either in written communications or in talks to lay groups
- A *researcher*, who instigates research studies, particularly action research
- A *change agent*, a catalyst for helping teachers to change and improve
- A *master teacher*, who can demonstrate effective teaching and can teach teachers

Although supervisors have other roles, these show the scope of their job in today's schools. Obviously, a special kind of person is required to be a supervisor, one with extended training and experience.

Once appointed, the supervisor must not assume that the training period is over. As with the teachers he or she supervises, the supervisor must keep up with developments in the field of supervision. To remain up-to-date and to maintain effectiveness, the supervisor should (1) participate in in-service activities for professional development, (2) regularly and systematically evaluate himself or herself, and (3) regularly and systematically request teachers to evaluate his or her effectiveness.

Supervisors can improve themselves by participating in some of the workshops, institutes, and conferences sponsored by both teacher education institutions and professional associations. They can take part in the activities of state and national organizations of particular service to supervisors, such as the Association for Supervision and Curriculum Development and the National Staff Development Council. In large school systems, supervisors can meet periodically to discuss mutual problems to which they are seeking solutions. Formal course work during the year or during the summer at a teacher education institution is another means of self-improvement. Supervisors can keep up with current developments by establishing their own professional libraries and reading regularly the professional journals that have the most significance for them and the teachers they supervise.

Supervisors may learn some of the skills of supervision by on-the-job training. For example, they may become adept at writing curriculum guides by participating with a group of teachers in that activity. They may polish their research skills by participating in research study under the direction of a specialist. They may develop the skills of organizing in-service activities by drafting plans for specific activities and putting them to the test. Supervisors should not become so complacent about their own professional development or so busy directing the professional development of teachers that they ignore their own growth. Nothing can be more incongruous in a school system than to see a faculty experiencing professional growth while the supervisory staff remains stagnant. The supervisor must continue to develop professionally if for no other reason than to set an example for teachers, thus communicating to them that professional growth is an expected part of the life of a professional.

EVALUATION OF THE SUPERVISOR

Supervisors should continuously evaluate their effectiveness. In seeking evaluation, supervisors serve as models to teachers, demonstrating a personal need for continuous evaluation of their performance. Feedback on performance is necessary for all professionals if they are to grow and develop. Supervisors can gain feedback on their performance in three ways. First, they are ordinarily evaluated by their administrators. Second, they can evaluate their own performance. Third, they can survey the perceptions of teachers about their work.

Evaluation by Superordinates

It is rather general practice for administrators and supervisors to be evaluated by their superordinates. Central office supervisors and principals are evaluated by their supervisors in the central administration. Principals assess the performance of assistant principals, lead teachers, department heads, grade coordinators, team leaders, and other supervisory personnel of the school.

Administrators and supervisors who rise through the ranks often hold tenure as teachers. They do not, as a rule, have tenure in administrative or supervisory positions. They serve in leadership positions at the discretion of their superordinates. Even the superintendent is evaluated one way or another by his or her superordinates: the public. If the superintendent is elected to office, the people may vote for a rival candidate at the next election. An appointed superintendent serves at the pleasure of the people's representatives, the local board of education. If the board is dissatisfied with the performance of the superintendent, it may refuse to renew a contract. If the board becomes dissatisfied enough with the superintendent during the period of the contract, it may buy up the remaining time of the contract and discharge the administrator.

Thus, school personnel are evaluated by their superordinates. Administrators and supervisors are evaluated for two purposes: (1) to provide them with feedback so they can improve their performance, and (2) to provide their superiors with data on which to base personnel decisions, such as whether to retain them in their administrative or supervisory positions.

Many school systems rate their administrative and supervisory personnel through instruments that detail the specific criteria considered important in those systems. Some school systems use the same instrument to rate both administrators and supervisors without distinguishing between these two types of personnel. In that respect, they emulate those preservice training programs of professional education institutions that stipulate the same course requirements for administrators and supervisors.

The evaluation instrument of the Clarke County (Georgia) Public Schools, shown in Figure 14.1, provides an illustration of the kinds of criteria supervisory personnel may be expected to demonstrate. Prospective administrators and supervisors should examine the criteria on which they will be evaluated before accepting a leadership position so they can decide whether they wish to or could fulfill the requirements of the position.

In selecting people for administrative or supervisory positions, especially those with no previous track record in administration or supervision, the employing officials need to gather as much evidence as they can to predict whether the applicants will be successful in the job. They should certainly investigate whether the prospective administrators and supervisors were successful as teachers, whether they were, in fact, superior teachers. They should learn something of their philosophy of education; their organizational and problem-solving skills; and especially, their skills in communicating and working with people.

Self-evaluation

A conscientious supervisor will stop periodically for self-assessment. This person will raise questions about the effectiveness of the help he or she provides teachers, look for evidence of the kind of assistance rendered, and gauge his or her competencies against some standards of performance such as those described in the literature on supervision. Supervisors look at the objectives they have specified for the year or other period of time and determine whether the objectives have been met. Not only do they assess the effectiveness of the supervisory program per se, but they also evaluate the quality of the roles they have played in that supervisory program.

CLARKE COUNTY SCHOOL DISTRICT-SUPERVISOR-COORDINATOR ASSESSMENT RECORD

NAME _____ SCHOOL _____

ASSESSOR _____ SUBJECT OR GRADE _____ DATE _____

THREE COPIES FOR: PART ① - PERSONNEL FILE   PART ② STAFF MEMBER   PART ③ ASSESSOR'S FILE

PLEASE USE BLACK BALL POINT PEN FOR THIS FORM

RATING

RATING

A. PERSONAL QUALITIES

1. Demonstrates sufficient stamina and energy to perform assignment at an effective level.

2. Demonstrates punctual and regular attendance.

3. Manifests poise and self control.

4. Dresses in a manner appropriate to the particular role.

5. Demonstrates competency in language usage.

6. Voice Quality: Speaks with clarity, appropriate tone and volume.

B. HUMAN AND INTERPERSONAL RELATIONSHIPS

1. Accepts constructive criticism positively.

2. Establishes and maintains positive relationships with teachers.

3. Establishes and maintains positive relationships with co-workers.

4. Establishes and maintains positive relationships with the community.

5. Is supportive of the school program.

C. PROFESSIONAL QUALITIES

1. Takes pride in teaching and is supportive of the profession.

2. Demonstrates cooperation in areas of assigned responsibilities within the school and/or school system.

3. Actively pursues a program of self-improvement.

4. Recognizes an obligation to understand and support administrative policies and procedures while offering dissent in a constructive manner.

D. PROFESSIONAL PERFORMANCE

1. Demonstrates adequate knowledge of area of responsibility.

2. Diagnoses strengths and weaknesses of persons/programs supervised or coordinated.

3. Provides appropriate assistance to teachers for the improvement of their performance.

4. Communicates clearly and effectively with school staff and co-workers.

5. Creates an atmosphere which stimulates interest and enthusiasm for teaching.

6. Supports the adopted policies and procedures of the school system.

7. Demonstrates ability to organize and manage area of responsibility.

E. COMMENTS (OPTIONAL)

Staff Member's Comments _____

_____

_____

Assessor's Comments _____

_____

_____

* SIGNATURE OF STAFF MEMBER _____ DATE _____

* SIGNATURE OF ASSESSOR _____ DATE _____

* This signature does not necessarily imply agreement; it indicates that the person has seen it.

If any area is checked as "improvement necessary" the "PERFORMANCE IMPROVEMENT PLAN" must be filled out by the assessor and the person being assessed.

1

PERSONNEL FILE

SPEEDIPLY> Patent Pending. Mt P- Patented 1,421,827, 1,016,108. Moore Business Forms, Inc. A

Figure 14.1. Clark County District-Supervisor-Coordinator Assessment Record. *Source: Clarke County Public Schools, Clarke County District-Supervisor-Coordinator Assessment Record, Athens, Ga. Reprinted with permission of the Clarke County Public Schools.*

579

Rate yourself on each of the items below by checking the appropriate number. 1 is the lowest and 5 highest. NA is not applicable.

Characteristics	1	2	3	4	5	NA
1. I provide assistance as needed.						
2. I am open to communication.						
3. I show concern for the individual teacher.						
4. I transmit pertinent information.						
5. I am receptive to others' ideas.						
6. I interact effectively with teachers.						
7. I communicate clearly.						
8. I provide leadership in curriculum development.						
9. I am up-to-date on curriculum developments.						
10. I am effective as a demonstration teacher.						
11. I am skillful in diagnosing instructional difficulties.						
12. I am skillful in prescribing measures for instructional improvement.						
13. I am effective as a group leader.						
14. I involve teachers in decision making.						
15. I am skillful in conducting conferences with teachers.						
16. I plan in-service activities in response to teachers' needs.						
17. I perceive my primary role as a helper to teachers.						

Figure 14.2. Self-assessment Instrument.

While encouraging teachers to evaluate themselves, supervisors can do no less than practice what they preach, evaluate their own traits and accomplishments, and make changes as a result of self-discovery. A checklist or inventory, such as the one in Figure 14.2, can be helpful in directing a self-appraisal.

Instead of following a checklist the supervisor could keep in mind a few basic questions to which he or she could periodically and privately respond:

- Am I meeting my objectives?
- Am I providing any real help to teachers?
- Where are the gaps in my help?

- Am I using my time wisely?
- In what areas do I need in-service education?
- Am I behaving like a supervisor or like an administrator?

Professional supervisors evaluate their own performance continuously.

Evaluation by Teachers

Although supervisors are commonly evaluated by their superiors in the educational hierarchy, much rarer but obviously necessary are opportunities for teachers to evaluate administrators and supervisors. Administrative and supervisory personnel at all levels of the educational spectrum commonly omit what could be a vital source of feedback—evaluation by "the troops."

Although there is a growing movement toward having teachers evaluate the performance of those who administer and supervise their work, evaluation of superiors by subordinates is a relatively recent development. The traditional and commonly held point of view has been that the administrators and supervisors were immune from evaluation by those lower on the table of organization. Historically, the bureaucratic approach to administration and supervision has dominated most formal organizations. Authority and communication in bureaucratic organizations usually proceed from the top down, with no upward flow.

With a growing emphasis on the democratic or collegial approach to administration, however, and the burgeoning move toward empowerment of teachers, superordinates have begun to permit and encourage subordinates to participate in the administration of the organization. In school settings, the evaluation of administrators and supervisors by the subordinates, the teachers, is analogous to the evaluation of teachers by their students and by the parents of their students. As administrators and supervisors suggest or require student evaluations and often recommend parents' evaluations of teachers, they should set an example by seeking teachers' perceptions of their performance.

The accountability movement, which has rubbed off not only on teachers but also on their administrators and supervisors, and the power of teachers' organizations have also contributed to the notion that administrators and supervisors are accountable to their subordinates as well as to their superiors. New supervisors can forge a strong link in the chain of rapport with teachers by promptly and voluntarily instituting a process by which the teachers supervised can periodically—at least annually—evaluate their performance. Feedback from the teachers is the best way for supervisors to learn whether they are accomplishing the mission. The teachers whom the supervisors serve are in a real sense the consumers of the product brought to them, and they are in the best position to judge whether that product is effective.

With the assistance of teachers, the supervisor may design an instrument that teachers can fill out toward the end of the year. To obtain valid results, the instrument should be administered in a threat-free environment. The best way to accomplish this is to have teachers fill out the instrument anonymously and turn it in to an elected committee of their colleagues. This committee will tabulate the data and furnish the supervisor with a summary of the data, after which the original evaluations will be destroyed.

With some minor changes, the self-evaluation instrument in Figure 14.2 can be transformed into an instrument by which teachers can evaluate the performance of the supervisor (Figure 14.3). Descriptive terms are used in place of numbers. A space is provided for the response "no information" if teachers feel they have inadequate data on which to base a judgment. Appropriate directions on how to complete the instrument and who would collect it would accompany the evaluation form.

Please rate your supervisor on the following characteristics.

Characteristics	Outstanding	Very Good	Good	Fair	Poor	No information
1. Provides assistance as needed.						
2. Is open to communication.						
3. Shows concern for the individual teacher.						
4. Transmits pertinent information.						
5. Is receptive to others' ideas.						
6. Interacts effectively with teachers.						
7. Communicates clearly.						
8. Provides leadership in curriculum development.						
9. Is up-to-date on curriculum developments.						
10. Is effective as a demonstration teacher.						
11. Is skillful in diagnosing instructional difficulties.						
12. Is skillful in prescribing measures for instructional improvement						
13. Is effective as a group leader.						
14. Involves teachers in decision making.						
15. Is skillful in conducting conferences with teachers.						
16. Plans in-service activities in response to teachers' needs.						
17. Perceives his or her primary role as a helper to teachers.						

Figure 14.3. Teacher Evaluation of the Supervisor.

EVALUATION OF THE SUPERVISORY PROGRAM

In addition to assessing their success in fulfilling prescribed roles, supervisors should assess the results of the supervision program. Evaluation should reveal not only how well the supervisor functions but also what results have been achieved. Two approaches to evaluation of the supervisory program have proved helpful. We call them (1) evaluation by objectives and (2) evaluative questioning.

Evaluation by Objectives

In keeping with the approach to administration referred to as management by objectives, supervision by objectives requires the supervisor to establish at the beginning of the year specific objectives that are to be pursued during the year. Just as the specification of instructional (behavioral) objectives simplifies the task of evaluating student achievement, the specification of supervisory objectives does the same for evaluating the success of the supervisory program.

Assume for the moment the role of assistant principal for curriculum and instruction in an elementary school. In this school, the principal, assistant principal, grade coordinators, and central office supervisors regularly visit and observe teachers. During the summer, the assistant principal drafts the following objectives, which will become his or her supervisory job targets for the ensuing academic year:

- By September 30, times and dates of staff-development workshops based on last year's survey of teachers will have been scheduled.
- By December 1, a videotaping system will have been put in place for teachers to evaluate their own performance.
- By January 1, each tenured teacher will have been visited once and each non-tenured teacher twice; conferences will have been held with each teacher.
- By February 1, assessment tests in the basic skills of fifth graders will have been completed.
- By March 1, a curriculum mapping study will have been completed at each grade level.
- By April 1, curriculum guides in social studies and science will have been completed.
- By May 1, the in-service needs of teachers will have been surveyed for purposes of planning next year's staff-development program.
- By May 31, the workshops scheduled in September will have been offered.
- By June 5, each teacher will have had the opportunity to visit and observe for one day another teacher in the school system.

The foregoing objectives are typical of those that might be specified by a school-based supervisor. In evaluating the supervisory program, the supervisor can readily determine which objectives have been achieved. Establishing the objectives in advance is an earmark of sound planning. Specifying objectives clarifies the program directions in the supervisor's own mind, communicates the targets to others, and eases the problem of evaluating the program.

Evaluative Questioning

The supervisor who employs evaluative questioning uses it to measure the results achieved. John T. Lovell and Kimball Wiles illustrated this approach by suggesting the following questions, which might be asked by the supervisor:

1. How many more teachers are experimenting?
2. Has there been an increase in the calls for help in thinking through problems?
3. Has there been a change in the nature of the problems presented?
4. Is there an increased demand in the staff for professional materials?
5. Is there more sharing of materials among members of the staff?
6. Is the faculty identifying the problems it has to face further ahead, so that it isn't confronted with so many emergencies?
7. Is there a greater use of evidence in deciding issues?
8. Is there within the faculty a greater acceptance of difference?
9. How many more parents are involved in the school?
10. How many rooms are attractive?
11. How many more teachers are active in professional organizations?
12. How many more teachers are seeking in-service experience?
13. How many more teachers are planning with other teachers?
14. How many more pupils are being included in planning and evaluating?
15. Is a larger percentage of the staff assuming responsibility for the improvement of the program?
16. Are staff meetings becoming more faculty directed?
17. How many more teachers are using a wider range of materials?
18. How are students scoring on achievement tests?[1]

Answers to questions like these will reveal a great deal about the effectiveness of the supervisory program. If the two approaches to program evaluation are both followed—that is, if prespecified objectives are assessed and if probing, evaluative questions are answered—a thorough assessment of the program may be made. Where deficiencies are uncovered, the supervisor must make plans to overcome them.

FUTURE DIRECTIONS IN SUPERVISION

It is almost pro forma for the author of an education textbook to gaze into a crystal ball and prophesy what he or she sees for the future. We have seen the emergence of an academic specialty called Futurism. It has its own organization composed of Futurists, whose writings appear in the organization's journal, *The Futurist*.[2] We can identify any number of books and films that predict what life will be like in the twenty-first century and beyond. The beauty of prophesying is that no one can prove the prophet wrong. Not until the future arrives can the prophecies be pronounced "right" or "wrong," or perhaps judged on the scale employed by some of those tough standardized-test items, "more right than wrong" or "more wrong than right."

So we cannot resist becoming a bit delphic and very briefly playing the game Prophecy. We'd like to consider this question with you: What will supervision be like ten years from now?

Domains of Supervision

Supervisory tasks will continue to fall in the three domains: instructional, curriculum, and staff development. In some cases, one supervisor may fulfill roles in all three domains. In other cases, separate supervisors will be charged with responsibility in one or two domains. School systems will continue to employ a part-time or full-time person to coordinate staff-development activities and a limited number of generalist and specialist coordinators.

Clarification of Approaches, Functions, and Roles

The first edition of this textbook (1976) optimistically predicted that the supervisor's role would be clarified in ten years. However, that prediction fell far short of complete realization. Supervision remains in a state of uncertainty and flux. Would that we could say the many issues discussed in Chapter 2 have been resolved!

A lack of clarity about the functions, roles, and practices of supervision permeates the field. The Association for Supervision and Curriculum Development, for example, devoted its 1992 Yearbook to *Supervision in Transition.*[3] Sergiovanni and Starratt[4] and Glickman et al.[5] called for redefinition of supervision. In fact, Sergiovanni, in speaking of "the regeneration of supervision," expressed the hope that as the twenty-first century approaches, schools will be "learning communities" where "supervision will no longer be needed."[6]

In seeking clarification of the function, roles, and practices of supervision, both practitioners and theorists face a number of conflicting approaches that command their attention. Multiple questions remain to be answered, for example:

- To which approach shall we subscribe: the scientific? the human relations? the human resources development? the artistic? the hermeneutic? the ecological-cultural?
- Shall supervisors work primarily with individual teachers? with groups? with neither, serving instead as a broker-impresario?
- Shall supervisors be primarily colleagues and teaching mentors or shall they be drawn from the central office staff or regional educational service agencies?

Perhaps no national resolution of the issues can ever be made. Instead, issues will be addressed locality by locality, school system by school system, school by school. By the very nature of the task, we may never see complete and unequivocal clarification.

For the immediate future, supervision in its clinical mode will continue to follow the scientific approach with primary emphasis on helping individual teachers and secondarily working with groups. Emphasis is shifting from service provided by supervisors from outside the school to help from staff members within the school.

Instructional supervisors will continue to put into practice the results of over thirty years' research on teacher evaluation, generic teaching skills, objective data collection, conferencing based on observable data, effective teaching practices, and instrumentation.

In the not-too-distant future, we can expect to see some synthesis of the scientific and artistic, interpretive, and ecological approaches. Elements of qualitative analysis of what goes on in the classroom will accompany quantitative analysis of observable teaching behaviors. We will see a heightened concern with the multicultural nature of teaching and learning and increased sensitivity to the school's culture and to the ecology of the classroom.

Supervisors will encourage teachers to perfect strategies, try out different models of teaching, and examine their teaching styles. They will lead teachers toward achieving loyalty to the group, commitment to the organization, positive attitudes toward themselves and their job, mutual trust, and effective communications within the system. They will become more perceptive of the goal of teacher satisfaction as expressed in the human resources approach to supervision. They will be concerned about the effectiveness and health of both the organization and the individuals who make up the organization.

Eclecticism is almost a way of life in the field of education. More and more we are coming to realize that there is no single approach to supervision that guarantees success under all conditions. Therefore, we expect to see the best features of the scientific and other approaches selected, combined, and implemented.

James Nolan and Pam Francis set forth several principles defining a "new mindscape on supervision":

> The primary purpose of supervision is to provide a mechanism for teachers and supervisors to increase their understanding of the learning-teaching process through collaborative inquiry with other professionals.
>
> Teachers should not be viewed only as consumers of research but as generators of knowledge about learning and teaching.
>
> Supervisors must see themselves not as critics of teaching performance, but rather as collaborators with teachers in attempting to understand the problems, issues, and dilemmas that are inherent in the process of learning and teaching.
>
> Acquiring an understanding of the learning-teaching process demands the collection of many types of data over extended periods of time.
>
> The focus for supervision needs to be expanded to include content-specific as well as general issues and questions.
>
> Supervision should focus not only on individual teachers but also on groups of teachers who are engaged in ongoing inquiry concerning problems, issues, and questions.[7]

With the exception of those supervisors who reject one approach or the other outright, most supervisors will likely adopt a combination of approaches. Some will follow a scientific approach with added artistic, interpretive, ecological, and qualitative dimensions; others will adopt artistic, interpretive, ecological, and/or qualitative approaches with added scientific and quantitative dimensions.

Clearly stating the premises undergirding an ecological approach to teaching with its inferences for supervision, Bowers and Flinders left some room for other ways of working:

> Our purpose is to help establish a new conceptual foundation for thinking about effective classroom practices, effective in the sense of being justified on sound pedagogical and political grounds. We shall thus incorporate the insights and classroom practices from other paradigms, including classroom management, when they can be reconciled with our more culture- and language-sensitive orientation.[8]

A new mindscape or redefinition of supervision should allow for multiple approaches within a given setting.

Some clarification, however, has taken place. We can be optimistic and predict that the profession will continue to clarify supervisory roles and responsibilities. Increasingly, school districts have written job descriptions for supervisors (as they have for all school personnel), delineating duties and differentiating responsibilities among various types of supervisors. If there are school systems that have not yet developed job descriptions, we anticipate that they will certainly do so in the near future.

Unfortunately, supervision still exists, as it has for many years, between teaching and administration. Some sharpening of focus for both supervision and administration is taking place and will continue to do so. In all but the smallest schools, we will see two types of supervisors: the staff specialist whose role is to help teachers improve instruction, and the line administrator, or school principal, whose task is to evaluate teachers for the purposes of making personnel decisions.

Training programs for instructional specialists have been modified by the professional education institutions. However, many programs for supervisors still reflect heavy orientation toward administration. Institutions will continue to develop training programs for staff specialists, better tailored to the needs of those who see their careers as instructional supervisors, not administrators-in-waiting or teachers once-removed. In addition to the more general background needed by professional personnel, training components for instructional specialists will emphasize such areas as curriculum development, instructional design, microteaching, human relations, communications skills, measurement and evaluation, and use of technology.

Instructional supervision will become increasingly important for the line supervisor. "The principal as instructional leader" has already become a cliché, implying that today's school administrators must give instructional supervision a higher priority. School administrators must be skilled in evaluating teacher performance for the purpose of making personnel decisions. To be effective, school administrators must have sufficient training in the techniques of instructional supervision.

Teacher Empowerment

Teachers will play an increasingly more vital role in the operation of the school's programs. As we learned in Chapter 9, their preferences for staff-development activities, for example, will take preference over supervisors' and administrators' wishes. As control of schools becomes more decentralized, apparently the current trend, school faculties will be charged with greater responsibility for making curricular and instructional decisions. If parental choice of school becomes universal practice, administrators, supervisors, and teachers will be forced to work even more closely together and share decision making in order to assure successful programs that will attract and retain students.

In the not-too-distant future, we should see teachers playing key roles in selecting administrators, supervisors, and teachers for their schools. Though they may not have final say on hiring, their input will be sought and heeded through a formalized process. It is a paradox of the educational system that higher education institutions have long involved faculty (and even students) in hiring both faculty members and college administrators, yet public school teachers have little or no say in the hiring of superintendents, principals, supervisors, or faculty. Employment of personnel remains largely the highly guarded prerogative of school principals, the superintendent, and, of course, the school board.

School-Based Supervision

The companion movements of school- or site-based management and shared decision making or shared governance will continue to spread and grow. As detailed state mandating holds constant or diminishes and as the empowerment movement grows in strength, school-based management will increase in intensity. Some school districts have for years granted principals a degree of authority to control their own budgets. In recent years, authority and responsibility have been extended to principals and their staffs in matters of administration, curriculum, instruction, and supervision.

An ERIC search of documents on school-based management will quickly reveal a multitude of school systems engaged in site-based management and shared governance. Dade County (Florida)[9] and the District of Columbia[10] provide examples.

The individual school is rapidly becoming the locus of school reform; states and districts are encouraging the formation of councils composed of teachers, parents, and other laypeople to work with principals and staffs to determine goals of the school and means for achieving those goals. Chicago made news in 1989 with its efforts to grant considerable decision-making authority to eleven-member school councils made up of the principal, two teachers from the school, six parents of children in the school, and two laypeople without children in the school.[11] Chicago's efforts have not been without conflict and litigation, some of which comes from within the educational system. Salt Lake City's practice of shared governance dates back to the 1970s.[12]

Both Florida and Kentucky have mandated shared decision making. In 1976, the Florida legislature required school boards to establish a district "advisory committee . . . composed of teachers, students, parents, and other citizens" and allowed similar committees for each school. In 1991, the legislature more specifically mandated school boards to "establish an advisory council for each school in the district composed of teachers, students, parents, and other citizens who are representative of the ethnic, racial, and economic community served by the school." Although it encouraged the creation of advisory councils at every school, the legislature permitted districts with 10,000 or fewer students to "establish a district advisory council comprised of a representative of each school in the district." The advisory councils assist the principal and staff in preparing and evaluating plans for school improvement.[13] The Kentucky Education Reform Act of 1990 made provision for school-based decision making; professional development of school employees, including administrators; and statewide assessment of student achievement, among other reforms.[14]

School-based management and shared decision making are natural concomitants of efforts to empower teachers, students, parents, and other members of the community. As a result of the thrust toward school-based management, individual schools will assume greater responsibility for providing instructional supervision for their faculties. Schools will seek to develop teachers' supervisory skills so they may aid each other. A significant portion of curriculum and instructional leadership is now performed by persons in the individual schools, namely lead teachers, assistant principals for curriculum and instruction, resource specialists, peers, coaches, and mentors. More of the day-to-day, one-on-one supervision conducted for improving instruction will become the province of school-based supervisors.

With greater responsibility placed on the individual school, the role of the central-office supervisor will change. Typically, the services of the central-office supervisors have been spread thin throughout the system. These personnel have tried, with varying degrees of success, to meet the supervisory needs of all the schools in their districts. As school-based personnel take over some of the tasks of instructional supervision, central-office supervisors can give more attention to facilitating and coordinating programs among the various schools and providing back-up help to school-based supervisory personnel who encounter problems. They will be consultants to teachers in some of the specialized subject areas. They will be staff development presenters. They will serve as trainers of lead teachers, team leaders, department heads, grade coordinators, peer supervisors, coaches, and mentors. They will keep teachers informed of significant developments in curriculum and instruction. They will serve as third-party evaluators of teacher performance. They will provide liaison between the school district and the state and nation on curricular and instructional matters.

Peers, Coaches, and Mentors

Whether they are called supervisors, coaches, mentors, or master teachers, peers will be more and more engaged in helping each other with the improvement of instruction. Master teachers and mentors will help induct beginning teachers into the profession. With the generally favorable predisposition of teachers to accept help from their colleagues, the use of peers in the supervisory process may be expected to increase. Programs in which peers assist each other eliminate or minimize the difference in status between the supervisor and teacher and allow schools to provide human resources beyond their current supervisory staffs.

The peer supervision movement responds to teachers' preferences for turning to their colleagues for help before looking elsewhere. School-based supervisors will work with central-office supervisors in training classroom teachers, team leaders, grade coordinators, and department heads to analyze their own performance and the performance of other teachers so they can assist their colleagues. We will see a greater camaraderie developing among faculty members when they work together in a supportive manner.

Teachers within departments, grades, and teams will develop skills and attitudes of willingness to help each other. More school systems will be willing to place some of their supervisory dollars into training teachers and providing released time for them to help their peers, especially assisting those peers who may be having difficulties.

Schools may institute coaching models in which teams of two teachers help each other develop new teaching strategies, as advocated by Bruce Joyce and Beverly

Showers, among others.[15] They may establish mentoring programs, as various states and districts have done, providing stipends and released time for experienced teachers ("mentors") to assist beginning teachers.

Problems abound in establishing and operating mentoring, coaching, and peer supervisory programs. Among these are funding and provision of released time for supervisory duties. Mentors should not be expected to perform supervisory tasks on top of a full teaching load, even if there is additional pay for mentoring responsibilities. Although some school-based supervisors—for example, lead teachers—may serve full-time in supervisory roles, mentor teachers, as a rule, should maintain responsibility for teaching some classes, thereby preserving their peer status and continuing to demonstrate their forte—effective teaching.

Teacher Incentives/Career Ladder/Merit Pay

Schools will constantly seek to identify incentives for teachers that promote pupil learning and staff growth. Rewarding teachers for outstanding performance in the classroom gained momentum during the 1980s as some two-thirds of the states including Arizona, California, Florida, Georgia, Iowa, North Carolina, Tennessee, Texas, and Virginia either adopted or considered incentive programs in the form of career ladders or merit pay.[16]

The Governor's Review Commission of Georgia, for example, stated the intention of a career ladder program as follows: "It is intended that a professionally competitive base salary coupled with career development incentives will provide a framework for a balanced and comprehensive system of teacher compensation that will recognize proficient and productive performance of teachers and to reward them for it."[17]

Tennessee gained considerable recognition in the 1980s for its career ladder program consisting of five levels.[18] Through a combination of state and local assessments the Tennessee plan called for evaluation of teachers on six basic areas of competence ("domains"):

- Planning for instruction
- Delivery of instruction (teaching strategy)
- Evaluation of student progress
- Classroom management
- Professional leadership
- Basic communication skills[19]

Data came from seven sources:

- Observation of classroom performance
- Students
- Supervisors (principals or immediate supervisors)
- Peers
- The teacher being evaluated
- Materials created by and for the teacher
- Test results[20]

The Tennessee plan made use of state-appointed peer evaluators with at least twelve years of experience to conduct the state's evaluations and to submit the results of their evaluations to the State Testing and Evaluation Center for scoring. Through provisions of the career ladder, Tennessee's teachers could become eligible for extended eleven- and twelve-month contracts and, depending on the level of the ladder, could earn substantial additional compensation. Mississippi, Oklahoma, and North Carolina tied incentives to certification by the National Board of Professional Teaching Standards, which began in 1994–95 to certify teacher attainment of national standards.[21]

The profession has flirted with teacher incentive programs in the form of merit pay systems in the past, as in New York State in the 1940s. Rewarding individual teachers with additional compensation for performance deemed outstanding has been attempted off and on in various states and localities from the early 1900s to the present. The concept regained popularity in the 1980s as states engaged in school-reform movements to improve student achievement and the image of public education.

Neither career ladders nor merit pay systems have proved particularly popular with teachers. In recent years, states have rescinded incentive programs and abandoned efforts to implement them. Criticisms of both career ladders and merit pay programs center on competitiveness and divisiveness which lower the group's morale. Although the public overwhelmingly endorses the concept of merit pay, surveys of teachers' attitudes toward the public schools reveal widespread disapproval of such systems.[22]

Distrust of administration is rampant in the merit pay issue. Teachers' groups raise the questions of subjectivity and unreliability in evaluation of teacher performance. They question whether teachers can be evaluated fairly. They object to plans that impose quotas on the numbers of teachers who can be rewarded, thus eliminating some deserving teachers. They frown on the efforts they must make to apply for and participate in the incentive programs. They view the customary small salary increments as just enough to exacerbate the situation. Faculty in institutions of higher education where merit pay systems have long been in effect wrestle with the same problems identified by public school teachers.

At this time, the movements toward career ladders and merit pay programs have crested. Speaking of career ladder plans, Lynn M. Cornett observed, "With the exception of Arizona, Missouri, Tennessee, and Utah, states with such plans never implemented all of the career levels their plans called for."[23] Although extrinsic forms of incentives like career ladders and merit pay provide recognition and status to a limited number of teachers, whether these systems enhance student achievement is problematic and doubted by many teachers.[24]

A further deficiency of many career ladder and merit plans, especially the early ones, is the exclusive focus on teacher performance without assessment of student achievement. Several states, including Kentucky, South Carolina, Tennessee, and Texas, did give some consideration to student achievement, although not all retained student achievement as a criterion. "Only Arizona," said Cornett, "made student achievement an integral part of its comprehensive career ladder system."[25] Recent plans in Kentucky, South Carolina, Tennessee, and Texas, however, factor student progress into decisions on individual or school merit.[26]

Newer directions in teacher incentives will include group merit pay systems that reward schools and faculty as a group on the basis of student achievement, creating competition among *schools* as opposed to competition among *individuals*. Rewarding the faculty as a whole is more palatable to most teachers than attempting to attribute superior merit to individual teachers.

Other incentives, like nonmonetary professional recognition and acclaim for work well done, will appeal to teachers' intrinsic motivation. Extrinsic rewards for all teachers will consist of opportunities for teachers to observe each other and work together, to participate in professional development activities designed around their individual needs and interests, and to receive administrative logistical support in the form of equipment and supplies necessary for promoting student achievement.

Distinction should be made between teacher incentive programs in the form of merit pay and career ladders and master teacher and mentoring programs that do offer some recognition, status, and additional pay to a limited number of teachers. The purposes of these two types of programs are far different—the former, a means of rewarding teachers who do their job well; the latter, a means of offering supervisory help to teachers.

In the evaluation of teachers for merit pay and position on the career ladder, the role of the instructional supervisor, as opposed to the role of the administrator, needs to be carefully defined. Because application for advancement on the ladder is a choice for teachers to make, the teacher choosing to apply may want the instructional supervisor to participate in the evaluation process.

Emphasis on Observable Teaching Competencies

In spite of some educators' recommendations to the contrary, continuing emphasis will be placed on the identification and development of specified, measurable, and observable competencies of teachers. Supervisors at the state and local levels will work with teachers to identify those competencies and devise strategies for achieving and evaluating them.

The principle of accountability will continue taking root with joint efforts by teachers and supervisors to ascertain whether the demonstrated instructional competencies of the teacher make a difference in the product of instruction—the students. In this respect, teacher competency will be considered effective when teachers succeed in helping learners to reach instructional objectives.

Distinction will be made in the competencies to be evaluated for formative purposes and those to be assessed for summative purposes. In working with teachers in a formative setting, supervisors will collect and interpret data exclusively on classroom performance. Those supervisors charged with the responsibility of making summative evaluations will expand the range of competencies they will judge to include not only classroom performance but also personal and professional attributes. In all cases, competencies will be assessed on the basis of observable indicators of the teacher behaviors considered to be important to a school system. Teachers will have agreed in advance with school administrators on which behaviors will be assessed, how they will be measured, and how the results will be used.

Increasingly, school systems, sometimes with pressure from the state level, will give attention in teacher evaluations to product—that is, the achievement of learners. Incorporating some way to relate teacher success to pupil success is not likely to displace completely current efforts to judge teaching process and selected teacher characteristics. Enough momentum has been generated throughout the country for the assessment of teachers on process criteria that this approach to teacher evaluation is not likely to disappear in the immediate future. Some judicious mixture of assessment of process, product, and attributes will no doubt be the key to successful teacher evaluation.

The profession may even make a breakthrough in answering this question: What is effective teaching? The advent of national standards for teachers will heighten the debate on what constitutes effective teaching.

Clinical Supervision

Clinical supervision will occupy a central place in the total supervisory program. Instructional supervisors will increase the help they give individual teachers in their classrooms. We believe the prevailing model for delivery of classroom supervision will continue to be the clinical model of supervisor and teacher working on a one-to-one basis. Supervisors and teachers working together will identify specific behaviors with which the teacher would like assistance. They will collect ample data following a cycle of supervision that includes observation and pre- and postobservation conferences. Clinical supervisors will focus on the improvement of instruction and will avoid rating teachers for personnel purposes. Teachers named to assist their peers will be trained in clinical techniques of supervision. Supervisors may explore with teachers linguistic, social, and cultural patterns in their classrooms. They may engage in discussion with teachers on the learning-teaching process.

The one-to-one model does not eliminate staff development activities in which a supervisor or group of supervisors work with groups of teachers. The Orange County (Florida) school district, for example, has formed an Institute for Professional Development. Under the Institute's auspices, teachers who have been referred or who refer themselves receive assistance with improving specific teaching and/or classroom management strategies.

Goal-Oriented Supervision

Goal-oriented supervision will be a viable alternative to or a supplement to across-the-board, or global, evaluation of teacher competencies. Supervisors and teachers will identify specific job targets on which the teachers will focus during a particular period of time, usually a year. The supervisor will help the teacher delimit areas in which they agree the teacher needs improvement. Teacher self-appraisal will be increasingly used as a technique for identifying areas needing improvement and for selecting job targets.

Supervisory Teams

Some teachers will be aided by supervisory teams. Although we do not see school systems deploying teams of supervisors to work with individual teachers generally throughout the system, we do see increased use of teams to help teachers who are having serious instructional difficulties. At least one member of each supervisory team will be a professional colleague trained and experienced in the teacher's field of specialization. The other members of the team may be school administrators, central office supervisors, or regional educational service agency specialists. Further, the teacher to be assisted will have some say in the composition of the supervisory team.

Use of Technology

More teachers will be willing to have their lessons videotaped so they and their supervisors may carefully analyze the teachers' performance. Media will become less of a mystery and more of an aid to both teachers and supervisors. Teachers will feel less threatened and students less distracted by the repeated appearance of video equipment in the classroom.

Enterprising school systems will create a professional library of videotaped protocol materials to be used for the analysis of teaching. We are just beginning to realize the implications of using computers in education. Supervisors will need sophistication in the application of computers, not only to help them do their own jobs more effectively but also to enable them to help teachers use computers and other types of technology for instructional purposes.

Needed Research

The supervisory profession needs continuing and repeated research on all three of the major domains of supervision: instructional, curriculum, and staff development. Supervisors must sharpen their knowledge and skills for performing their various roles.

Beyond conducting or examining research on improving knowledge and skills, supervisors should frequently survey teachers' perceptions about the supervisory program and processes. They should seek answers to questions such as these:

- What type of supervision do *teachers* want?
- Which do *teachers* prefer: individual help or help in collaborative groups?
- Are teachers, already hard-pressed to keep up with demands on their time, willing to allocate the time necessary for group deliberations?
- Do "most teachers," as Sergiovanni states, "consider supervision to be a non-event—a ritual they participate in according to well-established scripts without much consequence"?[27]
- What kinds of help from supervisors would make supervision a meaningful event?

Professional Education

Training programs for instructional specialists have been modified to a limited extent by the professional education institutions. However, many programs for supervisors still reflect heavy orientation toward administration. Previous editions of this text contained the prediction that preparation for instructional supervisors would become more distinguishable from programs designed for the preparation of administrators. Perhaps that was wishful thinking. We have seen few efforts except at the doctoral level to distinguish programs for training administrators from programs for training instructional supervisors. Supervisory programs are often lumped under the rubric of educational leadership. In fact, a set of guidelines developed for the National Council for Accreditation of Teacher Education (NCATE) encompasses both administration and supervision. Proposed by the National Policy Board for Educational Administration and composed of ten prestigious educational associations, these guidelines consist of eleven domains in five areas. Entitled *NCATE Curriculum Guidelines: Advanced Programs in Educational Leadership for Principals, Superintendents, Curriculum Directors, and Supervisors,* the guidelines were adopted by NCATE in October 1995.[28] Professional education institutions that seek accreditation from NCATE will be required to tailor their programs so those in training for administrative and supervisory positions will achieve competence in the eleven domains of the five areas presented in the *Guidelines*.

It is our hope, if not prophecy, that preparation programs for instructional supervisors will become more distinguishable from programs designed for the preparation of administrators. Prospective supervisors need to gain greater depth in curriculum, instruction, and staff development. The National Policy Board's guidelines leave an opening for some differentiation of programs while at the same time calling for uniformity of programs:

> While the emphasis in preparation programs may shift among the domains depending upon specific leadership roles (i.e., potential superintendents may focus more on finance and policy development while potential principals may focus more on instructional programs and student personnel), it is important for all school leaders to be familiar with all eleven domains presented in the Guidelines as well as to participate in an extensive internship.[29]

Training in understanding the ecology of the classroom with its social and cultural patterns and the cultural dimension of language—oral, written, and nonverbal—will become a part of the teacher education curriculum. Bowers and Flinders, for example, addressed the necessity of training in cultural and language processes of the classroom.[30] We may expect teacher education programs to increase efforts to develop an awareness of cultural, ethnic, and gender biases in the classroom. In so doing, programs will enable teachers to sense their own biases, attitudes, values, and cultural patterns.

Proposals for the reform of teacher education made by the Holmes Group,[31] and the Carnegie Forum on Education and the Economy's Task Force on Teaching as a Profession[32] contain a number of implications for supervision. Their recommendations, if brought to fruition, will impact undergraduate and graduate education of teachers, induction of new teachers into the profession, staff development of in-service teachers, and certification.

The Holmes Group, for example, would eliminate majors in education at the undergraduate level. In addition to gaining a background in general education, prospective secondary school teachers will pursue a major in an academic field; prospective elementary school teachers would engage in multiple areas of concentration in subject fields. Prospective teachers would earn a master's degree in education and would be required to complete successfully a year's internship in a school.

"Supervised by clinical faculty, interns teach children half of their time, engage in action research, and study curriculum."[33]

The Task Force on Teaching as a Profession recommended that prospective teachers obtain a bachelor's degree in the arts and sciences as "a prerequisite for the professional study of teaching"[34] and a Master in Teaching degree with an internship in the schools. It recommends employment of lead teachers to take leadership in redesigning schools and in exercising instructional supervisory functions. On the task force's agenda is the restructuring of the schools to grant teachers more autonomy and enhance their professionalism while at the same time holding them accountable for student achievement.

One of the task force's more controversial proposals was the recommendation for the establishment of a National Board for Professional Teaching Standards whose "primary function would be to establish standards for high professional teaching competence and issue certificates to people who meet those standards."[35] Created in 1987 by the Carnegie Forum on Education and the Economy, the National Board for Professional Teaching Standards would offer a voluntary means of certification that would not supplant state licensing.

The board calls for assessment of teachers on the standards, using newer measures such as interviews, portfolios, and videotaping of teacher performance, after they have earned a bachelor's degree and have at least three years of teaching experience. Rather than controlling the entry into the profession as does state licensing, the national certificate will bestow a mark of distinction on experienced teachers and recognition that they demonstrate high and rigorous standards.[36]

Changes in restructuring of the schools and reforming of teacher education are bound to affect the roles, responsibilities, and training programs of the instructional supervisor.

SUMMARY

Today's supervisor plays a number of varied roles. Throughout this text, his or her primary role is presented as that of a service-oriented helper to teachers in the areas of curriculum, instruction, and staff development. While giving attention to the in-service needs of teachers, supervisors must not neglect their own in-service training.

Supervisors are regularly evaluated by their supervisors. Conscientious supervisors regularly engage in self-evaluation and seek evaluation of their performance by the teachers being served. The supervisory program may be evaluated by determining whether objectives have been met and by responding to searching questions about the effects of the program.

The field of supervision is undergoing numerous changes. Among developments that might be predicted are the following:

- Supervisors will continue to work in three domains: curriculum, instruction, and staff development.
- Supervisory roles will be clarified and differentiated.
- Teachers will assume more responsibility in decision making in their schools.

- School-based supervisors will assume primary responsibility for day-to-day instructional supervision.
- Colleagues, in roles of coaches and mentors, will be instrumental in helping each other.
- The number of school systems establishing career ladders and individual merit pay programs will taper off and schools will resort to more group-oriented merit systems and appeal to intrinsic motives.
- Emphasis will continue on observable teaching competencies with some added attention to product.
- Clinical supervision will be widely practiced.
- Goal-oriented supervision will be an alternative to, or supplement to, global assessment of teaching performance.
- Supervisory teams will evaluate and assist teachers who are experiencing difficulties.
- Supervisors will make greater use of technological aids.
- There will be some synthesis of scientific and other approaches to supervision.
- Teacher education will continue to undergo modifications that will in turn affect the roles and responsibilities as well as the training programs of instructional supervisors.

QUESTIONS FOR DISCUSSION

1. How will instructional supervision change in the next ten years?
2. How can schools reward effective teachers?
3. What social forces may change the tasks of the supervisor?
4. How will training programs for supervisors differ in the next ten years?
5. What do you see as the main problems with instructional supervision?

ACTIVITIES FOR FURTHER STUDY

1. Create a self-evaluation instrument for supervisors.
2. Create an instrument by which administrators may evaluate supervisors' performance.
3. Create an instrument by which teachers may evaluate supervisors' performance.
4. Locate and report on one or more self-evaluation instruments for supervisors that are in use in school systems.
5. Locate and report on one or more instruments in use in school systems by which administrators rate their supervisors' performance.
6. Locate and report on one or more instruments in use in school systems by which teachers may evaluate supervisors' performance.
7. Obtain and analyze a set of objectives for a year that have been drawn up by one or more of the following:
   a. Assistant principal
   b. Department head
   c. Grade coordinator

    d. Lead teacher

    e. Team leader

    f. Central office supervisor (coordinator)

8. Obtain and analyze a set of objectives for a year that have been drawn up by a principal. Identify which objectives pertain to instructional supervision.

9. Make a list of probable questions you would ask as a supervisor to assess the results of your supervisory program.

10. Interview a supervisor (preferably in the type of position to which you aspire) and construct a job analysis of that supervisor's duties.

11. Survey at least ten teachers to learn whether they have ever had the opportunity to evaluate an administrator or supervisor.

12. Talk with a number of supervisors and report on in-service activities in which they have participated for their own professional department in the past twelve months.

13. Write a paper on how computers might be used in the field of supervision.

14. Draw up your own list of prophecies concerning what developments are likely to take place in the field of supervision within the next ten years.

15. Analyze the future directions in supervision discussed in this chapter and state whether you agree or disagree with each position and why.

16. Locate and report on several articles or books that make predictions for changes that may occur within the next ten years in curriculum and instruction.

17. Identify professional organizations and their major publications that are of special significance to the development and growth of the supervisor.

18. Compile a bibliography of books on supervision copyrighted within the past five years that would be suitable as the nucleus of a professional library for supervisors.

19. Debate this proposition: Teacher salary schedules should make provision for salary increments based on merit. If you take the affirmative side of this issue, suggest how merit will be defined and determined.

20. Describe a merit pay system that is in place. If your state or school system has a merit pay plan, tell how teachers are selected for merit increments.

21. Describe a career ladder program. Tell how teachers are selected for the career ladder and how they progress up the ladder. If your state or school system has a career ladder program, describe that one. If not, locate information in the literature.

22. Prepare a report on the pros and cons of a system of national certification of teachers. State your position.

23. Critique the following reports showing implications for instructional supervision:

    a. The Holmes Group, *Tomorrow's Teachers: A Report of the Holmes Group.*

    b. National Board for Professional Teaching Standards, *Toward High and Rigorous Standards for the Teaching Profession.*

    c. Task Force on Teaching as a Profession, *A Nation Prepared: Teachers for the 21st Century.*

NOTES

1. John T. Lovell and Kimball Wiles, *Supervision for Better Schools*, 5th ed. (Englewood Cliffs, N.J.: Prentice-Hall, 1983), pp. 287–90.

2. See *The Futurist: A Journal of Forecasts, Trends, and Ideas about the Future.* (Published by World Future Society, 7910 Woodmont Avenue, Suite 450, Bethesda, MD 20814.)

3. Carl D. Glickman, ed., *Supervision in Transition*, 1992 Yearbook (Alexandria, Va.: Association for Supervision and Curriculum Development, 1992).

4. Thomas J. Sergiovanni and Robert J. Starratt, *Supervision: A Redefinition*, 5th ed. (New York: McGraw-Hill, 1993).

5. Carl D. Glickman, Stephen P. Gordon, and Jovita M. Ross-Gordon, *Supervision of Instruction: A Developmental Approach*, 3rd ed. (Boston: Allyn & Bacon, 1995).

6. Thomas J. Sergiovanni, "Moral Authority and the Regeneration of Supervision," in *Supervision in Transition*, 1992 Yearbook, ed. Carl D. Glickman (Alexandria, Va.: Association for Supervision and Curriculum Development, 1992), pp. 211–12.

7. James Nolan and Pam Francis, "Changing Perspectives in Curriculum and Instruction," in *Supervision in Transition*, 1992 Yearbook, ed. Carl D. Glickman (Alexandria, Va.: Association for Supervision and Curriculum Development, 1992), p. 58.

8. C. A. Bowers and David J. Flinders, *Responsive Teaching: An Ecological Approach to Classroom Patterns of Language, Culture, and Thought* (New York: Teachers College Press, 1990), p. 29.

9. Robert A. Collins and Marjorie K. Hanson, *School-Based Management/Shared Decision Making Project 1987–88 through 1989–90, Summative Evaluation Report* (Miami, Fla.: Dade County Public Schools, 1991), ERIC Document ED 331 922 UD 028 023.

10. Zollie Stevenson, Jr., *Local School-Based Management in the District of Columbia Public Schools: First Impressions of Pilot Sites* (Washington, D.C.: District of Columbia Public Schools, 1990), ERIC Document ED 331 188 EA 022 974.

11. Maxey Bacchus and Bruce Marchiafava, "Implementing School Reform in Chicago: The System Perspective" (Paper presented at the annual meeting of the American Educational Research Association, Chicago, 1991), ERIC Document ED 331 887 TM 016 473.

12. Betty Malen and Rodney T. Ogawa, *The Implementation of the Salt Lake City School District's Shared Governance Policy: A Study of School-Site Councils* (Salt Lake City, Utah: Salt Lake City School District, 1985), ERIC Document ED 274 099 EA 018 864.

13. See *Florida Statutes*, Section 229.58 (1976 and 1991).

14. Mary Helen Miller et al., *A Guide to the Kentucky Education Reform Act of 1990* (Frankfort: Kentucky Legislative Research Commission, 1990), ERIC Document ED 327 352 RC 017 896. See also Eddy J. Van Meter, "The Kentucky Mandate: School-Based Decision Making," *NASSP Bulletin* 75 (February 1991): 52–62; Wallace G. Wilkinson, "Kentucky Education Reform: Schools Held Responsible and Accountable," *Appalachia* 23 (Summer 1990): 7–9.

15. See Bruce Joyce and Beverly Showers, "The Coaching of Teaching," *Educational Leadership* 40 (October 1982): 4–10; and Beverly Showers, "Teachers Coaching Teachers," *Educational Leadership* 42 (April 1985): 43–48.

16. Larry E. Frase and William K. Poston, Jr., "Teacher Incentive Programs: Diversity and Effectiveness without State Funding," *The Clearing House* 64 (November–December 1990): 95–98.

17. Georgia Department of Education, *The Georgia Career Ladder for Public Elementary and Secondary School Professional Personnel* (Atlanta: Georgia Department of Education, 1987), p. 1.

18. Tennessee Department of Education, *Teacher Career Ladder: Better Schools Program: Teacher Orientation Manual, 1984–85* (Nashville: Tennessee Department of Education, 1984), pp. 1, 4–7.

19. Ibid., p. 13.

20. Ibid., p. 19.

21. Lynn M. Cornett, "Lessons from 10 Years of Teacher Improvement Reforms," *Educational Leadership* 52, no. 5 (February 1995): 29.

22. See, for example, Stanley M. Elam, "The Second Gallup/Phi Delta Kappa Poll of Teachers' Attitudes toward the Public Schools," *Phi Delta Kappan* 70 (June 1989): 790.

23. Cornett, "Lessons," p. 29.
24. See Mark A. Smylie and John C. Smart, "Teacher Support for Career Enhancement Initiatives: Program Characteristics and Effects on Work," *Educational Evaluation and Policy Analysis* 12 (Summer 1990): 139–55.
25. Cornett, "Lessons," p. 29.
26. Ibid.
27. Sergiovanni, "Moral Authority," p. 203.
28. The Educational Leadership Constituent Council (c/o Association for Supervision and Curriculum Development, 1250 N. Pitt St., Alexandria, VA 22314), *NCATE Curriculum Guidelines: Advanced Programs in Educational Leadership for Principals, Superintendents, Curriculum Directors, and Supervisors*, 1995.
29. Ibid., p. F-1.
30. Bowers and Flinders, *Responsive Teaching*, p. 22.
31. The Holmes Group, *Tomorrow's Teachers: A Report of the Holmes Group* (East Lansing, Mich.: The Holmes Group, Inc., 1986).
32. Task Force on Teaching as a Profession, *A Nation Prepared: Teachers for the 21st Century* (Washington, D.C.: Carnegie Forum on Education and the Economy, 1986).
33. The Holmes Group, *Tomorrow's Teachers*, p. 95.
34. Task Force on Teaching as a Profession, *A Nation Prepared*, p. 55.
35. Ibid., p. 66.
36. National Board for Professional Teaching Standards, *Toward High and Rigorous Standards for the Teaching Profession* (Detroit, Mich.: National Board for Professional Teaching Standards, 1989). See discussion of national standards as an issue in Chapter 2.

BIBLIOGRAPHY

Alfonso, Robert J., and Lee Goldsberry. "Colleagueship in Supervision." In *Supervision of Teaching*. 1982 Yearbook, edited by Thomas J. Sergiovanni. Alexandria, Va.: Association for Supervision and Curriculum Development, 1982.

Bacchus, Maxey, and Bruce Marchiafava. "Implementing School Reform in Chicago: The System Perspective." Paper presented at the annual meeting of the American Educational Research Association, Chicago, 1991. ERIC Document ED 331 887 TM 016 473.

Bang-Jensen, Valerie. "The View from Next Door: A Look at Peer 'Supervision.' " In *Improving Teaching*. 1986 Yearbook, edited by Karen K. Zumwalt. Alexandria, Va.: Association for Supervision and Curriculum Development, 1986.

Bowers, C. A., and David J. Flinders. *Culturally Responsive Teaching and Supervision: A Handbook for Staff Development*. New York: Teachers College Press, 1991.

———. *Responsive Teaching: An Ecological Approach to Classroom Patterns of Language, Culture, and Thought*. New York: Teachers College Press, 1990.

Brandt, Ronald S. "On Teachers Coaching Teachers: A Conversation with Bruce Joyce." *Educational Leadership* 44 (February 1987): 12–17.

Collins, Robert A., and Marjorie K. Hanson. *School-Based Management/Shared Decision Making Project 1987–88 through 1989–90, Summative Evaluation Report*. Miami, Fla.: Dade County Public Schools, 1991. ERIC Document ED 331 922 UD 028 023.

Cornett, Lynn M. "Lessons from 10 Years of Teacher Improvement Reforms." *Educational Leadership* 52, no. 5 (February 1995): 26–30.

———. "Trends and Emerging Issues in Career Ladder Plans." *Educational Leadership* 43 (November 1985): 6–10.

Cornett, Lynn M., and G. Gaines. *Reflecting on Ten Years of Incentive Programs*. Atlanta: Southern Regional Education Board, 1994.

De Bevoise, Wynn. "Synthesis of Research on the Principal as Instructional Leader." *Educational Leadership* 41 (February 1984): 14–20.

Duke, Daniel L. *School Leadership and Instructional Improvement.* New York: Random House, 1987.

Dull, Lloyd W. *Supervision: School Leadership Handbook.* Columbus, Ohio: Merrill, 1981.

Edelfelt, Roy A. "Career Ladders: Then and Now." *Educational Leadership* 43 (November 1985): 62–66.

Elam, Stanley M. "The Second Gallup/Phi Delta Kappa Poll of Teachers' Attitudes toward the Public Schools." *Phi Delta Kappa*n 70 (June 1989): 785–98.

Franseth, Jane. *Supervision as Leadership.* Evanston, Ill.: Row, Peterson, 1961.

Frase, Larry E., and William K. Poston, Jr. "Teacher Incentive Programs: Diversity and Effectiveness without State Funding." *The Clearing House* 64 (November–December 1990): 95–98.

Furtwengler, Carol. "Tennessee's Career Ladder Plan." *Educational Leadership* 43 (November 1985): 50–56.

"The Future Preparation of Supervisors." *Wingspan: The Pedamorphosis Communique* 3 (December 1986).

Gallup, Alec. "The Gallup Poll of Teachers' Attitudes toward the Public Schools." *Phi Delta Kappan* 66 (October 1984): 97–107.

Georgia Department of Education. *The Georgia Career Ladder for Public Elementary and Secondary School Professional Personnel.* Atlanta: Georgia Department of Education, 1987.

Glatthorn, Allan A. *Differentiated Supervision.* Alexandria, Va.: Association for Supervision and Curriculum Development, 1984.

Glickman, Carl D., ed. *Supervision in Transition.* 1992 Yearbook. Alexandria, Va.: Association for Supervision and Curriculum Development, 1992.

Glickman, Carl D., Stephen P. Gordon, and Jovita M. Ross-Gordon. *Supervision of Instruction: A Developmental Approach,* 3rd ed. Boston: Allyn & Bacon, 1995.

Gray, William A., and Marilynne M. Gray. "Synthesis of Research on Mentoring Teachers." *Educational Leadership* 43 (November 1985): 37–43.

Grimmett, Peter P., Olaf P. Rostad, and Blake Ford. "The Transformation of Supervision." In *Supervision in Transition.* 1992 Yearbook, edited by Carl D. Glickman, pp. 185–202. Alexandria, Va.: Association for Supervision and Curriculum Development, 1992.

Hanes, Robert C., and Kay F. Mitchell. "Teacher Career Development in Charlotte-Mecklenburg." *Educational Leadership* 43 (November 1985): 11–13.

Hawley, Willis. "Designing and Implementing Performance-Based Career Ladder Plans." *Educational Leadership* 43 (November 1985): 57–61.

The Holmes Group. *Tomorrow's Teachers: A Report of the Holmes Group.* East Lansing, Mich.: The Holmes Group, Inc., 1986.

Joyce, Bruce, and Beverly Showers. "The Coaching of Teaching." *Educational Leadership* 40 (October 1982): 4–10.

Kent, Karen M. "A Successful Program of Teachers Assisting Teachers." *Educational Leadership* 43 (November 1985): 30–33.

Lavely, Carolyn, et al. "Role and Duties of Lead Teachers in Career Ladder Programs." *Education* 110 (Spring 1990): 388–96.

Little, Judith Warren. "Teachers as Teacher Advisors: The Delicacy of Collegial Leadership." *Educational Leadershi*p 43 (November 1985): 34–36.

Lovell, John T., and Kimball Wiles. *Supervision for Better Schools,* 5th ed. Englewood Cliffs, N.J.: Prentice-Hall, 1983.

Malen, Betty, and Rodney T. Ogawa. *The Implementation of the Salt Lake City School District's Shared Governance Policy: A Study of School-Site Councils.* Salt Lake City, Utah: Salt Lake City School District, 1985. ERIC Document ED 274 099 EA 018 864.

McIntyre, Kenneth E. "The Merits and Demerits of Merit Pay." *NASSP Bulletin* 68 (November 1984): 100–104.

Miller, Mary Helen, et al. *A Guide to the Kentucky Education Reform Act of 1990*. Frankfort: Kentucky Legislative Research Commission, 1990. ERIC Document ED 327 352 RC 017 896.

Moffett, Kenneth L., Jane St. John, and Jo Ann Isken. "Training and Coaching Beginning Teachers: An Antidote to Reality Shock." *Educational Leadership* 44 (February 1987): 34–36.

National Board for Professional Teaching Standards. *Toward High and Rigorous Standards for the Teaching Profession*. Detroit, Mich.: National Board for Professional Teaching Standards, 1989.

Neubert, Gloria A., and Elizabeth C. Bratton. "Team Coaching: Staff Development Side by Side." *Educational Leadership* 44 (February 1987): 29–32.

Nolan, James, and Pam Francis. "Changing Perspectives in Curriculum and Instruction." In *Supervision in Transition*. 1992 Yearbook, edited by Carl D. Glickman. Alexandria, Va.: Association for Supervision and Curriculum Development, 1992.

Peterson, Ken, and Anthony Mitchell. "Teacher-Controlled Evaluation in a Career Ladder Program." *Educational Leadership* 43 (November 1985): 44–47.

"Redefining Supervision." *Educational Leadership* 46, no. 8 (May 1989): 2–64.

Rosenholtz, Susan J. "Political Myths about Education Reform: Lessons from Research on Teaching." *Phi Delta Kappan* 66 (January 1985): 349–55.

Schlechty, Phillip C. "Evaluation Procedures in the Charlotte-Mecklenburg Career Ladder Plan." *Educational Leadership* 43 (November 1985): 14–19.

Sergiovanni, Thomas J. "Moral Authority and the Regeneration of Supervision." In *Supervision in Transition*. 1992 Yearbook, edited by Carl D. Glickman, pp. 203–214. Alexandria, Va.: Association for Supervision and Curriculum Development, 1992.

———, ed. *Supervision of Teaching*. 1982 Yearbook. Alexandria, Va.: Association for Supervision and Curriculum Development, 1982.

Sergiovanni, Thomas J., and Robert J. Starratt, *Supervision: A Redefinition*, 5th ed. New York: McGraw-Hill, 1993.

Showers, Beverly. "Teachers Coaching Teachers." *Educational Leadership* 42 (April 1985): 43–48.

Smylie, Mark A., and John C. Smart. "Teacher Support for Career Enhancement Initiatives: Program Characteristics and Effects on Work." *Educational Evaluation and Policy Analysis* 12 (Summer 1990): 139–55.

Stevenson, Zollie, Jr. *Local School-Based Management in the District of Columbia Public Schools: First Impressions of Pilot Sites*. Washington, D.C.: District of Columbia Public Schools, 1990. ERIC Document ED 331 188 EA 022 974.

Suhor, Charles. "Teacher Advancement—Myth or Reality?" *English Education* 22 (May 1990): 135–39.

Task Force on Teaching as a Profession. *A Nation Prepared: Teachers for the 21st Century*. Washington, D.C.: Carnegie Forum on Education and the Economy, 1986.

Tennessee Department of Education. *Tennessee Career Ladder: Better Schools Program: Teacher Orientation Manual, 1984–85*. Nashville: Tennessee Department of Education, 1984.

Thompson, J. C. *On Models of Supervision in General and on Peer Clinical Supervision in Particular*. 1979. ERIC Document Reproduction Service No. ED 192 462.

Van Meter, Eddy J. "The Kentucky Mandate: School-Based Decision Making." *NASSP Bulletin* 75 (February 1991): 52–62.

Wilkinson, Wallace G. "Kentucky Education Reform: Schools Held Responsible and Accountable." *Appalachia* 23 (Summer 1990): 7–9.

Zumwalt, Karen K., ed. *Improving Teaching*. 1986 Yearbook. Alexandria, Va.: Association for Supervision and Curriculum Development, 1986.

Exit Competencies

Listed here are the major competencies (objectives) of this textbook. After studying this book, you should be able to demonstrate each of these competencies, thus indicating that you possess a repertoire of knowledge and skills needed by successful supervisors. The number after each competency shows the chapter in which the competency is discussed.

DOMAIN: INSTRUCTIONAL DEVELOPMENT

1. Write a working definition and draw a working model of supervision. — 1
2. Describe minimal qualifications of a supervisor. — 1
3. Identify several unresolved problems (issues) in supervision and show your position on each. — 2
4. Describe and apply a model of instruction. — 3
5. Demonstrate the ability to write instructional goals and objectives in a particular discipline. — 3
6. Write behavioral objectives for each major category of the taxonomies of the three domains of learning. — 3
7. Demonstrate the ability to describe learning tasks. — 3
8. Demonstrate the ability to construct a unit plan. — 3
9. Demonstrate the ability to construct a lesson plan. — 3
10. Select instructional resources, applying appropriate criteria. — 4
11. Select instructional strategies, applying appropriate criteria. — 4
12. Demonstrate selected generic teaching skills. — 4
13. Describe principal causes of behavior. — 5
14. Describe ways in which a teacher can promote self-discipline. — 5
15. Recommend corrective measures for students, appropriate to specific age levels. — 5
16. Demonstrate the ability to specify entry skills for study of topics in your discipline. — 6

53. Train teachers to gather parent evaluations of their performance. 12

SUMMATIVE DIMENSION OF TEACHER EVALUATION
    54. Select or create and apply an instrument by which an administrator can evaluate teacher performance. 13

INSTRUCTIONAL SUPERVISION: EVALUATION AND CHANGE
    55. Select or create and apply an instrument by which an administrator can evaluate the supervisor's performance. 14
    56. Select or create and apply an instrument by which you can evaluate your own performance as a supervisor. 14
    57. Select or create and apply an instrument by which teachers can evaluate the supervisor's performance. 14
    58. Describe ways to evaluate the supervisory program. 14
    59. Describe features and problems of career ladder and merit pay programs. 14
    60. Describe trends and predict future developments in the field of supervision. 14
    61. Write job descriptions for supervisory personnel (Appendix B).

Examples of Descriptions of Supervisory Positions

JOB DESCRIPTION 1

TITLE: Assistant Superintendent for Instruction

QUALIFICATIONS:
1. A Doctor's Degree (in an area of Instructional Leadership preferred). Master's Degree in area of Instructional Leadership required.
2. At least six years of successful elementary and secondary teaching; at least three years of experience in administration or supervision.
3. Certification in Administration/Supervision; elementary education and/or a secondary subject area.

REPORTS TO: Superintendent

SUPERVISES: Division for Instruction Directors and Supervisory Support Staff

POSITION GOAL: To assist the Superintendent substantially and effectively in the tasks of providing leadership and developing, achieving, and maintaining the best possible educational programs and services.

PERFORMANCE RESPONSIBILITIES:
1. Directs the overall activities of planning, developing, implementing, and evaluating all district instructional and staff development programs.
2. Assists in the determination of types of programs needed by the schools and makes appropriate recommendations.
3. Directs the planning for and coordinates implementation of special, federal, and state-funded projects to ensure compliance and to meet students' needs.
4. Coordinates the selection of textbooks, materials, and equipment needed in the instructional programs.
5. Contributes to evaluation of principals as requested.

6. Coordinates the local and state student assessment program for the district and directs assistance to schools to improve student performance.
7. Coordinates the regional accreditation process.
8. Recommends and directs committees and task teams as needed.
9. Assists in the preparation of the School Board meeting agendas, preparing instructional services action items of routine and priority nature as well as timely reports.
10. Provides leadership to schools in area of curriculum.
11. Provides leadership to schools in area of instruction.
12. Monitors leave requests and purchase orders.
13. Directs the development and implementation of grants, policies, and procedures.
14. Coordinates the annual development/revision of the Division's District Comprehensive Educational Plan, Compensatory Education Plan, Pupil Progression Plan.
15. Supervises the development, implementation, and monitoring of summer school plans and procedures.
16. Directs the development and implementation of the district master plan for inservice education, Beginning Teacher Plan, Merit Teacher Plan, Merit Schools Plan, and other state mandates to ensure compliance.
17. Interprets the programs, philosophy, and policies of the district to staff, students, and the community at large.
18. Reports on the status of district programs and services at the request of the Superintendent.
19. Maintains liaison with social, professional, civic, volunteer, and other community agencies and groups having an interest in the schools.
20. Establishes necessary procedures for referral and cooperative planning with other agencies, both local and state.
21. Plays a significant leadership role in fostering professional growth and in building staff morale throughout the district.
22. Develops, recommends, and administers the division budget.
23. Recommends policy which is applicable to position responsibilities.
24. Assists in the preparation for and conduct of collective bargaining negotiations.
25. Assists the Superintendent in organizational analysis and development.
26. Coordinates all instructional services in the district.
27. Establishes and maintains a program of consultant services to schools.
28. Serves on the Superintendent's administrative team.
29. Performs other duties assigned by the Superintendent.

TERMS OF EMPLOYMENT: Twelve months. Salary to be based on the board-adopted administrative salary.

EVALUATION: Performance of this job will be evaluated annually by Superintendent in accordance with School Board policy for evaluation of administrative personnel.

Source: Volusia County Public Schools, DeLand, Florida. Reprinted with permission.

JOB DESCRIPTION 2

TITLE: Director—Curriculum and Instruction

JOB GOAL: To administer the development, implementation and evaluation of the curricula and instructional programs for the School District.

QUALIFICATIONS: Master's degree (Doctorate preferred). Extensive experience in school administration. Relevant state certification. Expertise in area of specialization.

REPORTS TO: Associate Superintendent, Educational Programs and Student Services

SUPERVISES: Various professional and non-professional personnel

RESPONSIBILITIES:
1. Administers, plans, and analyzes the development of curriculum.
2. Interprets and reports to the Associate Superintendent the needs of the unit.
3. Serves as consultant to school system personnel regarding curriculum and instruction.
4. Establishes goals and objectives for curriculum and instruction and develops long- and short-range plans for meeting goals and objectives.
5. Reviews and develops allocation and priorities of funds for curriculum and instruction unit.
6. Reviews and approves assignment of staff and evaluates their effectiveness.
7. Recommends policy statements regarding curriculum and instruction.
8. Directs the planning and coordination of staff and program development.
9. Evaluates program effectiveness system-wide and coordinates site evaluation of program effectiveness.
10. Reviews research related to curriculum.
11. Interprets curriculum to Board, administration, staff, and general public.
12. Coordinates development of educational specifications for school construction as it relates to curriculum and instruction.
13. Ensures that programs within curriculum and instruction unit are in accordance with established Board policy and state and federal regulations and guidelines.
14. Performs such other duties as may be required.

EVALUATION: In accordance with Board Policy.

Signature: _____   Date: _____

Source: New Orleans Public Schools, New Orleans, Louisiana. Reprinted with permission.

JOB DESCRIPTION 3

JOB TITLE: Area Director

REPORTS TO: Superintendency

SUPERVISES: Area level principals, assistant principals

RATIONALE: The Boise School District is organized on the Pre K–12 concept in which the Superintendent is responsible for maintaining effective interrelationships with the community, obtaining and developing personnel, and providing and maintaining funds and facilities. In a school district the size of Boise, the Superintendent must delegate authority for much of the administration and supervision of educational programs. The Area Director is responsible to the Superintendency for the character and quality of the total educational program in his/her assigned area of the District. It is his/her responsibility to provide quality educational leadership that will result in a superior educational program.

JOB SUMMARY: Directs and exercises leadership in planning, budgeting, implementing, supervising and evaluating educational programs in assigned areas of the District, Pre K–12.

MAJOR DUTIES AND REPONSIBILITIES:

Definitions for Columns:

FREQUENCY: (A) Annually   (Q) Quarterly   (M) Monthly   (W) Weekly   (D) Daily

IMPORTANCE: (1) Critically Important   (2) Significant   (3) Of Minor Importance

CAN THESE SKILLS BE LEARNED ON THIS JOB?   (Y) Yes   (N) No

The Area Director works under the direction of the Superintendency. The Area Director has the following duties:

Q 1 Y   1. In conjunction with the Human Resources Administrator, is responsible for the selection and placement of all staff in assigned schools.

A 1 Y   2. Projects certificated and non-certificated instructional staff needs.

D 2 Y   3. Manages personnel matters in assigned schools, including: a) building staff assignments; b) building and itinerant staff evaluation and supervision; c) intensive staff development, probation, and termination of staff; d) school staff transfers; e) approval of non-paid leave requests; and f) hearing officer for grievances, when requested.

W 1 Y   4. Regularly visits each assigned school to maintain contact and to assess the learning climate. Makes building and room visits necessary for understanding, counseling, and supervising the teaching/learning process.

D 2 Y   5. Has overall responsibility for planning, implementing, controlling and evaluating the budgets of assigned schools. This will include all Federal funds, staff development funds, appropriated capital outlay, instructional supplies and equipment funds, area travel funds, and other appropriate funds.

A 1 Y   6. Cooperates in preparation of the total District budget.

M 2 Y   7. Recommends to Coordinator of Educational Services the development, implementation and evaluation of a thorough and continuous staff development program for all staff members, including orientation of new personnel.

M 2 Y   8. Serves as a member of the Superintendent's Council and the Executive Council.

Q 2 Y   9. Coordinates assigned schools for program planning, committee assignments, administrative policies, enrollment and attendance, including graduation exercises of the senior high schools.

A 2 Y   10. Has overall responsibility for school boundaries in assigned area and works with other Area Directors in making recommendations concerning attendance area changes.

A 3 Y   11. In cooperation with other Area Districts, has overall responsibility for handling the requests for student transfers from one school to another school within the District.

M 2 Y   12. Attends all regular and special meetings of the Board of Trustees.

M 3 Y   13. Participates on various committees as assigned by the Superintendency.

M 3 Y   14. Schedules and holds principal meetings and prepares agenda for same.

D 1 N 15. Keeps members of the Superintendency advised of all major developments in assigned schools and promptly advises them of all major problems.

D 1 Y 16. Handles all special problems involving students in assigned schools including tuition waiver requests and hearings for students who have been suspended for truancy or other violations of the District's discipline policy, and in conjunction therewith, establishes relationships with the court and state and community agencies.

A 1 Y 17. In cooperation with the Coordinator of Educational Services, coordinates and assigns curriculum content placement, subject to the approval of the Superintendency.

D 2 Y 18. Performs all other job related duties and accepts other responsibilities as assigned by the Superintendency.

QUALIFICATIONS: Valid Idaho Administrator's Certificate.

A minimum of five years' successful experience in teaching and school administration/supervision.

Demonstrated competency required to perform the major duties and responsibilities of this position.

Demonstrated leadership ability in working with students, staff, parents, and the general public.

TERMS OF EMPLOYMENT:

Length of Contract—twelve months.

Salary—According to existing schedule for this position. Benefits are determined by the Board of Trustees.

Three weeks vacation per year after a full year's employment and such holidays as determined by the Board of Trustees.

This position is classified as administrative, which will require more time than a forty-hour week. The Area Director will be subject to call by the Superintendency for special meetings and to carry out necessary duties beyond the regular work day.

This job description may be changed by the Superintendent as the need arises. The job incumbent shall be promptly advised of any changes made in the job description.

EVALUATION: By the Superintendency.

Signature: _____   Date: _____

       (Employee)

_____

       (Supervisor)

Source: Independent School District, Boise City, Idaho. Reprinted with permission of Boise Independent School District, Boise City, Boise, Idaho.

JOB DESCRIPTION 4

BISMARCK PUBLIC SCHOOL DISTRICT NO. 1 BISMARCK, NORTH DAKOTA, 58501	DESCRIPTOR CODE: CGBA-R	ISSUED DATE: 01-10-91
ADMINISTRATIVE RULE: ASSISTANT SUPERINTENDENT OF INSTRUCTIONAL SERVICES JOB DESCRIPTION	RESCINDS: CGBA-R	ISSUED: 03-27-87

TITLE: Assistant Superintendent of Instructional Services and Secondary Schools.

QUALIFICATIONS: North Dakota and North Central Association Standards. Preference will be given, but not limited to, persons with the following background:

1. Doctorate with emphasis in curriculum, instruction supervision and/or measurement; or in educational administration with a strong emphasis in one or more of the preceding areas.
2. Experience as a school administrator.

REPORTS TO: Superintendent of Schools

SUPERVISES: Directly supervises the following:

1. Secondary Principals
2. Athletic Program
3. Chapter II, Title II, Bilingual Program, Chemical Health Program
4. Library Media
5. Special Education Director
6. Vocational Education Program

JOB GOAL: Direct the day-to-day operation of the instructional program for the entire school system.

PERFORMANCE RESPONSIBILITIES:

1. Recommend and prepare policy changes related to curriculum, instruction, and students.
2. Interpret and conduct both credit and inservice programs related to curriculum, instruction, and student policies and practices to contracted personnel, students, and the community at large.
3. Resolve difficulties including unresolved instructional or curricular conflicts referred to the Central Office involving faculty, paraprofessionals, teacher aides, students and parents.
4. Assure compliance to Title IX as it relates to curriculum and athletics.
5. Serve as the general resource person to all administrators and staff involved with curriculum, instruction and students.
6. Work with the Assistant Superintendent for Personnel in prioritizing all instructional staff needs in developing recommendations to the Superintendent and in the assignment of contract personnel.
7. Assist in the maintenance of high student and staff morale.
8. Direct curriculum development, including reduction and expansion. Recommend changes to the Superintendent.

9. Conduct an annual audit of the instructional program relative to content and student achievement. Develop recommendations as a result of the audit for consideration by the Superintendent.
10. Review all state and federal evaluation and accreditation requirements and reports and develop recommendations regarding our status to the Superintendent.
11. Direct an evaluation program for all contract staff with emphasis on improved performance and personal growth.
12. Assist the Superintendent in developing an evaluation program for all administrators and assist in that evaluation.
13. Direct the entry of all students into the system; make certain that all students comply with entry requirements including that of being properly immunized.
14. Make recommendations regarding school attendance boundaries to the Superintendent.
15. Make final administrative decisions regarding student transfer requests.
16. Conduct population studies and project student enrollment district wide and by school. Utilize community resource persons in this task.
17. Supervise the development of educational specifications for each level—elementary, junior high, and secondary—for future building needs.
18. Assume general responsibility for coordination of all federal instructional programs. Direct the preparation of proposals for all federal programs.
19. Consult and advise the Superintendent in determining the budgetary needs for each fiscal year.
20. Represent the school system before the media and the public on educational matters as requested by the Superintendent.
21. Attend Board meetings and prepare Board reports as requested by the Superintendent.
22. Act as Superintendent in the absence of the Superintendent and the other Assistant Superintendent.
23. Administer practice teacher agreements and placement between the District and participating colleges and universities.
24. Develop and administer community lifelong learning and adult basic education program.
25. Perform such other tasks which may from time to time be assigned by the Superintendent.

TERMS OF EMPLOYMENT: Twelve Month. Salary to be determined by the Board.

EVALUATION: Evaluation by Superintendent.

Approved by: _____   Date: _____

Reviewed and agreed to by: _____   Date: _____

Source: Bismarck Public School District No. 1, Bismarck, North Dakota. Reprinted with permission.

JOB DESCRIPTION 5

PRINCIPAL, ELEMENTARY

DUTIES AND RESPONSIBILITIES OF ELEMENTARY SCHOOL PRINCIPALS

I. SUPERVISION
  A. Personnel
    1. Supervise, direct, and evaluate through observation and written evaluation, the activities of the professional and non-professional staff assigned to the building(s).

2. Evaluations should be conducted in a manner to offer suggestions for improvement, if performance is less than satisfactory, and also to increase efficiency or effectiveness in fulfilling designated responsibilities.

B. Pupils
   1. Assist in the development and supervision of all activities related to an effective and appropriate educational program for students.
   2. Develop and maintain a positive school climate that will enhance the students' learning and success within a framework of appropriate behavioral and academic expectations.
   3. Appropriately develop and maintain students' permanent personal academic and attendance records.

II. INSTRUCTION
   A. Curriculum
   1. Assist in the development, revision, and evaluation of elementary curricular objectives.
   2. Provide time for appropriate schedules, materials, and equipment to implement the agreed-upon curriculum.
   3. Assist the Director of Curriculum, Reading Supervisor, and Computer Coordinator/Math Supervisor in developing the elementary curriculum.

   B. Staff
   1. Provide opportunities for professional growth through attendance at in-service meetings, workshops, seminars, conferences, or graduate coursework.
   2. Interview prospective employees, recommend for employment, and/or the transfer of staff.

III. FINANCE
   A. Budget
   1. Prepare budget proposals that include supplies, materials, and equipment needed to implement the agreed-upon elementary curriculum.
   2. Supervise and monitor the preparation of purchase orders that reflect expenditures from the Board-approved budget.
   3. Prepare budgetary transfers which will allow for maximum benefit from the approved budget.
   4. Maintain an inventory of all supplies, materials, and equipment.

IV. COMMUNICATION
   A. District
   1. Maintain effective communications with the Board, Central Administration and Principals by attending appropriate Board meetings, Administrative Council meetings, and Principals' meetings.
   2. Prepare and distribute memorandums to appropriate staff members that will ensure the effective functioning of the agreed-upon instructional programs.
   3. Prepare reports as required by the PDE or local School Board.

   B. Community
   1. Encourage and maintain effective participation by parents and the PTA in school activities by timely distribution of notices or newsletters.
   2. Meet with students, parents or the PTA to explain policies and procedures on the instructional programs in order to develop and maintain an effective home/school relationship.
   3. Attend school-related activities as a means of communicating to students and parents that these activities are an important part of the educational program.

V. OTHER DUTIES AND RESPONSIBILITIES
   A. Support Staff
   1. Supervise and work cooperatively with all members of the support staff to ensure appropriate services are provided students that have been identified as requiring additional help.

    2. Participate in MDT meetings to effectively administer mainstreaming, retention and placement policies.

 B. Discipline

    1. Provide support and guidance to students, parents and staff in developing and enforcing effective discipline policies.

    2. Work cooperatively with appropriate personnel to monitor positive student behavior on school buses.

 C. Miscellaneous

    1. Supervise the development and practice of evacuation or fire drills.

    2. Assist in the appropriate maintenance of building(s) by reporting maintenance needs to appropriate staff.

    3. Develop and maintain appropriate procedures for recording staff absences, employing effective substitutes when necessary.

Source: Northampton Area School District, Northampton, Pennsylvania. Reprinted with permission.

JOB DESCRIPTION 6

POSITION TITLE: Assistant Principal, Middle School

PRIMARY FUNCTION: Assists the principal in providing effective leadership in the organization, administration and supervision of the educational program of a middle school within the school system.

QUALIFICATIONS:

Educational: Master's Degree in addition to the educational requirements prescribed by the State of Indiana for an administrator's certificate. Advanced degree preferred.

Experience: A minimum of three (3) years of successful classroom teaching of 10- to 15-year-old students required. Administrative experience preferred.

Certification: Indiana Administration and Supervision license, Elementary or Secondary level.

JOB DUTIES:

1. Understands the Middle School philosophy; demonstrates a compassionate understanding of the characteristics and needs of the developing adolescent.
2. Assists the principal and staff in developing a special climate responsive to the developmental and intellectual needs of young adolescents.
3. Assists in the development and communication of a vital school philosophy based on the needs of early adolescents.
4. Assists the principal in the implementation of a model of shared decision making that involves stakeholders in close collaboration on decisions, solutions, and policies that direct the school toward the realization of its vision.
5. Supports and facilitates a process for continuous school improvement.
6. Serves in coordination with the principal as an instructional leader with individual teachers, teams, and team leaders.
7. Assists the principal in the administration of all employee resolutions and labor laws.
8. Assists in the development of transition plan to aid students in both the transition from elementary to middle school and from middle school to high school.
9. Works in collaboration with the community to provide opportunities for student service and leadership.

10. Assists in the development of a master schedule consistent with the philosophy of middle schools and the development of early adolescents.
11. Facilitates the establishment and maintenance of an effective parent involvement program appropriate to parents of middle school students.
12. Keeps abreast of developments, trends, and research concerning middle schools, their programs, and their administration.
13. Coordinates with the school staff under the direction of the principal a program of student management consistent with the development of a positive self-image for each student and the development of constructive social skills and attitudes.
14. Responds to all communications promptly, courteously, and efficiently, and submits all reports in a timely manner.
15. Assumes other duties or responsibilities as directed.

ORGANIZATIONAL RELATIONSHIP: Reports to the principal of the middle school
Source: Indianapolis Public Schools, Indianapolis, Indiana. Reprinted with permission.

JOB DESCRIPTION 7

POSITION GUIDE: Instructional Program Facilitator

ACCOUNTABLE TO: Principal

BROAD FUNCTION:
As a faculty member of the local school, the Instructional Program Facilitator will assist the school principal and the classroom teachers in effectively implementing the prescribed curriculum and instructional program as designed systemwide for the Crisp County School System. A portion of the day will be spent in classroom instructional activities which provide for direct services to students such as working with small groups of students with special needs in reading, mathematics, and other identified areas.

PROFESSIONAL QUALIFICATIONS AND PERSONAL CHARACTERISTICS:
Any person employed as an Instructional Program Facilitator must possess a T-5 certificate.
Any person employed as an Instructional Program Facilitator should have the capacity to build and maintain effective interpersonal relationships with co-workers and central office personnel.
Any person employed as an Instructional Program Facilitator should have the ability to work cooperatively with classroom teachers, interpret adopted curriculum to the faculty, and to train new and beginning teachers in the use of adopted materials.
Any person employed as an Instructional Program Facilitator should exhibit the organizational skills necessary to facilitate the school's instructional program and to balance his/her time between direct teaching activities and other instruction-related activities.
The Instructional Program Facilitator should be knowledgeable of current trends and practices in the teaching of reading and/or mathematics.

PRINCIPAL RESPONSIBILITIES:

A. TOTAL READING AND MATHEMATICS PROGRAM
   1. To assist the classroom teacher with the teaching of specific reading and mathematics groups.
   2. To test students for placement in the reading and mathematics program.
   3. To assist the classroom teacher in charting progress in the reading and mathematics program.

4. To assist with maintenance of the student's reading and mathematics folder.
5. To design and duplicate reteaching lessons for the basal reading and mathematics program.
6. To orient new teachers to the reading and mathematics program.
7. To establish and maintain a mathematics materials resource center.
8. To inventory and order reading and mathematics materials.
9. To develop materials for an individual student in the classroom.
10. To assist with preparing materials for parents to use at home with students.
11. To develop strategies for content area teachers to improve student achievement.
12. To provide the link between teachers of special education and regular classroom teachers, to assist with referral paperwork, staffings, and IEP implementation and review.
13. To assist with the coordination of the Title I teacher and the state-paid teacher.
14. To assist classroom teachers in scheduling Title I and Special Education services.

B. TESTING PROGRAM:
1. To inventory, schedule and distribute practice CRT [Criterion-Referenced Test] materials (grades 2, 3, 4, and 6).
2. To assist teachers in determining deficient skill areas on CRT.
3. To assist teachers in designing and/or acquiring materials to work on deficient CRT objectives.
4. To inventory and distribute CRT materials to teachers.
5. To assist teachers in administering the Metropolitan Readiness Tests and the Metropolitan Achievement Tests.
6. To begin the initial screening for special education services by administering the Slosson Intelligence Test and/or other diagnostic measures.
7. To assist teachers in understanding and utilizing test results.
8. To assist in the implementation of the promotion policy.

C. STAFF DEVELOPMENT:
1. To plan and assist with staff development in the schools.
2. To provide support to teachers in their classrooms through visitation, demonstration teaching, and problem solving.
3. To assist the principal in monitoring classroom organization (management, placement, and grouping).
4. To train and coordinate parent volunteers.
5. To assist in aide orientation and training.
6. To attend staff development sessions conducted by the central office.
7. To assist in workshops with parent groups, grade level meetings, and systemwide curriculum development activities, etc.

D. OTHER RESPONSIBILITIES:
1. To enhance school-community relations by assisting with a school newsletter or providing articles for the local paper.
2. To cooperate with and assist the school media specialist with media center motivational activities such as Book Week, Media Fairs, Book Fairs, etc.
3. To assist the principal and teachers with parent conferences.

Source: Crisp County Public Schools, Cordele, Georgia. Reprinted with permission.

JOB DESCRIPTION 8

INSTRUCTIONAL TEACHER LEADER

The instructional teacher leader as *liaison* between teachers and supervisors, building administrators, and the community will:
1. work with teachers, supervisors, and building administrators to establish and implement district and school goals;
2. provide information to teachers in regard to Board of Education and building administration policy, programs, scheduling, etc.;

3. participate in the instructional cabinet of the school;
4. communicate department policy, goals, curriculum offerings, etc., to the community, when appropriate;
5. communicate teacher concerns to board administrators and building administrators.

The instructional teacher leader as collegial *monitor of instruction* will:
1. ensure proper curriculum implementation;
2. demonstrate various teaching strategies, knowledge of PRISM and content;
3. analyze data to plan, pace and improve instruction;
4. observe and utilize the principles of conferring, coach teachers in the implementation of PRISM and knowledge of content;
5. provide human, material, and cultural resources;
6. provide leadership in professional development by informing teachers of current trends, educational research, professional publications, and by participating in conferences, workshops, and professional organizations;
7. offer guidance to permanent staff, substitute teachers, parents, and students.

The instructional teacher leader as department, grade, team or program *coordinator* will:
1. manage curricular activities within the department, team, program or grade, e.g., field trips, speakers;
2. identify the needs of the department, team, program or grade and develop programs, activities, materials, etc., to meet these needs;
3. assist the principal in developing schedules of students and teachers;
4. plan and conduct departmental, team, program or grade level meetings and inservice sessions. (The makeup of such groups will be determined by the size and nature of school, department, program or grade);
5. contribute to the development and administration of the school budget;
6. facilitate interdisciplinary planning;
7. provide orientation for new staff members.

The Instructional Teacher Leaders (ITL) belong to each school's instructional cabinet. As members they are involved in shared decision-making with regard to all instructional matters.

Although ITLs do not rate teachers, they provide instructional leadership for all teachers and observe and confer with all teachers. They work with the teachers who may be experiencing difficulty, help them to improve, and participate in the determination of whether improvement has been achieved. ITLs, along with special mentor teachers, also assist and work with teachers.

Source: From the Collective Bargaining Agreement between the Board of Public Education and the Pittsburgh Federation of Teachers, Pittsburgh, Pennsylvania. Reprinted with permission.

JOB DESCRIPTION 9

TITLE: Department Chairperson

QUALIFICATIONS:
1. Bachelor's degree with major in assigned curricular area
2. A valid Illinois teacher's certificate
3. Minimum of five years' teaching experience
4. Such alternatives to the above qualifications as the Board may find appropriate and acceptable

REPORTS TO: Principal

SUPERVISES: Department curriculum

JOB GOAL: Provide leadership, coordination, and innovation in assigned curricular area, so that each student may derive maximum benefit from the continuing pursuit of the subject area involved.

PERFORMANCE RESPONSIBILITIES:

A. INSTRUCTIONAL PLANNING AND SUPERVISION

1. Prepares and maintains a schedule of classes and teaching assignments for the department.
2. Prepares and presents formal proposals for study, revision, and improvement of curriculum, including recommendations for textbook and instructional material adoption.
3. Arranges for teacher substitutes.
4. Studies current curricular trends in the subject area and disseminates relevant information.
5. Recommends inservice topics within guidelines of district.
6. Coordinates the development and evaluation of courses of study, including course outlines, course requirements and objectives.
7. Facilitates development of department goals and objectives that are in keeping with those of the school and the District and the evaluation of same.
8. Recommends educationally sound field trips, meetings, and guest speakers.
9. Reviews and analyzes results of district testing program and implements changes in curriculum and assignments as needed.
10. Informs staff members about student placement criteria.
11. Maintains an awareness of student placement problems as determined by department members and discusses with administrators.
12. Provides input to the principal or designee concerning the content area qualifications of needed additional staff.
13. Acts as a resource person for department teachers on curriculum questions.
14. Uses standard rules of spelling, punctuation, and grammar in written communication.
15. Uses grammatically correct English in verbal communications.

B. DEPARTMENTAL MANAGEMENT

1. Prepares, maintains and updates an inventory of books, equipment, and other necessary instructional materials used in the department's educational program.
2. Requests staff input in the preparation and maintenance of department budget.
3. Plans for and presides at monthly department meetings; keeps and provides to the principal appropriate records of department business, including department meeting minutes.
4. Supervises the care, use and maintenance of equipment and materials.
5. Conducts periodic and end-of-year inspection of department facilities and makes recommendations as needed.
6. Initiates and facilitates inter- and intra-school department communications.
7. Delegates responsibilities for performing departmental tasks.
8. Handles the ordering and distribution of departmental textbooks.
9. Collects and forwards equipment repair requests to the administration.
10. Orients new staff members to the curriculum and the operation of the department.
11. Recommends department staff members for committee assignments.
12. Meets with counterparts at other buildings at least once per semester.
13. Facilitates communications by serving as liaison between the administration and staff.
14. Consults with principal on approved budget and bid preparation.

    15. Assists in the recruitment, training, and assigning of department personnel.
    16. Utilizes community resources for department needs.
    17. Assists department teachers in the handling of day-to-day problems of instruction.

C. STAFF AND PROFESSIONAL RESPONSIBILITIES

    1. Is punctual.
    2. Maintains and submits accurate and timely records/reports as required by law, Board policy, and administrative guidelines.
    3. Follows building and district rules, procedures, and policies.
    4. Actively participates in building, professional, and district level committees.
    5. Represents the department at building and district curriculum meetings.
    6. Promotes public relations by requesting possible press releases from department staff and interpreting instructional program to parents and the community.
    7. Assists in building/district responsibilities as directed by principal.

TERMS OF EMPLOYMENT: Wages, hours, terms, and conditions of employment pursuant to negotiated agreement.

EVALUATION: Performance in the position will be evaluated once every two years in accordance with the District's plan for evaluation of contractual continued service staff.

Source: Champaign Community Schools, Unit District No. 4, Champaign, Illinois. Reprinted with permission.

JOB DESCRIPTION 10

Team Coordinator—Elementary

a. Serves as an Educational Cabinet representative. The responsibilities as a Cabinet representative are:

    1. Assist in the establishment of school-wide goals and objectives.
    2. Coordinate curricular development to be consistent with the educational goals and learning objectives throughout the school.
    3. Plan, monitor, and assess program implementation in terms of non-graded continuous progress.
    4. Assure consistency of program implementation across teams.
    5. Jointly plan for and coordinate:
        a) Use of space (e.g., gym, all-purpose room, small group rooms) among teams.
        b) Communication among units.
        c) Use of instructional materials (e.g., books, audio-visual equipment).
        d) Use of library space and materials.
        e) Use of assessment devices.
        f) Research among the teams.
    6. Provide a channel of two-way communication by:
        a) Encouraging team and individual staff members to express their opinions, problems and concerns.
        b) Encouraging team and individual staff members to submit topics for Cabinet agendas.
        c) Distributing to all staff members Cabinet agendas in advance of each meeting to secure opinions of each staff member.
        d) Distributing to all staff members the minutes of each Cabinet meeting.
    7. Assist in the coordination and development of school-wide inservice programs.

8. Cooperatively monitor and evaluate the school's home-community relations program.
9. Cooperatively develop and implement plans for:
   a) Interpreting the school concepts to parents and residents of the school attendance area.
   b) Utilization of volunteer community personnel (e.g., parents, other adults, high school and college students, people with special expertise) in the instructional program and other school activities.

b. Team Coordinator as a team chairperson. The responsibilities as a team chairperson are:
   1. Schedule and chair team meetings.
   2. Develop agenda to include the discussion of individual students, the sharing of ideas, suggestions relative to rules and procedures for students, curriculum development, in-service programs, stated goals and objectives.
   3. See that meetings have appropriate follow-through, including written statements of agreed activities, suggestions or recommendations.
   4. Facilitate communications between administration and staff.
   5. Assist principal in coordinating schedules and duties of school aides.

c. To facilitate the above job description, instructional team coordinators will:
   1. Attend approximately 10 Cabinet meetings.
   2. Conduct approximately 15 team meetings.
   3. Participate in committee and/or individual work to meet Cabinet, instruction team, and school-wide objectives.
   4. Spend one day, or, if necessary, two days, in pre-school planning.

d. The instructional team coordinators will be paid an agreed amount with the Superintendent of Schools.

Source: Lake George School District, Lake George, New York. Reprinted with permission.

JOB DESCRIPTION 11

LANGUAGE ARTS CONSULTANT

QUALIFICATIONS:

1. A master's degree or higher with a major in English or reading or the equivalent
2. A valid state certificate to teach in Georgia
3. An Instructional Supervision Certificate (within one year) or an AS [Administration and Supervision certificate]
4. At least three years of successful teaching experience
5. Ability to work with individuals and groups in a consultative capacity

REPORTS TO: Language Arts Coordinator

JOB GOAL: To assist client systems in program development and staff development, primarily in Language Arts.

PERFORMANCE RESPONSIBILITIES:

I. Program Development
   A. Needs Assessment
      1. Assist with selection and/or development of instruments for needs assessment.
      2. Assist with development of procedures and plans for carrying out needs assessment.
      3. Assist with implementation of needs assessment plan.
      4. Assist with analyzing and prioritizing needs.
      5. Assist with identifying and evaluating programs to meet needs.

      6. Assist with testing students for placement.
  B. Planning
      1. Assist with development and/or revision of curriculum materials or guides.
      2. Assist with reviewing and selecting programs and materials.
      3. Recommend implementation strategies.
      4. Assist with identifying resources for implementing programs.
      5. Assist with the development of project proposals.
  C. Comprehensive Planning
  D. Program Implementation
      1. Visit classrooms at request of local personnel.
      2. Assist with organizing materials.
      3. Assist with evaluation of program implementation.
II. Staff Development
  A. Professional
      1. Plan staff development.
      2. Assist teachers in selecting and acquiring materials.
      3. Conduct and/or coordinate in-service workshops.
  B. Non-Professional
      1. Coordinate and/or conduct staff development programs for aides/parents/volunteers/substitutes.
III. Internal Operations
  A. Office Maintenance—Reports
      1. Assist in maintaining division and personal files, materials, and equipment.
      2. Record activities and complete activity-travel reports.
  B. Professional Growth
      1. Participate in staff meetings with other RESA [Regional Educational Service Agency] personnel.
      2. Participate in staff development activities.
      3. Attend professional meetings and conferences.

TERM OF EMPLOYMENT: 190 work days with the dates specified to include 195 days, five of which the consultant may take as unspecified holidays based upon the approval of the division coordinator.

EVALUATION: Performance of the job will be evaluated annually by the coordinator and the consultant. The results will be discussed and signed by both parties.

Approved by: _____ Date: _____

Reviewed and agreed to by: _____ Date: _____

Source: First District Regional Educational Service Agency, Statesboro, Georgia. Reprinted with permission.

JOB DESCRIPTION 12

TITLE: Administrative Assistant to the District Superintendent for Instructional Support Services, Staff and Curriculum Development

JOB GOAL:
To provide leadership in the ongoing development and improvement of the entire instructional and support program, and provide leadership in the development, implementation and coordination of curriculum and staff development with the component schools through the creation and guidance of an administrative curriculum council. To assure that all instructional programs meet the expressed needs of all component schools and BOCES.

PERFORMANCE RESPONSIBILITIES:

Duties would include, but not be limited to, the following:

- Plans with the county-wide Curriculum Advisory Council in developing programs to meet the needs of county schools.
- Guides development, implementation and evaluation of staff/curriculum and instructional services.
- Assists in the formulation of a philosophy and objectives for the instructional program of BOCES and component districts.
- Serves as a resource to component district administrators in organizing their staff training and curriculum development.
- Maintains liaison with The State Education Department in the areas of staff and curriculum development.
- Offers hands-on assistance to districts involved in various staff development and curricular activities.
- Acts as a staff developer in particular areas of expertise.
- Works with directors and building principals in the improvement of individual staff competencies.
- Communicates the approved curriculum to the superintendent, principal and professional staff, and maintains a list of approved instructional materials. Relates and coordinates state initiatives in syllabus dissemination for component schools.
- Directs creation of and edits for publication all curriculum guides and materials prepared by and to be distributed among the superintendent, principals, and instructional staff.
- Maintains a current curriculum manual to show graduation requirements, approved courses, credit allowed, and any pertinent information useful to students and staff.
- Maintains a curriculum library for staff use.
- Assumes a leadership role in developing staff development and curriculum for any course newly mandated by The State Education Department or the Board.
- Coordinates all formal efforts of cooperative projects relating to Staff and Curriculum Development.
- Participates in the work of state and national staff and curriculum associations and study groups.
- Maintains liaison and active participation with educational leaders in staff, curriculum and instruction at state, regional, and national levels.
- Develops proposals for funding from appropriate agencies.
- Supervises all programs within the instructional and support service area, i.e., SETRC, Gifted & Talented, Library System, and coordinates with Teacher Center and Statewide Health Advocacy Office.
- Takes a leadership role and promotes communication on all matters related to instructional services beginning with providing information to the superintendent.
- Meets regularly with component school superintendents.
- Performs such other tasks and assumes such other responsibilities as may from time to time be assigned by the District Superintendent or Assistant Superintendent.

Source: Sullivan County Board of Cooperative Educational Services, Liberty, New York. Reprinted with permission.

JOB DESCRIPTION 13

TITLE: Director of Planning, Testing and Program Evaluation

QUALIFICATIONS: **(1)** Master's Degree and certification in Education, Supervision and/or Administration or Educational Leadership.

> **(2)** Intensive course work and/or experience in testing, statistics and research designs.
>
> **(3)** Minimum of three years' successful experience in an educational supervisory and administrative position directly related to the instructional process.
>
> **(4)** Experience in individual and group test administration and interpretation.

KNOWLEDGE, SKILLS AND ABILITIES:

Knowledge of tests and measurements, assessment procedures, data analysis and evaluation design. Knowledge of statistical procedures. Knowledge of software programs used in scanning and scoring of data forms. Knowledge of state, regional and national research studies, trends and results as pertains to testing. Successful presentation and communications skills, both oral and written. Ability to maintain effective working relationship with other employees. Ability to communicate effectively to targeted audiences.

REPORTS TO: Assistant Superintendent for Instructional Services

JOB GOAL: Plan, organize and coordinate the various testing programs for the district; design and conduct evaluation projects to support the improvement of the instructional program and provide support to schools and district departments on test analysis.

SUPERVISES: Data Management Specialist.

*PERFORMANCE RESPONSIBILITIES:

> **(1)** Coordinate administration of the district-adopted achievement testing program and the Florida Statewide Student Assessment program.
>
> **(2)** Prepare reports of results of various testing programs, including SAT/8, SAT and ACT, PSAT and HSCT.
>
> **(3)** Assist in the correlation of testing programs with the district-adopted instructional program.
>
> **(4)** Assist district- and school-level personnel in the interpretation and utilization of testing data.
>
> **(5)** Make presentations to groups with varied interests and backgrounds.
>
> **(6)** Interface with appropriate divisional personnel, area superintendents, principals, teachers, students, parents and others in identifying curriculum areas in need of evaluation.
>
> **(7)** Conduct evaluations of district-adopted programs and other areas of need.
>
> **(8)** Maintain an awareness of state, regional and national research studies, trends and results and disseminate information to appropriate district personnel.
>
> **(9)** Conduct inservice training and technical assistance for administrators, teachers, students and parents on the planning process and the needs assessment for individual school improvement plans.
>
> **(10)** Represent the school district at state, regional and/or national research conferences, conventions and workshops.
>
> **(11)** Prepare and review budget performance for the department.
>
> **(12)** Use computers, software, scanners and other appropriate technological tools.
>
> **(13)** Use effective interpersonal communication skills.
>
> **(14)** Perform other incidental tasks or services consistent with the job goal of this position.

*Essential Performance Responsibilities.

PHYSICAL REQUIREMENT:
Light work: Exerting up to 20 pounds of force occasionally and/or up to 10 pounds of force frequently.

TERMS OF EMPLOYMENT: Nonbargaining Unit Compensation Plan.

Twelve months,   8.0 hours per day,   Pay Grade 16

EVALUATION:
Performance of this job will be evaluated in accordance with provisions of the Board's policy on evaluation of personnel.
Source: Brevard County Public Schools, Brevard County, Florida. Reprinted with permission.

JOB DESCRIPTION 14

POSITION TITLE: Coordinator of Staff Development

QUALIFICATIONS: **1.** Master's degree or higher in education or subject area.
2. Missouri certification as a teacher or administrator with appropriate graduate training in the area of service.
3. Successful experience as a teacher–administrator or teacher training experience helpful; comprehensive knowledge of the teaching-learning process; strong in strategies of inservice training and instructional improvement.
4. Effective interpersonal relations and communication skills.

REPORTS TO: Assistant Superintendent for Human Resources

LENGTH OF CONTRACT: 220 Days

JOB RESPONSIBILITIES:

1. Implements a comprehensive staff development program for all certified staff.
2. Works cooperatively with employees to determine development needs.
3. Recommends courses, workshops and other experiences for District staff.
4. Coordinates the use of District staff in teaching critical concepts.
5. Coordinates with building principals to meet the unique needs of staff.
6. Works cooperatively with the Professional Development Committee.
7. Manages the teacher mentor program.
8. Supervises student teaching.
9. Provides support as needed for hiring selection, recruitment, and evaluation work in the Human Resources Office.
10. Coordinates the Chapter I Program.
11. Responsible for the coordination of the Language Arts Curriculum for grades K–5.
12. Performs other duties and responsibilities as may be required by the Assistant Superintendent for Human Resources.

Source: Rockwood School District, Ellisville, Missouri. Reprinted with permission.

JOB DESCRIPTION 15

SYRACUSE MENTOR PROGRAM ACTIVITY/INTERACTION REPORT

I.D. # of Mentor _____ Period ____, ____, 19____ to ____, ____, 19____

ACTIVITY/AREA OF INTERACTION	COMMENTS
	Scheduled Meetings
	Needs to be Addressed
	Other Information
(A)	Student Grading
(B) Student Attendance/Reporting	
(C) Interpretation of Standardized Tests	
(D) State Testing Programs	
(E) Promotional Practices Policy	
(F) Referrals to Special Education, Alternative Programs, Support Services	
(G) Textbooks/Materials/Equipment	
(H) Visitations/Classrooms -Mentor to Resident -Resident to Mentor -Other	
(I) Demonstration Lessons	
(J) Parent Conferencing	
(K) Individualization of Instruction/General Curriculum/Group Work	
(L) Other _____	

TOPICS FOR ELEMENTARY CURRICULUM MENTORS TO COVER WITH NEW TEACHERS

I. Content of Curriculum
   - Review Curriculum Guides
   - Stress Importance of Teaching Curriculum
   - Discuss/Give Examples of Integration of Curriculum

II. Strategies for Long and Short Term Planning
   - Plan For the Year/Marking Period
   - Develop Weekly Schedule
   - Sample Lessons
   - Use of Plan Books
   - Actually Plan One or Two Weeks of Lessons

III. Texts, Supplemental Materials and Other Resources
   - Compare Texts and Curriculum
   - Review Supplemental Materials
   - Emphasize Importance of Using "Hands-On" Materials
   - Review Other Resources (Computer Room, Film Library, MECC Catalog, etc.)
   - Teacher Center
   - Other Staff
   - Sources of Money
   - Ordering Materials/Equipment
   - Bulletin Boards as Instructional Tools and as Showcases for Student Work

IV. Other
   - Testing
   - Equipment—Obtaining, Proper Use of, Repairing
   - If Relevant, Working With An Assistant

TOPICS FOR SECONDARY CURRICULUM MENTORS TO COVER WITH NEW TEACHERS

I. Content of Curriculum
- Review Curriculum Bulletin
- Stress Importance of Teaching Curriculum

II. Strategies for Long and Short Term Planning
- Sample Lessons
- Plan For Year/Marking Period
- Actually Plan Two Weeks of Lessons
- Use of Plan Books

III. Texts, Supplemental Materials and Other Resources
- Compare Texts and Curriculum
- Review Supplemental Materials, Check Catalogues
- Review Other Resources (Computer Room, Film Library, MECC Lists)
- Teacher Center
- Other Staff
- Departmental Procedures
- Sources of Money
- Equipment

IV. Other
- Exams, Testing
- Ordering, Catalogues
- Equipment
- Study Skills
- Bulletin Boards

Source: Syracuse City School District, Syracuse, New York. Reprinted with permission.

CREDITS

Name Index

Subject Index